W9-ADX-282

The Acts of Jesus

REPORTS OF THE JESUS SEMINAR

The Five Gospels:
The Search for the Authentic Words of Jesus

John the Baptist and Jesus

The Gospel of Mark: Red Letter Edition

The Parables of Jesus: Red Letter Edition

ALSO BY ROBERT W. FUNK

Honest to Jesus

Jesus as Precursor

The Poetics of Biblical Narrative

Parables and Presence

New Gospel Parallels

Language, Hermeneutic, and Word of God

A Beginning-Intermediate Grammar of Hellenistic Greek

The Acts of Jesus

The Search for the Authentic Deeds of Jesus

Robert W. Funk
and the Jesus Seminar

A Polebridge Press Book

HarperSanFrancisco
A Division of HarperCollins*Publishers*

HarperCollins Web Site: http://www.harpercollins.com

FIRST EDITION

Library of Congress Cataloging-in-Publication Data

The acts of Jesus : The Search for the Authentic Deeds of Jesus / Robert W. Funk.
p. cm.
Includes bibliographical references and index.
ISBN 0-06-062978-9 (cloth)
ISBN 0-06-062979-7 (pbk.)
1. Jesus Christ—Biography—History and criticism. 2. Jesus Christ—Historicity. 3. Bible. N.T. Gospels—Criticism, interpretation, etc. 4. Jesus Seminar. I. Funk, Robert Walter
BT301.9.A37 1998
232.9'08—dc21 97-44696
CIP

98 99 00 01 02 ❖/RRD(C) 10 9 8 7 6 5 4 3 2 1

This report is dedicated to all those

who have wrestled patiently with their doubts
through a long, dark night of discontent
anxiously awaiting a glimmer of honest illumination

and to those

who have dared to pioneer the way
across a minefield of theological issues

Contents

PREFACE

The Acts of Jesus, like *The Five Gospels,* has many authors. The Fellows of the Jesus Seminar labored together over a six-year period to produce this collaborative report. In the course of their work they examined 387 reports of 176 events and 69 versions of 47 narrative summaries, transitions, asides, general ized settings, and lists. Dozens of analytical papers were prepared in advance of the twice-yearly Seminar sessions, and hundreds of polls were taken after debate and discussion on a wide array of texts and issues. The seventy-nine Fellows of the Seminar are the real authors of this their second report.

The Jesus Seminar is sponsored by the Westar Institute, a scholarly think tank headquartered in Santa Rosa, California. The Fellows have paid their own ways to the twice-yearly meetings over the years, and the Associate members have been generous in their support of the meetings. Charlene Matejovsky has staged the meetings to everyone's pleasure and delight.

Individual Fellows contributed written drafts that went directly into this volume. I am grateful to them for their contributions: Andries G. van Aarde, Edward F. Beutner, Sterling Bjorndahl, Marcus Borg, Marvin E. Cain, Kathleen E. Corley, J. Dominic Crossan, Arthur J. Dewey, Robert T. Fortna, Julian V. Hills, Roy W. Hoover, Glenna S. Jackson, F. Stanley Jones, Perry V. Kea, Karen L. King, Lane C. McGaughy, Edward J. McMahon II, Marvin W. Meyer, Robert J. Miller, Stephen J. Patterson, Daryl D. Schmidt, Chris Shea, Dennis E. Smith, Mahlon H. Smith, W. Barnes Tatum, and Robert L. Webb.

Julian Hills and Daryl Schmidt corrected my initial drafts. Tom Hall attempted to decode my tortured sentences. Mary and John Dosier ran every statement through their fuzziness-finder. In spite of the keen efforts of these friendly critics, I am sure I have left a large residue of imperfections.

Daryl Schmidt deserves additional credit. His mental radar is especially attuned to detail. He has discovered and corrected hundreds of minor and major errors that would otherwise have been overlooked. He is the functional editor of this report.

Our Polebridge Press editor, Geneviève Duboscq, hovered over many drafts and versions in a gallant attempt to bring her order into our chaos. I hope she has succeeded sufficiently well to make this volume accessible to every literate reader.

Mark Chimsky, our Harper editor, has again taken a report of the Jesus Seminar and shepherded it patiently, skillfully into print.

POXY 2949, A FRAGMENT OF THE GOSPEL OF PETER

Scholars continue to debate whether the Gospel of Peter is independent of or dependent on the canonical gospels. The 1972 publication of Papyrus Oxyrhynchus 2949 introduced two tiny fragments into the discussion. While little can be made of the contents of the smaller fragment, the larger relates the story of Joseph of Arimathea's request to Pilate for the body of Jesus. This request appears to occur before the execution, contradicting the order of events in the canonical gospels, but closely resembling Pet 2:1–3a. These fragments date from the late second or the early third century, and are housed in the Ashmolean Museum, Oxford. (Photograph reprinted courtesy of the Committee of the Egypt Exploration Society, London.)

The Scholars Version Translation Panel

Editor in Chief

Robert W. Funk
Westar Institute

General Editors

Daryl D. Schmidt
Texas Christian University

Julian V. Hills
Marquette University

Editors, Apocryphal Gospels

Ron Cameron
Wesleyan University

Karen L. King
Harvard Divinity School

Translation Panel

Harold Attridge
Yale University

Edward F. Beutner
Westar Institute

J. Dominic Crossan
DePaul University, Emeritus

Jon B. Daniels
Defiance College

Arthur J. Dewey
Xavier University

Robert T. Fortna
Vassar College, Emeritus

Ronald F. Hock
University of Southern California

Roy W. Hoover
Whitman College

Arland D. Jacobson
Concordia College

John S. Kloppenborg
University of St. Michael's College

Helmut Koester
Harvard University

Lane C. McGaughy
Willamette University

Marvin W. Meyer
Chapman University

Robert J. Miller
Midway College

Stephen J. Patterson
Eden Theological Seminary

Bernard Brandon Scott
Phillips Theological Seminary

Philip Sellew
University of Minnesota

Chris Shea
Ball State University

Mahlon H. Smith
Rutgers University

THE SCHOLARS VERSION

The translators of the Scholars Version—SV for short—have taken as their motto this dictum: a translation is artful to the extent that one can forget, while reading it, that it is a translation at all. Accordingly, rather than attempt to make SV a thinly disguised guide to the original language, or a superficially modernized edition of the King James Version, the translators worked diligently to produce in the American reader an experience comparable to that of the first readers—or listeners—of the original. It should be recalled that those who first encountered the gospels did so as listeners rather than as readers.

Why a new translation?

Foremost among the reasons for a fresh translation is the discovery of new gospels and gospel fragments in the twentieth century. The scholars responsible for the Scholars Version determined that all the gospels had to be included in any primary collection.

Traditional English translations make the gospels sound like one another. The gospels are leveled out, presumably for liturgical reasons. In contrast, the Greek originals differ markedly from one another. The SV translators attempt to give voice to the individual evangelists by reproducing the Greek style of each in English.

The translators agreed to employ colloquialisms in English for colloquialisms in Greek. When the leper comes up to Jesus and says, "If you want to, you can make me clean," Jesus replies, "Okay—you're clean!" (Mark 1:40–41). They wanted to make aphorisms and proverbs sound like such. The SV panelists decided that "Since when do the able-bodied need a doctor? It's the sick who do" (Mark 2:17) sounds more like a proverb than "Those who are well have no need of a physician, but those who are sick." They shunned pious terms and selected English equivalents for rough language. Matt 23:13 reads:

> You scholars and Pharisees, you impostors! Damn you! You slam the door of Heaven's domain in people's faces. You yourselves don't enter, and you block the way of those trying to enter.

Contrast the New Revised Standard Version:

> But woe to you, scribes and Pharisees, hypocrites! For you lock people out of the kingdom of heaven. For you do not go in yourselves, and when others are going in, you stop them.

"Woe" is not a part of the average American's working vocabulary. If a person wants to curse someone, that person would not say "woe to you," but "damn you." Moreover, the diction of New Revised Standard Version strikes the ear as faintly Victorian. In sum, the translators abandoned the context of polite religious discourse suitable for a Puritan parlor and reinstated the common street language of the original.

Modern translations, especially those made by academics and endorsed by church boards, tend to reproduce the Greek text, more or less word-for-word. English words are taken from an English-Greek dictionary—always the same English word for the same Greek word—and set down in their Greek order where possible.

In Mark 4:9 and often elsewhere, this admonition appears in the King James Version: "He who has ears to hear, let him hear." In addition to being sexist, that is the rendition of a beginning Greek student who wants to impress the instructor by reproducing the underlying Greek text in English. One scholar among the SV translators proposed to make this substitution: "A wink is as good as a nod to a blind horse." The panel agreed that this English proverb was an excellent way to represent the sense of the Greek text. However, the translators did not want to substitute an English expression for one in Greek. They decided, rather, to represent not only the words, phrases, and expressions of the Greek text, but also to capture, if possible, the tone and tenor of the original expression. As a consequence, SV translates the admonition: "Anyone here with two good ears had better listen!" "Two good ears" is precisely what "ears to hear" means, except that it is said in English, and "had better listen" replaces the awkward English "let him hear." "Had better listen" sounds like something parents might say to inattentive children; "let him hear" would strike the youngster as permission to eavesdrop.

The New Revised Standard Version also sounds quaint by comparison: "Let anyone with ears to hear listen." But then, the New Revised Standard Version is a revision of the King James Version.

In addition, SV has attempted to reproduce the assonance of the Greek text. The term "here" is a homophone of "hear": because the two words are pronounced alike, one reminds the English ear of the other. "Anyone *here* with two good ears" has the succession sounds *-ere, ear,* which suggests the assonance of the Greek text, which may be transliterated as *ota akouein akoueto* (the succession of *akou-, akou-* and of *ota, -eto,* with a shift in vowels). The panelists were not always this successful, but this example does illustrate what they were trying to achieve.

Grammatical form is also an important function of translation. The New Revised Standard Version renders Luke 10:15 this way:

> And you Capernaum,
> will you be exalted to heaven?
> No, you will be brought down to Hades.

The question in Greek is a rhetorical question, anticipating a negative response. Consequently, SV translates:

> And you, Capernaum,
> you don't think you'll be exalted to heaven, do you?
> No, you'll go to Hell.

It is clear that the town of Capernaum could not, in the speaker's judgment, expect to be exalted to heaven. SV also replaces the archaic "Hades" with "Hell": in American English we don't tell people to "go to Hades," unless we want to soften the expression in polite company; we tell them to "go to Hell." That is what the Greek text says.

Style is another significant aspect of translation. The style of the Gospel of Mark, for example, is colloquial and oral; it approximates street language. Mark strings sentences together by means of simple conjunctions and hurry-up adverbs, which gives his prose a breathless quality. Both sentences and events follow each other in rapid succession. His account of Peter's mother-in-law is typical (Mark 1:29–31):

> They left the synagogue right away and went into the house of Simon and Andrew accompanied by James and John. Simon's mother-in-law was in bed with a fever, and they told him about her right away. He went up to her, took hold of her hand, raised her up, and the fever disappeared. Then she started looking after them.

The Gospel of Luke, on the other hand, will sound more literary to the English ear than Mark, because Luke writes in a more elevated Greek style.

Mark often narrates in the present tense rather than in the simple past. He also frequently switches back and forth. Mark makes use of what is called the imperfect tense in Greek, which is used to introduce the typical or customary. By turning Mark's present and imperfect tenses into simple past tenses, translators in the King James tradition misrepresent and mislead: Mark's typical scenes are turned into singular events and the oral quality of his style is lost. In contrast, Mark 4:1–2 is translated in SV as:

> Once again he started to teach beside the sea. An enormous crowd gathers around him, so he climbs into a boat and sits there on the water facing the huge crowd on the shore.
>
> He would then teach them many things in parables. In the course of his teaching he would tell them. . . .

This translation faithfully reproduces Mark's present tenses. The imperfect is represented by "would teach" and "would tell," which in English connotes the usual, the customary. This is a typical scene for Mark, one that happened on more than one occasion. On such occasions, Jesus would teach in parables. Among the parables he uttered on those occasions was the parable of the sower.

At the conclusion of the parable, Mark adds: "And as usual he said, 'Anyone here with two good ears had better listen!'" According to Mark, Jesus habitually appended this admonition to his parables.

The Scholars Version attempts to capture Mark's oral style and to represent Mark's scenes as typical and repeated rather than as specific and singular.

The translators believe that excessive capitalization gives the gospels an old-fashioned look. Pronouns referring to God are no longer capitalized as they once were. The term "son" is not capitalized when referring to Jesus. The word "messiah" is not capitalized in ordinary use; SV employs "the Anointed" when it is used as a Christian epithet for Jesus. (The translators decided to avoid "Jesus Christ," since many readers take "Christ" as a last name.) Similarly, "sabbath" is always left in lowercase, as is "temple," even when referring to the Jerusalem temple. The translators saw no reason to capitalize "gentile," which, after all, in contrast to "Jew," means "foreigner, or stranger, or non-Jew." (We capitalize "Greek," but not "barbarian"; the two terms represent a comparable division of humankind into two categories.) Part of the rationale in avoiding overcapitalization was the desire to desacralize terms that in the original were common and secular; English translators have given them an unwarranted sacred dimension by capitalizing them.

The Scholars Version has been formatted in accordance with modern editorial practice. Paragraphing is employed to set off the change in speakers in dialogue. Lengthy quotations, such as parables, are extracted and made to stand out from the surrounding narrative terrain. Punctuation follows modern practice. The goal of the panel was to make SV look and sound like a piece of contemporary literature.

For readers' ears only

The translators have made readability the final test of every sentence, every paragraph, every book. They have read the text silently to themselves, aloud to one other, and have had it read silently and aloud by others. Every expression that did not strike the ear as native was reviewed and revised, not once but many times.

Translation is always a compromise, some say even a betrayal. If translators strive to make the Greek of the Gospel of Mark sound as familiar to the modern American ear as the original did to its first readers, will they not have translated out many cultural expressions unfamiliar to contemporary readers? Will they not have eliminated the archaic in the interests of readability?

The panel agreed at the outset not to translate out the social and cultural features of the text that are unfamiliar—worse yet, distasteful—to the modern reader. That would be to deny the contemporary reader any direct experience of the world, the social context, of the original. On the contrary, they have tried to put those features, as alien and as distasteful as they sometimes are, into plain English. So there are still slaves in the text, the Pharisees and the Judeans are often turned into uncomplimentary stereotypes, Jesus gets angry and exasperated, the disciples are dim-witted, and the society of the Mediterranean world is male-dominated, to mention only a few. At the same time, the translators have avoided sexist language where not required by the original. Male singulars are occasionally turned into genderless plurals. The language of SV is inclusive wherever the text and its social context refer to people, not to a specific male or female.

The tradition of translations

Translations of the Bible become necessary when users no longer read the original languages with ease.

Early Christian communities adopted the Greek version of the Old Testament as their own because most members who were literate read Greek, but not Hebrew. The New Testament was composed in Greek because that was the common language of the day, the *lingua franca*, of the Roman world. But the Western church soon lost its facility with Greek and so switched to Latin, which then became the sacred language of both Bible and liturgy. The Eastern church has continued the ancient Greek tradition.

One central issue in the Reformation was whether the Bible was to be made accessible to the general population, or whether it was to remain the private province of theological scholars and the clergy. Martin Luther's translation of the Bible into German marked a radical departure from the Latin tradition. His translation had one other major consequence: it provided the German people with a single, unifying language for the first time in their history.

The appearance of the version authorized by King James in 1611 continued and advanced the tradition of translations into English, and it also put the English church on a firm political and cultural footing. The King James Version helped canonize Shakespearean English as the literary norm for English-speaking people everywhere. It also united English speakers worldwide.

The beauty and cadence of the King James Bible has retarded any interest in replacing it with a more accurate rendering. Theological conservatism also functioned as a retarding factor, since many cardinal points rested on the English vocabulary of that version. However, even the elevated English of the King James Version could not dam up progress forever. Toward the close of the nineteenth century, numerous English translations and revisions appeared. The tide became a flood in the twentieth century.

The English Bible tradition has been firmly established. Many English-speaking people do not even know that the original languages of the Bible were Hebrew (Old Testament) and Greek (New Testament). Hebrew, Greek, and Latin are in use primarily among scholars and a decreasing number of clergy. Many seminaries no longer require candidates for ordination to learn either biblical language. As a consequence, the English Bible has rapidly become the only version of the Bible known to most English-speaking people, including many clergy. The Bible in English occupies the same position today that the Greek Bible did for the early Christian movement and the Latin Bible did for the Roman Catholic church at an earlier time. Greek and Latin were replaced first by German and then by English.

Based on ancient languages

The Scholars Version is based on the ancient languages in which the gospels were written or into which they were translated at an early date: Greek, Coptic, Latin, and other exotic tongues. In some instances, the only primary source is a translation into a secondary language. The Gospel of Thomas, for example, has survived in full form only in Coptic, though its original language was Greek. In other cases, derivative versions are the means of checking the understanding of the original language.

Authorized by scholars

The Scholars Version is free of ecclesiastical and religious control, unlike other major translations into English, including the King James Version and its descendants (Protestant), the Douay-Rheims Version and its progeny (Catholic), and the New International Version (Evangelical). The Scholars Version is authorized by scholars.

The Complete Gospels

The Scholars Version of the gospels has been published as *The Complete Gospels* (revised and expanded edition. Santa Rosa, CA: Polebridge Press, 1994). The Scholars Version of the complete letters and the complete acts of the apostles is being prepared by the Fellows of the Westar Institute.

ABBREVIATIONS

Acts	Acts
Amos	Amos
Bar	Baruch
Barn	Barnabas
B.C.E.	before the Common Era
C.E.	of the Common Era
1–2 Chr	1–2 Chronicles
Clem	Clement
1–2 Cor	1–2 Corinthians
Dan	Daniel
Deut	Deuteronomy
Did	Didache
EgerG	Egerton Gospel
Esth	Esther
Exod	Exodus
Ezek	Ezekiel
Gal	Galatians
GEbi	Gospel of the Ebionites
Gen	Genesis
GHeb	Gospel of the Hebrews
GNaz	Gospel of the Nazoreans
GosFr 840	Gospel Oxyrhynchus 840
GosFr 1224	Gospel Oxyrhynchus 1224
Heb	Hebrews
Hos	Hosea
InJas	Infancy Gospel of James
InThom	Infancy Gospel of Thomas
Isa	Isaiah
Jas	James
Jer	Jeremiah
Job	Job
Joel	Joel
John, Jn	Gospel of John
Jonah	Jonah
Judg	Judges
1–2 Kgs	1–2 Kings
L	Special Luke
Lev	Leviticus
Luke, Lk	Gospel of Luke
LXX	the Septuagint, the Greek translation of the Hebrew scriptures
M	Special Matthew

1–2 Macc	1–2 Maccabees
Mal	Malachi
Mark, Mk	Gospel of Mark
Mary	Gospel of Mary
Matt, Mt	Gospel of Matthew
Mic	Micah
ms(s)	manuscript(s)
Nah	Nahum
Num	Numbers
1–2 Pet	1–2 Peter
Pet	Gospel of Peter
Phil	Philippians
POxy	Papyrus Oxyrhynchus
Prov	Proverbs
Ps(s)	Psalm(s)
PsMk	Pseudo-Mark
Q	Sayings Gospel Q
11QTemple Scroll	the Temple Scroll from Qumran Cave 11
Rev	Revelation
Rom	Romans
1–2 Sam	1–2 Samuel
SecMk	Secret Mark
Sir	Sirach
SV	the Scholars Version
1–2 Thess	1–2 Thessalonians
Thom, Th	Gospel of Thomas
1–2 Tim	1–2 Timothy
Zech	Zechariah

The treatment of biblical references:

// In the commentary, parallel bars are used to connect passages that are verbally parallel to each other, without implying dependence on a common source.

In the marginal notations:

cf. The notation cf. indicates a comparable saying that is not, strictly speaking, a parallel.

In the Scholars Version translation:

< > Pointed brackets enclose a subject, object, or other element implied by the original language and supplied by the translator.

[ ] Square brackets enclose words that are textually uncertain. In Peter, such words have been restored from a missing portion of the manuscript; in the other gospels, such words are lacking in some important manuscripts.

[...] Square brackets with dots for missing letters represent a hole or gap in the manuscript where the words cannot be satisfactorily restored.

( ) Parentheses are used in the usual sense, and also to indicate parenthetical remarks and narrative asides in the original text.

According to Mark, Jesus entered Jerusalem from the east, from the Mount of Olives, which overlooked the city and the temple area. The prophets had speculated that "the Lord" would go forth in final battle against Israel's enemies from this point (Zech 14:4). This made the Mount of Olives a popular site for organizing freedom rallies against the Romans during the first century C.E. For his part, Jesus made it clear that he was entering Jerusalem to face death (10:33). In that case, the "triumphal entry" as Mark depicts it is a satire of revolutionary processions and of the kind of triumphal entry the Romans enjoyed making into cities they had conquered. The Romans celebrated their victories with horse, chariot, and a show of arms—with a military parade. In contrast, Jesus ... st of burden. Thus Jesus was not making a stater... hship, but contrasting God's imperial rule ("Co... d's domain belongs to you") with Roman impe...

Th... ces of Jesus entering Jerusalem, in the judgment ... is difficult to isolate those traces, the story as a wh... accompanying narrative statement was colored gray.

Gospel with color coding (see pp. 36–37 for the significance of colors) followed by explanatory commentary.

11 [12]**On the next day, as they were**
gry. [13]So when he spotted a fig tree in t
on it, he went up to it expecting to fin
he got right up to it, he found nothing
see, it wasn't 'time' for figs.) [14]And he r
so much as taste your fruit again!" **And**

Title → **Fig tree without figs**
Primary text → Mk 11:12–14, 20–25
Parallel(s) → Mt 21:18–22
Source(s) → Source: Mark
Cf. indicates a comparable event, summary or setting that is not, strictly speaking, a parallel. → Cf. Lk 13:6–9

Fig tree without figs. The commentary f... continuation below, in Mark 11:20–25.

11

he turned the bankers' tables
the pigeon merchants, [16]**and h**
tainer through the temple area.

In the marginal notations, semicolons separate parallels from different sources: Mk 11:15–19//Mt 21:12–17 //Luke 19:45–48 from Mark → Jn 2:13–22 from John →

Temple incident
Mk 11:15–19
Mt 21:12–17, Lk 19:45–48;
Jn 2:13–22
Sources: Mark, John

Chapter 11 of the gospel resumes.

...es say, 'My house is to be regarded as a
...'—but you have turned it into 'a hide-

[18]**And the ranking priests and the s**
looking for a way to get rid of him. (T
fear of him, and that the whole crowd
ing.) [19]And when it grew dark, they ma

Jesus' words were colored in *The Five Gospels*.

Temple incident. The Fellows of the Jesus Seminar approved on three different occasions over a ten-year period the statement that Jesus performed

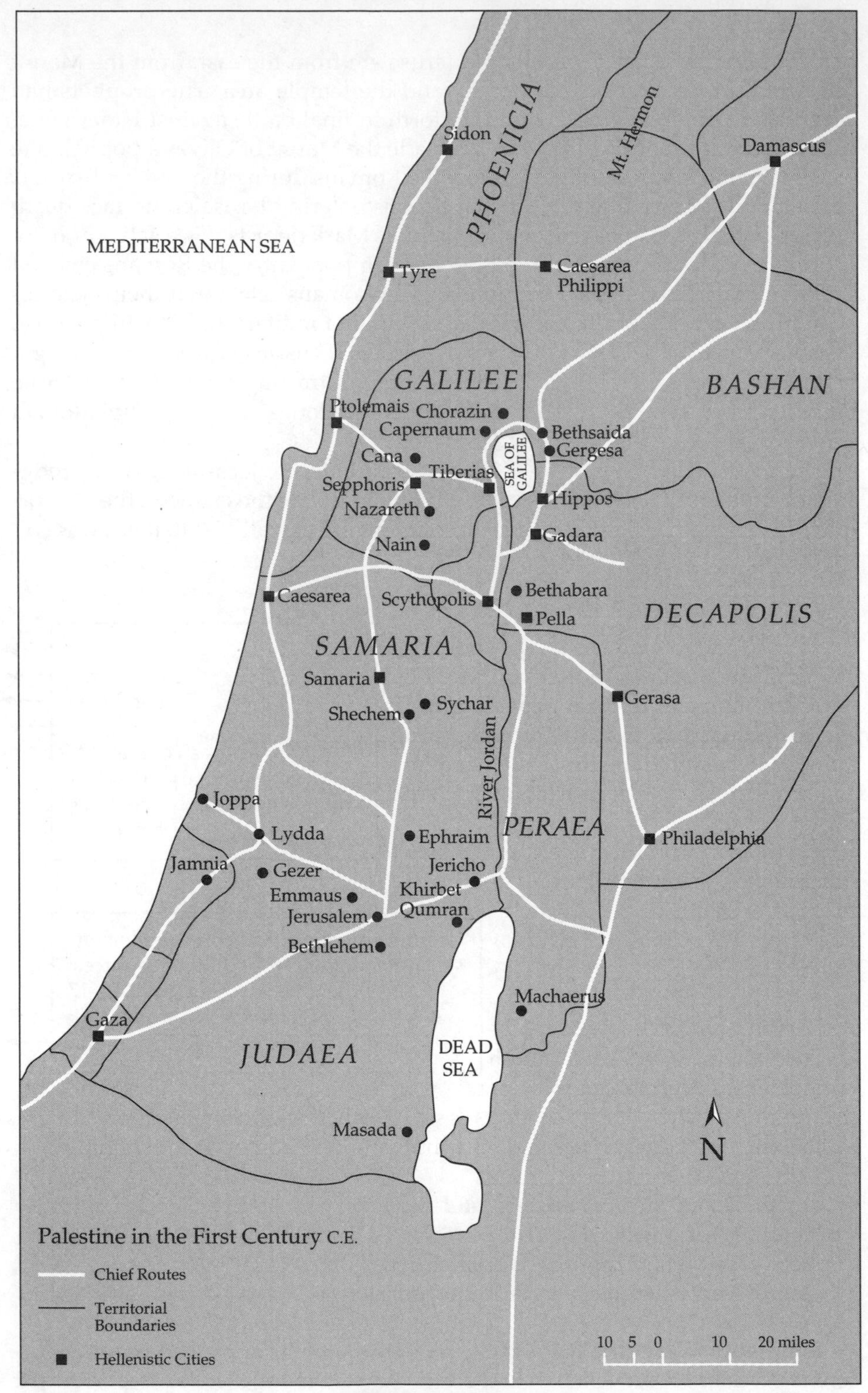

MAP OF PALESTINE

The Acts of Jesus

INTRODUCTION

The Acts of Jesus is an assessment of the reports in the ancient gospels of what Jesus of Nazareth did and what was done to him. These events together constitute the acts of Jesus.

THE ACTS OF JESUS IN COLOR

During the second phase of the Jesus Seminar, which lasted from 1991 to 1996, the Fellows examined 387 reports of 176 events, in most of which Jesus is the principal actor, although occasionally John the Baptist, Simon Peter, or Judas is featured. Of the 176 events, only ten were given a red rating (red indicates that the Fellows had a relatively high level of confidence that the event actually took place). An additional nineteen were colored pink (pink suggests that the event probably occurred). The combined number of red and pink events (29) amounts to 16% of the total (176). That is slightly lower than the 18% of the sayings—primarily parables and aphorisms—assigned to the red and pink categories in *The Five Gospels*.

For those who believe the Bible to be the word of God a 16% historical accuracy rate may seem ridiculously low. Why did the Seminar end up with so many black (largely or entirely fictive) and gray (possible but unreliable) reports? The results should not be surprising to critical scholars—those whose evaluations are not predetermined by theological considerations. Nevertheless, it is important to both the general reader and the scholars who participated in the Seminar to be as clear as possible about the reasons for this result.

The reason the Fellows colored so many of the events (84%) gray or black lies in the character of the gospels themselves. Although some twenty gospels have survived either in whole or in part from the first three centuries of the common era, only four were eventually included in the New Testament. The earliest tiny scraps of papyrus fragments are from a copy of the Gospel of John and the Egerton Gospel (consult the Dictionary of Terms & Sources for a description), and can be dated no earlier than about one hundred years after Jesus' death. The earliest substantial physical evidence for the gospels comes from the end of the second century C.E., about 170 years after Jesus' demise.

In the absence of hard information, scholars theorize that the New Testament gospels were composed during the last quarter of the first century by third-generation authors on the basis of folk memories preserved in stories that had circulated by word of mouth for decades. The oral stories the four evangelists recorded had been shaped, reshaped, augmented, and edited by numerous storytellers for a half century or more before achieving their final written forms.

Scholars also believe that written collections of sayings ascribed to Jesus had appeared perhaps as early as two decades after Jesus' death. One such collection, known as the Sayings Gospel Q, seems to have been incorporated into the gospels of Matthew and Luke. In addition, Matthew and Luke adopted the Gospel of Mark, the first of the narrative gospels, as the basis for their revised works. In revising Mark, they had very little new or more reliable information to assist them, other than the sayings they took from Q. The written gospels were then copied and recopied, modified, corrected, and augmented for the next century or more before reaching the physical state in which modern scholars know them.

As they retrace the trail that leads backward from the earliest surviving papyrus records to the earliest written gospels, to the first storytellers and collectors of Jesus lore, scholars hope to isolate some traces of the historical Jesus of Nazareth. It is a long and faint trail often obscured by myth and legend. The quest for the historical Jesus is a subtle, often frustrating, but not entirely hopeless enterprise that requires an open mind and a reservoir of patience.

THE FIRST STORYTELLERS

The followers of Jesus no doubt began to repeat his witticisms and parables during his lifetime. They soon began to recount stories about him, perhaps about his encounters with critics or about his amazing way with the sick and demon-possessed. As time went by, the words were gathered into compounds and clusters suggested by common themes or by catchwords to make them easier to remember and quote. His parables were retold and adapted to new audiences with each performance. The stories were likewise repeated by individual storytellers, who retold them in their own words, sometimes adding or omitting details as imagination or memory dictated. The gospel tradition was a living, breathing body of lore whose outside dimensions continued to grow.

Since the gospels consist of individual tales that were formed and circulated within this highly fluid body of lore, scholars find it necessary to analyze the structure of the simple anecdote.

A story or anecdote is the verbal representation of an event. To tell a story the narrator must bring two or more persons together in the same time and space and allow something to happen. That something is an event. In the gospels, the report of an event nearly always involves Jesus as the central character, although some anecdotes feature John the Baptist, Simon Peter, or Judas.

Storytellers sometimes report events on their own authority: they insert themselves between the event and the listener as though to say, "This is what happened; take my word for it." When storytellers frame their stories this way, literary critics call it "recounting." As an alternative, storytellers may take their listeners to the time and place of the event and allow them to see and hear what went on—all by means of words, of course. In that case, critics say the storyteller is "enacting" the scene. Because enactment seems more realistic—the words of participants in the story are quoted and their actions are described, sometimes in graphic detail—it is often assumed to be more historically reliable. That assumption is misleading: writers of fiction know how to narrate realistically by enactment, and when they do a good job of it, readers willingly accept as true what they are being told. To be convincing, writers of fiction must of course achieve a high level of plausibility. Recounting, on the other hand, appears less convincing because it seems to depend on the reliability of the narrator. If an evangelist assures us that something happened, and we are inclined to think the evangelist is reliable, we conclude that the evangelist was telling the historical truth. That conclusion can also be deceptive. In determining whether a story depicts fact or fiction, plausibility and the distinction between enactment and recounting are not trustworthy guides. In historical reconstruction, caution and skepticism are always in order.

How do we know when a storyteller is telling the historical truth? How do we know whether the narrator is recording a legend or myth or simply embellishing a tale with imaginative touches? How can we tell when a storyteller is concocting a composite "typical" event out of bits and pieces of historical lore? While scholars rarely achieve absolute certainty about historical facts, they are guided in the sorting process by their knowledge of how human beings acquire and record information.

Knowledge of the real world

The foundation of our knowledge of the real world is the face-to-face encounter. We get to know people and things through contact with them. The level of our knowledge improves if we have repeated contact with the same persons or events. It is difficult to determine what actually happened during an automobile accident, for example, because the event is fleeting and not repeatable. It is less difficult for a scientist to make an accurate measurement during an experiment that can be reenacted numerous times, or for one person to form a firm estimate of another through extended contact. Much of the reliable information human beings acquire about each other and the physical world comes to them through repeated direct observations.

In the everyday world, however, human beings interpret their encounters with persons as well as with things largely in terms of typifications they have previously acquired from their family, society, or culture. When crystallized, typifications become stereotypes. Many judgments people make about each other, especially when one party views another from a distance, are based on stereotypes. The more removed people are from personal encounters, the more their knowledge of others becomes generalized, the more their knowledge depends on shared typifications that neither originate with nor are corrected by face-to-face contact. It is for this reason that someone has said that all enemies are faceless: it is more difficult to hate someone who has a real face. And it is for the same reason that Jesus' admonition "love your enemies" is often a paradox: one cannot love someone who is faceless. The ultimate form of remote, anonymous knowledge is information that is mostly or wholly dependent on "they say . . . "or "it is said. . . ." Information derived from what nameless or unnamed people say is called "hearsay."

The foundation of the critical approach to the gospels is the recognition that much of the information in the gospels is based on hearsay. The historical figure of Jesus has been assimilated to a set of typifications developed over time by those who shared their convictions about him with each other through storytelling. Believers reinforced their convictions by subtly molding their stories—without being conscious of doing so—to conform to their beliefs. They domesticated their information by fitting their stories to a Procrustean bed of received conviction. Thus Jesus' critics, the Pharisees, are pictured in caricature in the gospels—as those who make stereotypical and mindless responses to things Jesus says and does. At the time the first written gospel was being produced, this shaping process was not, and could not be, corrected by additional evidence supplied, for example, by written documents (there were very few during the first couple of decades) or by recourse to the memories of eyewitnesses (they were no longer on the scene). That is the reason later gospel writers are dependent on earlier documents for much of their information.

The author of Mark, the earliest of the narrative gospels, was not an eyewitness: he is reporting information conveyed to him by a third person or persons, who themselves were quite possibly not eyewitnesses. (First and second persons would have been involved directly in the events being reported.) Since he doesn't name those from whom he gets his information, his sources are anonymous. The evangelist given the name Matthew reports a rumor that was circulating in his day (Matt 28:15): the guards at the tomb were bribed to say that Jesus' disciples stole his body. When the evangelist writes that the gossip was being passed around "until this very day," he is inadvertently betraying the chronological distance that separates him from events in the more remote past.

These views are not pure speculation. In such oblique ways, the authors tell us much about how they composed their gospels.

A pyramid of gospels

The author of the Gospel of Luke makes it explicit in his prologue (1:1–4) that he took his information from gospel writers who preceded him.

> Since so many have undertaken to compile an orderly narrative of the events that have run their course among us, [2]just as the original eyewitnesses and ministers of the words transmitted them to us, [3]it seemed good that I, too, after thoroughly researching everything from the begin-

ning, should set them systematically in writing for you, Theophilus, [4]so that Your Excellency may realize the reliability of the teachings in which you have been instructed.

From this prologue, we learn that Luke is at least a third-generation Christian scribe, writing at some remove from the events he is reporting (v. 2). We learn further that he knows of other gospels (v. 1), which he used in preparing his own version (v. 3). His prologue, which follows the pattern of those of other hellenistic historians, suggests that he has adopted their practice of freely copying from earlier sources and rearranging the borrowed materials in some new and interesting order ("systematically," v. 3). (Clearly, plagiarism had not yet been conceived as a violation of authorship and copyright.) Luke's claim to have researched everything should not be understood in the modern sense: he was not an academic historian attempting to achieve an historically accurate picture. Rather, he was creating his gospel in order to reassure his patron, Theophilus, of the correctness of the Christian faith imparted to him (v. 4). In other words, Luke's aim is fundamentally theological rather than historical.

Luke's method as a hellenistic historian prompts the modern historian to check how accurate Luke's information about his own world is. In Luke 2:1, for example, the author tells his readers that Mary and Joseph had to travel to Bethlehem to be enrolled in a census ordered by Quirinius, the governor of Syria. A partial census under Quirinius did take place in 6 C.E. However, according to Matthew (2:16), Jesus was born when Herod the Great was still king. Herod died in 4 B.C.E., about a decade earlier than Quirinius' census. Jesus could not have been born both in 6 C.E. and 4 B.C.E. In contradiction to the connection Luke makes with Quirinius, he also indicates that Jesus' birth was probably connected with Herod the Great (in Luke 1:5), where he sets the birth of John the Baptist in the time of Herod. It is evident that Luke did not know the date of Jesus' birth.

In another allusion, he refers to the high priesthood of "Annas and Caiphas" in connection with the appearance of John the Baptist (Luke 3:2). Annas and his son-in-law Caiaphas were not high priests at the same time, since the temple cult permitted only one high priest at a time. Moreover, they were not high priests consecutively. Luke is here confusing two generations of high priests.

Since Luke's knowledge of events in the larger world is faulty, the historian approaches his knowledge of events in the more restricted world of Jesus—events that took place a half century earlier—with considerable caution.

Folklore

Since much of the lore about Jesus was created and transmitted by word of mouth for a few decades before it was written down, it is folklore. How folklore is generated and takes root is illustrated by an incident that is alleged to have taken place at Roswell, New Mexico, in 1947. That incident is believed by a rather significant number of people to have involved the crash of a "flying saucer."

In its recent report entitled "The Roswell Incident: Case Closed," the U.S. Air Force attempted to put to rest the folklore that had gathered around that event. The original event, according to the Air Force, was simply the crash of a high-level surveillance balloon. Then, during the years 1954–59, the Air Force conducted a series of tests on dummies that were propelled from aircraft at high altitudes to determine the likelihood of survival of pilots forced to eject. Some of these dummies also fell to earth in New Mexico. According to the military, memories of the crash of the surveillance balloon were conflated with the appearance of dummies in the New Mexico desert to produce the rumor that the earth was being invaded by alien life-forms. Other observers have suggested that the rumor of an alien invasion was inspired by the science fiction that filled books, films, and television programs during the 1940s and the following decades. In addition, the genuine exploration of space and the search for intelligent life elsewhere in the universe had begun. The cultural air was filled with talk of deep space, aliens, and UFOs. The convergence of these factors produced the myth of a visit of aliens from outer space to planet Earth near Roswell, New Mexico.

Is it possible that memory plays such tricks on human beings when intrigued by a mystery and fired by the imagination? "Undoubtedly," is the answer folklorists unhesitatingly give.

In the manufacture and maintenance of folklore, memory does not function like a videotape. It is not possible to rewind and replay one's memories. On the contrary, memories are constantly edited, deleted, augmented, and combined with other memories as persons call them to mind. And when one adds the element of fear, or paranoia, or conviction, or nostalgia, those memories can become more vivid and powerful than everyday life. Parents tell their children, "When I was your age, I walked twenty miles through the snow to school." A bumper sticker reads: "The older I get, the better I was." Nostalgia is a great editorial assistant. Given the circumstances of the Roswell phenomenon, it is very difficult to determine what really happened and when.

Scholars of the gospels are faced with a similar problem: Much of the lore recorded in the gospels and elsewhere in the Bible is folklore, which means that it is wrapped in memories that have been edited, deleted, augmented, and combined many times over many years. Sorting out the fact from the fiction is a task for the well-informed and patient sleuth.

For many readers of the Bible, it is incomprehensible that the evangelists would have recorded stories that were the product of the Christian imagination, that well-intentioned believers would have invented tales about Jesus. Yet they seem to have done so. Under what circumstances would this have happened?

There are at least five conditions that might have prompted them to employ their imaginations. They might have created stories to fulfill a prophecy or to match scriptural language. They might have invented stories to assist in marketing the messiah to the larger world. They might have made up tales to give expression to their own convictions about who Jesus was and what he did and said. They might have imagined scenes to justify practices adopted by themselves or their communities. And they might have put into a fictive story form claims that they were making on their own behalf or on behalf of their leaders. In so doing they did not, of course, willfully distort the historical truth; rather, they were merely indulging the human proclivity to adjust inherited oral traditions to their own controlling perceptions born of faith.

Scripture as narrative catalyst

The first of the conditions under which believers might have allowed their imaginations to dictate the lineaments of a story is the promise/fulfillment scheme. The Gospel of Mark opens with a scripture citation derived from Malachi and Isaiah but tailored to serve its purposes:

> Here is my messenger,
> whom I send on ahead of you
> to prepare your way!
> A voice of someone shouting in the wilderness:
> "Make ready the way of the Lord,
> make his paths straight."

In the mind of the evangelist (and his community), those words constitute a forecast made in the sixth/fifth centuries B.C.E. that was fulfilled in the appearance of John the Baptist more than four hundred years later. The author of Mark makes the connection clear as he continues: "So, John the Baptizer appeared in the wilderness calling for baptism. . . ." That "messenger" from God, in turn, is made to forecast that someone "more powerful than I" will succeed him and that someone is none other than Jesus of Nazareth.

This is the classic promise/fulfillment scheme employed by the writers of the gospels and other biblical authors. In this case, an ancient prophecy is fulfilled in John the Baptist, who then makes another prophecy that is satisfied by the appearance of Jesus. That scheme functions frequently in the Gospel of Mark.

Mark alerts his readers to the role the scriptures played in shaping the passion narrative. Mark has Jesus himself declare: "the scriptures must come true" (Mark 14:49); Matthew enhances Mark's statement: "All of this happened so the writings of the prophets would come true" (Matt 26:56). In the Gospel of Luke, the author has Jesus reappear to his disciples after his death and remind them that everything written "in the Law of Moses and the Prophets and the Psalms is destined to come true" (Luke 24:44). As a consequence of this overwhelming conviction, the entire Bible (in its Greek rather than Hebrew version, since the early Christian community worked primarily with the Greek form of scripture) became source material for Christian scribes as they labored to fashion the gospel story, especially the passion narrative. The scriptural references and allusions are not to be understood as scholarly footnotes documenting events, but as promises that required narrative fulfillment. Accordingly, the evangelists took numerous clues from those ancient biblical texts that they then used as guidelines in imagining the story of Jesus. The task of the critical scholar, in such cases, is to determine which events in the story of Jesus were created merely to fulfill prophecy and which actually occurred.

A particularly poignant example of prophetic forecast creating narrative detail occurs in the Gospel of John (19:32–37). The soldiers have come to break the legs of three who have been crucified. When they come to Jesus, they notice that he is already dead, so they don't break his legs. Instead, one of the soldiers jabs Jesus in the side with his spear and water and blood pour out. Then the evangelist tells his readers:

> 36This happened so the scripture that says, "No bone of his shall be broken," would come true, 37as well as another scripture that says, "They shall look at the one they have pierced."

No other source within a hundred years of Jesus' death mentions the wound in the side, according to Raymond E. Brown.[1] Yet the ancient writer appears to insist in a parenthetical remark that the event is supported by eyewitness testimony:

> (35The one who observed this has given this testimony and his testimony is true. He knows he is telling the truth, so you too will believe.)

It is not altogether clear what the eyewitness is swearing to. He may be confirming only that "water and blood" came from the body of Jesus to form the two basic Christian sacraments, baptism and the eucharist. The evangelist certainly does not have independent confirmation of the failure to break Jesus' legs and the spear thrust in the side, yet he gives the impression that he does. The two details are probably the product of the Christian imagination as it has been prompted by scripture.

DISMANTLING THE WRITTEN GOSPELS

It is essential in assessing the historical reliability of the gospels to bear in mind that sayings ascribed to Jesus and individual stories told about him circulated orally for two decades or more before the first written records were created. It was another two decades or more before the first narrative gospel was composed. And then it was another decade or two before the derivative gospels were composed. In round numbers, the chronology of the written gospels may be divided into twenty-year periods:

30 C.E.	death of Jesus
50+ C.E.	written collections of sayings (Q)
70+ C.E.	first narrative gospel (Mark)
90+ C.E.	derivative gospels (Matthew, Luke, John)

In order to isolate the lore about Jesus during the oral period, scholars are compelled to dismantle the written gospels and sort the narrative components into two broad categories: (1) basic elements derived from the oral tradition and (2) framing stories and connective tissue used to mold the oral elements into a continuous narrative.

Clusters of the words of Jesus and stories told about him once circulated as independent units—without connection to each other—prior to the creation of the written gospels. The words of Jesus were assembled first of all into a written collection of sayings in the Sayings Gospel Q, while the stories were later gathered in the Gospel of Mark, with some sayings added. It is also possible that an early gospel of miracles was assembled out of miscellaneous traditions (this possibility is explored in a cameo essay, "A Gospel of Miracles?" pp. 388–89). Then the words and stories from Q and Mark were combined to create the gospels of Matthew and Luke. Each evangelist arranged the ingredients—words and stories—in more or less arbitrary clusters and sequences.

Individual evangelists also framed those clusters and sequences with legends that turned the whole into coherent narratives and gave the gospels overarching plots. When the framing stories and connective tissue are removed, the gospels turn out to be collections of individual parables and aphorisms, often assembled in compounds and clusters, and then alternated with discrete anecdotes in arbitrary sequences. Scholars who specialize in form criticism sort the individual anecdotes into story types: call stories, pronouncement stories, controversy stories, healing stories, exorcisms, nature wonders, and epiphanies. These constitute the lore about Jesus that circulated prior to the creation of the written gospels. Such discrete stories are the oral components of the gospel tradition. It is to these individual stories that scholars primarily look for historical data.

THE ORAL COMPONENTS

Stories told about Jesus are sorted into types based on form and content. The study of story types is known as form criticism; form criticism has to do with the formation and transmission of folklore or oral tradition. When people tell stories they tend to follow certain story patterns depending on the type of story and the content.

Because story patterns overlap at certain points, it is not possible to create an inventory with entirely clean lines. We will describe the various types of stories found in the gospels, provide some examples of each, and then refer the reader to more complete inventories at the back of this volume (pp. 556–68).

Parables and aphorisms

The parables and aphorisms form the bedrock of the tradition. They represent the point of view of Jesus himself. Jesus did not tell stories about what he did; he is not the subject of his own discourse. When he told stories, he talked about prodigal sons, dinner parties, lost sheep, travelers who had been mugged, and similar events in his everyday world. Stories about what Jesus did represent the perspective of others, usually third persons, who are mostly anonymous in the gospel tradition.

There is a fundamental difference between the sayings of Jesus and stories about Jesus. The transmission of the sayings of Jesus was achieved by what was, in effect, a repetition of the original spoken event. Apart from questions of accuracy of quotation, attribution, and meaning suggested by the clustering and re-contexting of the sayings, there is intrinsically no difference between the original speaking of a saying and subsequent quotations of it. To be sure, subsequent "performances" of a parable or cluster of sayings involved a change in audience, which usually meant a change in the way the words were heard and understood.

In the case of anecdotes told *about* Jesus, on the other hand, the situation is quite different. In a miracle story, for example, the event is not *repeated* (enacted a second time) but *reported*. We are confronted not with repeated reenactment but with a report that has a history because reports involve interpretation (this is how I see it; that is how you see it). The history of "reports" in gospel scholarship is the attempt to reconstruct the various stages through which a report may have passed, including its "original" form. (The original form of a report is always a hypothetical reconstruction, since there is no way to ascertain the precise words first used to describe an event.)

Since form criticism, as a subspecies of the study of folklore, rests on the premise that stories told about figures like Jesus tend to follow certain story patterns, gospel scholars analyze the stories in order to determine to what degree particular stories adhere to the standard paradigm and how those stories are modified over a period of time. In this respect, form criticism is the study of the properties of folklore. It is helpful only for reconstructing the history of oral stories; it is of no direct use in deciding whether a story reports an actual historical event or is a fiction. To decide whether a particular story reports an historical event, the critic must employ a variety of other tools, to be sketched later.

Pronouncement stories

One small step away from the sayings are the pronouncement stories. A pronouncement story is a brief anecdote that climaxes in the pronouncement of a famous person.

An example of a very brief pronouncement story is found in Luke 9:57–58:

> As they were going along the road, someone said to him, "I'll follow you wherever you go."
>
> And Jesus said to him, "Foxes have dens, and birds of the sky have nests; but the son of Adam has nowhere to rest his head."

Lucian tells this story about Demonax, a second-century C.E. Cynic philosopher:

> On seeing two philosophers ignorantly debating a subject, one asking silly questions and the other giving answers that were not at all to the point, Demonax said, "Doesn't it seem to you, friends, that one of these fellows is milking a he-goat and the other is holding a sieve for him?"[2]

Both of these stories are examples of stories told for the sake of the witticism of a famous teacher.

The term the Greek rhetoricians used for the pronouncement story is *chreia*. *Chreiai* with famous persons as their subject were extremely common in the hellenistic age, which extends from the death of Alexander the Great in 323 B.C.E. to the Council of Nicea in 325 C.E.

The pronouncement stories are inherently more plausible historically than other kinds of stories about Jesus, since we are reasonably certain that Jesus was a sage who taught in parables and aphorisms and made use of irony and wit. Beyond the authentic parables and sayings, scholars tend to look to the pronouncement stories for traces of the historical figure of Jesus. There are thirty-one of these anecdotes in the Gospel of Mark alone. A selection of them may be found in Table 1.

Table 1

Pronouncement Stories

1. John's inquiry
   Luke 7:18–23, Matt 11:2–6
2. Praise of John
   Luke 7:24–28, Matt 11:7–11
3. Beelzebul controversy
   Luke 11:14–23, Matt 12:22–32; Mark 3:20–30
4. Foxes have dens
   Luke 9:57–62, Matt 8:18–22
5. Jesus tours Galilee
   Mark 1:35–39, Luke 4:42–44
6. Dining with sinners
   Mark 2:15–17, Matt 9:10–13, Luke 5:29–32, GosFr 1224 5:1–2
7. Question of fasting
   Mark 2:18–22, Matt 9:14–17, Luke 5:33–39
8. Sabbath observance
   Mark 2:23–28, Matt 12:1–8, Luke 6:1–5
9. True relatives
   Mark 3:31–35, Matt 12:46–50, Luke 8:19–21; Thom 99:1–3
10. No respect at home
   Mark 6:1–6, Matt 13:54–58
11. Eating with defiled hands
   Mark 7:1–13, Matt 15:1–9
12. Demand for a sign
   Mark 8:11–13, Matt 16:1–4; Matt 12:38–40, Luke 11:29–30
13. Elijah as precursor
   Mark 9:9–13, Matt 17:9–13
14. Dispute about greatness
   Mark 9:33–37, Matt 18:1–5, Luke 9:46–48
15. By what authority?
   Mark 11:27–33, Matt 21:23–27, Luke 20:1–8
16. Emperor & God
   Mark 12:13–17, Matt 22:15–22, Luke 20:21–26, Thom 100:1–4, EgerG 3:1–6
17. On the resurrection
   Mark 12:18–27, Matt 22:23–33, Luke 20:27–40
18. Most important commandment
   Mark 12:28–34, Matt 22:34–40; Luke 10:25–29
19. Son of David
   Mark 12:35–37, Matt 22:41–46, Luke 20:41–44
20. Widow's pittance
   Mark 12:41–44, Luke 21:1–4

Table 2

Controversy Stories

1. Paralytic and four
   Mark 2:1–12, Matt 9:1–8, Luke 5:17–26
2. Question of fasting
   Mark 2:18–22, Matt 9:14–17, Luke 5:33–39
3. Sabbath observance
   Mark 2:23–28, Matt 12:1–8, Luke 6:1–5
4. Man with crippled hand
   Mark 3:1–6, Matt 12:9–14, Luke 6:6–11, GNaz 4
5. Is divorce permitted?
   Mark 10:2–12, Matt 19:3–8
6. The man with money
   Mark 10:17–31, Matt 19:16–30, Luke 18:18–23, GNaz 6:1–5
7. By what authority?
   Mark 11:27–33, Matt 21:23–27, Luke 20:1–8
8. Emperor & God
   Mark 12:13–17, Matt 22:15–22, Luke 20:19–26, Thom 100:1–4, EgerG 3:1–6
9. On the resurrection
   Mark 12:18–27, Matt 22:23–33, Luke 20:27–40
10. Most important commandment
    Mark 12:28–34, Matt 22:34–40; Luke 10:25–29
11. Disputed inheritance
    Luke 12:13–15, Thom 72:1–3
12. Afflicted woman
    Luke 13:10–21
13. Man with dropsy
    Luke 14:1–6f

Controversy stories

Another kind of anecdote is the controversy story. Such stories are occasioned by the cures Jesus performs, by his behavior or that of his disciples, or by questions put to Jesus. They are often a variation on the pronouncement story. An example of a controversy prompted by a cure is the account of the man with the crippled hand (Mark 3:1–6):

> Then he went back to the synagogue, and a fellow with a crippled hand
> was there. [2]So they kept an eye on him, to see whether he would heal the
> fellow on the sabbath day, so they could denounce him. [3]And he says to
> the fellow with the crippled hand, "Get up here in front of everybody."
> [4]Then he asks them, "On the sabbath day is it permitted to do good or to
> do evil, to save life or to destroy it?"
>
> But they maintained their silence. [5]And looking right at them with
> anger, exasperated at their obstinacy, he says to the fellow, "Hold out
> your hand!"
>
> He held it out and his hand was restored. [6]Then the Pharisees went
> right out with the Herodians and hatched a plot against him, to get rid of
> him.

The memorable "pronouncement" of Jesus is the question posed in v. 4. The controversy turns on whether it is permitted to cure a crippled hand on the sabbath. This controversy story is thus a pronouncement story combined with a cure. A selection of these controversy stories may be found in Table 2.

Miracle stories

Stories of Jesus' exorcisms, miraculous cures, and nature wonders are often grouped together as *miracle stories.* Like the pronouncement story, or *chreia,* the miracle story was borrowed from the wider cultural repertoire, both Jewish and pagan. Similar stories were told about other charismatic teachers and healers, including many Christian heroes in the book of Acts and other later documents. We shall have reference to several of these stories in the commentary and cameos.

Exorcisms and cures are occasionally framed as pronouncement stories, so there is the combination of miracle and pronouncement, creating a mixed type. The cure of the paralytic in Mark 2:1–12 exhibits a miracle story combined with a pronouncement story.

The gospels report six exorcisms performed by Jesus (Table 3), although one of them, Matt 9:32–34, may be no more than a duplicate of Matt 12:22–23, which will serve as a brief example:

> Then they brought to him a blind and mute person who was demon possessed, and he cured him so the mute was able both to speak and to see. And the entire crowd was beside itself and would say, "This fellow can't be the son of David, can he?"

No exorcisms are reported in the Fourth Gospel.

There are nineteen stories of cures and resuscitations in the gospels (Table 4). Resuscitations are grouped with cures because it is sometimes difficult to tell whether a patient has died and is being resuscitated, or is in a coma (Jesus says of Jairus' daughter, for example, that she is not dead but sleeping, Mark 5:39, whereas observers report that she had died, Mark 5:35). The same ambiguity pertains to the revival of the young man at Bethany in Secret Mark (1:1–13).

One example of a cure is this brief account (Mark 1:29–31):

Table 3

Exorcisms

1. Blind mute
   Luke 11:14–15, Matt 12:22–23
2. Unclean demon at Capernaum
   Mark 1:23–28, Luke 4:33–37
3. Gerasene demon
   Mark 5:1–20, Matt 8:28–34, Luke 8:26–39
4. Greek woman's daughter
   Mark 7:24–30, Matt 15:21–28
5. Man with mute spirit
   Mark 9:14–29, Matt 17:14–20, Luke 9:37–43
6. Man with mute demon
   Matt 9:32–34

> They left the synagogue right away and entered the house of Simon and Andrew along with James and John. Simon's mother-in-law was in bed with a fever, and they told him about her right away. He went up to her, took hold of her hand, raised her up, and the fever disappeared. Then she started looking after them.

Stories of Jesus' cures commonly follow standard patterns. In addition to the mixed pattern mentioned earlier, there is a common form that consists of the introduction of the patient, often with some mention of the gravity of the malady, followed by some contact with the healer or thaumaturge or exorcist, including a healing word or the use of a healing technique. The story climaxes with a demonstration on the part of the patient that a cure has in fact taken place. In the story just quoted, Peter's mother-in-law demonstrates her cure by serving her guests.

Table 4

Cures and Resuscitations

1. Officer's slave/son
   Luke 7:1–10, Matt 8:5–13, John 4:45–54
2. Peter's mother-in-law
   Mark 1:29–31, Matt 8:14–15, Luke 5:38–39
3. Leper
   Mark 1:40–45, Matt 8:1–4, Luke 5:12–16, EgerG 2:1–4
4. Paralytic
   Mark 2:1–12, Matt 9:1–8, Luke 5:17–26
5. Man with a withered hand
   Mark 3:1–6, Matt 12:9–14, Luke 6:6–11
6. Jairus' daughter
   Mark 5:21–24a, 35–43, Matt 9:18–19, 23–26, Luke 8:40–42a, 49–55
7. Woman with a vaginal hemorrhage
   Mark 5:24b–34, Matt 9:20–22, Luke 8:42b–48
8. Deaf mute
   Mark 7:31–37
9. The blind man of Bethsaida
   Mark 8:22–26
10. Revival of the young man at Bethany
    SecMark 1:1–13
11. Blind Bartimaeus
    Mark 10:46–52, Matt 20:29–34, Luke 18:35–43
12. Two blind men
    Matt 9:27–31
13. Widow's son at Nain
    Luke 7:11–17
14. Afflicted woman
    Luke 13:10–17
15. Man with dropsy
    Luke 14:1–6
16. Ten lepers
    Luke 17:11–19
17. Paralytic by the pool
    John 5:1–9
18. Man born blind
    John 9:1–7
19. Raising of Lazarus
    John 11:1–44

Table 5

Nature Wonders

1. Stilling the storm
   Mark 4:35–41, Matt 8:23–27, Luke 8:22–25
2. Loaves & fish for 5,000
   Mark 6:35–44, Matt 14:15–21, Luke 9:12–17, John 6:1–15
3. Walking on the water
   Mark 6:47–52, Matt 14:24–33, John 6:16–21
4. Loaves & fish for 4,000
   Mark 8:1–10, Matt 15:32–39
5. Fig tree without figs
   Mark 11:12–14, 20–25, Matt 21:18–22
6. Miraculous catch of fish
   Luke 5:1–11
7. Water into wine
   John 2:1–11

The nature wonders are usually assigned to a special class. They do not follow the standard pattern of the healing story or exorcism. And they are readily distinguished by their content. Among the best known of these tales are the stilling of the storm (Mark 4:35–41), Jesus walking on the water (Mark 6:47–52), and the transformation of water into wine (John 2:1–11). The gospels relate accounts of at least seven nature wonders. An inventory of these nature wonders appears in Table 5.

Call and commissioning stories

Another type of story found in the gospels is the call or commissioning story. Examples abound in the Hebrew bible. The call of Isaiah in Isa 6:1–13 is a classic example. In the gospels Jesus is represented as enlisting disciples (Mark 1:16–18):

> As he was walking along by the Sea of Galilee, he spotted Simon and Andrew, Simon's brother, casting their nets into the sea—since they were fishermen—and Jesus said to them: "Become my followers and I'll have you fishing for people!"
>
> And right then and there they abandoned their nets and followed him.

That is a call story at its simplest. Matt 28:16–20 is a commissioning story of a somewhat more complex nature. Table 6 (p. 16) provides a partial catalogue of the call and commissioning stories.

Legends

A sixth group of stories may be termed legends. Legends may be subdivided into two sub-types: biographical legends and cult legends. A biographical legend is a story that casts a supernatural aura around the hero. The temptation story is a biographical legend. A cult legend accounts in story form for the

Table 6

Call and Commissioning Stories

1. Call of Simon and Andrew
   Mark 1:16–18, Matt 4:18–20
2. Call of James and John
   Mark 1:19–20, Matt 4:21–22
3. Call of Levi
   Mark 2:13–14, Matt 9:9, Luke 5:27–28, GEbi 2:4
4. Call of the twelve
   Mark 3:13–19, Matt 10:1–4, Luke 6:12–16, GEbi 2
5. Mission of the twelve
   Mark 6:7–13, Matt 10:1, 5–15, Luke 9:1–6; Luke 10:1–16
6. Fishing for people
   Luke 5:1–11
7. Call of Andrew & Peter
   John 1:35–42
8. Call of Philip & Nathanael
   John 1:43–51
9. Appearance to the eleven
   Matt 28:16–20; Luke 24:36–49; John 20:19–23; PsMk 16:14–18
10. Appearance to seven
    John 21:1–14
11. Call of Paul
    Acts 9:1–19; Acts 22:3–16; Acts 26:9–19

establishment of some ritual practice in the Jesus movement. The depiction of the last supper is just such a cult legend.

Legends also include what are known as epiphanies. The transfiguration, where Jesus is seen walking and talking with Moses and Elijah in a transformed state, and the baptism of Jesus, at which the spirit descends from the sky and comes to rest on Jesus, are epiphanies. Epiphanies are stories in which the divine is represented as coming in contact with or becoming visible to the human. Both of these epiphanies are biographical legends. A partial catalogue of legends may be found in Table 7.

Our understanding of the characteristics of each of the story types has evolved over the last century, with the result that we now see the gospel tradition as more complex and varied than did the early form critics.

THE COMPOSITION OF THE GOSPELS

In evaluating the gospel tradition, the first critical step scholars take is to ascertain the relationship of the written gospels to each other. The second, equally important step is to segregate the oral traditions from the framing stories employed by Christian scribes to turn the collection of individual events into a continuous narrative. The third step in the critical process is to classify the oral stories into story types and reconstruct the history of each.

We have begun with the third step. Before proceeding to the question of the reconstruction of the history of individual stories, we must pause and consider the first and second steps.

Table 7

Legends

1. John baptizes Jesus
   Mark 1:9–11, Matt 3:13–17, Luke 3:21–22; John 1:29–34; GNaz 2; GEbi 4; GHeb 3
2. The temptation of Jesus
   Luke 4:1–13, Matt 4:1–11; Mark 1:12–13
3. Rejection at Nazareth
   Luke 4:16–30
4. Fishing for people
   Luke 5:1–11
5. Peter's confession
   Mark 8:27–30, Matt 16:13–20, Luke 9:18–22
6. Jesus predicts his death
   Mark 8:31–33, Matt 16:21–23, Luke 9:18–22
7. Transfiguration
   Mark 9:2–8, Matt 17:1–8, Luke 9:28–36
8. Jesus predicts his death again
   Mark 9:30–32, Matt 17:22–23, Luke 9:43–45
9. Jesus predicts his death a third time
   Mark 10:32–34, Matt 20:17–19, Luke 18:31–34
10. The last supper
    Mark 14:22–26, Matt 26:26–30, Luke 22:14–20; 1 Cor 11:23–26
11. Gethsemane
    Mark 14:32–42, Matt 26:36–46, Luke 22:39–46
12. Empty tomb
    Mark 16:1–8, Matt 28:1–8, Luke 24:1–12; John 20:3–10; Pet 12:1–13:3
13. Bribing of the guards
    Matt 28:11–15; Pet 11:1–7
14. Appearance to Mary of Magdala
    Matt 28:9–10; John 20:11–18; Pseudo-Mark 16:9–11
15. Appearance to two in the country
    Luke 24:13–35, Pseudo-Mark 16:12–13
16. Appearance to the eleven
    Matt 28:16–20; Luke 24:36–49; John 20:19–23; Pseudo-Mark 16:14–18
17. Doubting Thomas
    John 20:24–29
18. Appearance to seven
    John 21:1–14
19. Appearance to James, Jesus' brother
    GHeb 9:1–4
20. Ascension
    Luke 24:50–53; Pseudo-Mark 16:19–20; Acts 1:1–11
21. Birth & infancy stories
    Matt 1:18–2:23; Luke 1:7–2:52

Gospel relationships

Mark is believed to be the earliest of the narrative gospels. As previously noted, Mark was probably created out of oral stories and clusters of sayings (Figure 1, p. 18), although the author of Mark may have had access to some fragmentary written traditions. Scholarly opinion is divided on what, if any, those written sources might have been.

Matthew and Luke made use of Mark as the narrative outline for their com-

Figure 1

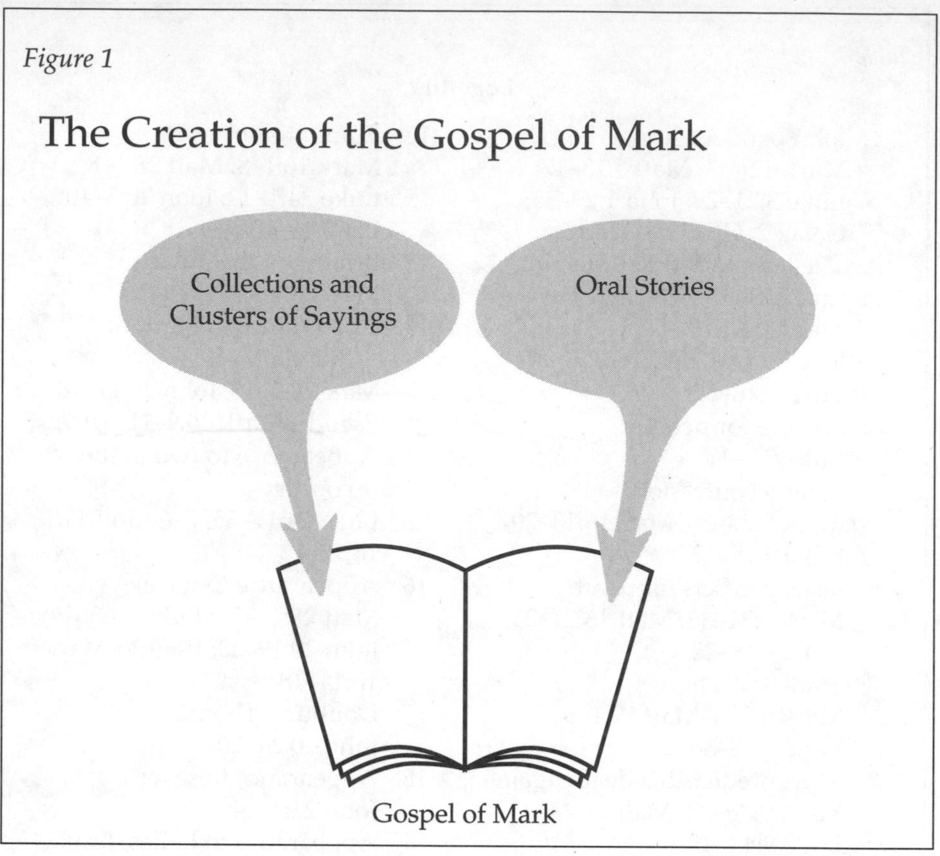

positions. When Mark is subtracted from Matthew and Luke, there remains a substantial body of common lore, mostly sayings, that the two evangelists must have borrowed from another written source. That source is now referred to as the Sayings Gospel Q. Q did not survive as a separate written gospel, so its contents have to be reconstructed from Matthew and Luke. At a few points Q seems to have overlapped with the Gospel of Mark. It is probable that Matthew and Luke also drew on oral tradition to a limited extent in augmenting the material they had taken from Mark and Q.

This theory is known as the two-source theory and is represented graphically in Figure 2.

Some scholars have argued that Matthew and Luke may also have had access to two fragmentary written collections of sayings and stories. These special sources known to Matthew and Luke respectively brings the number of sources to four. The four-source theory is merely a modest modification of the two-source theory.

Most of the Fellows of the Jesus Seminar subscribe to either the two-source or the four-source theory. They are therefore a part of a broad scholarly consensus. Because Matthew and Luke are derivative gospels—dependent on earlier written gospels—the Fellows assume that Matthew and Luke are not providing additional historical information when they are copying from Mark or

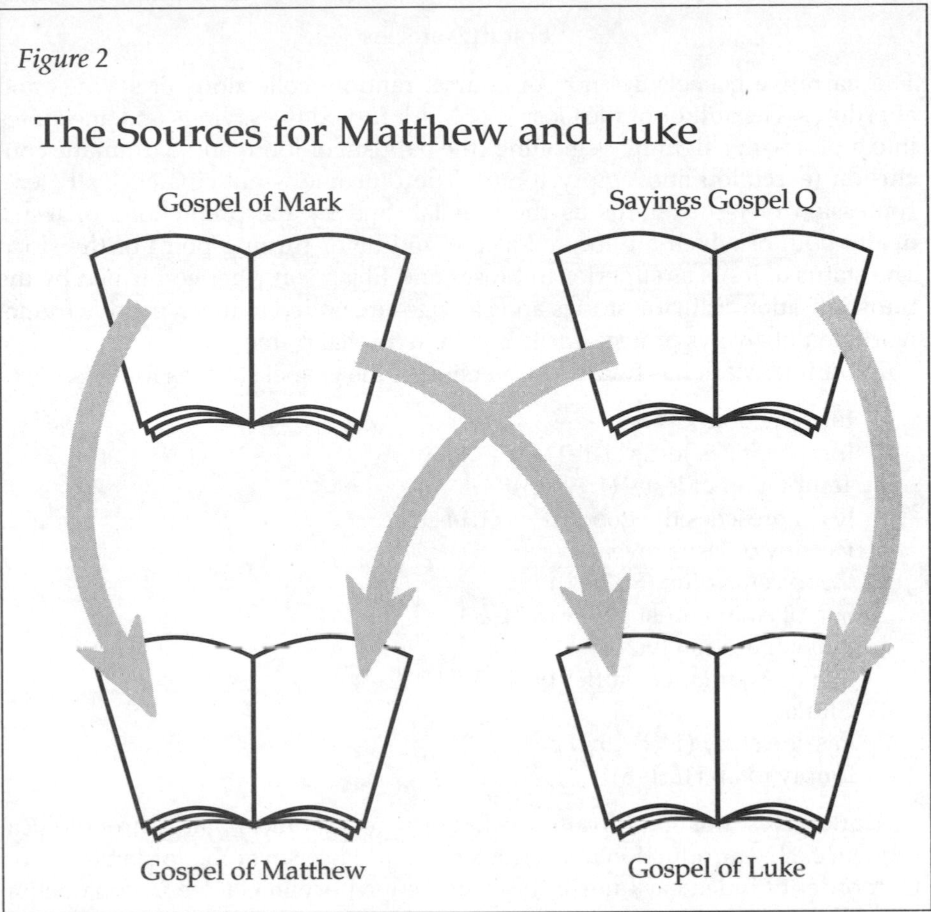

from Q. The occasional traditions not derived from Mark and Q have to be evaluated independently.

The present state of scholarly opinion on the relation of the Gospel of John to other written gospels is in flux. Some scholars claim that the author of John knew Mark and perhaps Luke; others take the view that the present gospel is based on an earlier gospel of "signs" that had a number of stories in common with the synoptic gospels. This particular view is elaborated in the cameo, "A Gospel of Miracles?" (pp. 388–89). Whatever the compositional theory, however, the Fourth Gospel is not thought to provide independent historical attestation of events in the life of Jesus. The narrative terrain of this gospel is accordingly black territory for the most part.

The situation with respect to the Gospel of Peter is even more uncertain. Some scholars have concluded that Peter is an epitome of the canonical passion stories. Other experts claim that Peter is composite—made up of both earlier and later strata. The earlier layers antedate the New Testament gospels; the later strata are dependent on the New Testament gospels. In either case, Peter does not appear to provide independently attested historical data. Its reports, like those of the Gospel of John, the Fellows frequently colored black.

Framing stories

The narrative gospels are not, of course, random collections of sayings and anecdotes. The author of the Gospel of Mark turned the sayings and anecdotes into a plot with a definite beginning (the baptism of John) and a dramatic conclusion (execution and empty tomb). The outcome is anticipated by Peter's confession of Jesus' status as the messiah and by the predictions of Jesus' death, both of which are located at the middle or turning point of the story. The status of Jesus as superior to Moses and Elijah is further confirmed by the transfiguration. Still, the stories and sayings embedded in this narrative framework do not always or necessarily cohere with that frame.

In outline, Mark has framed his version of the gospel story as follows:

1. Introduction
   John baptizes Jesus (1:1–11)
   Temptation of Jesus (1:12–13)
   Jesus preaches the good news (1:14–15)
2. Destiny of Jesus revealed
   Good confession (8:27–30)
   Son of Adam must suffer (8:31–33)
   Transfiguration (9:2–8)
   Son of Adam must suffer (9:30–32, 10:32–34)
3. Climax
   Passion story (14:1–15:47)
   Empty tomb (16:1–8)

Mark gives this plot framework both geographical and chronological sequence. His introduction takes Jesus from his baptism at the Jordan River on the border of Judea back north to his home territory in Galilee in conjunction with the arrest of the Baptist. The turning point at the Transfiguration in the middle of the story reveals Jesus' destiny just as he begins his journey south to arrive in Jerusalem at the time of Passover.

Matthew and Luke follow this overall plot development, but the Fourth Gospel shares only the beginning and ending events—Jesus' encounter with John the Baptist and his death in Jerusalem. After Jesus' contact with John—Jesus' baptism is not narrated and John has not yet been put in prison—Jesus returns momentarily to Galilee before he heads to Jerusalem for Passover. Jesus returns to Galilee briefly twice more, but soon returns to Jerusalem each time for major festivals. He is still in Jerusalem when the next Passover approaches, but is executed before it begins.

Both the synoptic sequence of events and the arrangement of the Fourth Gospel cannot be equally historical. Jesus cannot have spent most of his public life in Galilee and made one final, fatal trip to Jerusalem, and yet also have spent most of his final two years in Jerusalem with only brief trips to Galilee.

Within his plot structure, Mark groups the various kinds of vignettes and connects them together largely in accordance with his own theological interests and without regard to chronological sequence. For example, he has collected parables into a long cluster in Mark 4:1–34 and given them an artificial

ASCLEPIUS, GOD OF HEALING

Ancient Greece popularized both the science of medicine and the art of faith healing. Many doctors, in the tradition of Hippocrates (died fourth c. B.C.E.), offered medicinal diagnoses to patients. Those not cured were attracted to sacred locations associated with faith healers.

The most famous legendary healer was Asclepius, son of Apollo, the god of healing. His symbol was the staff with a snake wrapped around it. Numerous spas and temples were built in honor of Asclepius around the Mediterranean world. The sick bathed in the natural springs and slept in the temple, waiting for Asclepius to visit them in a dream. Once cured, patients left offerings with inscriptions describing their miraculous healing. The statue seen here is a replica from the best-known healing center, Epidauros, near Corinth, which was alleged to be his birthplace.

The Gospel of Mark also pictures Jesus as a healer of those without hope from doctors (Mark 5:25–26). Jesus was noted, however, as an itinerant who refused to be associated with special locations. Instead he told those healed to become healers themselves (Luke 10:9; Thom 14:4).

Asclepius, like Jesus, later became the subject of anecdotes. Lucian tells this one involving Demonax, a second-century C.E. Cynic philosopher:

> When one of his friends said, "Demonax, let's go to the Asclepeion and pray for my son," he replied, "You must think Asclepius very deaf, that he can't hear our prayers from where we are!"

Photo courtesy of Ambrose Edens.

narrative setting. The anecdotes themselves are frequently grouped into sequences exhibiting the same or similar form or subject matter. A series of controversy stories has been assembled in Mark 2:1–3:6. Needless to say, Jesus did not have all of his controversies in one unrelieved sequence, any more than he spoke an unrelieved string of parables on a single occasion. In similar fashion, the other evangelists modified Mark and Q to suit their special concerns. Matthew has assembled a lengthy compendium of Jesus' teachings into a single discourse, known as the sermon on the mount (Matt 5:1–7:28). To cite yet another example of clustering, Luke has constructed a travelogue of Jesus' journey from Galilee to Jerusalem, into which he has gathered numerous materials (9:51–19:27), the final part of which he has borrowed from Mark (18:15–19:27). Very little in the grouping and sequencing of materials contains reliable chronological information.

Narrator asides, transitions, and summaries

In addition to drawing on oral reports and written materials, the narrator occasionally intrudes directly into the story. Such an intrusion may take the form of an aside in which the narrator addresses the reader directly in order to supply a piece of necessary or interesting information. When Mark relates that Jesus' relatives came to get him, he explains: "You see, they thought he was out of his mind" (Mark 3:21). Or, the narrator may decide, at an appropriate point in the story, to sum matters up:

> And Jesus went about all the towns and villages, teaching in their synagogues and proclaiming the gospel of Heaven's imperial rule and healing every disease and ailment. Matt 9:35

Since such asides and summaries are the work of the individual evangelists, they have to be assessed independently. To pass muster as reliable historical data, the information they contain has to be corroborated by direct evidence found in segments that could have been derived from oral tradition. Table 8 furnishes an abbreviated inventory of such narrator contributions.

In the summary just quoted, for example, Jesus is represented as an itinerant. The Fellows of the Jesus Seminar, in concert with many other scholars, think that is a correct observation: nearly all the individual stories told about Jesus indicate that he wandered about teaching and healing. Scholars also generally agree that Jesus spoke about "Heaven's imperial rule." Nevertheless, Matthew's summary in the text cited exaggerates: Jesus probably did not visit *all* the towns and villages, and he probably did not cure *every* disease and ailment. Because of the exaggerations, the Fellows colored this summary pink rather than red.

Three other components have gone into the composition of the narrative gospels: the passion narrative, stories of the empty tomb and appearances of the risen Jesus, and birth and infancy tales. These components have a different status than the individual anecdotes comprising the gospel tradition. They were developed rather late in the emerging gospel tradition and present the historian with difficulties peculiar to themselves.

Table 8

Transitions and Summaries

1. Cures & exorcisms
   Mark 1:32–24, Matt 8:16–17, Luke 4:40–41
2. Jesus tours Galilee
   Matt 4:23–25
3. Jesus heals the multitudes
   Mark 3:7–12, Matt 12:15–21, Luke 6:17–19
4. Many sick are cured
   Mark 6:53–56, Matt 14:34–36
5. Jesus departs for Judea
   Mark 10:1, Matt 19:1–2
6. Narrative summary
   Matt 9:35
7. Narrative transition
   Matt 11:1
8. Jesus heals many
   Matt 15:29–31
9. Woman companions of Jesus
   Luke 8:1–3
10. Jesus' daily routine
    Luke 21:37–38
11. Many miracles
    John 2:23–25
12. Narrative recap
    John 12:37–43

Passion narrative

The passion narrative—the story of Jesus' arrest, trial, execution, and burial—is actually an appendix to the assemblage of materials that forms the body of the gospel. It was once thought that the passion narrative was the first part of the gospels to have been reduced to writing. At the end of the nineteenth century, the narrative gospels were described as passion narratives with lengthy introductions. In the judgment of many scholars, the chronological relationship between the two has been reversed: the narrative gospels are now regarded as collections of anecdotes, parables, and sayings with an extended appendix depicting the passion. In other words, the passion narrative was not the first part of the gospels to be developed.

The passion is regarded as the work of scribes, who were probably not part of the original circle of illiterate peasant followers and believers. The passion was created by scripturally sophisticated apologists sitting at their writing desks creating a narrative largely out of the fact of Jesus' execution coupled with suggestions derived from prophetic texts and the Psalms and inspired by tales of the suffering righteous heroes of Israel. Scholars have not been able to agree on the ingredients that made up the first passion story, nor is there a consensus on the relationship of one passion story to another. In general, however, beyond the basic facts—arrest, execution—very little in the passion narrative is now believed to be based on historical memory.

Empty tomb and appearance stories

The passion is followed by stories of the empty tomb, the appearances of the risen Jesus, and the ascension. The story of the empty tomb and depictions of the appearances of the risen Jesus to his followers come late in the emergence of the gospels. The Gospel of Mark has an empty tomb, but the author does not narrate any appearances of the risen Jesus. Indeed, the telltale evidence pointing to the priority of Mark is that the agreement between Matthew and Luke begins where Mark begins (Mark has no birth and childhood stories) and ends where Mark ends (Mark has no appearance stories). The five gospels that report appearances (Matthew, Luke, John, Peter, Gospel of the Hebrews) go their separate ways when they are not rewriting Mark; their reports cannot be reconciled to each other. Hard historical evidence is sparse.

Birth and infancy stories

Matthew and Luke have prefaced their gospels with two sets of birth and infancy stories that cannot readily be reconciled with each other. The birth and infancy narratives were developed last in the creation of the gospels. A little later, two other infancy gospels were composed: The Infancy Gospel of Thomas, which depicts a precocious young Jesus working miracles on every hand, and the Infancy Gospel of James, which relates the story of Mary's birth and childhood, before telling of the birth of Jesus. There is virtually no historical information in any of these tales.

Put in the broadest possible terms, the narrative gospels are made up of layered traditions, some oral, some written, piled on top of each other. At the bottom—in the earliest stratum—Jesus talks about the kingdom of God. Nearly all scholars consent to this generalization. In the same texts we find the disciples of Jesus talking about Jesus talking about God's imperial rule. At the next level, members of the early Jesus movement tell stories about the disciples talking about Jesus talking about God's domain. At the last stage in the written gospels, the evangelists represent their own communities reflecting on their appropriation of what the disciples had said about Jesus, who himself talked about God's kingdom in parables and aphorisms. Close observations regarding the layering of the tradition lie at the base of most critical assessments of the historical reliability of each gospel segment.

TRACKING THE ORAL TRADITION

The dismantling of the gospels and the isolation of units of oral tradition is the first huge step in the process of tracking the tradition back to its beginnings. When confronted with lists of stories that presumably circulated in oral form, scholars must next ask, How do we know we are dealing with oral stories? Even when it has been determined that a particular story antedates the composition of the written gospels, scholars face yet another question: How do we recover or reconstruct the earliest version of individual stories? Early versions, or what are thought to be early versions, must pass a further test: Are the scenes depicted in these stories historically plausible? And finally, the bottom line for scholars engaged in the quest of the historical Jesus is to determine how they can extract reliable historical information from their reconstructed tales.

These questions run through the detailed analyses prepared by the Fellows of the Jesus Seminar as they examined story after story over a six-year period.

The marks of oral stories

Seminar members searched among their inventories for stories that were clearly older than the written sources in which they are preserved. One way to ascertain whether stories antedate their written sources is to ask whether those stories appear in two or more independent sources. That fact would establish that such stories were older than the sources in which they are preserved. In *The Acts of Jesus* the marginal notations for each segment indicate what is believed to be the source or sources for that segment. The notation for the Beelzebul controversy, for example, reads:

Mk 3:20–30
Mt 12:22–32, Lk 11:14–23
Sources: Mark, Q

which tells the reader that the story is found in both Mark and Q. Since Mark and Q are believed to be independent sources for the Jesus tradition, it is highly probable that some account of the Beelzebul controversy circulated in the oral period.

Outside the passion narrative that presents a special set of problems, the inventory of the acts of Jesus (pp. 556–68) contains only eleven stories that are doubly attested:

1. The temptation of Jesus (Q, Mark)
2. Officer's son/slave (Q, John)
3. Beelzebul controversy (Q, Mark)
4. The leper (Mark, Egerton)
5. Dining with sinners (Mark, GosFr 1224)
6. True relatives (Mark, Thomas)
7. Mission of the twelve (Mark, Q)
8. Walking on the water (Mark, John)
9. Loaves and fish for 5,000/4,000 (Mark, John)
10. Jesus enters Jerusalem (Mark, John)
11. Temple incident (Mark, John)

Even in this short list, the double attestation of the last four events rests on the assumption that the author of the Fourth Gospel did not know the Gospel of Mark, and that walking on the water and loaves and fish for 5,000/4,000 did not derive from a gospel of miracles known to both Mark and John.

In addition to the eleven stories doubly attested, four are triply attested:

1. A voice in the wilderness (Mark, Q, John)
2. Demand for a sign (Mark, Q, John)
3. Emperor & God (Mark, Thomas, Egerton Gospel)
4. Anointing of Jesus (Mark, Luke, John)

It is unfortunate for the historian that most of the stories listed in the inventory of acts are attested solely by the Gospel of Mark.

In the case of the sayings of Jesus, it is sometimes claimed that attestation in more than one context is also prima facie evidence that the saying is older than the written gospel in which it is preserved. Not many acts fall into this category, but the temple incident is one example. It appears at the beginning of Jesus' public ministry in the Gospel of John (2:13–22) and near the close of Jesus' public life in Mark (14:15–19). The anointing of Jesus also appears in different contexts in Mark (14:3–9) and Luke (7:36–50). The temple incident is also doubly attested, the anointing triply attested.

There are also internal criteria that help scholars identify oral tradition. Oral stories tend to be short, compact, narrated with a parsimony of words. They have simple plots, involving no more than three characters. They are also self-contained: they do not require any information provided by the narrative sequence in which they appear. To be sure, the individual evangelists often link such stories to the preceding or following episodes to give their narratives greater coherence. A close comparison of the way synoptic writers handle the beginning and end of stories often points to the origin of stories.

Performance as gist; nucleus as core

It is a general rule in the study of folklore that oral storytellers reproduce the gist of stories in their oral performances; they do not memorize and repeat tales word for word. This rule is supported by observing how Matthew and Luke treat stories taken from their source, Mark: they tend to reproduce the nucleus of a story—the core event—with greater fidelity than the introduction or conclusion. They often rewrite the introductions to link particular stories to their own narrative contexts, and they revamp conclusions to accommodate their specific sequence of events or theological interpretations. As a consequence, historical reminiscence is likely to be found in the nucleus of stories, if anywhere; particular performances of the introductions and conclusions will tend to reflect the storyteller's or narrator's interests, convictions, and audience.

Reconstructing the earliest version

Form critics attempt to map the history of oral stories by reconstructing their hypothetical earliest performance. This is a difficult task under the best of circumstances. However, it is much easier when two versions of the same story derive from independent sources. The story of the official's son or slave (Luke 7:1–10//Matt 8:5–13; John 4:45–54) is illustrative of the problems faced.

The story is attested in two sources, Q and the Gospel of John. Most scholars assume that the two versions are variants of the same event. Yet the versions differ widely in details—in setting, in participants, even in core event.

Matthew and Luke agree in calling the petitioner a centurion (a Roman officer); for John he is a royal official. In Matthew and Luke, Jesus has just entered Capernaum when the centurion/official approaches him; in John, Jesus is located in Cana and the official has come there from Capernaum to enlist his help. The centurion is a gentile in Matthew and Luke; in John, it is possible that he is a Jew. The victim is a slave or servant in Luke; in Matthew, he is referred to ambiguously as a "boy"; the version in the Fourth Gospel pictures him as the son of the royal official.

The illness suffered by the victim varies: In Matthew the servant is paralyzed; in Luke the illness is unspecified, although the slave is on the point of death; in John the son is afflicted with a fever. Since there is no direct encounter between Jesus and the victim, the story is not, strictly speaking, a healing story. A conventional miracle story requires some contact and some word about healing technique. Finally, neither the petitioner nor the patient confirms that a cure has taken place; a cure is reported only indirectly by others—servants or friends or the narrator. The "cure" could be understood as a coincidence: the boy or slave got well while his father or owner was talking to Jesus miles away. The coincidence was of course reported by the evangelists and storytellers before them as a miracle.

The historian's suspicions are aroused when it is observed that the narrative appears to give voice to a christological confession based on the model of the Roman patronage system. Jesus is acclaimed as a healer because he, like the centurion, is viewed as the broker of a higher power. By asking Jesus to heal his boy and then describing the patronage system in Roman Palestine, the centurion reveals his belief that Jesus occupies the same mediating function vis-à-vis God as he, the centurion, occupies with respect to Caesar. Jesus is amazed that the centurion has come to view him as he does: "Let me tell you, not even in Israel have I found such trust" (Luke 7:9). Because the story expresses a confession of faith in the powerful brokerage function of Jesus, it has crossed the line from a bare report of a miraculous cure to reflection on the status of Jesus. As a result, some scholars have concluded that the story is neither a simple miracle story nor a report about an event in the life of the historical Jesus, but a story created to justify a mission to the gentiles (assuming that the centurion was a gentile).

In view of the difficulties in establishing even a hypothetical first form of the story, the Fellows decided to designate the Q version black in both its Matthean and Lukan forms. They gave a gray rating to the account in the Fourth Gospel on the grounds that the Johannine story was slightly more plausible than the Q account. The core event probably consisted of this: An official asked Jesus to cure his son (or servant) and the patient recovered.

Showing and telling

The distinction between enactment and recounting was introduced earlier. The two can also be termed "showing" and "telling." The story of Jesus' baptism in Mark 1:9–11 will illustrate the difference:

> 9During that same period Jesus came from Nazareth, Galilee, and was baptized in the Jordan by John. 10And just as he got up out of the water, he saw the skies torn open and the spirit coming down toward him like a dove. 11There was also a voice from the skies: "You are my favored son—I fully approve of you."

The baptism of Jesus is reported or recounted in v. 9: the storyteller does not depict the actual baptism. We do not know whether John administered baptism or whether Jesus immersed himself. But the story suddenly switches from reporting to showing in v. 10. Now we learn that Jesus was in the water and as he got up out of the water, he saw the skies split open and the spirit descend toward him or into him "like a dove." That sentence whisks the listener or reader away to the scene at the Jordan and allows him or her to witness what happened. Mark does not appear to take the metaphor of the dove entirely literally; Matthew moves more in that direction by having the dove light upon Jesus, while Luke adds that it was "in bodily form." In all three cases, Jesus "sees" the spirit descending.

The showing technique continues in v. 11: in addition to something seen, there is also something heard. As Matthew has it (3:17), a voice comes from the skies with an announcement: "This is my son. I fully approve of him." The hearing is not limited to Jesus; the voice is for everyone who witnessed Jesus' baptism. The voice is reproduced: the readers get to hear the actual words.

The Fellows of the Jesus Seminar decided to color v. 9 red, but they designated vv. 10–11 black. The fact that Jesus was baptized by John appears in more than one form in the gospels and is therefore probably based on historical reminiscence. On the other hand, the sights and sounds of vv. 10–11 are being supplied by the storyteller who imagines that is how the baptism of Jesus happened. The storyteller could not have known what Jesus saw, and it is doubtful that those standing around at the time heard those precise words in Greek (the tongue of the original observers at the event was Aramaic). Recall, too, that this is the form of the story that Mark knew or related almost fifty years after the event.

Dramatic plausibility

For enacted scenes to be convincing historically, they must be dramatically plausible. Dramatic plausibility requires that the coincidence of setting, participants, and action be realistic. In addition, anachronisms—the incorporation of elements that belong to a different time and place—strain and even invalidate dramatic plausibility.

The brief story of Jesus eating with toll collectors and sinners (Mark 2:15–17) will serve to illustrate these issues and the ways in which the Fellows elected to deal with them.

> [15]Then Jesus happens to recline at table in <Levi's> house, along with many toll collectors and sinners and Jesus' disciples. (Remember, there were many of these people and they were all following him.)
>
> [16]And whenever the Pharisees' scholars saw him eating with sinners and toll collectors, they would question his disciples: "What's he doing eating with toll collectors and sinners?"
>
> [17]When Jesus overhears, he says to them: "Since when do the able-bodied need a doctor? It's the sick who do. I did not come to enlist religious folks but sinners!"

In form this narrative segment is a pronouncement story: the brief narrative provides a setting for the sayings in v. 17. Form critics have customarily concluded that the setting is a fiction created to provide a narrative context for the sayings. They do so because the components of the scene do not fit realistically together. Anomalies involve two items: the set of participants and the continuity of time and place.

There are three participants at the dinner party: Jesus, toll collectors and sinners, and disciples. (Groups count as one if they function collectively.) Scholars who are Pharisees also appear as a fourth participant. The scene thus violates the rule of three, mentioned earlier.

There is ample evidence in both sayings and anecdotes that Jesus' original followers were regarded by his critics as "toll collectors and sinners," a stereotypical label indicating that they were thought of as socially inferior. Toll collectors were in the service of the Romans and "sinners" were those who did not observe purity codes and were thus excluded from conformist Judean society. Conformists regarded Jesus himself as a social deviant. The juxtaposition of Jesus with toll collectors and sinners is therefore historically plausible.

The category "disciples," on the other hand, appears to be an anachronism: the storyteller (or the evangelist) has added them (v. 15) in order to distinguish the disciples he knows from the "undesirables" who constituted part of the earliest circle around Jesus. As the tradition matured, the "authentic" followers of Jesus wanted to put distance between themselves and those who were regarded as "unworthy." A modern analogy would be the citizens of old penal colonies like Georgia and Australia, who no longer want to think of themselves as descendants of those who were transported to the new world as criminals. In this story as Mark tells it, the disciples are extraneous: they have no real function at the dinner party because the narrator is supplying them from his own context.

The sentence in parentheses in v. 15 is a storyteller's aside to his or her listeners. Since it is obviously the creation of the storyteller, we must be prepared to evaluate the information it provides independently of the rest of the segment.

The Pharisaic scholars are introduced in v. 16. The reader is told that they saw Jesus eating with sinners and toll collectors and so questioned his disciples about this practice. The form critic is prompted to ask: Why are they represented as questioning Jesus' disciples, when Jesus is available (in the story) for interrogation? And why is it Jesus, in fact, who answers their query? The answer form critics give is that the Pharisees in this story are a fiction. They are introduced because in the time of the storyteller the Pharisees and the disciples were at odds about whether "Christians" should eat with sinners, with those who do not observe kosher. Accordingly, both the Pharisees and the disciples are believed to belong to a later performance of this story. Nevertheless, since Jesus is the authority the disciples quote, the reply is put on his lips, as though the Pharisees had been there on the original occasion. (We do not know for sure whether there were Pharisees in Galilee in Jesus' day, or if there were, what they were like.)

An additional flaw in the narrative picture involves continuity of place: Where were the Pharisees during the dinner Jesus was allegedly eating with sinners? Were they lurking outside the room, perhaps peeking in through a window? The storyteller has not accommodated them in the space in which the event is set.

It is possible that the Pharisees heard the rumor that Jesus often dined with such folk and raised the question only later. Or perhaps they represent criticism of the practices of Jesus' followers long after Jesus' death, perhaps in the community of the evangelist. That the Pharisees did not belong to the original scene is hinted at in v. 16 by the "whenever," which suggests that incidents like this took place on more than one occasion.

In v. 17, the storyteller relates that Jesus "overhears" the Pharisees as they question his disciples. How are we to understand that scene? Are we still at the dinner party depicted in v. 15? Or is the narrator thinking of another occasion on which the Pharisees may have questioned the suitability of Jesus' table partners? Or does the evangelist merely introduce the notion that Jesus is omniscient—that he knows everything his disciples and critics are thinking and saying? This notion also adds to the implausibility of the tale.

Narrative information

As a result of anomalies of the type found in the account of Jesus eating with sinners, the Seminar was faced with a dilemma: Were the Fellows obliged to vote black on the entire story because some aspects of the scene were not historically plausible? Or could they devise a way to segregate reliable historical information in the scene from the flights of the storyteller's imagination? In order to escape from that dilemma, the Seminar had to resort to narrative analysis at a deeper level.

In such cases where a narrative scene combined incongruent elements, the Fellows extracted narrative statements from the story. Each statement contained only one piece of narrative information. Narrative statements are of two kinds: status statements (is-statements) and action statements (do-statements). The resolution of this brief narrative into status and action statements results in the following inventory (the statements are numbered for convenience of reference; A refers to actions, S to status).

A1 Jesus eats a meal in <Levi's> house.
S1 Toll collectors and sinners are present.
S2 Disciples of Jesus are also present.
S3 Toll collectors and sinners are followers of Jesus.
A2 Pharisaic scholars observe Jesus eating with toll collectors and sinners.
A3 Pharisaic scholars ask Jesus' followers about this practice.
A4 Jesus overhears the scholars.
A5 Jesus responds with an aphorism to justify his behavior.

The nucleus of this story consists of the report that Jesus ate with toll collectors and sinners, that he was criticized for it, and that he responded to such criticisms in aphorisms justifying his behavior. The narrative analysis made it possible for the Fellows to assess as fact or fiction each feature of the story along with a judgment about the historical reliability of the nucleus.

In making such judgments, the Seminar had to examine other reports and stories about Jesus' table practice and compare those reports with parables and aphorisms believed to be authentic. In so doing, they looked for evidence that the gospel tradition over its entire face supported the view that Jesus did participate in common meals with social outcasts, that he broke purity codes in so doing, and that he defended his behavior in parable and aphorism. The results of such assessments, initially prepared by individual Fellows, then reviewed and finally voted on by all the Fellows, are presented in this report as the findings of the Jesus Seminar. For convenience the narrative we have just analyzed is colored below as it appears later in this volume.

> [15]**Then Jesus happens to recline at table in <Levi's> house, along with many toll collectors and sinners and Jesus' disciples. (Remember, there were many of these people and they were all following him.)**
>
> [16]**And whenever the Pharisees' scholars saw him eating with sinners and toll collectors, they would question his disciples, "What's he doing eating with toll collectors and sinners?"**
>
> [17]**When Jesus overhears, he says to them:** "Since when do the able-bodied need a doctor? It's the sick who do. I did not come to enlist religious folks but sinners!"

"In <Levi's> house" is colored black because it is unclear that the meal in question was eaten in a particular house (the name Levi is in pointed brackets indicating that it is being supplied from the preceding narrative segment). The phrase "Jesus' disciples" is also designated black because, when distinguished from "toll collectors and sinners," it is an anachronism in the time of Jesus. The statement about Pharisees observing Jesus is colored pink, rather than red, because while we are relatively certain that Jesus had his critics in Galilee, it is uncertain that they were Pharisees.

The first part of v. 17 is again in black because it lacks dramatic plausibility—it is contrived to bring Jesus and the Pharisees into narrative proximity and to assert what was thought to be Jesus' clairvoyance. The other narrative statements were given the highest ranking (red) because they are confirmed by numerous other pieces of evidence in the gospel tradition. Even the narrator's aside in v. 15 was colored pink because it is very likely accurate, although the second half in particular is exaggerated (exaggerations are regularly reduced one color).

This extended analysis illustrates the painstaking detail with which the Fellows examined dozens of such anecdotes. It also illustrates the practice of color coding both the narrative text of the gospels and independently formulated narrative statements. Of course, it was not possible to treat every story in this detailed fashion; in many instances, the intertwining of fact and fiction made an overall gray the only viable option.

Stories told in the recounting mode were treated similarly. Narrative reports of this type are based on typifications. The stories of John the Baptist in the opening paragraphs of the synoptic gospels (Mark 1:1–8 and parallels) are all in the recounting mode—they consist of generalizations made about John: he did this, he said that. Yet the Fellows were inclined to view these reports as mostly reliable because they could be confirmed both by the sayings tradition

(Matt 11:7–8, for example) and by the testimony of Josephus, the first-century Jewish historian. Historians convict, so to speak, only on the testimony of two or more independent witnesses.

ADDITIONAL TESTS FOR HISTORICITY

The evaluation of the stories recorded by the gospels is the result of a series of criteria or tests that form a cross-hatched pattern. The criteria sketched above feature the vertical dimension of the tradition: the lines that run from written story to earliest account and original event. The Seminar also employed tests that run horizontally to the chronological line of development: they compared reports, details across the gospels. Chief among such horizontal tests was the congruence of act and word.

Words and actions

The Jesus Seminar made the assumption that Jesus was a reasonably well integrated person, that his behavior was more or less congruent with his words. On that assumption, the Seminar adopted as confirming evidence certain clues provided by his authentic speech as reported in *The Five Gospels.* From these clues a profile of the historical figure of Jesus began to emerge. A compendium of such clues derived from his sayings proved to be of inestimable help in evaluating the reports of Jesus' behavior.

The following is a checklist of things we think we know about the historical Jesus on the basis of his parables and sayings. These characteristics served as links to narratives that depicted the same or similar features.

Jesus as itinerant Several sayings suggest that Jesus was an itinerant. The Q saying "Foxes have dens, and the birds of the sky have nests; but the son of Adam has nowhere to lay his head" (Luke 9:58) is one example. Jesus' advice "Whenever you enter a town and they welcome you, eat whatever is set before you" indicates that he and his followers were frequently on the road. Typifications in the narrative portions of the gospels about Jesus wandering about from village to village appear to confirm the sayings.

Family ties that don't bind A harsh saying such as, "If any of you comes to me and does not hate your own father and mother and wife and children and brothers and sisters—yes, even your own life—you're no disciple of mine" (Luke 14:26) hints that Jesus may not have enjoyed the support of his family. Mark reports that Jesus' family thought him mad and at one point came to take him home (Mark 3:20–21, 31–35). The attitude of Jesus' family appears to be linked to his notion that conventional family ties, often extending to three or four generations, thwarted relationships in the kingdom of God.

Jesus as demon-possessed It was not just Jesus' family who thought him mad; others may also have regarded him as demon-possessed. He responds to such an accusation in Matt 12:27–29 and it is reflected elsewhere in the gospel tradition (for example, John 8:48). The convergence of the sayings with the accusation leveled against him in Mark 3:22 ("He is under the control of Beelzebul") is what induced the Fellows to color that report pink.

Jesus as exorcist The charge that Jesus was demon-possessed is connected also with the memory that he practiced exorcism. He was not the only exorcist in his day, to be sure. Yet sayings like Luke 11:19–20 ("If by God's finger I drive out demons, . . .") and Luke 10:18 ("I was watching Satan fall like lightning from heaven . . .") tended to reinforce the narrative affirmation that Jesus was an exorcist. Yet the Fellows could not identify a single report of an exorcism that they believe to be an accurate report of such an event.

Jesus as social deviant The sayings also provide substantial evidence that Jesus was a social deviant in other respects. He seems not to have observed kosher: he instructs his disciples to "eat whatever is set before you" as they wander around (Luke 10:8). That instruction is confirmed by another aphorism: "What goes into you can't defile you; what comes out of you can" (Mark 7:15). Jesus' public fraternizing with "sinners," the presence of women in his entourage, his apparent indifference to sabbath observance all mark him as a non-conformist.

An entourage of undesirables Like Jesus himself, his retinue appears to have included people who were otherwise regarded as on the social fringe. He speaks affectionately of the poor, hungry, and grieving. He seems to have had a special regard for children. Several stories reflect his contact with women in public, something that most people of his time would have regarded as deviant behavior. Examples are the story of the Greek woman's daughter (Mark 7:24–30), the woman with the internal hemorrhage (Mark 5:24–34), and the account of Jesus' concern for Jairus' daughter (Matt 9:18–19, 23–26). As a consequence of this general picture, the Seminar was inclined to view the tradition that Mary of Magdala was a member of Jesus' inner circle as historically credible.

Embracing the unclean Parables like the dinner party (Luke 14:16–23; Thom 64:1–11) provide evidence that Jesus endorsed table fellowship with the unclean—with those who had not observed the purity rituals or who were for other reasons regarded as unclean.

Jesus and the sabbath When Jesus says that the sabbath was created for Adam and Eve, not Adam and Eve for the observance of the sabbath (Mark 2:27), he appears to be taking liberties with sabbath observance. That liberty is depicted in the story about harvesting grain on a sabbath day in Mark 2:23–28.

Jesus and his critics Jesus quotes the proverb, "No prophet is welcome on his home turf" (Thom 31:1, Luke 4:24). Folks in his home village apparently didn't regard him highly. There is plenty of reason to think that Jesus had his critics. That fact squares with the story of Jesus' negative reception in the synagogue at Nazareth (Mark 6:1–6). He also seems to have functioned as a critic, for example, when he caricatures the scholars (Luke 20:46).

To judge by his mode of discourse, he appears to have attracted crowds: it is public, not private, discourse. The later claim that he instructed his disciples privately is undoubtedly an attempt to claim special privilege for the inner circle of teachers.

Jesus as healer Curiously enough, there is very little support in Jesus' authentic words for stories that depict him as a charismatic healer. One might point to a saying such as "Since when do the able-bodied need a doctor? It's the sick who do" (Matt 9:12). But he may not have meant that literally. Healing miracles could have been, and probably were, regarded by his contemporaries as signs of the arrival of the kingdom. Yet Jesus probably insisted that he would not provide his critics with a sign (Mark 8:10–13). In this respect, the miracle stories are inimical to the teachings of Jesus on signs.

Jesus and nature wonders There seems to be nothing in his sayings that suggest Jesus was prepared to perform miracles in the natural world. Even if authentic, sayings such as Matt 18:20 ("If you had trust no larger than a mustard seed, you will say to this mountain, 'Move from here to there,' and it will move. And nothing will be beyond you.") scarcely indicate that Jesus was ready to relocate mountains.

Jesus on Jesus The sayings regarded as authentic by the Seminar indicate that Jesus did not speak about himself. There were three generalizations that emerged from this fact:

- **Jesus does not as a rule initiate dialogue or debate, nor does he offer to cure people.**
- **Jesus rarely makes pronouncements or speaks about himself in the first person.**
- **Jesus makes no claim to be the Anointed, the messiah.**

For example, Jesus uncharacteristically interrupts the funeral procession of the only son of the widow from Nain (Luke 7:11–17). In initiating the contact first with the bier and then with the widow, he departs from his customary disposition to remain aloof unless asked. That feature alone raises the question whether Luke invented this story; in addition, the story is attested only by Luke.

On the basis of the second and third characteristics listed above, the Fellows concluded that stories in which Jesus makes claims on his own behalf are unlikely to be historical.

The biographical legends in which Jesus elicits the good confession from his followers (Mark 8:27–30) or predicts his passion and indicates its significance (Mark 10:32–34) are examples of stories that consistently drew black votes. The words of Jesus in those stories were designated black in *The Five Gospels;* the narrative settings given to those words were judged to reflect the convictions of the evangelists rather than the views of Jesus.

In this connection, stories in which Jesus is represented as other than a laconic sage are not likely to be historical. In the Fourth Gospel Jesus is not infrequently pictured as a philosopher or lecturer in dialogue with his students and critics as though leading a seminar on his ideas and personal significance. Jesus' lecture following the cure of the paralytic by the pool in John 5:1–47 is a good example of the Johannine Jesus. The dialogue of Jesus with his disciples and critics in John 7:10–52 and 8:12–59 furnishes another example. The Fellows designated both words and narrative framework black as improbable representations of the historical figure.

These observations on the sayings led the Seminar to generalize: The representation of social conditions and circumstances in the narrative material should correspond closely to the perception of social reality in the authentic sayings and parables. Any discrepancy between the two automatically raises suspicion about the accuracy of the narrative representation.

Christian interests

A further test involved monitoring stories for intrusive Christian interests. Features of stories that serve Christian convictions directly are likely to be the product of the Christian imagination. Christian orthodoxy did not emerge immediately after the death of Jesus but developed over decades. As a consequence, traces of later Christian orthodoxy attributed to Jesus or his first followers are anachronistic.

On the other hand, narrative data that might have been an embarrassment to the Jesus movement has a greater claim to historicity precisely because it survived in spite of being unfavorable to the Christian cause. The baptism of Jesus at the hands of John the Baptist is problematic from the Christian point of view: Why would God's son have submitted to the baptism of an "inferior" prophet who was calling on him to repent? For that reason, scholars usually conclude that Jesus' baptism was almost certainly an historical event.

The claim that Jesus died in accordance with the scriptures, in contrast, serves Christian interests directly. Christian scholars searched the scriptures diligently looking for reasons why God would have allowed this tragedy to happen. Those reasons were not spelled out until decades after the event, although the principle was given voice earlier; they are the result of Christian conviction that Jesus' death was foreordained.

Christian interests were also served by having Jesus imitate the heroes of Israel and of the hellenistic world. Elijah, Elisha, and Moses served as models for stories told about Jesus: Moses fed the Israelites in the wilderness, so Jesus is represented as feeding the multitude on five loaves and a few fish. Elisha heals Naaman, the Syrian leper, so Jesus heals a leper too. Jesus walks on the water because the Greek god Poseidon can walk on the water. Stories echoing Israelite and pagan heroes were strategies in the program to market the messiah to the wider world, and their historicity is thus seriously undermined.

Stories were developed to give authority to the ritual practices of the budding church. These are called cult legends. Accounts of Jesus' baptism and his last meal with his disciples function as cult legends. The practice of Christian baptism begins with the baptism of Jesus; the ritual of the eucharistic meal was inaugurated by Jesus at his last meal with his followers. Even though both the baptism and last meal were probably historical events, their narrative representations were given paradigmatic significance: they were turned into models of later Christian practice.

Other stories were invented to "Christianize" Jesus—to represent him as endorsing the beliefs and convictions of later Christians. This was another way of claiming the authority of Jesus for those convictions. For a related reason, the Fellows were skeptical of stories that undergirded the authority of particular leaders of the Christian movement. The story, for example, that an inner circle of disciples was privately instructed by Jesus gave that group a privileged position in the movement; at the same time, it contradicts Jesus' practice of speaking openly to everyone.

Beware of a congenial Jesus

The Fellows of the Jesus Seminar admonished themselves repeatedly to be wary of finding a Jesus that is entirely congenial or congruent with the interests and concerns of the present age. One Fellow of the Seminar restated this rule to read: "If you want it, you can't have it, especially if you want it very badly." The pre-eminent danger faced by Christian scholars assessing the gospels is the temptation to find what they would like to find. As a consequence, the inclination to fudge tends to be high—even among critical scholars—when working with traditions that have deep emotional roots and whose critical evaluation has sweeping consequences for the religious community.

BEADS & BOXES

As in the first phase (1985–1991), the Fellows of the Jesus Seminar continued the practice of voting. Voting is the most efficient way of determining whether a consensus currently exists among the Fellows on a given point. The usual scholarly procedure is to make up one's mind privately, publish opinions arrived at in some scholarly journal, and then wait to see whether other specialists agree. The process is glacially slow, painful, and usually indecisive.

Voting also makes it possible to make a report that is readily understood by a broad public; that public, after all, may not be interested in the arcane details and extended arguments that went into those votes. The Seminar once again employed colored beads for voting purposes. As in the first phase, the four colors—red, pink, gray, and black—represent degrees of judgment. The Fellows again adopted two optional ways of understanding the four categories:

Option 1

- red: **I would include this narrative information unequivocally in the database for determining who Jesus was.**
- pink: **I would include this narrative information with reservations (or modifications) in the database for determining who Jesus was.**
- gray: **I would not include this narrative information in the primary database, but I might make use of some of the content in determining who Jesus was.**
- black: **I would not include this narrative information in the primary database for determining who Jesus was.**

Option 2

- red: **The historical reliability of this information is virtually certain. It is supported by a preponderance of evidence.**
- pink: **This information is probably reliable. It fits well with other evidence that is verifiable.**

gray: This information is possible but unreliable. It lacks supporting evidence.

black: This information is improbable. It does not fit verifiable evidence; it is largely or entirely fictive.

To be sure, the categories are not precise. They allow for some flexibility. Fellows who are uncertain of their judgment often vote gray on something they consider a "gray area." Pink is the fall-back color for those who are more skeptical of the historical accuracy of stories but who believe a particular account to be generally reliable. Red is not often chosen, except in instances where the information is regarded as virtually unassailable. And because the Seminar works with weighted averages, a red consensus is not easy to achieve.

The weighting system works like this:

red = 3
pink = 2
gray = 1
black = 0

Each Fellow casts a ballot on each item on the agenda. The numbers of colored beads are multiplied by their corresponding points, the points are added up and then divided by the number of votes in order to determine the weighted average. We then divide by 3 to convert the scale to percentages—to yield a scale of 1.00 rather than a scale of 3.00. The result is a scale we divide into four quadrants:

red: .7501 and up
pink: .5001 to .7500
gray: .2501 to .5000
black: .0000 to .2500

This system seems superior to one that relies on majorities or pluralities of one type or another. In a system that made the dividing line between pink and gray a simple majority, nearly half of the Fellows would lose their vote in a close contest. There would be only winners and losers. By using weighted averages, all votes count. Black votes in particular readily pull an average down, as students know who have one "F" in a course along with several "A's." Yet this feature seems consonant with the methodological skepticism that was a working principle of the Seminar: when in doubt, leave it out. The weighted average also gave Fellows good reason to weigh their votes carefully: the end result could be dramatically affected by a single deviant vote.

In this report we have introduced another practice: we have sporadically reported the opinions of colleagues who were not members of the Jesus Seminar. It is customary in the scholarly world to document studies with references to the published work of others, both those with whom one agrees and those who represent contrary views. So we have introduced "footnotes" to report the views of other contemporary scholars.

The scholars whose work is reported in this volume are critical scholars:

they distinguish the historical Jesus from the Christ of faith at least in some particulars. Put differently, they think some narrative data in the gospel accounts should be colored black. Yet, in concert with many of their colleagues, these scholars are not always prepared to make and report historical judgments. Very few scholars have attempted to achieve the precision to which the Jesus Seminar has aspired.

We have chosen to report the conclusions of John P. Meier on the miracle stories. In his exhaustive work, *A Marginal Jew. Rethinking the Historical Jesus.* Volume 2: *Mentor, Message, and Miracles,* Meier has examined each of the miracle stories in detail and given his considered judgment. We have attempted to interpret his conclusions in terms of the four-color scheme we employ in the Seminar and have reported his opinions on more than thirty miracle stories.

We elected also to report the judgments of E. P. Sanders as expressed in his *The Historical Figure of Jesus.* Unfortunately, Sanders does not consistently tell his readers whether he regards a particular story as historical or not. He is selective, moreover, in the stories he cites in his study. Consequently, his judgments are cited less frequently.

The report on the Gospel of John and the passion narrative takes note of the work of Raymond E. Brown, *The Gospel According to John* and *The Death of the Messiah.* Although Brown often raises the question of historicity, he is usually reluctant to answer the question unequivocally. Much of the gospel and the passion seems "not implausible" to him, which he would probably want understood as a pink vote, but which could well be interpreted as an unenthusiastic gray vote. Brown sometimes reluctantly acknowledges that the gospel tradition passes "from history to parable"—a polite but indecisive way to say "fiction"—and thus deserves a black vote.

These modest checks on the conclusions of the Fellows of the Jesus Seminar should reassure our readers that a broad consensus on both method and result does exist among critical scholars.

ORGANIZATION OF THIS BOOK

The gospels that report acts of Jesus are the four New Testament gospels—Mark, Matthew, Luke, John—along with the Sayings Gospel Q, the Gospel of Thomas, and the Gospel of Peter.

The Sayings Gospel Q reports very few deeds of Jesus, as its name suggests. Yet the few acts it does record are among the earliest written stories about Jesus that have survived. Because Q is believed to be the earliest of the gospels, Q stories of Jesus' activities are treated first in *The Acts of Jesus.*

Since we do not have a reliable reconstructed text of Q, the Fellows elected to print both the Lukan and Matthean versions of the relevant Q passages in double columns for ready comparison. Scholars work with Q parallels in just this form, except that their texts are in the original language, Greek. In accordance with scholarly convention, Luke's version is in the left column (it is commonly held that Luke best preserves the order of Q).

Like Q, the Gospel of Thomas contains very little narrative material. Where it does include a brief narrative or narrative framework, we have cited and color-coded it in connection with parallels in the New Testament gospels. We have not reproduced Thomas in its entirety as a separate gospel.

In *The Acts of Jesus,* as in *The Five Gospels,* the New Testament gospels appear in an unconventional order. Mark is placed first because most scholars (inside and outside the Seminar) believe that Matthew and Luke used Mark as the narrative base for their gospels. As a consequence, the three share a common view of the words and acts of Jesus and so are called synoptic gospels. Mark is followed by Matthew and Luke. The Gospel of John with its many eccentricities and deviations from the synoptic picture comes next.

The Gospel of Peter follows the Gospel of John. The fragmentary remains of the Gospel of Peter consist of the concluding events of Jesus' trial and execution, along with a depiction of the resurrection and the story of the empty tomb. This gospel, discovered only in 1886 as a part of a small papyrus codex, at many points parallels the passion story reported by the New Testament gospels. It is also attested in two tiny Greek fragments that came to light more recently and were published in 1972.

We have introduced two further innovations into this report. We have detached the empty tomb and appearance stories from the gospels and collected them into a self-contained section following, with their own introduction. We have also gathered the birth and infancy stories into the final section of the report, again with their own introduction. By locating accounts of the resurrection and the miraculous birth after stories about the public life of Jesus, we are simply reflecting the chronological order in which these elements developed.

The order of development is betrayed in part by the fact that agreement among the synoptic gospels ceases with the end of the Gospel of Mark. When Mark is no longer the common source for Matthew and Luke, they go their separate ways in reporting appearances. Similarly, Mark's lack of birth and infancy stories is the primary reason for the widely diverging accounts in Matthew and Luke. Furthermore, some early editions of Matthew and Luke may have existed without those tales of Jesus' conception.

In the case of reports of the resurrection, the Gospel of John offers yet another set of variants when compared with Matthew and Luke. The Gospel of Peter adds additional and somewhat startling elements to those reports. As a means of imposing some order on apparent chaos, reports of the appearances in all the sources are grouped together, arranged in parallels and analyzed systematically.

Both the letters of Paul and the book of Acts—written by the author of Luke's gospel—also provide information essential to scholars assessing the historical foundation of the appearance stories. Since Paul's letters provide the earliest testimony of the resurrection, his evidence is crucial in evaluating the reports found in the narrative gospels. It seemed wise to integrate Pauline evidence into the analysis of stories derived from Acts and from the gospels.

In grouping the Seminar's evaluations of the empty tomb/appearance stories and the birth and infancy tales into their own sections at the end of the volume, we have made this report conform as closely as possible to the actual procedures the Fellows followed. During its second phase, the Jesus Seminar worked through the dozens of narrative segments that make up the body of the narrative gospels, including the few incidents in Q, and then turned penultimately to reports of the resurrection since they constitute a distinct part of the gospel tradition. The birth and childhood stories were evaluated late in the agenda of the Seminar, in accordance with the chronological history of the gospels. The overall organization of *The Acts of Jesus* itself thus conveys fundamental aspects of the historian's view of the gospels.

In addition to the seven gospels already mentioned, there are eight very fragmentary gospels that contain acts: the Egerton Gospel, the First Stone Gospel, Gospel Oxyrhynchus 840, Gospel Oxyrhynchus 1224, the Secret Gospel of Mark, the Gospel of the Hebrews, the Gospel of the Ebionites, and the Gospel of the Nazoreans. Because these ancient texts are so fragmentary, they are evaluated as parallels or near parallels to episodes reported in the basic six. Their location in *The Acts of Jesus* can be discovered by consulting the Index of Fragmentary Gospels. A description of them will be found in the Dictionary of Terms and Sources.

If the fragmentary gospels are included in the number, this volume is a report based on fifteen gospels.

The Gospel of Mary, the Secret Book of James, and the Dialogue of the Savior report very little about the deeds of Jesus. For that reason they were omitted from this report. The two infancy gospels, Infancy Thomas and Infancy James, have also been omitted. Scholars generally agree that they contain virtually no historical data. Since they are late and legendary, it seemed pointless to include them.

The Sayings Gospel Q

The Sayings Gospel Q reports very few activities of Jesus. Q was principally a collection of the *wisdom* of Jesus; it did not contain a passion narrative; it lacked stories of Jesus' resurrection; and, like Mark, it did not contain stories of Jesus' infancy. More important, Q did not attempt to provide a narrative setting for Jesus' teachings; indeed, Q was virtually devoid of significant narrative connectives. Nevertheless, five segments in Q depict Jesus in action. It is therefore appropriate to include the acts of Jesus in Q in this volume.

Specialists have not yet determined the original text of Q. As a consequence, the Q stories are printed in parallel columns, with Luke on the left, Matthew on the right. This arrangement complies with scholarly convention: Because Luke more frequently preserves the order of Q (in the judgment of most Q scholars), references to Q are customarily given as chapter and verse in the Gospel of Luke.

The temptation of Jesus
Lk 4:1–13
Mt 4:1–11; Mk 1:12–13
Sources: Q, Mark

Luke 4:1–13	Matt 4:1–11
Jesus departed from the Jordan	
full of the holy spirit	
and was guided	Then Jesus was guided
by the spirit into the wilderness,	into the wilderness by the spirit
2 where he was put to the test	**to be put to the test**
by the devil	**by the devil.**
for forty days.	
He ate nothing that whole time;	2 And after he had fasted
	'forty days and forty nights,'
and when it was all over,	
he was famished.	he was famished.
	3 And the tester confronted him
3 The devil said to him,	**and said,**

"To prove you're God's son,
order this stone to turn
into bread."
4Jesus responded to him,
"It is written,
'Human beings are not to live on
bread alone.'"

9Then he took him
to Jerusalem,
set him on the pinnacle
of the temple,
and said to him,
"To prove you're God's son,
jump off from here;
10remember, it is written,
'To his heavenly messengers he
will give orders about you,
to protect you,'
11and 'with their hands
they will catch you,
so you won't even stub your toe on
a stone.'"
12And in response
Jesus said to him,
"It is said,
'You are not to put the Lord your
God to the test.'"
5Then he took Jesus up,
and in an instant of time
showed him all the empires
of the civilized world.

6The devil said to him,
"I'll bestow on you authority over
all this and the glory that comes
with it; understand, it has been
handed over to me, and I can give
it to anyone I want.
7So, if you will pay
homage to me,
it will all be yours."
8Jesus responded,

"It is written,
'You are to pay homage

"To prove you're God's son,
order these stones to turn
into bread."
4He responded,
"It is written,
'Human beings are not to live on
bread alone,
but on every word that comes out of
God's mouth.'"
5Then the devil conducts him
to the holy city,
sets him on the pinnacle
of the temple,
6and says to him,
"To prove you're God's son,
jump off;
remember, it is written,
'To his heavenly messengers he
will give orders about you,'

and 'with their hands
they will catch you,
so you won't even stub your toe on
a stone.'"

7Jesus said to him,
"Elsewhere it is written,
'You are not to put the Lord your
God to the test.'"
8Again the devil takes him
to a very high mountain
and shows him all the empires
of the world
and their splendor,
9and says to him,
"I'll give you all these,

if you will kneel down and pay
homage to me."

10Finally Jesus says to him,
"Get out of here, Satan!
Remember, it is written,
'You are to pay homage

to the Lord your God,
and you are to revere him alone.'"
**13 So when the devil had tried every kind of test,
he let him alone
for the time being.**

to the Lord your God,
and you are to revere him alone.'"
11 Then the devil leaves him,

and heavenly messengers arrive out of nowhere and look after him.

The temptation of Jesus. The temptation story is a legend: a story based on what his followers imagined Jesus did when he was alone in the desert. In any case, his temptations as they are represented here would have been internal struggles and not acted-out scenes that could have been observed by others had others been present. The temptation story reminds one of Jesus' prayers in Gethsemane: there he withdraws from the disciples three times and prays alone, yet his prayers are reported verbatim by the storyteller.

In spite of the fact that these stories are legends, the Fellows were about evenly divided on whether Jesus went on a vision quest in the desert, or whether he fasted for an extended period and got hungry as a result. It seems plausible that he did so as he worked out his relation to John the Baptist and contemplated the future of his own work. Simple plausibility, however, can be a cruel friend in historical reconstruction, tempting the historian to assert facts when there is only speculation. Plausibility in this case merits no more than a gray designation.

In each temptation Jesus quotes from Deuteronomy (the Greek version known as the Septuagint, abbreviated LXX) where Moses is described as receiving the Law from Yahweh on Mount Sinai. The temptation story is thus a retelling of that ancient story but substituting Jesus for Moses. Just as Moses and Israel were tempted during their forty years in the wilderness, so Jesus was tempted during his forty days in the wilderness. Israel was tempted by hunger; that hunger was sated by the "manna that fell from heaven" each day. Jesus is tempted by hunger, but refuses to turn stones into bread. Israel was tempted by idolatry; Jesus is tempted to worship Satan. In Jewish lore, this kind of retelling, or reimagining, is called *haggadah*.

In Matthew, the temptations of Jesus are arranged in a spatial progress from low to high: first he is taken to the desert, then placed on the pinnacle of the temple, then carried to a high mountain. This corresponds to the progression in Matthew's gospel: Jesus' ministry begins in the desert and ends on a mountain in Galilee from which he ascends. Luke has altered the order of the temptations in order to have Jesus wind up in Jerusalem: for Luke Jerusalem is the navel of the earth, where the story begins and ends.

Matthew and Luke have placed the legend of Jesus' temptations between their accounts of his remarkable birth and the beginning of his career as a way of forecasting the kind of life he would lead. Yet they do not follow the prescriptions they have just narrated: in spite of Jesus' refusal to turn stones into bread, the evangelists have Jesus multiply loaves and fishes to satisfy the hunger of a multitude. And although Jesus refuses to jump off the pinnacle of the temple to prove he is God's son, they have him perform miracles to demonstrate that he is the messiah.

Officer's slave/son
Lk 7:1–10
Mt 8:5–13; Jn 4:45–54
Sources: Q, John

Luke 7:1–10

1 After he had completed
all he had to say to his audience,
he went into Capernaum.

2 An officer had a slave he was very
fond of but who was sick and about
to die. 3 So when he heard about
Jesus, the officer sent some Jewish
elders to him, and asked him to
come and cure his slave. 4
When they came to Jesus, they
pleaded with him urgently, saying,
"He deserves to have you do this for
him. 5 As you probably know, he
loves our people, and even built a
synagogue for us."
6 So Jesus went with them.
When he got close to the house,
the officer dispatched friends to
say to him,
"Don't trouble yourself, sir,
for I don't deserve to have you in
my house;
7 that's why I didn't presume to
come to you in person.
Just say the word,
and let my boy be cured.
8 After all, I myself am under
orders,
and I have soldiers under me.
I order one to go, and he goes;
I order another to come, and he
comes;
and <I order> my slave to do
something, and he does it."
9 As Jesus listened to this
he was amazed at him.
He turned and

Matt 8:5–13

5 When he had entered Capernaum,
an officer approached him and
pleaded with him: 6 "Sir, my servant
boy was struck down with paralysis
and is in terrible pain."

7 And he said to him, "I'll come and
cure him."

8 And the officer replied,
"Sir, I don't deserve to have you in
my house,

but only say the word
and my boy will be cured.
9 After all, I myself am under
orders,
and I have soldiers under me.
I order one to go, and he goes;
I order another to come, and he
comes;
and <I order> my slave to do
something, and he does it."
10 As Jesus listened
he was amazed and

said to the crowd that followed,
"Let me tell you,
not even in Israel have I found such trust."

said to those who followed,
"I swear to you,
I have not found such trust in a single Israelite!
11I predict that many will come from east and west and dine with Abraham and Isaac and Jacob in Heaven's domain, 12but those who think Heaven's domain belongs to them will be thrown where it is utterly dark. There'll be weeping and grinding of teeth out there."
13**And Jesus said to the officer,** "Be on your way. Your trust will be the measure of the results."
And the boy was cured at that precise moment.

10**And when the emissaries returned to the house, they found the slave in good health.**

Officer's slave/son. The two versions of this story—the account derived from the Sayings Gospel Q and the report preserved by the Fourth Gospel—differ in almost every detail, yet they agree that Jesus effected a cure at a distance.

In the Q version, Jesus is in Capernaum along with the patient; in the Fourth Gospel, Jesus is in Cana of Galilee. John has perhaps moved the location to Cana in order to link this miracle with the changing of the water into wine, which also takes place at Cana. The Fellows were inclined to the view that Jesus was probably in Capernaum along with the petitioner and the patient.

In the Q version, the petitioner is a Roman officer (centurion) with soldiers under his command; in the Fourth Gospel, he is an official appointed, presumably, by Herod Antipas (but not a person of royal blood, as some translations of the term suggest). Part of the point of the story is that the petitioner was a gentile. If a gentile, then Jesus is represented as being open to gentile followers and addresses an extremely complimentary remark to the official in Luke 7:9//Matt 8:10, a remark that Matthew expands into a sweeping inclusion of gentiles (8:11–12). The Fellows agreed that the intent of the Q version was to justify the Christian mission to the gentiles (vote: red).

The three accounts differ on the status of the patient. In Luke, the sufferer is a slave; in Matthew, he is a servant boy; in John, he has been elevated to the rank of son.

The ailment is also indeterminate. In Matthew, the servant has been struck down with paralysis and is in terrible pain; in Luke, the slave is near death; in John, the son is also near death of a fever. Again, it is impossible to ascertain what particular ailment was involved in the original story.

The Seminar decided to color the two Q versions black, but to put the Johannine version in gray. It did so as a consequence of decisions the Fellows took about the history of the tradition, based on a close analysis of the three versions. The two written reports (Q and John) were derived, in the view of a majority of the Fellows, from a common oral tradition (vote: pink). Of the two written versions, the Johannine one is closer to the original form (vote: pink). The Johannine story is derived from the Signs Gospel, a collection of wondrous deeds performed by Jesus underlying the Fourth Gospel. A reconstruction of that source suggests that Jesus simply told the official that his son or slave would live and coincidentally the lad recovered. In other words, the original version seems not to have claimed that Jesus healed the child—although the story was obviously told to imply that Jesus did perform a miracle. All of these conclusions are of course disputed as the bare majorities among the Fellows indicate.

The conclusions of John P. Meier, following a long and detailed discussion, do not differ from those reached by the Jesus Seminar. He thinks there is a historical core to the story, but given the variations in the three versions of the story, he is unable to stipulate which details are authentic. Had he been a member of the Seminar, he might have voted for a pink core with gray or even black details.[3] E. P. Sanders hedges his bets by summarizing the story without passing judgment on its historical reliability. He does, however, mention that Hanina ben Dosa, a Galilean healer who lived a little after Jesus, is reported to have effected a cure very similar to the one attributed to Jesus.[4]

John's inquiry
Lk 7:18–23
Mt 11:2–6
Source: Q

Luke 7:18–23

18 The disciples of John brought
reports of all these things to him.
19 John summoned a couple of his
disciples
and sent them to the Lord
to ask:
"Are you the one who is to come,
or are we to wait for someone else?"
20 And when the men came to
<Jesus>, they said, "John the Baptist
sent us to you to ask: 'Are you the
one who is to come, or are we to
wait for someone else?'"
21 Jesus had just cured many of their
diseases and plagues and evil
spirits, and restored sight to many
who were blind.
22 And so he answered them,
"Go report to John what you have
seen and heard:
the blind see again,
the lame walk,

Matt 11:2–6

2 While John was in prison
he heard about what the Anointed
had been doing
and he sent his disciples
3 to ask,
"Are you the one who is to come
or are we to wait for another?"
4 And so Jesus answered them,
"Go report to John what you have
heard and seen:
5 The blind see again
and the lame walk;

lepers are cleansed,
the deaf hear,
the dead are raised,
and the poor have the good news
preached to them.
[23]Congratulations to those who don't
take offense at me."

lepers are cleansed
and the deaf hear;
the dead are raised,
and the poor have the good news
preached to them.
[6]Congratulations to those who don't
take offense at me."

John's inquiry. John the Baptist probably did expect something apocalyptic to happen in the near future. Whether for John the Coming One meant a Davidic messiah, an apocalyptic son of Adam, or perhaps just the direct intervention of God in history is unclear. As it is represented in Q, the structure of the exchange is a Christian ploy: John's followers are made to play the straight man to Jesus by asking an innocent question to which Christians can give an unequivocal reply: "Yes, Jesus is the Coming One" (understood by Christians as the expected messiah). For his part, John the Baptist is pictured as uncertain about the status of Jesus, contrary to the way his testimony to Jesus is presented in the Gospel of John (1:29–34).

The Sayings Gospel Q does not, however, narrate stories that give warrant to the reply of Jesus in Luke 7:22. Q reports only one healing, that of the Roman officer's servant (Luke 7:1–10), and one exorcism (Luke 11:14–15). That is hardly sufficient to justify the list given in Luke 7:22. Luke has apparently expanded the narrative context in vv. 20–21 to cover the deficiency; the shorter form in Matthew may be the more original. Nevertheless, the Sayings Gospel Q presupposes that Jesus caused the blind to see, the lame to walk, and the deaf to hear; that he cleansed lepers, raised the dead, and preached the good news to the poor.

The narrative frame for the sentences taken from the ancient prophets in Luke 7:22//Matt 11:5 (Isa 26:19, 35:5–6, 61:1) is undoubtedly a Christian construction and merits the color black.

Praise of John
Lk 7:24–28
Mt 11:7–11
Source: Q
Cf. Th 78:1–3; Th 46:1–2

Luke 7:24–28

[24]After John's messengers had left,

<Jesus> began to talk about John to the crowds:
"What did you go out to the
wilderness to gawk at?
A reed shaking in the wind?
[25]What did you really go out to see?
A man dressed in fancy clothes?
But wait!
Those who dress fashionably
and live in luxury are found in
palaces.

Matt 11:7–11

[7]After <John's disciples> had departed,
Jesus began to talk about John to the crowds:
"What did you go out to the
wilderness to gawk at?
A reed shaking in the wind?
[8]What did you really go out to see?
A man dressed in fancy <clothes>?
But wait!
Those who wear fancy <clothes>
are found in regal quarters.

[26]Come on, what did you go out to see? A prophet? Yes, that's what you went out to see, yet someone more than a prophet. [27]This is the one about whom it was written: Here is my messenger, whom I send on ahead of you to prepare your way before you. [28]I tell you, among those born of women none is greater than John; yet the least in God's domain is greater than he."	[9]Come on, what did you go out to see? A prophet? Yes, that's what you went out to see, yet someone more than a prophet. [10]This is the one about whom it was written: Here is my messenger, whom I send on ahead of you to prepare your way before you. [11]I swear to you, among those born of women no one has arisen who is greater than John the Baptist; yet the least in Heaven's domain is greater than he."

Praise of John. The notice in Luke 7:24 and Matt 11:7 that Jesus began to talk about John after John's disciples had departed belongs to the narrative context created by the followers of Jesus who formed the Q community. It is of a piece with the narrative context given in Luke 7:18–23//Matt 11:2–6 in the preceding narrative segment. It is therefore a fiction. The appropriate designation is black.

Beelzebul controversy
Lk 11:14–23
Mt 12:22–32; Mk 3:22–30
Sources: Q, Mark

Luke 11:14–23	Matt 12:22–32
[14]Jesus was driving out a demon that was mute,	**[22]Then they brought to him a blind and mute person who was demon-possessed,**
and when the demon had departed the mute man spoke.	**and he cured him so the mute was able both to speak and to see.**
And the crowds were amazed.	**[23]And the entire crowd was beside itself and would say, "This fellow can't be the son of David, can he?"**
[15]But some of them said, "He drives out demons in the name of Beelzebul, the head demon."	**[24]But when the Pharisees heard of it, they said, "This fellow drives out demons only in the name of Beelzebul, the head demon."**
[16]Others were testing him by demanding a sign from heaven.	
[17]But he knew what they were thinking, and said to them:	**[25]But he knew how they thought, and said to them:**

"Every government divided against
itself is devastated,
and a house divided
against a house falls.
18 If Satan is divided against himself
—since you claim I drive out
demons in Beelzebul's name—
how will his domain endure?
19 If I drive out demons
in Beelzebul's name,
in whose name do your own people
drive <them> out?
In that case, they will be your
judges.
20 But if by God's finger
I drive out demons,
then for you God's imperial rule has
arrived.
21 "When a strong man is fully armed
and guards his courtyard, his
possessions are safe.
22 But when a stronger man attacks
and overpowers him, he takes the
weapons on which he was relying and
divides up his loot.
23 "The one who isn't with me is
against me,
and the one who doesn't gather
with me scatters."

"Every government divided against
itself is devastated,
and every town or household
divided against itself won't survive.
26 So if Satan drives out Satan,
he is divided against himself.
In that case,
how will his domain endure?
27 "Even if I drive out demons in
Beelzebul's name,
in whose name do your own people
drive <them> out?
In that case, they will be your
judges.
28 But if by God's spirit
I drive out demons,
then for you God's imperial rule has
arrived.
29 "Or how can someone enter a
powerful man's house and steal his
belongings,
unless he first ties him up?
Only then does he loot his house.
30 "The one who isn't with me is
against me,
and the one who doesn't gather
with me scatters.
31 That's why I tell you: Every offense
and blasphemy will be forgiven
humankind, but the blasphemy
of the spirit won't be forgiven.
32 And the one who speaks a word
against the son of Adam will be
forgiven; but the one who speaks a
word against the holy spirit won't be
forgiven, either in this age or in the
one to come."

Beelzebul controversy. It is perhaps striking that only here in the Sayings Gospel Q is there a saying referring to exorcism, and it is introduced by a very brief account of an exorcism. Since narratives in Q are rare, scholars have wondered whether this skeleton of a narrative was not created to go with the sayings that follow. In Luke the person possessed is only mute; in Matthew he is both mute and blind. There is some consensus that Luke's version more likely represents the form of the story that appeared in Q. Matthew liked the story so much he duplicates it in 9:32–34.

The Seminar decided to color-code the story of the mute gray (Luke 11:14//Matt 12:22–23) to suggest that it may reflect the memory of a specific event; however, the uncertainty quotient is high. Part of the hesitation owes to the fact that Mark provides a different introduction to the Beelzebul controversy (Mark 3:20–22). John P. Meier concludes that the historical value of the story is difficult to judge: it could have been based on an actual incident or it might have been a literary creation.[5]

The Beelzebul controversy (vv. 15–23//Matt 12:24–32) turns on the accusation that Jesus was mad. To say that Jesus was mad was to say that he "had a demon," that he was demon-possessed. Anyone who had the spirit of divination was also thought to be demon-possessed. Consequently, prophets and those who delivered oracles were regarded as "mad." Odd behavior of any kind could be covered by the same designation, just as it is in all human societies.

John the Baptist was said to be demon-possessed because he was an ascetic. In the book of Acts, a girl who possessed the spirit of divination is cured by Paul, who exorcized her demon (Acts 16:16–18). Paul reminds the Corinthians that outsiders will think the members of the congregation mad if they speak in tongues (1 Cor 14:23). Paul himself is accused of being mad, an accusation Paul denies (Acts 26:24–25).

It is not surprising that Jesus of Nazareth was regarded by some as mad. The Fellows thought the evidence warranted a red vote on the narrative statement:

- **Some who saw Jesus thought he was mad.**

They agreed that to say Jesus was demon-possessed was to say the same thing. They also agreed to this statement:

- **Some who saw Jesus said he was an agent of Beelzebul.**

These charges go together with his behavior as an exorcist: those who had control of demons were sometimes thought to be demon-possessed themselves. Accordingly, the accusation in v. 15 was voted red. The corresponding statement in Matt 12:24 was colored pink only because it is less certain that the Pharisees in particular laid this charge against Jesus. In the Fourth Gospel, it is the crowd (7:20) or the Judeans generally (8:48, 52, 10:20) who say that Jesus is crazy.

The evangelists may have understood the claim in v. 17 (//Matt 12:25) to mean that Jesus had supernatural powers in reading people's minds. But as they stand the sentences need mean no more than that Jesus was aware of how people tended to think about deviant behavior, especially when linked to the power to exorcize. These sentences were therefore given a pink rating as part of a plausible setting for the controversy.

Additional discussion of the issues involved will be found in the commentary on Mark 3:20–30, 31–35.

THE GOSPEL OF MARK

1 The good news of Jesus the Anointed begins 2with something
Isaiah the prophet wrote:

> Here is my messenger,
> whom I send on ahead of you
> to prepare your way!
> 3A voice of someone shouting in the wilderness:
> "Make ready the way of the Lord,
> make his paths straight."

4So, John the Baptizer appeared in the wilderness calling for bap-
tism and a change of heart that lead to forgiveness of sins. 5And
everyone from the Judean countryside and all the residents of
Jerusalem streamed out to him and got baptized by him in the
Jordan river, admitting their sins. 6And John wore a mantle made of
camel hair and had a leather belt around his waist and lived on
locusts and raw honey. 7And he began his proclamation by saying:
"Someone more powerful than I will succeed me, whose sandal
straps I am not fit to bend down and untie. 8I have been baptizing
you with water, but he will baptize you with holy spirit."

A voice in the wilderness
Mk 1:1–8
Mt 3:1–12, Lk 3:1–20;
Jn 1:19–28; GEbi 1, 3
Sources: Mark, Q, John

A voice in the wilderness. The Fellows were virtually unanimous in their judgment that there was a real person named John the Baptist who was a contemporary of Jesus. They agreed, moreover, that John called for repentance and practiced baptism—in flowing water—as a ritual expression of repentance. They think the evidence supports the claim that he was very popular, that he attracted crowds of people streaming out to him in the wilderness area around the Jordan River.

The evidence for the existence of John is overwhelming. John the Baptist appears in the two principal sources underlying the synoptic Gospels (Q, Mark): Mark, whose gospel is employed as the narrative frame by both Matthew and Luke; and Q, a document now lost that consisted almost entirely of sayings. References to John also appear in traditions known only to Matthew or Luke (dubbed M and L, respectively, to indicate special materials whether oral or written). John the Baptist also appears in the Gospel of John and in the Gospel of Thomas (46:1–2), both of which are literarily independent of the synoptic gospels and Q.

There are sayings *by* John the Baptist and sayings *about* him. Josephus, a Jewish author of the first century C.E., also makes reference to John in his *History of the Jews* (18.116–19):

> To some of the Jews it appeared that the destruction of Herod's troops by God had been divine retribution, and just retribution at that, for his treatment of John who was also known as the Baptist. It will be recalled that Herod put John to death; John was a good man who had admonished the Jews to practice virtue and to treat each other justly, with due respect to God, and to join in the practice of baptism. John's view was that correct behavior was a necessary preliminary to baptism, if baptism was to be acceptable to God. Baptism was not to gain pardon for sins committed, but for the purification of the body, which had already been consecrated by righteousness. Herod became alarmed at the crowds that gathered around John, who aroused them to fever pitch with his sermons. Eloquence that had such a powerful effect on people might lead to sedition, since it seemed that the people were prepared to do everything he recommended. Herod decided that it would be better to take preemptive measures and be rid of John before his influence led to rebellion than to wait and perceive the danger too late. Because Herod was suspicious of John, he sent John fettered to Machaerus, the fortress we mentioned earlier, and had him executed there. But the Jews were of the opinion that the destruction of Herod's forces was the price God willed that Herod had to pay for what he did to John.

Mark, the earliest narrative gospel, cites Isa 40:3 (v. 3) in Greek, not Hebrew, in which a voice crying in the wilderness is the messenger preparing the way for the return of the Israelite exiles following the Babylonian captivity in the sixth century B.C.E. Mark interprets this as applying to John the Baptist in the first century C.E. Mark understands John to be the messenger whose voice in the wilderness prepares the way for the coming of the lord—the messiah, whereas Isaiah understood the Lord who was coming to be God.

Normally, an allusion of this order would prompt scholars to doubt that the locale of John's activity was really the wilderness. Yet, the evidence is again overwhelming that John actually carried out his mission in the region around the Jordan, which was viewed as a part of that semi-arid territory, largely uninhabited, that constituted the "wilderness" of the Jordan valley. At the same time, the Jordan River afforded "living" water—water on the move—for the practice of baptism, probably in the form of immersion.

The evidence in support of the wilderness as the site of John's activity comes from independent sources, both narratives and sayings: the synoptics and John, the Sayings Gospel Q and the Gospel of Thomas (78:1–2). While Josephus does not explicitly mention the locale of John's activity, he tells us that John was imprisoned and then executed in the wilderness fortress of Machaerus, which belonged to Herod Antipas, John's enemy. Located east of the Dead Sea, only a few miles from the Jordan region where John presumably conducted his public ministry, Machaerus would have been an appropriate prison and execution site for John.

Our ancient sources also report that the two activities characteristic of John the Baptist were proclamation and water baptism. The Sayings Gospel Q understandably presents the preaching of John as his defining activity, whereas Mark combines the call to repentance with baptism as an initiation rite. In the Gospel of John, the tendency to turn the Baptist into a witness to Jesus as the messiah is part of the Christian overlay that obscures the original mission of John. In fact, the two movements—the Baptist movement and the Jesus movement—were competitors after Jesus left John, and especially after the deaths of John and Jesus.

In the judgment of the Fellows, John probably administered baptism himself; it was apparently not a self-administered rite as was usually the case with Jewish rites of purification. John's baptismal rite was almost certainly understood by him and others to be an outward expression of repentance—the desire to change one's ways. Less certainly, in the opinion of the Fellows, baptism was understood by John to mediate God's forgiveness. About half of the Fellows thought John's baptism constituted a protest against the temple establishment. Like other Judean rites of purification, John's baptism also functioned as a rite of purification, but this was not its primary purpose.

By a substantial majority the Fellows agreed that John was probably an ascetic and, by a narrow margin, they affirmed that he ate locusts and raw honey. However, the claim that John wore a camel hair mantle and had a leather belt around his waist corresponds to the description of Elijah in 2 Kgs 1:8 and recalls the description of a prophet's attire in Zech 13:4. As a consequence, the Fellows viewed this bit of information with suspicion: the gospel writers often adjust the details of a story to match corresponding features in Old Testament narratives. The Fellows accordingly designated this statement gray as something possible but not certain.

The Seminar agreed, by a very slim majority, that John probably did look forward to the one who was to come, and said so publicly. The debate in this case was over whether or not the statement of John, in v. 7, had been created by Mark to serve Christian interests. As in many other cases, the Fellows were divided on their interpretation of the evidence. Some Fellows argued that as an apocalyptic prophet John probably did think that a messiah would soon appear. Others emphasized how the Jesus and Baptist movements competed with each other after the deaths of their founders; and they saw here an attempt by the Christian community to demonstrate that John the Baptist had endorsed Jesus as the expected messiah. The result was a pink designation for v. 7 and a gray designation for v. 8. The Seminar thinks it probable that John the Baptist did talk about a coming messianic figure, that he compared himself with that figure, and that he believed the messiah would be more powerful than himself. On the other hand, the Fellows doubted that John contrasted his own water baptism with the messiah's spirit baptism. Jesus did not, in fact, baptize with holy spirit, at least not in the gospel records that have survived. He didn't baptize with water either, although his disciples seem to have taken up the practice after Jesus' death (cf. John 4:1–2).

The baptism of Jesus
Mk 1:9–11
Mt 3:13–17, Lk 3:21–22
Source: Mark
Cf. Jn 1:29–34; GNaz 2;
GEbi 4; GHeb 3

1 [9]**During that same period Jesus came from Nazareth, Galilee, and was baptized in the Jordan by John. [10]And just as he got up out of the water, he saw the skies torn open and the spirit coming down toward him like a dove.[11]There was also a voice from the skies: "You are my favored son—I fully approve of you."**

The baptism of Jesus. Very few of the Fellows of the Jesus Seminar doubt that John the Baptist baptized Jesus. The early Christian movement and the evangelists would have lacked motivation for making up such a story: it makes Jesus subservient to John. This in itself is strong evidence that the fact of Jesus' baptism by John came to them in the oral tradition. In all probability, Jesus was at one time a follower of John and like many others received baptism at John's hands.

The debate among the Fellows centered around the kind of experience Jesus may have had and the implications of his having presented himself to John for baptism.

Mark, followed by Matthew and Luke, represents Jesus as both seeing and hearing something. But the Fellows believe that this description owes its details to the imagination of Mark or storytellers in the early Christian movement. The Fellows denied, with black votes, that Jesus actually saw the heavens open and the spirit descend like a dove. They denied that Jesus heard a voice from heaven saying, "You are my favored son." Nonetheless, the memory of this event as having occurred at the outset of Jesus' public activity suggested to the Fellows that Jesus probably did have some kind of powerful religious experience. They affirmed that Jesus, in all likelihood, had visionary experiences on occasion, and they did not rule out the possibility that his baptismal experience involved a vision of some kind.

Neither Mark nor any other early source explicitly claims that Jesus became a disciple of John the Baptist. Given this silence, some Fellows hesitated to describe Jesus as a "disciple" of John in the sense of his being John's student and an itinerant follower. But most Fellows thought that Jesus' acceptance of baptism at the hands of John did make him a "disciple" in the broad sense that Jesus accepted what John was up to and thereby belonged to the movement initiated by him (Mark 11:27–33). They also affirmed that at some point Jesus deliberately separated himself from John's movement (Mark 1:14;

John 3:22–24) and that some of John's disciples became followers of Jesus (John 1:35–51).

The temptation of Jesus
Mk 1:12–13
Mt 4:1–11, Lk 4:1–13
Sources: Mark, Q

1 [12]And right away the spirit drives him out into the wilderness,
[13]where he remained for forty days, **being put to the test by Satan.**
While he was living there among the wild animals, **the heavenly messengers looked after him.**

The temptation of Jesus. The Fellows were fairly evenly divided on whether Jesus underwent a period of testing in the wilderness such as Mark depicts here. The weighted average fell just below the line separating pink and gray. They were much firmer in their convictions that he did not have an actual encounter with Satan. The forty-day period is likewise symbolic: It rained for forty days and forty nights in the story of Noah; the Israelites wandered for forty years in the wilderness; David and Solomon reigned for forty years. Forty expresses a relatively long but indefinite time. Forty is often connected with events that have special religious significance.

In response to more general statements, the majority of the Fellows believe Jesus spoke *of* Satan, but they are fairly dubious that he ever spoke *to* Satan.

Jesus proclaims the good news
Mk 1:14–15
Mt 4:12–17
Source: Mark
Cf. Lk 4:14–15, 16–30

1 [14]After John was locked up, **Jesus came to Galilee proclaiming God's good news.** [15]**His message went:**

"The time is up: God's imperial rule is closing in. Change your ways, and put your trust in the good news!"

Jesus proclaims the good news. There is no reason to doubt that Herod Antipas imprisoned John the Baptist and then had him executed, probably by beheading, at Machaerus, a fortress palace located in the wilderness east of the Jordan. The Jewish historian Josephus, writing toward the end of the first century (about the time the gospels were being composed), confirms the execution of John at Machaerus east of the Dead Sea.

Jesus had been a disciple of John. According to the Gospel of Mark, Jesus left the Jordan and returned to Galilee at the time John the Baptist was imprisoned. The Fellows were dubious that this chronology is completely reliable; some scholars think it possible that the public activities of John and Jesus overlapped, as represented by the Fourth Gospel (3:22–24).

In any case, when Jesus returns to Galilee, he continues the work of John by announcing the good news—the gospel. In *The Five Gospels,* the Jesus Seminar reported that the summary in Mark 1:15 reflected more the perspective of Mark—and the former followers of John the Baptist—than it did of Jesus. Thus, while the narrative statement in 1:14 is believed to contain reliable historical information, the summary of Jesus' preaching in v. 15 was deemed not to reflect accurately the content of Jesus' own message. For that reason the narrative introduction was colored black.

Call of the first disciples
Mk 1:16–18, 19–20
Mt 4:18–20, 21–22
Source: Mark
Cf. Lk 5:1–11; Jn 1:35–42; 43–51; GEbi 2

1 [16]As he was walking along by the Sea of Galilee, he spotted
Simon and Andrew, Simon's brother, casting <their nets> into the
sea—since they were fishermen—[17]and Jesus said to them: "Become
my followers and I'll have you fishing for people!"
[18]And right then and there they abandoned their nets and fol-
lowed him.
[19]When he had gone a little farther, he caught sight of James,
Zebedee's son, and his brother John mending their nets in the boat.
[20]Right then and there he called out to them as well, and they left
their father Zebedee behind in the boat with the hired hands and
accompanied him.

Call of the first disciples. These are twin anecdotes: the second reproduces the first almost word-for-word. They are classified as pronouncement stories, although the second does not report a pronouncement; it assumes the repetition of the call issued in the first story. Anecdotes of this type are usually stereotypical constructs rather than reports of actual events. They are, as Rudolf Bultmann, the pre-eminent German form critic, used to say, idealized scenes that honor a teacher or sage by portraying him in a favorable light. It is even possible that the metaphor "fishing for people" (on the part of fishermen) functioned as the nucleus around which the stories of the call of the first disciples developed.

The model for enlisting a successor is the story of Elijah's recruitment of Elisha (1 Kgs 19:19–21). Elisha was in the field ploughing with twelve yoke of oxen when Elijah came by and threw his mantle over his potential successor. Elisha asked permission to kiss his father and mother good-bye before he became a disciple. One of Jesus' potential disciples asked permission to bury his father before he took up his new vocation (Luke 9:59). The Elijah/Elisha cycle of stories in the scriptures undoubtedly influenced the construction of stories about Jesus.

No one believes that the call of Simon and Andrew happened exactly as Mark depicts it. If Jesus enlisted the four followers formally at all, they became disciples only after a period of time. Mark has preserved a story from the oral tradition that was designed to convey the essence of discipleship to all prospective followers: If you want to become a follower of Jesus, you must abandon your work, your family, give up all previous attachments and help enlist others. In the anecdote, it is not the historical Jesus, but Jesus the Master, Jesus the Lord—the Christ of the later movement who issues the call to one and all to go fishing for people.

There seems to be little reason to doubt that Jesus attracted followers—students or devotees—who wandered around with him on his teaching circuit. Although these stories in Mark do not mention them, those followers almost certainly included women, since women appear, almost unnoticed, in gospel stories (Mark 15:40–41, Luke 8:1–3), but assume a central role in the Gospel of Mary. It would not have been unusual for a sage to attract students—it was one of the most common ways in which teaching/learning took place—

but it would have been unusual for a teacher's retinue to include women. The basic issue, however, is whether Jesus actually took the initiative in recruiting disciples as depicted in these twin stories in Mark. The Fellows doubted that the stories reflected actual events, but held out the possibility that there was enough truth in them to warrant a gray designation.

The unclean demon at Capernaum
Mk 1:21–28
Lk 4:31–37
Source: Mark

1 [21]**Then they come to Capernaum,** and on the sabbath day he
went right to the synagogue and started teaching. [22]They were aston-
ished at his teaching, since he would teach them on his own author-
ity, unlike the scholars.
[23]Now right there in their synagogue was a person possessed by
an unclean spirit, which shouted,[24] "Jesus! What do you want with
us, you Nazarene? Have you come to get rid of us? I know you, who
you are: God's holy man!"
[25]But Jesus yelled at it, "Shut up and get out of him!"
[26]Then the unclean spirit threw the man into convulsions, and let-
ting out a loud shriek it came out of him. [27]And they were all so
amazed that they asked themselves, "What's this? A new kind of
teaching backed by authority! He gives orders even to unclean spir-
its and they obey him!"
[28]So his fame spread rapidly everywhere throughout Galilee and
even beyond.

The unclean demon at Capernaum. Mark opens the body of his gospel by having Jesus return to Galilee and begin to proclaim his message (1:14–15). Jesus next enlists four followers (1:16–20). With this passage, Mark narrates the first of Jesus' wondrous deeds: an exorcism. Mark is constructing a picture of the typical features of Jesus' public life by having him do a variety of things on the first day of his new life.

The introduction in vv. 21–22 is the narrative framework Mark has provided for the nucleus of the story in vv. 23–26. We cannot be certain that this story was originally set in Capernaum, since Mark is constructing an artificial sequence of events that extends from the entry into Capernaum in 1:21 to Jesus' departure on a tour in 1:39. Moreover, the characterization of Jesus in v. 22 is Christian reflection on the style of Jesus' teaching and goes with part of v. 27: "What's this?" Jesus' audience asks. "A new kind of teaching backed by authority!" they exclaim in response to their own rhetorical question. Mark has introduced the theme of teaching into the framework of a story that really has to do with an exorcism. The appropriate response is preserved, however, in the balance of v. 27: "And they were all amazed. . . . He gives orders even to unclean spirits and they obey him!" Verse 28 is Mark's conclusion.

With the elimination of the elements supplied by Mark, the story becomes a standard account of an exorcism with four parts: the demon recognizes the exorcist and struggles against him (vv. 23–24); the exorcist orders the demon to depart with a loud voice command (v. 25); the demon obeys but makes a scene in departing (v. 26); bystanders react appropriately to the feat (v. 27a, c). The

CAPERNAUM

The town of Capernaum figures prominently in the gospels. There is good reason to believe that Jesus made it the hub of his Galilean teaching and healing activities. Located on the northern shore of the Sea of Galilee—really only a lake—the town is situated just west of where the Jordan River flows into the lake (see map, p. 000). Capernaum is also only a couple of miles from an important east-west trade route connecting Egypt and India. Archaeologists have estimated that during the first century C.E. the town consisted of about 250 acres and had a population of approximately one thousand.

Mark makes Capernaum the site of a typical day in the life of Jesus (1:16–39). On the sabbath Jesus goes to the synagogue where he teaches "with authority" (1:21) and also exorcises an unclean spirit (1:23–27). The likelihood that Peter resided there (Mark 1:29–31) supports the Matthean assertion (4:13) that at some point in his life Jesus moved away from Nazareth and took up residence in Capernaum. The Gospel of John locates the walking on the water miracle near Capernaum (6:17). And both Matthew (11:23) and Luke (10:15) have Jesus curse the town: "And you, Capernaum, you don't think you'll be exalted to heaven, do you? No, you'll go to Hell."

The picture of Capernaum we get from the gospels gives us two pieces of information about life in northern Galilee. The first is that Capernaum was a center for commercial fishing. The second is that the Romans employed local residents as toll collectors (Matt 17:24). Some of the people who lived in Capernaum made their living on the lake. A few of the others worked for Rome and collected the money that supported the occupation army and the imperial governors, administrators, and officials. Those who caught fish for a living worked in a socially honorable trade. Those who collected tolls were considered pariahs because they collaborated with Rome.

Nearby were the towns of Chorazin, Magdala (home of Mary), and Bethsaida (hometown of Peter), Andrew, and Philip [John 1:44] three towns that appear to have been hostile to the Jesus movement (Luke 10:15//Matt 11:23). Not far away were Sepphoris and Tiberias, both of which had been built or rebuilt by Herod Antipas, the tetrarch of Galilee and Perea, who beheaded John the Baptist. He used the first as his capital for a time and then moved the capital to Tiberias. The combination of the trade route, commercial fishing, and the collection of Roman tolls made Capernaum a bustling place.

question is whether this story is the report of a specific event or a tale of the sort of thing Jesus often did. John P. Meier is inclined to think it is a Christian creation.[6] The Fellows of the Seminar came to the same conclusion, but allowed for the possibility that it reflected a particular event by coloring it gray. At the same time, the Fellows endorsed the statement that Jesus practiced exorcism with a red vote. The stories that report specific examples of his activities as an exorcist have so many embellishing elements, however, that no story received a stronger vote than pink. Other stories, such as this one, were colored gray. John P. Meier concluded that while this story could not be pressed for details, it is representative of the sort of thing Jesus did.[7] That is about what gray means for the Fellows of the Jesus Seminar. E. P. Sanders does not pass judgment on whether this particular story is historical or not, but he does admit that "the authors of the gospels . . . expanded on Jesus' reputation as an exorcist."[8]

Because the Fellows are virtually certain that Capernaum was one of the centers of Jesus' activity, they colored the opening statement red. It should be recalled, however, that Jesus was basically an itinerant and probably did not settle down in any one place. (For additional information about Capernaum, consult the cameo, p. 58.)

1 [29]**They left the synagogue right away and entered the house of Simon and Andrew along with James and John.** [30]**Simon's mother-in-law was in bed with a fever, and they told him about her right away.** [31]**He went up to her, took hold of her hand, raised her up, and the fever disappeared. Then she started looking after them.**

Peter's mother-in-law
Mk 1:29–31
Mt 8:14–15, Lk 4:38–39
Source: Mark

Peter's mother-in-law. Simon Peter undoubtedly had a mother-in-law since he was married. Paul, who knew Peter personally, said that Peter had a wife (1 Cor 9:5). Later church writers (Clement of Alexandria, Eusebius, and the author of the Pseudo-Clementines) also refer to the wife of Peter and even claim that the couple had children. As a consequence, the Fellows were all but unanimous that this bit of narrative information was reliable.

The evidence is overwhelming that Jesus was regarded as a healer during his public career. However, it is difficult to identify stories in the gospels that are reports of actual healing events. This brief vignette comes as close as any to qualifying as a report of an actual happening. The version Mark records lacks most of the features that are characteristic of stereotyped healing stories: there is no comment on the gravity of the malady; Jesus gives no command; the faith of the recipient is not remarked; and there is no one present to register amazement and confirm the cure. Further, there are no precedents in Hebrew scripture of which this story could be the imitation. And there are no allusions to stories involving Elijah and Elisha and no reference to cures of this type in catalogues of eschatological healings, such as we find in Isa 29:18–19, 35:5–6, 42:18. In sum, this simple tale appears to reflect the memory of a cure worked upon someone close to the inner circle of Jesus' followers; it does not appear to be fictive. Accordingly, the Fellows designated the gist of the story pink.

The affirmation of the core of this story does not, however, extend to all its details. The Fellows were dubious that the location of the cure was Simon's house in Capernaum. The specification of locale, especially when occurring in narrative introductions and conclusions, is often the contribution of the storyteller and does not necessarily reflect historical data. In this case, Mark has linked together a string of stories to form a picture of Jesus' typical activities on a single day (Mark 1:16–39): the call of disciples; an exorcism in a synagogue; the cure of Peter's mother-in-law; a gathering of sick and demon-possessed around his door; Jesus' withdrawal to pray. The grouping is artificial, so the narrative links between and among the stories must also be artificial. The Fellows agreed that the cure occurred at an unknown location.

They were even more skeptical that the cure took place on a sabbath as reported in Mark 1:21. The temporal location also belongs to Mark's artificial narrative framework and therefore may not be accurate. Controversies related to sabbath observance were characteristic of the period after the fall of Jerusalem in 70 C.E. when tension between the Jesus movement and emerging rabbinic Judaism was at its height. Narrative features that reflect such tensions have probably been adapted to the post-70 context of the storyteller and the Christian community—the end of second temple Judaism and the rise of Christian sect.

Doubt about the reliability of location and time prompted the Fellows to color the introductory sentence gray.

John P. Meier concludes that a judgment about the historical reliability of the story is not possible. His *non liquet* ("it is not clear") translates into a Jesus Seminar gray.[9] In other words, on this report he is more skeptical than the Fellows of the Seminar.

Cures & exorcisms
Mk 1:32–34
Mt 8:16–17, Lk 4:40–41
Source: Mark

1 **[32]In the evening, at sundown, they would bring all the sick and demon possessed to him. [33]And the whole town would crowd around the door.** [34]On such occasions he cured many people afflicted with various diseases and drove out many demons. **He would never let the demons speak, because they realized who he was.**

Cures & exorcisms. This summary, which is the creation of Mark, presumably brings the first day of Jesus' public acts to a close, a day that began with the enlistment of the first followers and ended with the cure of Peter's mother-in-law. Mark represents these activities as occurring on a particular occasion, when, in fact, he is generalizing on the basis of memories of the kind of public acts Jesus performed: Jesus healed folk and exorcized demons. He may have done so on a particular occasion in Capernaum, at sunset, at the door of Simon Peter's house. However, Mark does not have a particular story to tell, so he creates a typical scene out of many faceless and nameless participants and out of activities characteristic of Jesus.

The Fellows of the Seminar agreed that Jesus healed people and drove away what were thought to be demons. This much of Mark's report reflects historical reminiscence. As a possibility, that much of Mark's summary deserves a gray designation, but no more than that on account of Mark's tendency to exaggerate (the whole town was there!). The balance of the information has been supplied by Mark's imagination. This is particularly true of Mark's view that Jesus forbade the demons to speak because they knew who he was and Jesus wanted to keep that fact a secret for the time being. While Mark's summary reflects some vague historical memories, the connection with events of the first day, the time and the setting, and the number of patients are undoubtedly fictions.

Jesus tours Galilee
Mk 1:35–39
Mt 4:23–25, Lk 4:42–44
Source: Mark

1 **35 And rising early, while it was still very dark, he went outside
and stole away to an isolated place, where he started praying. 36 Then
Simon and those with him hunted him down. 37 When they had
found him they say to him, "They're all looking for you."**
38 But he replies: "Let's go somewhere else, to the neighboring vil-
lages, so I can speak there too, since that's what I came for."
**39 So he went all around Galilee speaking in their synagogues and
driving out demons.**

Jesus tours Galilee. Mark has constructed an anecdote to accommodate the saying of Jesus in v. 38: 'I came to speak in the villages of Galilee.' The anecdote is really a narrative introduction to a tour of Galilee. But the only event Mark seems to assign to this tour is the cure of the leper in the next episode (1:40–45), a tale that could go almost anywhere in his gospel. It lacks definition of place and time; it is not connected to other events, either earlier or later. It is possible that Mark has created this incident about Jesus' withdrawal, prayer, and Galilean tour as a way to extend the events of the first day for an indefinite period—Jesus goes on a tour to preach the kingdom, duration unspecified.

The Fellows of the Seminar, in concert with many scholars, doubt that this episode represents a particular historical occasion. They therefore designated it black. However, they are equally confident that Mark's anecdote reflects some bits of reliable information, which might be formulated in the form of narrative statements:

- **Jesus practiced prayer in seclusion.**
- **Jesus preached in the synagogues of Galilee.**
- **Jesus drove out what were thought to be demons.**

The Fellows believe these statements to be generally representative of activities of the historical Jesus. They are accordingly color coded red.

The leper
Mk 1:40–45
Mt 8:1–4, Lk 5:12–16;
EgerG 2:1–4
Sources: Mark, Egerton Gospel

1 **40 Then a leper comes up to him, pleads with him, falls down on
his knees, and says to him, "If you want to, you can make me clean."**
**41 Although Jesus was indignant, he stretched out his hand,
touched him, and says to him,** "Okay—you're clean!"
42 And right away the leprosy disappeared, and he was made clean.
43 And Jesus snapped at him, and dismissed him curtly 44 with this
warning: "See that you don't tell anyone anything, but go, have a
priest examine <your skin>. Then offer for your cleansing what Moses
commanded, as evidence <of your cure>."
**45 But after he left, he started telling everyone and spreading the
story, so that <Jesus> could no longer enter a town openly, but had
to stay out in the countryside. Yet they continued to come to him
from everywhere.**

The leper. The cure of the leper is attested in two independent sources: Mark and the Egerton Gospel (2:1–4).

> **Just then a leper comes up to him and says, "Teacher, Jesus, in wandering around with lepers and eating with them in the inn, I became a leper myself. [2]If you want to, I'll be made clean." [3]The master said to him, "Okay—you're clean!" And at once his leprosy vanished from him. [4]Jesus says to him,** "Go and have the priests examine <your skin>. Then offer your cleansing what Moses commanded—and no more sinning." [. . .]

Matthew and Luke both borrow and modify Mark's text without providing any new information. The version found in the Egerton Gospel is derived from oral tradition and, while it has much in common with its canonical counterpart, it does not reproduce any of the idiosyncrasies found in Mark. It is not therefore dependent on the synoptic account.

There are only two stories involving the cure of leprosy in the gospels: this tale and the cure of the ten lepers found in Luke 17:11–19. Leprosy played a significant role in the Hebrew scriptures because skin diseases of various kinds made their victims unclean—unable to participate in the temple cult and ostracized from society. Of course, they were also thought to be contagious. In all human societies, visible ailments such as skin lesions carry with them a certain social stigma that often gets interpreted religiously. In ancient Israel, the leper was required to rend his clothes, bare his head, cover his upper lip, and call out "Unclean! Unclean!" as he went about (Lev 13:45).

Jesus did not cure this leper of Hansen's disease—the ailment known to modern medicine as leprosy. In biblical times the term leprosy embraced a wide range of disorders, including rashes, acne, eczema, psoriasis, and other forms of dermatitis. Biblical leprosy consisted of scaly or flaking skin, accompanied by white spots and white hairs; the skin may also have developed red spots or streaks and may have been broken. Leprosy was sometimes regarded as divine punishment for sin, but it was not considered an incurable disease.

The Fellows of the Jesus Seminar agreed by a narrow margin that Jesus cured the "leper" of some form of dermatitis. They were much more certain that Jesus declared the leper clean. Under conventional circumstances, only a priest could declare a leper clean and thus eligible to reenter society. Jesus seems to have usurped this priestly function. Whether Jesus actually cured the ailment is less certain.

If Jesus were merely performing a priestly function in declaring the victim clean, his advice in v. 44 seems inappropriate or even contradictory. Why would Jesus send the leper to a priest to confirm the cure, unless, of course, he was recommending that the leper follow the letter of the law? Yet such advice appears to contradict Jesus' apparent disregard for purity regulations, as evident in his association with lepers, his disregard for kosher, and his failure to wash his hands properly before eating. The tension between the two parts of the narrative has led some scholars to speculate that v. 44 should be interpreted negatively: "Show yourself to a priest to demonstrate that you were in fact cured, in which case the priest will be obliged to affirm what has happened here." The last phrase of v. 44 could even be translated: "as evidence against them" (if "them" refers to the priests). This understanding is paralleled by Mark 6:11: "Shake the dust off your feet in witness *against them.*"

In the first phase of the Seminar, the words of Jesus in v. 44 were designated black, indicating that they probably did not originate with Jesus. The Fellows remain confident that the admonition, "See that you don't tell anyone anything" is the creation of Mark or a storyteller before Mark. But a review of the second part of Jesus' advice in the second phase of the Seminar produced a gray vote: the Fellows now allow the possibility that Jesus may have suggested to the leper that he get a clean bill of health from a priest and offer the appropriate sacrifice. The Fellows were not agreed, however, on how to interpret this second piece of advice. The difficulties accompanying the close analysis of these stories reveal once again how difficult it is to sort out the various strata in stories that have been told and retold for decades before achieving written form (and multiple written forms at that).

Verse 45 is Mark's narrative conclusion. It contains the narrator's estimate of Jesus' popularity rather than a report of actual responses to this single event. It is appropriately colored black.

John P. Meier is again somewhat more skeptical about the historical roots of this story than are the Fellows of the Jesus Seminar. He avers that Jesus claimed to have healed lepers and that others thought he had done so. Beyond that he is unwilling to go. Had he been a member of the Seminar, he might have voted black, or he might have settled for a gray.[10]

Paralytic & four
Mk 2:1–12
Mt 9:1–8, Lk 5:17–26
Source: Mark
Cf. Jn 5:1–9

2 **Some days later he went back to Capernaum and was rumored
to be at home. [2]And many people crowded around so there was no
longer any room, even outside the door. Then he started speaking to
them. [3]Some people then show up with a paralytic being carried by
four of them. [4]And when they were not able to get near him on
account of the crowd, they removed the roof above him. After dig-
ging it out, they lowered the mat on which the paralytic was lying.
[5]When Jesus noticed their trust, he says to the paralytic,** "Child, your
sins are forgiven."

**[6]Some of the scholars were sitting there and silently wondering:[7]
"Why does that fellow say such things? He's blaspheming! Who can
forgive sins except the one God?"**

**[8]And right away, because Jesus sensed in his spirit that they were
raising questions like this among themselves, he says to them:** "Why
do you entertain questions about these things? [9]Which is easier, to say
to the paralytic, 'Your sins are forgiven,' or to say, 'Get up, pick up
your mat and walk'?" **[10]But so that you may realize that on earth the
son of Adam has authority to forgive sins, he says to the paralytic,**
[11]"You there, get up, pick up your mat and go home!"

**[12]And he got up, picked his mat right up, and walked out as every-
one looked on. So they all became ecstatic, extolled God, and
exclaimed, "We've never seen the likes of this!"**

Paralytic & four. It is evident that this story had a checkered history. A simple healing story was expanded at some point, possibly by Mark himself, by the insertion of a controversy over the right to forgive sins. The middle section, vv. 5b–10, has evidently intruded into a simple healing story, vv. 3–5a, 11–12. If one skips from v. 5a to v. 11, the story becomes a conventional healing: The condition of the paralytic is evident from the fact that he has to be carried; Jesus cures the paralytic with a command to rise and walk; the man, now cured, does so and the crowd testifies to the miracle.

The controversy about the right to forgive sins reflects the interests of the later Christian community, which claimed that prerogative for its leaders. For this reason a majority of the Fellows of the Seminar voted to designate the middle section either gray or black on the grounds that the story has been modified to support those later interests.

A minority, on the other hand, argued that the controversy over the forgiveness of sins was integrally related to the cure: physical handicaps were regarded in those days as the consequence of sin and therefore as divine punishment. It may have been a matter of indifference to Jesus whether he said, "You there, get up, pick up your mat, and go home" or "Your sins are forgiven." The cure canceled the consequences of sin.

A critical point of interpretation is how to understand the phrase "the son of Adam" in v. 10: Does "son of Adam" refer to Jesus himself (meaning: "so that you may realize that on earth *I* have the authority . . . ")? Or is it used in the sense of any human being, any child of Adam? Understood as a reference to Jesus as the son of Adam (God's special emissary on earth), the middle section is clearly a later insertion. Understood as a reference to any child of Adam, it suggests that Jesus himself may have equated the cure of paralysis with the forgiveness of sin.

There can be no doubt that the author of the Gospel of Mark took son of Adam as a messianic title. However, Matthew evidently had intimations of a different and perhaps earlier view when he wrote at the conclusion of the story: "They glorified God who had given such authority to humans" (Matt 9:8). Of course, it is also possible to understand Matthew's conclusion as an allusion to a special group of human beings, namely those in charge of the budding church. Interpreters are often faced with different levels of interpretation of just this sort, a problem that makes it inordinately difficult to pinpoint the time frame of the story.

When the Fellows voted on the story as a whole, the weighted average came out gray. By segregating vv. 5b–10 from vv. 3–5a, 11–12, a very substantial majority agreed to a pink color for the core healing story. Pink does not affirm all the details of the story, but it does indicate that the story reflects an incident in the public life of Jesus. John P. Meier apparently concurs in this judgment; like the Fellows, he thinks the story has undergone considerable development in its pre-Markan history.[11] E. P. Sanders cites the story of the paralytic in the synagogue as though it were historical, although he does not make a specific claim to that effect.[12]

The narrative connective in v. 1 that locates the event in Capernaum the Fellows took as Mark's way of locating this story in his sequence of events comprising a typical day in Jesus' life. Both Matthew and Luke do not hesitate to modify Mark's setting. The core story, however, locates the cure in a house, so the link to a home, perhaps Jesus' own or that of a follower, is plausible (v. 1b–2). Recent archaeological work in Capernaum has unearthed a house dating to the first century C.E. The claim has been made that this house is Simon Peter's house, the very house referred to in the story of the paralytic. (Further, see the cameo on "Capernaum," p. 58.)

2 [13]**Again he went out by the sea. And, with a huge crowd gathered around him, he started teaching.**

[14]**As he was walking along, he caught sight of Levi, the son of Alphaeus, sitting at the toll booth, and he says to him,** "Follow me!"

And Levi got up and followed him.

Call of Levi
Mk 2:13–14
Mt 9:9, Lk 5:27–28; GEbi 2:4
Source: Mark

Call of Levi. Mark 2:13 is one of Mark's editorial connectives. It functions as a narrative introduction to the following story and, in a looser sense, to the following cluster of stories. It contains three pieces of information: Jesus goes out by the sea; a crowd gathers around him; he teaches them. The *again* of the first statement suggests that Jesus went out by the sea on more than one occasion. The Greek verbs in the second and third statements express habitual activity. In other words, this cluster of narrative statements describes some of Jesus' typical or habitual activities. Mark's narrative statements in this instance can be termed *typifications.*

We have no reason to doubt that Jesus taught crowds of people by the Sea of Galilee from time to time. After all, he numbered fishermen among his followers and we are confident that Capernaum on the Sea of Galilee was a center of his public activity. Yet critical scholars have resisted designating these statements as bits of historical lore. Why is that? In their narrative context and in most English translations, these statements are understood to refer to one specific occasion when Jesus enlisted a follower whose name was Levi or Matthew. Moreover, they occur in a transitional narrative splice created by Mark. As a consequence, scholars have understandably been reluctant to regard them as history. Nevertheless, as typifications, they probably accurately reflect frequent activities of Jesus. They represent traces in the folk memory of those who told stories about Jesus. We are relatively certain that this is the case because the typifications—Jesus teaching crowds by the sea—appear elsewhere in the gospel tradition.

The story about the call of some toll collector to become a follower of Jesus (v. 14) does not arouse the suspicions of the gospel scholar in the same way. It is the fact that this toll collector has been given a specific name, and the fact that the name varies in the Greek manuscripts, that make it difficult to accept the account as it stands as pure history.

Among Jesus' followers there were undoubtedly toll collectors—so the tradition remembers. One of them may well have been named Levi or Matthew. But the Fellows of the Seminar are dubious that the tradition remembers the occasion on which one particular toll collector joined the group. The story is again an example of the storyteller's license to particularize a well-known bit of lore. But we cannot be sure that the name Levi belonged in the original Greek text of Mark. While the Fellows designated the call of a toll collector pink, the variations in manuscript evidence would not permit them to endorse that toll collector's name.

Dining with sinners
Mk 2:15–17
Mt 9:10–13, Lk 5:29–32;
GosFr 1224 5:1–2
Sources: Mark, Gospel
Fragment 1224
Cf. Lk 15:1–2

2 [15]**Then Jesus happens to recline at table in <Levi's> house, along with many toll collectors and sinners and Jesus' disciples. (Remember, there were many of these people** and they were all following him.)

[16]**And whenever the Pharisees' scholars saw him eating with sinners and toll collectors, they would question** his disciples: "What's he doing eating with toll collectors and sinners?"

[17]**When Jesus overhears, he says to them:** "Since when do the able-bodied need a doctor? It's the sick who do. I did not come to enlist religious folks but sinners!"

Dining with sinners. There are three participants in this scene, not counting Jesus. There are the toll collectors and sinners with whom Jesus is eating; there are the Pharisees who question this practice; and then there are the silent disciples.

Scholars generally agree that the scene is a fiction. Jesus eating with a group of persons with dubious reputations is credible enough, but where were the Pharisees during the meal? Were they peeking in through the window? And if the Pharisees crashed the party in order to be critical, why didn't they address their queries to Jesus rather than to his disciples? And how does it happen that Jesus overhears them? Moreover, the storyteller makes a distinction between the disreputables who are dining companions of Jesus and the disciples. Yet many of the original followers of Jesus were from the peasant class and so were regarded as socially inferior. The gratuitous distinction between disciples and toll collectors and sinners hints that the Markan form of the story looks back on some hypothetical original scene from a great distance.

The fiction the storyteller has created juxtaposes elements from different stages of the tradition. This practice is not uncommon in ancient storytelling. Jesus shares a table with groups of people considered unclean by purity standards. This practice is criticized by the Pharisees on various occasions. Jesus defends it with witticisms and parables on other occasions. After the death of Jesus, the Pharisees and the disciples squabble over the practice. The disciples no longer consider themselves "toll collectors and sinners," so they distinguish themselves from the socially inferior companions of Jesus' past. They and the Pharisees clash. The brief story in Mark mixes all these different phases of the development of the tradition in one not entirely plausible narrative.

Does this brief narrative preserve any historical data? The Fellows extracted four narrative statements from the story that they were willing to endorse:

- **Jesus consorted openly with social outcasts.**
- **One label for social outcasts was "toll collectors and sinners."**

- **Jesus was criticized for eating with social outcasts.**
- **Jesus justified his practice of sharing an open table in aphorism (and parable).**

All four propositions received a red designation. The effort was then made to color-code the sentences in the story itself in accordance with these conclusions. Thus, while the story itself is considered to be a fiction embodying several levels of the tradition, the Fellows agreed that it preserved some reliable historical information. They were confident of its reliability, however, only because the information contained in the story was confirmed elsewhere in gospel lore about Jesus.

2 **18 John's disciples and the Pharisees were in the habit of fasting,**
and they come and ask him, "Why do the disciples of John fast, and
the disciples of the Pharisees, but your disciples don't?"
19 And Jesus said to them: "The groom's friends can't fast while the
groom is around, can they? So long as the groom is around, you can't
expect them to fast. 20 But the days will come when the groom is taken
away from them, and then they will fast, on that day.
21 "Nobody sews a piece of unshrunk cloth on an old garment, other-
wise the new, unshrunk patch pulls away from the old and creates a
worse tear.
22 "And nobody pours young wine into old wineskins, otherwise the
wine will burst the skins, and destroy both the wine and the skins.
Instead, young wine is for new wineskins."

Question of fasting
Mk 2:18–22
Mt 9:14–17, Lk 5:33–39
Source: Mark

Question of fasting. John the Baptist was an ascetic: he neither ate bread nor drank wine, and people accused him of being demented. Jesus, on the other hand, probably did not practice fasting himself. According to a saying preserved in the Sayings Gospel Q, Jesus both ate and drank and people accused him of being a glutton and a drunk, a friend of toll collectors and sinners (Luke 7:33–35). The style of Jesus' public life therefore contrasted with the style of John the Baptist, as well as with that of the Pharisees, who also practiced fasting. The first part of v. 18 was colored pink on the grounds that the followers of John the Baptist and the Pharisees probably did fast. The second part of the verse was designated gray because the question concerns the behavior of the disciples rather than the behavior of Jesus, which suggests that the question was framed—or reframed—long after Jesus was gone. The question originally must have had to do with Jesus' practice and the aphorism in v. 19 with the justification of his behavior. Verse 20 was tacked on as the justification for the Christian return to the practice of fasting.

2 **23 It so happened that he was walking along through the grain-**
fields on the sabbath day, and his disciples began to strip heads of
grain as they walked along. 24 And the Pharisees used to argue with

Sabbath observance
Mk 2:23–28
Mt 12:1–8, Lk 6:1–5
Source: Mark

him: "See here, why do they do what's not permitted on the sabbath day?"

[25]**And he says to them:** "Haven't you ever read what David did when he found it necessary, when both he and his companions were hungry? [26]He went into the house of God, when Abiathar was high priest, and ate the consecrated bread, and even gave some to his men to eat. No one is permitted to eat this bread, except the priests!"

[27]**And he continued:**

> The sabbath day was created for Adam and Eve,
> not Adam and Eve for the sabbath day.
> [28]So, the son of Adam lords it even over the sabbath day.

Sabbath observance. The two-part aphorism recorded in vv. 27–28 was judged by the Fellows to be an authentic formulation of Jesus. They further reasoned that such a sweeping reversal of priorities—invoking even the creation story—had probably been provoked by a concrete situation or a specific challenge. The setting provided by vv. 23–24 seemed entirely appropriate: Jesus and his disciples were itinerants, so a journey on the sabbath as a group is in character; Jesus and his disciples depended on the providence of God for food, one day at a time, so harvesting grain by hand to satisfy immediate hunger is historically plausible.

Scholars often object that this story must be an artificial construction because Pharisees would not have been monitoring the grainfields on a sabbath to catch Jesus and his followers. However, Mark does not represent this series of events as a single scene: the Pharisaic challenge of v. 24 did not necessarily take place at the time the disciples harvested grain. Rather, the story paints a picture of typical activities: Jesus and his disciples poach grain on sabbath journeys; the Pharisees criticize Jesus, who, as the disciples' teacher, must assume the responsibility for their behavior; Jesus responds with a witty reply. Exchanges of this type may have taken place on more than one occasion.

The Fellows earlier judged vv. 25–26 to be a Christian scribal insertion. In the controversies that arose between the Pharisees and Christian separatists after the death of Jesus, the tendency was for Christians to buttress their position by reference to the scriptures. Jesus was apparently not given to this practice.

These considerations led the Fellows to designate vv. 23–24 pink as a plausible scenario for the authentic Jesus aphorism preserved in vv. 27–28.

Man with crippled hand
Mk 3:1–6
Mt 12:9–14, Lk 6:6–11
Source: Mark
Cf. GNaz 4

3 **Then he went back to the synagogue, and a fellow with a crippled hand was there. [2]So they kept an eye on him, to see whether he would heal the fellow on the sabbath day, so they could denounce him. [3]And he says to the fellow with the crippled hand,** "Get up here in front of everybody." [4]**Then he asks them,** "On the sabbath day is it permitted to do good or to do evil, to save life or to destroy it?"

But they maintained their silence. [5]And looking right at them with anger, exasperated at their obstinacy, he says to the fellow, "Hold out your hand!"

He held it out and his hand was restored. [6]Then the Pharisees went right out with the Herodians and hatched a plot against him, to get rid of him.

Man with crippled hand. The story of the man with the withered hand brings to a close the cycle of controversy stories that began with the paralytic in the synagogue (2:1–12). Indeed, Mark seems to have thought of this story as the counterpart to the earlier controversy: there the right to forgive sins was in dispute, here the authority of Jesus to abrogate sabbath restrictions is at issue. In any case, Mark has designed this complex of stories to advance his plot, the conspiracy against Jesus' life. At the same time, he enhances the status of Jesus as son of Adam and Lord. These features are part of the Christian overlay he and the other evangelists are superimposing on their material.

The problem the Fellows (and many other scholars) found with this story may be summarized in this way: The plot against Jesus described in v. 6 is widely regarded as a Markan fiction. Nothing in the way Jesus treats the withered hand would have called for an attempt on his life.

If the plot is a Markan invention, then the authenticity of the saying in v. 4 becomes problematic: the rhetorical question Jesus poses is designed for this particular story. It sets up the option of saving life, in this case, the hand of the man, or destroying life—Jesus' own. Moreover, the rhetorical query is a typical way of responding to the charge in v. 2. In short, it is difficult to isolate any elements in the story that are not a part of Mark's compositional scheme that climaxes in the plot of v. 6. As John Meier puts it, when the story begins to unravel with v. 6, it continues unraveling with v. 4, until one wonders whether anything is left.[13]

Questions about the basis of the sabbath controversy depicted by the story produce further skepticism about its historicity. While the strict interpretation of the sabbath code prohibited the practice of medicine, various rabbis found ways around that restriction. In the story, Jesus does nothing beyond telling the fellow to hold out his hand. He gives no other word of command; he doesn't touch the man or perform some other act of healing. The response on the part of the Pharisees is trumped up by the storyteller.

In addition to all these problems, the story does not follow the pattern of other healing stories. In fact, the healing is incidental to the conflict over the sabbath. No mention is made of the gravity of the affliction; the victim does not solicit the help of Jesus; Jesus does nothing to effect a cure; and there is no confirmation of the cure by observers. Jesus takes the initiative throughout, which raises the suspicion that the story was created to support growing christological interests in the Christian community.

Considering the gravity of these problems, gray was a generous designation.

John P. Meier vacillates in his judgment about the historicity of this story. He is relatively certain that the sabbath controversy does not go back to an event in Jesus' life. Even without that feature, he is uncertain about its reliability. His *non liquet* ("it is not clear") can probably be translated into a Jesus Seminar gray in concert with the Fellows.[14] E. P. Sanders cites the story but is unclear about its status as a historical report.[15]

Jesus heals the crowds
Mk 3:7–12
Mt 12:15–21, Lk 6:17–19
Source: Mark

3 **[7]Then Jesus withdrew with his disciples to the sea, and a huge crowd from Galilee followed. When they heard what he was doing, a huge crowd from Judea, [8]and from Jerusalem and Idumea and across the Jordan, and from around Tyre and Sidon, collected around him. [9]And he told his disciples to have a small boat ready for him on account of the crowd, so they would not mob him. ([10]After all, he had healed so many that all who had diseases were pushing forward to touch him.) [11]The unclean spirits also, whenever they faced him, would fall down before him and shout out, "You son of God, you!"**

[12]But he always warned them not to tell who he was.

Jesus heals the crowds. Mark has constructed three rather full summaries of the activities of Jesus in his gospel: 1:32–24, 6:53–56, and this passage. In summaries of this type, ancient storytellers tended to exaggerate the success of their heroes. Here a huge crowd gathers from all the surrounding regions. It is so huge that Jesus must have a boat ready so he can escape. He has healed so many that everyone is pushing forward in order to touch him. Touch alone effects the cure. And the demons blurt out who he is in spite of his warning that they should not do so. All of this hyperbole is to be expected of the ardent fan of the wandering holy man.

Exaggeration is the rule among devoted reporters of famous sages, as this sample from Philostratus' life of Apollonius of Tyana indicates:

> When it became certain that he had arrived, people flocked to him from all over Greece aglow with anticipation; never had so many gathered for an Olympic festival as on this occasion. People came straight from Elis and Sparta, from as far away as Corinth; even the Athenians came, although they are not from the Peloponnesus. . . . And there were people from Megara who were then lodging at Olympia, together with many from Boeotia, and from Argos, as well as leading citizens of Phocis and Thessaly. Some of these folks had already made Apollonius' acquaintance, but were anxious to acquire additional knowledge from him.
>
> *Life of Apollonius,* 8.15

Both Mark and Philostratus belonged to the storytellers' guild of the hellenistic world.

Call of the twelve
Mk 3:13–19
Mt 10:1–4, Lk 6:12–16;
GEbi 2
Source: Mark
Cf. Acts 1:12–14, 15–26

3 **[13]Then he goes up on the mountain and summons those he wanted, and they came to him. [14]He formed a group of twelve to be his companions, and to be sent out to speak, [15]and to have authority to drive out demons.**

[16]And to Simon he gave the nickname Rock, [17]and to James, the son of Zebedee, and to John, his brother, he also gave a nickname, Boanerges, which means "Thunder Brothers"; **[18]and Andrew and**

Philip and Bartholomew and Matthew and Thomas and James, the son of Alphaeus; and Thaddeus and Simon the Zealot; [19]and Judas Iscariot, who, in the end, turned him in.

Call of the twelve. There is no question that Jesus attracted followers who accompanied him on his travels. The Fellows were divided on whether Jesus actively recruited disciples. But there was general agreement among the Fellows that the number "twelve" in connection with an inner circle of disciples is a fiction.

Twelve symbolizes the twelve tribes of Israel, which represent the descendants of Jacob. The twelve disciples of Jesus would thus have symbolized the new "Israel" being created by Jesus. According to Mark, the twelve were commissioned to exorcize demons and to speak, following the example of Jesus.

In addition to the reference here in Mark, the twelve are mentioned once in the Sayings Gospel Q (Luke 22:30//Matt 19:28) and once in Paul's first letter to the Corinthians (15:5), both of which date to the decade of the 50s, in all probability. The identification of Judas as one of the twelve (Mark 14:10, John 6:70), if historical, must have been an embarrassment to the early community. Other members of this circle are portrayed unfavorably: Peter deserts Jesus at his arrest; Thomas doubts; James and John, sons of Zebedee, the Thunder brothers, want special positions in the coming kingdom. At other times, the twelve argue about which of them is greatest and are represented as dense and without understanding. In view of this derogatory evidence, many scholars outside the Jesus Seminar have accepted as historical the tradition that Jesus did select twelve disciples to be with him, to accompany him on his travels, and to perform exorcisms and cures.

The Jesus Seminar, on the other hand, has tended to be skeptical about the existence of a special group designated "The Twelve." A group called the twelve is not mentioned in the earliest layer of the Sayings Gospel Q nor in the Gospel of Thomas; it appears in the title of the Didache but not in the body of that document (the title "The Teachings of the Twelve Apostles" was undoubtedly added later); the letter of Clement to the church at Corinth written about 96 C.E. does not mention the twelve, and neither do the letters of Ignatius composed between 110–117 C.E. Support for this highly symbolic designation depends on the Gospel of Mark, a reference in the later layer of Q, and a single reference in Paul's letters. However, Paul does not seem to know the twelve as an actual group of leaders with special authority. Instead, he is acquainted with an inner circle of "pillars," to which he refers in his letter to the Galatians (2:1–10).

Most important, the role of the "twelve" is associated with the eschatological self-consciousness of the Christian community, which thought of itself as the new Israel living at the endtime, just before the final judgment. The Seminar doubts that such a notion originated with Jesus.

In addition, the references to the twelve in Mark all occur in Mark's editorial work rather than in the body of anecdotes. The references to Judas as "one of the twelve" must also be regarded as a fabrication if the figure of Judas is a fiction, as many scholars think. Whether Judas was a real person or a fiction will be explored in the commentary on Mark 14:10–11.

To these reservations must be added the fact that it is impossible to establish a firm list of twelve names that constituted this special group. Matthew reproduces Mark's list (Matt 10:2–4); Luke replaces Thaddeus with a second Judas (Luke 6:16, Acts 1:13). No other gospel even has a list. However, the Fourth Gospel mentions as part of Jesus' intimate circle the names of Simon Peter and Andrew, his brother; the sons of Zebedee (although unnamed, presumably James and John); Philip, Thomas, Judas Iscariot, Judas (not Iscariot), Nathanael, and the "beloved disciple" (if not one of those named), for a total of ten. The symbolic number was apparently more important than the actual persons who made up the group.

Beelzebul controversy
Mk 3:20–30
Mt 12:22–32, Lk 11:14–23
Sources: Mark, Q

3 **[20]Then he goes home, and once again a crowd gathers, so they**
could not even grab a bite to eat. [21]When his relatives heard about it,
they came to get him. (You see, they thought he was out of his mind.)
[22]And the scholars who had come down from Jerusalem would say,
"He is under the control of Beelzebul" and "He drives out demons
in the name of the head demon!"
[23]And after calling them over, he would speak to them in riddles:
"How can Satan drive out Satan? [24]After all, if a government is divided
against itself, that government cannot endure. [25]And if a household is
divided against itself, that household won't be able to survive. [26]So if
Satan rebels against himself and is divided, he cannot endure but is
done for.
[27]"No one can enter a powerful man's house to steal his belongings
unless he first ties him up. Only then does he loot his house.
[28]"I swear to you, all offenses and whatever blasphemies human-
kind might blaspheme will be forgiven them. [29]But whoever blas-
phemes against the holy spirit is never ever forgiven, but is guilty of
an eternal sin."
([30]Remember, it was they who had started the accusation, "He is
controlled by an unclean spirit.")

Beelzebul controversy. Mark has framed the Beelzebul controversy (vv. 22–30) with a story about true relatives (vv. 20–21, 31–35). The Sayings Gospel Q also contained a version of the Beelzebul controversy (Luke 11:15–23//Matt 12:24–30), but it was introduced by an exorcism (Luke 11:14//Matt 12:22–23) rather than by a story about Jesus' relatives. The Gospel of Thomas preserves parallels to individual sayings in the Beelzebul complex (Thom 35:1–2, 44:1–3). The three sources indicate that one story developed in several different directions in the course of transmission.

The pink rating given to the role Jesus' family played in the charge that he was mad will be discussed in the commentary on the next section. The Fellows were persuaded that evidence scattered through the gospels sustains the claim that some authorities thought Jesus demon-possessed. That evidence is assembled in the next section.

3 [31]Then his mother and his brothers arrive. While still outside,
they send in and ask for him. [32]A crowd was sitting around him, and
they say to him, "Look, your mother and your brothers and sisters
are outside looking for you."

[33]**In response he says to them:** "My mother and brothers—who ever
are they?"

[34]**And looking right at those seated around him in a circle, he says,**
"Here are my mother and my brothers. [35]Whoever does God's will,
that's my brother and sister and mother!"

True relatives
Mk 3:31–35
Mt 12:46–50, Lk 8:19–21;
Th 99:1–3
Sources: Mark, Thomas

True relatives. Mark has elected to frame the Beelzebul controversy with a narrative about how Jesus' relatives thought him demented, or mad, or demon-possessed, and about how Jesus treated them when they came to get him. Two questions served as the focal points of the debate among Fellows: Did Jesus' relatives think him mad? Did Jesus' mother and brothers come to take him home as a result? A substantial majority of Fellows gave a positive answer to both questions.

In the controversy that follows the cure of the man born blind in the Gospel of John (9:1–10:42), there appears this paragraph:

> 10 [19]Once more there was a rift among the Judeans because he made these claims. [20]Many of them were saying, "He's out of his mind and crazy. Why pay any attention to him?" [21]Others would say, "These aren't the words of someone who is demon-possessed. A demon can't open the eyes of the blind, can it?"

The memory that some thought Jesus demon-possessed is thus supported by the Fourth Gospel. To be sure, the thought is not attributed to Jesus' relatives there, but to Judeans generally. Since it is unlikely that such a rumor was invented by the Christian community, who would not have regarded it as flattering, it appears to have some foundation in fact. Matthew and Luke both learned about it from their source, Mark, but both of them chose to suppress it. Later, in copying the manuscript of Mark some scribes modified the text of verse 21 so as to eliminate the reference to Jesus' family and substituted instead "When the scholars and others heard. . . ." It was evidently inconceivable to some in the early Christian community that Jesus' family could have regarded him as mad.

The Gospel of John also reports that Jesus' brothers did not believe in him (7:5). Again, the memory that there was a time when Jesus did not have the support of his mother and siblings was undoubtedly distasteful to the Christian community. Yet Mark is clear on that point. It was only later that Jesus' brother James changed his mind and became a leader in the Jerusalem church, possibly as a consequence of a vision he had of the risen Jesus (1 Cor 15:7).

In parables
Mk 4:1–34
Mt 13:1–53, Lk 8:4–18
Source: Mark

4 **Once again he started to teach beside the sea. An enormous crowd gathers around him, so he climbs into a boat and sits there on the water facing the huge crowd on the shore.**

2**He would then teach them many things in parables. In the course of his teaching he would tell them:**

3Listen to this! This sower went out to sow. 4While he was sowing, some seed fell along the path, and the birds came and ate it up. 5Other seed fell on rocky ground where there wasn't much soil, and it came up right away because the soil had no depth. 6But when the sun came up it was scorched, and because it had no root it withered. 7Still other seed fell among thorns, and the thorns came up and choked it, so that it produced no fruit. 8Finally, some seed fell on good earth and started producing fruit. The seed sprouted and grew: one part had a yield of thirty, another part sixty, and a third part one hundred.

9**And as usual he said:** "Anyone here with two good ears had better listen!"

10**Whenever he went off by himself, those close to him, together with the twelve, would ask him about the parables.** 11**And he would say to them:** "You have been given the secret of God's imperial rule; but to those outside everything is presented in parables, 12so that

They may look with eyes wide open
but never quite see,
and may listen with ears attuned
but never quite understand,
otherwise they might turn around and find forgiveness!"

13**Then he says to them:** "You don't get this parable, so how are you going to understand other parables? 14The 'sower' is 'sowing' the message. 15The first group are the ones 'along the path': here the message 'is sown,' but when they hear, Satan comes right along and steals the message that has been 'sown' into them. 16The second group are the ones sown 'on rocky ground.' Whenever they listen to the message, right away they receive it happily. 17Yet they do not have their own 'root' and so are short-lived. When distress or persecution comes because of the message, such a person becomes easily shaken right away. 18And the third group are those sown 'among the thorns.' These are the ones who have listened to the message, 19but the worries of the age and the seductiveness of wealth and the yearning for everything else come and 'choke' the message and they become 'fruitless.' 20And the final group are the ones sown 'on good earth.' They are the ones who listen to the message and take it in and 'produce fruit, here thirty, there sixty, and there one hundred.'"

21**And he would say to them:** "Since when is the lamp brought in to

be put under the bushel basket or under the bed? It's put on the lamp-
stand, isn't it?
22"After all, there is nothing hidden except to be brought to light,
nor anything kept secret that won't be exposed.
23"If anyone here has two good ears, use them!"
24**And he went on to say to them:** "Pay attention to what you hear!
The standard you apply will be the standard applied to you, and then
some.
25"In fact, to those who have, more will be given, and from those
who don't have, even what they do have will be taken away!"
26**And he would say:**

God's imperial rule is like this: Suppose someone sows seed on
the ground, 27and sleeps and rises night and day, and the seed
sprouts and matures, although the sower is unaware of it. 28The
earth produces fruit on its own, first a shoot, then a head, then
mature grain on the head. 29But when the grain ripens, all of a
sudden <that farmer> sends for the sickle, because it's harvest
time.

30**And he would say:**

To what should we compare God's imperial rule, or what para-
ble should we use for it? 31Consider the mustard seed: When it is
sown on the ground, though it is the smallest of all the seeds on
the earth, 32—yet when it is sown, it comes up, and becomes the
biggest of all garden plants, and produces branches, so that the
birds of the sky can nest in its shade.

33**And with the help of many such parables he would speak his
message to them according to their ability to comprehend. 34Yet he
would not say anything to them except by way of parable, but
would spell everything out in private to his own disciples.**

In parables. Mark has formed a rather lengthy discourse dealing with Jesus' use of parables as a teaching instrument. The authenticity of the various sayings components incorporated into this discourse was considered in *The Five Gospels.* The parables of the sower, seed and harvest, and mustard seed were designated pink, along with the saying about the lamp and bushel, and the remark about those who have and have not; the remainder of the sayings were colored gray and black. It remained for the Jesus Seminar to consider the sketchy narrative frame Mark has provided for these materials.

Two types of questions were involved in the evaluation of this narrative frame. The first is whether Mark represents this discourse as something that took place on a particular occasion, and, if so, whether that occasion is plausible historically. If he does not represent it as a singular event, does he depict things that Jesus *typically* did?

It is clear that the parables assembled in this complex were transmitted in the oral tradition as separate items. And Mark so represents them. His framework is composed in sentences that indicate: this is the sort of thing Jesus often or sometimes did. The Scholars Version has taken care to translate the Greek verbs into the English that conveys that sense. Most English translations misrepresent the Greek text and turn habitual activity into single events.

Even though Mark depicts what Jesus customarily does, the way Mark represents him may not be historical. In this complex, Jesus' teaching beside the sea, from a boat, to a huge crowd is entirely probable (v. 1). That he taught customarily in parables is indisputable (v. 2); that he taught exclusively in parables is highly dubious. Moreover, it is very unlikely that Jesus' public parables were intended to convey hidden meanings that he revealed only in private to his disciples (v. 10). The concluding remark (v. 33–34) combines these two aspects: Jesus did teach in parables (pink), but he did not teach exclusively in parables and did not provide his followers with a private interpretation (black). This distinction is correlative, of course, with the decisions regarding the teachings and explanations taken in *The Five Gospels:* Where the teachings and explanations are colored black, the corresponding narrative setting is usually colored black.

Jesus stills the storm
Mk 4:35–41
Mt 8:23–27, Lk 8:22–25
Source: Mark

4 [35]**Later in the day, when evening had come, he says to them,**
"Let's go across to the other side."
[36]**After sending the crowd away, they took him along since he was**
in the boat, and other boats accompanied him. [37]**Then a great squall**
comes up and the waves begin to pound against the boat, so that the
boat suddenly began to fill up. [38]**He was in the stern sleeping on a**
cushion. And they wake him up and say to him, "Teacher, don't you
care that we are going to drown?"
[39]**Then he got up and rebuked the wind and said to the sea,** "Be
quiet, shut up!"
The wind then died down and there was a great calm.
[40]**He said to them,** "Why are you so cowardly? You still don't trust,
do you?"
[41]**And they were completely terrified and would say to one**
another, "Who can this fellow be, that even the wind and the sea
obey him?"

Jesus stills the storm. Mark's account of the stilling of the storm brings us to the first of the so-called nature wonders. It also introduces a new and different sense of who Jesus is into the gospel story. The stories of Jesus as an exorcist (1:21–28) and Jesus as a healer of Peter's mother-in-law (1:29–31), of the leper (1:40–45), of the paralytic (2:1–12), of the man with a crippled hand (3:1–6) identify Jesus as simply another charismatic sage with healing powers; but a Jesus who has the power to calm the seas and still the wind puts him in a category with the other gods—with Yahweh, with Zeus, with Poseidon. In other words, the "christology" of this story is that of the early Christian community. For this reason alone, many scholars have concluded that the tale is the fictional product of the believing community.

The Fellows of the Jesus Seminar were unanimous in their judgment that the stilling of the storm is not based on an event in the life of Jesus. John P. Meier reached the same conclusion independently.[16] E. P. Sanders thinks the Christian tradition "augmented and enhanced" the miracle stories in order to make them impressive; he is also inclined to the view that Jesus' miracles were "relatively minor and excited the public only temporarily." He does not, however, come to a firm conclusion about this particular story.[17]

The Jesus Seminar began its evaluation with the observation that the sequence of events in Mark 4:35–5:43 is not historical but the result of Markan arrangement: the stilling of the storm (4:35–41); the demon of Gerasa (5:1–20); Jairus' daughter and the woman with a vaginal hemorrhage (5:21–43). In addition, there are a number of Markan touches in the storm story itself. The accusation in v. 40 that the disciples are cowardly and without trust is a Markan theme. The introduction (vv. 35–36) is probably the work of Mark, although the mention of "other boats" is inexplicable since they immediately disappear from the story. And surely v. 41 is a curious conclusion in view of the story Mark has been telling: Do the disciples not yet have an inkling of who Jesus is? Have they not been paying attention?

Some scholars have suggested that Mark's tale has been influenced by themes in the Hebrew bible, particularly the story of Jonah. The description of the storm echoes the opening of Jonah's adventure: a great storm comes up, the boat begins to founder, Jonah is asleep. The stilling of the storm is depicted in language borrowed from the Greek version of Ps 105:8–9: "The Lord . . . rebuked the Red Sea and it dried up." Also Ps 106:24–25 (LXX): "The Lord commanded the storm and it calmed to a breeze and the waves were still." Others have pointed to parallels in Greek and Roman literature, especially the *Odyssey* of Homer. Apollonius of Tyana, a contemporary of Jesus, also a charismatic sage and wonder worker, was regarded as the master of storms, of fire, and of perils of all kinds; people considered him to be a valuable traveling companion, no doubt because they thought his presence would protect them from danger at sea.[18] After all, making a sea voyage was a risky business, especially in winter. As in other instances, Christian storytellers may well be honoring Jesus by associating him with other heroes.

For the theory that the stilling of the storm may have been part of a gospel of miracles, see the related cameo (pp. 388–89).

5 **And they came to the other side of the sea, to the region of the**
Gerasenes. [2]And when he got out of the boat, suddenly a person con-
trolled by an unclean spirit came from the tombs to accost him. [3]This
man made his home in the tombs, and nobody was able to bind him,
not even with a chain, [4]because, though he had often been bound
with fetters and with chains, he would break the fetters and pull the
chains apart, and nobody could subdue him. [5]And day and night he

Demon of Gerasa
Mk 5:1–20
Mt 8:28–34, Lk 8:26–39
Source: Mark

would howl among the tombs and across the hills and keep bruising himself on the stones. [6]And when he saw Jesus from a distance, he ran up and knelt before him [7]and, shouting at the top of his voice, he says, "What do you want with me, Jesus, you son of the most high God? For God's sake, don't torment me!" [8]—because he had been saying to it: "Come out of that fellow, you filthy spirit!"

[9]And <Jesus> started questioning him: "What's your name?"

"My name is Legion," he says, "for there are many of us."

[10]And it kept begging him over and over not to expel them from their territory.

[11]Now over there by the mountain a large herd of pigs was feeding. [12]And so they bargained with him: "Send us over to the pigs so we may enter them!"

[13]And he agreed. And then the unclean spirits came out and entered the pigs, and the herd rushed down the bluff into the sea, about two thousand of them, and drowned in the sea. [14]And the herdsmen ran off and reported it in town and out in the country.

And they went out to see what had happened. [15]And they come to Jesus and notice the demoniac sitting with his clothes on and with his wits about him, the one who had harbored Legion, and they got scared. [16]And those who had seen told them what had happened to the demoniac, and all about the pigs. [17]And they started begging him to go away from their region. **[18]And as <Jesus> was getting into the boat, the ex-demoniac kept pleading with him to let him go along. [19]And he would not let him, but says to him,** "Go home to your people and tell them what your patron has done for you—how he has shown mercy to you."

[20]And he went away and started spreading the news in the Decapolis about what Jesus had done for him, and everybody would marvel.

Demon of Gerasa. The story of the demoniac of Gerasa is the most elaborate of all the tales of healing and exorcism. Mark's version savors florid detail, some of which both Matthew and Luke found distasteful. Scholars have long been troubled by its rambling complexities. A close but less elaborate approximation is found in the story of the man with a mute spirit in Mark 9:14–29.

The Fellows of the Jesus Seminar concluded that some vague historical event might lie behind the present narrative, but that was about all one could say. They were certain that Jesus did not have the conversation with the demon named Legion as reported in the story (vv. 9–12). John P. Meier regards that conversation as something "that strains credulity."[19] And they were equally certain that Jesus did not send the demons into a herd of pigs that subsequently stampeded into the lake and drowned (vv. 11–14). That feature of the story was probably developed for a Jewish audience that would have appreciated a demon named Legion—the term always suggested the Roman army—taking possession of a herd of swine that drowned in the lake, just as the Pharaoh's army was drowned in the Red Sea (Exod 15:4). An appropriate end for both the Legion and the swine (which were considered "unclean" animals, Lev 11:7)! But of course the allusion had to be made discreetly.

Mark, or some storyteller before him, tacked on vv. 18–20 as a model missionary discourse: Jesus urges the demoniac, now cured, to become a missionary to the cities of the Decapolis—the ten Greek cities—and report what his patron, Jesus, has done for him. This touch was added, no doubt, to validate the early Christian mission to the gentiles.

The opening verse (v. 1) is another Markan touch: Jesus crosses the Sea of Galilee and comes to the country of the Gerasenes. Sea crossings seem to be Mark's speciality: He reports a second in 6:45. Gerasa is located approximately thirty miles southeast of the Sea of Galilee, not exactly a convenient location for the drowning of the pigs. Matthew relocates the demoniac to Gadara, which is only six miles from the lakeshore. Later scribes tried other remedies to accommodate the pigs.

Verses 2–8 and 15–17 were designated gray, rather than black, only by a slim majority. On the other hand, more than half of the Fellows voted either red or pink on the narrative statement that Jesus exorcised a demon from someone who thought he was demon-possessed. Even that vote was not enough to raise the level to pink. Once again, the Seminar had no trouble believing that Jesus practiced exorcism; it had considerable reservations, however, about whether this particular story preserved memories of a specific historical event.

John P. Meier thinks that some historical event lies behind this story, but that it is difficult to say precisely what that event was because "too many layers of literary activity and theological imagination have been superimposed."[20] E. P. Sanders lists but does not evaluate this particular story.[21]

For information about the cycle of miracle stories that Mark may have had at his disposal, consult the cameo "A Gospel of Miracles?" (pp. 388–89).

5 **21 When Jesus had again crossed over to the other side, a large**
crowd gathered around him, and he was beside the sea. 22 And one of
the synagogue officials comes, **Jairus by name,** and as soon as he sees
him, he falls at his feet 23 and pleads with him and begs, "My little
daughter is on the verge of death, so come and put your hands on her
so she may be cured and live!"
24 And <Jesus> set out with him.

Jairus' daughter
Mk 5:21–24a, 35–43
Mt 9:18–19, 23–26,
Lk 8:40–42a, 49–56
Source: Mark

Jairus' daughter. The evangelist has interrupted the story of Jairus' daughter in order to tell the story of the woman with an internal hemorrhage. The commentary on vv. 21–24a will be found below, in conjunction with the commentary on continuation of the story in vv. 35–43.

5 **And a large crowd started following and shoving against him.**
25 And there was a woman who had had a vaginal flow for twelve
years, 26 who had suffered much under many doctors, and who had
spent everything she had, but hadn't been helped at all, but instead

Woman with
a vaginal hemorrhage
Mk 5:24b–34
Mt 9:20–22, Lk 8:42b–48
Source: Mark

had gotten worse. 27When <this woman> heard about Jesus, she
came up from behind in the crowd and touched his cloak. (28No
doubt she had been figuring, "If I could just touch his clothes, I'll be
cured!") 29And the vaginal flow stopped instantly, and she sensed in
her body that she was cured of her illness.

30And suddenly, because Jesus realized that power had drained
out of him, he turned around and started asking the crowd, "Who
touched my clothes?"

31And his disciples said to him, "You see the crowd jostling you
around and you're asking, 'Who touched me?'"

32And he started looking around to see who had done this.
33Although the woman got scared and started trembling—she real-
ized what she had done—she came and fell down before him and
told him the whole truth.

34He said to her, "Daughter, your trust has cured you. Go in peace,
and farewell to your illness."

Woman with a vaginal hemorrhage. The gist of this story in its earliest form must have been something like this:

- **There was a woman who suffered from vaginal hemorrhaging. She touched Jesus' cloak and the bleeding stopped instantly.**

The rest of the story appears to be an expansion of this core event.

Verse 24b is Mark's narrative introduction. Mark introduces the crowd pressing in on Jesus in order to prepare for the surreptitious touching that occurs later. Since no historical information is involved, black is the correct color.

The storyteller now expands on the woman's condition: she has suffered for twelve years, which provides a catchword association with the *twelve*-year-old girl in the Jairus story (v. 42), and she has exhausted her fortune in seeking help from physicians. She had heard about Jesus and was determined to touch him in the hopes of being cured. Much of the detail in vv. 25–27 no doubt derives from the storyteller's imagination. Yet the problem and the prospect of cure may reflect a historical event. Pink with gray catches the mixture of fact and fiction.

Verse 28 is a Markan explanatory note: only an omniscient storyteller can know what was going on in the woman's mind. Black is the appropriate color.

The woman appears to have had a recurrent somatic complaint that did not yield to medical treatment of any kind. Yet her contact with Jesus brings her complaint to an abrupt end. That suggests she did not have a physical disorder, but suffered from a psychosomatic malady. Touching was an effective therapy. Verse 29 is therefore the key narrative statement and deserves a pink designation.

The author of the Gospel of Mark is acquainted with touching as a healing technique. Jesus touches the leper as a part of the cure (1:41). After he heals the fellow with a crippled hand (3:1–6), those with diseases push forward to touch him (3:10). In another narrative summary, Mark describes the sick stretched out in marketplaces in the hopes of touching the fringe of Jesus' cloak (6:56). Jesus touches the tongue of the deaf-mute in another healing story (7:33). Jesus also touches the blind man of Bethsaida in another Markan story (8:22). Touching therapy is almost universal in its practice and has strong advocates even in societies that have espoused modern medicine.

Surprisingly, no mention is made of the woman's ritual condition: as a result of her hemorrhage, she would have been considered unclean. According to Leviticus, a woman was unclean during her menstrual period for seven days and anyone who touched her during that time was unclean until that evening (15:19). The bed and chair on which she lies and sits during this period are also unclean, and anyone touching either one must wash his or her clothes and bathe, *and* remain unclean for the balance of the day (15:20–24). And, of course, a woman with vaginal bleeding other than during her regular menstrual cycle was equally unclean (15:25).

Ezekiel can even compare the way Israel has profaned the land with words and deeds to the defilement occasioned by a woman during her menstrual period (Ezek 36:16).

In the Temple Scroll found at Qumran among the Dead Sea Scrolls, the restrictions on those considered unclean were strict. Israel was to set aside areas for those stricken with leprosy and other skin diseases, along with those having a discharge, and menstruating women, so that they would not enter the cities and towns and profane them (11QTemple Scroll, col. 48).

Yet nothing in the story of the afflicted woman suggests that she has defiled Jesus with her touch and that he objects to her touch for that reason. And no one in the surrounding throng seems to have noticed. Nevertheless, her act must have been considered brazen, which is a way, perhaps, for the storyteller to underscore the trust required for her to break a social taboo and touch Jesus.

The balance of the story, vv. 30–34, was colored black as part of the imaginative elaboration of the storyteller. The reference to power being drained out of Jesus moves the story into the realm of magic: Jesus has a limited fund of power and knows when it has been diminished. Mark then adds a small human touch: When Jesus wants to know who touched him, the disciples remind him that the throngs have been jostling him on every side (vv. 30–31). Jesus' ability to peer into the minds of other people, especially his opponents (as in the case of the paralytic, Mark 2:8), seems to have deserted him on this occasion.

The story of the woman with the hemorrhage does not have a demonstration as its conclusion: the onlookers do not attest to her new condition and she does nothing to indicate that she has been cured. In place of the customary demonstration, the woman becomes frightened when Jesus looks around to see who has robbed him of power and confesses. This permits Mark to add his own interpretive touch: her trust is responsible for her cure.

The Fellows agreed that the core story deserved a pink rating. John P. Meier is unwilling to go that far. He concludes that a firm judgment about its historical value is not possible. That is probably the equivalent of a gray vote.[22] E. P. Sanders describes but does not evaluate this story.[23]

Jairus' daughter
Mk 5:21–24a, 35–43
Mt 9:18–19, 23–26,
Lk 8:40–42a, 49–56
Source: Mark

5 [35]**While he was still speaking,** the synagogue official's people
approach and say, "Your daughter has died; why keep bothering the
teacher?"

[36]When Jesus overheard this conversation, he says to the syna-
gogue official, "Don't be afraid, just have trust!"

[37]**And he wouldn't let anyone follow along with him except Peter
and James and John, James' brother.** [38]When they come to the house
of the synagogue official, he notices a lot of clamor and people cry-
ing and wailing, [39]and he goes in and says to them, "Why are you car-
rying on like this? The child hasn't died; she's sleeping."

[40]And they started laughing at him. But he runs everyone out and
takes the child's father and her mother **and his companions** and goes
in where the child is. [41]And he takes the child by the hand and says
to her, *"talitha koum"* (which means, "Little girl," I say to you, "Get
up!"). [42]And the little girl got right up and started walking around.
(Incidentally, she was twelve years old.)
And they were downright ecstatic. [43]**And he gave them strict
orders that no one should learn about this, and he told them to give
her something to eat.**

Jairus' daughter. The Fellows of the Jesus Seminar were uncertain as a group that there was a synagogue ruler named Jairus, that he had a twelve-year-old daughter, and that Jesus healed her or raised her from the dead. The weighted averages all fell into the gray category. What were the reasons for this uncertainty?

The story of Jairus' daughter is interrupted at v. 24 and the account of the woman with a continuous vaginal hemorrhage inserted. The predominant view in the Seminar is that Mark is the one who performed the intercalation—inserting one story into another. He does so at other points in his gospel. For example, he inserts an argument about who can forgive sins into the story of the paralytic (Mark 2:1–12: vv. 5–10), and he surrounds the temple incident with the cursing of the fig tree, as though to say that what happened to the withered fig tree has also happened to the temple (Mark 11:12–25: vv. 15–18). The first step in the analysis, then, is to untangle the two stories.

Untangling the two stories entails identifying Mark's editorial work. Verse 21 is Mark's narrative transition; the sequencing of events in the gospels has no historical value, except in very rare instances. Similarly, v. 24a is Mark's device for splicing the two stories together: Jesus sets out with Jairus for the latter's home and a crowd starts jostling the pair as they walk along. Verse 35a is the way Mark has elected to resume the story of Jairus' daughter: the news comes that Jairus' daughter has died just as Jesus finishes talking with the woman. Furthermore, the mention of the intimate three in v. 37 (Peter, James, and John) is probably another Markan insertion to give some continuity to his gospel. The further reference to Jesus' companions in v. 40 is another Markan touch; they play no active role in the narrative. Mark has also translated the Aramaic command for his readers in v. 41. The narrative aside in v. 42b—the girl was twelve years old—is another storyteller's touch. Finally, the conclusion in v. 43a is a standard Markan motif: tell no one about what has happened. And the final proof of the resuscitation of the daughter is to give her something to eat (v. 43b): just as the risen Jesus will ask for something to eat to prove that he is no ghost (Luke 24:41–43), so the daughter is given food to prove that she is alive and well.

The oral form of the story that Mark has edited and adapted to its present literary context consisted of the three customary parts: (1) Jesus is petitioned by an important Jewish official to come and heal his daughter (vv. 22–23); while they are on their way, the report reaches them that she has died, indicating the gravity of the case (v. 35b). (2) Jesus revives the daughter by taking her by the hand and raising her up (v. 41). (3) Those who had gathered to mourn the passing of the little girl are ecstatic—their reaction confirms the miracle (v. 42).

What originally may have been a relatively simple healing story has developed into an elaborate resuscitation tale. Even in the final form of the story it is not at all clear that a resuscitation is involved. In v. 39 Jesus insists that the girl is not dead but sleeping. The story does not resolve the ambiguity. A similar thing occurs, when Paul allegedly raises Eutychus back to life. After examining the young man, Paul notes that he still has life in him (Acts 20:7–12). Other resuscitation stories also note such ambiguities. In view of the difficulty in determining when persons were really dead, it is disquieting to think how many people may have been buried alive in ancient times. The possibility of undetected life seems to be the reason mourning rites and final burial in rock-cut tombs took place only after a three-day wait.

Several features that serve to enhance the literary appeal of the story and heighten the miracle have been added. The interruption of the story of Jairus' daughter to tell about the woman with vaginal bleeding functions to heighten the tension. Jesus dramatically excludes everyone from the death chamber, except his intimates and the parents. Those gathered to mourn with the family are derisive of Jesus. The Aramaic "talitha koum" is reported as though it were a magical formula. Following her revival, the girl starts walking around (v. 42) as though she had been a paralytic. Her age is noted. Jesus' command to tell no one makes no sense as a conclusion to this story (Jesus has not been identified by demons as the messiah). Jesus orders the parents to give the girl something to eat to prove she is not a ghost. All these features strike the wary critic as fictional embellishments rather than as details of a historical report. The difficulties attendant upon recovering something approximating the original oral form of the story again led the Seminar to adopt gray as the appropriate color for the core story. Mark's obvious editorial touches are colored black.

As is so often the case in his book *The Historical Figure of Jesus,* E. P. Sanders summarizes the story of Jairus' daughter but does not say whether he thinks it is a historical report.[24] John P. Meier, on the other hand, concludes that the story is not the pure invention of the early church, although it has been "expanded and reinterpreted by Christian faith." His detailed discussion points to the same assessment that the Fellows reached: gray.[25]

No respect at home
Mk 6:1–6
Mt 13:54–58
Source: Mark
Cf. Lk 4:16–30

6 **Then he left that place, and he comes to his hometown, and his**
disciples follow him. **2When the sabbath day arrived, he started**
teaching in the synagogue; and many who heard him were
astounded and said so: "Where's he getting this?" and "What's the
source of all this wisdom?" and "Who gave him the right to perform
such miracles? 3This is the carpenter, isn't it? Isn't he Mary's son?
And who are his brothers, if not James, Joses, Judas, and Simon?
And who are his sisters, if not our neighbors?" And they were
resentful of him.

4**Jesus used to tell them:** "No prophet goes without respect, except
on his home turf and among his relatives and at home!"

5**He was unable to perform a single miracle there, except that he**
did cure a few by laying hands on them, 6though he was always
shocked at their lack of trust. And he used to go around the villages,
teaching in a circuit.

No respect at home. This narrative segment provides a great deal of hard information about Jesus and his home village—if, in fact, the details are historically accurate.

Verse 1 is Mark's narrative connective that links Jesus' visit to Nazareth to the preceding events. Since Mark, writing more than thirty years after Jesus' death, did not know the sequence of events in Jesus' life, the linkage is Mark's invention.

The evidence scattered through the gospels suggests that Jesus did teach in synagogues from time to time, if not in actual synagogue buildings, at least in houses used for such gatherings. The Seminar is fairly certain that this information is reliable and so voted pink. Of course, Mark here represents Jesus' appearance in a synagogue as linked to a specific series of events. That aspect of Mark's story may well be fictional. The Fellows elected to understand the events and remarks in vv. 2–3 as representative of things done and said on various occasions.

It is probably no exaggeration to say that Jesus' friends and neighbors from his home village were impressed with his wisdom, and surprised at the same time. They knew him to be an uneducated peasant and so wondered where he had acquired his knowledge and teaching skills. They had also heard of the wondrous things he had done elsewhere—probably performing exorcisms and curing some patients of skin diseases, paralysis, deafness, or blindness. These generalizations all fit what is otherwise known or can be inferred about Jesus.

The remark in v. 3 that Jesus was a carpenter, or woodworker, may be accurate, although it is difficult to verify. Nowhere else in the extant records is Jesus so designated. In addition, one might conclude from the stories Jesus told that he was a peasant farmer; his metaphors are mostly agricultural. Justin Martyr writing around the middle of the second century C.E. depicts Jesus as a woodworker fashioning plows and yokes. The same tradition is reported of Joseph in the Infancy Gospel of Thomas (13:1), a gospel that probably originated late in the second century. But that tradition is undoubtedly legend and may be based solely on Mark.

Mary was undoubtedly the name of Jesus' mother. Furthermore, Jesus was known as the son of Mary, which is striking in view of the fact sons were usually identified by reference to their fathers. Various explanations have been given for this oddity: Joseph was already dead; Joseph's name is omitted to protect the doctrine of the virgin birth; Jesus was actually illegitimate.

The doctrine of the perpetual virginity of Mary has impeded the recognition that Jesus had brothers and sisters. Except for James, the brothers are named only here and in the Matthean parallel in early Christian literature: James, probably the eldest of the four, Joses or Joseph (a variant), Judas, and Simon. The sisters are never named.

James is well known from his later role as a leader of the Jerusalem community (Gal 1:19, 2:9), although he apparently did not support Jesus during Jesus' lifetime (John 7:5). Nothing is known of the other three brothers. The attribution of letters to James and Judas (Jude) has no historical basis; the letters were written anonymously.

Jesus probably provoked resentment on the part of both his family and his Nazareth neighbors: They perhaps thought he had exceeded his position and place in their society. The remark in v. 3 is supported by the proverb in v. 4, which Jesus probably quoted.

His neighbors in Nazareth apparently regarded Jesus incapable of exorcisms and cures (v. 5). While not verifiable, this information is historically probable. The remark in v. 6 that Jesus was shocked at the lack of trust on the part of his family and friends in Nazareth echoes a Markan theme and therefore does not represent Jesus. Since Jesus was an itinerant and worked in lower Galilee, the final sentence in v. 6 is an accurate typification.

6 7**Then he summoned the twelve and started sending them out
in pairs and giving them authority over unclean spirits.** 8**And he
instructed them** not to take anything on the road, except a staff: no
bread, no knapsack, no spending money, 9but to wear sandals, and to
wear no more than one shirt. 10**And he went on to say to them:**
"Wherever you enter someone's house, stay there until you leave
town. 11And whatever place does not welcome you or listen to you, get
out of there and shake the dust off your feet in witness against them."
12**So they set out and announced that people should turn their
lives around,** 13**and they often drove out demons, and they anointed
many sick people with oil and healed <them>.**

Mission of the twelve
Mk 6:7–13
Mt 10:5–15, Lk 9:1–6; 10:1–16
Sources: Mark, Q
Cf. Mk 3:13–19, Mt 10:3–4, Lk 6:12–16

Mission of the twelve. The Fellows agreed that Jesus exorcized what were thought to be demons and that Jesus' disciples also exorcized demons. They further agreed that outsiders also cast out demons in Jesus' name. And, of course, there were still others who exorcized demons on their own. Yet the

Fellows doubt that Jesus authorized a particular *twelve* disciples to perform this function. That skepticism is born of the symbolic function of the number twelve: the twelve apostles represent the twelve tribes of Israel and thus symbolize a "new" Israel. In addition, the number twelve suggests the formation of a special community, the reconstitution of the twelve tribes of Israel, and thus an "eschatological" community, one that is readying itself for the end of the age. The Fellows doubt that this notion originated with Jesus.

Jesus probably did not dispatch a group of disciples on a particular mission during his public life. His followers undoubtedly did travel about on their own from time to time, and when they did so, Jesus may have instructed them on how to behave. Although Jesus himself probably did not contemplate a comprehensive mission to his own people or to the gentiles, some of his followers no doubt preached as they wandered about, and exorcized demons, and treated the sick when they could. Missions designed to call to repentance or to conversion are more in the style of the early Christian community, which regarded a world mission as its role prior to the return of the son of Adam. For these reasons, gray is the appropriate designation for the action part of this narrative segment of Mark.

Herod beheads John
Mk 6:14–29
Mt 14:1–12, Lk 9:7–9
Source: Mark

6 **[14]King Herod heard about it—by now, <Jesus'> reputation had
become well known—and people kept saying that John the Baptizer
had been raised from the dead and that, as a consequence, miraculous powers were at work in him. [15]Some spread the rumor that he
was Elijah, while others reported that he was a prophet like one of
the prophets.**

**[16]When Herod got wind of it, he started declaring, "John, the one I
beheaded, has been raised!"**

**[17]Earlier Herod himself had sent someone to arrest John and put
him in chains in a dungeon, on account of Herodias, his brother
Philip's wife, because he had married her. [18]You see, John had said to
Herod, "It is not right for you to have your brother's wife!"**

**[19]So Herodias nursed a grudge against him and wanted to eliminate him, but she couldn't manage it, [20]because Herod was afraid of
John. He knew that he was an upright and holy man, and so protected him, and, although he listened to him frequently, he was very
confused, yet he listened to him eagerly.**

**[21]Now a festival day came, when Herod gave a banquet on his
birthday for his courtiers, and his commanders, and the leading citizens of Galilee. [22]And the daughter of Herodias came in and captivated Herod and his dinner guests by dancing. The king said to the
girl, "Ask me for whatever you wish and I'll grant it to you!" [23]Then
he swore an oath to her: "I'll grant you whatever you ask for, up to
half my domain!"**

**[24]She went out and said to her mother, "What should I ask for?"
And she replied, "The head of John the Baptizer!"**

**25She promptly hastened back and made her request: "I want you
to give me the head of John the Baptizer on a platter, right now!"
26The king grew regretful, but, on account of his oaths and the
dinner guests, he didn't want to refuse her. 27So right away the king
sent for the executioner and commanded him to bring his head. And
he went away and beheaded <John> in prison. 28He brought his
head on a platter and presented it to the girl, and the girl gave it to
her mother. 29When his disciples heard about it, they came and got
his body and put it in a tomb.**

Herod beheads John. This narrative segment consists of two parts. The first reports how Jesus' fame spread, as a consequence of which he was thought to be John the Baptist raised from the dead, or Elijah, or one of the prophets (vv. 14–16). The second part relates how Herod Antipas had arrested and executed John the Baptist (vv. 17–29).

The Fellows of the Jesus Seminar were relatively certain that both Jesus and John the Baptist had acquired public reputations (v. 14a, pink). The question was: Of what did those reputations consist? The Seminar considered it probable (pink) that Jesus' followers thought of him as John's successor, although they did not think it as likely that the general public so regarded Jesus (gray). It seems clear that the Sayings Gospel Q and the Gospel of Mark identified John the Baptist as Elijah returned. It is not so clear that John's earlier followers, and Jesus, and Jesus' followers regarded John as Elijah. It is thus equally uncertain that Jesus, as John's successor, was regarded as a second Elijah. The fog surrounding the evidence produced a gray designation for v. 15. On the other hand, all the speculation about Jesus being John the Baptist raised from the dead is post-Easter rhetoric created by the early Christian movement. The appropriate color for that speculation is black.

Two independent sources report the events surrounding the demise of John the Baptist—the gospels and the Jewish historian Josephus. The two reports differ, of course, but they also confirm the basic facts: Herod Antipas (a son of Herod the Great was not actually a king but held the title of tetrarch) had John imprisoned; he then had John executed. Herod did so ostensibly because John had publicly criticized his marriage to Herodias, which may have led Herod to consider John as a threat to public order and tranquility. John was probably beheaded in Herod's wilderness fortress of Machaerus.

Herodias was Herod Antipas' second wife, he her second husband. She had been married to another Herod, by whom she had borne a daughter, Salome. (Mark incorrectly reports that she had been married to Philip, Herod Antipas' brother.) For his part, Herod Antipas had been married to a Nabatean princess whom he abandoned in favor of Herodias. John had apparently taken Herod Antipas to task for his part in this Hollywood-like wife-swapping scene. The parts of Mark's report having to do with these events the Fellows colored red as virtually certain.

The Seminar was less sanguine about the historical reliability of Herodias' role in the execution of John. Although her manipulative role in Mark seems consistent with her characterization by Josephus, the particulars of her conniving to rid herself of John at a private party appear only in Mark—not in Josephus. Herodias may, in fact, have requested the execution of John. She may have used her daughter Salome to get John executed. Her daughter may have danced for Herod and his court. But these details sound too much like fiction to warrant any stronger color than gray.

Three details in the text are implausible. The first is Herod's sympathetic protection of John (v. 20). The second is Herodias' request for the head of John on a platter (v. 25). The third is the dutiful burial of John by his followers (v. 29)—a pious proper burial story. All three were designated black.

The gospels generally, and Mark in particular, reflect a political apologetic in which they excuse Roman authorities for the treatment of leaders of the Jesus movement, especially Pilate for his role in the crucifixion of Jesus. Since Christianity in the early days was an illicit religion, this strategy was intended to curry favor with the Romans. In the story of John's death, too, the behavior of the Roman vassal Herod Antipas seems too good to be true, in other words, highly exaggerated.

The twelve report
Mk 6:30–34
Mt 14:13–14, Lk 9:10–11
Source: Mark

6 [30]Then **the apostles** regroup around Jesus and they reported to him everything that they had done and taught.

[31]**And he says to them,** "You come privately to an isolated place and rest a little."

(Remember, many were coming and going and they didn't even have a chance to eat.)

[32]**So they went away in the boat privately to an isolated place.**
[33]**But many noticed them leaving and figured it out and raced there on foot from all the towns and got there ahead of them.** [34]**When he came ashore, he saw a huge crowd and was moved by them, because they 'resembled sheep without a shepherd,' and he started teaching them at length.**

The twelve report. Mark has narrated the mission of the twelve in 6:7–13, followed by the beheading of John the Baptist in 6:14–29. Now he creates a narrative transition to the next phase of Jesus' public life in 6:30–34.

The twelve regroup around Jesus, according to Mark, and then withdraw with Jesus to an isolated place, to the wilderness, which will function as the setting for the next event, the multiplication of loaves and fish for the five thousand pilgrims. The motivation for withdrawal, although not formally expressed, is provided by the narrative context: the execution of John the Baptist. Although Mark's chronology places this event earlier, he reports it at this point to set the stage for increasing opposition and danger.

Most scholars regard the sequence of events in this section as Mark's fiction. And, of course, some of the events themselves are fictive.

The Seminar decided to color v. 30 gray on the grounds that Jesus' followers did come and go frequently. The reference to "apostles," however, is anachronistic—Jesus' followers were not known until later as apostles—so that phrase was colored black. Some of them followed him about on a regular basis. Others were probably with him for shorter or longer periods. Some may have left him temporarily to attend to their own affairs, and some may have ventured out on teaching tours of their own. We have only the sketchiest knowledge of the daily life of Jesus and his retinue.

The words attributed to Jesus in the first part of v. 31 were colored black in *The Five Gospels,* so the framing device is also colored black. The second half of v. 31 is a remark the author addresses to the reader (or listener). The balance of the passage is Mark's fiction to set the stage for the feeding in the wilderness that follows. Black is the suitable designation for these verses.

6 [35]**And when the hour had already grown late, his disciples**
would approach him and say, "This place is desolate and it's late.
[36]**Send them away so that they can go to the farms and villages**
around here to buy something to eat."

[37]**But in response he said to them,** "Give them something to eat
yourselves!"

And they say to him, "Are we to go out and buy half a year's
wages worth of bread and donate it for their meal?!"

[38]**So he says to them,** "How many loaves do you have? Go look."

And when they find out, they say, "Five, and two fish."

[39]**Next he instructed them all to sit down and eat, some over here,**
some over there, on the green grass. [40]**So they sat down group by**
group, in hundreds and in fifties. [41]**And he took the five loaves and**
the two fish, looked up to the sky, gave a blessing, and broke the
bread apart, and started giving it to his disciples to pass around to
them, and even the two fish they shared with everybody. [42]**Every-**
body had more than enough to eat. [43]**Then they picked up twelve**
baskets full of leftovers, including some fish. [44]**And the number of**
men who had some bread came to five thousand.

Loaves & fish for 5,000
Mk 6:35–44
Mt 14:15–21, Lk 9:12–17;
Jn 6:1–15
Sources: Mark, John
Cf. Mark 8:1–9, Mt 15:32–39

Loaves & fish for 5,000. Stories of the feeding of multitudes in the wilderness pose multiple problems for the critical reader and scholar. A sketch of those problems will prove helpful as we attempt to assess the first of six versions.

First, there are two feeding stories in Mark: the present text and Mark 8:1–10. What is the relation between the two? Second, there is a parallel story in the Gospel of John (6:1–15) that looks to be the twin of Mark 6:35–44. Is one story dependent on the other, or were they both derived from some common ancestor? Third, there is a remarkable resemblance between the New Testament stories and the feeding of one hundred men by Elisha in 2 Kgs 4:42–44. Did the Elisha story function as the generative model for stories about Jesus? Fourth, stories of the miraculous supply of bread in the wilderness and the narrative contexts of water crossings or water miracles recall epic events connected with the Exodus and the Sinai wilderness. Do the Christian stories attempt to depict Jesus as a new Moses? Fifth, reports of a meal of bread and fish are linked very closely to the early Christian eucharist. Which came first, bread and fish or bread and wine? Sixth, and finally, do these stories preserve some distant trace of the behavior of Jesus? Are they linked in any way to his practice of eating with "toll collectors and sinners"?

Rather than attempt to summarize Seminar views on these questions as part of the commentary on this first version, we will distribute the discussion of these six issues among the six versions (two in Mark, two in Matthew, one in Luke, and one in John).

It will be more efficient to state the general conclusions of the Seminar at the outset. By a fairly substantial majority, the Fellows of the Seminar concluded that none of these stories is a report of an actual miraculous multiplication of loaves and fish to feed a crowd in the wilderness. There were no red votes on any of these stories, and only a scattering of pink votes to suggest that there is a historical core in the story. In almost every case more than fifty percent of the Fellows voted black.

Some of the Fellows argued, however, that the meal practices of Jesus gave rise to these stories in conjunction with the suggestive power of stories about Elisha and Moses. We will return to this point subsequently.

Robert Fowler takes the view that Mark has deliberately doubled the stories about a miraculous feeding in the wilderness; Mark 6:35–44 and 8:1–10 are thus duplicate stories of the same hypothetical event. Other members of the Seminar took the view that the two Markan stories are derived from independent traditions already in existence at the time Mark wrote his gospel. Of the two, these Fellows argued that Mark 8:1–10 was the older, or more primitive, less sophisticated, account. Mark 6:35–44, on the other hand, reflected another version of the story that was also the source for John 6:1–15. To put matters simply, the version in Mark 6 is closer to John 6 than it is to Mark 8.

These theories of the history of the feeding story tradition are connected to theories about a gospel of miracles (more about this in the cameo essay on the subject, pp. 388–89). Those who believe that Mark found two feeding stories in a source he was using take the view that there was a gospel of miracles consisting of five parallel events:

1a	Jesus rebukes the wind and sea (Mark 4:35–42)	1b	Jesus walks on the sea (Mark 6:47–52)
2a	The demon of Gerasa (Mark 5:1–20)	2b	Jesus cures a blind man (Mark 8:22–26)
3a	Jesus cures Jairus' daughter (Mark 5:21–24a, 35–43)	3b	Jesus cures the Greek woman's daughter (Mark 7:24b–30)
4a	Jesus cures the woman with an internal hemorrhage (Mark 5:24b–34)	4b	Jesus cures a deaf mute (Mark 7:31–37)
5a	Loaves and fish for five thousand (Mark 6:35–44)	5b	Loaves and fish for four thousand (Mark 8:1–9)

The twin cycles began with a water miracle and ended with a miraculous feeding in the wilderness. The affinity of those two items with the Old

Testament story of the crossing of the Sea of Reeds—popularly known as the Red Sea—and the manna in the wilderness is striking. The alternative view, proposed by Robert Fowler, is that Mark himself is responsible for doubling the sequence, in some cases repeating stories he had already told, and in others using other materials from the oral tradition.

Whatever the source of this gospel story, the Fellows found it highly implausible as the report of an actual event. Mark states that the place they were in was "desolate" (a wilderness, v. 35), yet it was possible for them to go to nearby farms and villages and buy something to eat (v. 36). Nowhere in the story is it claimed that Jesus wrought a miracle; there is no acclamation or expression of wonder at the end, as one expects in the standard miracle story. Rather, he took the five loaves and two fish, said a blessing, and handed fragments to the disciples to distribute. There was plenty for everybody. Indeed, twelve baskets of bread and fish were left over. Where did the baskets come from? Why so much waste? These implausibilities have led countless interpreters to give the story a naturalistic interpretation: Jesus induced the people to share their food with each other in an egalitarian picnic.

The feeding story in particular, and the nature wonders in general, belong to a different category than the healings and exorcisms. The latter are understandable, even in a modern worldview, given what is known about psychosomatic illness and therapy. The multiplication of loaves and fish is magic: it is the equivalent of changing base metals into gold, if taken literally. The Fellows agreed on black for the story as a literal report.

John P. Meier concludes that "some especially memorable communal meal of bread and fish" lies behind this story. The evidence, he says, does not permit us to decide whether something miraculous took place.[26] E. P. Sanders wonders why the gospels report so little response to the major nature miracles. He responds to his own wonderment: perhaps because there were only a few major miracles. Jesus' actual miracles were possibly relatively minor, he reasons, and aroused interest only temporarily. Yet Sanders does not pass historical judgment on the feeding stories.[27]

6 **45And right away he made his disciples embark in the boat and go ahead to the opposite shore toward Bethsaida, while he himself dispersed the crowd. 46And once he got away from them, he went off to the mountain to pray.**

Departures
Mk 6:45–46
Mt 14:22–23
Source: Mark

Departures. Mark has here constructed another narrative link that connects two lake crossings, one in 6:32 ("So they went away in the boat privately to an isolated place."), the second here. The first crossing to "an isolated place" provided the wilderness setting for the feeding of the five thousand (6:35–44). The second crossing serves as preparation for the sea miracle to follow (6:47–52): his disciples embark in a boat from that unidentified "isolated place" intending to head for Bethsaida, which lies at the head of the lake. They eventually land at Gennesaret, which is located on the western rather than northern side of the lake. Mark's geography is hazy at best. Meanwhile, Jesus dismisses the crowd, as he does in the earlier boat trip (4:36), and goes off to a mountain to pray.

All of this consists of Markan themes woven together to provide some narrative continuity. The appropriate color is black.

Walking on the water
Mk 6:47–52
Mt 14:24–33; Jn 6:16–21
Sources: Mark, John

6 **[47]When evening came, the boat was in the middle of the sea,**
and he was alone on the land. [48]When he saw they were having a
rough time making headway, because the wind was against them, at
about three o'clock in the morning he comes toward them walking
on the sea and intending to go past them. [49]But when they saw him
walking on the sea, they thought he was a ghost and they cried out.
[50]By now they all saw him and were terrified. But right away he
spoke with them and says to them, "Take heart, it's me! Don't be
afraid." **[51]And he climbed into the boat with them, and the wind died**
down. By this time they were completely dumbfounded. ([52]You see,
they hadn't understood about the loaves; they were being obstinate.)

Walking on the water. Mark has two sea stories, one in which Jesus calms a storm (4:35–41), the other in which he walks on the water. Matthew reproduces both of them (8:23–27; 14:22–33). Luke makes use of the first (8:22–25), but omits the second. The Fourth Gospel reports the second (6:16–21), but seems not to know the first. The network of relationships between and among these stories and other related miracle stories poses one of the most difficult problems in gospel scholarship.

Rudolf Bultmann took the view that the two sea tales are variants of the same story.[28] He noted that the tale of walking on the water also contains hints that a storm was involved, which the presence of Jesus in the boat immediately calmed (vv. 48, 51). A trace of that theme is still present in the Johannine version (John 6:18). Yet John abandons the storm theme and replaces it with the miracle of the sudden arrival of the boat at their destination the minute Jesus steps into the boat (John 6:21). And the fact that both Luke and John report only one of the stories may give some credence to Bultmann's view that one story became two.

In both Mark and the Gospel of John, the miraculous feeding of the multitude in the wilderness is followed by a sea miracle—Jesus walking on the water. That intriguing sequence has elicited a wide variety of attempts to explain their connection. The one most widely adopted by scholars is that Mark and John are drawing on two different sources for their information. What those sources contained is a matter of dispute. (For a sketch of the possibilities, consult the cameo on "A Gospel of Miracles?" pp. 388–89.) If there were two sources, then the account of walking on the water is attested in at least two independent texts. However, there are alternative explanations. One is that Mark and John were making use of the *same* antecedent document, which contained the sequence: feeding in the wilderness, sea miracle. Another is that

John was simply dependent on Mark for this sequence of events. If John, like Matthew, is using the Gospel of Mark as his source, then the historical reliability of the account rests solely on Mark's version of the event.

A decision about sources does not seem to affect the scholarly assessment of the historicity of the tale. Historical reliability is affected, however, by the recognition of the kind of story involved. On almost any reckoning, walking on the water is an epiphany story. An epiphany is the appearance of God, a god, or a divine being such as an angel, to mortals, often suddenly and unexpectedly. Other epiphany stories include the miraculous catch of fish in Luke (5:1–11), the appearance of the risen Jesus following another miraculous catch in the Fourth Gospel (21:1–14), and the transfiguration (Mark 9:2–8). The unexpected appearance of Jesus to the disciples as they struggle, in the middle of the night, against the wind and the waves fits that definition. In this scene Jesus is not an ordinary Galilean sage; he is the manifestation of a divine being, whom the disciples mistake for a phantom (v. 49), until he reassures them that it is he. In so doing he uses a Greek formula *ego eimi*, "It's me!" that is reminiscent of other "I am" sayings in the Gospel of John ("I am the way, the truth, the life"; "I am the bread of life," etc.), as well as the "I am" saying of God in the Hebrew bible (Exod 3:14: "I am" is the name of God, which in Hebrew is Yahweh; cf. Isa 43:1–13, in which this wordplay is developed).

The Fellows of the Jesus Seminar agreed that walking on the water was not based on a historical event and that it originated as an epiphany and not as a miracle story. Almost to a person, the Fellows doubted that Jesus actually walked on the water. As a consequence, the story in Mark was designated black.

In his recent book on Jesus, E. P. Sanders corroborates the Seminar's judgment: Sanders concludes that perhaps Jesus did not actually perform many great miracles since the response to them seems not to have been overpowering, either on the part of the public or on the part of the disciples. But he is unclear whether this particular miracle has a historical base.[29] John P. Meier, on the other hand, concludes, in concert with the Seminar, that the story is not based on historical fact.[30]

Many sick are cured
Mk 6:53–56
Mt 14:34–36
Source: Mark

6 [53]**Once they had crossed over to land, they landed at Gennesaret and dropped anchor.** [54]**As soon as they had gotten out of the boat, people recognized him right away,** [55]**and they ran around over the whole area and started bringing those who were ill on mats to wherever he was rumored to be.** [56]**And wherever he would go, into villages, or towns, or onto farms, they would lay out the sick in the marketplaces and beg him to let them touch the fringe of his cloak. And all those who managed to touch it were cured!**

Many sick are cured. Luke 1:32–34 and 3:7–12, this narrative summary is wholly the work of Mark. He has constructed it out of elements borrowed from neighboring narrative terrain: crossing the sea and walking on the water;

the cure of the woman with the vaginal flow who had touched the hem of Jesus' garment; other healing stories. Exorcism is strangely absent from this summary. We expect exorcism to be mentioned because Mark has done so in previous summaries, which were designated gray. The role of Jesus as folk healer is greatly exaggerated here: the ill from over the entire region are brought to him; they are laid out in the marketplaces in the hope of being able to touch his garment; all who touch it are cured. It is as though Jesus' role has been reduced to the function of a thaumaturge—a worker of magic. Black is the appropriate color for the entire summary.

Eating with defiled hands
Mk 7:1–13
Mt 15:1–9
Source: Mark

7 The Pharisees gather around him, along with some of the
scholars, who had come from Jerusalem. **2When they notice some of
his disciples eating their meal with defiled hands, that is to say,
without washing their hands (3you see, the Pharisees and the
Judeans generally wouldn't think of eating without first washing
their hands in a particular way always observing the tradition of the
elders, 4and they won't eat when they get back from the marketplace
without washing again, and there are many other traditions they
cherish, such as the washing of cups and jugs and kettles), 5the
Pharisees and the scholars start questioning him: "Why don't your
disciples live up to the tradition of the elders, instead of eating
bread with defiled hands?"**
6And he answered them, "How accurately Isaiah depicted you
phonies when he wrote:

> This people honors me with their lips,
> but their heart stays far away from me.
> 7Their worship of me is empty,
> because they insist on teachings that are human commandments.

8You have set aside God's commandment and hold fast to human
tradition!"
9Or he would say to them, "How expert you've become at putting
aside God's commandment to establish your own tradition. 10For
instance, Moses said, 'Honor your father and your mother' and 'Those
who curse their father or mother will surely die.' 11But you say, 'If
people say to their father or mother, "Whatever I might have spent to
support you is *korban*"' (which means "consecrated to God"), 12you no
longer let those persons do anything for their father or mother. 13So
you end up invalidating God's word with your own tradition, which
you then perpetuate. And you do all kinds of other things like that!"

Eating with defiled hands. The Fellows of the Jesus Seminar concluded that the narrative picture provided by vv. 1–5 was reasonably accurate: The Pharisees in Jesus' day did observe the traditions of the elders; after returning from the marketplace, they did not eat until they washed their hands in a particular way. This picture is confirmed by the Jewish historian Josephus and by later rabbinic traditions that probably reach back into the first century C.E. The rabbinic schools of Hillel and Shammai, for example, debated whether hands should be washed before handling produce that had been tithed to the Jerusalem temple. This debate indicates that the issue was not hygiene, but ritual purity. However, it is clear that there was a division of opinion among the rabbis. We cannot say that all first-century Pharisees strictly observed the practice of ritual handwashing; we simply do not know how widespread the practice was.

Jesus and his disciples apparently did not observe handwashing in the Pharisaic tradition. Since Galilee was at some remove from Judea and Jerusalem where most Pharisees lived, it is difficult to know how deeply Pharisaic ways had penetrated Galilean customs. Nevertheless, it seemed likely to the Seminar that there was conflict on this and related points: just as Jesus and his disciples did not always observe kosher, they also did not practice ritual purity by washing their hands on appropriate occasions. In this they probably did not deviate greatly from common Galilean practice.

In v. 4 Mark indicates that the Pharisees also observed the proper cleansing of cups, jugs, and kettles in accordance with purity regulations. The basis for this practice is Lev 11:29–47. That part of the law concerns animals such as the mouse, the weasel, various kinds of lizards, and the chameleon. These are said to defile not only by ingestion (they are not to be eaten), but also by touch. Since they are often found in the kitchen in tropical climates, the possibilities for defilement are great. According to Leviticus, contact between one of these creatures and a kitchen vessel defiles the container along with its contents. Because it is earthenware and porous, it has to be broken. Rabbinic traditions suggest that the Pharisees were exceptionally scrupulous about purity and probably followed strict practices.

While the Fellows of the Seminar regarded the differences between Jesus and the Pharisees as historically probable, they regarded his reply in vv. 6–13 as improbable. His response does not really have to do with purity; rather, he accuses the Pharisees of interpreting the law so as to avoid some of its basic precepts. This is the opposite of Pharisaic intent: they were interested in applying the law to all areas of life. Accordingly, in *The Five Gospels*, vv. 6–13 were colored black.

Private interpretation
Mk 7:14–23
Mt 15:10–20
Source: Mark

7 [14]**Once again he summoned the crowd and would say to them:**
"Listen to me, all of you, and try to understand! [15]What goes into you
can't defile you; what comes out of you can. [16]If anyone has two good
ears, use them!"

[17]**When he entered a house away from the crowd, his disciples
started questioning him about the riddle. [18]And he says to them:**
"Are you as dim-witted as the rest? Don't you realize that nothing
from outside can defile by going into a person, [19]because it doesn't get
to the heart but passes into the stomach, and comes out in the out-
house?" **(This is how everything we eat is purified.)**

[20]**And he went on to say,** "It's what comes out of a person that

defiles. [21]For from out of the human heart issue wicked intentions: sex-
ual immorality, thefts, murders, [22]adulteries, envies, wickedness,
deceit, promiscuity, an evil eye, blasphemy, arrogance, lack of good
sense. [23]All these evil things come from the inside out and defile the
person."

Private interpretation. The narrative frame for this set of sayings has been termed a didactic scene by Philip Sellew, a Fellow of the Jesus Seminar. A didactic scene is one in which Jesus gives public teaching and then is asked to explain its meaning to his disciples in private. This particular scene may have come to Mark in its present form from the oral tradition or Mark may have created it himself. There are five such complexes in Mark's gospel: 4:3–20, 8:11–21, 9:14–29, 10:1–12, and the present segment. None of these complexes is likely to represent the practice of the historical Jesus. The Fellows of the Jesus Seminar reject the notion that he taught in puzzles and enigmas publicly and then gave his intimate followers a private interpretation. On the contrary, Jesus seems to have taught almost exclusively in parables and aphorisms; everyone had equal access to what he said and meant.

The Fellows designated the first half of v. 14 pink because it is a generalization on the way Jesus behaved. The notion of a private interpretation arose as a way to portray the disciples as privileged insiders: Jesus explained privately to the disciples, so they were in a position to interpret his words authoritatively for others. Verse 17 represents that development and so was colored black. The remark in parentheses in v. 19 is Mark's explanatory aside to his readers. The sayings in this complex (vv. 14–19) were colored either pink or gray in *The Five Gospels*.

Greek woman's daughter
Mk 7:24–30
Mt 15:21–28
Source: Mark

7 **[24]From there he got up and went away to the regions of Tyre.
Whenever he visited a house he wanted no one to know, but he
could not escape notice. [25]Instead, suddenly a woman whose daugh-
ter had an unclean spirit heard about him, and came and fell down
at his feet. [26]The woman was a Greek, by race a Phoenician from
Syria. And she started asking him to drive the demon out of her
daughter. [27]He responded to her like this:** "Let the children be fed
first, since it isn't good to take bread out of children's mouths and
throw it to the dogs!"

**[28]But as a rejoinder she says to him, "Sir, even the dogs under the
table get to eat scraps <dropped by> children!"**

[29]Then he said to her, "For that retort, be on your way, the demon
has come out of your daughter."

**[30]She returned home and found the child lying on the bed and the
demon gone.**

Greek woman's daughter. The story of the Greek woman's daughter again illustrates the difficulty the Fellows had in identifying particular stories as reports of specific incidents in the life of Jesus. By a narrow margin, the Fellows concluded that there was probably a historical core to Mark's version (fifty-seven percent of the group voted red or pink). They also agreed that a Greek woman regarded Jesus as an exorcist. They agreed that Jesus probably had a conversation with that woman and that their conversation involved an exchange of witticisms in which the woman got the better of Jesus. The majority of Fellows thought it unlikely that early Christian storytellers would have invented such an incident. The Fellows consequently concluded that the story has a historical core.

When it came to particular items in the story, however, the consensus dissolved. The following narrative statements could muster no more than a gray weighted average:

- **Jesus visited the region of Tyre in southern Lebanon.**
- **Jesus viewed foreigners as "dogs."**
- **Jesus said: "It isn't good to take bread out of children's mouths and throw it to the dogs."**
- **Jesus said: "Let the children be fed first."**
- **A demon left the girl because of her mother's wit.**
- **A demon left the girl because her mother trusted Jesus.**

The words ascribed to Jesus were given a black rating in *The Five Gospels*. In a review of the story in the second phase of the Seminar devoted to the acts of Jesus, the words ascribed to Jesus and to the mother of the girl were given a gray rating, even though the Fellows awarded some hypothetical core of the story a pink weighted average.

The Fellows themselves could not account for the apparent inconsistency between the affirmation that there was a historical core to the story and the inability to identify specific features of the tale as references to actual occurrences. They may have had confidence in the gist of the story: the verbal exchange between Jesus and the woman is reminiscent of the authentic sayings tradition of aphorisms and parables. Yet the Seminar could not agree that Jesus would have used the metaphor "dogs" to refer to Greeks, which cast doubt on the balance of the exchange. The consequence was, of course, that the story as a whole fell into the gray category, even though there was a fairly strong conviction that the story reflected the vague memory of some event.

This picture is complicated somewhat by the fact that about twenty percent of the Fellows took the view that the story was a Christian invention to justify the church's mission to the gentiles. Their black vote is endorsed by John P. Meier.[31] A steady input of black votes on a variety of specific details made it very difficult to achieve a positive consensus. E. P. Sanders, on the other hand, depicts the story as though it were historical.[32]

The encounter with the Greek woman takes place on foreign soil as does the story of the demon of Gerasa (Mark 5:1–20). The cure of the daughter involves exorcism at a distance, much like the story of the official's son (Luke 7:1–10//Matt 8:5–13; John 4:46–54). In all three cases, it is a gentile seeking help from a Jewish thaumaturge (miracle worker). The Fellows were inclined, on balance, to conclude that upon occasion Jesus did respond positively to requests from gentiles: They agreed that Jesus talked with a Greek woman, that she turned his clever words against him, and that he accepted her witty retort.

Deaf-mute
Mk 7:31–37
Source: Mark
Cf. Mt 15:29–31

7 **[31]Then he left the regions of Tyre and traveled through Sidon to
the Sea of Galilee, through the middle of the region known as the
Decapolis.**
**[32]And they bring him a deaf-mute and plead with him to lay his
hand on him. [33]Taking him aside from the crowd in private, he stuck
his fingers into the man's ears and spat and touched his tongue.
[34]And looking up to the sky, he groaned and says to him, "*ephphatha*"**
(which means, "Be opened!"). **[35]And his ears opened up, and right
away his speech impediment was removed, and he started speaking
properly. [36]Then he ordered them to tell no one. But no matter how
much he enjoined them, they spread it around all the more.**
**[37]And they were completely dumbfounded. "He's done every-
thing and has done it quite well," they said; "He even makes the
deaf hear and the mute speak!"**

Deaf-mute. The story of the deaf-mute was omitted by both Matthew and Luke, probably because it smacked too much of magic to suit the tastes of the Jesus movement toward the close of the first century, which had already begun, in some quarters at least, to lose its penchant for the miraculous cure. The core story has numerous primitive touches. Jesus takes the man aside in private before he performs the cure; he sticks his fingers into the man's ears; he spits on his finger and touches his tongue; and he looks up into the sky and pronounces the magical Aramaic incantation, "*ephphatha*," which of course means "Be opened!" These features were evidently too much for Matthew and Luke to swallow.

The holy man in the ancient world performed his wonders in private presumably because it was not advisable to "see" the god or God at work. Sticking fingers into the ear was a symbolic gesture intended to open the ear up. Spittle was known to have medicinal properties; in this case the combination of spittle and touching was supposed to loosen the tongue. And, of course, the Markan inclusion of an ordinary Aramaic word in a Greek text must have sounded to the Greek ear as a word of magic.

Mark probably did not invent this story. Several words appear in it that do not belong to Mark's standard vocabulary. And the bizarre elements just mentioned make it stand out from other miracle stories in Mark's gospel. In form, the story is made up almost entirely of the healing technique, which is itself unusual for Mark. Mark probably took the story over from oral tradition, where it had developed a life of its own. It may have originated as a story not about Jesus but about some other charismatic healer.

The Seminar agreed, by a very small margin, that Jesus used spittle and mud in his cures. At the same time, the Seminar did not find evidence that Jesus used traditional methods of treatment, such as medicinal plants, animals and animal products, minerals, oils, and spirits. Whether Jesus employed the combination of techniques depicted in this story is uncertain. The uncertainties are multiplied when corroborating evidence is lacking. Gray was the inevitable result.

Verse 36 is the standard response Mark has Jesus give: don't tell anyone. According to Mark, Jesus advocated a conspiracy to keep his messianic powers secret. The response of the crowds in v. 37 corresponds to Isaiah's description of the miracles that will accompany the restoration of Israel (Isa 35:5–6). Since these verses are the creation of Mark, they are colored black.

John P. Meier presumably agrees with the Fellows of the Jesus Seminar that the story of the deaf-mute reflects an actual event in the public life of Jesus, but he is unwilling to endorse the details as historical. That probably means a gray vote.[33] E. P. Sanders reports the event as though it were historical.[34]

Loaves & fish for 4,000
Mk 8:1–10
Mt 15:32–39
Source: Mark
Cf. Mk 6:35–44, Mt 14:15–21, Lk 9:12–17, Jn 6:1–15

8 **And once again during that same period, when there was a**
huge crowd without anything to eat, he calls the disciples aside and
says to them, 2"I feel sorry for the crowd, because they have already
spent three days with me and now they've run out of food. 3If I send
these people home hungry, they will collapse on the road—in fact,
some of them have come from quite a distance."

4**And his disciples answered him, "How can anyone feed these**
people bread out here in this desolate place?"

5**And he started asking them,** "How many loaves do you have?"

They replied, "Seven."

6**Then he orders the crowd to sit down on the ground. And he**
took the seven loaves, gave thanks, and broke them into pieces, and
started giving <them> to his disciples to hand out; and they passed
them around to the crowd. 7**They also had a few small fish. When he**
had blessed them, he told them to hand those out as well. 8**They had**
more than enough to eat. Then they picked up seven big baskets of
leftover scraps. 9**There were about four thousand people there. Then**
he started sending them away.

10**And he got right into the boat with his disciples and went to the**
Dalmanoutha district.

Loaves & fish for 4,000. Loaves and fish for four thousand appears to be a duplicate of the feeding of the five thousand: the two stories have much in common, although they differ in some details. The view that there were two similar events has not found much favor among critical scholars. It is difficult to believe, for example, that the disciples would be so obtuse as to ask, in v. 4, "How can anyone feed these people bread out here in this desolate place?" after just having witnessed the feeding of the five thousand. Scholars have preferred, by and large, to think that one story is a duplicate of the other. Either Mark deliberately replicated a story he found in his oral repertoire, or the story had already been duplicated prior to Mark and Mark merely inherited twin versions. (The possibility that Mark knew a gospel of miracles is discussed in a cameo essay, pp. 388–89.)

Mark has provided a new introduction to the feeding of the four thousand. He first of all recognizes that he has told a similar story earlier in his narrative (v. 1). This time Jesus takes the initiative with his disciples (vv. 1–3); in the previous version, the disciples raise the question of food for the crowd with Jesus, who gives them a sarcastic reply (6:35–37): "Give them something to eat yourselves!" In both versions, however, he discusses the problem with the disciples.

In both versions, the discussion between Jesus and the disciples ends with a query on the part of Jesus: "How many loaves do you have?" In the present story, the answer is seven (v. 5); we learn later there were also a few small fish (v. 7). In the previous story, there were five loaves and two fish. In both stories there are bread and fish, and the quantity adds up to the perfect number seven. In both versions, the crowd is instructed to sit down on the ground or grass (v. 6; 6:39). And in both stories Jesus takes the loaves (and fish), gives a blessing, breaks the bread, and gives the pieces to the disciples to distribute. Everyone was satisfied, according to the storyteller (v. 8; 6:42).

So far nothing has occurred that is obviously miraculous. In place of the usual testimony of witnesses, in the present story, seven big baskets of scraps are filled (v. 8); in the earlier version, it was twelve baskets full (6:43). In the version in the Gospel of John, it is also twelve baskets (John 6:13). The number of satisfied customers also varies: five thousand in the previous story (6:44) and in the Johannine version (John 6:10); in the story in Mark 8, it is four thousand (v. 9). Only in the Fourth Gospel, however, is the miracle explicitly proclaimed: The people recognize Jesus as the prophet who is to come and want to make him king (John 6:14–15).

The variation in detail indicates once again how free the evangelists were to alter or invent introductions, draw conclusions, and tinker with detail. They did not feel that they were obligated to ascertain facts or stick to the stories they had received. For this reason, it is very difficult to identify stories that are accurate reports of actual events.

As suggested earlier in the commentary on the feeding of the five thousand, members of the Jesus Seminar were inclined to the view that Mark had inherited two different versions of the same story. He included them both in his gospel because he had no aversion to duplicate accounts. Luke, on the other hand, did not like duplicate stories, so he omitted one version. John apparently knew of only one version. None of the versions is a report of an actual event, so black is the correct color. On the other hand, quite a few Fellows took the view that the feeding stories are historicized accounts of a later Christian ritual—sharing bread and fish, or bread and wine, in a common meal.

Demand for a sign
Mk 8:11–13
Mt 16:1–4; 12:38–40,
Lk 11:29–30
Sources: Mark, Q
Cf. Jn 2:18, 6:30

8 [11]**The Pharisees came out and started to argue with him. To test**
him, they demanded a sign in the sky. [12]He groaned under his breath
and says, "Why does this generation insist on a sign? I swear to God,
this generation won't get any sign!"

[13]**And turning his back on them, he got back in the boat and**
crossed over to the other side.

Demand for a sign. In discussing this and related passages about the demand for a sign, the Fellows voted on the following propositions with the indicated results:

- **The Pharisees probably did expect heavenly signs related to the coming of God's kingdom.**
- **The crowds who came to hear Jesus expected a sign related to the coming of God's kingdom.**
- The Pharisees asked Jesus for a sign.
- **Jesus refused to provide heavenly signs.**

It is fairly certain that Jesus addressed the question of "signs." It is also relatively certain that Jesus refused to provide a sign or at least circumscribed what might constitute a sign. Since Jesus addressed the question, it is very likely that he was asked for a sign. The problem the Seminar had to face was whether the gospel reports correctly identified those who asked Jesus for a sign. This is how the Fellows went about their analysis.

In the Gospel of Thomas, the disciples ask Jesus when God's imperial rule will come. This is Jesus' response:

> **His disciples said to him, "When will the <Father's> imperial rule come?"**
>
> "It will not come by watching for it. It will not be said, 'Look, here!' or 'Look, there!' Rather, the Father's imperial rule is spread out upon the earth, and people don't see it." Thom 113:1–4

A similar saying is recorded in the Gospel of Luke 17:20–21. The Fellows designated both of these sayings pink as approximations of something Jesus said. In both versions of the saying, Jesus refuses to point to some external evidence that the kingdom is arriving; he suggests that the kingdom is already present but not subject to naive observation. That would appear to make the question of accompanying signs moot so far as Jesus is concerned.

Who is likely to have confronted Jesus with a challenge to provide a sign of the kingdom's approach or presence? According to Mark 8:11, the Pharisees make the request. In Matthew's parallel version (16:1), it is the "Pharisees and Sadducees." In Matt 12:38, it is the scholars and Pharisees together who ask for a sign. In Luke 17:20 it is the Pharisees. In Thom 113, on the other hand, it is the disciples. In John 6:30, it is the crowd; in John 2:18, it is "the Judeans." In Luke 11:16 and 11:29, it is apparently the crowd that raises the question.

The evidence provided by Jesus' response, however, indicates that it was "this generation" that asked for a sign. In other words, it was a question that was in the air, on people's lips, a part of everyone's expectations. That is supported by Jesus' response in v. 12. Of course, in keeping with the general expectations of the times, the disciples, the Pharisees, and the crowds would all have anticipated some sign from heaven.

There is a tendency in the gospels to identify Jesus' opponents as Pharisees. We have noted that it is the disciples who ask Jesus about the coming of the kingdom in Thom 113:1; in Luke's version it is the Pharisees. In Thom 100:1, an anonymous "they" give Jesus a gold coin and ask about paying taxes; in the parallel in Mark 12:13, it is the Pharisees who put Jesus to this test. Luke 3:7 has John the Baptist address the crowd as "You spawn of Satan! Who warned you to flee from the impending doom?" The exact same words in Matt 3:7 are addressed not to the crowds in general but to the Pharisees and Sadducees.

These details led the Fellows to conclude that the request for a sign probably came most often from the crowds that surrounded Jesus as he taught. Later versions tended to substitute the Pharisees because they were the debating partners of the Jesus movement decades later, after the fall of Jerusalem and the temple.

These considerations prompted the Seminar to color v. 11 gray: the information is possible but not probable. Verse 13 is a part of Mark's narrative linkage; it is not based on the memory of a specific sequence of events but on Mark's imagination.

Bread & leaven
Mk 8:14–21
Mt 16:5–12, Lk 12:1
Source: Mark

8 [14]**They forgot to bring any bread and had nothing with them in the boat except one loaf.** [15]**Then he started giving them directives:** "Look," **he says,** "watch out for the leaven of the Pharisees and the leaven of Herod!"

[16]**They began looking quizzically at one another because they didn't have any bread.** [17]**And because he was aware of this, he says to them:** "Why are you puzzling about your lack of bread? You still aren't using your heads, are you? You still haven't got the point, have you? Are you just dense? [18]Though you have eyes, you still don't see, and though you have ears, you still don't hear! Don't you even remember [19]how many baskets full of scraps you picked up when I broke up the five loaves for the five thousand?"

"Twelve," they reply to him.

[20]"When I broke up the seven loaves for the four thousand, how many big baskets full of scraps did you pick up?"

And they say, "Seven."

[21]**And he repeats,** "You still don't understand, do you?"

Bread & leaven. It was determined, in the first phase of the Jesus Seminar, that this complex is a retrospective construction of Mark. The author is looking back on the two accounts of the feeding of the crowd in the wilderness (6:35–44; 8:1–9) and developing one of his favorite themes—the obtuseness of the disciples. The saying about the leaven of the Pharisees in v. 15 probably suggested the idea to Mark. Matthew has simply reproduced Mark, while Luke decided to omit the entire segment because he held a higher opinion of the disciples than did Mark. Black is the correct designation for the narrative frame of this complex.

8 [22]They come to Bethsaida, **and they bring him a blind person,**
and plead with him to touch him. [23]He took the blind man by the
hand and led him out of the village. And he spat into his eyes, and
placed his hands on him, and started questioning him: "Do you see
anything?"

[24]When his sight began to come back, the first thing he said was:
"I see human figures, as though they were trees walking around."

[25]Then he put his hands over his eyes a second time. And he
opened his eyes, and his sight was restored, and he saw everything
clearly. [26]And he sent him home, saying, "Don't bother to go back to
the village!"

The blind man of Bethsaida
Mk 8:22–26
Source: Mark
Cf. Mk 10:46–52; Jn 9:1–7

The blind man of Bethsaida. The Fellows by a narrow majority concluded that Jesus cured at least one blind person. By a similar majority they were inclined to the view that he employed either mud or spittle, or both, to effect the cure, in addition to the more customary touch. Jesus did not use spittle or mud as a kind of primitive medicine, but as a part of the ritual employed by the charismatic healer in the ancient world. The Seminar took the view that the blindness Jesus was able to cure was subject to psychosomatic therapy. In arriving at these conclusions, the Fellows were drawing on the evidence provided by three stories: the blind man at Bethsaida, blind Bartimaeus (Mark 10:46–52), and the man born blind (John 9:1–7).

In this story, the Fellows were dubious that locating the cure in Bethsaida reflected historical information (v. 22). They were relatively certain that v. 26 represented Mark's narrative conclusion: the dismissal—the order to go home—appears in other healing stories (2:11, 5:19).

Jesus performs the cure in private after leading the man out of the village (v. 23). The motif of privacy appears frequently in other healing and resuscitation stories (for example, Mark 5:40, 7:33, Acts 9:40, 1 Kgs 17:19, 2 Kgs 4:4, 4:33). The story is unusual for Jesus in that he uses spittle rather than a command or a magical word to effect the cure. Because it is rare for Jesus to effect a cure by degrees, the Fellows decided to color v. 24 gray, and because Mark evidently created v. 25 to contrast the blind man's recovered sight with that of the disciples, they elected to color that verse black. To the core of the story (vv. 22–23), however, the Fellows gave a pink rating.

According to John P. Meier, the core of the story is probably historical. However, the tale has been "worked up" in the oral tradition and "exploited" by Mark in reaching its present form.[35] E. P. Sanders again summarizes this story without indicating whether he thinks it is historical or not.[36]

8 **[27]Jesus and his disciples set out for the villages of Caesarea**
Philippi. On the road he started questioning his disciples, asking
them, "What are people saying about me?"

Peter's confession
Mk 8:27–30
Mt 16:13–20, Lk 9:18–22
Source: Mark

[28]**In response they said to him, "<Some say, 'You are> John the Baptist,' and others, 'Elijah,' but others, 'One of the prophets.'"**

[29]**But he continued to press them,** "What about you, who do you say I am?"

Peter responds to him, "You are the Anointed!" [30]**And he warned them not to tell anyone about him.**

Peter's confession. In *The Five Gospels,* the exchange pictured here was described as a stylized scene shaped by Christian motifs. It is atypical of Jesus to initiate a dialogue in which his own identity is the focus, although he does so frequently in the Fourth Gospel. Indeed, this way of representing Jesus is alien to his fundamental disposition, which was to regard himself as the servant or slave of all. He recommended that posture to his followers as well. The Fellows did not hesitate to designate the entire episode black.

Jesus predicts his death
Mk 8:31–33
Mt 16:21–23, Lk 9:22
Source: Mark
Cf. Mk 9:30–32, Mt 17:22–23, Lk 9:43b–45; Mk 10:32–34, Mt 20:17–19, Lk 18:31–34

8 [31]**He started teaching them that** the son of Adam was destined to suffer a great deal, and be rejected by the elders and the ranking priests and the scholars, and be killed, and after three days rise. [32]**And he would say this openly. And Peter took him aside and began to lecture him.** [33]**But he turned, noticed his disciples, and reprimanded Peter verbally:** "Get out of my sight, you Satan, you, because you're not thinking in God's terms, but in human terms."

Jesus predicts his death. The gospel story was transmitted in the oral period in individual anecdotes and compounds, clusters, collections, and complexes of sayings and parables. These stories and the sayings materials were retold as the need and occasion arose. A connected story had not yet been formed until the creation of the Gospel of Mark, the first of the narrative gospels.

As Mark began to link individual stories together to form a sequence of events, he created a narrative framework for the whole. His framework stories appear at the beginning, middle, and end of his gospel. The first group of framework stories covers Jesus' relation to John the Baptist, Jesus' baptism, his sojourn in the wilderness, and a summary of his message (1:1–15). This sequence forms the introduction to the gospel.

A second group of stories forms the turning point of the gospel. This group is made up of Peter's confession (8:27–30), three predictions of Jesus' suffering and death (8:31–33, 9:30–32, 10:32–34) and the epiphany of the transfiguration (9:2–8). These stories elicit the first "Christian" confession and provide an ominous forecast of the tragedy to come.

A third cluster of stories serves as the conclusion to the gospel. The passion narrative (14:1–15:47) and the tale of the empty tomb (16:1–8) detail Jesus' arrest, trial, and execution, and forecast his resurrection.

These stories are by and large the creation of Mark. That does not mean that in every case they are pure fictions. Jesus' baptism at the hands of John, for example, is almost certainly historical. Yet there was a tendency on the part of

Christian storytellers to read back into the life of Jesus convictions they had acquired in the period after his death.

The words of Jesus in this first prediction of his death were voted black by common consent in the first phase of the Jesus Seminar. The narrative frame in which those words are set was designated black in the second phase. The forecast of the passion, together with the complex of sayings on discipleship that follows (8:34–9:1) is a "defining moment" in Mark's gospel story.

Way of the cross
Mk 8:34–9:1
Mt 16:24–28, Lk 9:23–27
Source: Mark

8 34**After he called the crowd together with his disciples, he said**
to them, "If any of you wants to come after me, you should deny your-
self, pick up your cross, and follow me! 35Remember, by trying to save
your own life, you're going to lose it, but by losing your life for the
sake of the good news, you're going to save it. 36After all, what good
does it do to acquire the whole world and pay for it with life? 37Or,
what would you give in exchange for life?

38"Moreover, if any of you are ashamed of me and my message in
this adulterous and sinful generation, of you the son of Adam will
likewise be ashamed when he comes in his Father's glory accompa-
nied by holy angels!"

9 1**And he used to tell them,** "I swear to you: Some of those stand-
ing here won't ever taste death before they see God's imperial rule set
in with power!"

Way of the cross. This compendium of sayings is the work of Mark. The Fellows decided to color the narrative reference in v. 34 black simply because it specifies a particular occasion: Mark has imagined that occasion and what Jesus said at that time. The typification in v. 1, however, was designated gray to match the color given to the saying it introduces.

Transfiguration
Mk 9:2–8
Mt 17:1–8, Lk 9:28–36
Source: Mark

9 2**Six days later, Jesus takes Peter and James and John along and**
leads them off by themselves to a lofty mountain. He was trans-
formed in front of them, 3and his clothes became an intensely bril-
liant white, whiter than any laundry on earth could make them.
4Elijah appeared to them, with Moses, and they were conversing
with Jesus. 5Peter responds by saying to Jesus, "Rabbi, it's a good
thing we're here. In fact, why not set up three tents, one for you, and
one for Moses, and one for Elijah!" (6You see, he didn't know how
else to respond, since they were terrified.)

7And a cloud moved in and cast a shadow over them, and a voice
came out of the cloud: "This is my favored son, listen to him!"
8Suddenly, as they looked around, they saw no one, but were alone
with Jesus.

Transfiguration. The transfiguration of Jesus is reported in all three synoptic gospels and alluded to in 2 Peter. These accounts and this allusion are dependent on the Gospel of Mark, directly or indirectly.

The allusion to the transfiguration in 2 Pet 1:16–18 is almost certainly based on the account in Matt 17:1–8. This is allegedly Peter speaking of a past experience:

> [16]We were not merely repeating clever tales when we told you about the glory and coming of our Lord Jesus Christ; we saw his majesty with our own eyes. [17]When honor and glory were bestowed on him from God the Father, a voice came to him from the sublime presence: "This is my favorite son. I am very pleased with him." [18]We heard this voice wafting down from heaven when we were with him on the holy mountain.

The words that come from heaven in v. 17 follow Matthew's version rather than Mark's. 2 Peter was not written until well into the second century C.E.; its author was not Peter the fisherman and confidant of Jesus of Nazareth, in the judgment of most scholars.

The transfiguration, along with the confession of Peter (8:27–30) and the three predictions of the passion (8:31–33, 9:30–32, 10:32–34), serves as the turning point in the Gospel of Mark. The transfiguration looks back to the baptismal scene with its voice from heaven confirming who Jesus is ("You are my favored son," 1:9–11) and forward to the resurrection (16:1–8). The scene on the mountain also confirms Peter's confession (8:27–30): Jesus is the expected messiah and as such is superior to Moses and Elijah, the two ancient heroes of Israel.

At the same time, the transfiguration recalls many of the features that characterized Moses' experience on Mt. Sinai when he encountered Yahweh and received the ten commandments (Exod 24:9–18). In the next narrative segment, Mark will indicate that John the Baptist is Elijah returned, the fulfillment of another prophecy (Mal 4:5–6). In the present scene, Mark pictures Jesus as the new Moses. All of this belongs to the Christian interpretive overlay of the gospel story, the overlay that depicts John the Baptist as the new Elijah and Jesus as the messiah and new Moses. However, it is Matthew who specializes in parallels between Jesus and Moses (for further information on this theme, consult the commentary on Matt 17:1–8).

The transfiguration fits with Mark's understanding of Jesus as God's son (1:11, 15:39) and provides the reader with a preview of Jesus' supernatural glory, which Mark does not otherwise narrate. In the account of Jesus' baptism, God had declared Jesus to be his son (1:11), and Mark reaffirms that role here at a crucial point in the gospel's plot, just after Jesus' first prediction that he will suffer and die (8:31–33). The command to "listen to him," rather than to Moses or Elijah, underscores the grim prediction of Jesus' passion that Mark has just reported.

Mark was apparently the first to formulate this story in its present form. The other versions and allusions are dependent on him. Even if it originated as a story of an appearance of the risen Jesus, Mark has transformed it in adapting it to its present place in his sequence of events. As an invention of Mark, it merits a black designation.

Elijah as precursor
Mk 9:9–13
Mt 17:9–13
Source: Mark

9 **9And as they were walking down the mountain he instructed
them not to describe what they had seen to anyone, until the son of
Adam rise from the dead.**
**10And they kept it to themselves, puzzling over what this could
mean, this 'rising from the dead.' 11And they started questioning
him: "The scholars claim, don't they, that Elijah must come first?"**
12He would respond to them, "Of course Elijah comes first to
restore everything. So, how does scripture claim that the son of Adam
will suffer greatly and be the object of scorn? 13On the other hand, I tell
you that Elijah in fact has come, and they had their way with him, just
as the scriptures indicate."

Elijah as precursor. This story is an anecdote that Mark has linked editorially to the transfiguration, which just precedes it (9:2–8). The editorial linkage (vv. 9–10) is Mark's own creation.

The early Christian community identified John the Baptist with Elijah in accordance with the prophecy of Malachi:

> Look, I will send Elijah to you before the great and terrible day of the Lord comes. He will redirect a father's heart towards his son and the hearts of everyone towards their neighbor, so I won't have to come and give the earth a devastating blow. Mal 4:5–6 (LXX)

Verses 12–13 may therefore be the product of early Christian speculation based on Old Testament prophecy. (However, the second part of v. 12 is regarded as a gloss—a marginal note that was copied by mistake into a manuscript.) The death of John the Baptist was thus considered preparation for the death of Jesus.

The words ascribed to Jesus were colored black in *The Five Gospels*. The Markan narrative frame was considered fictive in the second phase of the Jesus Seminar.

Man with mute spirit
Mk 9:14–29
Mt 17:14–20, Lk 9:37–43
Source: Mark

9 **14When they rejoined the disciples, they saw a huge crowd sur-
rounding them and scholars arguing with them. 15And all of a sud-
den, when the whole crowd caught sight of him, they were alarmed
and rushed up to meet him. 16He asked them,** "Why are you bother-
ing to argue with them?"
**17And one person from the crowd answered him, "Teacher, I
brought my son to you, because he has a mute spirit. 18Whenever it
takes him over, it knocks him down, and he foams at the mouth and
grinds his teeth and stiffens up. I asked your disciples to drive it
out, but they couldn't."**
19In response he says, "You distrustful lot, how long must I asso-
ciate with you? How long must I put up with you? Bring him over
to me!"

**[20]And they brought him over to him. And when the spirit noticed
him, right away it threw him into convulsions, and he fell to the
ground, and kept rolling around, foaming at the mouth. [21]And
<Jesus> asked his father,** "How long has he been like this?"

**He replied, "Ever since he was a child. [22]Frequently it has thrown
him into fire and into water to destroy him. So if you can do any-
thing, take pity on us and help us!"**

[23]Jesus said to him, "What do you mean, 'If you can'? All things are
possible for the one who trusts."

**[24]Right away the father of the child cried out and said, "I do trust!
Help my lack of trust!"**

**[25]When Jesus saw that the crowd was about to mob them, he
rebuked the unclean spirit, and commands it,** "Deaf and mute spirit,
I command you, get out of him and don't ever go back inside him!"

**[26]And after he shrieked and went into a series of convulsions, it
came out. And he took on the appearance of a corpse, so that the
rumor went around that he had died. [27]But Jesus took hold of his
hand and raised him, and there he stood.**

**[28]And when he had gone home, his disciples started questioning
him privately: "Why couldn't we drive it out?"**

[29]He said to them, "The only thing that can drive this kind out is
prayer."

Man with mute spirit. Jesus has twice earlier been confronted by a demon, once in the synagogue at Capernaum (1:21–28), and a second time in Gerasa (5:1–20). He also is reported to have exorcized a demon from the daughter of a Greek woman, but he did so at a distance. Now for a third time he encounters a demon, this time one that renders its victim mute and deaf.

Mark's version is an elaborate, wandering tale replete with repetitive graphic descriptions of the symptoms (vv. 18, 20, 21–22, 26). In this respect, it resembles the story of the Gerasene demoniac (Mark 5:1–20). Rudolf Bultmann was of the opinion that two stories had been put together: one featuring the failure of the disciples to drive out a demon, and a second one focusing on the father of the epileptic. In any case, it is an elaborate tale that both Matthew and Luke feel obligated to shorten.

This story, however, has some unique features. Unlike the earlier stories, here the failure of the disciples to perform the requested exorcism is a framing device. In the earlier stories Jesus converses directly with the demon; in this story since the demon is mute and deaf and the victim speechless, Jesus converses with the father of the boy. Here trust is made a factor in the exorcism (vv. 23–24), probably as a consequence of Mark's editing; elsewhere Mark tacks that motif on the end of his stories—for example, in the cure of the woman with vaginal bleeding (8:34) and the cure of blind Bartimaeus (10:52).

Mark has provided a narrative introduction of his own devising in vv. 14–16 and added a conclusion featuring his own theme: a private exchange with the disciples following the incident (vv. 28–29).

The Jesus Seminar has endorsed the view that Jesus was known as an exorcist. It is possible that the account of the deaf and mute epileptic boy harbors some reference to an actual event. The core of the story is therefore designated gray. However, the Markan embellishments, insofar as they can be identified, are colored black. John P. Meier, like the Fellows of the Jesus Seminar, thinks that some vague historical remembrance lies behind the Markan account.[37]

9 [30]**They left there and started going through Galilee, and he did**
not want anyone to know. [31]**Remember, he was instructing his dis-**
ciples and telling them: "The son of Adam is being turned over to his
enemies, and they will end up killing him. And three days after he is
killed he will rise!" [32]**But they never understood this remark, and**
always dreaded to ask him <about it>.

Jesus predicts his death again
Mk 9:30–32
Mt 17:22–23, Lk 9:43b–45
Source: Mark
Cf. Mk 8:31–33, Mt 16:21–23, Lk 9:22; Mk 10:32–34, Mt 20:17–19, Lk 18:31–34

Jesus predicts his death again. Jesus is now represented as making the second formal prediction of his passion, the first being the prediction he gave in Mark 8:31–33. Actually, however, Mark has slipped in another forecast of the future treatment of the son of Adam in the exchange about Elijah (9:9–13; in v. 12 the son of Adam is to suffer and be the object of scorn). Nevertheless, this is the second formal statement. The third prediction is to follow when they are on their way south to Judea and Jerusalem.

These predictions of Jesus' death and resurrection encapsulate Mark's "gospel"—the proclamation of the early Christian community as Mark understood it. To distinguish this "gospel" from the continuous narrative or story the term gospel usually conjures up, scholars often employ the term "kerygma," which is simply the Greek term for proclamation or message. The basic ingredients of Mark's kerygma, or proclamation, were the same as Paul's. The first formulation of the Christian message known to us is the one Paul records in 1 Cor 15:3–4:

> Among the very first things I handed on to you was what I myself also received as tradition:
>
> Christ died for our sins according to the scriptures,
> and was buried,
> and rose on the third day according to the scriptures.

Paul's formulation features the death and resurrection of Jesus, just as do Mark's three predictions of the passion of Jesus. In the view of the Jesus Seminar, Mark has summarized the Christian message and placed it on the lips of Jesus as a prediction. It is therefore a prediction after the fact. As such, it merits a black designation.

The narrative setting for the prediction is the creation of Mark. Verse 30 indicates that Jesus and his followers had left the region of Caesarea-Philippi (8:27) and were moving south through Galilee. But this, of course, is a movement conceived in Mark's imagination, since Mark did not know the sequence of events. The concluding verse (v. 32) is Mark's editorial comment. Both are appropriately black.

Dispute about greatness
Mk 9:33–37
Mt 18:1–5, Lk 9:46–48
Source: Mark

9

[33]And they came to Capernaum. When he got home, he started
questioning them, "What were you arguing about on the road?"
[34]They fell completely silent, because on the road they had been
bickering about who was greatest.

[35]He sat down and called the twelve and says to them, "If any of
you wants to be 'number one,' you have to be last of all and servant of
all!"

[36]And he took a child and had her stand in front of them, and he
put his arm around her, and he said to them, [37]"Whoever accepts a
child like this in my name is accepting me. And whoever accepts me is
not so much accepting me as the one who sent me."

Dispute about greatness. The setting and saying in vv. 33–35 are the creation of Mark, in all probability. When the gospel writers portray Jesus initiating conversation with his disciples about something they have done, it is usually to address a problem in one of their own communities, rather than an issue Jesus intended to address. In this case, the saying in v. 35 most likely reflects a leadership or pecking-order dispute in the Markan community. While the saying itself may derive from Jesus (the Fellows designated it gray in *The Five Gospels*), the setting Mark has given the saying is his invention.

Various sayings about welcoming the sender, accepting a representative, or receiving a child are preserved in the gospels (v. 37 with parallels in Matt 18:5 and Luke 9:48a; a Q version found in Luke 10:16//Matt 10:40; variations on the theme in John 5:23, 12:44, 13:20). In v. 37, Mark has remodeled some early version of welcoming a representative—anyone who is sent or dispatched—into a saying about receiving a child and given it a narrative setting in v. 36. Both the saying and the setting were designated black by the Seminar.

The strange exorcist
Mk 9:38–41
Lk 9:49–50
Source: Mark

9

[38]John said to him, "Teacher, we saw someone driving out
demons in your name, so we tried to stop him, because he wasn't
one of our adherents."

[39]Jesus responded, "Don't stop him! After all, no one who performs
a miracle in my name will turn around the next moment and curse me.
[40]In fact, whoever is not against us is on our side. [41]By the same token,
whoever gives you a cup of water to drink because you carry the name
of the Anointed, I swear to you, such a person certainly won't go unrewarded!

[42]"And any of you who misleads one of these little trusting souls
would be better off if you had a millstone hung around your neck and
were thrown into the sea!

[43]"And if your hand gets you into trouble, cut it off! It's better for
you to enter life maimed than to wind up in Gehenna, in the
unquenchable fire, with both hands!

[45]"And if your foot gets you into trouble, cut it off! It's better for you
to enter life lame than to be thrown into Gehenna with both feet!

[47]"And if your eye gets you into trouble, rip it out! It's better for you
to enter God's domain one-eyed than to be thrown into Gehenna with
both eyes, [48]where the worm never dies and the fire never goes out!
[49]"As you know, everyone there is salted by fire.
[50]"Salt is good <and salty>—if salt becomes bland, with what will
you renew it?
"Maintain 'salt' among yourselves and be at peace with one
another."

The strange exorcist. The saying in v. 40 is proverbial and was cited by Cicero, a Roman statesman and orator who lived in the first century B.C.E. Cicero accused Caesar of counting everyone an adherent who was not against him. The Fellows thought it possible that Jesus may have quoted the proverb on some occasion; they designated it gray in *The Five Gospels*. The saying in v. 41, on the other hand, is clearly the product of the early Christian movement; its designation of Jesus as the Anointed made the Seminar wary of the entire complex. The setting Mark has given to the proverb and a cluster of related sayings is probably fictional. As a fiction it is appropriately black.

10 **And from there he gets up and goes to the territory of Judea and across the Jordan, and once again crowds gather around him. As usual, he started teaching them.**

Jesus departs for Judea
Mk 10:1
Mt 19:1–2
Source: Mark

Jesus departs for Judea. Jesus undoubtedly did go from Galilee to Judea at some point in his career, perhaps more than once. However, Mark's geography leaves much to be desired. To get from Capernaum to Judea, Jesus would have to cross the Jordan twice or not at all. (For help with the geography of Palestine, consult the map, p. xxiv.)

Matthew did not improve matters in his revision (". . . went to the territory of Judea across the Jordan"). Had Mark written (as some manuscripts of Mark read): "And from there he gets up and goes to Judea by way of Perea . . ." there would have been no problem. But because Mark's geography is askew, the Seminar decided that gray was the appropriate designation.

Either Mark did not know the layout of the provinces—Galilee, Samaria, Judea, Perea—or his text became garbled in transmission. None of Judea lies on the east side of Jordan. Pilgrims going to Jerusalem often did cross the Jordan into Perea and head south on the eastern side before crossing back into Judea farther south. In so doing, they were able to avoid Samaria, which separated Galilee (to the north) from Judea and Jerusalem (to the south), and remain in territory that was governed by Herod Antipas, the ruler of Galilee. The Galileans who elected to follow the central ridge south through Samaria, which was a more direct route, would have found that the Samaritans were not always hospitable to them. After all, the Samaritans had built their own temple atop Mt. Gerizim as a rival to Jerusalem, and there were centuries of bad blood between the two groups, especially after the Judeans destroyed that temple in the second century B.C.E. Contacts between Galileans and Samaritans sometimes turned violent.

Luke tells the story of one trip Jesus made south through Samaria (9:51–56): Advance scouts sent on ahead to prepare for an overnight stay were ill-received; James and John suggested that they call down fire from heaven to teach the Samaritans a lesson; Jesus refused. The story may be apocryphal, but it does aptly illustrate the friction that often developed between the two peoples.

Is divorce permitted?
Mk 10:2–12
Mt 19:3–9
Source: Mark

10 [2]**And Pharisees approach him and, to test him, they ask whether a husband is permitted to divorce his wife. [3]In response he puts a question to them:** "What did Moses command you?"

[4]**They replied, "Moses allowed one to prepare a writ of abandonment and thus to divorce the other party."**

[5]**Jesus said to them,** "He gave you this injunction because you are obstinate. [6]However, in the beginning, at the creation, 'God made them male and female.' [7]'For this reason, a man will leave his father and mother and be united with his wife, [8]and the two will become one person,' so they are no longer two individuals but 'one person.' [9]Therefore those God has coupled together, no one else should separate."

[10]**And once again, as usual, when they got home, the disciples questioned him about this. [11]And he says to them,** "Whoever divorces his wife and marries another commits adultery against her; [12]and if she divorces her husband and marries another, she commits adultery."

Is divorce permitted? In several sources Jesus is reported to have said something about divorce (Mark, Q, 1 Cor 7:1–11). It is difficult to determine what that teaching was. However, the narrative frame provided for the dialogue in this passage is Mark's invention. Mark has created another of his didactic scenes in which Jesus makes a public statement and then is asked about its interpretation in private. Other examples are: Mark 4:3–20, 7:14–23, 8:11–21, and 9:24–29. In addition, either Mark or the oral tradition before him probably created the dialogue with the Pharisees in vv. 2–5. The Fellows of the Seminar are dubious that Jesus had many exchanges of this type with the Pharisees. The storyteller has created a plausible though fictive context for the pronouncement in v. 9.

Children in God's domain
• Mk 10:13–16
Mt 19:13–15, Lk 18:15–17;
Th 22:1–3
Sources: Mark, Thomas

10 [13]**And they would bring children to him so he could lay hands on them, but the disciples scolded them. [14]Then Jesus grew indignant when he saw this and said to them:** "Let the children come up to me, don't try to stop them. After all, God's domain belongs to people like that. [15]I swear to you, whoever doesn't accept God's imper-

ial rule the way a child would, certainly won't ever set foot in <his domain>!" [16]**And he would put his arms around them and bless them, and lay his hands on them.**

Children in God's domain. Jesus likely made some pronouncement about God's domain belonging to children, similar to his promise to the poor, the hungry, and the mournful. It is also likely that Jesus endorsed this new status for children by welcoming them into his circle, as suggested by vv. 13–14. However, the conflict Mark reports between Jesus and his male disciples when parents did bring their children to him, may well be the creation of Mark. Because it may be fictive, the Fellows decided to color it gray.

The narrative conclusion in v. 16 reflects a later development in the Christian community, when blessing the children and laying hands on them followed Christian baptism. It was therefore designated black.

The man with money
Mk 10:17–31
Mt 19:16–30, Lk 18:18–30; GNaz 6:1–5
Source: Mark

10

[17]**As he was traveling along the road, someone ran up, knelt before him, and started questioning him: "Good teacher, what do I have to do to inherit eternal life?"**

[18]**Jesus said to him,** "Why do you call me good? No one is good except for God alone. [19]You know the commandments: 'You must not murder, you are not to commit adultery, you are not to steal, you are not to give false testimony, you are not to defraud, and you are to honor your father and mother.'"

[20]**He said to him, "Teacher, I have observed all these things since I was a child!"**

[21]**Jesus loved him at first sight and said to him,** "You are missing one thing: make your move, sell whatever you have, and give <the proceeds> to the poor, and you will have treasure in heaven. And then come, follow me!"

[22]**But stunned by this advice, he went away dejected, since he possessed a fortune.**

[23]**After looking around, Jesus says to his disciples,** "How difficult it is for those who have money to enter God's domain!" [24]**The disciples were amazed at his words.**

In response Jesus repeats what he had said, "Children, how difficult it is to enter God's domain! [25]It's easier for a camel to squeeze through a needle's eye than for a wealthy person to get into God's domain!"

[26]**And they were very perplexed, wondering to themselves, "Well then, who can be saved?"**

[27]**Jesus looks them in the eye and says,** "For mortals it's impossible, but not for God; after all, everything's possible for God."

[28]**Peter started lecturing him: "Look at us, we left everything to follow you!"**

29 **Jesus said,** "I swear to you, there is no one who has left home, or
brothers, or sisters, or mother, or father, or children, or farms on my
account and on account of the good news, 30 who won't receive a hun-
dred times as much now, in the present time, homes, and brothers, and
sisters, and mothers, and children, and farms—including persecu-
tions—and in the age to come, eternal life.
31 "Many of the first will be last, and of the last many will be first."

The man with money. Verses 17–22 form a pronouncement story—an anecdote that climaxes in a saying of Jesus—to which Mark has appended further sayings about money (vv. 23–31).

The simple narrative connective in v. 17 ("As he was traveling along the road") is the way Mark links this episode to the sequence of events that takes place on the road to Jerusalem. Mark has assembled the sayings in vv. 23–31 and provided them with a narrative framework. Since all of this is the work of Mark, it merits a black designation.

The core anecdote about the man with money may possibly reflect an incident in the life of Jesus. Nevertheless, the Fellows were skeptical that the words attributed to Jesus in the exchange with the rich man were really spoken by Jesus, since they are not memorable epigrams. And they were equally dubious that the anecdote should be viewed as a historical report; it is probably an idealized scene in which Jesus gives advice to a wealthy person to the delight of his disciples. Nevertheless, the content of the anecdote is compatible with such sayings as "It is easier for a camel to squeeze through the eye of a needle than for a wealthy person to get into God's domain" (Mark 10:25). As a consequence, they colored both sayings and narrative frame gray.

Jesus predicts his death a third time
Mk 10:32–34
Mt 20:17–19, Lk 18:31–34
Source: Mark
Cf. Mk 8:31–33, Mt 16:21–23, Lk 9:22; Mk 9:30–32, Mt 17:22–23, Lk 9:43–45

10 32 **On the road going up to Jerusalem, Jesus was leading the
way, they were apprehensive, and others who were following were
frightened. Once again he took the twelve aside and started telling
them what was going to happen to him:**
33 "Listen, we're going up to Jerusalem, and the son of Adam will be
turned over to the ranking priests and the scholars, and they will sen-
tence him to death, and turn him over to foreigners, 34 and they will
make fun of him, and spit on him, and flog him, and put <him> to
death. Yet after three days he will rise!"

Jesus predicts his death a third time. This is the third forecast of death that Mark puts on the lips of Jesus. In this version, Mark actually anticipates many of the details of the passion story he is about to relate—Jesus' trial before the priests and Romans, the mocking, the spitting, and the flogging prior to execution. The Fellows of the Seminar agreed that this prediction was a "prophecy after the fact" and therefore the creation of Mark or the oral tradition prior to Mark. Since the prophecy is largely Mark's work, the narrative setting for it is also his invention. Both are appropriately black.

Revival of the young man at Bethany
SecMk 1:1–13
Jn 11:1–44
Sources: Secret Mark, John
Cf. Jn 11:1–44

And they come into Bethany, and this woman was there whose brother
had died. 2She knelt down in front of Jesus and says to him, "Son of
David, have mercy on me." 3But the disciples rebuked her.

4And Jesus got angry and went with her into the garden where the
tomb was. 5Just then a loud voice was heard from inside the tomb. 6Then
Jesus went up and rolled the stone away from the entrance to the tomb.

7He went right in where the young man was, stuck out his hand,
grabbed him by the hand, and raised him up. **8The young man looked**
at Jesus, loved him, and began to beg him to be with him.

9Then they left the tomb and went into the young man's house.
(Incidentally, he was rich.)

10Six days later Jesus gave him an order; 11and when evening had
come, the young man went to him, dressed only in a linen cloth. 12He
spent that night with him, because Jesus taught him the mystery of
God's domain.

13From there <Jesus> got up and returned to the other side of the
Jordan.

Revival of the young man at Bethany. For information about the discovery of the fragments of Secret Mark, consult the cameo "Secret Mark" (pp. 116–17).

This story, which was allegedly located between verses 34 and 35, has a close parallel in the tale of the raising of Lazarus (John 11:1–44). However, no traces of the special features of the Johannine story appear in Secret Mark, which suggests but does not prove that the version in Secret Mark was transmitted independently of the Fourth Gospel. (Comparisons are examined further in the commentary on John 11:1–44.)

This story has intriguing connections with other parts of the Gospel of Mark. In SecMk 1:1, Jesus and his followers arrive at Bethany; Jesus arrives at Bethany in Mark 11:1 after they leave Jericho in 10:46. SecMk 1:13 has Jesus "return to the other side of the Jordan"; in Mark 10:1, Jesus goes "to the territory of Judea and across the Jordan." The names and places are comparable but given in a different sequence.

The sister of the young man pleads with Jesus, "Son of David, have mercy on me"; those are the precise words blind Bartimaeus employs in Mark 10:47.

The person Jesus resuscitates is a young man (SecMk 1:7, 8, 9, 10); that same term is used to describe the young man who fled naked in the garden the night of Jesus' arrest (Mark 14:51–52).

Jesus grabs the young man by the hand and raises him up (SecMk 1:7), just as he does others he heals (Mark 1:31, 5:41, 9:27).

The young man Jesus revives is rich, and when the youth sees Jesus, he loves him (SecMk 1:8). The young man Jesus encounters in 10:17–22 is rich, and when Jesus sees him, he loves him. The direction of love has changed, but the motif persists.

The young man begs Jesus to permit him to be with Jesus (SecMk 1:8). After Jesus exorcizes the demonic of Gerasa, the man begs to be allowed to accompany Jesus (Mark 5:18).

These and other ties to other stories in the Gospel of Mark may be merely

SECRET MARK

The Secret Gospel of Mark is an expanded version of the Gospel of Mark. It is called Secret Mark because it was presumably intended only for insiders, for those who had attained a higher level of knowledge than the ordinary Christian. So far as we now know, Secret Mark contained only two additional items. One is an account of the resuscitation of a young man, the other a brief reference to the young man, his mother, and Salome. But these two fragments have intriguing ties to other parts of the gospel tradition.

The story of the discovery is shrouded in mystery. In 1958, Morton Smith, a professor at Columbia University, discovered the two excerpts from Secret Mark in a fragment of a letter of Clement of Alexandria (ca. 150–215 C.E.), which was copied into the flyleaf of an edition of the letters of Ignatius of Antioch (ca. 35–107 C.E.) published in 1646. At the time of the discovery, Smith was living at the monastery of Mar Saba between Jerusalem and the Dead Sea, where he was making an inventory of the ancient books and manuscripts in the monastery library. Unfortunately, the volume disappeared before other scholars could examine the flyleaf. However, Smith did publish a facsimile of the letter in 1973.

Clement had addressed his letter to a certain Theodore, otherwise unknown, who had come in contact with a group of Carpocratians from whom he had learned about a secret version of Mark. Clement alleges that Mark, after migrating from Rome to Alexandria upon the death of Simon Peter, revised his gospel to include secret teachings. This new version of Mark was intended for a select circle of initiates who were prepared for the "higher mysteries."

The story of the resuscitation of the young man was placed in the secret edition of Mark between 10:34 and 10:35 of canonical Mark. It exhibits striking parallels to the account of the resuscitation of Lazarus in John 11:1–44. The Fellows of the

fortuitous, or they may be storytelling traits of Mark, in which case they represent the transmigration of motifs from one story to another. John Dominic Crossan has advanced the hypothesis that when the gospel of Mark was stripped of its secret elements, some of these motifs were distributed to other parts of the gospel.[38]

The Fellows of the Jesus Seminar agreed that the core story of the revival of a youth considered dead might reflect an actual event in the life of Jesus. Accordingly, they colored the key verses (4–7) gray to correspond to the gray designation they gave to the core of the Lazarus story (John 11:33–44).

Request for precedence
Mk 10:35–45
Mt 20:20–28, Lk 22:24–27
Source: Mark

10 [35]**Then James and John, the sons of Zebedee, come up to him, and say to him, "Teacher, we want you to do for us whatever we ask!"**

[36]**He said to them,** "What do you want me to do for you?"

[37]**They reply to him, "In your glory, let one of us sit at your right hand, and the other at your left."**

[38]**Jesus said to them,** "You have no idea what you're asking for. Can

Jesus Seminar are convinced that this story in Secret Mark is not a revision of the Johannine story but an independent version. The two versions are believed to stem from a common written source or to be dependent upon oral tradition.

The second excerpt mentioned by Clement is too brief to provide much additional information. It consists of only one sentence that is located between the first and second parts of Mark 10:46.

The young man whom Jesus loved and resuscitated seems to be related to the young man who fled naked from the garden the night of Jesus' arrest (Mark 14:51). The fact that neither Matthew nor Luke mentions this young man prompts an intriguing question: Was that reference deliberately omitted by the two later evangelists, or was it not present in the copy of Mark that they used? The incident in canonical Mark is itself baffling, unless of course it is somehow connected to an initiation rite like the one depicted in Secret Mark (1:11–12):

> . . . when evening had come, the young man went to him, dressed only in a linen cloth. He spent that night with him, because Jesus taught him the mystery of God's domain.

Another intriguing question is which of the two editions of the Gospel of Mark came first. A number of scholars have argued convincingly that, contrary to the opinion expressed by Clement in his letter, canonical Mark is a revision of Secret Mark. It appears that Matthew and Luke did not make use of Secret Mark, but based their gospels on public or canonical Mark. If so, canonical Mark is a gospel from which the esoteric passages have been deleted. That knowledge in itself casts important new light on the transmission of the gospel texts: Since Mark went through at least two editions, other gospels may also have done so. We are certain that the Gospel of Thomas appeared in at least two versions, and many scholars are convinced that the Gospel of John was known in two, perhaps three, different editions.

you drink the cup that I'm drinking, or undergo the baptism I'm undergoing?"

39**They said to him, "We can!"**

Jesus said to them, "The cup I'm drinking you'll be drinking, and the baptism I'm undergoing you'll be undergoing, 40but as for sitting at my right or my left, that's not mine to grant, but belongs to those for whom it has been reserved."

41**When they learned of it, the ten got annoyed with James and John. 42So, calling them aside, Jesus says to them:** "You know how those who supposedly rule over foreigners lord it over them, and how their strong men tyrannize them. 43It's not going to be like that with you! With you, whoever wants to become great must be your servant, 44and whoever among you wants to be 'number one' must be everybody's slave. 45After all, the son of Adam didn't come to be served, but to serve, even to give his life as a ransom for many."

Request for precedence. This segment is another anecdote in two parts. In the first part, James and John, the sons of Zebedee, request that they be awarded places of honor in the coming kingdom. Jesus responds in vv. 39–40 with sayings that the Fellows concluded were not authentic sayings of Jesus. They colored the sayings black in *The Five Gospels*. The narrative setting, they decided, should also be designated black as a creation of Mark or someone in the oral tradition before him.

In the second part, Mark gathers additional sayings related to the basic theme in part one. While some of the sayings Mark has collected in vv. 42–45 may go back to Jesus (they were labeled gray in *The Five Gospels*), the narrative setting provided for them in vv. 41–42 is a fiction of the author of Mark.

Blind Bartimaeus
Mk 10:46–52
Mt 20:29–34, Lk 18:35–43
Source: Mark
Cf. Mt 9:27–31; Jn 9:1–7

10 [46]**Then they come to Jericho. As he was leaving Jericho with**
his disciples and a sizable crowd, Bartimaeus, a blind beggar, the
son of Timaeus, was sitting alongside the road. [47]**When he learned**
that it was Jesus the Nazarene, he began to shout: "You son of
David, Jesus, have mercy on me!"

[48]**And many kept yelling at him to shut up, but he shouted all the**
louder, "You son of David, have mercy on me!"

[49]**Jesus paused and said, "Tell him to come over here!"**

They called to the blind man, "Be brave, get up, he's calling you!"
[50]**So he threw off his cloak, and jumped to his feet, and went over to**
Jesus.

[51]**In response Jesus said, "What do you want me to do for you?"**

The blind man said to him, "Rabbi, I want to see again!"

[52]**And Jesus said to him,** "Be on your way, your trust has cured
you." **And right away he regained his sight, and he started follow-**
ing him on the road.

Blind Bartimaeus. In evaluating this story, the Seminar affirmed once again that the narrative introductions to episodes are likely to have been the inventions of storytellers. Consequently, they colored v. 46 gray, with the exception of the description of the afflicted person. The location in Jericho, the name Bartimaeus, explained for a Greek audience as "son of Timaeus," and a blind beggar strategically situated on the road taken by pilgrims on their way to Jerusalem, are all details supplied by a narrator.

The elaborate prelude to the contact between Jesus and the blind beggar is unusual, except in stories in which a representative of the patient is petitioning Jesus (for example, the official's son, Luke 7:1–10, and the Greek woman's daughter, Mark 7:24–30). In this realistic prelude, the blind man calls Jesus "son of David," which may mean that he is regarded as Solomon's equal in being able to effect cures. But to the evangelist Mark, it was almost certainly a messianic title, meaning that Mark took Jesus to be the expected Davidic messiah. In color coding it pink, the Fellows elected to understand the title as a reference to Solomon as a renowned healer.

The connection of trust with the cure (v. 52) is a Markan motif that appears elsewhere in Mark's stories (for example, 5:34 and 9:19). The notice that the blind man, now cured, became a follower of Jesus is probably also a Markan touch. The core story, however, drew a pink weighted average. As John P. Meier puts it, considering the theological freight the story is made to bear in Mark, "it would be naive to treat the story as a videotape replay of an event in A.D. 30." Yet he takes the view that the story does reflect a specific deed of the historical Jesus.[39]

A second excerpt from the Secret Gospel of Mark (2:1–2) was found in a letter of Clement of Alexandria discovered in 1958. (For the details of the discovery, consult the cameo "Secret Mark," pp. 116–17). It is to be located, according to Clement, between two phrases in Mark 10:46: "Then they came to Jericho" and "As he was leaving Jericho." This is how the excerpt reads:

> **1The sister of the young man whom Jesus loved was there, along with his mother and Salome, 2but Jesus refused to see them.**

Verse 46 in canonical Mark has long been considered a riddle by scholars. Why mention entering and leaving Jericho, unless something happened in Jericho? Secret Mark provides an answer to that riddle. The young man Jesus loved was there, along with his mother and Salome. However, Jesus refused to see them, although he had just recently revived the young man when he was thought to be dead (the commentary on the resuscitation of the young man appears above, between Mark 10:34 and 10:35). Secret Mark thus fills a blank in the text of the Gospel of Mark.

Salome appears elsewhere in the Gospel of Mark at 15:40 and 16:1. In the first passage she observes the crucifixion of Jesus from a distance, along with Mary of Magdala and Mary the mother of James and Joses. In the second, she joins the two Marys on Sunday morning when they go to the tomb to embalm Jesus. Salome is thus connected with tomb stories twice in Mark's gospel.

The Fellows were of the opinion that this fragment of Secret Mark does not provide any significant additional historical information about Jesus. The result was a black designation.

Jesus enters Jerusalem
Mk 11:1–11
Mt 21:1–11, Lk 19:28–40; Jn 12:12–19
Sources: Zech 9:9, Ps 118:25–26, Mark, John

11 When they get close to Jerusalem, near Bethphage and Bethany at the Mount of Olives, he sends off two of his disciples
2with these instructions: "Go into the village across the way, and right after you enter it, you'll find a colt tied up, one that has never been ridden. Untie it and bring it here.
3If anyone questions you, 'Why are you doing this?' tell them, 'Its master has need of it and he will send it back here right away.'"

4They set out and found a colt tied up at the door out on the street, and they untie it.
5Some of the people standing around started saying to them, "What do you think you're doing, untying that colt?"
6But they said just what Jesus had told them to say, so they left them alone.

7So they bring the colt to Jesus, and they throw their cloaks over it; then he got on it.
8And many people spread their cloaks on the road, while others cut leafy branches from the fields.
9Those leading the way and those following kept shouting,

"Hosanna! Blessed is the one
who comes in the name of the Lord!"
10Blessed is the coming kingdom of our father David!
"Hosanna" in the highest!

11And he went into Jerusalem to the temple area and took stock of everything, but, since the hour was already late, he returned to Bethany with the twelve.

Jesus enters Jerusalem. After a lengthy debate, the Fellows took a poll on the following proposition:

- **Jesus rode into Jerusalem on an ass as a symbolic act.**

The weighted average was gray as the result of a divided vote. In a second vote, the Fellows were virtually unanimous in rejecting a messianic interpretation of such an event:

- **Jesus rode into Jerusalem on an ass in order to declare his messiahship in fulfillment of Zech 9:9.**

The Seminar thus rejected the interpretation suggested by Mark in vv. 8–10 that Jesus is entering Jerusalem in triumph as its expected savior.

About a third of the Fellows argued for the view that the story of the triumphal entry was a fiction inspired in part by Ps 118:25–26, but especially by the prophecy in Zech 9:9, which Mark does not cite but Matthew and John do (from the LXX):

> Tell the daughter of Zion,
> Look, your king comes to you in all modesty
> and mounted on a donkey and on a colt,
> the foal of a pack animal.

About two-thirds of the Fellows held out for some historical kernel lurking behind the gospel accounts. The compromise solution eventually settled on was the first proposition, cited above; it elicited a gray weighted average. In other words, the Seminar could not come to a clear-cut conclusion.

On the way to this compromise the Seminar also rejected the possibility that Jesus entered Jerusalem at the time of one of the festivals as a pilgrim (but not mounted on an ass) and was greeted with acclamations. The vote was black.

According to Mark, Jesus entered Jerusalem from the east, from the Mount of Olives, which overlooked the city and the temple area. The prophets had speculated that "the Lord" would go forth in final battle against Israel's enemies from this point (Zech 14:4). This made the Mount of Olives a popular site for organizing freedom rallies against the Romans during the first century C.E. For his part, Jesus made it clear that he was entering Jerusalem to face death (10:33). In that case, the "triumphal entry" as Mark depicts it is a satire of revolutionary processions and of the kind of triumphal entry the Romans enjoyed making into cities they had conquered. The Romans celebrated their victories with horse, chariot, and a show of arms—with a military parade. In contrast,

Jesus entered Jerusalem on a beast of burden. Thus Jesus was not making a statement about his own messiahship, but contrasting God's imperial rule ("Congratulations, you poor! God's domain belongs to you") with Roman imperial rule.

The Markan story preserves traces of Jesus entering Jerusalem, in the judgment of some Fellows, but since it is difficult to isolate those traces, the story as a whole was designated black. The accompanying narrative statement was colored gray.

Fig tree without figs
Mk 11:12–14, 20–25
Mt 21:18–22
Source: Mark
Cf. Lk 13:6–9

11 [12]**On the next day, as they were leaving Bethany, he got hungry.** [13]**So when he spotted a fig tree in the distance with some leaves on it, he went up to it expecting to find something on it. But when he got right up to it, he found nothing on it except some leaves. (You see, it wasn't 'time' for figs.)** [14]**And he reacted by saying:** "May no one so much as taste your fruit again!" **And his disciples were listening.**

Fig tree without figs. The commentary for this segment is to be found in its continuation below, in Mark 11:20–25.

Temple incident
Mk 11:15–19
Mt 21:12–17, Lk 19:45–48; Jn 2:13–22
Sources: Mark, John

11 [15]**They come to Jerusalem. And he went into the temple and began chasing the vendors and shoppers out of the temple area, and he turned the bankers' tables upside down, along with the chairs of the pigeon merchants,** [16]**and he wouldn't even let anyone carry a container through the temple area.** [17]**Then he started teaching and would say to them:** "Don't the scriptures say, 'My house is to be regarded as a house of prayer for all peoples'?—but you have turned it into 'a hideout for crooks'!"

[18]**And the ranking priests and the scholars heard this and kept looking for a way to get rid of him. (The truth is that they stood in fear of him, and that the whole crowd was astonished at his teaching.)** [19]**And when it grew dark, they made their way out of the city.**

Temple incident. The Fellows of the Jesus Seminar approved on three different occasions over a ten-year period the statement that Jesus performed some anti-temple act and spoke some word against the temple. More than a hundred scholars participated in these affirmations. In spite of the confidence that some historical event underlies the report of Mark, the Fellows have had serious difficulties in pinpointing what Jesus actually did.

One source of difficulties is the size of the area in which Jesus' anti-temple behavior is alleged to have taken place. The entire temple mount covered more than thirty-five acres. That is a space big enough to accommodate thirty-four football fields, each measuring fifty by one hundred yards. Into that space during the three great festivals—Passover, Pentecost, and Tabernacles—were crowded thousands of pilgrims, together with tables of money changers, stalls for the sale of sacrificial animals, and temple priests and police, all milling around. Owing to the magnitude of the scene, the Fellows thought it possible that Jesus chased some vendors and patrons out of the area, but they doubt that he was able to drive all the pigeon merchants from the temple precincts. They were also uncertain that he overturned some of the tables of money changers for the simple reason that he would probably have been arrested on the spot by the temple police. And they doubted that he could have prevented people from carrying vessels through the area.

That he also began speaking in a way critical of the temple and its bureaucracy seems likely, yet the Fellows gave a gray designation to the quotation that is a mixture of Isa 56:7 and Jer 7:11 (v. 17). The quotation from scripture was probably supplied by early Christian interpreters. Jesus probably said something like what he is reported to have said in Mark 13:2: In reference to the monumental buildings that adorned the temple mount, he may have remarked, "Not one stone will be left on top of another."

The checkered color coding of the passage suggests how difficult it was for the Fellows to agree on specifics. The pink of v. 15 is intended to indicate that Jesus precipitated some kind of temple incident by his aggressive criticism of the commercialization of the temple cult. The statement about the bankers' tables and the pigeon merchants was given a gray ranking on the basis of the improbability of such actions: there were probably dozens of each in the temple area. Verse 16 was voted black again because of the virtual impossibility of carrying out such a program among thousands of pilgrims. The remark in v. 17 that Jesus said something negative about the temple is probably accurate: he did say something, but what is reported in the rest of the verse is not what he said. Verses 18 and 19 are a narrative conclusion conceived by Mark as a transition to the next day during the passion week.

Fig tree without figs
Mk 11:12–14, 20–25
Mt 21:18–22
Source: Mark
Cf. Lk 13:6–9

11 [20]**As they were walking along early one morning, they saw
the fig tree withered from the roots up. [21]And Peter remembered and
says to him: "Rabbi, look, the fig tree you cursed has withered up!"**
[22]**In response Jesus says to them:** "Have trust in God. [23]I swear to
you, those who say to this mountain, 'Up with you and into the sea!'
and do not waver in their conviction, but trust that what they say will
happen, that's the way it will be. [24]This is why I keep telling you, trust
that you will receive everything you pray and ask for, and that's the
way it will turn out. [25]And when you stand up to pray, if you are holding anything against anyone, forgive them, so your Father in heaven
may forgive your misdeeds."

Fig tree without figs. The cursing of the fig tree is derived from a single source, the Gospel of Mark. Matthew reproduces it in a somewhat different form, but Luke omits it, probably because he didn't think it appropriate. There is nothing comparable in the Gospel of John or any of the other gospels. It has puzzled interpreters of the gospels for centuries.

Causing an unproductive fig tree to wither seems uncharacteristic of the historical Jesus. A senseless miracle of retribution, triggered by a petty, even petulant, response, is scarcely a mode of behavior that comports with the Jesus who restored a withered limb, declared a leper clean, ate openly with undesirables, and embraced the poor, hungry, and grieving. What then did the author of the gospel have in mind in recording this story?

In the judgment of many scholars, the story of the fig tree without figs is an allegory intended to interpret Jesus' pronouncements on and response to the temple cult: since the temple cult no longer "bears fruit," it is to wither and die—not one stone will be left on top of another. This—so the argument goes—is the reason Mark sandwiches the temple incident between the two halves of the fig tree tale: the literary envelope—the barren fig tree—is designed to explain Jesus' temple action. The story may in fact have been inspired by the parable of the fig tree recorded by Luke (13:6–9). In that parable, however, the vinekeeper pleads with the owner to allow him to cultivate the fig tree for one more year in the hope that it will finally bear fruit. In any case, the Fellows were clear that the cursing of the fig tree does not reflect an event in the life of Jesus and is incongruent with acts he is known to have performed. Black is the appropriate rating. John P. Meier, for a related set of reasons, comes to the same conclusion.[40]

The cursing of the fig tree is sometimes classified as a cursing or punitive miracle: the tree is punished, presumably because it had not produced fruit, even though it was not the season for fruit.

There are other miracles of punishment recorded in the Bible. God brings ten plagues on Egypt through the hand of Moses because the Pharaoh would not let the Israelites go (Exod 7:1–12:32). God causes the waters of the Red Sea to engulf the Egyptian army as it pursues the fleeing Israelites (Exod 14:26–29). Elisha transfers the leprosy of Naaman the Syrian, whom he has just cured, to his servant Gehazi because Gehazi accepts a reward from Naaman behind Elisha's back (2 Kgs 5:19–27).

In the New Testament, Ananias and Sapphira drop dead when Peter accuses them of holding back some proceeds from the sale of property (Acts 5:1–12). Paul blinds the sorcerer Bar-Jesus on the island of Cyprus when he turns the governor away from the faith (Acts 13:4–12). The Infancy Gospel of Thomas is filled with vindictive miracles wrought by the boy Jesus. The cursing of the fig tree is just one punitive miracle among many reported in the Bible and other ancient texts.

Mark has assembled in vv. 22–25 the sayings that he took from other sources of the Jesus tradition. The saying about mountains into the sea in v. 23 is attested also in the Sayings Gospel Q and the Gospel of Thomas. The saying about asking and receiving is found also in the Fourth Gospel. The remark about prayer and forgiveness is recorded also in Q. The Jesus Seminar studied and evaluated these sayings individually as reported in *The Five Gospels*. Scholars in general are firm in their judgment that Mark is responsible for gathering them and appending them to the story about the withered fig tree.

By what authority?
Mk 11:27–33
Mt 21:23–27, Lk 20:1–8
Source: Mark

11 **[27]Once again they come to Jerusalem. As he walks around in the temple area, the ranking priests and scholars and elders come up to him [28]and start questioning him: "By what right are you doing these things?" or, "Who gave you the authority to do these things?"**

[29]But Jesus said to them: "I have one question for you. If you answer me, then I will tell you by what authority I do these things. [30]Tell me, was the baptism of John heaven-sent or was it of human origin? Answer me that."

[31]And they conferred among themselves, saying, "If we say 'heaven-sent,' he'll say, 'Then why didn't you trust him?' [32]But if we say 'Of human origin . . . !'" They were afraid of the crowd. (You see, everybody considered John a genuine prophet.) **[33]So they answered Jesus by saying, "We can't tell."**

And Jesus says to them: "I'm not going to tell you by what authority I do these things either!"

By what authority? The sequence of events reported by the Gospel of Mark at the beginning of the passion week includes the entry into Jerusalem, the cursing of the fig tree, the temple incident, and the question posed by "the ranking priests and scholars and elders" about his authority for "doing these things." "These things" in the mind of the evangelist must have been the three preceding events: the question about authority was evidently triggered by the boldness of Jesus in making a "royal" entry into the city, cursing a fig tree, and acting against the temple. Since Mark did not know the sequence of events, he was creating a sequence that suited his narrative purpose, which was to demonstrate Jesus' authority, on the one hand, and, on the other, to prepare the way for his eventual arrest and execution.

In *The Five Gospels* the Fellows reported that the sayings ascribed to Jesus in this story did not originate with him: Since they are neither a parable nor an aphorism, they would not have survived oral transmission as independent sayings. And it is unlikely that the present anecdote with its clever exchange of repartee reflects an actual incident in the life of Jesus. It is more likely that Mark, or some storyteller before him, invented this scene to go with the sequence of events that precedes it.

The leased vineyard
Mk 12:1–12
Mt 21:33–46, Lk 20:9–20
Source: Mark

12 **And he began to speak to them in parables:**

Someone planted a vineyard, put a hedge around it, dug a winepress, built a tower, leased it out to some farmers, and went abroad. [2]In due time he sent a slave to the farmers to collect his share of the vineyard's crop from them. [3]But they grabbed him, beat him, and sent him away empty-handed. [4]So once again he sent another slave to them, but they attacked him and abused him. [5]Then he sent another, and this one they killed; many others followed, some of whom they beat, others of whom they killed.

6He still had one more, a son who was the apple of his eye.
This one he finally sent to them, with the thought, "They will
show this son of mine some respect."
7But those farmers said to one another, "This fellow's the heir!
Come on, let's kill him and the inheritance will be ours!" 8So they
grabbed him, and killed him, and threw him outside the vine-
yard.

9What will the owner of the vineyard do? He will come in person,
and do away with those farmers, and give the vineyard to someone
else.
10Haven't you read this scripture,

> A stone that the builders rejected
> has ended up as the keystone.
> 11It was the Lord's doing
> and is something you admire?

**12<His opponents> kept looking for some opportunity to seize
him, but they were still afraid of the crowd, since they realized that
he had aimed the parable at them. So they left him there and went
on their way.**

The leased vineyard. Mark has supplied a narrative frame for this parable, as he did for many other parables, sayings, and anecdotes. The generalization in v. 1 rings true to Jesus' method of teaching, so it is colored pink.

The narrative conclusion in v. 12, however, is the author's way of advancing the plot: Jesus' opponents are now looking for some way to arrest him, but they are still afraid of the crowd. Mark did not know when Jesus spoke this parable or what kind of response it evoked—it came to him in the oral tradition without narrative context. Verse 12 as Mark's fiction deserves a black rating.

Emperor & God
Mk 12:13–17
Mt 22:15–22, Lk 20:21–26;
Th 100:1–4; EgerG 3:1–6
Sources: Mark, Thomas,
Egerton Gospel

12 **13And they send some of the Pharisees and the Herodians to
him to trap him with a riddle. 14They come and say to him, "Teacher,
we know that you are honest and impartial, because you pay no
attention to appearances, but instead you teach God's way forth-
rightly. Is it permissible to pay the poll tax to the Roman emperor or
not? Should we pay or should we not pay?"**
15But he saw through their trap, and said to them, "Why do you
provoke me like this? Let me have a look at a coin."
16They handed him a silver coin, and he says to them, "Whose pic-
ture is this? Whose name is on it?"
They replied, "The emperor's."
17Jesus said to them: "Pay the emperor what belongs to the
emperor, and God what belongs to God!" **And they were dumb-
founded at him.**

Emperor & God. Verses 13–15a are part of Mark's narrative design for the passion week: intrigue against Jesus that leads to his arrest, trial, and execution. For this fiction, black is the relevant designation.

The saying about paying the emperor what is due the emperor and God what is due God was evidently transmitted as an independent pronouncement of Jesus in the oral tradition. It is preserved in the Gospel of Thomas without the long introduction provided by Mark. The minimal narrative framework provided for the basic saying in vv. 16–17 is very close to the context given in the Gospel of Thomas (100:1–4):

> **They showed Jesus a gold coin and said to him, "The Roman emperor's people demand taxes from us."**
>
> **He said to them,** "Give the emperor what belongs to the emperor, give God what belongs to God, and give me what is mine."

That part of the narrative context may well reflect an actual incident in the life of Jesus. The final remark about the impression Jesus made on his interlocutors, however, is a pious exaggeration on the part of the storyteller.

On the resurrection
Mk 12:18–27
Mt 22:23–33, Lk 20:27–40
Source: Mark

12 **[18]And some Sadducees—those who maintain there is no**
resurrection—come up to him and they start questioning him.
[19]"Teacher," they said, "Moses wrote for our benefit, 'If someone's
brother dies and leaves his widow childless, his brother is obligated
to take the widow as his wife and produce offspring for his brother.'
[20]There were seven brothers; now the first took a wife but left no
children when he died. [21]So the second married her but died without
leaving offspring, and the third likewise. [22]In fact, all seven <mar-
ried her but> left no offspring. Finally, the wife died too. [23]In the res-
urrection, after they rise, whose wife will she be?" (Remember, all
seven had her as wife.)

[24]Jesus said to them: "You've missed the point again, haven't you,
all because you underestimate both the scriptures and the power of
God. [25]After all, when men and women rise from the dead, they do not
marry, but resemble heaven's messengers. [26]As for whether or not the
dead are raised, haven't you read in the book of Moses in the passage
about the bush, how God spoke to him: 'I am the God of Abraham and
the God of Isaac and the God of Jacob'? [27]This is not the God of the
dead, only of the living—you're constantly missing the point!"

On the resurrection. Most of the Fellows were of the opinion that this anecdote developed well after the death of Jesus. The sayings of Jesus cannot be isolated from the fabric of the debate and so would not have been transmitted as individual sayings. The story is an anecdote in the style of rabbinic debate. It reflects conflicts between the early Christian community and its Jewish counterpart. Nevertheless, because some of the Fellows thought the ideas were not alien to Jesus, the weighted average fell into the gray category.

SILVER DENARIUS OF EMPEROR TIBERIUS

The bust of Tiberius is surrounded by the words TI CAESAR DIVI AVG F AVGVSTVS, which stand for "Tiberius Caesar Divi August Filius Augustus." Tiberius is both "Caesar Augustus," as each emperor was called, and "Divi Augusti Filius," son of Divine (or Deified) Augustus. Tiberius was the stepson and heir of Augustus. At his death in 14 C.E., the Roman Senate declared Augustus a god, as it had his adopted father, Julius Caesar. Augustus had popularized coins that proclaimed himself "son of the Divine." (See a coin of "Divine Julius," p. 128.) Tiberius merely adjusted the claim now to apply to himself, "son of the Divine Augustus."

On the reverse are the words PONTIF MAXIM, which stand for "Pontifex Maximus," the title given to Julius Caesar as head of the Roman religion (the Greek equivalent is translated "high priest"). Tiberius became Pontifex Maximus on 10 March, 15 C.E.

The seated female figure was common on coins of Augustus. She holds an olive branch and a scepter, representing PAX, peace. She is also often identified as Tiberius' mother Livia, wife of Augustus.

This coin was the most widely distributed one in the Roman Empire in Jesus' day. A number of them have been discovered in what was the Roman province of Palestine. The inscriptions on the coin epitomize Roman political and religious beliefs popular at that time. This is almost certainly the coin depicted in the anecdote in Mark 12:13–17.

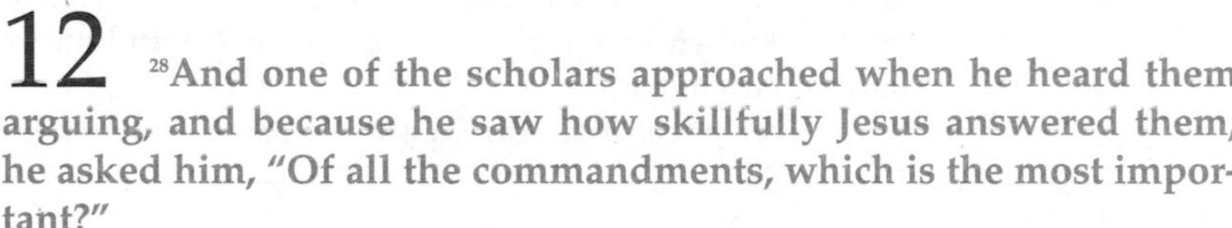

Most important commandment?
Mk 12:28–34
Mt 22:34–40
Source: Mark
Cf. Lk 10:25–29

12

28 And one of the scholars approached when he heard them
arguing, and because he saw how skillfully Jesus answered them,
he asked him, "Of all the commandments, which is the most important?"

29 Jesus answered: "The first is, 'Hear, Israel, the Lord your God is
one Lord, 30 and you are to love the Lord your God with all your heart
and all your soul and all your mind and with all your energy.' 31 The
second is this: 'You are to love your neighbor as yourself.' There is no
other commandment greater than these."

32 And the scholar said to him, "That's a fine answer, Teacher. You
have correctly said that God is one and there is no other beside him.
33 And 'to love him with all one's heart and with all one's mind and
with all one's energy' and 'to love one's neighbor as oneself' is
greater than all the burnt offerings and sacrifices put together."

SILVER DENARIUS OF DIVINE JULIUS

The coin shows a bust of Augustus surrounded by the words CAESAR AVGVSTVS ("Caesar Augustus"), and on the reverse a comet with the words DIVVS IVLIVS, meaning "Divus (Divine or Deified) Julius."

A comet, most often called a star then, appeared shortly after the death of Julius Caesar and quickly came to symbolize his proclaimed divinity.

In 46 B.C.E. Julius had begun annual games dedicated to Venus, whom the Julian family claimed as their ancestor. After the death of Julius in March 44, his adopted son Octavian staged the annual weeklong games in July and dedicated them in honor of Julius Caesar. A comet appeared "about the eleventh hour" the day the games began. In popular lore it was seen as Caesar's soul ascending to heaven.

On New Year's Day in 42 B.C.E., the Senate declared Julius Caesar to be a god. That same year Virgil wrote: "Behold, the star of Caesar came forth as a sign" (*Eclogue* 9.47). The "Julian star" became a popular literary image. Horace (c. 24 B.C.E.) declared: "The Julian star outshines all others just as the Moon outshines the lesser lights" (*Odes* 1.12.46–48).

Octavian, named "Augustus" by the Senate in 27 B.C.E., issued a series of coins, such as the one above, commemorating the comet as the symbol of "Divine Julius." Augustus thus promoted himself as "son of the Divine." The above coin has been dated to 17 B.C.E., likely commemorating the tenth anniversary of Octavian becoming "Augustus."

When Matthew, a century later, describes a star associated with a newborn king (Matt 2:2), it was by then a widely known image to associate "a star" with both royalty and divinity.

Photograph copyright British Museum, used by permission.

34 **And when Jesus saw that he answered him sensibly, he said to him,** "You are not far from God's domain."

And from then on no one dared question him.

Most important commandment? A friendly scholar now approaches Jesus with a standard question for the period: Which is the greatest commandment? The response Jesus gives is one any Judean faithful to his or her tradition could have given, had he or she been informed by Rabbi Hillel, a contemporary of Jesus. The ideas expressed in the exchange are therefore not inimical to those Jesus embraced. Nevertheless, the Fellows observed that the words ascribed to Jesus and the narrative frame must have been conceived together as question and answer in a kind of catechetical exchange. They were inclined to the view that the anecdote expresses the ideas of a very young Jesus movement and so colored the words and narrative framework gray.

The final note in v. 34 is Mark's comment, bringing to a close the series of exchanges that began in 11:27. Jesus is first challenged by priests, scholars, and elders (11:27), then by Pharisees and Herodians (12:13), and finally by Sadducees (12:18). Mark permits a friendly scholar to ask Jesus the last public question.

12 35**And during the time Jesus was teaching in the temple area,**
he would pose this question: "How can the scholars claim that the
Anointed is the son of David? 36David himself said under the influence
of the holy spirit, 'The Lord said to my lord, "Sit here at my right, until
I make your enemies grovel at your feet."' 37David himself calls him
'lord,' so how can he be his son?"
And a huge crowd would listen to him with delight.

Son of David
Mk 12:35–37
Mt 22:41–46, Lk 20:41–44
Source: Mark

Son of David. In this anecdote Jesus uncharacteristically initiates an exchange with a clever question. By demonstrating that the Anointed could not be David's son on the basis of scripture (Ps 110:1), was Jesus supposed to be carrying on a polemic against the concept of a Davidic messiah? While that seems entirely within the realm of possibility for Jesus, it seems unlikely that the Christian community would have been interested in transmitting an exchange that contradicted its own views. As a consequence, it is difficult to know what the point of the story is, unless it was Mark's intention to redefine the meaning of "the Anointed." The Fellows colored the words of Jesus black in *The Five Gospels,* and now follow suit in designating the minimal narrative frame in vv. 35 and 37 black.

12 38**During the course of his teaching he would say:** "Look out
for the scholars who like to parade around in long robes, and insist on
being addressed properly in the marketplaces, 39and prefer important
seats in the synagogues and the best couches at banquets. 40They are
the ones who prey on widows and their families, and recite long
prayers just to put on airs. These people will get a stiff sentence!"

Scholars in long robes
Mk 12:38–40
Lk 20:45–47
Source: Mark

Scholars in long robes. Mark's generalization in v. 38 is an accurate typification of the behavior of Jesus. Since Mark claims no more specific knowledge than the typical, pink is a valid designation.

12 41**And he would sit across from the treasury and observe the**
crowd dropping money into the collection box. And many wealthy
people would drop large amounts in. 42Then one poor widow came
and put in two small coins, which is a pittance. 43And he motioned

Widow's pittance
Mk 12:41–44
Lk 21:1–4
Source: Mark

his disciples over and said to them: "I swear to you, this poor widow has contributed more than all those who dropped something into the collection box! [44]After all, they were all donating out of their surplus, whereas she, out of her poverty, was contributing all she had, her entire livelihood!"

Widow's pittance. This charming little story was told for the sake of Jesus' pronouncement in vv. 43–44. Jesus could not have known that the woman was indeed donating all her resources, unless, of course, he were omniscient. Yet his statement may have been nothing more than hyperbole suggested by the outward appearance of poverty. She placed her two tiny coins into one of the receptacles located against the wall of the Court of Women in the temple precincts.

Stories featuring the sacrifice of the poor in acts of worship are known the world over. There are parallels to this anecdote in Jewish, Buddhist, and Greek literature. It is possible that this story imitates the folk tradition that God is especially appreciative of the gifts of the poor. It is also possible that Jesus told such a story that was later converted into an incident in his own life. We cannot know for sure. Yet there is nothing in the story that is out of character with what we otherwise know of Jesus.

A gray designation is all the facts permit.

Temple's destruction
Mk 13:1–2
Mt 24:1–2, Lk 21:5–6
Source: Mark

13 **And as he was going out of the temple area, one of his disciples remarks to him, "Teacher, look, what magnificent masonry! What wonderful buildings!"**

[2]**And Jesus replied to him,** "Take a good look at these monumental buildings! You may be sure not one stone will be left on top of another! Every last one will certainly be knocked down!"

Temple's destruction. Mark is here creating a narrative context for his collection of apocalyptic materials (13:1–37). He has constructed two lengthy discourses in his gospel, this one and the collection of parables in 4:1–34, both of which are collections of individual units of oral tradition. He then provided each of them with a minimal narrative framework. The scene depicted in v. 1 is a Markan fiction and as such deserves a black designation. It is Mark's attempt to create a plausible setting for the saying in v. 2, which was colored gray in *The Five Gospels.* A majority of Fellows voted red or pink on the statement that Jesus predicted the destruction of the temple in this manner, but the gray and black votes pulled the weighted average into the gray range.

Signs of the end
Mk 13:3–37
Mt 24:3–42, Lk 21:7–36
Source: Mark

13 [3]**And as he was sitting on the Mount of Olives across from the temple, Peter would ask him privately, as would James and John and Andrew: [4]"Tell us, when are these things going to happen, and what will be the sign to indicate when all these things are about to take place?"**

5**And Jesus would say to them,** "Stay alert, otherwise someone
might just delude you! 6You know, many will come using my name
and claim, 'I'm the one!' and they will delude many people. 7When
you hear of wars and rumors of wars, don't be afraid. These are
inevitable, but it is not yet the end. 8For nation will rise up against
nation and empire against empire; there will be earthquakes every-
where; there will be famines. These things mark the beginning of the
final agonies.

9"But you look out for yourselves! They will turn you over to coun-
cils, and beat you in synagogues, and haul you up before governors
and kings, on my account, so you can make your case to them. 10Yet the
good news must first be announced to all peoples. 11And when they
arrest you to lock you up, don't be worried about what you should
say. Instead, whatever occurs to you at the moment, say that. For it is
not you who are speaking but the holy spirit. 12And one brother will
turn in another to be put to death, and a father his child, and children
will turn against their parents and kill them. 13And you will be univer-
sally hated because of me. Those who hold out to the end will be
saved!

14"When you see the 'devastating desecration' standing where it
should not (the reader had better figure out what this means), then the
people in Judea should head for the hills; 15no one on the roof should
go downstairs; no one should enter the house to retrieve anything;
16and no one in the field should turn back to get a coat. 17It'll be too bad
for pregnant women and nursing mothers in those days! 18Pray that
none of this happens in winter! 19For those days will see distress the
likes of which has not occurred since God created the world until now,
and will never occur again. 20And if the Lord had not cut short the
days, no human being would have survived! But he did shorten the
days for the sake of the chosen people whom he selected. 21And then if
someone says to you, 'Look, here is the Anointed,' or 'Look, there he
is!' don't count on it! 22After all, counterfeit messiahs and phony
prophets will show up, and they will provide portents and miracles so
as to delude, if possible, even the chosen people. 23But you be on your
guard! Notice how I always warn you about these things in advance.

> 24But in those days, after that tribulation,
> the sun will be darkened,
> and the moon will not give off her glow,
> 25and the stars will fall from the sky,
> and the heavenly forces will be shaken!

26"And then they will see the son of Adam coming on the clouds
with great power and splendor. 27And then he will send out messen-
gers and will gather the chosen people from the four winds, from the
ends of the earth to the edge of the sky!

28"Take a cue from the fig tree. When its branch is already in bud
and leaves come out, you know that summer is near. 29So, when you

THE PASSION NARRATIVE: INTRODUCTION

The sequence of events in the passion narrative is as follows:

The conspiracy against Jesus (Mark 14:1–2)
The anointing (Mark 14:3–9)
Judas' betrayal (Mark 14:10–11, 43–52)
The last supper (Mark 14:12–26)
Peter's denial (Mark 14:27–31)
Gethsemane (Mark 14:32–42)
The arrest (Mark 14:43–52)
Trial before the Council (Mark 14:53–72)
Trial before Pilate (Mark 15:1–15)
Mocking and crucifixion (Mark 15:16–41)
Burial (15:42–47)

A considerable amount of the passion narrative in all the gospels is colored black. Why are the Fellows of the Jesus Seminar skeptical of the historical reliability of these stories surrounding the final events of Jesus' life?

The Fellows are convinced that the male disciples of Jesus forsook him at his arrest and fled. The women disciples may have observed from a distance, and they are the only eyewitnesses among Jesus' followers to the *public* events of the passion. There were of course no eyewitnesses to the *private* events, such as the prayers in Gethsemane and the agreement Judas is alleged to have made with the priests.

The individual episodes that make up the passion narrative are not the types of stories that lend themselves to oral repetition: they make little sense as isolated anecdotes; they gain their meaning only as part of a longer, connected narrative. The passion narrative, unlike the body of the narrative gospels, was therefore not made up of discrete anecdotal "scenes" strung together, but was an extended, sequential composition from the beginning. It betrays its origins as a scribal composition prepared by those who were "searching the scriptures" for clues about why Jesus of Nazareth was crucified. If this view is correct, oral storytellers told few, if any, independent anecdotes about the final days of Jesus' life during the formative years of the tradition.

A third factor that contributed to the emergence of a passion story was the influence of "prophetic" scriptures. As Jesus' followers reflected on the events of the past, they asked themselves why these things had to happen. They became convinced, because of their regard for Jesus, that God had foreordained these events. They therefore began looking for prophecies that would help them understand the arrest, trial, and execution of Jesus. What they found contributed in a fundamental way to the stories that came to be told.

A final reason for skepticism arises from the fact that the five versions of the passion narrative that have survived exhibit a single, relatively coherent narrative. This suggests that all of those versions are derived from one source. That source may be one of the five surviving accounts, or it may be some hypothetical source no longer extant. In either case, we are dependent on a single source for all our data; the versions dependent on that source do not provide additional information. The basic issue for scholars is to identify the primary source of information about the passion of Jesus.

By solid majority, the Fellows of the Jesus Seminar held to the generally accepted view that Mark created the first *written* passion story. If the Gospel of Mark, which was composed probably in the decade of the 70s, is the earliest written version of the connected narrative, and if the passion narrative was not built up out of individual anecdotes, it follows that the first attempt to narrate the story did not come until four decades or more after Jesus' death. The lengthy delay and the absence of individual oral anecdotes connected with the final events make it even more likely that scripture and theological imagination contributed to the contours and details of the story.

The skepticism of the Fellows, and scholars generally, does not mean that there are no historical data in the passion story. However, what we have is limited to a few basic points.

It is all but certain, because attested also by Josephus and Tacitus, two ancient historians, that:

- **There was a person named Jesus, who was executed by the authorities during the prefecture of Pontius Pilate (26–36 C.E.).**

The Seminar was also convinced, on the basis of the evidence—the persistent connection of Jesus' arrest with the temple incident—that some Jewish officials, probably the high priest and his associates, urged Pilate to execute Jesus as a threat to public order. For his part, Pilate needed little convincing.

The execution of Jesus took place at a site called Golgotha, in all likelihood. In accordance with Roman practice, Jesus may well have been flogged as a preliminary to his crucifixion. The Fellows were again relatively certain that:

- **The disciples fled when Jesus was arrested.**

But of course the Jesus movement did not die. In the weeks and months following the crucifixion, Jesus' followers became convinced that Jesus was still with them. As a consequence, they began to organize themselves into a community in order to put into practice what Jesus had taught them about the kingdom of God.

In the course of their deliberations the Seminar also arrived at certain negative conclusions about the composition and reliability of the passion story. Two of these influenced their decisions on individual narrative segments.

- **The assertion that the Romans were innocent of Jesus' death and the Jews responsible is pure Christian propaganda.**
- **The underlying structure of the passion story was suggested by prophetic scriptures taken from the Greek Bible (the Septuagint).**

The first of these conclusions is based on the tendency in the stories themselves to shift the blame, a tendency encouraged initially by the conflict between the Jesus sect and other forms of Judaism. It was later aggravated by the fact that the Jesus movement soon became a gentile movement. Gentile Christians interpreted what was originally an intra-Jewish conflict as an anti-Jewish one; in addition, they were eager to convince new gentile converts that the Roman rulers were not their enemies.

The second conclusion was suggested by the observation that detail after detail in the passion story meshed with suggestions derived from scripture. These details are noted in the commentary on individual passages.

see these things take place, you ought to realize that he is near, just outside your door. [30]I swear to you, this generation certainly won't pass into oblivion before all these things take place! [31]The earth will pass into oblivion and so will the sky, but my words will never be obliterated!

[32]"As for that exact day or minute: no one knows, not even heaven's messengers, nor even the son, no one, except the Father.

[33]"Be on guard! Stay alert! For you never know what time it is. [34]It's like a person who takes a trip and puts slaves in charge, each with a task, and enjoins the doorkeeper to be alert. [35]Therefore, stay alert! For you never know when the landlord returns, maybe at dusk, or at midnight, or when the rooster crows, or maybe early in the morning. [36]He may return suddenly and find you asleep. [37]What I'm telling you, I say to everyone: Stay alert!"

Signs of the end. Verses 3–4 are a continuation of the fictive setting Mark began to set out in 13:1. The compendium of apocalyptic materials in 13:1–37 is a creation of Mark and the narrative setting is also his creation. As a fiction it merits a black designation.

The conspiracy
Mk 14:1–2
Mt 26:1–5, Lk 22:1–2; Jn 11:45–57
Sources: Mark, John

14 Now it was two days until Passover and the feast of Unleavened Bread. **And the ranking priests and the scholars were looking for some way to arrest him by trickery and kill him. [2]For their slogan was: "Not during the festival, otherwise the people will riot."**

The conspiracy. Mark sets the stage for his version of the passion story by concocting a conspiracy against Jesus on the part of the higher-ranking priests and scholars. According to Mark, these folks were convinced that Jesus was so popular that to arrest him publicly at festival time would produce a riot (v. 2).

The conspiracy theory is an invention of Mark, in all probability. It is played out in subsequent events and allusions in Mark's passion story. It is renewed next in the story of how Judas makes a deal with the ranking priests to turn Jesus in for money (Mark 14:10–11). The next mention takes place at the last supper, when Jesus predicts that one of his meal partners will turn him in (Mark 14:17–21). It is further alluded to at the conclusion of the Gethsemane scene, when Jesus observes that his betrayal is at hand (14:42). Then comes the arrest proper with the kiss of betrayal (14:43–51). The conspiracy continues as the priests, scholars, and elders attempt to assemble evidence against Jesus that warrants the death penalty (14:53, 55–65, 15:1, 3, 10) and then as they incite the crowd and taunt him (15:11, 31–32).

While the Fellows of the Jesus Seminar concluded that high-ranking Jewish officials probably urged Pilate to execute Jesus, they were dubious of Mark's account of the conspiracy. One reason for their skepticism is the obvious tendency on the part of the evangelists to increase the blame assigned to the Jews, coupled with the Christian missionary interest, in the period after the fall of

Jerusalem, in claiming that the Romans found nothing illegitimate about their movement. In a decisive vote, the Seminar agreed to this statement: that the Romans were innocent of and the Jews responsible for the death of Jesus is nothing more or less than a Christian fiction.

The temporal notice that the events connected with Jesus' execution took place in conjunction with Passover was voted gray (v. 1): the Fellows were about equally divided on the question. The pre-eminent issue here is the inconclusive dating of the last meal and the crucifixion: the synoptics make the last meal the Passover meal, while the Fourth Gospel has Jesus being crucified at the time the synoptics are preparing for the last meal—at the moment the Passover lambs were being slaughtered. They cannot both be right. Lack of conclusive evidence breeds skepticism. In addition, there are intriguing suggestions that the crucifixion may have taken place in the fall, perhaps at the time of the Feast of Booths or Tabernacles. The presence of leafy branches (Mark 11:8) or palms (John 12:13) during the entry into Jerusalem and the story of the fig tree out of season (Mark 11:12–14) hint at a fall date. In this, as in other matters, caution is the rule for historians seeking to determine the facts.

The anointing
Mk 14:3–9
Mt 26:6–13; Lk 7:36–50;
Jn 12:1–8
Sources: Mark, Luke, John

14 [3]When he was in Bethany at the house of Simon the leper,
he was just reclining there, and a woman came in carrying an
alabaster jar of myrrh, of pure and expensive nard. She broke the jar
and poured <the myrrh> on his head.
[4]Now some were annoyed <and thought> to themselves: "What
good purpose is served by this waste of myrrh? [5]For she could have
sold the myrrh for more than three hundred silver coins and given
<the money> to the poor." And they were angry with her.
[6]Then Jesus said, "Let her alone! Why are you bothering her? She
has done me a courtesy. [7]Remember, there will always be poor around,
and whenever you want you can do good for them, but I won't always
be around. [8]She did what she could—she anticipates in anointing my
body for burial. [9]So help me, wherever the good news is announced in
all the world, what she has done will also be told in memory of her!"

The anointing. This story has been recorded by all four narrative gospels. There are significant variations in the four versions, yet there is also remarkable agreement on the basic ingredients of the tale. The setting of all versions is a meal, or symposium, at which the owner of the house is present. A woman anoints Jesus during the meal (not before or after it) with a jar of perfume. Members of the party object to the woman's action and Jesus defends her. The similarities in the setting and plot suggest that one incident or story lies behind the four versions. Yet because of the variation in other details, the Fellows of the Seminar decided that the original version of the incident is irretrievable. A divided vote on the historicity of the incident produced a gray weighted average for all forms of the story.

A symposium in the house of Simon the Leper is the setting in Mark for the appearance of the woman with her jar of expensive myrrh. Because she is assumed to be respectable, her appearance is a potential source of scandal. She pours the perfume on Jesus' head, she anoints him, which hints at his role as the Anointed, as the messiah, although the anointing of head and face, and the washing and anointing of feet, were commonplace at such banquets. The objection to the woman's action on account of the expense involved seems contrived, and the connection with Jesus' burial is an afterthought. In the original story the woman's act was probably interpreted by Jesus as a "courtesy," which Jesus would have expressed with the Greek term *kalon,* which can be understood as either a good or a beautiful act. The double meaning of the term would have been understood as a clever reply to the criticism leveled at Jesus by his disciples (vv. 4–5).

In view of the lack of agreement on the history of the story, the conclusion was the inevitable gray that accompanies indecision.

The contract
Mk 14:10–11
Mt 26:14–16, Lk 22:3–6
Source: Mark

14 **[10]And Judas Iscariot, one of the twelve, went off to the ranking priests to turn him over to them. [11]When they heard, they were delighted, and promised to pay him in silver. And he started looking for some way to turn him in at the right moment.**

The contract. While Paul reports that Jesus was "handed over" or "turned in" (1 Cor 11:23) on the same night that he ate his last meal with his disciples, the name of Judas is not connected with that event until the creation of the Gospel of Mark some two decades later. The first mention of Judas in Mark is in the list of the twelve (3:13–19), where he is identified as the one "who turned Jesus in" (v. 19). He next appears in the current passage where he volunteers his services as informer to the ranking priests, who promise to pay him in silver for his work. What he could provide was "the right moment," since the wrong moment might produce a riot (Mark 14:2).

Jesus brings up the matter of his being turned in during the last meal (Mark 14:18–21), although the name of Judas is not mentioned. However, Jesus declares that the betrayer is someone who is sharing the meal with him, and then pronounces a curse on the traitor to be.

At the conclusion of the Gethsemane scene, with the three disciples asleep, Jesus wakes them up with the announcement: "Here comes the one who is going to turn me in" (Mark 14:42). A crowd immediately appears, one that had been dispatched by the priests, scholars, and elders—the entire Jerusalem leadership—with Judas at its head. The fatal kiss and arrest follow (Mark 14:43–46). Judas is not mentioned thereafter in Mark's gospel.

Two-thirds of the Fellows of the Jesus Seminar took the view that both the role and the person of Judas in the betrayal and arrest of Jesus were entirely fictive. Bishop John Shelby Spong, who prepared the discussion paper for the group on this topic, argued that the traitor Judas was Mark's invention. A minority of Fellows dissented: most of this minority agreed with John Dominic Crossan that although Mark's story is a fiction, Judas was a real historical person. In either case, whether as a consequence of the majority vote that Judas is a fiction, or as a result of the minority opinion that although Judas was a real person, the story is a fiction, vv. 10–11 are to be colored black. The reasons for this conclusion are discussed in the commentary on Mark 14:17–21.

Preparation for Passover
Mk 14:12–16
Mt 26:17–19, Lk 22:7–13
Source: Mark

14 [12]**On the first day of Unleavened Bread, when they would
sacrifice the Passover lamb, his disciples say to him, "Where do you
want us to go and get things ready for you to celebrate Passover?"**
[13]**He sends two of his disciples and says to them,** "Go into the city,
and someone carrying a waterpot will meet you. Follow him, [14]and
whatever place he enters say to the head of the house, 'The teacher
asks, "Where is my guest room where I can celebrate Passover with
my disciples?"' [15]And he'll show you a large upstairs room that has
been arranged. That's the place you're to get ready for us."
[16]**And the disciples left, went into the city, and found it exactly as
he had told them; and they got things ready for Passover.**

Preparation for Passover. Mark launches his account of the final events with the conspiracy against Jesus (14:1–2). He continues that theme in 14:10–11 with his story of the compact between Judas and the ranking priests. Now he is ready to introduce the Passover theme with its focus on the last meal Jesus is to eat with his disciples.

The meal is the key event that brings together stories about how the disciples behaved in that crucial time—and probably prescribes how they were to behave in the time Mark was writing. At the meal Jesus predicts the betrayal of Judas: there is a traitor among the twelve. Just after the meal, as they are on their way to Gethsemane, Jesus predicts that Peter will disown him; Peter takes a strong oath that he will never do that. The Gethsemane scene follows. In that scene Peter, James, and John fall asleep, even though Jesus admonishes them to stand watch, presumably in anticipation of the arrest that is to follow. The last meal is thus the centerpiece in this series of events that have to do with discipleship.

Both the preparation for the triumphal entry (11:1–6) and the preparation for the Passover have been suggested, in all probability, by the story of the anointing of Saul by the prophet Samuel (1 Sam 10:1–8). Samuel first anoints Saul who is to become the first king of Israel, then kisses him. Samuel tells him that he will reign over Israel and that he will save his people from their enemies. Samuel advises Saul as he is about to leave that he will encounter two men by Rachel's tomb who will tell him that the donkeys he went to seek have been found. That will be a sign to him (1 Sam 10:2).

In preparation for the entry into Jerusalem, Jesus sends two disciples to find a colt under mysterious circumstances. When someone objects to the disciples' action in taking the colt, they reply that "its Master has need of it." They are permitted to lead the colt away (Mark 11:1–6).

In the earlier story, Samuel then advises Saul that he will also meet three men on their way to Bethel, to the house of God, who will have goats, bread, and wine with them. They will give Saul two loaves of bread (1 Sam 10:3–4). This will be a second sign. There is also a third sign involved: Saul will meet a band of prophets, and Saul will fall into a prophetic frenzy with them (1 Sam 10:5–6). When Saul encounters these signs, he is to do whatever he sees fit to do, since God is with him.

In preparing for the Passover, Jesus again sends two disciples into the city. There they will meet someone carrying a water jar. They are to follow that person, who will lead them to a house in which they are to celebrate Passover in an upper room.

In Mark's version, Jesus enters Jerusalem twice, once on Palm Sunday and once on the day of preparation for Passover (recall that the Jewish day began at sunset), was suggested by the anointing of Saul and its aftermath of "signs." Like Saul, Jesus was anointed, after which he acquired a donkey (under strange circumstances), and then found a place to eat Passover, which involved bread and wine (on equally mysterious terms). The acquisition of donkey and upper room were also in their way a kind of "sign."

We have already observed that Mark has created the string of events that lead up to Jesus' execution largely out of his imagination. He has invented the conspiracy against Jesus; he has fictionalized the story of Jesus' betrayal at the hands of Judas. Now he is setting the stage for the last meal by an equally fictitious account of the preparation for that meal. Both the words ascribed to Jesus and the narrative framework were designated black by the Seminar.

The betrayer
Mk 14:17–21
Mt 26:20–25, Lk 22:21–23; Jn 13:21–30
Sources: Mark, John

14 17**When evening comes, he arrives with the twelve.** 18**And as they reclined at table and were eating, Jesus said,** "So help me, one of you eating with me is going to turn me in!"

19**They began to fret and to say to him one after another, "I'm not the one, am I?"**

20**But he said to them,** "It's one of the twelve, the one who is dipping into the bowl with me. 21The son of Adam departs just as the scriptures predict, but damn the one responsible for turning the son of Adam in! It would be better for that man had he never been born!"

The betrayer. The plot against Jesus and Judas' role in it have been discussed in the commentary on Mark 14:1–2 and 10–11. The third time the betrayal of Jesus comes up is during the last meal (vv. 17–21). Although Judas is not mentioned by name, he is clearly the target of the prediction and the curse. The Seminar overwhelmingly voted to color this passage black, along with the earlier references to plot and betrayal. Why were the Fellows so confident that Mark's stories are fictions rather than history?

The name Judas is not introduced into the gospel tradition until the appearance of the Gospel of Mark in the decade of the 70s. Paul, who was writing his letters in the sixth decade, knows that Jesus was turned over to the authorities, but he doesn't mention any names. The name Judas may be nothing more or less than the personification of "the Jews"—Judas is the Greek form of Judah, the name of the tribe whose descendants are the Jews. The story of the betrayal of Joseph by eleven brothers in the book of Genesis (37–50) may have suggested the idea to an early Christian storyteller. Silver was involved in the sale of Joseph (Gen 37:25–28) just as it is in Mark's story of the betrayal of Jesus. Ps 41:9, usually translated "Even my bosom friend, whom I trusted, who ate of my bread, has raised his heel against me," has perhaps influenced Mark's report of the announcement of the betrayal at the meal. Even if Judas were a real person, the Fellows are convinced that the stories about his role in the arrest of Jesus are not historical.

The last supper
Mk 14:22–26
Mt 26:26–30, Lk 22:14–20
Source: Mark
Cf. Jn 13:1–20

14 [22]And as they were eating, he took a loaf, gave a blessing,
broke it into pieces and offered it to them. And he said, "Take some;
this is my body!" [23]He also took a cup, gave thanks, and offered it to
them, and they all drank from it. [24]And he said to them: "This is my
blood of the covenant, which has been poured out for many! [25]So help
me, I certainly won't drink any of the fruit of the vine again until that
day when I drink it for the first time in God's domain!"
[26]**And they sang a hymn and left for the Mount of Olives.**

The last supper. Jesus ate a meal with his disciples on the night he was betrayed, a meal involving the breaking of bread and the sharing of a cup of wine. This is the only story in the entire passion narrative for which there is evidence that antedates the writing of the gospels. In 1 Cor 11:23–26, written two decades or more earlier than the Gospel of Mark, Paul reports this tradition. The supper as Paul describes it probably originated in the communities of Asia Minor and Greece where Paul had established churches and not in Jerusalem where Jesus died.

In addition to the fact that the earliest mention of the meal is provided by Paul of Tarsus, a hellenistic Jew, two cultural norms or practices suggest that the meal had its origins in a pagan context. First of all, Jews of the first century usually observed the prescriptions in the law—in Leviticus—not to eat or drink blood. The suggestion that those who ate the bread and drank the cup were eating the body of Christ and drinking his blood would have been offensive to Jesus' Judean followers. The typical reaction of Judeans is indicated by the response Jesus gets when he says, in the Gospel of John, that only those who eat his flesh and drink his blood can be saved: the "Jews" and even his followers objected to that language and some dropped out of the movement as a result (John 6:48–66). While the story in the Fourth Gospel is probably fiction, it does accurately reflect the cultural conditioning of Palestinian Jews.

The ingenious proposal, made by one Fellow, that Jesus was himself reinterpreting what went on in the sacrificial cult in the temple in terms of his own body and blood, was rejected as improbable by the Seminar. The Seminar regarded it as much more likely that the symbolism of drinking the blood of a god arose in a pagan rather than a Jewish context.

The second of the cultural practices that influenced the decision of the Fellows was the custom of having a meal "in memory of" someone who had died. In the hellenistic world societies were formed, in fact, to hold meals in

THE GOSPEL OF MARK: LITERARY DNA

The Gospel of Mark preserves many characteristics of oral storytelling. Mark pulls the reader directly into the story by using the present tense of verbs rather than the more literary past tense (1:40):

> Then a leper *comes* up to him, *pleads* with him, *falls* down on his knees and *says* to him, "If you want to, you can make me clean."

Mark concludes the same story with a summary that typifies the activity around Jesus: the leper "started telling everyone and spreading the story" and people "continued to come to him from everywhere" (Mark 1:45). The storyteller's technique is to take the listeners to the scene—by means of words—and allow them to observe the movement of the characters.

As in folklore generally, Mark uses various forms of repetition, reiteration, or parallelism to give clear definition to his characters and as an aid to memory. Jesus begins in Capernaum with an exorcism (1:21–28), and then inaugurates the first trip into gentile territory with another exorcism (5:1–20). There are pairs of stories featuring healing by touch (1:40–45 and 5:25–34), miraculously feeding large crowds (6:30–44 and 8:1–10), and restoring sight to the blind (8:22–26 and 10:46–52). Mark also makes use of duplicate expressions on a smaller scale. He likes to say "early, while it was still dark" (1:35); "Be quiet, shut up!" (4:39); "now, in the present" (10:30); "the chosen people whom he selected" (13:20); "It's over! The time has come!" (14:41). Redundancy of this sort gives listeners (readers) breathing space—a better chance to take the story in.

Threefold repetition is a standard feature of folklore. Mark also makes use of this device. Jesus predicts his suffering three times (8:31, 9:31, 10:33); three disciples are three times found sleeping (14:32–42); Peter denies Jesus three times (14:66–72); and Jesus is mocked three times (14:65, 15:16–20, 15:29–32).

Mark is also fond of intertwining two stories. Early in the gospel Mark inserts disputes inside other stories: a dispute over who can forgive (2:5b–10a) is encased in a healing story about a paralytic (2:1–5a, 10b–12); a dispute over sabbath observance (3:4–5a) is placed inside an account of Jesus' cure of a crippled hand (3:1–3, 5b–6); a dispute about whether Jesus is in league with Beelzebul (3:22–29) is bracketed by two parts of a family conflict (3:20–21, 31–35).

In other cases Mark sandwiches one healing story inside another: the cure of the woman with a vaginal hemorrhage (5:24b–34) interrupts the story of the cure of Jairus' daughter (5:21–24a, 35–43). In the Jerusalem section of his gospel, Mark wraps the temple incident (11:15–18) in the cursing of the fig tree (11:12–14, 20–25). In employing this technique, Mark invites the reader to understand the inserted story with the help of its envelope.

remembrance of those who had died and to drink a cup in honor of some god. Socrates says to the jailer who has just given him the cup of hemlock to drink, "What do you say about making a libation out of this cup to some god?" (*Phaedo* 117).

Mark has modified the interpretation Paul had given to the story to fit more precisely with his own narrative aims. In Mark, Jesus does not ask that the meal be repeated "in memory" of him; instead, Mark has moved the remem-

Another notable literary device Mark uses is to predict incidents before they occur. Scripture is the most reliable source of such predictions, but the words of Jesus have much the same function. Once a prediction has been uttered, its fulfillment is inevitable. Mark features decisive predictions at the beginning, midpoint, and conclusion of his story.

Mark begins his gospel by quoting scripture: "The good news of Jesus the Anointed begins with something Isaiah the prophet wrote." Isaiah's "voice of someone shouting in the wilderness" (1:3) is fulfilled when John the Baptist appears in the wilderness (1:4). John, in turn, offers a new prediction: "someone more powerful than I will succeed me" (1:8). Then Mark introduces Jesus. Mark has now set up the prediction/fulfillment momentum that will govern the rest of his narrative.

The author of the gospel indicates the turning point of his story with this prediction: "The son of Adam is being turned over to his enemies, and they will end up killing him" (9:31). The rest of the gospel fulfills the prediction.

The most poignant moment at the end of the story is when the spotlight is turned on Peter (14:27–30):

> [27]Jesus says to them, "You will all lose faith. Remember, scripture says, 'I will strike the shepherd, and the sheep will be scattered.' [28]But after I'm raised, I'll go ahead of you to Galilee."
>
> [29]Peter said to him, "Even if everyone else loses faith, I won't!"
>
> [30]And Jesus says to him, "So help me, tonight before the rooster crows twice, you will deny me three times!"

Mark has woven three predictions into this scene. Jesus first indicates that all the disciples will abandon him. He next anticipates their reunion back in Galilee. Finally, Jesus predicts that Peter will deny him not once, but three times.

The first prediction is fulfilled at Jesus' arrest when the disciples flee (14:50). Peter is reminded of Jesus' prediction about his unfaithfulness when the rooster crows twice (14:72)—but only when it is too late. The narrator tells the reader all this happened because "the scriptures must come true!" (14:49).

Mark ends his narrative without fulfilling the final prediction that Jesus will precede his disciples to Galilee. The reader's attention is thus drawn to stories yet to be told.

These are some of the features that betray the literary proclivities of Mark's storytelling. His idiosyncrasies become literary DNA that enable scholars to trace Markan influence into the other gospels that employ him as a source.

brance theme to the meal at which Jesus is anointed by an unnamed woman (14:3–9), and where he predicts that his anointing will be told "in memory of *her*" (14:9). In addition, Mark has connected the final meal with the celebration of the arrival of the future eschatological kingdom, the kingdom beyond time (v. 25). That gives the symbolic meal a different sense than it has in Paul's letter to the Corinthians.

The last supper as it is depicted in Mark was not a historical event.

Nevertheless, the Fellows were clear that Jesus often ate meals with his disciples and others and that these meals had symbolic value. They were expressions of egalitarianism: Jesus ate indiscriminately with rich and poor, powerful and weak, clean and unclean. He undoubtedly taught at meals, in the manner of the symposium. His behavior at meals was viewed by outsiders as scandalous, so much so that he came to be known as "a glutton and a drunk." Since Jesus ate frequently with his followers, there must have been a last meal with them. Mark's narrative is not a report of that meal. But because the tradition is older than Mark, and because it reflects Jesus' well-known meal practice, the Fellows consented to color Mark's version gray by a very narrow margin.

The oath
Mk 14:27–31
Mt 26:31–35, Lk 22:31–34; Jn 13:36–38
Sources: Mark, John

14 [27]**And Jesus says to them,** "You will all lose faith. Remember,
scripture says, 'I will strike the shepherd and the sheep will be scat-
tered!' [28]But after I'm raised I'll go ahead of you to Galilee."
[29]**Peter said to him, "Even if everyone else loses faith, I won't!"**
[30]**And Jesus says to him,** "So help me, tonight before the rooster
crows twice you will disown me three times!"
[31]**But he repeated it with more bluster: "If they condemn me to die
with you, I will never disown you!" And they took the same oath—
all of them.**

The oath. The account of Peter's denial is divided into three parts: the first consists of this prediction on the way to the Mount of Olives; the second is the report of Peter following Jesus into the courtyard of the high priest (14:54); the third and final part is the triple disavowal that he knows Jesus, also set in the courtyard of the high priest (14:66–72).

One of the literary devices of Mark is the use of a prediction followed by a subsequent fulfillment (consult the cameo, "The Gospel of Mark: Literary DNA," pp. 140–41). He makes use of that device in this story. For Mark, as for folklore generally, things tend to come in threes. Mark has divided his story into three parts and Peter thrice denies that he knows Jesus. Another literary strategy of Mark is to nest one story in another. In this case he has nested the account of Jesus' trial before the high priest and Council in the tale of Peter's denial (14:53–65). By narrating the two "trials" simultaneously, so to speak, the author permits the reader to see the contrast between Jesus' response to his interrogation and that of Peter in the courtyard below. These devices prompt Burton Mack to conclude that nothing in the story of Peter's denial is based on historical reminiscence.[41] The Fellows of the Jesus Seminar concurred in that judgment.

How did they come to that decision? The story of Peter's denial, like other components of the passion, does not have the shape of an anecdote—a unit of oral storytelling—and therefore was not derived from the oral tradition. Peter's denial was invented by Mark at the time he composed his gospel. It was suggested to him by a number of factors. He here picks up the earlier theme of Peter's confession followed by Jesus' rebuke (Mark 8:27–33) and Jesus' teaching that discipleship requires denial and fortitude (8:34–38). The prediction in Zechariah ("Strike my shepherd and scatter my sheep; and I will turn my hand against my sheep," 13:7) may also have played a role in forming the story (v. 27). Peter's oath in v. 29 may have been suggested by the comparable oath on the part of Ittai to King David in 2 Sam 15:21 (for more on this topic consult the cameo "David and Jesus on the Mount of Olives," pp. 150–51). Moreover, Mark has aimed his tale not just at Peter but also at all the disciples (v. 31): the promise that Jesus would precede them to Galilee (14:28) anticipates the desertion of them all at the arrest (14:50).

Gethsemane
Mk 14:32–42
Mt 26:36–46, Lk 22:39–46
Source: Mark

14

32 **And they go to a place the name of which was Gethsem-**
ane, and he says to his disciples, "Sit down here while I pray."
33 **And he takes Peter and James and John along with him, and he**
grew apprehensive and full of anguish. 34 **He says to them,** "I'm so
sad I could die. You stay here and be alert!"
35 **And he would move on a little, fall on the ground, and pray that**
he might avoid the crisis, if possible. 36 **And he would say,** "Abba
(Father), all things are possible for you! Take this cup away from me!
But it's not what I want <that matters>, but what you want."
37 **And he returns and finds them sleeping, and says to Peter,**
"Simon, are you sleeping? Couldn't you stay awake for one hour? 38 Be
alert and pray that you won't be put to the test! Though the spirit is
willing, the flesh is weak."
39 **And once again he went away and prayed, saying the same**
thing. 40 **And once again he came and found them sleeping, since**
their eyes had grown very heavy, and they didn't know what to say
to him.
41 **And he comes a third time and says to them,** "You may as well
sleep on now and get your rest. It's all over! The time has come! Look,
the son of Adam is being turned over to foreigners. 42 Get up, let's go!
See for yourselves! Here comes the one who is going to turn me in."

Gethsemane. In the immediate sequence of events, according to Mark, Jesus has just predicted that one of his followers will betray him (14:17–21). After supper, they sing a hymn and depart for the Mount of Olives (14:26). On the way, Mark depicts Peter taking an oath to the effect that he will never deny Jesus (14:27–31). Then they arrive at a place called Gethsemane, which means the place of the oil press. Jesus asks the three members of the inner circle to stand watch, but they fall asleep. Jesus is deeply troubled; in his prayers he confesses that he is ready to accede to the will of God. His betrayer shows up and Jesus is arrested.

This sequence of events was inspired by the story of David in 2 Samuel 15–17. With his son Absalom in revolt, David flees across the Kidron and climbs the Mount of Olives. Ittai, a loyal servant, swears he will not forsake him. David is sorrowful and repentant. He has been betrayed by Ahithophel, who now proposes to pursue David at night. Ahithophel remarks that it is appropriate that one man die so the people can have peace. When Ahithophel's counsel is rejected by Absalom, Ahithophel hangs himself. (For additional details, consult the cameo on "David and Jesus on the Mount of Olives," pp. 150–51.) Mark, or some storyteller prior to Mark, has created a comparable sequence of events involving Jesus, Judas, Peter, and the Mount of Olives. The parallels are so striking that they cannot be merely fortuitous.

In any case, the scene in the garden would not have circulated as an independent anecdote during the oral period. Its viability as a story about Jesus depends on its present context. It is evidently the creation of the evangelist or his source, if he has one. Black is the correct designation.

The arrest
Mk 14:43–52
Mt 26:47–56, Lk 22:47–54a;
Jn 18:1–12
Sources: Mark, John

14 [43]And right away, while he was still speaking, Judas, one of
the twelve, shows up, and with him a crowd, **dispatched by the
ranking priests and the scholars and the elders,** wielding swords
and clubs. **[44]Now the one who was to turn him in had arranged a sig-
nal with them, saying, "The one I'm going to kiss is the one you
want. Arrest him and escort him safely away!" [45]And right away he
arrives, comes up to him, and says, "Rabbi," and kissed him.**

[46]And they seized him and held him fast. **[47]One of those standing
around drew his sword and struck the high priest's slave and cut off
his ear. [48]In response Jesus said to them,** "Have you come out to take
me with swords and clubs as though you were apprehending a rebel?
[49]I was with you in the temple area day after day teaching and you
didn't lift a hand against me. But the scriptures must come true!"

[50]And they all deserted him and ran away. **[51]And a young man was
following him, wearing a shroud over his nude body, and they grab
him. [52]But he dropped the shroud and ran away naked.**

The arrest. The sequence of events that leads up to Jesus' arrest, according to the author of Mark, consists of the preparation for Passover, the celebration of Passover, the prediction that Judas would turn Jesus in, the oath of Peter, the scene in the Garden of Gethsemane, and the arrest (14:12–52). The Fellows of the Jesus Seminar are dubious that the meal depicted in the passion story is the Passover Seder. They are equally skeptical that Jesus predicted that Judas would turn him in. They doubt that Peter took an oath not to deny Jesus, and they believe the scene in the Garden of Gethsemane is a fiction. As a consequence, numerous questions arise about what we can really know about the arrest: Was Jesus arrested in the garden? Was it night? Did Judas lead the arresting party? Did Judas kiss Jesus to identify him? Was Jesus alone when he was arrested? Did one or more disciples resist when the police attempted to arrest Jesus? Who was in the arresting party?

In sorting through the immediate sequence of events and after examining the larger picture, the Seminar came to this conclusion: The temple incident, the handing over of Jesus, and the arrest were linked. The temple incident is what precipitated the action against Jesus. Some person or persons must have assisted the authorities either in identifying Jesus or in locating him at the time of the arrest. Jesus was arrested and summarily executed. However, the narrative connection posited by Mark, or some storyteller before Mark, is evidently a fiction: Some individual items are fictitious links in the chain; other items, although reflecting some historical event, have evidently been adapted to the narrative frame into which they were made to fit.

About a third of the Fellows think Judas was a historical person and that his action in turning Jesus in is historical. However, if the name of Judas is eliminated from the story, the percentage of Fellows who think that *someone who knew Jesus* turned him in almost doubles. The remaining forty percent hold to the view that the entire betrayal scene is fictional. The Fellows who take this view have been influenced by the coincidence of language here and in Isaiah's prophecy about the suffering servant: "He was handed over to die" (Isa 53:12).

Aside from whether someone named Judas was involved, this problem has plagued scholars: What did the betrayer betray? Was it necessary to identify Jesus because he was unknown by sight to the authorities? Or was it necessary to inform the officials of his whereabouts on an occasion when the crowds were not present? The first seems improbable in view of the fact that Jesus was a public figure who was admired by the crowds; he had, after all, been teaching daily in the temple area. The second seems almost as improbable, unless Jesus went into hiding as the Fourth Gospel depicts (John 11:53–57; in John 18:1–3, the author depicts Judas as leading the officials to the secret place where Jesus met frequently with his followers). Mark depicts the function of Judas as identifying Jesus (he does so with a kiss, v. 44). That function, the Fellows agreed, is a Markan fiction.

Since the Seminar concluded that the scene in the garden was inspired by the story of David in 2 Samuel 15–17, many Fellows doubt that the arrest took place in the Garden of Gethsemane, or any garden, for that matter. That prompted them to question whether Jesus was arrested at night. That, too, may be a simple fiction designed to satisfy the requirements of the plot: the fear of a riot if Jesus were apprehended in public during the day. The Romans were probably not involved at this point; the arresting party, according to Mark, was a crowd with swords and clubs: the "crowd" probably consisted of temple police and perhaps those attached to the service of the high priest. The latter will have been involved because the offense Jesus had committed, after all, was against the temple.

The Fellows agreed that Jesus alone was arrested; there is no evidence that other members of his circle were taken. Although mentioned by all four canonical gospels, an attack on one of the police is not likely: The story was told and Peter's name attached to it perhaps to offset the shame of abandoning Jesus at the crucial moment. The Fellows were relatively certain that the disciples fled at the time of the arrest, as the reports indicate. This story would probably not have been made up by the disciples since it was an embarrassment to them (it is not beyond Mark, however, in view of the fact that he had a rather low opinion of the inner circle of followers). Several of the sources indicate that the disciples returned to Galilee following the arrest.

To recapitulate, in Mark's version of the arrest, the Fellows decided to color the two basic factual statements pink: the arrest and the flight of the disciples are highly probable but not entirely certain. The role of Judas in the arrest drew a gray weighted average owing to the division of opinion about Judas as a historical person. The remainder of Mark's version was designated black as the creative work of some early Christian storyteller, possibly the author of Mark.

Before the high priest
Mk 14:53–54
Mt 26:57–58, Lk 22:54;
Jn 18:13–14, 15–18
Sources: Mark, John

14 [53]And they brought Jesus before the high priest, **and all the ranking priests and elders and scholars assemble.**

[54]Peter followed him at a distance until he was inside the courtyard of the high priest, and was sitting with the attendants and keeping warm by the fire.

Before the high priest. Mark is here setting the stage for two intertwined events, the hearing before the Jewish authorities and the denial of Peter.

The statement in v. 53 is colored pink on the grounds that Jesus was certainly arrested and was almost certainly arrested by envoys of the high priest. If that is accurate, then those messengers of the temple bureaucracy would have brought him under arrest to the high priest. That may already be saying more than our historical knowledge allows. Everything else connected with the so-called "trial" is the product of Christian imagination.

Mark also introduces the story of the disavowal of Peter. Since that story is a fiction, its introduction here should be designated black.

Before the Council
Mk 14:55–65
Mt 26:59–68, Lk 22:66–71;
Jn 18:19–24
Sources: Mark, John

14 **[55]The ranking priests and the whole Council were looking for evidence against Jesus in order to issue a death sentence, but they couldn't find any. [56]Although many gave false evidence against him, their stories didn't agree. [57]And some people stood up and testified falsely against him: [58]"We have heard him saying,** 'I'll destroy this temple made with hands and in three days I'll build another, not made with hands!'" **[59]Yet even then their stories did not agree.**

[60]And the high priest got up and questioned Jesus: "Don't you have some answer to give? Why do these people testify against you?"

[61]But he was silent and refused to answer.

Once again the high priest questioned him and says to him, "Are you the Anointed, the son of the Blessed One?"

[62]Jesus replied, "I am! And you will see the son of Adam sitting at the right hand of Power and coming with the clouds of the sky!"

[63]Then the high priest tore his vestments and says, "Why do we still need witnesses? [64]You have heard the blasphemy! What do you think?" And they all concurred in the death penalty.

[65]And some began to spit on him, and to put a blindfold on him, and punch him, and say to him, "Prophesy!" And the guards abused him as they took him into custody.

Before the Council. The "trial" before the Council, as Mark represents it, consists of the sham of manufactured evidence produced by false witnesses (vv. 55–60), the effort to establish the identity of Jesus (vv. 61–62), the charge of blasphemy (vv. 63–64), and the abuse of Jesus (v. 65). There are three major reasons why scholars have found this scene problematic. The first consists of historical problems inherent in Mark's representation of events. In the second place, so much of the trial scene, like the passion story in general, seems to have been suggested by the Greek version of the Hebrew scriptures. The third has to do with discrepancies between Mark's version and the other gospel accounts of the same series of events.

We will treat the first and second reasons here in the commentary on Mark, to the extent required by the text of Mark. The discussion of discrepancies will be reserved for the commentary on the other gospels as their stories depart from Mark.

Jesus is pictured as the innocent sufferer—the suffering servant of Isaiah. The persecution of the innocent righteous representative of God is carried out in a trial. A trial thus becomes the centerpiece of the persecution. And because the righteous one is innocent, false charges and false witnesses are necessary ingredients. In this case, the false witnesses do not agree, so attention turns to the identity of Jesus: the high priest attempts to get Jesus to say something that will make it possible to convict him out of his own mouth. The result is the charge of blasphemy, which warrants the death penalty. That settles the matter. The guards may now begin to abuse the prisoner.

This picture is beset with improbabilities and problems. It is very unlikely that the hearing before the high priest was held the night Passover began—which is required by Mark's chronology, according to which the last supper was the Passover meal. Moreover, on this sacred night, when pious Judeans would have been celebrating Passover, the entire Council (or Sanhedrin) is gathered together to review the case—another improbability. To top it off, the hearing is a sham: the leading priests and indeed the whole Council deliberately set out to manufacture evidence to convict Jesus of a crime requiring the death sentence. Mark does not indicate what that false evidence was, except the report that Jesus had spoken some word against the temple (v. 58). The words attributed to Jesus in v. 58 are repeated by taunters in 15:29, but they are never spoken by Jesus himself in any of the synoptic gospels (the Gospel of John and the Gospel of Thomas are another matter). The only saying preserved by Mark that might give warrant for the charge is recorded in 13:2: "You may be sure not one stone will be left on top of another! Every last one will certainly be knocked down!" The Seminar voted a gray rating for that saying. However, it gave a pink rating to Jesus' action against the bankers and vendors in the temple area (11:15–16). Together these might constitute the basis for the accusation in v. 58. But Mark reports that the testimony of the false witnesses was not congruent.

The only explicit charge made against Jesus was the charge of blasphemy (vv. 63–64)—the most obvious capital offense available in a Jewish setting. That was also the first charge made against Jesus in Mark's gospel (2:7): the scholars accused Jesus of blaspheming when he told the paralytic that his sins were forgiven—something reserved for God alone. Yet the words uttered in both 2:7 and in v. 62 would scarcely warrant the death sentence. After all, messianic pretenders were not condemned for that pretense and prophetic criticism of the temple cult did not necessarily result in a death warrant. "Blasphemy" turns out to be a catchword that Caiaphas allegedly used in order to get the Council to support his denunciation of Jesus.

The entire proceeding is so implausible that it appears to be a fabrication designed by Mark merely to account for Jesus' execution and to lay the blame at the feet of Jesus' Jewish opponents connected with the temple. It is Christian revenge in spades.

That the trial before the Council is a fabrication is borne out by the details that have been suggested by the scriptures. The Psalms have played a large role in this process. For example, regarding false witnesses:

> Do not deliver me into the hands of those who oppress me,
> for false witnesses have arisen against me.
>
> Ps 26:12 (LXX 27:12)

and

> False witnesses have arisen
> who ask me things about which I have no knowledge.
>
> Ps 35:11 (LXX 36:11)

Psalm 37 (LXX; Hebrew 38) provides a number of suggestions:

> 12My friends and neighbors acted like my enemies,
> and those closest to me stood a long way off.
> 13Those who seek my life harassed me;
> those who desire harm for me uttered empty phrases.
> They practiced treachery all day long.
> 14I was like a deaf person unable to hear,
> like a mute whose mouth is closed.
> 15It is as though I lost my hearing,
> and there is no rebuttal in my mouth.

As Christian scribes combed the scriptures for reasons their Lord was crucified, they found psalms of this type not only comforting but also helpful in framing the story of Jesus' trial and execution. While the Jesus Seminar suspects that the priestly consortium played a role in Jesus' execution by the Romans, they regard Mark's account of the trial a Christian fabrication.

Peter's denial
Mk 14:66–72
Mt 26:69–75, Lk 22:54b–62;
Jn 18:15–18, 25–27
Sources: Mark, John

14 **66And while Peter was below in the courtyard, one of the high priest's slave women comes over, 67and sees Peter warming himself; she looks at him closely, then speaks up: "You too were with that Nazarene, Jesus!"**

68But he denied it, saying, "I haven't the slightest idea what you're talking about!" And he went outside into the forecourt.

69 And when the slave woman saw him, she once again began to
say to those standing nearby, "This fellow is one of them!"
70 But once again he denied it.
And a little later, those standing nearby would again say to Peter, "You really are one of them, since you also are a Galilean!"
71 But he began to curse and swear, "I don't know the fellow you're
talking about!" 72 And just then a rooster crowed a second time, and
Peter remembered what Jesus had told him: "Before a rooster crows twice you will disown me three times!" **And he broke down and started to cry.**

Peter's denial. Like the narrative of Judas' betrayal, Mark's story of Peter's denial is divided into three parts: first there is the prediction of his denial (14:27–31); then Mark has Peter follow Jesus at a distance until he gets into the courtyard of the high priest (14:53–54); finally, he relates the story of Peter's triple disavowal. Again, as in the way he handles the betrayal of Judas, Mark also has Jesus predict what will happen, followed by the fulfillment of that prediction, as though Jesus' words had the same status as scripture. Mark again indulges his folk preference for threes: He has Peter deny Jesus three times. He sandwiches Peter's denial between the two trials, the trial before the Council and the trial before Pilate; or, viewed differently, he nests the hearing before the high priest between the two parts of Peter's denial. The use of threes and the nesting technique are all clearly Markan literary devices.

One strand of the passion narrative treats the relation of the disciples to Jesus during this period of testing. They do not do well. Judas betrays Jesus, and Peter disavows him; all of them flee at the time of the arrest. Jesus is left alone to face his accusers. The account of Peter's denial is Mark's way of bringing his story of the disciples to a negative climax—they all desert Jesus—just at the crucial moment in Jesus' story—the trial. Burton Mack has pointed out the poignancy of this literary device: at the same time Jesus is upstairs being interrogated by the high priest in preparation for his execution, Peter is in the courtyard below contesting his association with his Galilean teacher.[42]

The Fellows of the Jesus Seminar are convinced that the tale of Peter's denial is a Markan invention. Peter did not deny Jesus because he was not there; he had fled with the rest of the disciples. Moreover, the narrative has Mark's literary fingerprints all over it (on this subject, consult the cameo "The Gospel of Mark: Literary DNA," pp. 140–41). Black was the designation.

15 And right away, at daybreak, the ranking priests, **after con-**
sulting with the elders and scholars and the whole Council, bound
Jesus and led him away and turned him over to Pilate, <the Roman
governor>. **2 And Pilate questioned him:** *"You* are 'the King of the
Judeans'?"
And in response he says to him, "If you say so."
3 And the ranking priests started a long list of accusations against

Before Pilate
Mk 15:1–15
Mt 27:1–2, 11–26, Lk 23:1–7, 13–25; Jn 18:28–19:16; Pet 1:1–2
Sources: Mark, John, Peter

DAVID & JESUS ON THE MOUNT OF OLIVES

Scriptural texts and stories influenced the way Jesus' early followers told stories about him. In some cases, scriptural precedents even suggested models on which fictions could be based. In other cases, ancient stories and texts provided details that could be used to fill in tales about actual incidents. Jesus was made to imitate models found in the Hebrew Bible in its Greek dress. The pre-eminent model in the minds of early Christian storytellers was King David.

David lived a thousand years before Jesus, but he was once again very much in the minds of the Judeans, especially following the successes of the Maccabean brothers in the second century B.C.E. Hopes were rekindled that the kingdom of David might be restored, and for a time it looked as though the Maccabees would succeed in doing just that. Then in 63 B.C.E. Pompey arrived in Palestine with his Roman legion and the dream was abruptly brought to an end. Domination descended once again on the land and its people.

Jesus' followers remembered him as a potential king. Although he had not assembled troops and amassed an army, he was somehow thought to be the fulfillment of the Davidic hope. The empire of which Jesus spoke so frequently was misunderstood in the popular mind as a renewal of the ancient Davidic kingdom.

One of the stories about King David that served as a model for stories about Jesus was the account of David's flight across the Kidron valley and up the Mount of Olives during the rebellion of Absalom, his son (2 Samuel 15–17). David had been betrayed, not just by his son, who launched his revolt by exchanging a kiss with David (2 Sam 14:33), but by Ahithophel, who had been one of David's counselors but had now become a co-conspirator with Absalom (2 Sam 15:12, 31). Ahithophel was to David what Judas was to Jesus.

When it became apparent that Absalom was about to attack Jerusalem, David fled across the Wadi Kidron with his company and ascended the Mount of Olives opposite (2 Sam 15:13–18, 23, 30). Jesus did the same on the night in which he, like David, was betrayed.

As David climbs the Mount of Olives to the place where God is worshiped, his head is covered and he is barefoot; he weeps because of the tragedy that looms before him (2 Sam 15:30). When Hushai, a loyal friend, comes to David, his clothes are torn and he has dirt on his head (2 Sam 15:32). These are outward signs of prayer and repentance. Jesus, too, becomes apprehensive and full of anguish; he says he is so sad he could die (Mark 14:33–34). On the Mount of Olives he falls on the ground and prays (Mark 14:35).

As David makes his exit from Jerusalem, Ittai the Gittite, a foreigner, follows him. David urges Ittai to return to Jerusalem. But Ittai refuses. Instead, he takes an oath that he will not forsake David (2 Sam 15:19–31). In similar fashion, as Jesus

him. [4]Again Pilate tried questioning him: "Don't you have some answer to give? You see what a long list of charges they bring against you!"

[5]But Jesus still did not respond, so Pilate was baffled.

[6]At each festival it was the custom for the Roman governor to set one prisoner free for them, whichever one they requested. [7]And one called Barabbas was being held with the insurgents who had com-

and his disciples leave the last meal together, after they had sung a hymn, Peter also takes an oath that he will not forsake his leader (Mark 14:27–31).

In the presence of Abiathar and Zadok, the two ranking priests, David confesses that he may or may not find favor in God's eyes; he is prepared to accept whatever destiny God has in mind for him (2 Sam 15:25–26). That is also the substance of Jesus' prayer in the garden: "It's not what I want, but what you want that matters" (Mark 14:36).

Ahithophel, David's betrayer, wants to go after David *at night;* if he overtakes him while he is weary, all the people will flee in panic. In making this proposal to Absalom, Ahithophel remarks: "You are only asking for the life of one man, which will bring peace to all the people" (2 Sam 17:1–3). Just as Jesus finishes his prayers, Judas arrives with a mob wielding swords and clubs (Mark 14:43). In the Gospel of John, Caiaphas remarks that it is prudent to let one person die for the whole nation (11:49–52).

Ahithophel's counsel was rejected by Absalom in favor of the counsel of Hushai, David's loyal friend. Having lost face, Ahithophel returns home and hangs himself (2 Sam 17:5–19, 23). Matthew has undoubtedly been influenced by this tale to augment Mark's story with the suicide of Judas by hanging (Matt 27:3–10). Judas repents his deed, according to Matthew, takes the thirty pieces of silver and flings them into the temple. Matthew's representation of this act was triggered by something in Zechariah: "They gave me thirty silver coins for my wages. I took the thirty silver coins and threw them into the treasury in the house of the Lord" (Zech 11:12–13). Both the amount of money and the action were suggested by Zechariah.

The ranking priests decide that keeping blood money for the temple would not be appropriate, so they take the thirty silver coins and buy the Potter's Field as a cemetery for foreigners. As a result, that field is known as the Bloody Field (Matt 27:8)—presumably because it was bought with blood money. Matthew has been influenced by Jeremiah's purchase of land (Jer 32:6–15) and his visit to the potter (Jer 18:1–3) in developing this story. Matthew has been prompted by yet another story in Jeremiah (19:1–6) in which the prophet renames the Hinnom Valley, where the Bloody Field is located, the Valley of Slaughter. The Hinnom Valley curves around the southern edge of the old city of Jerusalem and joins the Kidron Valley on the east. The Hinnom Valley was associated with child sacrifice and other pagan practices in the Hebrew Bible. It is known in the New Testament as Gehenna and came to be identified with hell.

The scriptures functioned as a rich deposit of hints and suggestions for narrating the story of Jesus. In some instances, details of actual incidents were generated by scriptural precedents. In other cases, the event itself blossomed in the imagination of the troubadour as a result of some Old Testament person or event. The passion narrative is constructed in large part out of such allusions and references.

mitted murder during the uprising. 8And when the crowd arrived, they began to demand that he do what he usually did for them.

9And in response Pilate said to them, "Do you want me to set 'the King of the Judeans' free for you?" 10After all, he realized that the ranking priests had turned him over out of envy.

11But the ranking priests incited the crowd to get Barabbas set free for them instead.

[12]But in response <to their request> Pilate would again say to them, "What do you want me to do with the fellow you call 'the King of the Judeans'?"

[13]And they in turn shouted, "Crucify him!"

[14]Pilate kept saying to them, "Why? What has he done wrong?"

But they shouted all the louder, "Crucify him!" [15]And because Pilate was always looking to satisfy the crowd, he set Barabbas free for them, had Jesus flogged, and then turned him over to be crucified.

Before Pilate. The Fellows agreed that Jesus was probably arrested on the authority of temple officials. Jesus was then in the custody of the priests and their police force. At some point in the course of events, they turned Jesus over to Pilate. The appropriate portions of v. 1 are therefore designated pink. The Fellows were dubious that the ranking priests consulted widely with the elders and scholars and they seriously doubted that the whole Council or Sanhedrin was involved. That part of v. 1 is accordingly colored black. The time was designated gray on the sole grounds that a morning transfer of Jesus from the temple authorities to Pilate was entirely plausible.

The only completely reliable piece of information in this segment is that Jesus was executed on the authority of Pilate (the vote was virtually unanimous). Both Josephus, the Jewish historian, and Tacitus, the Roman historian, attest to the reliability of this piece of information, as does 1 Tim 6:13. The relevant part of v. 15 was accordingly voted red. But the Fellows were almost as certain that no such trial took place as Mark represents it. A majority of Fellows considered the notion that Jesus was put "on trial" before "rulers" as a story generated by the suggestions in Psalm 2, where kings and rulers array themselves "against the Lord and his anointed" (Ps 2:2). The vast majority of Fellows approved this statement:

- **It is not just the content of the trial but the fact of a trial that lacks historical foundation.**

By a less robust majority the Seminar also approved this statement:

- **The trial narrative was created on the basis of Psalm 2.**

The credibility of the Christian account of Jesus' death required that there be a Roman trial and that it be presided over by Pilate, who was the governor or Procurator or Prefect (26–36 C.E.) at the time of Jesus' execution. For that reason Mark invented the story that appears in his gospel.

Pilate's administration was not noted for humanitarian measures, nor for accommodating the local populace. It is quite possible that he had issued a standing order for dealing with troublemakers, in which case the "trial" may have been a very brief discussion with the handiest local centurion.

Mark has crafted the scene with considerable ingenuity. The charge against Jesus is shifted away from the accusations made against him before the Council: those accusations include remarks he may have made against the temple and whether or not he claims to be the messiah and the son of the Blessed; the reference to blasphemy is also dropped (14:55–64). In the place of those charges, Pilate asks Jesus whether he regards himself as "King of the Judeans." Jesus' response is from Pilate's perspective: 'From your point of view that's what I am' (v. 2). As an official of the Roman government, Pilate can understand that: All too frequently in his experience pretenders to the Jewish throne have sought to get their claims to royalty certified by Rome. Since Jesus is not a threat from Pilate's point of view—the Romans make and break Jewish kings frequently—he seeks to release Jesus. In framing his story in this way, Mark has set the stage to assign the entire blame for Jesus' death to the Jewish authorities.

In v. 1, Mark represents the priests as leveling a series of charges against Jesus, but the author does not specify what those charges were. Pilate urges Jesus to answer (vv. 3–5).

The Barabbas segment is wholly fictional, in spite of the fact that the name Barabbas is actually attested on ossuaries (small stone coffins) from the period. Barabbas means "son of the father," the son (*bar* in Aramaic) of Abba, the Aramaic address Jesus uses for God in the Lord's Prayer. That "son" is substituted for Jesus, who in Christian minds is the "son of the Father."

When Pilate asks the crowd what he is to do with "the king of the Judeans," they call out to have him crucified (vv. 12–14). There is considerable irony in that scene: the Judeans are now to assume responsibility for the death of someone called their king (v. 12). Pilate gives way to the will of the crowd, has Jesus flogged in accordance with Roman practice, and turns Jesus over to his enemies to be crucified. That scene, although the product of Mark's vivid imagination, has wrought untold and untellable tragedy in the history of the relation of Christians to Jews. There is no black deep enough to symbolize adequately the black mark this fiction has etched in Christian history.

15 **16And the Roman soldiers led him away to the courtyard of
the governor's residence, and they called the whole company <of
Roman troops> together. 17And they dressed him in purple and
crowned him with a garland woven of thorns. 18And the soldiers
began to salute him: "Greetings, 'King of the Judeans'!" 19And they
kept striking him on the head with a staff, and spitting on him; and
they would get down on their knees and bow down to him. 20And
when they had made fun of him, they stripped off the purple and
put his own clothes back on him. And the Romans lead him out to
crucify him.**

Mocking
Mk 15:16–20
Mt 27:27–31; Jn 19:1–3;
Pet 3:1–4
Sources: Mark, John, Peter
Cf. Zech 3:3–5 (LXX)

Mocking. In Mark's account, the abuse of Jesus had already begun at the end of the trial before the Council: those assembled began to spit on Jesus. Then they put a blindfold on him and punched or hit him, taunting him to guess which of them had done it. And the guards also abused him as they took him into custody (14:65). At the end of the trial before Pilate, Pilate has Jesus flogged or scourged (15:15).

Mark supplied flogging, striking, and spitting as forms of abuse because they were suggested by Isa 50:6:

> I presented my back to the scourge,
> my cheeks to be slapped,
> and I did not avoid the shame of someone spitting in my face.

Spitting was one insult to which Jesus was earlier subjected, along with blows to the head; those insults are now repeated by the Roman soldiers (v. 19). Pilate had just now—in the narrative, v. 15—provided the flogging, so Mark does not have that form of abuse repeated.

The narrative framework of this story, however, was suggested to Mark by the royal ritual of investiture. When Joseph is installed as Pharaoh's vice-regent, Pharaoh has a signet ring put on Joseph's finger, arrays him in fine robes, puts a gold chain around his neck, and has his people kneel before Joseph as he passes (Gen 41:40–45). When the Persian king Ahasuerus wants to honor Mordecai in the book of Esther, he robes him in royal raiment, gives him a royal horse to ride, and puts a crown on his head. The king then has Mordecai paraded through the city to proclaim his new status (Esth 6:1–11). The robing ritual is also depicted by the prophet Zechariah, who envisions the high priest Joshua (Jesus in Greek) in a heavenly trial where he is disrobed of filthy garments, dressed in fine vestments and given a clean turban to wear (Zech 3:1–5). These standard investiture protocols undoubtedly suggested to Mark the way to represent the mocking of Jesus and yet through that very irony proclaim who he really was: the king of the Judeans.

Notice that Mark has assembled the whole company of soldiers (investiture is a public event), before whom some soldiers array Jesus in robes of royal purple and crown him with a mock crown of thorns. This ritual theatre is derisive, to be sure, but it is also ironic, and that is Mark's basic point: It proclaims the real truth but does so indirectly.

The Jesus Seminar voted consistently to designate these mocking scenes black because they were suggested by scriptures and standard protocol and also because they served Christian apologetic purposes. Jesus did not think of himself as a king; he did not refer to himself as a king; and he would have been inhospitable to the idea that he might have made a good king. The notion that Jesus was a king is a basic ingredient in the Christian myth.

Simon of Cyrene
Mk 15:21
Mt 27:32, Lk 23:26–32
Source: Mark

15 **[21]And they conscript someone named Simon of Cyrene, who was coming in from the country, the father of Alexander and Rufus, to carry his cross.**

Simon of Cyrene. Mark adds this odd bit of detail for his own narrative purposes, which have to do with another person named Simon. Mark has depicted *Simon* Peter's denial in three parts: a prediction (14:27–31); Peter following Jesus to trial but at a distance (14:53–54); the denial with an oath that he was not a disciple of Jesus (14:66–72). To lavish so much narrative space on this Simon evidently meant a great deal to Mark. Earlier, Jesus had advised his disciples that if they wanted to be his followers, they had to *deny themselves,* take up their crosses, and come after him (Mark 8:34). Since Simon Peter did not follow Jesus' instructions—he deserted Jesus along with the others when Jesus was arrested—Mark has another Simon do so. The other details have no historical value; they are included merely to give the scene plausibility. Writers of fiction scatter references to specific persons, places, and dates to enhance believability. Black is the correct color for this piece of Markan fiction.

Crucifixion
Mk 15:22–32
Mt 27:33–44, Lk 23:33–43;
Jn 19:17–24; Pet 4:1–5
Sources: Mark, John, Peter

15 22 **And the Roman soldiers bring him to the place Golgotha**
(which means "Place of the Skull"). 23 **And they tried to give him wine**
mixed with myrrh, but he didn't take it. 24 And the soldiers crucify
him, **and they divide up his garments, casting lots to see who would**
get what. 25 **It was 9 o'clock in the morning when they crucified him.**
26 And the inscription, which identified his crime, read, 'The King of
the Judeans.' 27 **And with him they crucify two rebels, one on his**
right and one on his left.
29 **Those passing by kept taunting him, wagging their heads, and**
saying, "Ha! You who would destroy the temple and rebuild it in
three days, 30 **save yourself and come down from the cross!"**
31 **Likewise the ranking priests had made fun of him to one**
another, along with the scholars; they would say, "He saved others,
but he can't save himself! 32 **'The Anointed,' 'the King of Israel,'**
should come down from the cross here and now, so that we can see
and trust for ourselves!"
Even those being crucified along with him would abuse him.

Crucifixion. In the collective judgment of the Fellows, the details of the crucifixion scene were inspired largely by Psalm 22 and related prophetic texts. In spite of that firm conviction, none of the Fellows doubts that Jesus was crucified (v. 24a). They are confident that he was crucified in Jerusalem, at a site outside the old city walls. Just about everything else in the story was inspired by some scripture.

Prior to crucifixion, the Roman soldiers offer Jesus wine mixed with myrrh as a kind of sedative (v. 23). That offer may have been inspired by Prov 31:6: "Give strong drink to those in grief, and wine to those in pain." Later, they will offer Jesus sour wine (15:36), which was probably suggested to the storyteller by Ps 69:21:

> They gave me something bitter for food,
> and for my thirst they offered me sour wine to drink.

After Jesus is crucified (the storyteller does not describe how crucifixion was carried out), the Roman soldiers gamble to see who will get his clothes (v. 24; he was apparently stripped naked before being affixed to the cross). That feature is derived from Ps 22:18:

> They divide my clothes among themselves,
> and for my clothing they cast lots.

Mark next mentions that it is 9:00 A.M., a bit of information that anticipates developments that will take place at high noon and at three o'clock in the afternoon (15:33, 34).

Crucifixion was a public execution; it was intended to warn others about certain offenses. It was the Roman custom to parade the convict around with a wooden placard around his neck, specifying the crime. On the grounds that the use of a placard was Roman practice, the Fellows granted the possibility that Jesus may have been similarly treated (v. 26). The Seminar was dubious, however, that proclaiming himself "king of the Judeans" was actually Jesus' crime. A gray vote was the result.

That Jesus was executed along with two rebels was inspired by Ps 22:17 LXX (16 in Hebrew and English):

> For many dogs have encircled me,
> and a host of evildoers has surrounded me.

in conjunction with Isa 53:12:

> His soul was handed over to death,
> and he was reckoned among the sinners.

It would of course not be surprising that other victims were crucified at the same time. For the Romans, the death of Jesus was probably a non-event, little noticed because they crucified thousands of people during the first century, particularly in connection with the siege of Jerusalem (66–70 C.E.).

Mark paints an elaborate scene of ridicule and taunting in vv. 29–32. The details of that scene are dependent on Ps 21:7–9 LXX (22:6–8 in Hebrew and English):

> But I am a worm, and not human;
> scorned by others, and despised by the people.
> All who set their eyes on me mock me;
> they make mouths at me, they shake their heads;
> He hoped in the Lord,
> so let the Lord rescue and save him,
> since he holds him dear.

All the ingredients of the Markan scene are present in the Psalm. All Mark had to do was to let his imagination roam in constructing the scene he did.

The picture of the crucifixion in Mark was constructed out of firsthand knowledge of crucifixions and scripture. There may be traces of historical reminiscence in it, but it isn't likely. Anecdotes about Jesus' execution had not been developed during the oral period, so whatever memories there may have been were not kept alive. Four decades or more later, Mark and the other evangelists had to reinvent the scene. As a consequence, the Jesus Seminar was unable to verify any of the details in this scene as a report of actual events. A black designation was the result.

The death of Jesus
Mk 15:33–41
Mt 27:45–56, Lk 23:44–49; Jn 19:25–37; Pet 5:1–6
Sources: Mark, John, Peter

15 **33 And when noon came, darkness blanketed the whole land
until mid-afternoon. 34 And at 3 o'clock in the afternoon Jesus shouted
at the top of his voice,** *"Eloi, Eloi, lema sabachthani"* (which means "My
God, my God, why did you abandon me?").

**35 And when some of those standing nearby heard, they would say,
"Listen, he's calling Elijah!" 36 And someone ran and filled a sponge
with sour wine, stuck it on a pole, and offered him a drink, saying,
"Let's see if Elijah comes to rescue him!"**

37 But Jesus let out a great shout and breathed his last.

**38 And the curtain of the temple was torn in two from top to bot-
tom! 39 When the Roman officer standing opposite him saw that he
had died like this, he said, "This man really was God's son!"**

40 Now some women were observing this from a distance, among
whom were Mary of Magdala, and Mary the mother of James the
younger and Joses, and Salome. 41 <These women> had regularly fol-
lowed and assisted him when he was in Galilee, along with many
other women who had come up to Jerusalem in his company.

The death of Jesus. The death of Jesus, like his trial and crucifixion, is depicted almost entirely in images taken from scripture. Mark begins with the congruence of cosmic omens: in the ancient world, cosmic signs were thought to accompany the death of a great person; the descent of darkness on the world for three hours, beginning at noon, is such a cosmic portent. This image was probably suggested by Amos 8:9 where on the day of judgment the Lord will make the sun go down at noon and will darken the earth in broad daylight. A comet is said to have crossed the sky when Caesar Augustus died; a coin showing that comet was minted in honor of the occasion (see p. 128). Jesus' birth was also accompanied by an astral sign (Matt 2:2), as were the births of other heroes of the time.

Mark has divided the period that begins with Peter's denial and ends with Jesus' burial into intervals of three hours:

3 A.M.	The cock crows (14:72)
6 A.M.	Jesus is taken to Pilate at daybreak (15:1)
9 A.M.	Jesus is crucified (15:25)
Noon	Darkness descends on the land (15:33)
3 P.M.	Jesus dies (15:34)
6 P.M.	Jesus is buried (15:42)

This scheme is obviously artificial: There was no hourly record available to the gospel writers when they composed their passion narratives four decades or more after Jesus' death.

Jesus' shout from the cross at 3:00 (v. 34) is a direct quotation of Ps 22:1. The Fellows designated that shout black in *The Five Gospels.* Mark adds a touch of realism, however, by quoting the words first in Aramaic, Jesus' native tongue, and then translating them into Greek for his readers.

The offer of sour wine to Jesus in v. 36 is again inspired by Ps 69:21:

> They gave me something bitter for food,
> and for my thirst they gave me sour wine to drink.

Mark had already made use of this allusion in 15:23.

Just as Jesus dies, the curtain of the temple is torn open from top to bottom (vv. 37–38). Josephus tells us that the curtain was embroidered with suns, moons, stars—with heavenly bodies; thus the "heavens were torn open" at Jesus' death to match the opening of the heavens at his baptism. The spirit descends at Jesus' baptism; it departs at his death. The destruction of the curtain at Jesus' death also signals that the age of the temple has come to an end and with it the separation between the sacred and the profane represented by the veil that shielded the temple sanctuary from the forecourt. The rupture of the veil was thought to be an act of God (God is the unexpressed agent of the action, termed the "divine passive" by grammarians). The tearing of the veil is also to be understood figuratively as the fulfillment of the first part of the saying attributed to Jesus: "I will destroy the temple and rebuild it in three days" (15:29). The crucifixion and the death of Jesus are accompanied in Mark by two portents: darkness at noon and the rending of the temple curtain.

The polemic embedded in the story of Jesus' crucifixion reaches its climax with the confession of the Roman centurion (v. 39). The Jerusalem authorities are not willing to acknowledge Jesus, but this unknown centurion is (further in the cameo "The Guard at the Tomb," p. 474). This feature expresses the underlying anti-Judaism of the Christian story: the Judeans scorn and mock, while the gentiles come to faith. That is also the sequence in Psalm 22. From the historian's point of view, the evangelists had no way of knowing what the Romans involved in Jesus' execution said at the time; the words attributed to both parties—Judeans and Romans—have been invented by the storytellers.

The only item in the Markan account of Jesus' death that has any claim to historical veracity is the presence of women followers at his execution. They are depicted as watching from a distance, which conforms to Roman practice: relatives and loved ones were not permitted to interfere with executions. The followers of Jesus, including the women, might well have been in danger had they attempted to become involved. The Fellows cannot be certain of the names of the women, but Mary of Magdala was probably one of them, perhaps the leader of the group. Even so, the mention of the women watching is tenuous in view of one of the psalms of lament, Ps 38:11: "My friends and companions stand afar from my affliction, those closest to me stand at a distance." The scene may have been suggested by that psalm, but also by the memory that the women alone remained behind when the male disciples fled at Jesus' arrest. On the other hand, Mark may have created the scene to account for how the women knew where the tomb was (15:47) so they could perform the burial rites (16:1). By voting this passage pink, the Fellows chose to err on the side of the women, whose role in these events was probably belittled and even repressed, as we learn from Mark 16:8.

15 [42]**And when it had already grown dark, since it was prepara-**
tion day (the day before the sabbath), [43]**Joseph of Arimathea, a re-**
spected council member, who himself was anticipating God's impe-
rial rule, appeared on the scene, and dared to go to Pilate to request
the body of Jesus. [44]**And Pilate was surprised that he had died so**
soon. He summoned the Roman officer and asked him whether he
had been dead for long. [45]**And when he had been briefed by the**
Roman officer, he granted the body to Joseph. [46]**And he bought a**
shroud and took him down and wrapped him in the shroud, and
placed him in a tomb that had been hewn out of rock, and rolled a
stone up against the opening of the tomb. [47]**And Mary of Magdala**
and Mary the mother of Joses noted where he had been laid to rest.

The burial
Mk 15:42–47
Mt 27:57–61, Lk 23:50–56; Jn 19:38–42; Pet 2:1–5, 6:1–4
Sources: Mark, John, Peter

The burial. The ultimate insult in the ancient world was to let someone go unburied. To honor one's father and mother meant seeing to their proper interment. That is why Jesus' saying was considered so radical: "Leave it to the dead to bury their own dead" (Luke 9:60). For Jesus, it seems, leaving someone without the customary burial rites was a possibility in view of the absolute demands of the kingdom. But what about his followers? Were they as liberated from convention?

We have observed over and over again that the passion narrative originated as a scribal composition some years, even decades, after the death of Jesus. We lack substantial evidence that anecdotes about Jesus' trial, crucifixion, and burial were circulated during the oral period. What then can we expect from this account of Jesus' burial, which the Fellows of the Seminar think is the earliest of the written versions?

Mark's story begins to take on the hues of fiction immediately with the mention of Joseph of Arimathea (v. 43). The Seminar concluded that Joseph was a Markan invention: after all, Mark describes him as "a respected member of the Council"—the Council that had just condemned Jesus—and as someone who was looking for the kingdom's arrival (v. 43). That is backhanded Christian apologetic: Jesus' opponents are refashioned into friends and supporters after the damage has been done. And Joseph is from an unidentified place, Arimathea. Storytellers like to invent names and places because they give verisimilitude to their fictions.

In Mark, Joseph is only a respected member of the Council and someone looking for the kingdom. In Matthew he takes on stronger hues: he is now a rich man and a disciple of Jesus, but not a member of the Council (Matthew evidently felt it incongruous to have someone who just voted for the death penalty reverse himself so completely: Matt 27:57). Luke retains Joseph's Council membership, but describes him as a decent and upright man, who was in reality a normal politician: he was a member of the Council but he did not go along with the Council's decision and action (Luke 23:51). Like Matthew, Luke is struggling to soften Mark's incongruities. Luke follows Mark in having Joseph anticipate the coming of the kingdom.

Joseph is bold enough to go to Pilate and ask for the body (v. 43), as though Pilate were likely to be concerned about the disposition of crucified bodies. Mark has an amazing amount of very specific information about all this: Pilate is surprised that Jesus died so quickly; Pilate interrogates the Roman officer in charge, and when satisfied, grants the body to Joseph. On what grounds could we imagine the transmission of such specific bits of information? The Fellows were inclined to the view that such information had not been transmitted in anecdote and story but was imagined by Mark.

Mark's narrative is the result of Christian reflection on the fate of their Lord and the hope that he was properly buried. That hope has to be set alongside Roman expectation and the protocol of crucifixion.

In Roman practice, those crucified were guarded while they slowly and painfully died lest friend and relative take them down and attempt to revive them or give them proper burial. (The Roman officer on duty during Jesus' crucifixion was probably there to prevent the women from helping Jesus: 15:39–40). The corpses were left to rot in the sun or serve as carrion for scavengers; if they were buried, it was in a shallow open pit where crows and dogs could get to them. The Jewish historian Josephus tells the story of his discovery of three friends who had been crucified during the siege of Jerusalem (66–70 C.E.). He reported his discovery to his friend General Titus (to become emperor 79–81 C.E.), who ordered the three friends to be taken down and given medical attention. Two of them died anyway; a third survived (*The Life*, 420).

During the same siege, Josephus reports that those seeking to escape from Jerusalem were taken prisoner by the Romans, flogged and tortured, then executed, then crucified—hung on crosses where they could be seen from the walls of the city as a warning to others. Five hundred or more were thus treated daily; the carnage grew to such a level that space could not be found for the crosses, nor crosses for the bodies. The Roman soldiers in a rage nailed their victims to the crosses in different postures to amuse themselves (Josephus, *Jewish War*, 5.449–51).

Josephus and other ancient sources attest to the fact that both the Romans and the ancient Israelites crucified both those who were alive and those who had already been executed. Both were intended to produce unrestricted shame: the victims were publicly exposed, naked, unburied, and left as carrion.

Not only does Joseph retrieve the body of Jesus, he also buys a shroud, wraps Jesus' body in it, and places it in a tomb hewn out of rock—the kind reserved for the nobility—and seals the opening with a stone (v. 46). The picture of the tomb was probably inspired by the story of Joshua's treatment of the five kings he had defeated (Josh 10:16–27). The relevant part of the story is when Joshua brings them out of the cave where they had been hiding and executes them (vv. 26–27):

> [26]Joshua killed them [the five kings] and hung them on five trees, and they hung there until evening. [27]And when the sun had set, Joshua gave the orders and they took them down from the trees and threw them into the cave where they had been hiding. And they rolled stones up against the cave, stones that remain to this day.

Earlier in the story Joshua had ordered his men to roll stones against the mouth of the cave where the kings had been hiding. They were thus imprisoned in their own hiding place.

The tomb sealed with a stone and the presence of the women are, of course, narrative preparation for what is to come. The details of Joseph's role in the burial make sense only as part of the story of the empty tomb to follow. The note about the women observers is cut from the same cloth: they need to know where Jesus was buried so they can perform the mourning and burial rites after the sabbath day of rest is past (v. 47). The burial is a fiction because it goes with the empty tomb story, which is the central fiction in Mark's passion narrative. There is nothing in Mark's narrative that can be colored anything other than black.

Note: Stories of the empty tomb, the appearance of the risen Jesus, and the ascension have been gathered into a separate section (pp. 449–95). Color coding and commentary on Mark 16:1–8, 9–11, 12–13, 14–18, and 19–20 will be found in that section.

CALENDAR OF EVENTS

B.C.E.	332	Alexander the Great conquers Palestine
		The hellenistic era begins
	ca. 250	Jews in Egypt translate the Torah into Greek (LXX)
	168	Judas Maccabeus leads revolt against Antiochus IV
	164	Jerusalem temple rededicated, celebrated as Hanukkah
	128	Samaritan temple on Mt. Gerizim destroyed by Judeans
	63	Roman general Pompey captures Jerusalem; Judean independence ends
	44	Julius Caesar is murdered; a comet said to reveal his divinity
	40	Herod the Great is appointed king of Judea by Roman Senate
	37	Herod takes control of Jerusalem
	27	Augustus becomes first Roman emperor
	ca. 6	Jesus of Nazareth born
	4	Death of Herod sparks revolts
		Herod's son Herod Antipas becomes ruler of Galilee, Archelaus of Judea
	ca. 1	Apollonius of Tyana born
C.E.	6	Roman prefects take control of Judea; zealots revolt in Galilee
	6–15	Annas is high priest in Jerusalem
	ca. 10	Rabbi Hillel dies; his followers become leaders of Pharisaic Judaism
	14	Augustus dies; his stepson Tiberius becomes emperor
	18–36	Caiaphas, Annas' son-in-law, is high priest
	ca. 29	Herod Antipas beheads John the Baptist
	ca. 30	Pontius Pilate crucifies Jesus
	ca. 33	Paul of Tarsus experiences visions of Jesus
	ca. 44	Herod Agrippa executes James son of Zebedee and imprisons Peter
	ca. 54	Paul writes letters to Corinthians
	ca. 62	James, brother of Jesus, martyred in Jerusalem
	ca. 65	Nero persecutes Christians in Rome; Paul and Peter may have been martyred
	66	Jewish revolt against the Romans begins
	67	Vespasian and his son Titus capture Galilee; Jewish commander Josephus surrenders, begins writing history of Jewish war
	68	Romans massacre thousands of Samaritans; Qumran destroyed, scrolls hidden in caves
	69	Vespasian becomes emperor
	70	Titus captures Jerusalem, destroys the temple
	79	Titus becomes Roman emperor
	ca. 107	Ignatius, Bishop of Antioch, martyred
	130	Papias, Bishop of Hierapolis, dies (born ca. 60)
	132–135	Second Jewish revolt against the Romans; Jerusalem completely destroyed
	ca. 200	Irenaeus of Lyons dies (born ca. 130)
	ca. 225	Tertullian dies (born ca. 160)
	ca. 254	Origen dies (born ca. 185)
	313	Emperor Constantine ends persecution of Christians
	325	Council of Nicea: Nicene Creed formulated
	340	Eusebius of Caesarea dies (born 260)
	420	Jerome dies (born 342)
	430	Augustine of Hippo dies (born 354)

The Gospel of Matthew

The birth and infancy narratives of Matthew and Luke were the last part of the gospel tradition to develop. The color-coded text and related commentary are accordingly placed last in *The Acts of Jesus*, following the empty tomb and appearance stories. The gospels of both Matthew and Luke may originally have begun with chapter 3.

A voice in the wilderness
Mt 3:1–12
Mk 1:1–8, Lk 3:1–20;
Jn 1:19–28; GEbi 1, 3
Sources: Mark, John

3 In due course John the Baptizer appears in the wilderness of
Judea, [2]calling out: "Change your ways because Heaven's imperial
rule is closing in."
[3]No doubt this is the person described by Isaiah the prophet:

> A voice of someone shouting in the wilderness:
> "Make ready the way of the Lord;
> make his paths straight."

[4]Now this same John wore clothes made of camel hair and had a
leather belt around his waist; his diet consisted of locusts and raw
honey. [5]Then Jerusalem, and all Judea, and all the region around the
Jordan streamed out to him, [6]and got baptized in the Jordan river by
him, admitting their sins.

[7]When he saw that many of the Pharisees and Sadducees were
coming for baptism, <John> said to them, "You spawn of Satan! Who
warned you to flee from the impending doom? [8]Well then, start pro-
ducing fruit suitable for a change of heart, [9]and don't even think of
saying to yourselves, 'We have Abraham for our father.' Let me tell
you, God can raise up children for Abraham right out of these rocks.
[10]Even now the axe is aimed at the root of the trees. So every tree not
producing choice fruit gets cut down and tossed into the fire.

JOHN THE BAPTIST & THE QUMRAN COMMUNITY

John the Baptist conducted a prophetic ministry in the Judean wilderness around 25–28 C.E. He got his nickname from a religious rite that involved immersing penitents in water. Shortly after the discovery of the Dead Sea Scrolls in 1947, scholars observed similarities between ideas and practices described in the Scrolls and those attributed to John the Baptist. These similarities suggested that John may have had some connection to the Qumran community, perhaps had even been a member.

Both John and the members of the Qumran community practiced ritual immersion. Both linked immersion to repentance, atonement for sins, a spirit of holiness, and the expectation of an eschatological cleansing. Both connected the location of their activities in the wilderness to Isa 40:3:

> A voice of one shouting in the desert: "Make ready the way of the Lord, make straight the paths of our God."

John also preached an imminent eschatological judgment and expected an eschatological figure who would be the agent of God's judgment and restoration. Similar ideas and expectations are found in the Dead Sea Scrolls, especially in the "Community Rule" or the "Manual of Discipline," as it is also known. These similarities are reinforced by the proximity of John's ministry to the Qumran community: both are located in the Jordan valley close to the point at which the Jordan River empties into the Dead Sea.

While intriguing, the similarities are not sufficient in the judgment of many scholars to support a direct connection between John and the Qumran community. Many of these ideas and practices were "in the air" at the time of John and Jesus, so they appear in one form or another in other forms of sectarian Judaism. The proximity of John and the Qumran group to each other in the wilderness was inspired in part by passages in the Hebrew Bible that linked the wilderness to the simpler religion of Israel's past, and in part by the desire to avoid the intrigues and compromises of urban life and the temple cult. The wilderness stood for "the good old days." The concern for purity and the expectation that God would intervene directly in history in eschatological judgment are part of a "wilderness mentality" that was widespread in first-century Judaism.

11"I baptize you with water to signal a change of heart, but some-
one more powerful than I will succeed me. I am not fit to carry his
sandals. He'll baptize you with holy spirit and fire. 12His pitchfork is
in his hand, and he'll make a clean sweep of his threshing floor, and gather his wheat into the granary, but the chaff he'll burn in a fire that can't be put out."

A voice in the wilderness. In creating this section on John the Baptist, Matthew has combined Mark with materials he derived from the Sayings Gospel Q. Matthew follows Mark closely in vv. 1–6; vv. 7–12 are derived from Q.

Matthew begins the narration of Jesus' activity as an adult by presenting

John the Baptist as the expected forerunner of the messiah—Jesus. The locale of John's work was the wilderness around the Jordan river, where he preached and baptized. He was popular; many responded favorably to his call for a baptism of repentance. He was an ascetic and probably lived on a diet that included locusts and raw honey. There is less likelihood that he actually dressed in camel hair with a leather belt, since those details recall the dress of Elijah (2 Kgs 1:8).

In v. 2 Matthew has offered a summary of John's message that betrays his own editorial work. The synoptic gospels generally report that the theme of Jesus' message was God's imperial rule (the kingdom of God), or, as Matthew would have it, heaven's imperial rule (Matthew substituted "heaven" for "God" out of respect for the divine name). Matthew has borrowed the summary of Jesus' message in 4:17 (//Mark 1:15) and placed it on the lips of John. Because the words in v. 2 preserve John's call to repentance, the Fellows decided to color it gray rather than black.

Matthew provides John with a brief sermon consisting of sayings taken from the Sayings Gospel Q. The Seminar thought it probable that Pharisees and Sadducees did come to hear John, if for no other reason than curiosity. The sayings in vv. 7b–10 are a scathing invective and a call for repentance in the light of the coming judgment. The Fellows were evenly divided on whether these remarks were correctly attributed to John; the result was a gray designation. The fact that the sayings were focused narrowly on the Pharisees and Sadducees struck some Fellows as the hand of Matthew rather than the voice of John. Had they been framed with a more general audience in view, they would readily have been designated pink or even red.

The words ascribed to John in v. 11 are the Q version that corresponds to Mark 1:7–8. John probably did anticipate the arrival of the messiah in the near future, but he probably did not contrast his own water baptism with the spirit baptism of his successor.

The saying in v. 12 is an agricultural image of the coming apocalyptic judgment. These words cohere with John's proclamation that the endtime had come and with his demeanor.

The Gospel of the Ebionites, like the Gospel of Mark, apparently opened with a reference to John the Baptist. There exist only seven fragments of this gospel. The fragments are in the form of quotations embedded in the works of Epiphanius of Salamis (ca. 315–403). They are attributed to the Ebionites merely because Epiphanius quotes them in a section of his work devoted to the Ebionites.

The Ebionites constituted a Christian sect that flourished for a time east of the Jordan. The name means "the poor." They apparently held that Jesus became the Christ only at his baptism; as a consequence, they disregarded the stories of Jesus' miraculous birth. They led an ascetic life, like John the Baptist, and held to the strict observance of the Mosaic law.

Epiphanius reports that their gospel begins like this (GEbi 1):

In the days of Herod, king of Judea, John appeared in the Jordan river baptizing with a baptism that changed people's hearts. [2]He was said to

be a descendant of Aaron the priest, a son of Zechariah and Elizabeth.
[3]And everybody went out to him.

The Gospel of the Ebionites thus begins like the Gospel of Mark. Most scholars hold that the Gospel of the Ebionites is derived from the canonical gospels, especially Matthew. The Fellows nevertheless designated red those sentences that repeat historical data regarding John. The ancestry of John and the names of his parents were probably created by Christian lore in the early days of the movement.

In a second fragment quoted by Epiphanius, John is represented much as he is in Matt 3:4–5, except that instead of locusts and raw honey he is supposed to have restricted his diet to wild honey, which tasted like manna (GEbi 3):

[1]It so happened that John was baptizing, and Pharisees and all
Jerusalem went out to him and got baptized. [2]And John wore clothes
made of camel hair and had a leather belt around his waist. [3]His food
consisted of raw honey that tasted like manna, like a pancake cooked
with oil.

Epiphanius regarded this modification of the canonical tradition by the Ebionites as a lie.

The baptism of Jesus
Mt 3:13–17
Mk 1:9–11, Lk 3:21–22
Source: Mark
Cf. Jn 1:29–34; GNaz 2; GEbi 4; GHeb 3

3 **[13]Then Jesus comes from Galilee to John at the Jordan to get**
baptized by him. [14]And John tried to stop him with these words:
"I'm the one who needs to get baptized by you, yet you come to
me?"
[15]In response, Jesus said to him, "Let it go for now. After all, in this way we are doing what is fitting and right."**Then John deferred to him.**
[16]After Jesus had been baptized, he got right up out of the water,
and—amazingly—the skies opened up, he saw God's spirit coming
down on him like a dove, perching on him, [17]and—listen!—there
was a voice from the skies, which said, "This is my favored son—I
fully approve of him!"

The baptism of Jesus. Matthew borrows the story of Jesus' baptism from Mark. The sentence reporting that fact is therefore designated red in accordance with its counterpart in Mark. The description of Jesus' experience at his baptism remains black.

Matthew has made an important addition to the story: he reports a conversation between John and Jesus (vv. 14–15). This verbal exchange obviously represents an attempt by the evangelist to explain "why" Jesus would allow himself to be baptized by John. These words show that the church was bothered by the fact that Jesus had submitted to John's baptism. The exchange is obviously a fiction formulated by the evangelist to soften the undesirable implication that Jesus was once subservient to John.

The Christian explanation of Jesus' baptism by John in Matthew is paralleled by another version in the Gospel of the Nazoreans. Jerome, a scholar of the ancient church who completed the translation of the Bible into Latin around 380 C.E., quotes this fragment (GNaz 2):

[1]**The mother of the Lord and his brothers said to him, "John the Baptist baptized for the forgiveness of sins. Let's go and get baptized by him."** [2]**But he said to them,** "How have I sinned? So why should I go and get baptized by him? Only if I don't know what I'm talking about."

The point of this fragment is to avoid the conclusion that Jesus got baptized because he was seeking the forgiveness of his sins. The fragment also hints that Jesus' mother and brothers were baptized by John. There is nothing in this fragment that rests on historical reminiscence; the appropriate color is black.

Another fragment from the Gospel of the Ebionites quoted by Epiphanius in a work he wrote in 375 C.E. relates this story of Jesus' baptism (GEbi 4):

[1]**When the people were baptized, Jesus also came and got baptized by John.** [2]**As he came up out of the water, the skies opened and he saw the holy spirit in the form of a dove coming down and entering him.** [3]**And there was a voice from the sky that said, "You are my favored son—I fully approve of you."** [4]**And again, "Today I have become your father."**

[5]**And right away a bright light illuminated the place. When John saw this, he said to him, "Who are you?"** [6]**And again a voice from the sky said to him, "This is my favored son—I fully approve of him."**

[7]**John knelt down in front of him and said, "Please, Lord, you baptize me."**

[8]**But he stopped him and said,** "It's all right. This is the way everything is supposed to be fulfilled."

The first verse echoes the synoptic report of Jesus' baptism by John and is therefore designated red. The balance of the fragment is a pastiche drawn from all three synoptic gospels. In vv. 2–6, the gospel quotes Mark, Luke, and then Matthew leaving the impression that the voice from heaven speaks three times.

Verses 7–8, on the other hand, are another version of the Christian explanation for Jesus' baptism given in the Gospel of Matthew. These attempts to account for Jesus' baptism may reflect the rivalry between the Baptist and Christian movements after Jesus' death.

The temptation of Jesus
Mt 4:1–11
Lk 4:1–13; Mk 1:12–13
Sources: Q, Mark

4 **Then Jesus was guided into the wilderness by the spirit to be put to the test by the devil.** [2]**And after he had fasted 'forty days and forty nights,' he was famished.**

[3]**And the tester confronted him and said, "To prove you're God's son, order these stones to turn into bread."**

[4]**He responded,** "It is written, 'Human beings are not to live on bread alone, but on every word that comes out of God's mouth.'"

5Then the devil conducts him to the holy city, sets him on the pin-
nacle of the temple, 6and says to him, "To prove you're God's son,
jump off; remember, it is written, 'To his heavenly messengers he
will give orders about you,' and 'with their hands they will catch
you, so you won't even stub your toe on a stone.'"
7Jesus said to him, "Elsewhere it is written, 'You are not to put the
Lord your God to the test.'"
8Again the devil takes him to a very high mountain and shows
him all the empires of the world and their splendor, 9and says to
him, "I'll give you all these, if you will kneel down and pay homage
to me."
10Finally Jesus says to him, "Get out of here, Satan! Remember, it is
written, 'You are to pay homage to the Lord your God, and you are to
revere him alone.'"
11Then the devil leaves him, and heavenly messengers arrive out
of nowhere and look after him.

The temptation of Jesus. The commentary for this segment will be found in the Sayings Gospel Q: Luke 4:1–13//Matt 4:1–11, (pp. 41–50).

The good news
Mt 4:12–17
Mk 1:14–15
Source: Mark
Cf. Lk 4:14–15, 16–30

4

12When Jesus heard that John had been locked up, he headed
for Galilee. 13He took leave of Nazareth to go and settle down in
Capernaum-by-the-sea, in the territory of Zebulun and Naphtali,
14so that the word spoken through Isaiah the prophet would come
true:

> 15Land of Zebulun and of Naphtali,
> the way to the sea,
> across the Jordan,
> Galilee of the pagans!
> 16You who languished in darkness have seen a great light,
> you who have wasted away in the shadow of death,
> for you a light has risen.

17From that time on Jesus began to proclaim: "Change your ways
because Heaven's imperial rule is closing in."

The good news. Matthew follows the lead of Mark in providing a transition from Jesus' trials in the wilderness to the beginning of Jesus' public activities. This transition also functions as the introduction of the body of Matthew's gospel story.

To Mark's information that Jesus began his public life in Galilee at the time John was imprisoned, Matthew adds that Jesus immediately left Nazareth and settled down in Capernaum. He introduces this note here apparently to satisfy the elements of the prophetic text he is about to quote in vv. 15–16. In so doing,

THE SYNAGOGUE

During the period of the Second Temple (520 B.C.E.–70 C.E.), the term synagogue did not refer primarily to a building but to an assembly. In the villages and towns of ancient Palestine, local affairs were governed by local people. The town or village assembly consisted of the townspeople who attended to a variety of matters—political, judicial, economic, as well as religious (there was no dividing line between religion and the state). The gospels sometimes speak of a "chief of the synagogue." Such a person may have presided over the full assembly or over the council, which represented the people.

In most villages and towns of first-century Palestine, the assembly probably gathered in the town square or at the city gate. There were also generic assembly halls for such gatherings. After the destruction of the temple, synagogue buildings were erected and those buildings became centers of public worship and study. The synagogue that a friendly Roman officer built for Jewish elders (Luke 7:5) reflects post-70 conditions. Luke's picture of Corinth with a house-church next door to a synagogue building (Acts 18:7) also fits the later archaeological evidence.

Archaeologists have now uncovered numerous synagogue sites in ancient Palestine. The majority of them are in Galilee and the Golan Heights. The presence of synagogue buildings reflects the growth of rabbinic Judaism in those areas following the destruction of the temple and the final defeat of Jewish forces in 135 C.E. After these events, the Jews were expelled from Judea, and Galilee became the dominant center of Judaism in the third century of the common era. Ruins of large synagogues from the third and fourth centuries exhibit decorative mosaic floors and Torah shrines.

The only New Testament writings that antedate the fall of Jerusalem, the letters of Paul, make no mention of synagogues. New Testament references to synagogue buildings are all from the gospels and Acts, written after 70 C.E. Readers of the gospels should be aware of anachronistic references to synagogue buildings in the time of Jesus (Mark 1:21, Matt 4:23, Luke 4:16–20).

In Jesus' day, the activities that took place in assembly halls were mostly social and educational. The "synagogue" was primarily a place of study where scripture (Torah and the Prophets) was read aloud and commented on. Luke describes such a typical scene in Nazareth at the beginning of Jesus' ministry (Luke 4:16–30), although some of the terminology he uses mirrors conditions in Luke's time. That such sessions could turn into heated arguments is attested also by Josephus. The typical gospel stories that picture Jesus as "teaching" in the synagogue as a school thus appear to be historically plausible.

he has given us another example of his inclination to match events with prophecy. His proclivity to join event and prophecy inevitably arouses the suspicions of scholars about his reliability as a reporter. But in this case Matthew is probably guilty of no more than representing Jesus as shifting from Nazareth to Capernaum in order to fulfill the prophecy. In fact, Jesus may have been entirely innocent of the Isaiah proclamation. It is for this reason alone that the Fellows have color-coded v. 13 black; the information that Capernaum was the center of Jesus' work during his Galilean period is probably correct. Consult the cameo on "Capernaum," p. 58, for additional references and archaeological information.

Call of the first disciples
Mt 4:18–20, 21–22
Mk 1:16–18, 19–20
Source: Mark
Cf. Lk 5:1–11; Jn 1:35–42; 43–51; GEbi 2

4 [18]**As he was walking by the Sea of Galilee, he spotted two broth-**
ers, Simon, also known as Peter, and Andrew his brother, throwing
their net in the sea, since they were fishermen. [19]**And Jesus says to**
them, "Become my followers and I'll have you fishing for people!" [20]**So**
right then and there they abandoned their nets and followed him.
[21]**When he had gone on a little farther, he caught sight of two**
other brothers, James, Zebedee's son, and his brother John, in the
boat with Zebedee their father, mending their nets, and he also
called out to them. [22]**They abandoned their boat and their father**
right then and there and followed him.

Call of the first disciples. The call to become a disciple echoes a theme found in stories told about sages other than Jesus. Diogenes Laertius told this story about Socrates:

> The story is told to the effect that Socrates met Xenophon in a narrow passageway and that he stretched out his staff to bar the way. He inquired of Xenophon where he could purchase various kinds of food. When he had received a reply, he put another question to Xenophon: "Where do men become good and honorable?" Xenophon was puzzled by the question, to which Socrates responded, "Then follow me and learn." From that time on he was a disciple of Socrates.
>
> *Lives of Eminent Philosophers*, 2.48

In this exchange the listener learns that Xenophon knows where to shop for food, but he is uncertain where to go to become good and honorable. Like many people, Xenophon has knowledge of trivial things but lacks knowledge of what is essential. Socrates, the master teacher, offers to teach him real knowledge. The anecdote is not the report of an actual event, but the depiction of an ideal scene, of something Socrates might have done. Yet it is also an account of the enlistment of a follower.

Matthew has copied Mark very closely in reproducing two anecdotes representing Jesus as recruiting disciples. The second story, the call of James and John, is an exact duplicate of the first account in which Peter and Andrew are recruited. The two stories are highly stylized: they echo a standard call scene of the type found elsewhere in the Bible (Jer 1:4–10, Ezek 2:1–3:3) and they provide the basis for the claims to leadership later made by Peter, James, and John. Eighty-five percent of the Fellows approved the statement that Jesus did not actively recruit disciples. At the same time, approximately the same number agreed that a group of disciples, including women, traveled with Jesus. The inclination of the storyteller was to turn volunteerism into a divine mandate in order to validate apostolic leadership.

**4 23 And he toured all over Galilee, teaching in their synagogues,
proclaiming the news of <Heaven's> imperial rule, and healing
every disease and every ailment the people had. 24 And his reputation
spread through the whole of Syria. They brought him everyone who
was ill, who suffered from any kind of disease or was in intense
pain, who was possessed, who was epileptic, or a paralytic, and he
cured them. 25 And huge crowds followed him from Galilee and the
Decapolis and Jerusalem and Judea and from across the Jordan.**

Jesus tours Galilee
Mt 4:23–25
Mk 1:35–39, Lk 4:42–44
Source: Mark

Jesus tours Galilee. This paragraph constitutes a narrative summary created by Matthew. It draws on remarks in the Gospel of Mark, but goes beyond them, once again indicating that the authors of gospels felt free to alter scenes and compose new transitions. But Matthew does more than summarize. He provides narrative continuity by linking stories he has just narrated, he expands the geographical reach of Jesus' fame, and he extends the time Jesus carries out his teaching, preaching, healing, and exorcisms—all of these are aspects of the "defocalizing" process by which storytellers bring a sequence to a conclusion, much as a musician brings a composition to its tonic resolution. In addition, these summaries reflect the principal themes of the gospel story as the authors conceive them. Matthew even lists the kinds of patients Jesus helps. To be sure, these summaries also tend to exaggerate: Matthew modestly remarks that they bring to Jesus *everyone who was ill.* That seems highly unlikely.

While the composition is the product of Matthew's imagination, we can isolate certain pieces of narrative information that probably reflect historical actualities. Among them are the following:

- **Jesus was an itinerant teacher in Galilee.**
- **Jesus proclaimed the kingdom of God.**
- **Jesus cured some sick people.**
- **Jesus drove out what were thought to be demons.**
- **Jesus enjoyed a certain amount of popularity in Galilee and surrounding regions.**

These observations are almost certainly historical.

**5 Taking note of the crowds, he climbed up the mountain, and
when he had sat down, his disciples came to him. 2 He then began to
speak, and this is what he would teach them:**

Great sermon
Mt 5:1–7:29
Lk 6:20–49
Source: Q

3 Congratulations to the poor in spirit!
Heaven's domain belongs to them.
4 Congratulations to those who grieve!
They will be consoled.
5 Congratulations to the gentle!
They will inherit the earth.

[6]Congratulations to those who hunger and thirst for justice!
They will have a feast.
[7]Congratulations to the merciful!
They will receive mercy.
[8]Congratulations to those with undefiled hearts!
They will see God.
[9]Congratulations to those who work for peace!
They will be known as God's children.
[10]Congratulations to those who have suffered persecution for the sake of justice!
Heaven's domain belongs to them.

[11]"Congratulations to you when they denounce you and persecute you and spread malicious gossip about you because of me. [12]Rejoice and be glad! In heaven you will be more than compensated. Remember, this is how they persecuted the prophets who preceded you.

[13]"You are the salt of the earth. But if salt loses its zing, how will it be made salty? It then has no further use than to be thrown out and stomped on. [14]You are the light of the world. A city sitting on top of a mountain can't be concealed. [15]Nor do people light a lamp and put it under a bushel basket but rather on a lampstand, where it sheds light for everyone in the house. [16]That's how your light is to shine in the presence of others, so they can see your good deeds and acclaim your Father in the heavens.

[17]"Don't imagine that I have come to annul the Law or the Prophets. I have come not to annul but to fulfill. [18]I swear to you, before the world disappears, not one iota, not one serif, will disappear from the Law, until that happens. [19]Whoever ignores one of the most trivial of these regulations, and teaches others to do so, will be called trivial in Heaven's domain. But whoever acts on <these regulations> and teaches <others to do so>, will be called great in Heaven's domain. [20]Let me tell you: unless your religion goes beyond that of the scholars and Pharisees, you won't set foot in Heaven's domain.

[21]"As you know, our ancestors were told, 'You must not kill' and 'Whoever kills will be subject to judgment.' [22]But I tell you: those who are angry with a companion will be brought before a tribunal. And those who say to a companion, 'You moron,' will be subject to the sentence of the court. And whoever says, 'You idiot,' deserves the fires of Gehenna. [23]So, even if you happen to be offering your gift at the altar and recall that your friend has some claim against you, [24]leave your gift there at the altar. First go and be reconciled with your friend, and only then return and offer your gift. [25]You should come to terms quickly with your opponent while you are both on the way <to court>, or else your opponent will hand you over to the judge, and the judge <will turn you over> to the bailiff, and you are thrown in jail. [26]I swear to you, you'll never get out of there until you've paid the last dime.

[27]"As you know, we once were told, 'You are not to commit adul-

tery.' 28But I tell you: Those who leer at a woman and desire her have
already committed adultery with her in their hearts. 29And if your
right eye gets you into trouble, rip it out and throw it away! You
would be better off to lose a part of your body, than to have your
whole body thrown into Gehenna. 30And if your right hand gets you
into trouble, cut it off and throw it away! You would be better off to
lose a part of your body, than to have your whole body wind up in
Gehenna.

31"We once were told, 'Whoever divorces his wife should give her a
bill of divorce.' 32But I tell you: Everyone who divorces his wife (except
in the case of infidelity) makes her the victim of adultery; and who-
ever marries a divorced woman commits adultery.

33"Again, as you know, our ancestors were told, 'You must not break
an oath,' and 'Oaths sworn in the name of God must be kept.' 34But I
tell you: Don't swear at all. Don't invoke heaven, because it is the
throne of God, 35and don't invoke earth, because it is God's footstool,
and don't invoke Jerusalem, because it is the city of the great king.
36You shouldn't swear by your head either, since you aren't able to turn
a single hair either white or black. 37Rather, your responses should be
simply 'Yes' and 'No.' Anything that goes beyond this is inspired by
the evil one.

38"As you know, we once were told, 'An eye for an eye' and 'A tooth
for a tooth.' 39But I tell you: Don't react violently against the one who is
evil: when someone slaps you on the right cheek, turn the other as
well. 40If someone is determined to sue you for your shirt, let that per-
son have your coat along with it. 41Further, when anyone conscripts
you for one mile, go along an extra mile. 42Give to the one who begs
from you; and don't turn away the one who tries to borrow from
you.

43"As you know, we once were told, 'You are to love your neighbor'
and 'You are to hate your enemy.' 44But I tell you: Love your enemies
and pray for your persecutors. 45You'll then become children of your
Father in the heavens. <God> causes the sun to rise on both the bad
and the good, and sends rain on both the just and the unjust. 46Tell me,
if you love those who love you, why should you be commended for
that? Even the toll collectors do as much, don't they? 47And if you greet
only your friends, what have you done that is exceptional? Even the
pagans do as much, don't they? 48To sum up, you are to be as liberal in
your love as your heavenly Father is.

6 "Take care that you don't flaunt your religion in public to be
noticed by others. Otherwise, you will have no recognition from your
Father in the heavens. 2For example, when you give to charity, don't
bother to toot your own horn as some phony pietists do in houses of
worship and on the street. They are seeking human recognition. I
swear to you, their grandstanding is its own reward. 3Instead, when

you give to charity, don't let your left hand in on what your right hand
is up to, 4so your acts of charity may remain hidden. And your Father,
who has an eye for the hidden, will applaud you.

5"And when you pray, don't act like phonies. They love to stand up
and pray in houses of worship and on street corners, so they can show
off in public. I swear to you, their prayers have been answered! 6When
you pray, go into a room by yourself and shut the door behind you.
Then pray to your Father, the hidden one. And your Father, with his
eye for the hidden, will applaud you. 7And when you pray, you should
not babble on as the pagans do. They imagine that the length of their
prayers will command attention. 8So don't imitate them. After all, your
Father knows what you need before you ask. 9Instead, you should
pray like this:

> Our Father in the heavens,
> your name be revered.
> 10Impose your imperial rule,
> enact your will on earth as you have in heaven.
> 11Provide us with the bread we need for the day.
> 12Forgive our debts
> to the extent that we have forgiven those in debt to us.
> 13And please don't subject us to test after test,
> but rescue us from the evil one.

14"For if you forgive others their failures and offenses, your heavenly
Father will also forgive yours. 15And if you don't forgive the failures
and mistakes of others, your Father won't forgive yours.

16"When you fast, don't make a spectacle of your remorse as the pre-
tenders do. As you know, they make their faces unrecognizable so
their fasting may be publicly recognized. I swear to you, they have
been paid in full. 17When you fast, comb your hair and wash your face,
18so your fasting may go unrecognized in public. But it will be recog-
nized by your Father, the hidden one, and your Father, who has an eye
for the hidden, will applaud you.

19"Don't acquire possessions here on earth, where moths and insects
eat away and where robbers break in and steal. 20Instead, gather your
nest egg in heaven, where neither moths nor insects eat away and
where no robbers break in or steal. 21As you know, what you treasure is
your heart's true measure.

22"The eye is the body's lamp. It follows that if your eye is clear,
your whole body will be flooded with light. 23If your eye is clouded,
your whole body will be shrouded in darkness. If, then, the light
within you is darkness, how dark that can be!

24"No one can be a slave to two masters. No doubt that slave will
either hate one and love the other, or be devoted to one and disdain
the other. You can't be enslaved to both God and a bank account!

25"That's why I tell you: Don't fret about your life—what you're
going to eat and drink—or about your body—what you're going to

wear. There is more to living than food and clothing, isn't there? 26Take a look at the birds of the sky: they don't plant or harvest, or gather into barns. Yet your heavenly Father feeds them. You're worth more than they, aren't you? 27Can any of you add one hour to life by fretting about it? 28Why worry about clothes? Notice how the wild lilies grow: they don't slave and they never spin. 29Yet let me tell you, even Solomon at the height of his glory was never decked out like one of them. 30If God dresses up the grass in the field, which is here today and tomorrow is thrown into an oven, won't <God care for> you even more, you who don't take anything for granted? 31So don't fret. Don't say, 'What am I going to eat?' or 'What am I going to drink?' or 'What am I going to wear?' 32These are all things pagans seek. After all, your heavenly Father is aware that you need them. 33You are to seek <God's> domain, and his justice first, and all these things will come to you as a bonus. 34So don't fret about tomorrow. Let tomorrow fret about itself. The troubles that the day brings are enough.

7 "Don't pass judgment, so you won't be judged. 2Don't forget, the judgment you hand out will be the judgment you get back. And the standard you apply will be the standard applied to you. 3Why do you notice the sliver in your friend's eye, but overlook the timber in your own? 4How can you say to your friend, 'Let me get the sliver out of your eye,' when there is that timber in your own? 5You phony, first take the timber out of your own eye and then you'll see well enough to remove the sliver from your friend's eye.

6"Don't offer to dogs what is sacred, and don't throw your pearls to pigs, or they'll trample them underfoot and turn and tear you to shreds.

7"Ask—it'll be given to you; seek—you'll find; knock—it'll be opened for you. 8Rest assured: everyone who asks receives; everyone who seeks finds; and for the one who knocks it is opened. 9Who among you would hand a son a stone when it's bread he's asking for? 10Again, who would hand him a snake when it's fish he's asking for? Of course no one would! 11So if you, worthless as you are, know how to give your children good gifts, isn't it much more likely that your Father in the heavens will give good things to those who ask him?

12"Consider this: Treat people in ways you want them to treat you. This sums up the whole of the Law and the Prophets.

13"Try to get in through the narrow gate. Wide and smooth is the road that leads to destruction. The majority are taking that route. 14Narrow and rough is the road that leads to life. Only a minority discover it.

15"Be on the lookout for phony prophets, who make their pitch disguised as sheep; inside they are really voracious wolves. 16You'll know who they are by what they produce. Since when do people pick grapes from thorns or figs from thistles? 17Every healthy tree produces choice fruit, but the rotten tree produces spoiled fruit. [18]A healthy tree cannot produce spoiled fruit, any more than a rotten tree can produce choice fruit. [19]Every tree that does not produce choice fruit gets cut down and tossed on the fire. [20]Remember, you'll know who they are by what they produce.

[21]"Not everyone who addresses me as 'Master, master,' will get into Heaven's domain—only those who carry out the will of my Father in heaven. [22]On that day many will address me: 'Master, master, didn't we use your name when we prophesied? Didn't we use your name when we exorcised demons? Didn't we use your name when we performed all those miracles?' [23]Then I will tell them honestly: 'I never knew you; get away from me, you subverters of the Law!'

[24]"Everyone who pays attention to these words of mine and acts on them will be like a shrewd builder who erected a house on bedrock. [25]Later the rain fell, and the torrents came, and the winds blew and pounded that house, yet it did not collapse, since its foundation rested on bedrock. [26]Everyone who listens to these words of mine and doesn't act on them will be like a careless builder, who erected a house on the sand. [27]When the rain fell, and the torrents came, and the winds blew and pounded that house, it collapsed. Its collapse was colossal."

[28]And so, when Jesus had finished this discourse, the crowds were astonished at his teaching, [29]since he had been teaching them on his own authority, unlike their <own> scholars.

Great sermon. Matthew has taken the basic scheme for the great sermon from the Sayings Gospel Q. His introduction in 5:1–2 is probably based on an introduction to the sermon in Q, but it has also been influenced by Mark 3:13 ("Then he goes up on the mountain and summons those he wanted . . . "). The analogy that hovers in the background is Moses' ascent to the mountain in Sinai to receive the ten words on stone—the ten commandments. In other words, the mountain is the mythical mountain of revelation. Jesus repeats what Moses had done before him.

Luke sets the same sermon, also derived from Q, on "a level place" as Jesus comes down from the mountain (6:17–20). The variation between Matthew and Luke, both of whom were presumably reading Q, makes it difficult to determine the setting of the sermon in Q. And of course Matthew has a greatly expanded version of the sermon in comparison with Luke. In any case, the introduction to the sermon in Matthew is the author's own construction and is therefore appropriately colored black.

The conclusion to the sermon on the mount in 7:28–29 is also the work of Matthew. It is one of five such narrative transitions found in Matthew's gospel: this one along with 11:1, 13:53, 19:1, and 26:1 create five "books," which some scholars have suggested parallel the five books of Moses or the Torah. To those five books are prefaced an account of Jesus' preliminary association with John the Baptist and appended an account of his trial and execution.

Although the conclusion to the great sermon is the creation of Matthew, it does preserve what many think may be an accurate reflection of Jesus' teaching technique. Jesus apparently did not quote and interpret scripture, he probably did not debate fine points of the law, and he almost certainly did not quote authorities to back up his views. On the contrary, he seems to have taught on his own authority—on the authority of his stories and aphorisms as self-evident truth. Because that strategy appears to be confirmed by the evidence of his authentic words, the Fellows decided to color the statement in v. 29 gray.

8 **When he came down from the mountain, huge crowds fol-**
lowed him. 2Just then a leper appeared, bowed down to him, and
said, "Sir, if you want to, you can make me clean."
3And he stretched out his hand, touched him, and says, "Okay—
you're clean!" **At once his leprosy was cleansed away.** 4Then Jesus
warns him: "See that you don't tell anyone, but go, have a priest
examine <your skin>. Then offer the gift that Moses commanded, as
evidence <of your cure>."

The leper
Mt 8:1–4
Mk 1:40–45, Lk 5:12–16; EgerG 2:1–4
Sources: Mark, Egerton Gospel

The leper. Matthew has taken the story of the leper from Mark and omitted from it the emotional features present in Mark 1:41, 43, and Mark's elaborate narrative conclusion in 1:45. However, Matthew has provided a narrative introduction in v. 1 that connects the story with the sermon on the mount that has just preceded.

Verses 2–3 are the heart of the story in all four of its versions. The Fellows believe these verses approximate some actual event in the career of Jesus and so colored them pink. They were less certain about v. 4, which appears to contradict the behavior of Jesus in other respects regarding the observance of formal aspects of the Mosaic code, and which does not comport well with the declaration of v. 3. Jesus has declared the leper "clean," which is the proper function of a priest. Jesus appears to be performing a priestly function in so doing. He may have sent the leper to the official priest to observe the proprieties or to oblige the real priests to acknowledge his curative powers. The Fellows colored that directive black in *The Five Gospels.*

Leprosy in biblical times was not, of course, what later came to be known as Hansen's disease; the bacterium causing that disease was isolated and identified for the first time in 1874. The biblical affliction covered a wide range of skin disorders.

8 **5When he had entered Capernaum, a Roman officer approached**
him and pleaded with him: 6"Sir, my servant boy was struck down
with paralysis and is in terrible pain."
7And he said to him, "I'll come and cure him."
8And the Roman officer replied, "Sir, I don't deserve to have you
in my house, but only say the word and my boy will be cured. 9After

Officer's slave
Mt 8:5–13
Lk 7:1–10; Jn 4:45–54
Sources: Q, John

all, I myself am under orders, and I have soldiers under me. I order
one to go, and he goes; I order another to come, and he comes; and <I
order> my slave to do something, and he does it."
10 **As Jesus listened he was amazed and said to those who fol-**
lowed, "I swear to you, I have not found such trust in a single
Israelite! 11 I predict that many will come from east and west and dine
with Abraham and Isaac and Jacob in Heaven's domain, 12 but those
who think Heaven's domain belongs to them will be thrown where it
is utterly dark. There'll be weeping and grinding of teeth out there."
13 **And Jesus said to the Roman officer,** "Be on your way. Your trust
will be the measure of the results." **And the boy was cured at that pre-**
cise moment.

Peter's mother-in-law
Mt 8:14–15
Mk 1:29–31, Lk 4:38–39
Source: Mark

14 **And when Jesus came to Peter's house, he noticed his mother-in-**
law lying sick with a fever. 15 He touched her hand and the fever dis-
appeared. Then she got up and started looking after him.

Officer's slave. The commentary for this story is found in the Sayings Gospel Q, Luke 7:1–10//Matt 8:5–13 (pp. 41–50).

Peter's mother-in-law. In his customary fashion, Matthew has abbreviated the story of the cure of Peter's mother-in-law he borrowed from Mark. In Mark, the disciples call Jesus' attention to the condition of the woman, while Matthew puts the initiative in the hands of Jesus. Indeed, Matthew omits any mention of Andrew, James, and John. Finally, rather than serve the disciples and Jesus, the woman serves Jesus alone. These changes are Matthew's maneuvers to focus attention exclusively on Jesus.

In spite of Matthew's alterations to the Markan account, the Fellows designated the gist of the story pink, as they did in the case of Mark. The initial clause they colored gray because they doubted that the location of the cure was historically accurate: Mark has Jesus leave the synagogue on the sabbath and enter the house of Peter in Capernaum as a part of his sequence of events forming a picture of an ideal day in Jesus' public career; these connectives are probably the invention of Mark.

Cures & exorcisms
Mt 8:16–17
Mk 1:32–34, Lk 4:40–41
Source: Mark

8 16 **In the evening, they brought many who were demon-**
possessed to him. He drove out the spirits with a command, and all
those who were ill he cured. 17 In this way Isaiah's prophecy came
true:

> He took away our illnesses
> and carried off our diseases.

Cures & exorcisms. Matthew employs this narrative summary to conclude the *second* sequence of public activities that began with Jesus climbing the mountain to deliver his great sermon. In addition to the sermon on the mount, Matthew includes in this sequence the cure of the leper, the healing of the Roman officer's servant boy, and the visit to the home of Simon Peter to doctor

Peter's mother-in-law. In the *first* series of events, Matthew includes Jesus' return to Galilee, his first preaching, and his enlistment of two pairs of followers. That short series is followed by a transitional summary in 4:23–25. The sequence of events according to Matthew is then:

First Sequence
1. Return to Galilee, commencement of preaching (4:12–17)
2. Call of the first pairs of followers (4:18–22)
3. Summary: Tour of Galilee (4:23–25)

Second Sequence
1. Sermon on the mount (5:1–7:29)
2. Cure of the leper (8:1–4)
3. Healing of the Roman officer's servant boy (8:5–13)
4. Cure of Simon Peter's mother-in-law (8:14–15)
5. Summary: Cures & exorcisms (8:16–17)

In contrast, Mark joins the following events into a chronological sequence:

1. Return to Galilee, commencement of preaching (1:14–15)
2. Call of the first pairs of followers (1:16–20)
3. Exorcism in the synagogue at Capernaum (1:21–28)
4. Cure of Simon Peter's mother-in-law (1:29–31)
5. Summary of concluding events of day one (1:32–34)
6. Tour of Galilee (1:35–39)

It is clear from this comparison of sequences that Matthew felt no obligation to follow the order of events he had before him in the Gospel of Mark. For this reason, scholars conclude that the authors of the gospels did not know the actual sequence of events. Since the gospels they were creating are basically travel narratives, aside from the passion story, they simply clustered events in sequences as oral storytellers are wont to do.

Matthew concludes his summary with a prophetic text drawn from the Greek version of Isa 53:4 that confirms Jesus as the one who "took away our illnesses and carried off our diseases."

Although Matthew's summary reflects the probability that Jesus healed the sick and drove out demons, the summary does not represent independent confirmation of those activities. It was accordingly color-coded black.

Foxes have dens
Mt 8:18–22
Lk 9:57–62
Source: Q

8 18**When Jesus saw the crowds around him, he gave orders to cross over to the other side.** 19**And one scholar came forward and said to him, "Teacher, I'll follow you wherever you go."**

20**And Jesus says to him,** "Foxes have dens, and birds of the sky have nests, but the son of Adam has nowhere to rest his head."

21**Another of his disciples said to him, "Master, first let me go and bury my father."**

22**But Jesus says to him,** "Follow me, and leave it to the dead to bury their own dead."

Foxes have dens. The narrative transition in v. 18 Matthew has taken from Mark 4:23, the parallel in Matthew's source. The exchange that follows, however, is derived from Q. The narrative introduction—Jesus crosses to the other side of the lake—does not preserve specific historical information, so it was designated black. The frame for the dialogue in vv. 19, 20, 21, 22 is the invention of the storyteller to give some setting to the witticisms of Jesus preserved in vv. 20 and 22. In other words, the sayings were remembered and quoted again and again, although the precise setting in which they were first uttered had long since been forgotten.

Jesus stills the storm
Mt 8:23–27
Mk 4:35–41, Lk 8:22–25
Source: Mark

8 [23]**When he got into a boat, his disciples followed him.** [24]**And**
just then a great storm broke on the sea, so that the boat was
swamped by the waves; but he was asleep. [25]**And they came and**
woke him up, and said to him, "Master, save us! We are going to
drown!"

[26]**He says to them,** "Why are you so cowardly? You have so little trust!" **Then he got up and rebuked the winds and the sea, and there was a great calm.**

[27]**And everyone marveled, saying, "What kind of person is this, that even the winds and the sea obey him?"**

Jesus stills the storm. Matthew has of course borrowed the story of the stilling of the storm from Mark. Verse 18 was Matthew's introduction to the event, parallel to vv. 35–36 in Mark, but Matthew interrupted the story to introduce some dialogue on discipleship in vv. 19–22. This dialogue is derived from the Sayings Gospel Q. In v. 23 Matthew returns to the sea voyage.

In the judgment of numerous scholars, the storm story was inspired by the tale of Jonah (Jonah 1:1–16), who, fleeing from the presence of God, elected to put to sea. In both stories there is a departure by boat, a violent storm at sea, sailors who fear the ship will founder, and a protagonist asleep while the storm rages. Something the protagonist does causes the storm to cease, and the sailors around him marvel. Of course, in Jonah's case, the sailors throw him into the sea (at his own request) and he is swallowed by a whale. Here, Jesus merely rebukes the wind and the sea, and a calm descends (v. 26).

The story has parallels in Greek and Roman texts as well. In Virgil's *Aeneid,* Aeneas sleeps during a storm at sea (4.553–83). Mention was made in the commentary on Mark's version of the reputation of Apollonius of Tyana: people liked to ship out with him because he was thought to be a master of unruly seas. According to Iamblichus, a third-century C.E. writer, Pythagoras, a sixth-century B.C.E. philosopher and mathematician, was believed to have powers to calm seas and rivers so his companions might cross over safely. Like Jesus, Pythagoras' life quickly became the subject of legend and speculation, probably because he was thought to be endowed with spiritual powers and learning. The theme, it seems, was commonplace in the tales of ancient heroes. As a hero with special spiritual powers, Jesus is made to conform to that tradition. The Fellows of the Jesus Seminar regard the tale as a piece of pious fiction.

Demon of Gerasa
Mt 8:28–34
Mk 5:1–20, Lk 8:26–39
Source: Mark

8 [28]**And when he came to the other side, to the region of the**
Gadarenes, he was met by two demoniacs who came out from the
tombs. They were so hard to deal with that no one could pass along
that road. [29]**And just then they shouted, "What do you want with us,**
you son of God? Did you come here ahead of time to torment us?"
[30]**And a large herd of pigs was feeding off in the distance.** [31]**And the**
demons kept bargaining with him: "If you drive us out, send us into
the herd of pigs."
[32]**And he said to them,** "Get out <of him>!"
And they came out and went into the pigs, and suddenly all the
herd rushed down the bluff into the sea and drowned in the water.
[33]The herdsmen ran off, and went into town and reported every-
thing, especially about the demoniacs. [34]And what do you know, the
whole town came out to meet Jesus. And when they saw him, they
begged him to move on from their district.

Demon of Gerasa. Matthew has reduced Mark's version of the Gerasene demoniac from twenty verses to seven. Matthew apparently did not like some features of Mark's version of ritual exorcism—for example, the request for the name of the demon and the command to leave. Matthew has also changed Gerasa to Gadara, perhaps in the interests of locating the exorcism closer to the Sea of Galilee. However, Gadara is still some six miles from the shore. The demons no longer speak of "the son of the most high God," but call Jesus simply "son of God." Matthew's version ends with the negative response of the townspeople (v. 34), whereas in Mark Jesus commissions the former demoniac to spread the word of his miraculous cure. Furthermore, Matthew has increased the number of demoniacs to two, who apparently converse with Jesus in unison. Matthew may have increased the number to two in order the more readily to eliminate Mark's first exorcism story set in the Capernaum synagogue (Mark 1:21–28). Matthew has Jesus heal two blind men at once (9:27–31) and omits one of Mark's stories of the cure of a blind man (Mark 8:22–26). It appears that Matthew made use of a "compression" technique: he increases the number of patients to two in order to eliminate some stories.

The color-coding of Matthew's story left the Fellows without a recognizable core: The Fellows regarded the exchange between the demons and Jesus and the exit of the demons into the swine as implausible (vv. 29–32). Those verses were designated black. And the Fellows also took the narrative introduction (v. 28a) to be fictive. The remnants designated gray are too fragmentary to constitute an independent tale. Nevertheless, the color suggests that some distant event lies behind the tale in the version Matthew has extracted from the Gospel of Mark.

The paralytic
Mt 9:1–8
Mk 2:1–12, Lk 5:17–26
Source: Mark
Cf. Jn 5:1–9

9 After he got on board the boat, he crossed over and came to his
own town. 2The next thing you know, some people were bringing
him a paralytic lying on a bed. When Jesus noticed their trust, he
said to the paralytic, "Take courage, child, your sins are forgiven."
3At that some of the scholars said to themselves, "This fellow
blasphemes!"
4Because he understood the way they thought, Jesus said, "Why
do you harbor evil thoughts? 5Which is easier: to say, 'Your sins are
forgiven,' or to say, 'Get up and walk'?" 6But so that you may realize
that on earth the son of Adam has authority to forgive sins, he then
says to the paralytic, "Get up, pick up your bed and go home."
7And he got up and went to his home. 8When the crowds saw this,
they became fearful, and extolled God for giving such authority to
humans.

The paralytic. Matthew has borrowed the story of the paralytic from the Gospel of Mark, situated it in a different sequence of events, and abbreviated it. Matthew omits the picturesque account of the four friends lowering the paralytic through the roof of the house (Mark 2:4). He also omits Mark's description of the setting: a house in Capernaum with a throng gathered about the door. And he changes the mat to a bed, which should be thought of as a stretcher.

The Fellows decided not to attempt to isolate a core story in Matthew's revision of Mark, even though they identified a core in Mark's account and colored it pink. Their refusal to do so does not, however, signal a different conclusion about the event itself: they agreed that Jesus did cure a paralytic. Their reluctance stems from the difficulty in segregating primary from secondary material, especially in revised versions such as Matthew's, and in evaluating the historical value of editorial changes. They decided to color Matthew's contrived narrative introduction—the boat crossing—in v. 1 black, and put the rest of the story in gray. Gray indicates that there may be a historical trace in the story, but the details are unreliable.

Call of Matthew
Mt 9:9
Mk 2:13–14, Lk 5:27–28;
GEbi 2:4
Source: Mark

9 9As Jesus was walking along there, he caught sight of a man sitting at the toll booth, one named Matthew, and he says to him,
"Follow me!" And he got up and followed him.

Call of Matthew. Matthew borrows this brief account from Mark but changes the name of the toll collector from Levi son of Alphaeus to Matthew. Some Greek manuscripts of Mark read James the son of Alphaeus instead of Levi. Scribes making copies of the gospels attempted at various times to harmonize the reports they had before them—make them agree with each other—or to solve problems. In this case the scribes who substituted James the son of Alphaeus wanted to identify this follower with someone in the list of the twelve (Mark 3:18). The author of Matthew, however, decided to change the name to Matthew, which may be the reason his gospel came to be known as the Gospel of Matthew.

The Gospel of the Ebionites, which is quoted by the fourth-century writer Epiphanius, also preserves the name Matthew in a version of this story (GEbi 2):

> **[4]Then I summoned you, Matthew, while you were sitting at the toll booth, and you followed me.**

The Gospel of the Ebionites is very close to the Gospel of Matthew to judge by the few fragments quoted by Epiphanius. That may account for the identification of the toll collector as Matthew (rather than Levi, as in Mark). However, there are only eight names in the list of the "twelve" that appears in the Gospel of the Ebionites. The confusion about the name of this toll collector mounts when we compare this evidence with that provided by the Gospel of Peter: In 14:3 reference is made to Levi the son of Alphaeus, which is what the Gospel of Mark has. Variations of this type indicate how unstable such specific information as names often was. We cannot avoid the conclusion that we do not know the name of the toll collector in Jesus' circle of followers; there may, in fact, have been more than one. In addition, we are not certain that the story Mark and Matthew tell reports a specific incident; it may be a fiction that reflects the presence of one or more toll collectors in Jesus' retinue. Nevertheless, we are reasonably confident that there was at least one toll collector in Jesus' company because this piece of information appears in several different contexts in the gospels.

9

[10]And it so happened while he was dining in <Matthew's>
house that many toll collectors and sinners showed up just then and
dined with Jesus and his disciples.
[11]And whenever the Pharisees saw this, they would question
his disciples: "Why does your teacher eat with toll collectors and
sinners?"
[12]When Jesus overheard, he said, "Since when do the able-bodied
need a doctor? It's the sick who do. [13]Go and learn what this means,
'It's mercy I desire instead of sacrifice.' After all, I did not come to
enlist religious folks but sinners!"

Dining with sinners
Mt 9:10–13
Mk 2:15–17, Lk 5:29–32; GosFr 1224 5:1–2
Sources: Mark, Gospel Fragment 1224
Cf. Lk 15:1–2

Dining with sinners. In this fictive scene, Jesus is represented as sharing a table with those of dubious social reputations, who were called toll collectors and sinners. He may have been criticized by Pharisees in his own day in Galilee for this practice. Later, after Jesus' death, the disciples were under fire from Pharisees for the same practice. Earlier, Jesus had defended his practice with the witticism recorded in v. 12, which Matthew has expanded in his usual fashion with a quotation from the scriptures. The fictive elements in the scene are color-coded black. The role of the Pharisees is colored pink rather than red because their presence on every occasion is exaggerated. The features that almost certainly reflect historical circumstance are colored red: Jesus did eat with toll collectors and sinners; he was criticized for it by Pharisees; Jesus justifies his practice with an aphorism.

The fragmentary gospel known as Gospel Oxyrhynchus 1224 was discovered in 1903 and published in 1914. It consists of two small fragments; the handwriting can be dated to the late third or early fourth century C.E. This gospel also reports the tradition that Jesus ate with sinners (5:1–2):

> [1]**When the scholars and Pharisees and priests observed him, they were**
> **indignant because he reclined <at table> in the company of sinners.**
> [2]**But Jesus overhead them and said,** "Those who are well don't need a
> doctor."

The Fellows of the Jesus Seminar took the view that this fragmentary gospel is not dependent on the New Testament gospels, since it does not betray any of the literary DNA characteristic of those gospels. This is the only segment that contains narrative. The Fellows colored the first part of v. 1 gray simply because Jesus' critics are expanded to include all classes of leaders and is therefore an exaggeration. On the other hand, it was very likely the case that some Jewish leaders were critical of Jesus for failing to discriminate in selecting his dining partners; that produced a pink rating for the second half of the verse. Jesus' witticism in response to the criticism is brief and to the point; it appears to reflect a more primitive stage of the tradition than Matthew.

Question of fasting
Mt 9:14–17
Mk 2:18–22, Lk 5:33–39
Source: Mark

9 [14]**Then the disciples of John come up to him, and ask: "Why do**
we fast, and the Pharisees fast, but your disciples don't?"
[15]**And Jesus said to them,** "The groom's friends can't mourn as long
as the groom is around, can they? But the days will come when the
groom is taken away from them,and then they will fast. [16]Nobody puts
a piece of unshrunk cloth on an old garment, since the patch pulls
away from the garment and creates a worse tear. [17]Nor do they pour
young wine into old wineskins, otherwise the wineskins burst, the
wine gushes out, and the wineskins are destroyed. Instead, they put
young wine in new wineskins and both are preserved."

Question of fasting. Jesus had once been a disciple of John the Baptist, according to the gospels. During that time he may well have followed the practices of John and observed a restricted diet and fasted upon occasion. When he left John and returned to Galilee to begin his public ministry, Jesus evidently abandoned those practices and began to eat and drink in normal fashion. A saying preserved in the Sayings Gospel Q contrasts this new form of behavior on Jesus' part with that of John: John, it was said, ate no bread and drank no wine, as a consequence of which people thought him demented; Jesus, on the other hand, both ate and drank, so that people accused him of being a glutton and a drunk, a friend of toll collectors and sinners, with whom he was frequently seen eating and drinking. Since the two movements—that of the Baptist and that of Jesus—became rivals after Jesus' departure from the Jordan valley, it is plausible that the disciples of John would have asked Jesus and his followers why they didn't fast, especially when fasting was endorsed by the Pharisees.

The question in v. 14 should have embraced the practice of Jesus as well as that of his disciples. Because it concerns only the habits of the disciples, the Fellows decided to color it gray: as it stands it reflects conditions after Jesus' death. Nevertheless, Jesus must have been reproached for eating and drinking without regard to fast days, to which the aphorism in v. 15 seems a likely response.

9 [18]**Just as he was saying these things to them,** one of the officials
came, kept bowing down to him, and said, "My daughter has just
died. But come and put your hand on her and she will live." [19]**And
Jesus got up and followed him, along with his disciples.**

Jairus' daughter
Mt 9:18–19, 23–26
Mk 5:21–24a, 35–43,
Lk 8:40–42a, 49–56
Source: Mark

Jairus' daughter. Matthew follows Mark in sandwiching the story of the woman with vaginal bleeding between the two parts of the account of Jairus' daughter. The commentary on the entire Jairus episode will be found below following the second half of the text.

9 [20]And just then a woman who had suffered from vaginal bleed-
ing for twelve years came up from behind and touched the hem of
his cloak. [21]**She had been saying to herself, "If I only touch his cloak,
I'll be cured."** [22]When Jesus turned around and saw her, he said,
"Take courage, daughter, your trust has cured you." And the woman
was cured right then and there.

Woman with a vaginal hemorrhage
Mt 9:20–22
Mk 5:24b–34, Lk 8:42b–48
Source: Mark

Woman with a vaginal hemorrhage. Matthew has greatly abbreviated the story of the woman with a vaginal hemorrhage, as he did the story of Jairus' daughter in which it is embedded. He has thereby reduced the Markan elaboration to the bare minimum. Matthew does not repeat the remark about power being drained out of Jesus (Mark 5:30). And nothing is said about Jesus wanting to know who it was who touched him. Furthermore, the woman doesn't have to confess that it was she (Mark 5:35). Matthew has reduced the story to the primary structure of a healing story: the victim is introduced with some indication of the gravity of the affliction; a cure is effected; it is asserted that a cure has taken place. In this instance, the customary demonstration of the cure by the patient has been replaced by a simple announcement.

The Fellows agreed to designate the core story pink. Verse 21 is an explanatory aside that Matthew took over from his Markan source; the correct color for that remark is black.

Jairus' daughter
Mt 9:18–19, 23–26
Mk 5:21–24a, 35–43,
Lk 8:40–42a, 49–56
Source: Mark

9 [23]And when Jesus came into the home of the official and saw the mourners with their flutes, and the crowd making a disturbance, [24]he said, "Go away; you see, the girl hasn't died; she's sleeping." And they started laughing at him. [25]When the crowd had been thrown out, he came in and took her by the hand and raised the little girl up. [26]**And his reputation spread all around that region.**

Jairus' daughter. Matthew has followed Mark in weaving the stories of Jairus' daughter and the woman with the vaginal hemorrhage together. However, Matthew has again greatly abbreviated Mark's version of the Jairus tale (he also shortens his rewrite of the demoniac in Gadara, Matt 8:28–34). Matthew's edited version is shorter by two-thirds and is less picturesque than Mark's. Matthew has provided a different setting: Jesus has evidently been in a house, presumably in Capernaum, when the synagogue officials arrive (9:10); in Mark Jesus has just crossed the lake and disembarked from a boat. In Matthew, the girl is dead from the beginning of the story; in Mark she dies while the rescue party is en route. Matthew reduces the magical element by omitting the Aramaic formula, *"talitha koum,"* found in Mark 5:41. In Matthew, Jesus simply takes the little girl by the hand and raises her up. In Mark, the girl gets up and walks; her age is specified as twelve; the response of observers is recorded (they are ecstatic); Jesus gives strict orders that no one should learn of this miracle; and Jesus tells them to give her something to eat. Matthew's version exhibits a huge reduction of detail in the concluding scene of the story. It is probable that Matthew has edited the story back in the direction of the oral form, which probably contained fewer details.

The Fellows decided to color the core of the story gray, given the difficulties in untangling the oral form of the story from Mark's elaborate version and Matthew's revision. Matthew's editorial touches were designated black.

Two blind men
Mt 9:27–31
Source: Matthew
Cf. Mt 20:20–34,
Mk 10:46–52, Lk 18:35–43,
Jn 9:1–7

9 [27]**And when Jesus left there, two blind men followed him, crying out, "Have mercy on us, son of David."**

[28]**When <Jesus> arrived home, the blind men came to him. Jesus says to them,** "Do you trust that I can do this?"

They reply to him, "Yes, master."

[29]**Then he touched their eyes, saying,** "Your trust will be the measure of your cure."[30]**And their eyes were opened. Then Jesus scolded them, saying,** "See that no one finds out about it."[31]**But they went out and spread the news of him throughout that whole territory.**

Two blind men. This story is unique to Matthew. It is almost certainly a fiction created by Matthew in the judgment of many modern scholars. The model for it may well have been the account of the healing of blind Bartimaeus given in Mark 10:46–52 with its Matthean parallel 20:29–34. In the latter, Jesus cures *two* blind men; in Matthew's version of the demoniac of Gadara (8:28–34), there are *two* demoniacs; and Matthew has put *two* blind men into the present story. Matthew apparently likes to have pairs cured at once.

The motivation for including an array of miracle stories was provided, however, by the words ascribed to Jesus in Matt 11:5:

> The blind see again and the lame walk;
> lepers are cleansed and the deaf hear;
> the dead are raised,
> and the poor have the good news preached to them.

The blind, deaf, and lame are mentioned in Isa 35:5–6. The deaf and blind are referred to in Isa 29:18–19. Isa 26:19 is the source of the promise that the dead will be raised. Good news for the poor was inspired by Isa 61:1. While there is no direct prophetic promise for the lepers, the cure of Naaman the Syrian leper arranged by Elisha may have served as a model (2 Kgs 5:1–19). In agreement with the Seminar, John P. Meier considers this story a Matthean fiction.[43]

Man with mute demon
Mt 9:32–34
No parallels
Source: Matthew
Cf. Mt 12:22–24, Lk 11:14–15

9 [32]Just as they were leaving, they brought to him a mute who was demon-possessed. [33]And after the demon had been driven out, the mute started to speak. And the crowd was amazed and said, "Nothing like this has ever been seen in Israel."
[34]But the Pharisees would say, "He drives out demons in the name of the head demon."

Man with mute demon. This story was created by Matthew. This is the judgment of many modern commentators as well as the opinion of the Fellows of the Jesus Seminar. The evangelist has simply doubled the story of the cure of the dumb demoniac that appears later in his gospel, a story he had before him in the Sayings Gospel Q (12:22–24). In Q the cure was the event that led to the Beelzebul controversy, which begins with an accusation that Jesus casts out demons in the name and on the authority of the head demon Beelzebul. Here v. 34 betrays the source of this duplication. John P. Meier agrees with many scholars that this story is a creation of Matthew.[44]

Why does Matthew create cures attributed to Jesus?

The answer to that question depends on how one understands Matthew's narrative strategies. In the judgment of many commentators, Matthew has structured chapters 8–9 of his gospel to accommodate three sets (or triads) of three miracle stories, accompanied by other material. If one counts individual miracles (Jairus' daughter and the woman with the vaginal hemorrhage as two), the number comes to *ten,* which is the number of miracles Moses performed in Egypt (Exod 7–12). And by locating the sermon on the *mount,* Matthew also hints that Jesus is the new Mosaic lawgiver (Moses brought down the ten commandments from his visit to the sacred mountain in Sinai). In any case, Matthew likes symmetry, so he completes his cycles by duplicating stories or creating new ones.

The three triads are:

1. the cure of the leper (8:1–4)
   the centurion's servant (8:4–13)
   Peter's mother-in-law (8:14–15)
2. stilling the storm (8:23–27)
   the Gadarene demoniacs (8:28–34)
   the paralytic (9:1–8)
3. the ruler's daughter (9:18–26)
   two blind men (9:27–31)
   the mute demoniac (9:32–34)

Many scholars have concluded that the cure of the two blind men in the third triad is a duplicate of the cure of blind Bartimaeus (20:29–34). To complete the triad, Matthew also duplicated the exorcism of the mute demoniac he knew from the Sayings Gospel Q (12:22–24).

The exclamation of the crowd in v. 33 functions as the climax to the third triad, which portrays Jesus as a healer. And the remark of Jesus' critics in v. 34 prepares for the mission speech to follow in 10:1–15, which emphasizes the opposition his followers will face in their missionary travels. In these small ways Matthew provides continuity in his narrative.

Sheep without a shepherd
Mt 9:35–38
No parallels
Source: Matthew

9 [35]And Jesus went about all the towns and villages, teaching in
their synagogues and proclaiming the gospel of <Heaven's> imper-
ial rule and healing every disease and ailment. **[36]When he saw the
crowd, he was moved by them because they were in trouble and
helpless, like sheep without a shepherd. [37]Then he said to his disci-
ples,** "Although the crop is good, still there are few to harvest it. [38]So
beg the harvest boss to dispatch workers to the fields."

Sheep without a shepherd. The narrative summary of vv. 35–36 is the creation of Matthew. He is drawing on Mark 6:6, 34 for his information. Because the information given in v. 35 was designated red in Mark, the Fellows decided to award Matthew's secondary version a pink rating. Verse 36, however, was colored black to accord with its source, Mark 6:34.

Call of the twelve
Mt 10:1–4
Mk 3:13–19, Lk 6:12–16;
GEbi 2
Source: Mark
Cf. Acts 1:12–14, 15–26

10 **And summoning his twelve disciples he gave them author-
ity to drive out unclean spirits and to heal every disease and every
ailment. [2]The names of the twelve apostles were these: first, Simon,
also known as Rock, and Andrew his brother, and James the son of
Zebedee and John his brother, [3]Philip and Bartholomew, Thomas,
and Matthew the toll collector, James the son of Alphaeus, and
Thaddaeus, [4]Simon the Zealot, and Judas of Iscariot, the one who, in
the end, turned him in.**

Call of the twelve. In his version of the mission charge, Matthew has conflated Mark's appointment of the twelve (3:13–19) with Jesus' charge to the group (Matt 10:5–15), much of which he derived from the Sayings Gospel Q.

Matthew's list includes Simon, also known as "Rock," along with Andrew his brother. A second pair of brothers consists of James and John, sons of Zebedee. Both of these pairs are known from Mark's call stories (Mark 1:16–20). The next pair of names is Philip and Bartholomew. In the synoptic gospels Philip is only a name, but in the Gospel of John he plays a more prominent role (John 1:43–51, 6:5, 12:20–22, 14:8). Philip is present in the upper room after the ascension of Jesus, when Matthias is elected to replace Judas (Acts 1:12–14). Bartholomew is a mere name in the synoptics and is not mentioned by John; he does appear in the Acts list (1:13).

A fourth pair consists of Thomas and Matthew the toll collector. Thomas is traditionally credited with carrying Christianity to India. He is known only by name in the synoptics, but appears more frequently in the Fourth Gospel (11:16, 14:5, 20:24–29, 21:2). He is three times referred to as the twin (the name Thomas actually means twin), but it is unclear whose twin he is. In the Acts of Thomas, a third- or fourth-century C.E. Syrian work, he is the twin brother of Jesus. Matthew is called a toll collector here in the Gospel of Matthew; in Mark 2:14 it is Levi the toll collector that Jesus enlists as a follower. It is unknown whether the two are the same person with two names or different persons. The simple name Matthew appears in Mark's list of the twelve (Mark 3:18) as it does in Acts 1:13.

The gospels tell us virtually nothing about James the son of Alphaeus; however, he is to be distinguished from James the Just, the brother of Jesus. Thaddaeus, too, is a name without a face. He appears in Mark's list but is absent from Luke and Acts. In some Greek manuscripts the name is Lebbaeus. In place of Thaddaeus, Luke and Acts have Judas the son of James. A Judas appears in the Gospel of John in Jesus' farewell discourses and is distinguished from Judas Iscariot.

Matthew's list is rounded out with a sixth pair of names, Simon the "Cananean" and Judas Iscariot. Simon the "Cananean" also appears in Mark's list (3:18); in Luke and Acts he is called Simon the "Zealot."

Epiphanius quotes a gospel that he claims was used by the Ebionites, a Palestinian Jewish wing of the Jesus movement. He characterizes the edition he knew as adulterated and mutilated. This is the story found in that nameless gospel to which scholars have given the title, the Gospel of the Ebionites (2:1–5):

> [1]**There was this man named Jesus, who was about thirty years old, who chose us.** [2]**And when he came to Capernaum, he entered the house of Simon, who was nicknamed Peter. He then began to speak as follows:**
>
> [3]"As I was walking along by the lake of Tiberias, I chose John and James, sons of Zebedee, and Simon and Andrew and Thaddaeus and Simon the Zealot and Judas the Iscariot. [4]Then I summoned you, Matthew, while you were sitting at the toll booth, and you followed me. [5]Therefore, I want you to be twelve apostles, to symbolize Israel."

The curious thing about this list is that it contains only eight names, yet in v. 5 the group is said to constitute the twelve apostles, which is a symbol of the twelve tribes of Israel. Epiphanius is a fourth-century C.E. Christian writer, so he is reporting a tradition that had grown stronger symbolically but weaker historically.

The evidence indicates that it is difficult to establish a single list of the twelve. Even if that were possible, very little is known about several of the names in the group. Matthew's list, like the one in Mark on which Matthew is drawing, is traditional and probably reflects a later idealization of the circle around Jesus. The list preserved in the Gospel of the Ebionites is probably dependent on earlier lists and of no independent historical value. The absence of reliable information allowed later imaginations to speculate freely about the composition of the inner circle of Jesus' disciples.

Mission of the twelve
Mt 10:5–15
Mk 6:7–13, Lk 9:1–6; 10:1–16
Sources: Mark, Q

10 [5]**Jesus sent out these twelve after he had given them these
instructions:** "Don't travel foreign roads and don't enter a Samaritan
town, [6]but go rather to the lost sheep of the house of Israel.
[7]"Go and announce: 'Heaven's imperial rule is closing in.'
[8]"Heal the sick, raise the dead, cleanse the lepers, drive out demons.
You have received freely, so freely give. [9]Don't get gold or silver or
copper coins for spending money, [10]don't take a knapsack for the road,
or two shirts, or sandals, or a staff; for 'the worker deserves to be fed.'
[11]"Whichever town or village you enter, find out who is deserving;
stay there until you leave. [12]When you enter a house, greet it. [13]And if
the house is deserving, give it your peace blessing, but if it is unwor-
thy, withdraw your peace blessing. [14]And if anyone does not welcome
you, or listen to your words, as you are going out of that house or
town shake the dust off your feet. [15]I swear to you, the land of Sodom
and Gomorrah will be better off on judgment day than that town."

Mission of the twelve. In Matthew's gospel, the beginning of the charge to the twelve is to be found in 10:1: "And summoning his twelve disciples he gave them authority to drive out unclean spirits and to heal every disease and every ailment." Matthew then lists the twelve. (For an analysis of the list, consult the commentary on Matt 10:1–4.) Now Matthew turns to their instructions. Most of the instructions given in this passage were colored black or gray in *The Five Gospels*.

Since the instructions reflect conditions in the later Jesus movement, the introduction to them in v. 5 can scarcely represent a specific historic event. The only remaining question is whether Jesus ever dispatched his followers on missionary journeys. About ninety-five percent of the Fellows considered it just possible that Jesus did invite his followers to imitate him in his role as itinerant sage, and so voted gray. There were no red or pink votes. At the same time, the Seminar was virtually unanimous in its judgment that Jesus did not appoint "twelve" as his special envoys.

10 16"Look, I'm sending you out like sheep to a pack of wolves. Therefore you must be as sly as a snake and as simple as a dove. 17And beware of people, for they will turn you over to the Council and in the synagogues they will scourge you. 18And you will be hauled up before governors and even kings on my account so you can make your case to them and to the nations. 19And when they lock you up, don't worry about how you should speak or what you should say. It will occur to you at that moment what to say. 20For it is not you who are speaking but your Father's spirit speaking through you. 21One brother will turn in another to be put to death, and a father his child, and children will turn against their parents and kill them. 22And you will be universally hated because of me. But those who hold out to the end will be saved. 23When they persecute you in this town, flee to another. I swear to you, you certainly won't have exhausted the towns of Israel before the son of Adam comes.

24"Students are not above their teachers, nor slaves above their masters. 25It is appropriate for students to be like their teachers and slaves to be like their masters. If they have dubbed the master of the house 'Beelzebul,' aren't they even more likely to malign the members of his household?

26"So don't be afraid of them. After all, there is nothing veiled that won't be unveiled, or hidden that won't be made known. 27What I say to you in darkness, say in the light, and what you hear whispered in your ear, announce from the rooftops.

28"Don't fear those who kill the body but cannot kill the soul; instead, you ought to fear the one who can destroy both the soul and the body in Gehenna. 29What do sparrows cost? A penny apiece? Yet not one of them will fall to the earth without the consent of your Father. 30As for you, even the hairs on your head have all been counted. 31So, don't be so timid: you're worth more than a flock of sparrows. 32Everyone who acknowledges me in public, I too will acknowledge before my Father in the heavens. 33But the one who disowns me in public, I too will disown before my Father in the heavens.

34"Don't get the idea that I came to bring peace on earth. I did not come to bring peace but a sword. 35After all, I have come

> to pit a man against his father,
> a daughter against her mother,
> and a daughter-in-law against her mother-in-law.
> 36Your enemies live under your own roof.

37"If you love your father and mother more than me, you're not worthy of me, and if you love your son or daughter more than me, you're not worthy of me. 38Unless you take your cross and come along with me, you're not worthy of me. 39By finding your life, you'll lose it, and by losing your life for my sake, you'll find it.

[40]"The one who accepts you accepts me, and the one who accepts me accepts the one who sent me. [41]The one who accepts a prophet as a prophet will be treated like a prophet; and the one who accepts a virtuous person as a virtuous person will be treated like a virtuous person. [42]And whoever gives so much as a cup of cool water to one of these little ones, because the little one is a follower of mine, I swear to you, such a person certainly won't go unrewarded."

Narrative transition
Mt 11:1
No parallels
Source: Matthew

11 **And so when Jesus had finished instructing his twelve disciples, he moved on from there to teach and proclaim in their towns.**

Narrative transition. This is the second of Matthew's standard narrative transitions that divides the body of his gospel into five major sections or "books." The other transitions are 7:28–29, 13:54, 19:1, and 26:1. Since these are Matthew's arbitrary markers, they are all designated black.

John's inquiry
Mt 11:2–6
Lk 7:18–23
Source: Q

11 **[2]While John was in prison he heard about what the Anointed had been doing and he sent his disciples [3]to ask, "Are you the one who is to come or are we to wait for another?"**

[4]And so Jesus answered them, "Go report to John what you have heard and seen:

[5]The blind see again and
the lame walk;
lepers are cleansed and the deaf hear;
the dead are raised,
and the poor have the good news preached to them.
[6]Congratulations to those who don't take offense at me."

Praise of John
Mt 11:7–11
Lk 7:24–28
Source: Q
Cf. Th 78:1–3; Th 46:1–2

[7]After <John's disciples> had departed, Jesus began to talk about John to the crowds: "What did you go out to the wilderness to gawk at? A reed shaking in the wind? [8]What did you really go out to see? A man dressed in fancy <clothes>? But wait! Those who wear fancy <clothes> are found in regal quarters. [9]Come on, what did you go out to see? A prophet? Yes, that's what you went out to see, yet someone more than a prophet.

[10]"This is the one about whom it was written:

Here is my messenger,
whom I send on ahead of you
to prepare your way before you.

[11]"I swear to you, among those born of women no one has arisen who is greater than John the Baptist; yet the least in Heaven's domain is greater than he."

John's inquiry. The color-coded text and commentary are to be found in the Sayings Gospel Q, Luke 7:18–23//Matt 11:2–6 (pp. 41–50).

Praise of John. This segment is likewise derived from the Sayings Gospel Q. The color-coded text and accompanying commentary will be found in the Q gospel, the first section of this volume (pp. 41–50).

11 12"From the time of John the Baptist until now Heaven's impe-
rial rule has been breaking in violently, and violent men are attempt-
ing to gain it by force. 13You see, the Prophets and even the Law pre-
dicted everything that was to happen up to John's time. 14And if you
are willing to admit it, John is the Elijah who was to come. 15Anyone
here with two ears had better listen!

16"What does this generation remind me of? It is like children sitting
in marketplaces who call out to others:

> 17We played the flute for you,
> but you wouldn't dance;
> we sang a dirge
> but you wouldn't mourn.

18Just remember, John appeared on the scene neither eating nor drink-
ing, and they say, 'He is demented.' 19The son of Adam appeared on
the scene both eating and drinking, and they say, 'There's a glutton
and a drunk, a crony of toll collectors and sinners!' Indeed, wisdom is
vindicated by her deeds."

Damn you, Chorazin!
Mt 11:20–24
Lk 10:13–15
Source: Q

20**Then he began to insult the towns where he had performed most
of his miracles, because they had not changed their ways:** 21"Damn
you, Chorazin! Damn you, Bethsaida! If the miracles done in you had
been done in Tyre and Sidon, they would have <sat> in sackcloth and
ashes and changed their ways long ago. 22So I tell you, Tyre and Sidon
will be better off on judgment day than you. 23And you, Capernaum,
you don't think you'll be exalted to heaven, do you? No, you'll go to
Hell. Because if the miracles done among you had been done in
Sodom, Sodom would still be around. 24So I tell you, the land of
Sodom will be better off on judgment day than you."

Damn you, Chorazin! The invectives recorded in vv. 21–24 are derived from Q and probably originated with the failure of the Christian mission to the towns mentioned—Chorazin, Bethsaida, and Capernaum. The curses were given a black rating in *The Five Gospels* because they do not reflect the disposition of Jesus. Matthew has provided them with a fictional narrative frame, which also deserves to be colored black.

Wise & untutored
Mt 11:25–30
Lk 10:21–22
Source: Q

11 25**At that point, Jesus responded:** "I praise you, Father, Lord of
heaven and earth, because you have hidden these things from the wise
and the learned but revealed them to the untutored; 26yes indeed,
Father, because this is the way you want it. 27My Father has turned

everything over to me. No one knows the son except the Father, nor
does anyone know the Father except the son—and anyone to whom
the son wishes to reveal him. 28All you who labor and are overbur-
dened come to me, and I will refresh you. 29Take my yoke upon you
and learn from me, because I am meek and modest and your lives will
find repose. 30For my yoke is comfortable and my load is light."

Wise & untutored. This compendium of sayings has been taken from the Sayings Gospel Q. Matthew has provided the briefest of narrative suggestion in v. 25, which may also have come from Q; in its present narrative context, it makes very little sense. Black is the appropriate color.

Sabbath observance
Mt 12:1–8
Mk 2:23–28, Lk 6:1–5
Source: Mark

12 **On that occasion Jesus walked through the grainfields on
the sabbath day. His disciples were hungry and began to strip heads
of grain and chew them. 2When the Pharisees saw this, they said to
him, "See here, your disciples are doing what's not permitted on the
sabbath day."**

3He said to them, "Haven't you read what David did when he and
his companions were hungry? 4He went into the house of God, and ate
the consecrated bread, which no one is permitted to eat—not even
David or his companions—except the priests alone! 5Or haven't you
read in the Law that during the sabbath day the priests violate the sab-
bath in the temple and are held blameless? 6Yet I say to you, someone
greater than the temple is here. 7And if you had known what this
means, 'It's mercy I desire instead of sacrifice,' you would not have
condemned those who are blameless. 8Remember, the son of Adam
lords it over the sabbath day."

Sabbath observance. In his customary fashion, Matthew has edited a story he took from the Gospel of Mark. The principal change he made was to turn typical activities of Jesus, his disciples, and the Pharisees into a specific scene by linking the harvesting of grain immediately to the objection of the Pharisees. In other words, Matthew has placed Pharisees in the grainfield—an unlikely place for them to be on a sabbath—where they challenged Jesus and his disciples. That is an implausible juxtaposition of personnel, and has prompted many scholars to conclude that the entire scene was a Christian construction.

Matthew's source, the Markan version of the story, does not make this mistake. As Mark has it, Jesus and his disciples made sabbath journeys since they were itinerants; and they made use of whatever food was at hand to satisfy their hunger because Jesus had taught them to depend on the providence of God. These practices were generally known and the Pharisees criticized Jesus for the behavior of his followers. Jesus responded to this criticism in his typical way—with an aphorism.

Matthew has preserved Mark's story for the most part. However, because Matthew creates a scene with Jesus and the Pharisees in a grainfield, the

Fellows decided to color v. 2 gray to indicate that some details are not historically correct. They colored v. 1 pink to match their decisions about the corresponding verse in Mark.

In *The Five Gospels* the Seminar had already determined that vv. 3–4 were a Christian interpolation developed after the death of Jesus to bolster the Christian argument by quoting scriptural precedent. And v. 5 preserves what is left of the two-line aphorism Jesus employed in his original response to the Pharisees (to be found in Mark 2:27–28).

Man with crippled hand
Mt 12:9–14
Mk 3:1–6, Lk 6:6–11
Source: Mark
Cf. GNaz 4

12 [9]**And when he had moved on, he went into their synagogue.**
[10]**Just then a fellow with a crippled hand appeared, and they asked**
him, "Is it permitted to heal on the sabbath day?" so they could dis-
credit him.

[11]**He asked them,** "If you had only a single sheep, and it fell into a
ditch on the sabbath day, wouldn't you grab it and pull it out? [12]A per-
son is worth considerably more than a sheep. So, it is permitted to do
good on the sabbath day!"

[13]**Then he says to the fellow,** "Hold out your hand!"**He held it out**
and it was restored to health like the other.

[14]**The Pharisees went out and hatched a plot against him to get rid**
of him.

Man with crippled hand. Matthew has followed Mark in including the story of the man with a crippled hand in his gospel. In fact, Matthew is here reproducing the middle panel of a triptych he has borrowed from Mark: the controversy over harvesting grain on the sabbath (Mark 2:23–28); the man with the withered hand (Mark 3:1–6); and a summary of Jesus' activities (Mark 3:7–12). Matthew reproduces the series in 12:1–8, 9–14, and 15–21.

Verses 9–10 and 12b–14 are based on the story Matthew found in Mark. Matthew has inserted the saying in v. 11 into Mark's story; he may have known it from oral tradition or he may have found it in the Sayings Gospel Q (a similar saying is found in Luke 14:5). Finally, v. 12a is his own addition.

Unlike Mark, Matthew has Jesus' critics take the initiative in raising the controversial question: "Is it permitted to heal on the sabbath day?" In Mark Jesus takes the initiative throughout. Matthew frames Jesus' response with the counterquestion about rescuing a sheep that has fallen into a ditch on the sabbath. He then argues from the lesser to the greater: If you would do as much for your sheep, you should be willing to do as much for a person who is worth more than a sheep. Then Matthew has Jesus draw the obvious conclusion: "So, it's permitted to do good on the sabbath," a conclusion to which even relatively strict Pharisees would have consented. Jesus thereby justifies his action in advance and is not in violation of the sabbath. In other respects Matthew has followed the text of Mark.

The Fellows gave a gray rating to Mark's version even though they regarded it as largely a fiction. Because Matthew had revised Mark's story and added further fictional elements, the rating of Matthew dropped to the line between gray and black. A weighted average falling on the dividing line is relegated to the lower rank.

According to the Gospel of the Nazoreans as quoted by the fourth-century C.E. scholar Jerome, the man with the crippled hand appeals to Jesus and explains who he is (GNaz 4):

> **"I was a stonemason making a living with my hands. I plead with you, Jesus, give me back my health so that I won't have to beg for my food in shame."**

If some incident involving a person with a crippled hand lies in the distant background of the story recorded by Mark and copied by Matthew and Luke, then this embellishment in the Gospel of the Nazoreans has some remote claim to historical veracity. But since the Markan version is probably fictional, this seems to be a further fictional particularization, illustrating once again how these stories took on a life of their own in the oral tradition.

Jesus heals the crowds
Mt 12:15–21
Mk 3:7–12, Lk 6:17–19
Source: Mark

12 [15]**Aware of this, Jesus withdrew from there, and huge crowds**
followed him, and he healed all of them. [16]**And he warned them not**
to disclose his identity, [17]**so what was spoken through Isaiah the**
prophet would come true:

[18]Here is my servant whom I have selected,
my favored of whom I fully approve.
I will put my spirit upon him,
and he will announce judgment for foreigners.
[19]He will not be contentious,
nor loud-mouthed,
nor will anyone hear his voice on main street.
[20]He is not about to break a crushed reed,
and he's not one to snuff out a smoldering wick,
until he brings forth a decisive victory,
[21]and foreigners will center their hope on him.

Jesus heals the crowds. This summary, inspired by the parallel passage in Mark and patterned on Matthew's earlier summary in 8:16–17, contains no reliable historical information about Jesus' public acts beyond what we learn from other discrete accounts of particular deeds. In addition, Matthew has expanded the summary with a quotation from scripture to confirm the contours of the picture he is painting. The appropriate color is therefore black.

Blind mute
Mt 12:22–32
Lk 11:14–23
Source: Q

12 [22]**Then they brought to him a blind and mute person who**
was demon-possessed, and he cured him so the mute was able both
to speak and to see. [23]**And the entire crowd was beside itself and**
would say, "This fellow can't be the son of David, can he?"

[24]**But when the Pharisees heard of it, they said, "This fellow drives out demons only in the name of Beelzebul, the head demon."**

[25]**But he knew how they thought, and said to them:** "Every government divided against itself is devastated, and every town or household divided against itself won't survive. [26]So if Satan drives out Satan, he is divided against himself. In that case, how will his domain endure?

[27]"Even if I drive out demons in Beelzebul's name, in whose name do your own people drive <them> out? In that case, they will be your judges. [28]But if by God's spirit I drive out demons, then for you God's imperial rule has arrived.

[29]"Or how can someone enter a powerful man's house and steal his belongings, unless he first ties him up? Only then does he loot his house.

[30]"The one who isn't with me is against me, and the one who doesn't gather with me scatters. [31]That's why I tell you: Every offense and blasphemy will be forgiven humankind, but the blasphemy of the spirit won't be forgiven. [32]And the one who speaks a word against the son of Adam will be forgiven; but the one who speaks a word against the holy spirit won't be forgiven, either in this age or in the one to come."

Blind mute. This is another segment Matthew and Luke have taken from the Sayings Gospel Q. The text with appropriate color-coding and commentary is to be found in the Q section of this volume (pp. 41–50).

12 [33]"If you make the tree choice, its fruit will be choice; if you make the tree rotten, its fruit will be rotten. After all, the tree is known by its fruit. [34]You spawn of Satan, how can your speech be good when you are corrupt? As you know, the mouth gives voice to what the heart is full of. [35]The good person produces good things out of a fund of good; and the evil person produces evil things out of a fund of evil. [36]Let me tell you: On judgment day people will have to account for every thoughtless word they utter. [37]Your own words will vindicate you, and your own words will condemn you."

Demand for a sign
Mt 12:38–40
Lk 11:29–30; Mk 8:11–13, Mt 16:1–4
Sources: Q, Mark
Cf. Jn 2:18, 6:30

[38]**Then some of the scholars and Pharisees responded to him, "Teacher, we would like to see a sign from you."**

[39]**In response he said to them,** "An evil and immoral generation insists on a sign, and no sign will be given it, except the sign of Jonah the prophet. [40]You see, just as 'Jonah was in the belly of a sea monster for three days and three nights,' so the son of Adam will be in the bowels of the earth for three days and three nights."

Demand for a sign. In this passage derived from Q, some scholars and Pharisees request a sign from Jesus, not just to know when the kingdom might come, but also to check Jesus' credentials. Jesus apparently rejected such requests, even insisting that the kingdom is already present although not observable by the everyday eye (Luke 17:20–21//Thom 113:1–4). In this passage, he connects the desire for a sign to an evil and immoral generation, a connection the Seminar believes does not represent Jesus' outlook but that of a subsequent generation of Christian folk. The only sign permitted for these later interpreters was the sign of Jonah, which is here explained as Jesus' descent into Hades for three days and nights—actually parts of three days and nights—between his death and resurrection. The Fellows were inclined to think that the demand for a sign originated with the crowds around Jesus and not specifically with the Pharisees and Pharisaic scholars, although they allowed for the latter as a possibility. For that reason the narrative introduction in v. 38 was designated gray rather than black.

12 [41]"At judgment time, the citizens of Nineveh will come back to life along with this generation and condemn it, because they had a change of heart in response to Jonah's message. Yet take note: what is right here is greater than Jonah.

[42]"At judgment time, the queen of the south will be brought back to life along with this generation, and she will condemn it, because she came from the ends of the earth to listen to Solomon's wisdom. Yet take note: what is right here is greater than Solomon.

[43]"When an unclean spirit leaves a person, it wanders through waterless places in search of a resting place. When it doesn't find one, [44]it then says, 'I will return to the home I left.' It then returns and finds it empty, swept, and refurbished. [45]Next, it goes out and brings back with it seven other spirits more vile than itself, who enter and settle in there. So that person ends up worse off than when he or she started. That's how it will be for this perverse generation."

True relatives
Mt 12:46–50
Mk 3:31–35, Lk 8:19–21; Th 99:1–3
Sources: Mark, Thomas

[46]**While he was still speaking to the crowds, his mother and brothers showed up outside; they had come to speak to him.** [47]**Someone said to him, "Look, your mother and your brothers are outside wanting to speak to you."**

[48]**In response he said to the one speaking to him,** "My mother and my brothers—who ever are they?" [49]**And he pointed to his disciples and said,** "Here are my mother and my brothers. [50]For whoever does the will of my Father in heaven, that's my brother and sister and mother."

True relatives. This story about true relatives is preceded in the Gospel of Mark with this introduction (3:20–21):

> [20]**Then he goes home, and once again a crowd gathers, so they could not even grab a bite to eat.** [21]**When his relatives heard about it, they came to get him. (You see, they thought he was out of his mind.)**

The Seminar voted the Markan introduction pink, while Matthew "voted" it black—not because it was not historical, but because he found it offensive. How could the mother who appears in his miraculous birth story (Matt

1:18–25) have thought her son demented? Matthew was also influenced by the arrangement he found in the Sayings Gospel Q. In Q the Beelzebul controversy was introduced by an exorcism (Matt 12:22–23//Luke 11:14) rather than by a notice that Jesus' family thought him mad. Matthew thus had the option of omitting Mark's introduction and employing the alternative provided by Q. But when he returned to his source, Mark, he found the segment in which Jesus' family actually came to get him and decided to incorporate it into his own gospel.

The Fellows decided to designate this story pink. The Fourth Gospel supports the rumor that some thought Jesus demon-possessed (John 8:48, 10:20) and the suggestion that his family did not believe in him (John 7:5). The fact that Matthew found the first distasteful undergirds the judgment that the early Christian community would not have invented such a rumor. And Matthew could understand the report that his mother and brothers were outside merely as the occasion for his remark about true relatives rather than as a reflection of Jesus' family's lack of faith. According to Matthew, Jesus' family had come only to speak to him (v. 46); in Mark they had come "looking for him" (Mark 3:32). In Matthew it is a matter of a family parley; in Mark the family has come to deprogram him.

In parables
Mt 13:1–53
Mk 4:1–34, Lk 8:4–18
Source: Mark

13

That same day, Jesus left the house and sat beside the sea.
2Huge crowds gathered around him, so he climbed into a boat and
sat down, while the entire crowd stood on the sea shore. 3He told
them many things in parables:

This sower went out to sow. 4While he was sowing, some seed
fell along the path, and the birds came and ate it up. 5Other seed
fell on rocky ground where there wasn't much soil, and it came
up right away because the soil had no depth. 6When the sun
came up it was scorched, and because it had no roots it withered.
7Still other seed fell among thorns, and the thorns came up and
choked them. 8Other seed fell on good earth and started producing fruit: one part had a yield of one hundred, another a yield of
sixty, and a third a yield of thirty.
9Anyone here with two ears had better listen!

10And his disciples came up and said to him, "Why do you
instruct them only in parables?"
11In response he said to them, "You have been given the privilege
of knowing the secrets of Heaven's imperial rule, but that privilege
has not been granted to anyone else. 12In fact, to those who have, more
will be given, and then some; and from those who don't have, even
what they do have will be taken away! 13That is why I tell them parables, because

When they look they don't really see
and when they listen they don't really hear or understand.

14Moreover, in them the prophecy of Isaiah comes true, the one which
says,

> You listen closely, yet you won't ever understand,
> and you look intently but won't ever see.
> 15For the mind of this people has grown dull,
> and their ears are hard of hearing,
> and they have shut their eyes,
> otherwise they might actually see with their eyes,
> and hear with their ears,
> and understand with their minds,
> and turn around
> and I would heal them.

16How privileged are your eyes because they see, and your ears
because they hear. 17I swear to you, many prophets and righteous ones
have longed to see what you see and didn't see it, and to hear what
you hear and didn't hear it.

18"You there, pay attention to the interpretation of the sower. 19When
anyone listens to the message of <Heaven's> imperial rule and does
not understand it, the evil one comes and steals away what was sown
in the heart: this is the one who is sown 'along the path.' 20The one who
is sown 'on rocky ground' is the one who listens to the message and
right away receives it happily. 21However, this one lacks its own 'root'
and so is short-lived. When distress or persecution comes because of
the message, such a person becomes easily shaken right away. 22And
the one sown 'into the thorns' is the one who listens to the message,
but the worries of the age and the seductiveness of wealth 'choke' the
message and it becomes 'fruitless.' 23The one who is sown 'on the good
earth' is the one who listens to the message and understands, who
really 'produces fruit and yields here a hundred, there sixty, and there
thirty.'"

24He spun out another parable for them:

> Heaven's imperial rule is like someone who sowed good seed in
> his field. 25And while everyone was asleep, his enemy came and
> scattered weed seed around in his wheat and stole away. 26And
> when the crop sprouted and produced heads, then the weeds
> also appeared. 27The owner's slaves came and asked him,
> "Master, didn't you sow good seed in your field? Then why are
> there weeds everywhere?" 28He replied to them, "Some enemy
> has done this." The slaves said to him, "Do you want us then to
> go and pull the weeds?" 29He replied, "No, otherwise you'll root
> out the wheat at the same time as you pull the weeds. 30Let them
> grow up together until the harvest, and at harvest time I'll say to
> the harvesters, 'Gather the weeds first and bind them in bundles
> to burn, but gather the wheat into my granary.'"

[31]He put another parable before them with these words:

Heaven's imperial rule is like a mustard seed that a man took
and sowed in his field. [32]Though it is the smallest of all seeds, yet,
when it has grown up, it is the largest of garden plants, and
becomes a tree, so that the birds of the sky come and roost in its
branches.

[33]He told them another parable:

Heaven's imperial rule is like leaven that a woman took and con-
cealed in fifty pounds of flour until it was all leavened.

[34]Jesus spoke all these things to the crowds in parables. And he
would not say anything to them except by way of parable, [35]so what
was spoken through the prophet would come true:

I will open my mouth in parables,
I will utter matters kept secret since the foundation of the world.

[36]Then he left the crowds and went into the house. His disciples
came to him with this request: "Explain the parable of the weeds in
the field to us."
[37]This was his response: "The one who 'sows the good seed' is the
son of Adam; [38]'the field' is the world; and 'the good seed' are those to
whom Heaven's domain belongs, but 'the weeds' represent progeny
of the evil one. [39]'The enemy' who sows <the weeds> is the devil, and
'the harvest' is the end of the present age; 'the harvesters' are the heav-
enly messengers. [40]Just as the weeds are gathered and destroyed by
fire—that's how it will be at the end of the age. [41]The son of Adam will
send his messengers and they will gather all the snares and the sub-
verters of the Law out of his domain [42]and throw them into the fiery
furnace. People in that place will weep and grind their teeth. [43]Then
those who are vindicated will be radiant like the sun in my Father's
domain. Anyone here with two ears had better listen!

[44]Heaven's imperial rule is like treasure hidden in a field:
when someone finds it, that person covers it up again, and out of
sheer joy goes and sells every last possession and buys that field.
[45]Again, Heaven's imperial rule is like some trader looking for
beautiful pearls. [46]When that merchant finds one priceless pearl,
he sells everything he owns and buys it.
[47]Once more: Heaven's imperial rule is like a net that is cast into
the sea and catches all kinds of fish. [48]When the net is full, they
haul it ashore. Then they sit down and collect the good fish into
baskets, but the worthless fish they throw away. [49]This is how the
present age will end. God's messengers will go out and separate
the evil from the righteous [50]and throw the evil into the fiery fur-
nace. People in that place will weep and grind their teeth.

51"Do you understand all these things?"
"Of course," they replied.
52**He said to them,** "That's why every scholar who is schooled in
Heaven's imperial rule is like some proprietor who produces from his
storeroom treasures old and new."
53**And so when Jesus had finished these parables, he moved on
from there.**

In parables. Matthew has reproduced a lengthy parables complex he found in the Gospel of Mark (4:1–34). It is possible that some of these parables had been linked already in the oral tradition. However, Matthew is dependent primarily on Mark, although he makes some minor adjustments in the complex.

Matthew particularizes Mark's setting by connecting the parables discourse with the preceding events: teaching in parables by the sea takes place on "that same day" (v. 1). In other respects he simply copies Mark (vv. 1–3). Because Matthew particularizes Jesus' customary activity, the designation was reduced from pink to gray.

The Fellows doubt that Jesus gave his disciples a private interpretation so that outsiders would not know what he was talking about. Verse 10, consequently, was colored black. Matthew had borrowed this idea from his source, Mark.

Verse 34a, on the other hand, represents Jesus as employing parables as his teaching instrument. The Fellows believe this statement is historically accurate, so they designated it pink. The balance of vv. 34–35 suggests that the parables contained secrets. It was not the intent of Jesus to shield his wisdom from the crowds, but to make it available to them. Matthew, following Mark, has perpetuated the idea that the meaning of the parables was for insiders only. Because this notion does not stem from Jesus, the Fellows labeled it black. Similarly, the request of the disciples in v. 36 to have Jesus explain the meaning of the parables to them privately contradicts what we otherwise know of Jesus' teaching habits. It, too, was given a black designation.

Verse 53 is a transitional narrative remark provided by Matthew to give his story some continuity. He creates such transitions after each of his major units of teaching material. It has no historical value.

No respect at home
Mt 13:54–58
Mk 6:1–6
Source: Mark
Cf. Lk 4:16–30

13 54**And he came to his hometown and resumed teaching them
in their synagogue, so they were astounded and said so: "What's the
source of this wisdom and these miracles? 55This is the carpenter's
son, isn't it? Isn't his mother called Mary? And aren't his brothers
James and Joseph and Simon and Judas? 56And aren't all his sisters
neighbors of ours? So where did he get all this?" 57And they were
resentful of him.** Jesus said to them, "No prophet goes without
respect, except on his home turf and at home!" 58**And he did not per-
form many miracles there because of their lack of trust.**

No respect at home. Matthew has borrowed this segment from Mark and revised it. Matthew has modified Mark's outright statement that Jesus was a carpenter; Jesus is now the son of a carpenter. Matthew may have found identifying Jesus as an artisan or woodworker was beneath the lofty titles now being bestowed upon him. But the shift may not be particularly significant: sons usually followed the trades of their fathers. Yet the change caused the Fellows to reduce the color to gray (Mark's statement was colored pink).

Matthew has also changed "Mary's son" to "his mother's name is Mary," which is significant: knowing the name of the mother was not shameful; being identified by one's mother probably meant that there was some question about one's paternity. In addition, the textual variant "Joses" in Mark has become "Joseph" in Matthew and the names of Judas and Simon are given in reverse order. Otherwise Matthew has simply copied Mark. The color is therefore pink as it is in Mark: the information provided is probably reliable.

Matthew has also copied Mark's notice that Jesus did not perform many miracles in Nazareth, but he then links Jesus' failure directly to the lack of faith on the part of Jesus' neighbors (v. 58). Matthew has here expanded on his source.

Herod beheads John
Mt 14:1–12
Mk 6:14–29, Lk 9:7–9
Source: Mark

14 On that occasion Herod the tetrarch heard the rumor about
Jesus [2]**and said to his servants, "This is John the Baptizer. He's been**
raised from the dead; that's why miraculous powers are at work in
him."

[3]Herod, remember, had arrested John, put him in chains, and
thrown him in prison, on account of Herodias, **his brother Philip's**
wife. [4]John, for his part, had said to him, "It is not right for you to
have her."

[5]And while <Herod> wanted to kill him, he was afraid of the
crowd because they regarded <John> as a prophet. [6]On Herod's
birthday, the daughter of Herodias danced for them and captivated
Herod, [7]so he swore an oath and promised to give her whatever she
asked.

[8]**Prompted by her mother, she said, "Give me the head of John the**
Baptizer right here on a platter."

[9]**The king was sad, but on account of his oath and his dinner**
guests, he ordered that it be done. [10]And he sent and had John
beheaded in prison. [11]**<John's> head was brought on a platter and**
presented to the girl, and she gave it to her mother. [12]**Then his disci-**
ples came and got his body and buried him. Then they went and
told Jesus.

Herod beheads John. Matthew has copied the story of John the Baptist's death from his source, Mark. In characteristic Matthean fashion, the evangelist tells the story in fewer words but retains its substance. The color-coding of the text thus follows that of Mark.

Because of the convergence of evidence provided by the Jewish historian Josephus and the gospels, the Fellows agreed on the major facts:

- **Herod Antipas had John arrested for having condemned his marriage to Herodias.**
- **John was popular with the people.**
- **Herod regarded John as a threat to his political control of the people.**
- **Herod had John beheaded at his fortress palace of Machaerus located in Perea, east of the Jordan River.**

Neither Mark nor Matthew identifies Machaerus as the place of execution. Josephus provides this bit of information. The Fellows thought it very probably accurate because of Machaerus' proximity to the place of John's baptizing activity in the Jordan valley.

The members of the Seminar were much less certain about other details in the story. Although they allowed for the possibility of Herodias' role in the execution, they dismissed as too novelistic the grotesque claim that John's head was served on a platter. Naturally, this image, although fictive, has captured the imagination of visual artists over the centuries.

The twelve report
Mt 14:13–14
Mk 6:30–34, Lk 9:10–11
Source: Mark

14 **[13]When Jesus got word of <John's death>, he sailed away
quietly to an isolated place. The crowds got wind of <his departure>
and followed him on foot from the towns. [14]When he stepped
ashore, he saw this huge crowd, took pity on them, and healed their
sick.**

The twelve report. The translation of v. 13 is uncertain: the words in pointed brackets have been supplied by the translators in order to make sense of the sentence. In both Mark and Matthew, the execution of John has just been reported, so the translators elected to understand what Jesus heard as the report of John's death. However, Matthew may have been editing what he found in the Gospel of Mark. According to Mark 6:30, the apostles regroup around Jesus and "report to him everything they had done and taught." Mark had narrated the mission of the twelve just prior to his account of John's execution. In contrast, Matthew had reported the mission of the twelve earlier in his chapter 10 (1–15). Since he could not very well follow Mark in reporting the return of the twelve, he may have taken Mark's remark about Jesus receiving the disciples' report and adapted it to his own narrative context. To mention so small a point seems incommensurate with the gravity often assigned to scripture, but scholars must make what they can of every detail in the text they have in front of them. In this case, they are attempting to account for Matthew's truncated remark in v. 13: "When Jesus got word of . . . ." What did Jesus hear? The report of the twelve when they returned (as in Mark, his source) or word of the execution of John the Baptist? In either case, Matthew's narrative transition is a shortened version of how Mark imagined the sequence of events, and accordingly was voted black.

Loaves & fish for 5,000
Mt 14:15–21
Mk 6:35–44, Lk 9:12–17;
Jn 6:1–15
Sources: Mark, John
Cf. Mk 8:1–9, Mt 15:32–39

14 **15 When it was evening the disciples approached him, and**
said, "This place is desolate and it's already late. Send the crowd
away so that they can go to the villages and buy food for them-
selves."
16 Jesus said to them, "They don't need to leave; give them some-
thing to eat yourselves!"
17 But they say to him, "We have nothing here except five loaves of
bread and two fish."
18 He said, "Bring them here to me." **19 And he told the crowd to sit**
down on the grass, and he took the five loaves and two fish, and
looking up to the sky he gave a blessing, and breaking it apart he
gave the bread to the disciples, and the disciples <gave it> to the
crowd.
20 And everybody had more than enough to eat. Then they picked
up twelve baskets full of leftovers. 21 The number of people who had
eaten came to about five thousand, not counting women and chil-
dren.

Loaves & fish for 5,000. Matthew has taken this story from Mark and, as was his custom, abbreviated it. He has also enhanced the parallels between this story and that of the last supper (Matt 26:20–29): in both accounts, it is evening, they sit down or recline, Jesus takes bread, says a blessing, breaks it, and gives it to his disciples.

Matthew undoubtedly also recognized the parallels to the miracle performed by Elisha recorded in 2 Kgs 4:42–44:

> 42 And a man came from Baithsarisa, and brought to the man of God, by way of first fruits, twenty barley loaves and fruit cakes, and told him, "Give it to the people and let them eat."
>
> 43 And his servant said, "How in the world can I set this before a hundred men?"
>
> He replied, "Give it to the people and let them eat. For the Lord says, 'they shall eat and have some left over.'"
>
> 44 And they ate and had some left over, just as the Lord had said.

The context of the Elisha story is that of a famine, which had left the company of prophets hungry (2 Kgs 4:38). So some food is brought—two kinds of food—and the amount is given in numbers (v. 42). Elisha commands them to give it to the people to eat. An objection is made to the amount of food in relation to the number to be fed (v. 43). The people eat and there is some left over (v. 44). Except for the famine, these are very close parallels to the story in Matthew and Mark.

Matthew undoubtedly also perceived some affinities with Moses, who fed the Israelites in the wilderness with manna "from heaven" (Exod 16:4–8).

Matthew has appended an interesting note at the conclusion of his version: the number came to five thousand men, "not counting women and children"

(v. 21). If Matthew is echoing some distant historical memory, the crowd was even larger than Mark stated and more diversified in age and gender than might have been expected in a public gathering (in that culture one expects public gatherings of any size to consist predominantly of males).

The Fellows of the Jesus Seminar are dubious that this story is a report of an actual event in the life of Jesus. They were agreed, however, that it may preserve some traces of Jesus' habit of eating openly with his followers and admirers, no matter what their rank or condition. Yet black is the only possible color for a story that poses as a historical report.

Departures
Mt 14:22–23
Mk 6:45–46
Source: Mark

14 [22]**And right away he made the disciples get in a boat and go ahead of him to the other side, while he dispersed the crowds.**
[23]**After he had dispersed the crowds, he went up to the mountain privately to pray. He remained there alone well into the evening.**

Departures. Matthew adopts the narrative transition Mark had created to link the feeding of the crowd in the wilderness with Jesus walking on the water. However, Matthew rightly omits Mark's reference to Bethsaida (Mark 6:45), which lies in a different direction from Gennesaret where they eventually come to shore (Matt 14:34). Matthew simply reproduces Mark with some editorial corrections and a few minor embellishments that emphasize Jesus' solitude, illustrating once again the freedom with which these authors treated their sources.

Walking on the water
Mt 14:24–33
Mk 6:47–52; Jn 6:16–21
Sources: Mark, John

14 [24]**By this time the boat was already some distance from land and was being pounded by waves because the wind was against them.** [25]**About three o'clock in the morning he came toward them walking on the sea.** [26]**But when the disciples saw him walking on the sea, they were terrified. "It's a ghost," they said, and cried out in fear.**

[27]**Right away Jesus spoke to them, saying,** "Take heart, it's me! Don't be afraid."

[28]**In response Peter said, "Master, if it's really you, order me to come across the water to you."**

[29]**He said,** "Come on."

And Peter got out of the boat and walked on the water and came toward Jesus. [30]**But with the strong wind in his face, he started to panic. And when he began to sink, he cried out, "Master, save me."**

[31]**Right away Jesus extended his hand and took hold of him and says to him,** "You have so little trust! Why did you hesitate?"[32]**And by the time they had climbed into the boat, the wind had died down.**

[33]**Then those in the boat paid homage to him, saying, "You really are God's son."**

Walking on the water. Matthew has taken over the story of Jesus walking on the water from Mark. But he has made two major changes in Mark's version. He has inserted an episode about Peter attempting to imitate Jesus; Peter fails because he lacks the requisite trust (vv. 28–31). The second change he makes is in the conclusion. Mark has the disciples "dumbfounded" as a result of the experience (Mark 6:51). Matthew refurbishes Mark's portrait of the disciples by having them declare in unison, "You really are God's son" (v. 33). Matthew thereby moves the story more in the direction of the conventional miracle story, in which the conclusion consists of testimony that a miracle has taken place.

Jesus' feat of walking on the water has its counterparts in other mythic lore. In Homer's *Odyssey* (5.44–46, 54), for example, the poet depicts the god Hermes' ability to glide over the sea:

> Right away he strapped onto his feet
> his beautiful sandals, immortal and golden,
> which were able to bear him quickly
> over the waters of the sea
> and over the limitless land
> like the blasts of the wind.
> . . . .
> Thus did Hermes ride on the myriad waves.

There is also the story of a disciple of the Buddha who wanted to visit his master one evening. When he came to the bank of the river Aciravati, he found the ferry boat missing. In deep meditation and trust, he stepped onto the water and walked as if on dry land to the middle of the river. Then he came out of his meditative mood, noticed the waves, became frightened, and began to sink. He forced himself to regain his concentration, resumed his meditation, and came safely to the opposite bank.

The disciple of the Buddha apparently encountered the same problem that Peter did when he attempted to imitate Jesus.

Matthew's revision of Mark's tale illustrates once again how freely the evangelists modified the stories they found in the gospel tradition. The three versions of the story vary in detail enough to warrant skepticism about the fidelity of the tradition to some hypothetical original version. However, the basic reason for coloring all three accounts black is that they are epiphany stories—manifestations of divine power that suspends the laws of nature.

14 **34Once they had crossed over they landed at Gennesaret.**
35And the local people recognized him and sent word into the whole
surrounding area and brought him all who were ill. 36And they
begged him just to let them touch the fringe of his cloak. And all
those who managed to touch <it> were cured!

Many sick are cured
Mt 14:34–36
Mk 6:53–56
Source: Mark

Many sick are cured. Matthew has borrowed the elements of this summary from Mark. He has greatly abbreviated Mark's account. Neither Mark nor

Matthew provides any additional reliable historical information about Jesus. The notice that Jesus healed throngs of people is not plausible in view of the relatively few individual stories of such cures.

Eating with defiled hands
Mt 15:1–9
Mk 7:1–13
Source: Mark

15 **Then the Pharisees and scholars from Jerusalem come to**
Jesus, and say, 2"Why do your disciples deviate from the traditions
of the elders? For instance, they don't wash their hands before they
eat bread."
3**In response he asked them,** "Why do you also break God's com-
mandment because of your tradition? 4You remember God said,
'Honor your father and mother' and 'Those who curse their father or
mother will surely die.' 5But you say, 'If people say to their father or
mother, "Whatever I might have spent to support you has been conse-
crated to God," 6they certainly should not honor their father or
mother.' So you end up invalidating God's word because of our tradi-
tion. 7You phonies, how accurately Isaiah depicted you when he said,

> 8This people honors me with their lips,
> but their heart strays far away from me.
> 9Their worship of me is empty,
> because they insist on teachings that are human regulations."

Eating with defiled hands. Matthew has substantially condensed the material he took from Mark. The basic charge against Jesus is that he and his disciples deviated from "the traditions of the elders," that is, from established purity regulations, in that they did not regularly wash their hands before eating. The Jesus Seminar concluded that this picture is, in general, probably valid historically. Jesus and his followers did not always observe purity codes; the Pharisees usually did. As a result the two groups occasionally clashed. As a consequence, the Fellows colored the narrative introduction pink.

The narrative framework, however, was designated gray. In *The Five Gospels*, the Fellows also colored Jesus' reply gray as vaguely appropriate to some hypothetical exchange with Pharisees.

Other stories were told about Jesus in conflict with the Pharisees over purity issues. One such story appears in a single page of an unidentified gospel discovered at the beginning of the twentieth century at Oxyrhynchus, Egypt, a site that has yielded numerous papyrus fragments of importance, including three Greek fragments of the Gospel of Thomas.

The fragment is distinctive in both size and material. It is made of vellum (animal skin) rather than papyrus and measures only 3.5 x 3 inches. The writing is confined to an area 2 inches square. The book was thus a miniature. Its size suggests that the fragment comes from a book that was used as an amulet by some early Christian. The style of handwriting is characteristic of the fourth century, but the text of the gospel was likely composed considerably earlier. Scholars know this gospel as Gospel Oxyrhynchus 840, but its popular name is the Miniature Gospel.

The text of the forty-five surviving lines on a single page reads (2:1–9):

> **And taking <the disciples> along, he led them into the inner sanctuary itself, and began walking about in the temple precinct.**
>
> **2This Pharisee, a leading priest, Levi by name, also entered, ran into them, and said to the Savior, "Who gave you permission to wander around in this inner sanctuary and lay eyes on these sacred vessels, when you have not performed your ritual bath, and your disciples have not even washed their feet? 3Yet in a defiled state you have invaded this sacred place, which is ritually clean. No one walks about in here, or dares lay eyes on these sacred vessels, unless they have bathed themselves and changed clothes."**
>
> **4And the Savior stood up immediately, with his disciples, and replied,** "Since you are here in the temple, I take it you are clean."
>
> **5He replies to <the Savior>, "I am clean. I bathed in the pool of David, you know, by descending into it by one set of steps and coming up out of it by another. 6I also changed to white and ritually clean clothes. Only then did I come here and lay eyes on these sacred vessels."**
>
> **7In response the Savior said to him:** "Damn the blind who won't see. You bathe in these stagnant waters where dogs and pigs wallow day and night. 8And you wash and scrub the outer layer of skin, just like prostitutes and dance-hall girls, who wash and scrub and perfume and paint themselves to entice men, while inwardly they are crawling with scorpions and filled with all sorts of corruption. 9But my disciples and I—you say we are unbathed—have bathed in lively, life-giving water that comes down from [. . .] But damn those [. . .]"

The purity issue in dispute in this fragment is reminiscent of the account preserved in Mark 7:1–13//Matt 15:1–9. However, instead of the Pharisees coming from Jerusalem to challenge Jesus in Galilee, Jesus here goes to Jerusalem and is confronted by a leading priest, named Levi, who is also a Pharisee; it is an unusual combination for a priest to be a Pharisee. Jesus and his disciples are challenged by Levi, who wants to know why they haven't taken their ritual baths and changed their clothes, or at least washed their feet. Jesus responds by asking the priest whether he is ritually clean. The priest's recitation of the prescribed rituals does not satisfy Jesus. He replies with a scathing denunciation of phony purity rites.

The exchange between Jesus and the priest (or Pharisee) seems quite contrived. The storyteller never actually uses the name Jesus, or even the designation "the Lord," but calls him "the Savior," which is typical of gnostic forms of Christianity. Pools like the one depicted in the Miniature Gospel have been excavated in the temple area, but no evidence exists for one called the Pool of David.

The sacred vessels referred to are probably objects employed by the priests in their rituals. They would have been stored in the temple itself and seen only by the priests. Jesus contrasts the ritual bathing practices in use in the temple area with Christian washing in "life-giving water," an echo of John 4:10–11.

The entire episode is filled with improbable features, including Jesus'

THE PURITY CODES

Purity is the condition of being free from physical, moral, or ritual contamination. The opposite of purity is defilement. Jesus lived in a social world where purity mattered; purity was a core social value. Purity and defilement structured Jesus' everyday world. Purity was therefore a political matter.

Purity codes were supposed to create a social world with clear boundaries. The inside of that world was holy; the world outside was defiled. Purity applied to places (the temple), times (the sabbath, the high holy days), things (food, corpses, bodily fluids, human waste), and certain forms of behavior (eating unclean food, touching a corpse, wearing a garment made of two kinds of material, planting two kinds of seed in the same field, having intercourse during menstruation, homosexual intercourse, and many others). Defilement meant that one was prevented temporarily from participation in the temple cult and from social contact with those who were ritually clean.

Defilement and cleansing

People could become defiled in many ways. Many forms of impurity were routine, easily dealt with, and not considered either reprehensible or sinful. Sexual intercourse, for example, because it involves the emission of semen, made men unclean; menstruation and childbirth made women unclean. In many cases, all that was required to become clean again was the passage of time, usually combined with ritual bathing. In other cases, sacrifice in the temple was also required.

Defilement was also associated with more or less permanent conditions. Some people were unclean because of a questionable ancestry, others because of birth defects or chronic physical conditions. In Jewish traditions first put into writing in the third and fourth centuries C.E., members of certain occupational groups were impure, and some of these distinctions seem to have gone back to the time of Jesus. The normal bodily processes of women seem to render them unclean more frequently than men.

There is reason to think that defilement was attached by association to the poor. Although one could be rich and ignore purity codes, purity seems to have been the ideology of the wealthy. Poverty itself was not defiling, of course. However, the routine observance of purity laws was difficult for peasants. Temple sacrifice was difficult or impossible for peasants living at a distance from Jerusalem. Recent archaeological evidence suggests that (ritual) bathing pools were common in the houses of the wealthy; peasants probably had little access to such pools.

The purity codes

The purity codes were formulated and promoted by the temple authorities, by the scribes, and by such groups as the Pharisees and Essenes.

In the social world of Jesus, purity was centered in the temple and temple elites. It was fundamental to temple theology, according to which the "holy of holies" in the temple was the dwelling place of God on earth, the place of greatest purity and the geographical center of purity. From it radiated outward concentric circles of decreasing degrees of purity. Moreover, the temple was the only place where sacrifices for certain kinds of sins and impurities could be offered. In an important sense, temple theology claimed for the temple a monopoly on access to God.

The temple was presided over by the high priest and chief priests. They were an economic elite as well. Together with their extended families and other aristocratic families who were frequently linked to them by marriage, they comprised one to two percent of the population, and to them flowed one half to two thirds of the agricultural production of peasants, extracted through taxes, tithes, and rent for land. The temple elites were thus not only the religious elites, but also the economic and political elites of the society.

Moreover, the elaboration of purity laws beyond what is found in the Pentateuch was done by scribes who were "retainers" of the temple elites. Central to this elaboration was a text from the purity code in the book of Leviticus: "You (Israel) shall be holy, for I the LORD your God am holy" (Lev 19:2). "Holy" was understood to mean separation from everything impure.

Purity was also central to the Pharisees and Essenes. The Pharisees were committed to extending priestly purity to the Jewish population in general. The Essenes were committed to observing even more rigorous standards of purity in their communal life; indeed, this commitment was primarily responsible for their virtual withdrawal from mainstream society. Both Pharisees and Essenes were scribal movements; their elaboration and extension of purity depended upon the exegesis of literate scribes. The emphasis on purity is not to be equated with Judaism as a whole, but was the result of reading the Jewish scriptures in a particular way. The purity society in which Jesus lived was the product of a scribal elaboration that saw and interpreted the Jewish tradition through the lens of purity. Purity was part of a religious ideology legitimating the social position of the temple elites.

Jesus on purity

When Jesus is heard to say (Mark 7:15), "What goes into you can't defile; what comes out of you can," he is subverting the purity code humorously. When he and his disciples eat with defiled hands (Mark 7:2), he is ignoring the code. When he and his disciples fail to observe the sabbath (Mark 2:23–28), he is infringing the rules. When he touches a bier (Luke 7:11–17) or a leper (Mark 1:40–45), he is violating purity. When he eats with toll collectors and sinners (Mark 2:15–17), he is demonstrating against the restrictions of the purity codes.

Those who protest purity restrictions either redefine the values inherent in the purity codes or reinterpret the basis for those values. Jesus appears to have employed both strategies. The saying about not what goes in but what comes out redefines what defilement means. He also reinterprets the Levitical holiness formula to mean,"Be compassionate as God is compassionate" (Luke 6:36).

The effect of Jesus' attitude toward and practice of purity was to subvert the dominant paradigm that was the special province of the elites in his society.

description of the ritual baths. Both the words of Jesus and the narrative setting were voted black as fictions.

Private interpretation
Mt 15:10–20
Mk 7:14–23
Source: Mark

15 [10]**And he summoned the crowd and said to them,** "Listen and try to understand. [11]What goes into your mouth doesn't defile you; what comes out of your mouth does."

[12]**The disciples came and said to him, "Don't you realize that the Pharisees who heard this remark were offended by it?"**

[13]**He responded:** "Every plant which my heavenly Father does not plant will be rooted out. [14]Never mind them. They are blind guides of blind people! If one blind person guides another, both will end up in some ditch."

[15]**Then Peter replied, "Explain the riddle to us."**

[16]**He said,** "Are you still as dim-witted as the rest? [17]Don't you realize that everything that goes into the mouth passes into the stomach and comes out in the outhouse? [18]But the things that come out of the mouth come from the heart, and those things defile a person. [19]For out of the heart emerge evil intentions: murders, adulteries, sexual immorality, thefts, false witnesses, blasphemies. [20]These are the things that defile a person. However, eating with unwashed hands doesn't defile anybody."

Private interpretation. Matthew has once again taken a passage from Mark and revised it. First of all, he has revised the words of Jesus. Mark reports Jesus as saying, "It's not what goes into a person from the outside that can defile; rather it's what comes out of the person that defiles" (Mark 7:14). Matthew has changed the words to match the interpretation in v. 18: It's what comes out of the mouth that defiles. Jesus had left open the question of which human orifice was involved, as v. 17 demonstrates.

Matthew has also introduced vv. 12–14 into this complex. This is an additional slam against the Pharisees, who by Matthew's time were locked in disputes with the leaders of the new Jesus movement.

Matthew has retained Mark's framework for the complex, however. That framework represents Jesus as using enigmatic expressions in his public teaching and then interpreting his dark sayings privately to insiders. That contradicts what the Seminar believes Jesus' practice actually was to teach always in aphorisms and parables to everyone, everywhere. Aside from the accurate generalization in v. 10, the narrative framework is fictive and misrepresents the historical Jesus. Black is the appropriate color.

Greek woman's daughter
Mt 15:21–28
Mk 7:24–30
Source: Mark

15 [21]**So Jesus left there, and withdrew to the district of Tyre and Sidon.**

[22]**And this Canaanite woman from those parts appeared and cried out, "Have mercy on me, sir, you son of David. My daughter is severely possessed."**

[23]**But he did not respond at all.**
And his disciples came and began to complain: "Get rid of her, because she is badgering us."
[24]**But in response he said,** "I was sent only to the lost sheep of the house of Israel."
[25]**She came and bowed down to him, saying, "Sir, please help me."**
[26]**In response he said,** "It's not right to take bread out of children's mouths and throw it to the dogs."
[27]**But she said, "Of course, sir, but even the dogs eat the scraps that fall from their master's table."**
[28]**Then in response Jesus said to her,** "My good woman, your trust is enormous! Your wish is as good as fulfilled." **And her daughter was cured at that moment.**

Greek woman's daughter. This story, like its Markan counterpart, consists of two parts. One part concerns the cure of the Canaanite woman's daughter (vv. 21–22, 28). The other involves the verbal exchange between the woman and Jesus (vv. 23–27).

The woman is a Greek in Mark's version, of Syrophoenician extraction (Mark 7:26); Matthew has altered the designation to "Canaanite," which suggests the ancient enemies of Israel who occupied the land prior to the settlement following the exodus. In either case, she is a gentile.

In comparison with his source, Mark, Matthew has expanded the dialogue section. First, he adds the complaint of Jesus' disciples about the persistence of the woman (vv. 23–24). In Jesus' response to the disciples, Matthew makes it clear that he does not regard Jesus' mission as extending beyond Israel (Tyre and Sidon, v. 21, are located in Phoenicia, modern-day Lebanon). If Mark's version is viewed as a justification for the church's mission to the gentiles, Matthew's revision would seem to be an effort to reinstate a narrower scope for Jesus' activity. Matthew also expands the woman's address to Jesus in v. 22 with a reference to Jesus as "son of David," presumably because David, like Solomon, was thought to have thaumaturgic powers—the power to perform wonders.

It is possible that this story was inspired by the account of Elijah's resuscitation of the widow of Zarephath's son (1 Kgs 17:17–24). The widow was a gentile, who lived in Sidon (the twin city of Tyre in Matt 15:21), and whose son, near death of some unspecified ailment, was miraculously healed. Moreover, in the tale (1 Kgs 17:8–16), Elijah asks the widow for a "morsel of bread," and suggests that it is important for him to be fed first; these same motifs appear in the exchange between Jesus and the woman. The second half of the Elijah story detailing the resuscitation of the widow's son (vv. 17–24) may have suggested the lineaments of the story about the Greek woman's daughter.

In the case of Mark's version, the Fellows on balance thought the story reflected a distant memory of an actual event, but were unable to identify precisely what that event was beyond the verbal battle between the woman and Jesus. Accordingly, they colored the story gray but allowed that it had a pink core. They followed suit in evaluating Matthew's version, except that they designated Matthew's additions black.

Jesus heals many
Mt 15:29–31
No parallels
Source: Matthew

15 **[29]Then Jesus left there and went to the sea of Galilee. And he
climbed up the mountain and sat there. [30]And huge crowds came to
him and brought with them the lame, the blind, the maimed, the
mute, and many others, and they crowded around his feet and he
healed them. [31]As a result, the crowd was astonished when they saw
the mute now speaking, the maimed made strong, and the lame
walking and the blind seeing. And they gave all the credit to the
God of Israel.**

Jesus heals many. Matthew has substituted this narrative summary for the story of the deaf-mute he found in his source, the Gospel of Mark. Matthew betrays his source, however, by having Jesus arrive at the sea of Galilee just as he does in Mark (7:31) and by having the crowd marvel at the mute who now speaks (v. 31), which is an oblique reference to Mark's story. Matthew omitted the account of the deaf mute because he evidently has an aversion to traces of magic, such as the use of spittle and the magical Aramaic word, "ephphatha" (Mark 7:33–34).

Verse 30 generalizes on scenes that must have been common during the public life of Jesus: surrounded by crowds, Jesus heals the sick (and casts out demons). It merits at least a gray rating.

In preparation for the feeding of the four thousand, Matthew has Jesus climb up a mountain and sit down (v. 29), just as he does in preparation for the great sermon (Matt 5:1). Matthew produces the four thousand by having huge crowds come with the lame, blind, maimed, and mute for Jesus to heal (vv. 30–31), but says nothing further about them in the story that follows. Matthew has constructed this narrative context out of his own imagination. Other than the typifications in v. 30, the rest is pure fiction and deserves a black rating.

Loaves & fish for 4,000
Mt 15:32–39
Mk 8:1–10
Source: Mark
Cf. Mk 6:35–44, Mt 14:15–21,
Lk 9:12–27, Jn 6:1–15

15 **[32]Then Jesus called his disciples aside and said:** "I feel sorry
for the crowd because they have already spent three days with me and
now they've run out of food. And I don't want to send these people
away hungry, for fear they'll collapse on the road."

**[33]And the disciples say to him, "How can we get enough bread
here in this desolate place to feed so many people?"**

[34]Jesus says to them, "How many loaves do you have?"

They replied, "Seven, plus a few fish."

[35]And he ordered the crowd to sit down on the ground.

**[36]And he took the seven loaves and the fish and gave thanks and
broke them into pieces, and started giving <them> to the disciples,
and the disciples <started giving them> to the crowds. [37]And every-**

**one had more than enough to eat. Then they picked up seven bas-
kets of leftover scraps. 38Those who had eaten numbered four thou-
sand, not counting women and children. 39And after he sent the
crowds away, he got into the boat and went to the Magadan region.**

Loaves & fish for 4,000. Matthew has followed Mark in relating a second feeding story that is parallel to one he had just told (14:15–22). Matthew has provided the second story with a different setting than had Mark (the story of the deaf-mute, 7:31–37, precedes the feeding in Mark, whereas in Matthew Jesus ascends a mountain and heals huge crowds, 15:29–31, just prior to the feeding). Matthew has modified the second feeding story slightly so that it agrees more closely with the first feeding than is the case in Mark. He has omitted a few minor details and made some slight improvements in style. These changes are hardly worthy of note. Matthew has in effect copied Mark.

The Fellows agreed that this report, like the other versions of the same story, is not the depiction of an actual event in the life of Jesus. So they designated it black also. However, they agreed that Jesus ate meals frequently with groups of people, some of whom were social outcasts and regarded as unclean. On these occasions Jesus induced his followers to share their food with each other in what one of the Fellows aptly described as a kind of egalitarian picnic. The meal customs of the ancient world dictated that different dishes be served to different social classes, with those higher up on the social scale naturally eating better than those lower down. In the gospel feeding stories, however, everyone gets the same simple but abundant fare. In the context of its time, this was a powerful message about what God's imperial rule was like.

The repetition of events of this sort eventually produces a ritual, in this case the eucharist. A ritual, on one definition, reenacts the crossing of social borders or boundaries. In this case, the common meal represented the collapse of the distinction between "toll collectors and sinners" and others—toll collectors and sinners being a semantic tag for those who had been socially marginalized. The reenactment of the common meal eventually led to the eucharist, in which the bread and wine came to symbolize the body and blood of Jesus. Somewhere along this trajectory the original function of the ritual was lost and the eucharist substituted. In its infancy the ritual was probably a common meal of bread and fish. Later it became a meal of bread and wine. Still later, the ritual was reduced to token amounts of bread and wine symbolizing the body and blood of the Christ.

16 **And the Pharisees and Sadducees came, and to put him to
the test they asked him to show them a sign in the sky.**
2**In response he said to them,** "When it's evening, you say, 'It'll be
fair weather because the sky looks red.' 3Early in the morning, <you
say, > 'The day will bring winter weather because the sky looks red
and dark.' You know how to read the face of the sky, but you can't dis-
cern the signs of the times. 4An evil and immoral generation seeks a

Demand for a sign
Mt 16:1–4
Mk 8:11–13; Mt 12:38–42,
Lk 11:29–30
Sources: Mark, Q
Cf. Jn 2:18, 6:30

sign, yet no sign will be given it except the sign of Jonah." **And he turned his back on them and walked away.**

Demand for a sign. The source for vv. 1, 4 is Mark 8:11–13. The words of Jesus in vv. 2–3 do not appear in some ancient manuscripts; they were probably inserted here by some scribe to make Jesus' reply square with Luke 12:54–56, a group of sayings derived from Q. Jesus' response in v. 4 has been modified from its Markan form. In Mark (8:12), Jesus' refusal is absolute: "I swear to God, no sign will be given this generation!" Here Matthew has provided for an exception: the sign of Jonah, which may refer to the preaching of Jonah to the city of Nineveh. Matthew's version was colored black in *The Five Gospels*.

The narrative framework in vv. 1–2 and 4 is not historical. It is dubious that an alliance between the Pharisees and Sadducees would ever have produced a common front against Jesus (v. 1), although it is possible that Jesus responded to a question about signs during his public life. In modifying Mark, Matthew moved away from history in the direction of fiction. Black is the result.

Bread & leaven
Mt 16:5–12
Mk 8:14–21, Lk 12:1
Source: Mark

16 [5]**And the disciples came to the opposite shore, but they forgot to bring any bread.** [6]**Jesus said to them,** "Look, take care and guard against the leaven of the Pharisees and Sadducees."

[7]**Now they looked quizzically at each other, saying, "We didn't bring any bread."**

[8]**Because Jesus was aware of this, he said,** "Why are you puzzled that you don't have any bread? You have so little trust! [9]You still aren't using your heads, are you? You don't remember the five loaves for the five thousand and how many baskets you carried away, do you? [10]Nor the seven loaves for four thousand and how many big baskets you filled? [11]How can you possibly think I was talking to you about bread? Just be on guard against the leaven of the Pharisees and Sadducees."

[12]**Then they understood that he was not talking about guarding against the leaven in bread but against the teaching of the Pharisees and Sadducees.**

Bread & leaven. Matthew has taken this complex over from Mark, as in so many other instances. He has abbreviated some of Mark's acerbic remarks about the denseness of the disciples and has shortened Mark's review of the two feeding stories, one of 5,000 in the wilderness, the other of 4,000. And he has provided a new conclusion in v. 11. Matthew wanted to make sure that the reader did not misunderstand: Jesus was not talking to them about bread; he intended "the leaven of the Pharisees" in some metaphorical sense.

Since the complex is Mark's invention, and since Matthew's information was limited to what he derived from Mark, black is the appropriate color for the narrative frame of the complex.

16 **13When Jesus came to the region of Caesarea Philippi, he started questioning his disciples, asking,** "What are people saying about the son of Adam?"

14They said, "Some <say, 'He is> John the Baptist,' but others, 'Elijah,' and others, 'Jeremiah or one of the prophets.'"

15He says to them, "What about you, who do you say I am?"

16And Simon Peter responded, "You are the Anointed, the son of the living God!"

17And in response Jesus said to him, "You are to be congratulated, Simon son of Jonah, because flesh and blood did not reveal this to you but my Father who is in heaven. 18Let me tell you, you are Peter, 'the Rock,' and on this very rock I will build my congregation, and the gates of Hades will not be able to overpower it. 19I shall give you the keys of Heaven's domain, and whatever you bind on earth will be considered bound in heaven, and whatever you release on earth will be considered released in heaven."

20Then he ordered the disciples to tell no one that he was the Anointed.

Peter's confession
Mt 16:13–20
Mk 8:27–30, Lk 9:18–22
Source: Mark

Peter's confession. Matthew has borrowed the basic story from Mark and then added vv. 17–19. The Seminar designated the words of Jesus black by common consent in *The Five Gospels.* The Markan framework was likewise voted black as the creation of the early Christian community.

There are other stories of this type, in addition to the Markan account and its synoptic parallels. The counterpart in the Gospel of Thomas (13:1–8) privileges Thomas above the other disciples: Jesus takes Thomas aside and speaks three sayings to him, which Thomas refuses to divulge to his friends, who include Simon Peter and Matthew.

> **Jesus said to his disciples,** "Compare me to something and tell me what I am like."
>
> **2Simon Peter said to him, "You are like a just angel."**
>
> **3Matthew said to him, "You are like a wise philosopher."**
>
> **4Thomas said to him, "Teacher, my mouth is utterly unable to say what you are like."**
>
> **5Jesus said,** "I am not your teacher. Because you have drunk, you have become intoxicated from the bubbling spring that I have tended."
>
> **6And he took him, and withdrew, and spoke three sayings to him.**
>
> **7When Thomas came back to his friends, they asked him, "What did Jesus say to you?"**
>
> **8Thomas said to them, "If I tell you one of the sayings he spoke to me, you will pick up rocks and stone me, and fire will come from the rocks and devour you."**

A similar story in the Fourth Gospel (1:35–42) portrays Andrew as the first to confess that Jesus is the messiah or Anointed. Nevertheless, in the Johannine story Jesus gives Simon the name Cephas, which in Aramaic means "Rock"; its Greek equivalent is Peter. The tradition giving Simon the nickname of Peter or "Rock" is likely to be quite old since it is reported in Mark 3:16 (with parallels in Matt 10:2, Luke 6:14), as well as here in 16:18; the apostle Paul refers to him as Cephas in his letter to the Galatians (1:18, 2:9, 11, 14), written two decades earlier than the Gospel of Mark. Furthermore, later on in the Fourth Gospel, Peter is credited with confessing that Jesus is "God's holy one" (6:66–68). Peter may well have been the first to confess that Jesus was the Anointed, most probably after the Easter event. But the stories that provide a narrative frame for that confession are the product, in all likelihood, of the Christian imagination. Accordingly, the narrative framework of this story is colored black.

Jesus predicts his death
Mt 16:21–23
Mk 8:31–33, Lk 9:22
Source: Mark
Cf. Mk 9:30–32, Mt 17:22–23, Lk 9:43b–45; Mk 10:32–34, Mt 20:17–19, Lk 18:31–34

16 [21]**From that time on Jesus started to make it clear to his disciples that he was destined to go to Jerusalem, and suffer a great deal at the hands of the elders and ranking priests and scholars, and be killed and, on the third day, be raised.**

[22]**And Peter took him aside and began to lecture him, saying, "May God spare you, master; this surely can't happen to you."**

[23]**But he turned and said to Peter,** "Get out of my sight, you Satan, you. You are dangerous to me because you are not thinking in God's terms, but in human terms."

Jesus predicts his death. The Fellows of the Jesus Seminar are of the opinion that Jesus did not have any special foreknowledge of his destiny. They agreed, of course, that as an astute sage, he might well have had some notion of the dangers to which he was exposing himself. But he was not a clairvoyant and certainly did not have the kind of detailed information about events shortly to transpire that is suggested by v. 21. The Seminar accordingly designated that verse black.

The predictions of the passion do not play the same role in Matthew and Luke that they do in Mark. Yet the death of Jesus soon came to be a central feature of the Christian gospel, as Paul makes clear in his first letter to the Corinthians (2:1–5 and 15:3–5, for example). So Matthew and Luke accepted Mark's view that the death of Jesus was inevitable and even anticipated by scripture. And they adopted Mark's view that the disciples did not at the time understand the role Jesus' death was to play in the gospel. That in itself is a clue to the time these predictions of the passion were formulated: long after Jesus' death. They are what is known as "predictions after the event."

The correct color is black.

Way of the cross
Mt 16:24–28
Mk 8:34–9:1, Lk 9:23–27
Source: Mark

16 [24]**Then Jesus said to his disciples,** "If any of you wants to come after me you should deny yourself, pick up your cross, and follow me!

[25]"Remember, by trying to save your own life, you are going to lose it, but by losing your own life for my sake, you are going to find it.

[26]After all, what good will it do if you acquire the whole world but forfeit your life? Or what will you give in exchange for your life?

[27]"Remember, the son of Adam is going to come in the glory of his Father with his messengers, and then he will reward everyone according to their deeds. [28]I swear to you: Some of those standing here won't ever taste death before they see the son of Adam's imperial rule arriving."

Way of the cross. Matthew has followed Mark in providing this sayings complex with an arbitrary narrative frame in v. 24. It tells us nothing about the actual setting of any of these sayings.

Transfiguration
Mt 17:1–8
Mk 9:2–8, Lk 9:28–36
Source: Mark

17 **Six days later, Jesus takes Peter and James and his brother John along and he leads them off by themselves to a lofty mountain. [2]He was transformed in front of them and his face shone like the sun, and his clothes turned as white as light. [3]The next thing you know, Moses and Elijah appeared to them and were conversing with Jesus.**

[4]Then Peter responded by saying to Jesus, "Master, it's a good thing we're here. If you want, I'll set up three tents here, one for you, one for Moses, and one for Elijah!"

[5]While he was still speaking, there was a bright cloud that cast a shadow over them. And just then a voice spoke from the cloud: "This is my favored son of whom I fully approve. Listen to him!"

[6]And as the disciples listened, they prostrated themselves, and were frightened out of their wits.

[7]And Jesus came and touched them and said: "Get up; don't be afraid." **[8]Looking up they saw no one except Jesus by himself.**

Transfiguration. Matthew has once again taken a story from Mark and modified it to suit his own designs.

Mark has Jesus conversing with Elijah and Moses; Matthew reverses that sequence in order to highlight Moses, which comports with his view of Jesus as the new Moses. Matthew has also carried over other features of Mark's account in order to link Jesus to Mount Sinai and Moses' encounter with God.

Moses takes three with him up the sacred mountain, Sinai (Exod 24:1), just as Jesus does in the transfiguration. Moses and Elijah have both talked with God on Sinai; in the transfiguration, a voice comes from heaven and confirms Jesus' status as God's son (v. 5). A cloud descends and overshadows Moses (Exod 24:15–18), just as it does Jesus (v. 5). Both Jesus and Moses become radiant (vv. 2–3; Exod 34:29–35). The transfiguration, like God's communication with Moses, takes place after six days (v. 1; Exod 24:16). Moses and Elijah were the only heroes of Israel who had talked with God (Deut 34:10; 2 Kgs 19:9–13); Jesus now joins their august company and even supersedes them, as the voice from the cloud indicates.

Matthew enhances the connection with the scene on Mount Sinai by adding that Jesus' "face shone like the sun" (v. 2), which is an allusion to Moses' face shining after he talked with God (Exod 34:29–35); Mark does not have this detail. Matthew also changes what the voice from heaven says: Mark has "This is my favored son" (Mark 9:7), while Matthew expands to match the words spoken at Jesus' baptism (Matt 3:17): "This is my favored son of whom I fully approve" (v. 5). Matthew is thereby adapting the voice to Isa 42:1: "Jacob my son, whom I will help; Israel my chosen, whom my soul approves." These are subtle changes, but they underscore the parallelism between Moses and Jesus.

Elijah is supposed to have been taken directly to heaven (2 Kgs 2:11) and the burial place of Moses was unknown (Deut 34:6). These traditions suggest that the two triumphed over death, just as Jesus will do at his resurrection and ascension. The luminous appearance of Jesus on this occasion has led a number of scholars to conclude that the transfiguration originated as an appearance story (of the risen Jesus) and then was remodeled by Mark to function as the turning point of his gospel. Since Matthew does not offer any information he has not derived from Mark or supplied from Old Testament allusions, his version was also designated black.

Elijah as precursor
Mt 17:9–13
Mk 9:9–13
Source: Mark

17 [9]**And as they came down from the mountain, Jesus ordered them:** "Don't tell anyone about this vision until the son of Adam has been raised from the dead."

[10]**And the disciples questioned him: "Why, in the light of this, do the scholars claim that Elijah must come first?"**

[11]**In response he said,** "Elijah does indeed come and will restore everything. [12]But I tell you that Elijah has already come, and they did not recognize him but had their way with him. So the son of Adam is also going to suffer at their hands."

[13]**Then the disciples understood that he had been talking to them about John the Baptizer.**

Elijah as precursor. Matthew has edited Mark's version of this anecdote. First of all, Matthew has exonerated the disciples by omitting v. 10 in Mark, which read: "And they kept it [the transfiguration] to themselves, puzzling over what this 'rising from the dead' could mean." Mark had represented the disciples as unable to comprehend what was about to happen. Matthew gives them credit for understanding.

Matthew has also added a conclusion in v. 13. This editorial comment indicates that the disciples understood that Jesus had been talking about John the Baptist. Finally, Matthew clarifies the second half of v. 12: the son of Adam will suffer and die just as John has suffered and died. The relationship is not altogether clear in Mark.

The Fellows designated the words of Jesus black in *The Five Gospels.* They followed suit by voting the narrative context black for *The Acts of Jesus.*

Man with mute spirit
Mt 17:14–20
Mk 9:14–29, Lk 9:37–43
Source: Mark

17 14 **And when they rejoined the crowd,** a person approached
and knelt before him 15 and said, "Master, have mercy on my son,
because he is epileptic and suffers great <pain>. For instance, he
often falls into the fire and just as often into the water. 16 So I brought
him to your disciples, but they couldn't heal him."
17 In response Jesus said, "You distrustful and perverted lot, how
long must I associate with you? How long must I put up with you?
Bring him here to me!" 18 And Jesus rebuked him and the demon
came out of him and the child was healed at that precise moment.
19 **Later the disciples came to Jesus privately and asked, "Why
couldn't we drive it out?"**
20 **So he says to them,** "Because of your lack of trust. I swear to you,
even if you have trust no larger than a mustard seed, you will say to
this mountain, 'Move from here to there,' and it will move. And noth-
ing will be beyond you."

Man with mute spirit. Matthew has cut Mark's account of the epileptic boy's cure in half. He has omitted Mark's elaborate repetitive description of the boy's symptoms, eliminated Jesus' dialogue with the father of the boy on the subject of trust, and skipped Mark's long narrative introduction. And Matthew doesn't repeat the description of the exorcism proper. It would seem that Matthew's community was less impressed by exorcism than Mark's audience had been at a somewhat earlier date.

In addition, Matthew has turned an exorcism in the direction of a pronouncement story: v. 20 is Matthew's addition of a climactic saying of Jesus in response to the disciples' query in v. 19, which Matthew has taken over from Mark. In other words, Matthew has thoroughly remodeled the story.

The Jesus Seminar took the view that Matthew's version, to the extent it imitates the core of Mark's account, also deserved a gray designation. Matthew's introduction (v. 14a) and his repetition of Mark's embellishment in v. 19 are colored black.

Note: Verse 21 does not appear in the best ancient manuscripts and so is not included in modern critical editions of the Greek New Testament.

Jesus predicts his death again
Mt 17:22–23
Mk 9:30–32, Lk 9:43b–45
Source: Mark
Cf. Mk 8:31–33, Mt 16:21–23, Lk 9:22; Mk 10:32–34, Mt 20:17–19, Lk 18:31–34

17 22 **And when they had been reunited in Galilee, Jesus said to
them,** "The son of Adam is about to be turned over to his enemies,
23 and they will end up killing him, and on the third day he'll be
raised." **And they were very sad.**

Jesus predicts his death again. Matthew has taken over Mark's second forecast of Jesus' death and modified it in accordance with his usual practice. Matthew edits the narrative line in v. 22, which, in any case, is fictive. And he tones down Mark's observation that the disciples did not understand Jesus' remark about being turned over to his enemies, dying, and being raised; for

Matthew the disciples do understand and that makes them sad. Matthew thus contradicts Mark's comment. Both the words of Jesus and the narrative framework are appropriately black.

Temple tax
Mt 17:24–27
No parallels
Source: Matthew

17 [24]**And when they came to Capernaum, those who collect the temple tax came to Peter and said, "Your teacher pays his temple tax, doesn't he?"** [25]**He said, "That's right."**

And when he got home, Jesus anticipated what was on Peter's mind: "What are you thinking, Simon? On whom do secular rulers levy taxes and tolls? Do they levy them on their own people or on aliens?"

[26]**Peter said, "On aliens."**

Jesus responded to him, "Then their own people are exempt. [27]Still, we don't want to get in trouble with them, so go down to the sea, cast your line in, and take the first fish that rises. Open its mouth and you will find a coin. Take it and pay them for both of us."

Temple tax. This story, which is reported only by Matthew, is undoubtedly apocryphal. The Fellows colored the words of Jesus black in *The Five Gospels,* so the narrative frame should be black as well. The question it poses is whether Christians should pay the "temple tax" imposed by the Emperor Vespasian (69–79 C.E.) to support the temple of Jupiter Capitolinus in Rome. The recommendation here is that Christians should be good citizens and pay the tax. Jesus is likely to have given an equivocal recommendation, as he does when asked the question directly (Matt 22:15–22).

The method of presenting the recommendation is contrived. Peter represents the Jesus movement, which was faced with the dilemma of the pagan tax. Jesus reads Peter's mind (v. 25)—the mind of the community—and provides the authorized solution. In addition, Matthew again presents Peter in an authoritative role as the mouthpiece for Jesus. After all, in Matthew's gospel Peter is given "the keys of Heaven's domain" (16:19).

Dispute about greatness
Mt 18:1–10
Mk 9:33–50, Lk 9:46–50
Source: Mark

18 **At that moment the disciples approached Jesus with the question: "Who is greatest in Heaven's domain?"**

[2]**And he called a child over, had her stand in front of them,** [3]**and said,** "I swear to you, if you don't do an about-face and become like children, you'll never enter Heaven's domain. [4]Therefore those who put themselves on a level with this child are greatest in Heaven's domain. [5]And whoever accepts one such child in my name is accepting me. [6]Any of you who misleads one of these little souls who trusts me would be better off to have a millstone hung around your neck and be drowned in the deepest part of the sea!

[7]"Damn the world for the snares it sets! Even though it's inevitable for snares to be set, nevertheless, damn the person who sets such

snares. [8]If your hand or your foot gets you into trouble, cut it off and
throw it away! It's better for you to enter life maimed or lame than to
be thrown into the eternal fire with both hands and both feet. [9]And if
your eye gets you into trouble, rip it out and throw it away! After all,
it's better for you to enter life one-eyed than to be thrown into
Gehenna's fire with both eyes. [10]See that you don't disdain one of these
little ones. For I tell you, their guardian angels constantly gaze on the
face of my Father in heaven."

Dispute about greatness. Matthew has created this complex on the basis of materials he found in Mark 9:33–50. His narrative setting was inspired by Mark 9:33–34, 36. Since Mark's setting was probably fictive, Matthew's is as well. Black is the correct designation.

Traps
Mt 18:12–35
Lk 15:3–7, 17:3–4
Source: Q

18 [12]"What do you think about this? If someone has a hundred
sheep and one of them wanders off, won't that person leave the
ninety-nine in the hills and go look for the one that wandered off?
[13]And if he should find it, you can bet he'll rejoice over it more than
over the ninety-nine that didn't wander off. [14]And so it is the intention
of your Father in heaven that not one of these little souls be lost.
[15]"And if some companion does wrong, go have it out between
the two of you privately. If that person listens to you, you have won
your companion over. [16]And if he or she doesn't listen, take one or two
people with you so that 'every fact may be supported by two or three
witnesses.' [17]Then if he or she refuses to listen to them, report it to the
congregation. If he or she refuses to listen even to the congregation,
treat that companion like you would a pagan or toll collector. [18]I swear
to you, whatever you bind on earth will be considered bound in
heaven, and whatever you release on earth will be considered released
in heaven. [19]Again I assure you, if two of you on earth agree on any-
thing you ask for, it will be done for you by my Father in heaven. [20]In
fact, wherever two or three are gathered together in my name, I will be
there among them."
**[21]Then Peter came up and asked him, "Master, how many times
can a companion wrong me and still expect my forgiveness? As
many as seven times?"**
[22]Jesus replies to him, "My advice to you is not seven times, but
seventy-seven times.

[23]This is why Heaven's imperial rule should be compared to a
secular ruler who decided to settle accounts with his slaves.
[24]When the process began, this debtor was brought to him who
owed ten million dollars. [25]Since he couldn't pay it back, the ruler
ordered him sold, along with his wife and children and every-
thing he had, so he could recover his money.

[26]At this prospect, the slave fell down and groveled before him: 'Be patient with me, and I'll repay every cent.' [27]Because he was compassionate, the master of that slave let him go and canceled the debt.

[28]As soon as he got out, that same fellow collared one of his fellow slaves who owed him a hundred dollars, and grabbed him by the neck and demanded: 'Pay back what you owe!'

[29]His fellow slave fell down and begged him: 'Be patient with me and I'll pay you back.'

[30]But he wasn't interested; instead, he went out and threw him in prison until he paid the debt.

[31]When his fellow slaves realized what had happened, they were terribly distressed and went and reported to their master everything that had taken place.

[32]At that point, his master summoned him: 'You wicked slave,' he says to him, 'I canceled your entire debt because you begged me. [33]Wasn't it only fair for you to treat your fellow slave with the same consideration as I treated you?' [34]And the master was so angry he handed him over to those in charge of punishment until he paid back everything he owed. [35]That's what my heavenly Father will do to you, unless you find it in your heart to forgive each one of your brothers and sisters."

Traps. Matthew has constructed this complex out of materials he has taken from Q. The brief narrative context provided by vv. 21–22 has been devised by Matthew, as a comparison with Luke 17:4 demonstrates: Luke does not have this exchange between Peter and Jesus. As a fictive setting, it is correctly colored black.

Jesus departs for Judea
Mt 19:1–2
Mk 10:1
Source: Mark

19 **And so when Jesus had finished this instruction, he took leave of Galilee and went to the territory of Judea across the Jordan. [2]And large crowds followed him and he healed them there.**

Jesus departs for Judea. Verse 1 is one of Matthew's formulaic breaks in his story. The Gospel of Matthew is sometimes said to consist of five panels, corresponding to the five books of Moses—the Torah—in the Hebrew Bible. At the end of each one of these panels Matthew has put a narrative break (7:28–9, 11:1, 13:53, 19:1, 26:1).

The geography of Matthew, like that of Mark in the parallel passage, is mistaken. No part of Judea lies east of the Jordan (consult the map, p. xxiv). Matthew has probably been misled by Mark into thinking that Judea extended eastward across the Jordan, although he appears to make the proper distinction in both 3:5 and 4:25 (crowds from "Judea and from across the Jordan"). It was only because of this geographical error that the Fellows of the Seminar thought it appropriate to color this passage gray instead of pink. In other respects it is generally accurate: Jesus did go to Judea on at least one occasion. Crowds probably followed him when he did so, and he may well have healed some people on his journey.

Is divorce permitted?
Mt 19:3–9
Mk 10:2–12
Source: Mark

19 **3 And the Pharisees approached him and, to test him, they**
ask, "Is <a husband> permitted to divorce his wife for any reason?"
4 In response he puts a question to them: "Have you not read that
in the beginning the Creator 'made them male and female,' 5 and that
further on it says, 'for this reason, a man will leave his father and
mother and be united with his wife, and the two will be one body'?
6 Consequently, from then on they are one body instead of two.
Therefore those whom God has coupled together, no one else should
separate."
7 They say to him, "Then why did Moses order 'a written release
and separation'?"
8 He says to them, "Because you are obstinate Moses permitted you
to divorce your wives, but it wasn't like that originally. 9 Now I say to
you, whoever divorces his wife, except for infidelity, and marries
another commits adultery."

Is divorce permitted? Matthew has taken over this segment from Mark and altered it slightly. Matthew has retained the dialogue format but omitted the private instruction to the disciples on the subject of divorce that appears in Mark 10:10–12. Since the private instruction along with the narrative framework is Mark's invention, the appropriate designation here in Matthew is also black.

Castration for heaven
Mt 19:10–12
No parallels
Source: Matthew

19 **10 The disciples say to him, "If this is how it is in the case of a**
man and his wife, it's better not to marry."
11 Then he said to them, "Not everyone will be able to accept this
advice, only those for whom it was intended. 12 After all, there are cas-
trated men who were born that way, and there are castrated men who
were castrated by others, and there are castrated men who castrated
themselves because of Heaven's imperial rule. If you are able to accept
this <advice>, do so."

Castration for heaven. The evangelist is exercising the storyteller's license here to provide a narrative setting for Jesus' sayings in vv. 11–12 and to furnish some minimal connection to the preceding segment on divorce. Black is the appropriate designation.

Children in God's domain
Mt 19:13–15
Mk 10:13–16, Lk 18:15–17;
Th 22:1–3
Sources: Mark, Thomas

19 **13 Then little children were brought to him so he could lay**
his hands on them and pray, but the disciples scolded them.
14 Now Jesus said, "Let the children alone. Don't try to stop them

from coming up to me. After all, Heaven's domain belongs to people
like that." 15**And he laid his hands on them and left that place.**

Children in God's domain. Matthew has again reproduced a segment he found in his source, the Gospel of Mark. Jesus probably did suggest that God's domain belonged to the children. It is doubtful, however, that Jesus' male disciples objected to the presence of children in the manner depicted in v. 13, if Jesus had expressed a positive disposition to their presence. For that reason, the first part of the narrative setting is colored gray. The concluding verse, in addition to repeating the act of Jesus laying his hands on children, provides a spatial connective (". . . left that place") that is Matthew's contribution. It is therefore black.

The man with money
Mt 19:16–30
Mk 10:17–31, Lk 18:18–30,
GNaz 6:1–5
Source: Mark

19

16**And just then someone came and asked him, "Teacher,
what good do I have to do to have eternal life?"**
17**He said to him,** "Why do you ask me about the good? There is
only One who is good. If you want to enter life, observe the commandments."
18**He says to him, "Which ones?"**
Jesus replied, "'You must not murder, you are not to commit adultery, you are not to steal, you are not to give false testimony, 19you are
to honor your father and mother, and you are to love your neighbor as yourself.'"
20**The young man says to him, "I have observed all these; what am I missing?"**
21**Jesus said to him,** "If you wish to be perfect, make your move, sell your belongings, and give <the proceeds> to the poor and you will have treasure in heaven. And then come, follow me!"
22**When the young man heard this advice, he went away dejected since he possessed a fortune.**
23**Jesus said to his disciples,** "I swear to you, it's difficult for the rich
to enter Heaven's domain. 24And again I tell you, it's easier for a camel
to squeeze through a needle's eye than for a wealthy person to get into God's domain."
25**When the disciples heard this, they were quite perplexed and said, "Well then, who can be saved?"**
26**Jesus looked them in the eye, and said to them,** "For mortals this is impossible; for God everything's possible."
27**In response Peter said to him, "Look at us, we left everything to follow you! What do we get out of it?"**
28**Jesus told them,** "I swear to you, you who have followed me, when the son of Adam is seated on his throne of glory in the renewal <of creation>, you also will be seated on twelve thrones and sit in
judgment on the twelve tribes of Israel. 29And everyone who has left
homes or brothers or sisters or father or mother or children or farms,

on my account, will receive a hundred times as much and inherit eternal life. [30]Many of the first will be last, and of the last many will be first."

The man with money. From Mark, Matthew has taken over the anecdote about the rich man (vv. 16–22), along with the compendium of sayings Mark had suffixed to that story (vv. 23–30).

The story of Jesus' dialogue with the rich man may reflect some incident in the life of Jesus, in the judgment of the Fellows. Their initial decision was based on the content of the sayings ascribed to Jesus. For that reason, they agreed to designate its narrative setting gray. Mark had already provided a narrative frame for the compendium of sayings, which Matthew has taken over and enhanced: in v. 28 he elevates the twelve to the position of cosmic judges who will eventually reign with Jesus; this is Matthew's addition to what he found in his source. The narrative context for that group of additional sayings is clearly fictive and therefore merits a black designation.

20 For Heaven's imperial rule is like a proprietor who went out the first thing in the morning to hire workers for his vineyard. [2]After agreeing with the workers for a silver coin a day he sent them into his vineyard.

[3]And coming out around 9 A.M. he saw others loitering in the marketplace [4]and he said to them, "You go into the vineyard too, and I'll pay you whatever is fair." [5]So they went.

Around noon he went out again, and at 3 P.M. he repeated the process. [6]About 5 P.M. he went out and found others loitering about and says to them, "Why did you stand around here idle the whole day?"

[7]They reply, "Because no one hired us."

He tells them, "You go into the vineyard as well."

[8]When evening came the owner of the vineyard tells his foreman: "Call the workers and pay them their wages starting with those hired last and ending with those hired first."

[9]Those hired at 5 P.M. came up and received a silver coin each. [10]Those hired first approached thinking they would receive more. But they also got a silver coin apiece. [11]They took it and began to grumble against the proprietor: [12]"These guys hired last worked only an hour but you have made them equal to us who did most of the work during the heat of the day."

[13]In response he said to one of them, "Look, pal, did I wrong you? You did agree with me for a silver coin, didn't you? [14]Take your wage and get out! I intend to treat the one hired last the same way I treat you. [15]Is there some law forbidding me to do as I please with my money? Or is your eye filled with envy because I am generous?"

[16]The last will be first and the first last.

Jesus predicts his death a third time
Mt 20:17–19
Mk 10:32–34, Lk 18:31–34
Source: Mark
Cf. Mk 8:31–33, Mt 16:21–23, Lk 9:22; Mk 9:30–32, Mt 17:22–23, Lk 9:43–45

[17]**On the way up to Jerusalem Jesus took the twelve aside privately and said to them as they walked along:** [18]"Listen, we're going up to Jerusalem, and the son of Adam will be turned over to the ranking priests and scholars, and they will sentence him to death, [19]and turn him over to foreigners to make fun of, and flog, and crucify. Yet on the third day he will be raised."

Jesus predicts his death a third time. Matthew has copied this third prediction of Jesus' death directly from the Gospel of Mark, just as he did in the first two instances. In so doing, he also copied Mark's narrative setting, thus reproducing Mark's view that Jesus gave this information to his disciples privately. Since the Fellows designated Mark's narrative setting black, they followed suit in rating Matthew's reuse of it.

Request for precedence
Mt 20:20–28
Mk 10:35–45, Lk 22:24–27
Source: Mark

20

[20]**Then the mother of the sons of Zebedee came up to him with her sons, bowed down before him, and asked him for a favor.**

[21]**He said to her,** "What do you want?"

She said to him, "Give me your word that these two sons of mine may sit one at your right hand and one at your left in your domain."

[22]**In response Jesus said,** "You have no idea what you're asking for. Can you drink the cup that I'm about to drink?"

They said to him, "We can!"

[23]**He says to them,** "You'll be drinking my cup, but as for sitting at my right or my left, that's not mine to grant, but belongs to those for whom it's been reserved by my Father."

[24]**And when they learned of it, the ten became annoyed with the two brothers.** [25]**And calling them aside, Jesus said,** "You know how foreign rulers lord it over their subjects, and how their strong men tyrannize them. [26]It's not going to be like that with you! With you, whoever wants to become great will be your slave, [27]and whoever among you wants to be 'number one' is to be your slave. [28]After all, the son of Adam didn't come to be served but to serve, even to give his life as a ransom for many."

Request for precedence. Matthew has taken over this anecdote from Mark, but has revised it slightly as he usually does. Rather than have the two brothers ask Jesus for places of honor, Matthew shifts the blame for the request to their mother (vv. 20–21). Matthew has perhaps done so because he thought such a request directly from the two brothers seemed excessively crass; to blame their doting mother perhaps seemed less objectionable. That Matthew has edited Mark is betrayed, however, by vv. 22–23. The "you" in v. 22 refers to the brothers, as their response in the same verse makes clear. Matthew has thus made a clumsy attempt to shift the blame and protect the reputations of the inner circle. The Fellows agreed without debate that the narrative context for the sayings in vv. 22–23 should be colored black.

The narrative frame for the second part of the anecdote was also designated black as a creation of Mark, Matthew's source.

Blind Bartimaeus
Mt 20:29–34
Mk 10:46–52, Lk 18:35–43
Source: Mark
Cf. Mt 9:27–31; Jn 9:1–7

20

**[29]And as they were leaving Jericho, a huge crowd followed
him. [30]There were two blind men sitting beside the road. When they
learned that Jesus was going by, they shouted, "Have mercy on us,
Master, you son of David."**
**[31]The crowd yelled at them to shut up, but they shouted all the
louder, "Have mercy on us, Master, you son of David."**
[32]Jesus paused and called out to them, "What do you want me to
do for you?"
[33]They said to him, "Master, open our eyes!"
**[34]Then Jesus took pity on them, touched their eyes, and right away
they regained their sight and followed him.**

Blind Bartimaeus. Matthew has omitted the name Bartimaeus and once again doubled the number of blind persons, as he does in the story he has created in Matt 9:27–31, where two blind men accost Jesus and ask to be cured. Because Matthew has so modified the story, the Fellows colored it gray rather than pink, which was the designation they gave to Mark's version.

Jesus enters Jerusalem
Mt 21:1–11
Mk 11:1–11, Lk 19:28–40;
Jn 12:12–19
Sources: Zechariah 9:9,
Psalm 118:25–26, Mark, John

21

**When they got close to Jerusalem, and came to Bethphage at
the Mount of Olives, then Jesus sent two disciples ahead [2]with these
instructions:** "Go into the village across the way, and right away you
will find a donkey tied up, and a colt alongside her. Untie <them> and
bring <them> to me. [3]And if anyone says anything to you, you are to
say, 'Their master has need of them and he will send them back right
away.'" **[4]This happened so the word spoken through the prophet
would come true:**

> [5]Tell the daughter of Zion,
> Look, your king comes to you in all modesty
> mounted on a donkey
> and on a colt, the foal of a pack animal.

**[6]Then the disciples went and did as Jesus instructed them, [7]and
brought the donkey and colt and they placed their cloaks on them,
and he sat on top of them. [8]The enormous crowd spread their cloaks
on the road, and others cut branches from the trees and spread them
on the road. [9]The crowds leading the way and those following kept
shouting,**

> **"Hosanna" to the son of David!**
> **"Blessed is the one who comes in the name of the Lord!"**
> **"Hosanna" in the highest.**

[10]**And when he entered into Jerusalem the whole city trembled, saying, "Who is this?"** [11]**The crowds said, "This is the prophet Jesus from Nazareth, Galilee!"**

Jesus enters Jerusalem. The citation from Zechariah in v. 5 appears to have been added to the versions of this story in Matthew and John; it does not appear in Mark. In Matthew and John the entry of Jesus into Jerusalem mounted on an ass thus becomes the fulfillment of an Old Testament prophecy and confirms the early Christian conviction that Jesus was the expected messiah. The Christianization of whatever event lay behind this story led the Fellows to declare the narrative a fiction based on prophecy. At the same time, they held out the possibility that Jesus may have entered Jerusalem astride a donkey as a symbolic act.

One can observe in Matthew's revision how prophetic texts tended to influence the telling of stories about Jesus. The parallelism of the poem from Zechariah permits the ancient prophet to state and then restate the same thought in two different ways:

> mounted on a donkey,
> and on a colt, the foal of a pack animal.

In Hebrew poetry, in the form known as synonymous parallelism, the second line reiterates the thought of the first line but in different words. However, Matthew takes the prophet quite literally and has Jesus mounted on both a donkey *and* a colt (v. 7), to make sure the prophecy is completely fulfilled. It is difficult to imagine how Jesus could have ridden two animals at the same time.

The citation from Psalm 118 has also played a role in the shaping of this story. Indeed, evangelists freely modify the text they are quoting to serve their own particular interests. In Mark, the quotation goes:

> Hosanna!
> Blessed is the one
> who comes in the name of the Lord!

To which Mark adds as though it were a part of the Psalm:

> Blessed is the coming kingdom of our father David!
> "Hosanna" in the highest!

The term *hosanna*, a transcription of an Aramaic word, means "save us" in Ps 118:25; it may also be a term of greeting. "The one who comes in the name of the Lord" in the Psalm is the pilgrim who is arriving in Jerusalem for one of the high festivals: pilgrims are blessed and are seeking blessing. The reference to the coming kingdom of our father is a Markan expansion, as is the phrase "in the highest."

Matthew has left out Mark's reference to the coming of the kingdom, but has substituted for the first line:

> "Hosanna" to the son of David!

which provides an explicit messianic reference. That reference does not appear in the Psalm. In other respects Matthew follows Mark. Luke makes yet other alterations, as does the author of the Fourth Gospel.

In vv. 10b–11, Matthew has added his own conclusion to the story, again suggesting that Jerusalem will never again be the same now that the prophet Jesus has arrived.

The Jesus Seminar was not inclined to view the narrative as the report of an actual event. Some Fellows argued that the story is a fiction generated by the prophecy of Zechariah and the Psalm, which was usually sung after the Passover meal. Others suggested that Jesus did enter Jerusalem astride a donkey to contrast his lowly entry into Jerusalem with the customary pomp and circumstance of Roman triumphal parades. In response to that proposition the Fellows produced a weighted average that fell into the gray category.

Temple incident
Mt 21:12–17
Mk 11:15–19, Lk 19:45–48;
Jn 2:13–22
Sources: Mark, John

21

12 And Jesus went into God's temple and chased all the ven-
dors and shoppers out of the temple area and he turned the bankers'
tables upside down, along with the chairs of the pigeon merchants.
13 Then he says to them, "It is written, 'My house is to be regarded
as a house of prayer,' but you're turning it into 'a hideout for crooks'!"
14 And some blind and lame people came to him in the temple
area, and he healed them. 15 Then the ranking priests and scholars
saw the remarkable feats he performed, and the children who kept
cheering in the temple area, shouting, "Hosanna to the son of
David," and they were infuriated. 16 And they said to him, "Do you
hear what these people are saying?"
Jesus says to them, "Of course. Have you never read 'You have pro-
duced praise for yourselves out of the mouths of babies and infants at
breast'?"
17 And leaving them behind, he went outside the city to Bethany
and spent the night there.

Temple incident. Matthew has abbreviated Mark's account of the temple incident: his version is compressed into vv. 12–13. Matthew has supplied out of his imagination the additional material found in vv. 14–16. In v. 17 he is following Mark's narrative transition.

While the Fellows agreed that Jesus performed some anti-temple act and spoke some anti-temple word, they disagreed on what specifically Jesus did and said. The statement in v. 12 was colored pink to indicate that Jesus acted in some hostile way against the vendors and pilgrims who contributed to the commercial atmosphere of the temple cult, although Matthew has overstated the case by saying "all the vendors and shoppers." Exaggeration is one of the ways the narrative incidents tend to get heightened as the stories are told and retold. The Fellows doubt that Jesus would have been physically able to overturn all the bankers' tables and the stalls of the pigeon merchants in an area so vast (the temple area was about thirty-five acres in extent). Consequently, they colored the balance of v. 12 gray to suggest that Jesus may have taken some action, the precise nature of which is unknown. The Seminar had already reported in *The Five Gospels* that the words ascribed to Jesus in v. 13 were probably put on his lips by early Christian storytellers. Yet the Fellows were convinced that Jesus openly criticized the temple cult, perhaps forecasting that its days were numbered.

Fig tree without figs
Mt 21:18–22
Mk 11:12–14, 20–25
Source: Mark
Cf. Lk 13:6–9

21 [18]**Early in the morning, as he was returning to the city, he got hungry.** [19]**And so when he spotted a single fig tree on the way, he went up to it, and found nothing on it except some leaves, and he says to it,** "You are never to bear fruit again!" **And the fig tree withered instantly.**

[20]**And when the disciples saw this, they expressed amazement: "How could the fig tree wither up so quickly?"**

[21]**In response Jesus said to them,** "I swear to you, if you have trust and do not doubt, not only can you do this to a fig tree but you can even say to this mountain, 'Up with you and into the sea!' and that's what will happen; [22]and everything you ask for in prayer you'll get if you trust."

Fig tree without figs. Matthew has taken the story of the barren fig tree over from Mark but has put the two parts back together (Mark used the allegory of the fig tree as an interpretive frame for the cleansing of the temple). In so doing, Matthew has heightened the miracle: the fig tree withers instantly (v. 19), rather than withering overnight, as it does in the Gospel of Mark. Matthew apparently does not understand the story as an allegory, but takes it quite literally as evidence that if one trusts, one can achieve anything (vv. 21–22). The Fellows were unanimous in their judgment that the story does not reflect an event in the life of Jesus. It was therefore colored black.

By what authority?
Mt 21:23–27
Mk 11:27–33, Lk 20:1–8
Source: Mark

21 [23]**And when he came to the temple area, the ranking priests and elders of the people approached him while he was teaching, and asked, "By what right are you doing these things?" and "Who gave you this authority?"**

[24]**In response Jesus said to them,** "I also have one question for you. If you answer me, I'll tell you by what authority I do these things. [25]The baptism of John, what was its origin? Was it heaven-sent or was it of human origin?"

And they conferred among themselves, saying, "If we say 'heaven-sent,' he'll say to us, 'Why didn't you trust him?' [26]**And if we say 'Of human origin . . . !' We are afraid of the crowd." (Remember, everybody considered John a prophet.)** [27]**So they answered Jesus by saying, "We can't tell."**

He replied to them in kind: "I'm not going to tell you by what authority I do these things either!"

By what authority? It is highly probable that both the words and the scene are the invention of some early Christian storyteller. The words ascribed to Jesus would not have survived oral transmission in their present form, and the story would have been transmitted only in outline. Because the anecdote fits so perfectly with the events that precede—the triumphal entry and the cleansing of the temple—it appears to have been contrived. To be sure, nothing in the content of the story contradicts what we otherwise know of Jesus. This is probably one of those many places in the gospels where a fiction represents Jesus accurately.

21 28 "Now what do you think?

Two sons
Mt 21:28–32
No parallels
Source: Matthew

A man had two children. He went to the first, and said, "Son,
go and work in the vineyard today."
29 He responded, "I'm your man, sir," but he didn't move.
30 Then he went to the second and said the same thing.
He responded, "I don't want to," but later on he thought bet-
ter of it and went <to work>.

31 "Which of the two did what the father wanted?"
They said, "The second."
Jesus said to them, "I swear to you, the toll collectors and prosti-
tutes will get into God's domain, but you will not. 32 After all, John
came to you advocating justice, but you didn't believe him; yet the toll
collectors and prostitutes believed him. Even after you observed
<this>, you didn't think better of it later and believe him."

Two sons. The evangelist has again exercised the storyteller's license in constructing a minimal dialogue to give a narrative context to the parable and the sayings. As a fictive exchange, black is the correct designation.

21 33 Listen to another parable:

The leased vineyard
Mt 21:33–46
Mk 12:1–12, Lk 20:9–20
Source: Mark

There once was a landlord who "planted a vineyard, put a hedge
around it, dug a winepress in it, built a tower," leased it out to
some farmers, and went abroad. 34 Now when it was about har-
vest time, he sent his slaves to the farmers to collect his crop.
35 And the farmers grabbed his slaves, and one they beat and
another they killed, and another they stoned.
36 Again he sent other slaves, more than the first group, and
they did the same thing to them.
37 Then finally he sent his son to them, with the thought, "They
will show this son of mine some respect."
38 But when the farmers recognized the son they said to one
another, "This fellow's the heir! Come on, let's kill him and we'll

have his inheritance!" [39]And they grabbed him, dragged him out-
side the vineyard, and killed him.

[40]"When the owner of the vineyard comes, what will he do to those
farmers then?"

**[41]They say to him, "He'll get rid of these wicked villains and lease
the vineyard out to other farmers who will deliver their produce to him
at the proper time."**

[42]Jesus says to them, "Haven't you read in the scriptures,

> A stone that the builders rejected
> has ended up as the keystone.
> It was the Lord's doing
> and is something you admire?

[43]Therefore I say to you, God's domain will be taken away from you and
given to a people that bears its fruit."

**[45]And when the ranking priests and Pharisees heard his parable,
they realized that he was talking about them. [46]They wanted to seize
him, but were afraid of the crowds, because everyone regarded him as
a prophet.**

The leased vineyard. The introductory remark in v. 33 accurately characterizes what Jesus often did—speak to his audience in parables. Pink is the appropriate color.

The question asked in v. 40 is in Mark's version a rhetorical question that Jesus answers without interruption. However, Matthew has introduced an exchange between Jesus and his listeners in v. 41, obviously a Matthean touch, in which Jesus' fictive listeners agree that the vineyard will be turned over to new proprietors. Since the exchange does not reflect history, black is the correct designation.

The narrative conclusion in vv. 45–46 Matthew has borrowed directly from Mark: this is how Mark imagined the plot of passion week developing. Black is again appropriate.

Wedding celebration
Mt 22:1–14
Lk 14:15–24; Th 64:1–12
Sources: Q, Thomas

22 **Jesus again responded to them and told them parables:**

[2]Heaven's imperial rule is like a secular ruler who gave a wed-
ding celebration for his son. [3]Then he sent his slaves to summon
those who had been invited to the wedding, but they declined to
attend.

[4]He sent additional slaves with the instructions: "Tell those
invited, 'Look, the feast is ready, the oxen and fat calves have
been slaughtered, and everything is set. Come to the wedding!'"

[5]But they were unconcerned and went off, one to his own farm,
one to his business, [6]while the rest seized his slaves, attacked and
killed them.

[7]Now the king got angry and sent his armies to destroy those

murderers and burn their city. 8Then he tells his slaves: "The wed-
ding celebration is ready but those we've invited didn't prove
deserving. 9So go to the city gates and invite anybody you find to
the wedding."
10Those slaves then went out into the streets and collected
everybody they could find, the good and bad alike. And the
wedding hall was full of guests.
11The king came in to see the guests for himself and noticed
this man not properly attired. 12And he says to him, "Look pal,
how'd you get in here without dressing for the occasion?"
And he was speechless.
13Then the king ordered his waiters: "Bind him hand and foot
and throw him where it is utterly dark. They'll weep and grind
their teeth out there. 14After all, many are called but few are
chosen."

Wedding celebration. Jesus often did tell parables, but Matthew has here particularized the setting in order to provide some continuity to his narrative: Jesus tells yet another parable to the ranking priests, Pharisees, and crowds mentioned in 21:13 and renewed most recently in 21:45. The persons Jesus addresses and the continuity are contrived. Black is the correct color.

Emperor & God
Mt 22:15–22
Mk 12:13–17, Lk 20:21–26; Th 100:1–4; EgerG 3:1–6
Sources: Mark, Thomas, Egerton Gospel

22 **15Then the Pharisees went and conferred on how to entrap**
him with a riddle. 16And they send their disciples to him along with
the Herodians to say, "Teacher, we know that you are honest and
that you teach God's way forthrightly, and are impartial, because
you pay no attention to appearances. 17So tell us what you think: Is it
permissible to pay the poll tax to the Roman emperor or not?"
18Jesus knew how devious they were, and said, "Why do you
provoke me, you pious frauds? 19Let me see the coin used to pay the
poll tax."
And they handed him a silver coin.
20And he says to them, "Whose picture is this? Whose name is on it?"
21They say to him, "The emperor's."
Then he says to them, "Pay the emperor what belongs to the
emperor, and God what belongs to God!"
22Upon hearing his reply, they were dumbfounded. And they
withdrew from him and went away.

Emperor & God. Matthew has followed Mark in providing a lengthy fictional introduction to the saying about emperor and God in v. 21. That introduction was designed to advance the plot against Jesus that eventually led to his arrest. As such, it is pure fiction. Black is the correct color.

The minimal exchange depicted in vv. 19b–21, however, may well represent something like the context in which Jesus originally spoke the saying. It was perhaps the image of the emperor on a Roman coin (see p. 127) that provoked the question. The context of the saying in the Gospel of Thomas (100:1–4) supports this view. Pink indicates an approximation of that context.

The conclusion in v. 22 is Mark's pious exaggeration of how impressive Jesus was in his response.

The Egerton Gospel preserves an alternate account of the same incident (3:1–6):

> **They come to him and interrogate him as a way of putting him to the test. [2]They ask, "Teacher, Jesus, we know that you are from God, since the things you do put you above all the prophets. [3]Tell us, then, is it permissible to pay to rulers what is due them? Should we pay them or not?" [4]Jesus knew what they were up to, and became indignant. [5]Then he said to them,** "Why do you pay me lip service as a teacher, but not do what I say? [6]How accurately Isaiah prophesied about you when he said, 'This people honors me with their lips, but their heart stays far away from me; their worship of me is empty, because they insist on teachings that are human commandments. . . .' "

The Egerton version of the question concerning tribute to Caesar fails to report the test, which consisted of the presentation of a coin bearing the image of Caesar, and the ambiguous response of Jesus. Both test and response are preserved by Mark and Thomas, and reproduced by Matthew and Luke. Instead, in response to the question Egerton has Jesus quote a passage from Isaiah (vv. 5–6), which in Mark appears in the context of eating with unwashed hands (Mark 7:6–8//Matt 15:7–9). It is unlikely that Jesus quoted Isaiah in either context. Egerton has apparently settled for Jesus' indignant response to his critics rather than record Jesus' teaching on the subject of imperial taxes. As a consequence, Egerton omits the core of the story and adds nothing historical to our knowledge of the incident.

On the resurrection
Mt 22:23–33
Mk 12:18–27, Lk 20:27–40
Source: Mark

22 **[23]That same day, some Sadducees—who maintain there is no resurrection—came up to him and questioned him. [24]"Teacher," they said, "Moses said, 'If someone dies without children, his brother is obligated to marry the widow and produce offspring for his brother.' [25]There were seven brothers we knew; now the first married and died. And since he left no children, he left his widow to his brother. [26]The second brother did the same thing, and the third, and so on, through the seventh brother. [27]Finally the wife died. [28]So then, in the resurrection, whose wife, of the seven, will she be?" (Remember, they had all married her.)**

[29]In response Jesus said to them, "You have missed the point again, all because you underestimate both the scriptures and the power of God. [30]After all, at the resurrection people do not marry but resemble heaven's messengers. [31]As for the resurrection of the dead, haven't you read God's word to you: [32]'I am the God of Abraham and the God of

Isaac and the God of Jacob.' This is not the God of the dead, only of the
living."
33And when the crowd heard, they were stunned by his teaching.

On the resurrection. Matthew has simply copied this anecdote from Mark and added his own conclusion in v. 33. Because the ideas expressed in the words attributed to Jesus in vv. 29–32 seemed to be consonant with Jesus' perspective, the vote produced a gray weighted average. The question and the response are a closely conceived unity, so the sayings would not have been circulated orally as an independent tradition. In other words, the anecdote and the sayings were created simultaneously.

Most important commandment?
Mt 22:34–40
Mk 12:28–34
Source: Mark
Cf. Lk 10:25–29

22 **34When the Pharisees learned that he had silenced the
Sadducees, they conspired against him. 35And one of them, a legal
expert, put him to the test: 36"Teacher, which commandment in the
Law is the greatest?"**
37He replied to him, "'You are to love the Lord your God with all
your heart and all your soul and all your mind.' 38This commandment
is first and foremost. 39And the second is like it: 'You are to love your
neighbor as yourself.' 40On these two commandments hangs every-
thing in the Law and the Prophets."

Most important commandment? Matthew has taken this anecdote from Mark and greatly abbreviated it. Moreover, in Mark the question is posed by a scholar friendly to Jesus; Matthew has converted the questioner to a legal expert who is a part of the conspiracy against Jesus. In Matthew's view, this suits the context of the passion week better. The Fellows accordingly designated Matthew's version black.

Son of David
Mt 22:41–46
Mk 12:35–37, Lk 20:41–44
Source: Mark

22 **41When the Pharisees gathered around, Jesus asked them,**
42"What do you think about the Anointed? Whose son is he?"
They said to him, "David's."
43He said to them, "Then how can David call him 'lord,' while
speaking under the influence of the spirit: 44'The Lord said to my lord,
"Sit here at my right, until I make your enemies grovel at your feet"'?
45If David actually called him 'lord,' how can he be his son?"
**46And no one could come up with an answer to his riddle. And
from that day on no one dared ask him a question.**

Son of David. Matthew has taken Mark's brief anecdote and converted it into a dialogue. As usual, the evangelists have made the Pharisees the opponents of Jesus in this exchange. Such a conversation, if it ever took place, is more likely located in the Christian community much later. Jesus is represented as a clever debater in the narrative conclusion, v. 46. He no doubt coined many memorable stories and couplets, but he was probably not the scribal debater suggested by that conclusion. Matthew's free conversion of Mark's text and the implausible exchange warrant a black rating.

Scholars & Pharisees
Mt 23:1–39
Mk 12:38–40, Lk 20:45–47, 11:37–44, 45–54, 13:34–35
Sources: Mark, Q, Matthew

23 **Then Jesus said to the crowds and to his disciples,** 2"The scholars and Pharisees occupy the chair of Moses. 3This means you're supposed to observe and follow everything they tell you. But don't do what they do; after all, they're all talk and no action. 4They invent heavy burdens and lay them on folks' shoulders, but they themselves won't lift a finger to move them. 5Everything they do, they do for show. So they widen their phylacteries and enlarge their tassels. 6They love the best couches at banquets and prominent seats in synagogues 7and respectful greetings in marketplaces, and they like to be called 'Rabbi' by everyone. 8But you are not to be called 'Rabbi'; after all, you only have one teacher, and all of you belong to the same family. 9And don't call anyone on earth 'father,' since you have only one Father, and he is in heaven. 10You are not to be called 'instructors,' because you have only one instructor, the Anointed. 11Now whoever is greater than you will be your slave. 12Those who promote themselves will be demoted and those who demote themselves will be promoted.

13"You scholars and Pharisees, you impostors! Damn you! You slam the door of Heaven's domain in people's faces. You yourselves don't enter, and you block the way of those trying to enter.

15"You scholars and Pharisees, you impostors! Damn you! You scour land and sea to make one convert, and when you do, you make that person more of a child of Hell than you are.

16"Damn you, you blind guides who claim: 'When you swear by the temple, it doesn't matter, but when you swear by the treasure in the temple, it is binding.' 17You blind fools, which is greater, the treasure or the temple that makes the gold sacred? 18You go on: 'When you swear by the altar, it doesn't matter, but when you swear by the offering that lies on the altar, it is binding.' 19You sightless souls, which is greater, the offering or the altar that makes the offering sacred? 20So when you swear by the altar, you swear by the altar and everything on it. 21And anyone who swears by the temple, swears by the temple and the one who makes it home, 22and anyone who swears by heaven swears by the throne of God and the one who occupies it.

23"You scholars and Pharisees, you impostors! Damn you! You pay tithes on mint and dill and cumin too, but ignore the really important matters of the Law, such as justice and mercy and trust. You should have attended to the last without ignoring the first. 24You blind leaders! You strain out a gnat and gulp down a camel.

25"You scholars and Pharisees, you impostors! Damn you! You wash the outside of cups and plates, but inside they are full of greed and dissipation. 26You blind Pharisee, first clean the inside of the cup and then the outside will be clean too.

27"You scholars and Pharisees, you impostors! Damn you! You are like whitewashed tombs: on the outside they look beautiful, but inside they are full of dead bones and every kind of decay. 28So you too look like decent people on the outside, but on the inside you are doing nothing but posturing and subverting the Law.

29"You scholars and Pharisees, you impostors! Damn you! You erect tombs to the prophets and decorate the graves of the righteous 30and claim: 'If we had lived in the days of our ancestors, we wouldn't have joined them in spilling the prophets' blood.' 31So, you witness against yourselves: You are descendants of those who murdered the prophets, 32and you're the spitting image of your ancestors. 33You serpents! You spawn of Satan! How are you going to escape Hell's judgment? 34Look, that is why I send you prophets and sages and scholars. Some you're going to kill and crucify, and some you're going to beat in your synagogues and hound from town to town. 35As a result there will be on your heads all the innocent blood that has been shed on the earth, from the blood of innocent Abel to the blood of Zechariah, son of Baruch, whom you murdered between the temple and the altar. 36I swear to you, all these things are going to rain down on this generation.

37"Jerusalem, Jerusalem, you murder the prophets and stone those sent to you! How often I wanted to gather your children as a hen gathers her chicks under her wings, but you wouldn't let me. 38Can't you see, your house is being abandoned as a ruin? 39I tell you, you certainly won't see me from now on until you say, 'Blessed is the one who comes in the name of the Lord.'"

Scholars & Pharisees. Matthew has assembled this complex of invectives against the scholars and Pharisees from a variety of sources and invented much of it himself. The minimal narrative context provided by v. 1 is Matthew's contribution to narrative continuity and tells us nothing historical. Black is appropriate.

Temple's destruction
Mt 24:1–2
Mk 13:1–2, Lk 21:5–6
Source: Mark

24

And Jesus was leaving the temple area on his way out, when his disciples came to him and called his attention to the sacred buildings.

2In response he said to them, "Yes, take a good look at all this! I swear to you, you may be sure not one stone will be left on top of another! Every last one will certainly be knocked down!"

Temple's destruction. Matthew has borrowed the narrative setting Mark invented for his collection of apocalyptic sayings and warnings. Since the setting

PHARISEES

Information about the Pharisees comes from three sources: Josephus, early Christian literature, and the rabbinic literature. The data these sources provide about the Pharisees in the period prior to the destruction of the temple in 70 C.E. are surprisingly scanty and frequently contradictory. As a consequence, scholars have developed divergent theories about who the Pharisees were and what they stood for. It is difficult to draw a sharply defined picture of them.

Since the New Testament gospels and Acts were written after the fall of Jerusalem in 70 C.E., the picture they give of the Pharisees has been influenced by the controversies between the sectarian Jesus movement and rabbinic Judaism, which began to take definitive shape in the wake of the destruction of the temple cult. In addition, the authors of these documents probably had no direct experience of conditions in Galilee and Judea during the time of Jesus and so were dependent on hazy memories for the pictures they draw of both Jesus and his critics. Scholars are wisely cautious in making use of the data.

In this cameo we will compare and contrast the evidence provided by the Sayings Gospel Q, the Gospel of Mark, and the Gospel of John, and will then sketch an overview based on evidence from all the sources.

The Pharisees appear in Q in a series of invectives directed against them (Luke 11:37–54; Matt 23:1–36). They also appear in the demand for a sign (Matt 12:38–42) and in the accusation that Jesus casts out demons with the assistance of Beelzebul, the chief demon (Matt 12:24–37; Luke 11:15–23). These two stories have overlapping counterparts in the Gospel of Mark.

According to Mark, the Pharisees appear primarily in Galilee and always in connection with controversies, features that are also characteristic of the Q references just listed. The Pharisees are critics of Jesus when he eats with "toll collectors and sinners" (Mark 2:15–17) and when he fails to fast (Mark 2:18–22). They are there when Jesus' disciples infringe the sabbath by harvesting grain (Mark 2:23–28). When Jesus heals the man with a crippled hand on the sabbath, the Pharisees hatch a plot against him (Mark 3:1–6). Jesus and the Pharisees are at odds over handwashing as a part of the purity codes (Mark 7:1–13), and the Pharisees demand a sign of Jesus to substantiate his authority (Mark 8:10–13). Jesus warns his disciples against the "leaven" of the Pharisees (Mark 8:14–21). The Pharisees also approach Jesus to ask about divorce, which Jesus turns into an occasion to depict the Pharisees as "obstinate" (Mark 10:2–9). Finally, Mark has some Pharisees and Herodians approach Jesus with a trick question about paying taxes (Mark 12:13–17). All these stories are set in Galilee, except the last two, which are located in Judea and Jerusalem. The Pharisees play no role at Jesus' trial and execution. For Mark, and for the synoptics generally, they appear primarily as those who opposed Jesus in Galilee.

The issues that formed the foci of the confrontations between Jesus and the Pharisees, according to Mark, were fasting, sabbath observance, divorce, the purification of hands, and eating with disreputable persons. These issues were probably legitimate Pharisaic concerns, since the Pharisees attempted to develop a code that defined their life-style in contrast to the pagan and rather lax Jewish context in which they lived. In other words, at a time when the temple cult was allied with the Roman authorities and much of Jewish Palestine was under pagan influence, the Pharisees sought to maintain a way of life that identified them more narrowly as Jews. However, the Pharisees were probably not at that time in charge of synagogues and probably did not form a religious sect. Rather, they were individuals who practiced stricter forms of piety within society, during the period when the temple cult was in decline and other groups, such as the Essenes, withdrew from society in order to maintain their group identity.

In the Gospel of John, in contrast to the synoptics, the Pharisees are represented as a Jerusalem group closely allied with the authorities, the ranking priests, and the Council. They are government officials and scholars of the law who repeatedly check up on whether Jesus is teaching the truth. They send a delegation to John the Baptist, presumably in the Jordan valley, to discover what authority he claimed for himself (John 1:19–28). In this scene, the Pharisees are headquartered in Jerusalem. And in John 4:1, their awareness of rumors about Jesus' success prompts him to depart for Galilee. Again they are located in Jerusalem. Nicodemus is identified as a Pharisee and a Judean leader (John 3:1). None of the authorities had become disciples of Jesus, according to John (7:48), but Nicodemus is uneasy about the wholesale condemnation of Jesus (John 7:50–51). In conjunction with the "authorities," the Pharisees send deputies to arrest Jesus (7:32–52). Jesus has a debate with the Pharisees in Jerusalem (John 8:13–30). The Pharisees interrogate the man born blind whom Jesus had healed and find that Jesus had broken the law (John 9:1–41).

The ranking priests and Pharisees call the Council together and propose arresting Jesus (John 11:47–57). The Pharisees fear Jesus' success (John 12:19), and those who became followers of Jesus feared the Pharisees, who are represented as having the authority to expel persons from the synagogue (John 12:42). Finally, the police sent to arrest Jesus are dispatched by the ranking priests and Pharisees (John 18:3). The Pharisees then drop out of the passion narrative, just as they do in the synoptics, and have nothing further to do with the prosecution of Jesus.

The author of John has undoubtedly conflated facets of stories about Jesus' opponents and merged them into a composite group to which the name "Pharisees" has been attached. As the Gospel of John represents them, they are not a plausible historical entity.

If the Pharisees can be regarded as a well-defined sect in the time of Jesus—and that is dubious—they are of the reforming type: They sought to maintain a form of life that was recognizably Jewish in the midst of waves of alien cultural and political influences. They were not an apocalyptic sect that anticipated the direct intervention of God in history, and they were not a separatist movement that withdrew from society in order to create a purified community, such as the one at Qumran. They were realists who formed alliances with authorities and institutions in society in order to achieve their goals. Jesus and his followers, while akin to the Pharisees in some respects, appear to have been less realistic and more utopian in orientation. The Jesus movement seems to have been concerned to lower social barriers and expand community boundaries in ways that may have excited Pharisaic opposition.

in Mark, his source, was a fiction, Matthew's edition of that setting is also imaginary. Black is the appropriate color.

Signs of the end
Mt 24:3–42
Mk 13:3–37, Lk 21:7–36
Source: Mark

24 [3]**As he was sitting on the Mount of Olives, the disciples came to him privately, and said, "Tell us, when are these things going to happen, and what will be the sign of your coming and the end of the age?"**

[4]**And in response Jesus said to them:** "Stay alert, otherwise someone might just delude you! [5]You know, many will come using my name, and claim, 'I am the Anointed!' and they will delude many people. [6]You are going to hear about wars and rumors of wars. See that you are not afraid. For these are inevitable, but it is not yet the end. [7]For nation will rise up against nation and empire against empire; and there will be famines and earthquakes everywhere. [8]Now all these things mark the beginning of the final agonies.

[9]"At that time they will turn you over for torture, and will kill you, and you will be universally hated because of me. [10]And then many will suffer a loss of faith, and they will betray one another and hate each other. [11]And many false prophets will appear and will delude many. [12]And as lawlessness spreads, mutual love will grow cool. [13]Those who hold out to the end will be saved! [14]And this good news of Heaven's imperial rule will have been proclaimed in the whole inhabited world, so you can make your case to all peoples. And then the end will come.

[15]"So when you see the 'devastating desecration' (as described by Daniel the prophet) standing 'in the holy place' (the reader had better figure out what this means), [16]then the people in Judea should head for the hills; [17]no one on the roof should go downstairs to retrieve anything; [18]and no one in the field should turn back to get a coat. [19]It'll be too bad for pregnant women and nursing mothers in those days! [20]Pray that you don't have to flee during the winter or on the sabbath day. [21]For there will be great distress, the likes of which has not occurred since the world began until now, and will never occur again. [22]And if those days had not been cut short, no human being would have survived. But for the sake of the chosen people, those days will be cut short.

[23]"Then if someone says to you, 'Look, here is the Anointed' or 'over here,' don't count on it! [24]After all, counterfeit messiahs and phony prophets will show up, and they'll offer great portents and miracles to delude, if possible, even the chosen people. [25]Look, I have warned you in advance. [26]In fact, if they should say to you, 'Look, he's in the wilderness,' don't go out there; 'Look, he's in one of the secret rooms,' don't count on it. [27]For just as lightning comes out of the east and is visible all the way to the west, that's what the coming of the son of Adam will be like. [28]For wherever there's a corpse, that's where vultures gather.

29"Immediately after the tribulation of those days

the sun will be darkened,
and the moon will not give off her glow,
and the stars will fall from the sky,
and the heavenly forces will be shaken!

30And then the son of Adam's sign will appear in the sky, and every
tribe of the earth will lament, and they'll see the son of Adam coming
on clouds of the sky with great power and splendor. 31And he'll send
out his messengers with a blast on the trumpet, and they'll gather his
chosen people from the four winds, from one end of the sky to the
other!

32"Take a cue from the fig tree. When its branch is already in bud
and leaves come out, you know that summer is near. 33So, when you
see all these things, you ought to realize that he is near, just outside
your door. 34I swear to God, this generation certainly won't pass into
oblivion before all these things take place! 35The earth will pass into
oblivion and so will the sky, but my words will never be obliterated!

36"As for that exact day and minute: no one knows, not even heaven's
messengers, nor even the son—no one, except the Father alone.

37"The son of Adam's coming will be just like the days of Noah.
38This is how people behaved then before the flood came: they ate and
drank, married and were given in marriage, until the day 'Noah
boarded the ark,' 39and they were oblivious until the flood came and
swept them all away. This is how it will be when the son of Adam
comes. 40Then two men will be in the field; one will be taken and one
will be left. 41Two women will be grinding at the mill; one will be taken
and one left. 42So stay alert! You never know on what day your lord
returns."

Signs of the end. Matthew has once again borrowed a narrative setting from Mark in connection with his use of the compendium of apocalyptic sayings Mark has assembled. Matthew's use of Mark is a mere repetition of a fiction, so black is the correct designation.

24
43"Mark this well: if the homeowner had known when the bur-
glar was coming, he would have been on guard and not have allowed
anyone to break into his house. 44By the same token, you too should be
prepared. Remember, the son of Adam is coming when you least
expect it.

45"Who then is the reliable and shrewd slave to whom the master
assigns responsibility for his household, to provide them with food at
the right time? 46Congratulations to the slave who's on the job when
his master arrives. 47I swear to you, he'll put him in charge of all his

property. 48But suppose that worthless slave says to himself, 'My master is taking his time,' 49and begins to beat his fellow slaves, and starts eating and drinking with drunkards, 50that slave's master will show up on the day he least expects and at an hour he doesn't suspect. 51He'll cut him to pieces, and assign him a fate fit for the other impostors. <Those who share this fate> will moan and grind their teeth.

25 When the time comes, Heaven's imperial rule will be like ten maidens who took their lamps and went out to meet the bridegroom. 2Five of them were foolish and five were sensible. 3You see, the foolish maidens took their lamps but failed to take oil with them, 4while the sensible ones took flasks of oil along with their lamps. 5When the bridegroom didn't come, they all dozed off and fell asleep.

6Then in the middle of the night there was a shout: 'Look, the bridegroom is coming! Let's go out to meet him.' 7Then the maidens all got up and trimmed their lamps.

8The foolish said to the sensible ones, 'Let us have some of your oil because our lamps are going out.'

9But the prudent maidens responded, 'We can't do that in case there isn't enough for both of us. Instead, you had better go to the merchants and buy some for yourselves.'

10While they were gone to get some, the bridegroom arrived and those who had come prepared accompanied him to the wedding; then the door was closed.

11The other maidens finally come and say, 'Master, master, open the door for us.'

12He responded, 'I swear to you, I don't recognize you.'

13So stay alert because you don't know either the day or the hour.

14You know, it's like a man going on a trip who called his slaves and turned his valuables over to them. 15To the first he gave thirty thousand silver coins, to the second twelve thousand, and to the third six thousand, to each in relation to his ability, and he left.

16Immediately the one who had received thirty thousand silver coins went out and put the money to work; he doubled his investment.

17The second also doubled his money.

18But the third, who had received the smallest amount, went out, dug a hole, and hid his master's silver.

19After a long absence, the slaves' master returned to settle accounts with them. 20The first, who had received thirty thousand silver coins, came and produced an additional thirty thousand, with this report: 'Master, you handed me thirty thousand silver coins; as you can see, I have made you another thirty thousand.'

21 His master commended him: 'Well done, you competent and reliable slave! You have been trustworthy in small amounts; I'll put you in charge of large amounts. Come celebrate with your master!'

22 The one with twelve thousand silver coins also came and reported: 'Master, you handed me twelve thousand silver coins; as you can see, I have made you another twelve thousand.'

23 His master commended him: 'Well done, you competent and reliable slave! You have been trustworthy in small amounts; I'll put you in charge of large amounts. Come celebrate with your master!'

24 The one who had received six thousand silver coins also came and reported: 'Master, I know that you drive a hard bargain, reaping where you didn't sow and gathering where you didn't scatter. 25 Since I was afraid, I went out and buried your money in the ground. Look, here it is!'

26 But his master replied to him, 'You incompetent and timid slave! So you knew that I reap where I didn't sow and gather where I didn't scatter, did you? 27 Then you should have taken my money to the bankers. Then when I returned I would have received my capital with interest. 28 So take the money away from this fellow and give it to the one who has the greatest sum. 29 In fact, to everyone who has, more will be given and then some; and from those who don't have, even what they do have will be taken away. 30 And throw this worthless slave where it is utterly dark. Out there they'll weep and grind their teeth.'

31 "When the son of Adam comes in his glory, accompanied by all his messengers, then he will occupy his glorious throne. 32 Then all peoples will be assembled before him, and he will separate them into groups, much as a shepherd segregates sheep from goats. 33 He'll place the sheep to his right and the goats to his left. 34 Then the king will say to those at his right, 'Come, you who have the blessing of my Father, inherit the domain prepared for you from the foundation of the world. 35 You may remember, I was hungry and you gave me something to eat; I was thirsty and you gave me something to drink; I was a foreigner and you offered me hospitality; 36 I was naked and you clothed me; I was ill and you visited me; I was in prison and you came to see me.'

37 "Then the virtuous will say to him, 'Lord, when did we see you hungry and feed you or thirsty and give you a drink? 38 When did we notice that you were a foreigner and offer you hospitality? Or naked and clothe you? 39 When did we find you ill or in prison and come to visit you?'

[40]"And the king will respond to them: 'I swear to you, whatever you did for the most inconspicuous members of my family, you did for me as well.'

[41]"Next, he will say to those at his left, 'You, condemned to the everlasting fire prepared for the devil and his messengers, get away from me! [42]You too may remember, I was hungry and you didn't give me anything to eat; I was thirsty and you refused me a drink; [43]I was a foreigner and you failed to offer me hospitality; naked and you didn't clothe me; ill and in prison and you didn't visit me.'

[44]"Then they will give him a similar reply: 'Lord, when did we notice that you were hungry or thirsty or a foreigner or naked or ill or in prison and did not attempt to help you?'

[45]"He will then respond: 'I swear to you, whatever you didn't do for the most inconspicuous members of my family, you didn't do for me.'

[46]"The second group will then head for everlasting punishment, but the virtuous for everlasting life."

Note: Introductory information regarding the passion story is provided by the cameo "The Passion Narrative: Introduction" (pp. 132–33), and by a second cameo essay, "Sources for the Passion Story."

SOURCES FOR THE PASSION STORY

The story of Jesus' arrest, trial, crucifixion, and burial is derived from five sources: the four canonical gospels and the Gospel of Peter.

The Gospel of Peter was discovered toward the end of the nineteenth century and consists of one large fragment dated to around 800 C.E. and two tiny fragments dated to approximately 200 C.E. The surviving text of the Gospel of Peter begins with Jesus' trial just as Pilate is washing his hands and ends with Peter and Andrew returning to their trade as fishermen.

One coherent and consecutive story runs through all five versions of the passion story, in spite of incidents that diverge from some hypothetical baseline or vary markedly from other accounts of the same incident. For scholars, that raises the crucial question of whether or not there was a single underlying narrative source for all five versions. It is inconceivable that five authors, working independently of each other, could each have fashioned one coherent story out of isolated oral traditions. The only viable alternative appears to be: all five accounts are creative adaptations of a single written original.

What is the present state of informed opinion about how the process of forming one coherent passion story may have taken place? There is a fairly strong scholarly consensus that Mark is the only source of the sequence of events for Matthew and Luke (Matthew and Luke may have had other sources for this or that detail or incident, but not for the narrative as a whole). This is more evident, and therefore less disputed, in the case of Matthew who follows Mark quite closely. It is less evident, and therefore more disputed, for Luke who makes use of Mark more creatively.

The real problem is the relation of the Fourth Gospel to the synoptics. Scholars

26 **And so when Jesus had concluded his discourse, he told his
disciples,** [2]"You know that Passover comes in two days, and the son of
Adam will be turned over to be crucified."
[3]**Then the ranking priests and elders of the people gathered in the
courtyard of the high priest, whose name was Caiaphas,** [4]**and they
conspired to seize Jesus by trickery and kill him.** [5]**Their slogan was:
"Not during the festival, so there won't be a riot among the people."**

The conspiracy
Mt 26:1–5
Mk 14:1–2, Lk 22:1–2;
Jn 11:45–57
Sources: Mark, John

The conspiracy. Matthew has Jesus once again repeat his prediction of the passion as an introduction to the passion narrative (vv. 1–2). Then, in vv. 3–5, he copies Mark's introduction to the conspiracy.

Matthew is faithful to his source, furthermore, in reproducing Mark's references and allusions to the conspiracy. In 26:14–16, Matthew reiterates Judas' contract with the priests. At the last supper, Jesus predicts that one of his followers will turn him in (26:20–25). Like Mark, Matthew concludes the Gethsemane scene with the observation that his betrayer is at hand (26:46). Then, too, Matthew narrates the arrest in the garden with Judas leading the way (26:47–56). The conspiracy continues when the arresting party brings Jesus before Caiaphas, the high priest (26:57). The priests and the Council then

are at present divided on whether John made use of Mark, or perhaps even Matthew or Luke. Current opinion is swinging once again in the direction of Johannine dependence on one or more of the synoptic accounts. If John's account of the passion is based on a source independent of the synoptics, that hypothetical source must also have been the basis for Mark's version, in order to account for two relatively consistent versions of the same sequence of events. Thus far scholars have been unable to reconstruct such a hypothetical common source for both Mark and John.

The recently discovered Gospel of Peter poses a further problem. It follows the common sequence of the other four accounts of the passion, but also includes material unique to each of them, as well as material found nowhere else. On the view of most scholars, Peter is a composite document: earlier sources were expanded to form what is presently the Gospel of Peter. Scholars are divided on whether those early sources in Peter preserve an early, independent source for the passion of Jesus or whether Peter is dependent on one or the other, or all four, of the canonical gospels.

About a third of the Fellows think that Matthew and Luke had access to information found only in Mark, their common source. The other two-thirds are of the opinion that Mark was not their sole source: Matthew and Luke, in that case, would have supplied what they did not get from Mark out of their imaginations and scriptural suggestions. A bare majority believes that the fourth evangelist knew and used Mark; the minority view is that the author of John had an independent source. Most of the Fellows hold to the traditional view that Mark is the oldest and therefore the first of the passion stories. In other words, the Seminar, like the scholarly world generally, has to work with divergent and often conflicting judgments about the history of the passion narrative.

conspire to collect false testimony against Jesus (26:59–68). The plot continues to unfold as the priests and elders turn Jesus over to Pilate and urge the death penalty (27:1, 12, 18, 20). The final manifestation of the conspiracy comes with the mocking (27:41–42).

Matthew has done little more than repeat what Mark, his source, had written. Matthew has not sought to correct the record, but in fact to enhance the conspiracy theory in minor ways. Because Mark's account of the conspiracy was deemed fictitious, the Fellows agreed that Matthew's version should also be colored black.

The anointing
Mt 26:6–13
Mk 14:3–9; Lk 7:36–50;
Jn 12:1–8
Sources: Mark, Luke, John

26 **[6]While Jesus was in Bethany at the house of Simon the leper,**
[7]a woman who had an alabaster jar of very expensive myrrh came up
to him and poured it over his head while he was reclining <at
table>. [8]When they saw this, the disciples were annoyed, and said,
"What good purpose is served by this waste? [9]After all, she could
have sold it for a good price and given <the money> to the poor."
[10]But Jesus saw through <their complaint> and said to them,
"Why are you bothering this woman? After all, she has done me a
courtesy. [11]Remember, there will always be poor around; but I won't
always be around. [12]After all, by pouring this myrrh on my body she
has made me ready for burial. [13]So help me, wherever this good news
is announced in all the world, what she has done will be told in memory of her."

The anointing. Matthew has copied Mark's version almost word-for-word. He places slightly more emphasis on the symbolic act of anointing Jesus' body in advance for burial (v. 12), so much so in fact, that Matthew does not later have the women bring spices to the tomb (Matt 28:1). Matthew notes that women were present at meals with Jesus (in the wilderness feeding stories he mentions women and children on both occasions: Matt 14:21, 15:38). And Matthew does not object to Jesus' association with women of ill repute (Matt 21:31): "toll collectors and prostitutes will get into God's domain, but you will not." Nevertheless, there is no sexual innuendo in Matthew's version of the story.

As in the case of Mark's account, the Fellows were almost evenly divided on whether the story had a historical kernel or not. The result was a gray weighted average.

The contract
Mt 26:14–16
Mk 14:10–11, Lk 22:3–6
Source: Mark

26 **[14]Then one of the twelve, Judas Iscariot by name, went to the**
ranking priests [15]and said, "What are you willing to pay me if I turn
him over to you?" They agreed on thirty silver coins. [16]And from that
moment he started looking for the right occasion to turn him in.

The contract. In Matthew's version of the compact Judas makes with the priests, it is Judas who takes the initiative in raising the money question (v. 15).

In Mark, Judas does not mention money; the initiative apparently lies with the priests (Mark 14:10). Matthew also supplies the figure agreed on: thirty pieces of silver. This figure may have its roots in ancient lore: the law governing personal injuries caused by an ox (Exod 21:28–32) provides that compensation in the amount of thirty shekels of silver must be paid to the owner of a slave who has been gored to death. That is also the wages the shepherd is to be paid when he annuls his contract with the sheep merchants in Zechariah (Zech 11:12). Matthew was undoubtedly influenced by Zechariah and perhaps Exodus in supplying the specific amount of money Judas was paid. Matthew has done no more than embellish the account he found in his source Mark and has done so on the basis of suggestions taken from the scriptures. Whether or not Judas is a historical figure, the Fellows agreed that this story, like its Markan counterpart, is a fiction. Accordingly, its designation is black.

26 [17]**On the first <day> of Unleavened Bread the disciples came to Jesus, and said, "Where do you want us to get things ready for you to celebrate Passover?"**

[18]**He said,** "Go into the city to so-and-so and say to him, 'The teacher says, "My time is near, I will observe Passover at your place with my disciples."'" [19]**And the disciples did as Jesus instructed them and they got things ready for Passover.**

Preparation for Passover
Mt 26:17–19
Mk 14:12–16, Lk 22:7–13
Source: Mark

Preparation for Passover. Matthew has followed Mark in the sequence of events that begins with the conspiracy against Jesus and ends with Jesus' arrest. Matthew has done no more than reproduce Mark, except that, in this case, he has again slightly abbreviated the story of the preparation for Passover by making the discovery of the upper room less mysterious. Matthew has perhaps not recognized the significance of the biblical account of the anointing of Saul (1 Sam 10:1–8) that has influenced Mark's version of the preparation for Passover. Because Mark's version was taken to be a fiction, the Fellows also designated Matthew's derivative account black.

26 [20]**When it was evening, he was reclining <at table> with his twelve followers.** [21]**And as they were eating, he said,** "So help me, one of you is going to turn me in."

[22]**And they were very upset and each one said to him in turn, "I'm not the one, am I, Master?"**

[23]**In response he said,** "The one who dips his hand in the bowl with me—that's who's going to turn me in! [24]The son of Adam departs just as the scriptures predict, but damn the one responsible for turning the son of Adam in. It would be better for that man had he never been born!"

[25]**Judas, who was to turn him in, responded, "You can't mean me, can you, Rabbi?"**

He says to him, "You said it."

The betrayer
Mt 26:20–25
Mk 14:17–21, Lk 22:21–23; Jn 13:21–30
Sources: Mark, John

The betrayer. In Mark's version of this story, the name of Judas is not mentioned. Matthew supplies the name in v. 25 in an exchange between Judas and Jesus. Matthew's revision of Mark illustrates two ways in which the authors of the gospels modified their sources: they supplied details not mentioned, and sometimes not even implied, in their sources; they created dialogue for both Jesus and those with whom he is in conversation. These practices, characteristic of the tellers of folk stories the world over, indicate how cautious the historian must be in determining whether details and dialogue reflect actual events.

The last supper
Mt 26:26–30
Mk 14:22–26, Lk 22:14–20
Source: Mark
Cf. Jn 13:21–30, 6:48–58;
1 Cor 11:23–26; Did 9:1–5

26

26 **As they were eating, Jesus took a loaf, gave a blessing, and**
broke it into pieces. And he offered it to the disciples, and said,
"Take some and eat; this is my body."
27 **He also took a cup and gave thanks and offered it to them, say-**
ing, "Drink from it, all of you, 28 for this is my blood of the covenant,
which has been poured out for many for the forgiveness of sins. 29 Now
I tell you, I certainly won't drink any of this fruit of the vine from now
on, until that day when I drink it for the first time with you in my
Father's domain!"
30 **And they sang a hymn and left for the Mount of Olives.**

The last supper. In line with his usual practice, Matthew has taken the account of the last meal Jesus ate with his disciples from Mark and added a touch here and there. For example, in v. 28 he has added the phrase "for the forgiveness of sins." Mark had associated the forgiveness of sins with baptism as practiced by John the Baptist (Mark 1:4); Matthew omitted mention of the forgiveness of sins when he reproduced the baptism story from Mark (Matt 3:2), but has added it here to the last supper. In most respects, however, Matthew is simply reproducing Mark.

The tradition of a last supper is reported by Paul in his first letter to the Corinthians (1 Cor 11:23–26). The text of Paul's report reads as follows:

> 23 For I received from the Lord what I also delivered to you, that **the Lord Jesus on the night when he was betrayed took bread, 24 and when he had given thanks, he broke it, and said, "This is my body which is for you. Do this in remembrance of me." 25 In the same way also the cup, after supper, saying, "This cup is the new covenant in my blood. Do this, as often as you drink it, in remembrance of me."**

The Seminar decided to color Paul's statement black: Paul certainly did not receive this information directly from Jesus, and the last meal Jesus ate with his disciples was not a memorial meal, contrary to what Paul says in v. 24. If anything, it was a meal celebrating the arrival of God's kingdom.

The Didache, a Christian manual composed at the end of the first century or the beginning of the second, is the first document to give explicit instruction regarding the celebration of "eucharist." The Didache makes no mention of a last supper, of Passover, nor does it connect eucharist with the passion of Jesus. These are the instructions of the Didache (9:1–5):

1 Concerning eucharist, this is how you are to conduct it: 2 First, concern-
ing the cup, "We thank you, our Father, for the sacred vine of David, your
child, whom you made known to us through Jesus, your child. To you be
glory forever." 3 Then concerning the fragments of bread: "We thank you,
our Father, for the life and knowledge that you made known to us
through Jesus, your child. To you be glory forever. 4 Just as this loaf was
scattered upon the mountains but was gathered into a unity, so your
church should be gathered from the ends of the earth into your domain.
Yours is the glory and the power through Jesus Christ forever." 5 No one
is to eat or drink from your eucharist except those baptized in the name
of the Lord. Recall what the Lord said about this: "Don't throw what is
sacred to the dogs."

John Dominic Crossan has argued forcefully that this version of the eucharist reflects the kind of meal Jesus frequently ate with his disciples and any others who cared to share his table. Jesus' open table gave expression to the inclusiveness he practiced. As it gradually came to be ritualized, the common meal first took the form preserved in the Didache. Then it was developed as Paul represents it in his letter to the Corinthians (cited above), and was finally formalized as Mark pictures it (Mark 14:22–26). Mark was of course copied by Matthew and Luke.

There are other reasons the Fellows thought the last supper as depicted by the gospels was not the report of a historical event. The earliest collection of Jesus' teachings, the Sayings Gospel Q, makes no mention of a last supper of Jesus. The Gospel of Thomas also lacks any reference to the last supper. Furthermore, the core teachings of Jesus do not portray Jesus as someone who focused on his own actions or death, contrary to the words of institution—"this is my body, this is my blood"—attributed to Jesus at the last supper.

The oath
Mt 26:31–35
Mk 14:27–31, Lk 22:31–34;
Jn 13:36–38
Sources: Mark, John

26 31 **Then Jesus says to them,** "All of you will lose faith in me
this night. Remember, it is written, 'I will strike the shepherd and the
sheep of his flock will be scattered!' 32 But after I'm raised, I'll go ahead
of you to Galilee."

33 **In response Peter said to him, "If everyone else loses faith in
you, I never will."**

34 **Jesus said to him,** "So help me, tonight before the rooster crows
you will disown me three times!"

35 **Peter says to him, "Even if they condemn me to die with you, I
will never disown you!" And all of the disciples took the same
oath—all of them.**

The oath. This story does not have the shape of an anecdote that was transmitted from person to person orally before it was written down. It is not a stand-alone story. Rather, it appears to have been composed for its present narrative context. Of course, Matthew has taken it over from Mark, his source. It was probably Mark's invention. The Fellows colored the words attributed to

Jesus black in *The Five Gospels.* They have now designated the narrative frame black as well.

Gethsemane
Matt 26:36–46
Mk 14:32–42, Lk 22:39–46
Source: Mark

26 [36]**Then Jesus goes with them to a place called Gethsemane,**
and he says to the disciples, "Sit down here while I go over there and
pray."
[37]**And taking Peter and the two sons of Zebedee, he began to feel**
dejected and full of anguish. [38]**He says to them,** "I'm so sad I could
die. You stay here with me and be alert!"
[39]**And he went a little farther, lay face down, and prayed,** "My
Father, if it is possible, take this cup away from me! Yet it's not what I
want <that matters>, but what you want."
[40]**And he returns to the disciples and finds them sleeping, and**
says to Peter, "Couldn't you stay awake with me for one hour? [41]Be
alert, and pray that you won't be put to the test! Though the spirit is
willing, the flesh is weak."
[42]**Again for a second time he went away and prayed,** "My Father, if
it is not possible for me to avoid this <cup> without drinking it, your
will must prevail!"
[43]**And once again he came and found them sleeping, since their**
eyes had grown heavy. [44]**And leaving them again, he went away and**
prayed, repeating the same words for a third time.
[45]**Then he comes to the disciples and says to them,** "Are you still
sleeping and taking a rest? Look, the time is at hand! The son of Adam
is being turned over to foreigners. [46]Get up, let's go! See for yourselves!
Here comes the one who is going to turn me in."

Gethsemane. Matthew has taken the Gethsemane story directly from Mark. Although he usually abbreviates and eliminates redundancies, in this case he expands the scene slightly. For the second prayer (v. 42), Mark states that Jesus repeats himself (Mark 14:39); Matthew supplies the words of the prayer Jesus is supposed to have prayed. And Matthew fills in the transition from the second to the third prayers, this time remarking that Jesus prays the same words (v. 44). Matthew has no new information that informs his editorial decision. He is revising only as his storyteller's instincts dictate.

The sequence of events beginning with the prediction of the betrayal by Judas, the oath Peter takes that he will not disavow Jesus, the crossing of the Kidron, and the movement up the Mount of Olives were all doubtless suggested to some early Christian scribe by the story of King David recorded in 2 Samuel 15–17. The details of that story and its Christian parallels are sketched in the cameo, "David and Jesus on the Mount of Olives" (pp. 150–51). Since this story is an invention of some Christian scribe, it does not reflect an actual event. Black is the correct color.

Raymond E. Brown doubts that the Christian scribes who passed on this tradition would have "claimed to retain memories of the wording" Jesus used. They wrote rather "in light of the psalms and of their own prayers."[45] That suggests a gray vote, perhaps even a black vote, for the narrative frame. Brown pictures Jesus as struggling in prayer about how his death fitted into the inbreaking kingdom.[46]

The arrest
Mt 26:47–56
Mk 14:43–52, Lk 22:47–54a;
Jn 18:1–12
Sources: Mark, John

26 47 **And while he was still speaking, suddenly Judas, one of**
the twelve, arrived and with him a great crowd wielding swords and
clubs, dispatched by the ranking priests and elders of the people.
48 **Now the one who was to turn him in had arranged a sign with**
them, saying, "The one I'm going to kiss is the one you want. Arrest
him!"
49 **And he came right up to Jesus, and said, "Hello, Rabbi," and**
kissed him.
50 **But Jesus said to him,** "Look friend, what are you doing here?"
Then they came and seized him and held him fast. 51 **At that**
moment one of those with Jesus lifted his hand, drew his sword,
struck the high priest's slave, and cut off his ear.
52 **Then Jesus says to him,** "Put your sword back where it belongs.
For everyone who takes up the sword will be done in by the sword.
53 Or do you suppose I am not able to call on my Father, who would put
more than twelve legions of heavenly messengers at my disposal?
54 How then would the scriptures come true that say these things are
inevitable?"
55 **At that moment Jesus said to the crowds,** "Have you come out to
take me with swords and clubs as though you were apprehending a
rebel? I used to sit there in the temple area day after day teaching, and
you didn't lift a hand against me."
56 **All of this happened so the writings of the prophets would come**
true. Then all the disciples deserted him and ran away.

The arrest. Matthew has taken over the lineaments of the story from Mark. Those Markan features include the arrival of Judas, the betrayer; the appearance of a crowd accompanying Judas; the act of betrayal (kiss); the arrest; resistance in the form of swordplay; Jesus' reaction; and the flight of the disciples. Matthew reproduces all seven of these features. He has also expanded Jesus' reaction to the resistance in vv. 52–54 with the addition of a saying in v. 52 and a reminder in v. 53 that he could call for heavenly help. As Raymond E. Brown notes, this expansion testifies to the "storytelling and reflectional development" that continued at work on the tradition first formulated by Mark.[47] Then, in characteristic fashion, Matthew concludes by reminding the reader that the course of events is fixed because it was predicted by the scriptures (v. 54).

The reliability of Matthew's account depends on the historical value of Mark's version, since Mark is Matthew's source of information. The arrest is a Markan fiction, in all probability. The arrest story does not have the shape of an isolated anecdote that could have been passed around by word of mouth for the four decades or more that intervened between the death of Jesus and the composition of Mark. On the contrary, the arrest story was created at the same time that the passion narrative was formed. The arrest is an integral part of that story. The arrest cannot be readily segregated from the story of Judas, the last supper, the crossing of Kidron, and the scene on the Mount of Olives. The ingredients and their combination are basically fictitious.

In spite of its fictive character as represented here by Matthew, and by Mark his source, Jesus was undoubtedly arrested. His execution implies that he was apprehended at some point prior to his crucifixion. And he may well have been turned in by someone who knew him well. While those incidents are almost certainly historical, the story that depicts them is largely invented.

The two statements colored pink in the Matthean text indicate the two points that are probably historical (vv. 50, 56). Less certain, and therefore gray, is the statement that Judas led the authorities to Jesus at some private or secret rendezvous (v. 47). The remainder of the Matthean story is black because its Markan counterpart is fictive.

Before the high priest
Mt 26:57–58
Mk 14:53–54, Lk 22:54;
Jn 18:13–14, 15–18
Sources: Mark, John

26 **57Those who had arrested Jesus brought him before Cai-
aphas the high priest, where the scholars and elders had assembled.
58But Peter followed him at a distance as far as the courtyard of the
high priest. He went inside and sat with the attendants to see how
things would turn out.**

Before the high priest. Matthew has done no more than reproduce Mark, his source, in introducing two events: the "trial" before the high priest and other Jewish authorities, and the denial of Peter. Since Jesus was probably arrested by representatives of the high priest or the temple bureaucracy, he was probably brought to the high priest. That much deserves a pink color. The story of Peter's denial, however, is wholly fictitious, so its introduction merits a black designation.

Before the Council
Mt 26:59–68
Mk 14:55–65, Lk 22:66–71;
Jn 18:19–24
Sources: Mark, John.

26 **59The ranking priests and the whole Council were looking
for false testimony against Jesus so they might issue a death sen-
tence; 60but they couldn't find many perjurers to come forward.
Finally, two persons came forward 61and said, "This fellow said,** 'I'm
able to destroy the temple of God and rebuild it within three days.'"

**62Then the high priest got up and questioned him: "Don't you
have something to say? Why do these people testify against you?"**

63But Jesus was silent.

**And the high priest said to him, "I adjure you by the living God:
Tell us if you are the Anointed, the son of God!"**

64Jesus says to him, "If you say so. But I tell you, from now on you
will see the son of Adam sitting at the right hand of Power and coming
on the clouds of the sky."

**65Then the high priest tore his vestment, and said, "He has blas-
phemed! Why do we still need witnesses? See, now you have heard
the blasphemy. 66What do you think?"**

In response they said, "He deserves to die!" 67Then they spit in his

face, and punched him and hit him, [68]saying, "Prophesy for us, you Anointed, you! Guess who hit you!"

Before the Council. Matthew is again dependent on Mark for the basic story of the trial before the Council, but as usual he augments or modifies here and there. Matthew identifies the high priest as Caiaphas (v. 57), who is unnamed in Mark, his source. Mark tells his readers that many perjurers came forward to bear false witness (14:56), while Matthew retreats from that position in asserting that the authorities could not find many who were willing to perjure themselves (v. 60). Matthew specifies that *two* witnesses testified (thus satisfying the legal requirement) that Jesus claimed he would destroy the temple and rebuild it in three days; Mark is less precise in stating that "some people" did so (14:57).

When the high priest asks Jesus if he is the messiah, Mark has him confess "I am!" (14:62). Matthew modifies Jesus' answer to: "If you say so" (v. 64). Matthew also has the mockers call Jesus "the Anointed" (v. 68). The strategy here and elsewhere in the passion story is to have those outside the Christian circle bear witness to the Christian truth, to indicate that Jesus' status was evident even to non-believers. For example, Sanhedrin members are made to ask Jesus if he was "the son of God" (v. 63), a title not used by anyone for Jesus during his lifetime, in the opinion of Raymond E. Brown and the Fellows of the Jesus Seminar. Brown puts the matter pointedly: the question of the high priest "was *not* the formulation in a Jewish interrogation of Jesus" at his trial.[48]

The trial scene was created by some Christian scribe, possibly the author of the Gospel of Mark, at some temporal distance—probably four decades or more—from the events depicted. The basis of the story was not an anecdote that had been formed and transmitted orally. Scholars have searched for a source or sources for the passion story that antedate the surviving written gospels, without any real success. That search should be understood as an effort to date the formation of the passion narrative closer to the events it depicts. Yet even those scholars who have identified a source or sources behind Mark or the Fourth Gospel agree that the passion is largely a Christian fiction inspired in large measure by scriptural allusions. An earlier date does not improve scholarly confidence in the historical reliability of the various accounts.

The problems and improbabilities noted in the commentary on Mark's version apply also to Matthew's revision. Even very conservative gospel scholars concede that the passion story was *partially* created out of scriptural texts, principally the Psalms having to do with the suffering righteous one and Second Isaiah's suffering servant (Isaiah 53). It is difficult to avoid the conclusion that a black designation is both necessary and appropriate.

Peter's denial
Mt 26:69–75
Mk 14:66–72, Lk 22:54b–62; Jn 18:15–18, 25–27
Sources: Mark, John

26 **[69]Meanwhile Peter was sitting outside in the courtyard, and one slave woman came up to him, and said, "You too were with Jesus the Galilean."**

[70]But he denied it in front of everyone, saying, "I don't know what you're talking about!"

[71]**After <Peter> went out to the entrance, another slave woman saw him and says to those there, "This fellow was with that Nazorene Jesus."**

[72]**And again he denied it with an oath: "I don't know the man!"**

[73]**A little later those standing about came and said to Peter, "You really are one of them; even the way you talk gives you away!"**

[74]**Then he began to curse and swear: "I don't know the fellow."**

And just then a rooster crowed. [75]**And Peter remembered what Jesus had said:** "Before the rooster crows you will disown me three times." **And he went outside and wept bitterly.**

Peter's denial. Matthew is dependent on Mark for his story of Peter's denial. He has done no more than make a few changes in detail. In Mark, the same slave woman twice accuses Peter of being a member of Jesus' party (14:69); Matthew attributes the second accusation to another woman (v. 71). Matthew represents Peter as denying the accusation a second time with an oath (v. 72); Mark reserves the oath for Peter's third denial (14:71). Mark has the rooster crow twice (14:72); in Matthew, once is enough (v. 75). Of course, since Matthew has the rooster crow only once, he had to modify the prediction in Matt 26:34 to accommodate this change in the fulfillment. Nevertheless, Matthew follows Mark in having Peter deny his affiliation with the group three times.

Having decided that the basic story was a Markan invention, the Fellows saw nothing in Matthew's text to warrant anything other than a black designation.

Of this story Raymond E. Brown writes: "The survival of the story without a basis in fact seems incredible; yet the Gospel narratives reflect strongly an imaginative storytelling style."[49] That could perhaps be interpeted as a pink vote for the core of the story, but a gray vote for the narrative as a whole.

Before Pilate
Mt 27:1–2
Mk 15:1, Lk 23:1; Jn 18:28
Sources: Mark, John

27 **When morning came, all the ranking priests and elders of the people plotted against Jesus to put him to death.** [2]**And they bound him and led him away and turned him over to Pilate the Roman governor.**

Before Pilate. Matthew introduces the next narrative stage of Jesus' trial and execution, then pauses to report the death of Judas (27:3–10). The Fellows of the Seminar agreed that police under the jurisdiction of the temple authorities—the leading priests—arrested Jesus and took him into custody. Since Jesus was in their custody, it was necessary for them to turn him over to Pilate. The relative certainty of this information prompted the Fellows to color v. 2 pink. The first verse, however, is part of the fictitious plot against Jesus' life. It is quite possible that Caiaphas, the high priest, denounced Jesus to Pilate, perhaps because Jesus threatened the temple cult with its many bankers and vendors; but Matthew's statement that all the ranking priests and elders were involved is a gross exaggeration.

The death of Judas
Mt 27:3–10
Acts 1:15–20
Source: popular lore

27 3Then Judas, who had turned him in, realizing that he had
been condemned, was overcome with remorse and returned the
thirty silver coins to the ranking priests and elders 4with this
remark, "I have made the grave mistake of turning in this blameless
man."
But they said, "What's that to us? That's your problem!"
5And hurling the silver into the temple he slunk off, and went out
and hanged himself.
6The ranking priests took the silver and said, "It wouldn't be right
to put this into the temple treasury, since it's blood money."
7So they devised a plan and bought the Potter's Field as a burial
ground for foreigners. 8As a result, that field has been known as
the Bloody Field even to this day. 9So the prediction Jeremiah the
prophet made came true: "And they took the thirty silver coins,
the price put on a man's head (this is the price they put on him
among the Israelites), 10and they donated it for the Potter's Field, as
my Lord commanded me."

The death of Judas. Alternate explanations arose about the fate of Judas the informer, one found in Matthew, the other in the book of Acts. Both are based on scripture in combination with the origin of a place name.

The amount Judas receives for handing Jesus over was the price an owner received for the loss of a slave (Exod 21:28–32) and the wages Zechariah received as a shepherd. When Zechariah receives his wages from "the sheep merchants," he takes the money and throws it into the temple treasury, as the Lord had instructed him (Zech 11:12–13). In addition, Ahithophel, who betrayed King David at the time Absalom revolted, ended his career by hanging himself (2 Sam 17:5–19, 23). Matthew evidently borrowed the essential elements from these earlier sources in arriving at his story of the repentance and demise of Judas. Verses 3–5 are part of the developing legend about the fate of Judas based on suggestions found in the scriptures. As a fiction, they deserve a black designation. Raymond E. Brown agrees that the story of Ahithophel is what prompted Christian storytellers to invent the tale of Judas' death by hanging.[50]

In the gospel account, the priests decided that Judas' blood money was not acceptable, so they used the money to buy a plot in Jerusalem for the burial of aliens. The field they bought became known, according to the legend, as the "Bloody Field," presumably because the priests had purchased it with "blood money." Etiological legends grew up in the ancient world as explanations for how and why places acquired their names. Black accurately reflects the Seminar's assessment that Judas was swept up into a whirlwind of popular lore and scribal activity with no basis in history.

In the book of Acts (1:15–20), the author Luke offers an entirely different explanation of Judas' fate, although that explanation is also connected with a field in Jerusalem called the "Bloody Field."

15And it was during this period that Peter got up before the assembled
brotherhood, about one hundred and twenty altogether, and began:

16"My brothers, the scripture was bound to come true, the one in
which the holy spirit used the mouth of David to foretell what
would happen to Judas who guided the police to Jesus when he
was arrested. 17Judas was one of our number and shared our com-
mon ministry."

**18(This Judas, it should be said, purchased a plot of ground
with the proceeds of his act of villainy, and fell headlong on the
ground so that he burst open in the middle and his entrails
poured out. 19This bit of information was common knowledge to
everyone in Jerusalem so that they named the place *Akeldema* in
their own language, which means 'plot <purchased with> blood
<money>.')**

**20The text to which I refer, Peter continued, is found in the
Book of Psalms:**

May his dwelling place become desolate,
and may no one else inhabit it.

Further,

Someone else should assume his office.

In this account, Judas, rather than the priests, takes the "blood money" and buys a plot of ground with it. He subsequently falls headlong on this ground and is eviscerated. It is unclear from Luke's story just how this happened. But the same explanation is given for the name of the field in Jerusalem: it was called *Akeldema,* which means "Bloody Field." According to Luke, the fate of Judas was to fulfill two different predictions in the Psalms, one an adaptation of Ps 69:25, the other a quotation from Ps 109:8. Luke's version is also a legend created out of the imagination fired by incidental phrases and sentences in the scriptures, allied with the desire to account for the origin of a place name.

The cameo "David and Jesus on the Mount of Olives" (pp. 150–51) provides additional details of the role played by the Greek scriptures in conceiving the events surrounding Jesus' betrayal and arrest, and Judas' fate.

Before Pilate
Mt 27:11–26
Mk 15:1–15, Lk 23:1–7,
13–25; Jn 18:28–19:16;
Pet 1:1–2
Sources: Mark, John, Peter

27

**11Jesus stood before the Roman governor, and the governor
questioned him: "You are 'the King of the Judeans'?"**
Jesus said, "If you say so."
**12And while he was being accused by the ranking priests and
elders, he said absolutely nothing.**
**13Then Pilate says to him, "Don't you have something to say to the
long list of charges they bring against you?" 14But he did not
respond to him, not to a single charge, so the governor was baffled.**
15At each festival it was the custom for the Roman governor to set

one prisoner free for the crowd, whichever one they wanted. 16<The
Romans> were then holding a notorious prisoner named Jesus
Barabbas. 17When the crowd had gathered, Pilate said to them, "Do
you want me to set Jesus Barabbas free for you or Jesus who is
known as 'the Anointed'?" 18After all, he knew that they had turned
him in out of envy.

19While he was sitting on the judgment seat, his wife sent a mes-
sage to him: "Don't have anything to do with that innocent man,
because I have agonized a great deal today in a dream on account
of him."

20The ranking priests and the elders induced the crowds to ask for
Barabbas but to execute Jesus. 21In response <to their request> the
Roman governor said to them, "Which of the two do you want me to
set free for you?"

They said, "Barabbas!"

22Pilate says to them, "What should I do with Jesus known as 'the
Anointed'?"

Everyone responded, "Have him crucified!"

23But he said, "Why? What has he done wrong?"

But they would shout all the louder, "Have him crucified!"

24Now when Pilate could see that he was getting nowhere, but
rather that a riot was starting, he took water and washed his hands
in full view of the crowd, and said, "Don't blame me for this fel-
low's blood. Now it's your business!"

25In response all the people said, "So, smear his blood on us and
on our children."

26Then he set Barabbas free for them, but had Jesus flogged, and
then turned him over to be crucified.

Before Pilate. Matthew has taken over his story from Mark, with some modifications and notable embellishments. Verse 11 is taken directly from Mark: Pilate asks Jesus whether he is the "King of the Judeans." Jesus responds, as he does in Mark, from Pilate's perspective, "If you say so." Later in the episode Matthew will refocus the question on whether Jesus is the Anointed (v. 22). Verses 12–14 are also taken directly from Mark with little or no change.

Matthew next comes to the Barabbas episode, which he has also borrowed from Mark, except that he has introduced a parallelism in names: Barabbas has become Jesus Barabbas to match Jesus the Anointed. Matthew has also abbreviated Mark's account slightly (vv. 15–18).

With v. 19 we come to the first of Matthew's amplifications: the message from Pilate's wife that she has learned in a dream that Jesus is innocent. Matthew believes God communicates with human beings through the medium of dreams and visions—the astrologers from the East, for example, are warned in a dream to return home by another way (Matt 2:12)—so this is his way of underscoring the innocence of Jesus. The dream of Pilate's wife is a Matthean fabrication.

In v. 22, Matthew shifts from the "King of the Judeans" to "Jesus known as the Anointed." This represents a change from Mark (14:12). But the result is the same: the crowd wants Jesus crucified and Barabbas released.

At this point Matthew makes another fateful addition to the Markan story: He has Pilate wash his hands as a way of declaring his own innocence in the death of Jesus—after all, Pilate wanted to release Jesus (v. 24). The washing of hands is the custom prescribed in Deuteronomy for those who seek to be free of blood guilt for a murder (Deut 21:1–9). Handwashing as a symbol of innocence is also mentioned in Psalm 26:6. The crowd—all the people—then accept the responsibility for Jesus' blood (v. 25). Thus Matthew has further aggravated the tragic fiction—which Mark invented with *mea culpas*—by having Judeans embrace collective guilt for themselves and their children, although many of them had been followers of Jesus and many others probably knew little or nothing about him. The blame that was supposed to last only for two generations has been extended by Christians for two millennia. Matthew has blatantly exonerated Pilate, the truly guilty party, and along with him, one presumes, all his Italian descendants.

As in the case of Mark, Matthew's version of the trial before Pilate, with the exceptions noted, is to be colored in the deepest hues of black.

Raymond E. Brown agrees that the underlying event narrated here deserves what the Jesus Seminar would interpret as a red vote: "Pilate sentenced Jesus to die on the cross on the charge of being 'the king of the Jews.'"[51] Yet he interprets the actual descriptions as dramatizations. Matthew has expanded the "romanticized characterizations" drawn from "popular reflection" in depicting the dream of Pilate's wife, the handwashing of Pilate, as well as the shared responsibility for Jesus' innocent blood.[52] That analysis would probably convert to a black vote. Brown does think that someone like Jesus Barabbas was arrested during a riot in Jerusalem but spared by Pilate (a gray vote?), despite the "frustrating" lack of any historical evidence.[53]

Mocking
Mt 27:27–31
Mk 15:16–20; Jn 19:1–3;
Pet 3:1–4
Sources: Mark, John, Peter

27 **[27]Then the Roman governor's soldiers took Jesus into the
governor's residence and surrounded him with the whole company
<of Roman troops>. [28]The Romans stripped him and dressed him in
a crimson cloak, [29]and they wove a crown out of thorns and put it on
his head. They placed a staff in his right hand, and bowing down
before him, they made fun of him, saying, "Greetings, 'King of the
Judeans'!"[30] And spitting on him, the Roman soldiers took the staff
and hit him on the head. [31]And when they had made fun of him, they
stripped off the cloak and put his own clothes back on him and led
him out to crucify him.**

Mocking. Matthew follows Mark closely in reproducing this piece of ritual theatre. In investiture protocol, it is important to invest a new leader before all the people so they will know who their leader is. Matthew follows Mark in having the whole company of soldiers assembled (v. 27).

They then enact a derisive investiture by stripping Jesus of his regular clothes and arraying him in a royal robe (v. 28); next they put a mock crown of thorns on his head and a staff of authority in his right hand, and bow down before him in jeering obeisance. Finally, they taunt him with the title "King of the Judeans" (v. 30). This piece of ritual theatre proclaims the truth—Jesus *is* king of the Judeans for Matthew—but does so ironically: the ritual says something like the opposite of what it ostensibly says.

The ironic scene complete, the soldiers reverse the procedure, strip Jesus of his royal vestments, and take him out to crucify him.

Like its Markan predecessor, Matthew's mockery is the product of the Christian imagination long after the events it is supposed to depict. From the distance of a half century, Jesus can be thought of as a kind of king, even though he had no aspirations in that direction. The theatre and the details were of course suggested by scripture and by standard protocol that goes with investing royalty. Black is the accurate designation.

27 [32]**As they were going out, they came across a Cyrenian named Simon. This fellow they conscripted to carry his cross.**

Simon of Cyrene
Mt 27:32
Mk 15:21, Lk 23:26–32
Source: Mark

Simon of Cyrene. Matthew does no more than copy Mark's note about Simon from Cyrene. Matthew apparently has no sense of Mark's narrative purpose, which was to depict a true Simon who, unlike the unfaithful Simon Peter, was ready to carry the cross of Jesus. Since that scene is the product of Mark's literary imagination, this one rightly deserves a black designation.

Raymond E. Brown rejects the proposal that Simon of Cyrene is a fiction. The "anomaly of one person carrying another's cross increases the odds that Simon was a historical figure." That might be translated as a Jesus Seminar gray or pink. But in that case, Brown has to vote black on John 19:17, which states that Jesus carried his own cross. He also has to account for the omission of Simon in the Gospel of Peter.[54]

27 [33]**And when the soldiers reached the place known as**
Golgotha (which means "Place of the Skull"), [34]**they gave him a drink**
of wine mixed with something bitter, and once he tasted it, he didn't
want to drink it. [35]After crucifying him, **the Romans divided up his**
garments by casting lots. [36]**And they sat down there and kept guard**
over him. [37]**And over his head** they put an inscription that identified
his crime: "This is Jesus the King of the Judeans."

[38]**Then the Roman soldiers crucified two rebels with him, one on**
his right and one on his left.

[39]**Those passing by kept taunting him, wagging their heads, and**
saying, [40]**"You who would destroy the temple and rebuild it in three**
days, save yourself; if you're God's son, come down from the cross!"

Crucifixion
Mt 27:33–44
Mk 15:22–32, Lk 23:33–43;
Jn 19:17–24; Pet 4:1–5
Sources: Mark, John, Peter

[41]Likewise the ranking priests made fun of him along with the scholars and elders; they would say, [42]"He saved others, but he can't even save himself! He's the King of Israel; he should come down from the cross here and now and we'll trust him. [43]He trusted God, so God should rescue him now if he holds him dear. After all, he said, 'I'm God's son.'"

[44]In the same way the rebels who were crucified with him would abuse him.

Crucifixion. Following his customary practice, Matthew has taken over the text of Mark and in the process has revised and amplified what he found in that earlier narrative of the crucifixion scene. The sequence of events in Mark was this:

arrival at Golgotha
drink of wine mixed with myrrh
crucifixion
division of garments
temporal reference: 9 A.M.
placard identifying the crime
crucifixion of two rebels, one on either side
taunting and making fun

Matthew follows this schedule closely, except that he omits the mention of the time and substitutes the observation that the Judean authorities kept guard over Jesus, probably in anticipation of his later notice that they also posted a guard at the tomb (27:62–66).

He has also made other minor alterations in Mark's version. For example, he revises the drink that Jesus was offered at the outset (Matt 27:34//Mark 15:23) to "wine mixed with something bitter" to bring the incident closer to Ps 69:21:

> They gave me something bitter for food,
> and for my thirst they offered me sour wine.

Raymond E. Brown has argued that there was only one offering of wine to Jesus while he was on the cross and that offering was the second one in 27:48//Mark 15:36. In his customary fashion, Mark doubled the incident, the first of which is the fictive version. Brown would thus presumably vote black on this verse in Matthew.[55]

Matthew also modifies Mark's suggestion that the Romans identified Jesus' offense by noting it on a placard; Matthew positions it over Jesus' head and thus suggests that it was attached to the cross (v. 37). There is no corroborating evidence that the Romans tacked placards to the crosses of their victims. The typical cross consisted of a simple crossbeam set on top of a post (like a capital T rather than a lowercase t). Matthew invents the tall cross with placard above the head so beloved by artists. The person being punished either carried the placard himself, or someone else carried it for him.

Brown insists there is "no convincing objection" to the charge on the basis of which the Romans executed Jesus and thus to the historicity of the placard.[56] It is difficult to know how Brown's vote should be interpreted. Does "no convincing objection" mean it probably occured (= pink) or does it mean it is possible that it occurred (= gray)? In his massive study of the passion, Brown consistently assumes the historicity of the details of one or the other of the gospels, and seeks only to determine whether there is solid evidence against such an assumption. This methodology lends itself to a high fudge factor.

There is some comparative evidence for the use of a placard in connection with punishment for some crime. Suetonius, the Roman historian (ca. 69–140 C.E.), tells the story of how the Emperor Domitian (ruled 81–96 C.E.) had a spectator dragged from his seat at the Colosseum because he made a remark about how the Thracian gladiator was an adequate match for his Gallic opponent. The spectator also said something disparaging about the emperor, the patron of the games. For his loose tongue, he had a placard tied around his neck reading, "A Thracian supporter who spoke evil of his Emperor," and was thrown to the dogs who tore him to pieces (Suetonius, *Domitian* 10.1).

The church historian Eusebius relates a similar incident about a certain Attalus who was destined for the arena to face wild beasts. He was led around the amphitheatre and a placard was carried in front of him which read, "This is Attalus the Christian" (*Ecclesiastical History* 5.1.43–44).

At the close of the mocking scene, Matthew extends the jibe by those jesting to include v. 43. The language of that addition directly imitates Ps 21:9 LXX (22:8 in Hebrew and English):

> He hoped in the Lord,
> so let the Lord rescue and save him,
> since he holds him dear.

And Matthew adds the editorial comment: "After all, he said, 'I'm God's son'" (v. 43). The attribution of the claim that he was God's son is put on the lips of the taunters. Matthew seems to enjoy making hostile witnesses bear unwitting witness to Christian convictions. In the temptation story, Matthew has Satan twice challenge Jesus with "If you are God's son, . . . " (4:3, 6). Jesus of course did not himself make such a claim.

Matthew has reproduced the scene in Mark, which had itself already been developed along lines suggested by Psalm 22 and Isaiah 53. (The additional references to scripture are discussed in the commentary on the parallel passage in Mark.) Like its Markan counterpart, the bulk of Matthew's version of the crucifixion scene was designated black.

The death of Jesus
Mt 27:45–56
Mk 15:33–41, Lk 23:44–49; Jn 19:25–37; Pet 5:1–6
Sources: Mark, John, Peter

27 [45]**Beginning at noon darkness blanketed the entire land
until mid-afternoon.** [46]**And about 3 o'clock in the afternoon Jesus
shouted at the top of his voice,** *"Eli, Eli, lema sabachthani"* (which
means, "My God, my God, why did you abandon me?")
[47]**When some of those standing there heard, they would say, "This**

fellow's calling Elijah!" [48]And immediately one of them ran and took a sponge filled with sour wine and stuck it on a pole and offered him a drink.

[49]But the rest would say, "Wait! Let's see if Elijah comes to rescue him."

[50]Jesus again shouted at the top of his voice and stopped breathing.

[51]And suddenly the curtain of the temple was torn in two from top to bottom, and the earth quaked, rocks were split apart, [52]and the tombs were opened and many bodies of sleeping saints came back to life. [53]And they came out of the tombs after his resurrection and went into the holy city, where they appeared to many. [54]The Roman officer and those keeping watch over Jesus with him witnessed the sign and what had happened, and were terrified, and said, "This man really was God's son."

[55]Many women were there observing this from a distance—those who had followed Jesus from Galilee to assist him, [56]among whom were Mary of Magdala, and Mary the mother of James and Joseph, and the mother of the sons of Zebedee.

The death of Jesus. As usual, Matthew follows Mark quite closely in rehearsing the death of Jesus. He narrates the events in the same sequence, and he sticks fairly close to the language of Mark, except at one point.

In vv. 51–53, Matthew has expanded on Mark's tale of the temple curtain: in addition to the veil being split, there is now an earthquake, rocks are split apart, tombs pop open and many saints are restored to life. Of course, Matthew adds with a red face, they did not come out of their tombs and appear in Jerusalem until after the resurrection of Jesus (they could not preempt Jesus by appearing prior to his resurrection!). This communal resurrection is similar to the account in the Gospel of Peter where a cross symbolizing the slain righteous of Israel accompanies Jesus from the tomb (Pet 10:1–5).

The expansion of the supernatural phenomena found in Mark—darkness at noon and the rending of the temple curtain—does not lend credence to Matthew's reputation as a historian: He is a religious propagandist representing these cosmic portents as acts of God. Except for the mention of the women in vv. 55–56, the text of Matthew, like that of Mark, was given a black rating.

Raymond E. Brown concedes that v. 53 is most likely "a Matthean development beyond" any earlier tradition Matthew is using.[57] The apocalyptic signs in vv. 51–52 come from "diverse popular traditions" used imaginatively by Matthew.[58] Of course, Brown prefers to read these signs as "theological interpretation"; to evaluate their "literal historicity," he counters, misses the point.[59] He would no doubt give their theological interpetation a red vote, but that does not obscure the fact that even on his guarded terms the signs deserve a black vote for their historical value.

Commentary on other features in Matthew's account may be found under the parallel passage in Mark.

27 **57 When it had grown dark, a rich man from Arimathea, by**
the name of Joseph, who himself was a follower of Jesus, appeared
on the scene, 58 and went to Pilate and requested the body of Jesus.
Then Pilate ordered it to be turned over <to him>. 59 And taking the
body, Joseph wrapped it in a clean linen shroud 60 and put it in his
new tomb, which had been cut in the rock. He rolled a huge stone in
the opening of the tomb and went away. 61 But Mary of Magdala and
the other Mary stayed there, sitting opposite the tomb.

The burial
Mt 27:57–61
Mk 15:42–47, Lk 23:50–56;
Jn 19:38–42; Pet 2:1–3, 6:1–4
Sources: Mark, John, Peter

The burial. Matthew has turned Joseph into a *rich* man and made him a *follower of Jesus* (v. 57), two pieces of information he did not find in his source, the Gospel of Mark. As the story develops, Joseph grows in stature. Eventually, in the Gospel of John, Joseph will be joined by another imaginary character, Nicodemus (John 19:39). Moreover, the shroud Mark had Joseph purchase has now become a *clean* shroud (v. 59), and the tomb has been turned into *his new* tomb (v. 60). The two Marys not only note where Jesus has been buried, Matthew has them sit opposite the tomb, as though guarding it (v. 61). This motif comports with Matthew's notice that a guard was posted at the tomb to keep his disciples from stealing the body of Jesus (27:62–66).

In other respects, Matthew is doing no more than copying Mark. Since Mark's account is fictitious, that of Matthew has to fall in the same category. The text is accordingly colored black.

27 **62 On the next day, which is the day after Preparation, the**
ranking priests and the Pharisees met with Pilate: 63 "Your Excel-
lency, we remember what that impostor said while he was still alive:
'After three days I am going to be raised up.' 64 So order the tomb
sealed for three days so his disciples won't come and steal his body
and tell everyone, 'He has been raised from the dead,' in which case,
the last deception will be worse than the first."

65 Pilate replied to them, "You have a guard; go and secure it the
best way you know how."

66 They went and secured the tomb by sealing <it with a> stone
and posting a guard.

The guard at the tomb
Mt 27:62–66
Pet 8:1–6
Sources: Matthew, Peter

The guard at the tomb. Matthew reflects the view that in some quarters the empty tomb story backfired as an attempt to demonstrate the historicity of Jesus' resurrection. Unbelievers countered the story of the empty tomb with the charge that the body had simply been removed from the tomb by the disciples. Matthew creates a story to counteract that charge and to buttress the account of the empty tomb. The posting of the guard is reported only by Matthew among the canonical gospels, but it is elaborated in the Gospel of Peter (8:1–11:7). (The version in Peter may well be based on the information found in Matthew.) The exchange between Jews and Jewish Christians involved the charge of deception on both sides: you Christians stole the body and claimed that he had risen from the dead; you Jewish critics bribed the guards not to tell what they really saw (Pet 11:5–7).

The implausibilities of the scenes about the guards at the tomb are so notable that even Raymond E. Brown acknowledges the complete lack of either internal or external evidence that would affirm their historicity.[60] Brown concedes that they belong in the same category with the massacre of the children in the birth narrative and the flight to Egypt. Since he seems to regard none of these events as historical, we may conclude that he would have cast a black vote had he been a member of the Jesus Seminar.

The Fellows of the Seminar concluded that the original story of the empty tomb was a Markan fiction and that the subsequent fiction of the guards at the tomb and the charge and countercharges were equally fictive. They decided to color the entire narrative black.

Note: Stories of the empty tomb, appearances of the risen Jesus, and the ascension have been gathered into a separate section (pp. 449–95). Color coding and commentary on Matt 28:1–8, 9–10, 11–15, 16–20 will be found in that section.

The Gospel of Luke

1 Since so many have undertaken to compile an orderly narrative
of the events that have run their course among us, [2]just as the original
eyewitnesses and ministers of the word transmitted them to us, [3]it
seemed good that I, too, after thoroughly researching everything from
the beginning, should set them systematically in writing for you,
Theophilus, [4]so that Your Excellency may realize the reliability of the
teachings in which you have been instructed.

Prologue
Lk 1:1–4
No parallels
Source: Luke

Prologue. Luke is the only gospel writer to preface his work with a formal prologue. In doing so, he imitates the style of the hellenistic historians. The key phrases are "an orderly narrative of events" (v. 1), "original eyewitnesses" and "ministers" (v. 2), "thoroughly researching everything" in order to "set them systematically in writing" (v. 3), and a dedication to a supporting patron, who can count on its "reliability" (v. 4).

The author betrays the fact that he is a second- or third-generation Christian who is aware of other gospels and seeks to improve on them. Ancient historians endeavored to be impartial in their perspectives, but they did not claim factual accuracy in the modern sense.

Luke also begins the book of Acts with a prologue that is parallel to this one. The author of Luke-Acts is the only author who wrote a sequel to his gospel.

Since Luke's prologue reports neither words nor acts of Jesus, the Fellows of the Jesus Seminar did not assess its historical reliability.

Note: The infancy narratives from the Gospel of Luke have been gathered together with those from the Gospel of Matthew and placed at the end of this volume. Their placement reflects the chronological development of the gospel traditions: the birth stories came last among the components of the written gospels.

JOHN THE BAPTIST

The disciples of John the Baptist formed a movement that continued after the ministry of Jesus began and even after John's death. The New Testament itself confirms this fact. Both the Gospel of Mark and the Sayings Gospel Q document the existence of the disciples of John during Jesus' public ministry. Mark notes that the disciples of John fast in contrast to the disciples of Jesus, who do not (Mark 2:18). When John is beheaded by Herod Antipas, John's disciples collect his body and bury it (Mark 6:29). The Sayings Gospel Q records that John sends his disciples to Jesus to determine who Jesus is (Luke 7:18). The Gospel of John reports that a dispute arose between the disciples of John and some Judeans over matters of purification (John 3:25). Evidently some of the key disciples of Jesus had once been followers of John (John 1:35–51).

Since the Baptist movement existed alongside the Jesus movement, to what extent did the Baptist influence the disciples of Jesus and perhaps even Jesus himself? This is a particularly pertinent question if Jesus had once been a follower of John (Mark 1:9–11). The notion that John the Baptist may have risen from the dead (Mark 6:14, 16, 8:28) probably originated with the disciples of John. This conviction of John's disciples may have established the pattern of expectation for the disciples of Jesus after his crucifixion.

The *Pseudo-Clementines,* a collection of fictitious tales concerning the conversion of Clement of Rome and his travels with Peter, suggests that the disciples of John may have prayed to John. It is possible that John's disciples thought of him as the messiah. This probably explains why the Fourth Gospel takes such pains to deny that the Baptist was the messiah (John 1:20, 25, 3:28) and why it represents him as expressly advising his followers to become disciples of Jesus (1:35–42). Some scholars think the birth story of John the Baptist preserved in Luke (1:5–25, 57–80) derives from John's followers and reflects their messianic understanding of him.

John the Baptist plays a key role in the New Testament gospels, in Q, and in the Gospel of Thomas. The followers of Jesus found it necessary to interpret Jesus in categories related to John. For that reason, it appears that John and his disciples provide several paradigms (messianic figure; special birth; resurrection) for their understanding of Jesus.

John was a major religious figure in the time of Jesus. In the public mind, John was very likely a much "bigger" presence than Jesus. Josephus, the Jewish historian, states flatly that Herod Antipas feared John on the grounds that the Baptist could instigate a revolution; as a consequence, he had John executed. The Jews later viewed the destruction of Herod's army as retribution for John's execution (*Antiquities* 18.118–19). The Gospel of Mark reports, probably with some exaggeration, that all the residents of Judea and Jerusalem were baptized by John (Mark 1:5) and that everybody considered John a prophet (Mark 11:32). Some of the supporters of John probably adopted the cause of Jesus' followers and introduced Johannine elements, such as fasting and baptism, into the nascent Christian movement.

Just as Jesus conducted his ministry in the shadow of John's public ministry, so Jesus' disciples competed with the followers of John the Baptist in developing their new movement.

A voice in the wilderness
Lk 3:1–20
Mk 1:1–8, Mt 3:1–12;
Jn 1:19–28; GEbi 1, 3
Sources: Mark, Q, John

3 In the fifteenth year of the rule of Emperor Tiberius, when
Pontius Pilate was governor of Judea, Herod tetrarch of Galilee, his
brother Philip tetrarch of the district of Iturea and Trachonitis, and
Lysanias tetrarch of Abilene, 2during the high-priesthood of Annas
and Caiaphas, the word of God came to John, son of Zechariah, in
the wilderness. 3And he went into the whole region around the
Jordan, calling for baptism and a change of heart that lead to for-
giveness of sins. 4As is written in the book of the sayings of Isaiah
the prophet,

> The voice of someone shouting in the wilderness:
> "Make ready the way of the Lord,
> make his paths straight.
> 5Every valley will be filled,
> and every mountain and hill leveled.
> What is crooked will be made straight,
> and the rough ways smooth.
> 6Then the whole human race will see the salvation of God."

7So <John> would say to the crowds that came out to get baptized
by him, "You spawn of Satan! Who warned you to flee from the
impending doom? 8Well then, start producing fruits suitable for a
change of heart, and don't even start saying to yourselves, 'We have
Abraham for our father.' Let me tell you, God can raise up children
for Abraham right out of these rocks. 9Even now the axe is aimed at
the root of the trees. So every tree not producing choice fruit gets cut
down and tossed into the fire."

10The crowds would ask him, "So what should we do?"

11And he would answer them, "Whoever has two shirts should
share with someone who has none; whoever has food should do the
same." 12Toll collectors also came to get baptized, and they would
ask him, "Teacher, what should we do?" 13He told them, "Charge
nothing above the official rates." 14Soldiers also asked him, "And
what about us?" And he said to them, "No more shakedowns! No
more frame-ups either! And be satisfied with your pay."

15The people were filled with expectation and everyone was try-
ing to figure out whether John might be the Anointed.

16John's answer was the same to everyone: "I baptize you with
water; but someone more powerful than I is coming. I am not fit to
untie his sandal straps. He'll baptize you with holy spirit and fire.
17His pitchfork is in his hand, to make a clean sweep of his threshing
floor and to gather his wheat into the granary, but the chaff he'll
burn in a fire that can't be put out."

18And so, with many other exhortations he preached to the people.
19But Herod the tetrarch, who had been denounced by John over the
matter of Herodias, his brother's wife, 20topped off all his other
crimes by shutting John up in prison.

A voice in the wilderness. Luke adds new material to the story as he found it in the Gospel of Mark (like Matthew, Luke borrowed heavily from Mark in composing his gospel). The additional material is found in vv. 1–2, 5–6, 10–14.

Luke has constructed an extended literary period in 3:1–2 as though he were beginning his gospel all over again. This elaborate sentence is the equivalent of a formal prologue to a book that reports the words and deeds of a prophet. In its Greek version, the book of Jeremiah begins: "The word of God came to Jeremias, son of Chelcias . . . in the thirteenth year of the rule of Josias, son of Amos, king of Israel." The fact that there are two prologues in Luke's gospel has led many scholars to think that the Gospel of Luke once began with 3:1–2, and that the birth and childhood stories in chapters 1–2 were added at a later time, along with a second formal prologue.

The prologue of 3:1–2 is used to date the inauguration of John's activity as an adult. Luke had set the dates of the birth of John and Jesus in the context of world history by referring to Herod the Great (38–4 B.C.E., Luke 1:5) and the Emperor Augustus (26 B.C.E.–14 C.E., Luke 2:1). He now locates the prophetic call of John as having occurred during the fifteenth year of the reign of the Emperor Tiberius (14–37 C.E.), which would place it in 28/29 C.E., depending on when the new year began; and during the governorship of Pontius Pilate (26–36 C.E.); and during the reign of Herod Antipas, tetrarch of Galilee (4 B.C.E.–39 C.E.); and during the tenure of Philip, another son of Herod the Great, who was tetrarch of regions beyond the Jordan (4 B.C.E.–34 C.E.); and during the tetrarchy of Lysanias of Abilene, an otherwise unknown official; and during the high priesthood of Annas (6–15 C.E.) and his son-in-law Joseph Caiaphas (18–36 C.E.). The Fellows colored all of this chronological information gray because of the ambiguities and uncertainties connected with the date of the ascension of Tiberius, the identity of Lysanias, and the mention of Annas and Caiaphas as in office at the same time. In fact, Luke may have borrowed some of these names from other documents and thus may not have been cognizant that his information was not entirely accurate. The Fellows were also dubious that Zechariah was the name of John's father (v. 2), since its only other mention is in the birth and childhood stories (further discussion in the commentary on the birth stories in Luke, pp. 497–526).

John's public ministry was undoubtedly located in the region about the Jordan, and he almost certainly called for baptism as a sign of repentance (v. 3), as both the gospels and the Jewish historian Josephus testify.

The sayings attributed to John in vv. 7–9 Luke has taken from the Sayings Gospel Q, as did Matthew. It is uncertain whether vv. 10–14 were also found in Q or whether they were supplied from another source. The Fellows agreed that the groups mentioned and the kinds of admonitions represented may well reflect the work of John; they were dubious that these specific sayings would have been remembered and transmitted over such a long period of time. The safe designation was gray, except for v. 9, which they took, together with v. 17 below, accurately to reflect John's eschatological preaching that the apocalyptic judgment was at hand.

On the basis of the evidence, the Fellows concluded that John anticipated that another figure—the expected one—would come (v. 16b), but that John did not contrast his own water baptism with the spirit baptism of that superior figure (v. 16a, c).

Luke decided not to incorporate into his gospel the dramatic Markan story of the death of John the Baptist (Mark 6:14–29). He substitutes the notice in vv. 19–20 that Herod incarcerated John for denouncing Herod's marriage to Herodias. Luke repeats Mark's mistake in stating that Herodias had been married to Herod's brother Philip, when in fact she had been the wife of another Herod and had borne a daughter, Salome, by him. In spite of this error, the Fellows concluded that the basic information about John's public criticism of Herod was accurate and probably the excuse for his imprisonment and ultimate execution (not reported by Luke).

3 [21]**And it so happened, when all the people were baptized, and**
after Jesus had been baptized **and while he was praying, that the sky**
opened up, [22]**and the holy spirit came down on him in bodily form**
like a dove, and a voice came from the sky, "You are my son; today I
have become your father."

The baptism of Jesus
Lk 3:21–22
Mk 1:9–11, Mt 3:13–17
Source: Mark
Cf. Jn 1:29–34; GNaz 2; GEbi 4; GHeb 3

The baptism of Jesus. Like Matthew, Luke has taken over the story of Jesus' baptism from Mark but in the process has again revised it. Luke has failed to mention that John the Baptist was the agent of Jesus' baptism, probably reflecting the embarrassment of the Christian movement over this fact. Indeed, if we follow Luke's chronology, John cannot have been the agent since he had already been put in prison (Luke 3:20). The pronouncement of the voice from the sky in v. 22 probably reflects an "adoptionist christology"—it is on this occasion that God adopts Jesus as son and messiah. Luke has noticed that Mark quotes the first part of Ps 2:7, "you are my son"; he has added the second part, "today I have become your father," which originally referred to the coronation of Israelite kings. The king was of course anointed—a messiah.

There is yet another version of the baptismal scene, this time in the Gospel of the Hebrews (3:1–4):

[1]**The whole fountain of the holy spirit comes down on him. For the Lord is the spirit and where the spirit is, there is freedom.**

[2]**And it happened that when the Lord came up out of the water, the whole fountain of the holy spirit came down on him and rested on him.** [3]**It said to him, "My Son, I was waiting for you in all the prophets, waiting for you to come so I could rest in you.** [4]**For you are my rest; you are my first-begotten Son who rules forever."**

In this version, the voice that comes from the sky is that of the holy spirit rather than that of God. Moreover, Jesus is not adopted as God's son and messiah on this occasion, but is represented as already the divine son.

The reference to the fountain of the holy spirit is derived from Isa 11:2 where the prophet is meditating on the ideal Davidic king. The holy spirit speaks like Sophia, Wisdom, in the Wisdom of Solomon, a book belonging to the Greek scriptures (LXX; it was composed around the time of Jesus): "In every generation Sophia enters holy souls and turns them into prophets and friends of God" (Wis 7:27). Divine Wisdom wanders the earth searching for someone or some place in which to rest, according to another book of wisdom, the Wisdom of Jesus son of Sirach, a treatise written at the beginning of the second century B.C.E.: "I have acquired something among every people and nation. Among all of them I sought rest. I sought to make my home in someone's land" (Sir 24:6–7). The account in the Gospel of Hebrews thus gathers up strands from numerous traditions and combines them in its brief account of Jesus as the wisdom of God.

Genealogy
Lk 3:23–38
Source: Luke
Cf. Mt 1:1–17

3

[23]Jesus was about thirty years old when he began his work. He
was supposedly the son of Joseph, son of Eli, [24]son of Matthat, son of
Levi, son of Melchi, son of Jannai, son of Joseph, [25]son of Mattathias,
son of Amos, son of Nahum, son of Hesli, son of Naggai, [26]son of
Maath, son of Mattathias, son of Semein, son of Josech, son of Joda,
[27]son of Johanan, son of Rhesa, son of Zerubbabel, son of Salathiel,
son of Neri, [28]son of Melchi, son of Addi, son of Cosam, son of
Elmadam, son of Er, [29]son of Joshua, son of Eliezer, son of Jorim, son
of Matthat, son of Levi, [30]son of Simeon, son of Judah, son of Joseph,
son of Jonam, son of Eliakim, [31]son of Melea, son of Menna, son of
Mattatha, son of Nathan, son of David, [32]son of Jesse, son of Obed,
son of Boaz, son of Sala, son of Nahshon, [33]son of Amminadab, son of
Admin, son of Arni, son of Hezron, son of Perez, son of Judah, [34]son
of Jacob, son of Isaac, son of Abraham, son of Terah, son of Nahor,
[35]son of Serug, son of Reu, son of Peleg, son of Eber, son of Shelah,
[36]son of Cainan, son of Arphachshad, son of Shem, son of Noah, son
of Lamech, [37]son of Methuselah, son of Enoch, son of Jared, son of
Mahalalel, son of Kenan, [38]son of Enosh, son of Seth, son of Adam,
son of God.

Genealogy. The commentary explaining the Jesus Seminar's evalutaion of the Lukan genealogy appears with the infancy narratives, which are located on pp. 497–526 of *The Acts of Jesus*.

The temptation of Jesus
Lk 4:1–13
Mt 4:1–11; Mk 1:12–13
Sources: Q, Mark

4

Jesus departed from the Jordan full of the holy spirit and was
guided by the spirit into the wilderness, [2]where he was put to the
test by the devil for forty days. He ate nothing that whole time; and
when it was all over, he was famished.

[3]The devil said to him, "To prove you're God's son, order this
stone to turn into bread."

[4]Jesus responded to him, "It is written, 'Human beings are not to
live on bread alone.'"

[5]Then he took Jesus up, and in an instant of time showed him all
the empires of the civilized world. [6]The devil said to him, "I'll
bestow on you authority over all this and the glory that comes with

it; understand, it has been handed over to me, and I can give it to anyone I want. 7So, if you will pay homage to me, it will all be yours."

8Jesus responded, "It is written, 'You are to pay homage to the Lord your God, and you are to revere him alone.'"

9Then he took him to Jerusalem, set him on the pinnacle of the temple, and said to him, "To prove you're God's son, jump off from here; 10remember, it is written, 'To his heavenly messengers he will give orders about you, to protect you,' 11and 'with their hands they will catch you, so you won't even stub your toe on a stone.'"

12And in response Jesus said to him, "It is said, 'You are not to put the Lord your God to the test.'"

13So when the devil had tried every kind of test, he let him alone for the time being.

The temptation of Jesus. Since Luke 4:1–13 appeared originally in the Sayings Gospel Q, the color-coded text of this section appears with other Q materials in the first section in *The Acts of Jesus* (pp. 41–50).

A voice in Galilee
Lk 4:14–30
Source: Luke
Cf. Mk 1:14–15, Mt 4:12–17

4 **14Then Jesus returned in the power of the spirit to Galilee. News about him spread throughout all the surrounding area. 15He used to teach in their synagogues, and was acclaimed by everyone.**

16When he came to Nazareth, where he had been brought up, he went to the synagogue on the sabbath day, as was his custom. He stood up to do the reading 17and was handed the scroll of the prophet Isaiah. He unrolled the scroll and found the place where it was written:

> 18The spirit of the Lord is upon me,
> because he has anointed me
> to bring good news to the poor.
> He has sent me to announce pardon for prisoners
> and recovery of sight to the blind;
> to set free the oppressed,
> 19to proclaim the year of the Lord's amnesty.

20After rolling up the scroll, he gave it back to the attendant, and sat down; and the attention of everyone in the synagogue was riveted on him.

21He began by saying to them, "Today this scripture has come true as you listen."

22And they all began voicing approval of him, and marveling at the pleasing speech that he delivered; and would remark, "Isn't this Joseph's son?"

23And he said to them, "No doubt you will quote me that proverb, 'Doctor, cure yourself,' and you'll tell me, 'Do here in your hometown what we've heard you've done in Capernaum.'"

[24]**Then he said,** "The truth is, no prophet is welcome on his home
turf. [25]I can assure you, there were many widows in Israel in Elijah's
time, when the sky was dammed up for three and a half years, and a
severe famine swept through the land. [26]Yet Elijah was not sent to any
of them, but instead to a widow in Zarephath near Sidon. [27]In addition,
there were many lepers in Israel in the prophet Elisha's time; yet none
of them was made clean, except Naaman the Syrian."

[28]**Everyone in the synagogue was filled with rage when they heard
this. [29]They rose up, ran him out of town, and led him to the brow of
the hill on which their town was built, intending to hurl him over it.
[30]But he slipped away through the throng and went on his way.**

A voice in Galilee. Luke has borrowed an incident reported in Mark 6:1–6, reconceived it, and made it the frontispiece of his gospel. Upon returning to Galilee from the Jordan Valley where he had been attending John the Baptist, Jesus centered his activities in Capernaum. That much seems clear. At some subsequent point, he returned to Nazareth where he was apparently not well received. That, too, may well be historical. However, Luke has imagined a scene in which Jesus' Nazareth reception is concentrated in a single appearance in a synagogue. That is very probably a fiction of Luke.

In addition, Luke has Jesus brag that the prophecy of Isaiah is being fulfilled right now in their midst—fulfilled by the miracles he has performed in Capernaum (v. 23), even though Luke has not reported any miracles as yet. This notice itself indicates that the Nazareth visit did not take place at the beginning of Jesus' public life as Luke represents it, but actually came after considerable activity elsewhere at an earlier date. Luke's fiction does not suit the context in which he has placed it. Jesus probably did teach in synagogues, so the first part of v. 16 is colored pink.

The Fellows of the Jesus Seminar are dubious that Jesus could read and write. That he was an oral sage is attested by ample evidence. But that does not mean that he had learned the scribal skills, in his day a rare achievement among peasants. It is by no means certain that Jesus could read Hebrew, so the remainder of v. 16 and all of vv. 17, 20 is probably a Lukan fiction. This is another way of saying that Luke did not have independent information about this incident; he is merely revising and enhancing Mark.

According to Luke, the response to Jesus is altogether positive at first (v. 22). (Luke has changed "Mary's son"—Mark 6:3—to "Joseph's son" to square with what he has in his genealogy at 3:23.) Then Jesus provokes his audience so that the congregation turns completely hostile. Luke has added his own theological touch in vv. 25–27: the widow of Zarephath, whose son Elijah brought back to life (1 Kgs 17:1–16), and Naaman the Syrian, whose leprosy Elisha cured (2 Kgs 5:1–14), were both gentiles; Jesus' rejection at Nazareth is Luke's symbolic foreshadowing of the church's mission to the gentiles in the book of Acts. Furthermore, vv. 28–30 are Luke's imaginative account of the first assault on Jesus and how he miraculously escaped. This conclusion discloses Luke's theme that religious leaders will reject Jesus' prophetic message, as they did those of the prophets of old. It is highly unlikely that any such response took place before Jesus launched his public career in Capernaum.

Luke's version of Jesus' visit to Nazareth lacks historical foundation. Black is the appropriate color.

4 **[31]He went down to Capernaum, a town in Galilee, and he**
would teach them on the sabbath day. [32]They were astonished at his
teaching because his message carried authority.
[33]Now in the synagogue there was a person who had an unclean
demon, which screamed at the top of its voice, [34]"Hey Jesus! What do
you want with us, you Nazarene? Have you come to get rid of us? I
know you, who you are: God's holy man."
[35]But Jesus yelled at it, "Shut up and get out of him!"
Then the demon threw the man down in full view of everyone
and came out of him without doing him any harm. [36]And so amaze-
ment came over them all and they would say to one another, "What
kind of message is this? With authority and power he gives orders to
unclean spirits, and they leave." [37]So rumors about him began to
spread to every corner of the surrounding region.

The unclean demon at Capernaum
Lk 4:31–37
Mk 1:21–28
Source: Mark

The unclean demon at Capernaum. Luke has borrowed and edited Mark's story as the first of twenty-one miracle stories he includes in his gospel. Luke has abbreviated Mark's introduction by omitting the comparison of Jesus' authoritative teaching with that of the scribes (v. 32). He has softened Mark's description of the convulsions the demon inflicts on his victim and the shriek he makes upon departure (v. 33): Luke apparently no longer understands that convulsions and outcries were signs that the demon was making an exit. Verse 37 is Mark's conclusion to the story, but reformulated by Luke.

It is difficult to decide whether the basic contours of this story reflect a specific event or whether Mark or Christian storytellers before him have created a typical event. Scholarly opinion generally is divided; so were the Fellows of the Jesus Seminar. The division of opinion is reflected in the gray vote: the story may have historical elements, but they are minimal.

4 **[38]He got up from the synagogue and entered the house of**
Simon. Simon's mother-in-law was suffering from a high fever, and
they made an appeal to him on her behalf. [39]He stood over her,
rebuked the fever, and it disappeared. She immediately got up and
started looking after them.

Peter's mother-in-law
Lk 4:38–39
Mk 1:29–31, Mt 8:14–15
Source: Mark

Peter's mother-in-law. Luke has taken over Mark's simple story of the cure of Peter's mother-in-law but has modified it in doing so. Like Matthew, Luke omits any mention of Andrew, Peter's brother, and James and John. The fever is now a "high" fever rather than just a fever. Rather than touch her hand to effect the cure, Luke has Jesus "rebuke" the fever, perhaps to imply that the fever may have been the result of demon possession. And, finally, in Luke's version the response of the woman is instantaneous. In spite of these aberrations from the account in Mark, the Fellows agreed to designate the gist of the story pink. They colored the introduction (v. 38a) gray because they were dubious that the event occurred in the house of Simon or that it followed immediately upon Jesus' exit from the synagogue, a connection that Luke has borrowed from Mark, and which in Mark was a link probably provided by the storyteller.

Cures & exorcisms
Lk 4:40–41
Mk 1:32–34, Mt 8:16–17
Source: Mark

4 [40]**As the sun was setting, all those who had people sick with various diseases brought them to him. He would lay his hands on each one of them and cure them.** [41]**Demons would also come out of many of them screaming, and saying, "You son of God, you!" But he would rebuke them and not allow them to speak, because they knew that he was the Anointed.**

Cures & exorcisms. Luke has created a narrative summary based loosely on Mark 1:32–34. He omits Mark's exaggeration that the whole town was collected at the door. He has Jesus lay hands on the sick as a gesture of healing. He supplies the title the demons use for Jesus as they exit their victims. He of course repeats Mark's theme that Jesus did not want the demons to broadcast who he was.

This summary is the product of Luke's storytelling craft. It provides no new historical information.

Jesus tours Galilee
Lk 4:42–44
Mk 1:35–39, Mt 4:23–25
Source: Mark

4 [42]**The next morning he went outside and withdrew to an isolated place. Then the crowds came looking for him, and when they got to him they tried to keep him from leaving them.** [43]**He said to them,** "I must declare God's imperial rule to the other towns as well; after all, this is why I was sent." [44]**And he continued to speak in the synagogues of Judea.**

Jesus tours Galilee. This narrative summary, which was inspired by Mark 1:35–39, is another of Luke's creations. However, Luke fails to mention here that Jesus withdrew to a secluded place in order to pray (he delays mention of this until 5:16); rather than Simon and his companions coming to find Jesus, Luke has crowds seeking him; he adds that the crowds attempted to keep Jesus from continuing his tour; he specifies that Jesus came to preach the kingdom of God. These alterations are part of the storyteller's license to modify and invent. Because the summary is Luke's creation, the Fellows colored it black.

Once again it is quite possible that some bits of historical information are preserved in this summary, as in other summaries of this type. Jesus probably did practice prayer in solitude (note Mark 1:35, 6:46, 14:35–36). He probably did attract crowds from time to time. He undoubtedly proclaimed God's imperial rule. He may well have spoken in assemblies (synagogues) of Galilee and perhaps Judea. Some of these individual statements could have been colored pink, some even red, had the Fellows elected to vote on them as extracted narrative statements.

Call of the first disciples
Lk 5:1–11
Source: Luke
Cf. Jn 21:1–14; Mk 1:16–20, Mt 4:18–22; Jn 1:35–51; GEbi 2

5 **On one occasion, when the crowd pressed him to hear the word**
of God, he was standing by the lake of Gennesaret. [2]He noticed two
boats moored there at the shore; the fishermen had left them and
were washing their nets. [3]He got into one of the boats, the one
belonging to Simon, and asked him to put out a little from the shore.
Then he sat down and began to teach the crowds from the boat.

[4]**When he had finished speaking, he said to Simon,** "Put out into
deep water and lower your nets for a catch."

[5]**But Simon replied, "Master, we've been hard at it all night and**
haven't caught a thing. But if you insist, I'll lower the nets."

[6]**So they did and netted such a huge number of fish that their nets**
began to tear apart. [7]They signaled to their partners in the other boat
to come and lend a hand. They came and loaded both boats until
they nearly sank.

[8]**At the sight of this, Simon Peter fell to his knees in front of Jesus**
and said, "Have nothing to do with me, Master, heathen that I am."
[9]**For he and his companions were stunned at the catch of fish they**
had taken, [10]as were James and John, sons of Zebedee and partners
of Simon.

Jesus said to Simon, "Don't be afraid; from now on you'll be catch-
ing people." [11]**They then brought their boats to shore, abandoned**
everything, and followed him.

Call of the first disciples. Luke was apparently dissatisfied with the call of the first four disciples as reported in Mark (1:16–20). He may have thought Mark had not provided adequate motivation for the recruitment of disciples: Jesus recruits them at the beginning of his public ministry, before he has established himself as a teacher and healer; there is no obvious reason why the four fishermen should have responded as they did. Luke remedies these deficiencies in two ways: He moves the recruitment of the first disciples to a slightly later position in the sequence of events; he then remodels the story as a miraculous catch of fish.

In concert with many scholars, the Fellows agreed that neither of Luke's modifications was based on historical memory. The color was black by a wide majority.

How Luke rearranges the events he has taken from Mark can be observed by comparing the order of the two gospels:

The Gospel of Mark has this order:

1. Jesus arrives in Galilee; summary of his gospel (1:14–15)
2. Jesus calls the first four disciples (1:16–20)

3. Jesus exorcizes an unclean spirit (1:21–28)
4. Jesus heals Peter's mother-in-law (1:29–31)
5. Jesus treats the sick and demon-possessed (1:32–34)
6. Jesus withdraws to an isolated place (1:35–39)

Luke simply detaches item 2 in Mark's order and moves it to a position after item 6. As a consequence, items 3 through 6 come *before* Jesus enlists the first disciples, providing them with some knowledge of who he is and what he is capable of doing. Luke's sequence is thus:

1. Return to Galilee (4:14–30)
2. Jesus exorcizes an unclean spirit (4:31–37)
3. Jesus heals Peter's mother-in-law (4:38–39)
4. Jesus treats the sick and demon-possessed (4:40–41)
5. Jesus withdraws to an isolated place (4:42–44)
6. Jesus calls the first disciples (5:1–11)

Luke made this transposition, not because he had better knowledge of the course of events, but because he was a better storyteller than Mark.

In addition to a shift in the sequence of events, Luke also substitutes a miraculous catch of fish as the basis for the attraction of Peter, James, and John to Jesus. How Luke manages the substitution is illustrative of the way in which the gospel writers not infrequently manipulated elements in the tradition in the interests of improving the story.

First of all, Luke borrows elements from different places in Mark to create a new context. Then, as the core of his revised story, he utilizes a miraculous catch of fish, which probably belonged originally to another setting. Upon close inspection, we can see where the relocation of materials has left traces in Luke's revised account.

The introduction in vv. 1–3 Luke has fashioned out of Mark 4:1—Jesus gets into a boat and teaches the crowd on the shore—and out of elements he found in Mark 1:16–20, accounts of the call of the fishermen who were casting their nets into the sea or mending their nets (Luke has them washing their nets, but that is a minor alteration). Luke has clearly borrowed these features from Mark and fashioned both his introduction and conclusion out of them (vv. 10–11).

Into the middle of this reconstructed situation, Luke has inserted another story (vv. 4–9). The affinities of this story with an appearance story preserved in the appendix to the Gospel of John (21:1–14) are unmistakable.

> Some time after these events, Jesus again appeared to his disciples by
> the Sea of Tiberias. This is how he did it: [2]When Simon Peter and Thomas,
> the one known as "the Twin," were together, along with Nathanael from
> Cana, Galilee, the sons of Zebedee, and two other disciples, [3]Simon Peter
> says to them, "I'm going to go fishing."
>
> "We're coming with you," they reply.
>
> They went down and got into the boat, but that night they didn't catch a thing.
>
> [4]It was already getting light when Jesus appeared on the shore, but his
> disciples didn't recognize that it was Jesus.

5“Lads, you haven’t caught any fish, have you?” Jesus asks them.
“No,” they replied.
6He tells them, “Cast your net on the right side of the boat and you’ll
have better luck.”
They do as he instructs them and now they can’t haul it in for the huge
number of fish. 7The disciple Jesus loved most exclaims to Peter, “It’s the
Master!”
When Simon Peter heard “It’s the Master,” he tied his cloak around
himself, since he was stripped for work, and threw himself into the
water. 8The rest of them came in the boat, dragging the net full of fish.
They were not far from land, only about a hundred yards offshore.
9When they got to shore, they see a charcoal fire burning, with fish
cooking on it, and some bread. 10Jesus says to them, “Bring some of the
fish you’ve just caught.”
11Then Simon Peter went aboard and hauled the net full of large fish
ashore—one hundred fifty-three of them. Even though there were so
many of them, the net still didn’t tear.
12Jesus says to them, “Come and eat.”
None of the disciples dared ask, “Who are you?” They knew it was the
Master. 13Jesus comes, takes the bread and gives it to them, and passes the
fish around as well.
14This was now the third time after he had been raised from the dead
that Jesus appeared to his disciples.

The points of contact are striking:

1. The disciples have fished all night and caught nothing (Luke 5:5//John 21:3).
2. Jesus instructs the disciples to cast their nets (Luke 5:4//John 21:6).
3. The result is an extraordinarily large catch (Luke 5:6–7//John 21:6).
4. Simon Peter (this is the only occasion when Luke refers to him by this double name) reacts to the catch (Luke 5:8//John 21:7).
5. The other disciples assist with the catch but say nothing in response (Luke 5:9–10//John 21:8).
6. The huge catch symbolizes the success of the missionary endeavors of the Jesus movement (Luke 5:9–10//John 21:11).
7. There is the notable failure in both Luke and John to mention Andrew, the brother of Peter, who appears in Mark’s version of the call story (Mark 1:16).

These points of contact have led scholars to conclude that the two stories are two versions of the same event. Both writers took it from the oral tradition, where it was a post-crucifixion epiphany. John has retained that setting. Luke, on the other hand, has reconceived it as an enlistment story and moved it back into Jesus’ public life. Yet Luke’s version has at least one trace of its origin as an appearance story: in Luke 5:8, Peter falls to his knees, refers to Jesus as “Master,” and confesses that he is unworthy. That response makes no sense in the context of a story in which Peter encounters Jesus for the first time. But it does make sense as a reaction to an appearance of the risen Jesus on the part of one who had recently denied Jesus three times.

The evidence seems incontrovertible: the story as it stands in Luke is fiction, not history. The correct designation is black. For further discussion, consult the commentary on the appearance story in John 21:1–14 (pp. 449–95).

The leper
Lk 5:12–16
Mk 1:40–45, Mt 8:1–4;
EgerG 2:1–4
Sources: Mark,
Egerton Gospel

5 12 **And it so happened while he was in one of the towns, there**
was this man covered with leprosy. Seeing Jesus, he knelt with his
face to the ground and begged him, "Sir, if you want to, you can
make me clean."
13 **Jesus stretched out his hand, touched him, and says,** "Okay—
you're clean!"
And at once the leprosy disappeared. 14 **He ordered him to tell no**
one. "But go, have a priest examine <your skin>. Then make an offer-
ing, as Moses commanded, for your cleansing, as evidence <of your
cure>."
15 **Yet the story about him spread around all the more. Great**
crowds would gather to hear him and to be healed of their sick-
nesses. 16 **But he would withdraw to isolated places and pray.**

The leper. Luke has drawn on Mark's version of the cure of the leper and revised it modestly to suit his own purposes. He has skipped over Mark's references to Jesus becoming "indignant" in Mark 1:41 and Jesus "snapping" and "dismissing" in Mark 1:43, characterizations that evidently seemed inappropriate in Luke's view. A growing awareness of Jesus' status as messiah in Luke's community toward the end of the first century may have dictated the omission of these allusions. In a similar vein, Luke adds that the leper bowed with "his face to the ground," a heightening of the reverence paid to Jesus: in Mark the leper only falls to his knees. Further, Luke has Jesus touch the leper, which Mark does not. Luke probably understands this as part of the healing technique, which often involved touching, but it could also be understood as a deliberate move on Jesus' part to identify with the leper and risk acquiring the disease. Such a gesture would have impressed any onlookers.

As in the case of the versions in Mark and Matthew, the Fellows designated the core story in Luke pink—it approximates an actual event in Jesus' public work. Luke has provided his own narrative introduction in v. 12 (Mark has none, while Matthew links the event to the conclusion of the sermon on the mount). It is therefore colored black.

The Seminar was divided on whether Jesus sent the leper to the priests for confirmation of the cure. In conventional healing stories confirmation by third parties is a standard feature. Yet this particular form of confirmation seems uncharacteristic of Jesus, who has just performed the function of a priest by declaring the leper clean. It is possible that Jesus sent the leper to the priests in order to induce them to confirm his cure and thus testify to his power. But that, too, seems unlike the one who refused to produce signs. This uncertainty on the part of the Fellows produced a gray designation for v. 14.

Verse 15 is Luke's edition of Mark's conclusion, which was colored black. But Luke has softened Mark's exaggeration, "Jesus could no longer enter a town but had to stay in the wilderness," to a simple statement of Jesus' popularity, which may well be historically accurate. Luke has thus edited Mark back in the direction of the historically probable. Finally, Luke failed to incorporate an earlier notice of Mark that Jesus withdrew to isolated places and prayed (Luke 4:42 corresponds to Mark 1:35). He now remedies that omission and includes it here.

Paralytic & four
Lk 5:17–26
Mk 2:1–12, Mt 9:1–8
Source: Mark
Cf. Jn 5:1–9

5 [17]And it so happened one day, as he was teaching, that the
Lord's healing power was with him. Now Pharisees and teachers of
the Law, who had come from every village of Galilee and Judea and
from Jerusalem, were sitting around. [18]The next thing you know,
some men appeared, carrying a paralyzed person on a bed. They
attempted to bring him in and lay him before <Jesus>. [19]But finding
no way to get him in on account of the crowd, they went up onto the
roof and lowered him on his pallet through the tiles into the middle
of the crowd in front of Jesus.
[20]When Jesus noticed their trust, he said, "Mister, your sins have
been forgiven you."
[21]And the scholars and the Pharisees began to raise questions:
"Who is this that utters blasphemies? Who can forgive sins except
God alone?"
[22]Because Jesus was aware of their questions, he responded to
them, "Why do you entertain such questions? [23]Which is easier: to say,
'Your sins have been forgiven you,' or to say, 'Get up and walk'?" [24]But
so that you may realize that on earth the son of Adam has authority
to forgive sins, he said to the paralyzed man, "You there, get up, pick
up your pallet and go home!"
[25]And immediately he stood up in front of them, picked up what
he had been lying on, and went home praising God. [26]They all
became ecstatic, and they began to extol God, but they were also
filled with fear and exclaimed, "We saw some incredible things
today!"

Paralytic & four. Luke has provided Mark's story of the paralytic with an elaborate narrative introduction of his own devising: he has assembled "Pharisees and teachers of the law" from every village in Galilee and Judea and from Jerusalem, as though a convention were being held in Capernaum. The presence of Pharisees and teachers of the law anticipates the controversy that is to take place in the story (vv. 21–24). Luke has thereby corrected a deficiency in the Markan version (in Mark the scribes appear from nowhere), a deficiency that has helped scholars to see that the controversy over forgiveness of sins is an intrusion into Mark's account. Luke's small improvements illustrate once again that Luke is a more sensitive storyteller than Mark. Yet because Luke's revision of Mark's setting is his own invention, the Fellows designated it black.

As in the case of Matthew, the Fellows colored the nucleus of Luke's story gray, even though they agreed that the core of Mark's story probably did reflect an actual event in the life of Jesus. They hesitated to take this step, however, because it is possible that editorial changes may have been introduced to achieve a more realistic picture. Yet secondary modifications ordinarily do not reflect better historical knowledge. In spite of these reservations, however, the Fellows endorsed two narrative statements that are derived from this and other versions of the story:

- **Jesus told a lame man to pick up his mat.**
- **Jesus cured a lame man.**

Call of Levi
Lk 5:27–28
Mk 2:13–14, Mt 9:9;
Gebi 2:4
Source: Mark

5 [27]**After these events he went out and observed a toll collector named Levi sitting at the toll booth. He said to him,** "Follow me!" [28]**Leaving everything behind, he got up, and followed him.**

Call of Levi. Luke's version of the story of the toll collector is directly dependent on the Gospel of Mark. Luke makes only minor editorial changes. We do not learn anything new from Luke. The color-coding matches that of Mark: Jesus encountered a toll collector during his walks along the seashore, that toll collector became one of his followers. In the manuscripts he is given various names, Levi son of Alphaeus, Matthew, James son of Alphaeus. We simply do not know the toll collector's name.

Dining with sinners
Lk 5:29–32
Mk 2:15–17, Mt 9:10–13;
GosFr 1224 5:1–2
Sources: Mark, Gospel
Fragment 1224
Cf. Lk 15:1–2

5 [29]**And Levi gave him a great banquet in his house, and a large group of toll collectors and others were dining with them.**

[30]**The Pharisees and their scholars would complain to his disciples: "Why do you people eat and drink with toll collectors and sinners?"**

[31]**In response Jesus said to them:** "Since when do the healthy need a doctor? It's the sick who do. [32]I have not come to enlist religious folks to change their hearts, but sinners!"

Dining with sinners. Luke has just sufficiently rewritten the story as reported by Mark to reduce it to the gray category. Luke has Levi giving a banquet (Luke likes banquets) at which both sinners and Pharisees are present. That is an unlikely scene in itself. But then the Pharisees direct a criticism at Jesus for his practice of socializing with the disreputable. Although the scene as depicted is a fiction, it retains elements that are historical: Jesus did consort openly with social outcasts; he was criticized for the practice; and he did defend his practice with aphorisms and parables.

5 **33 They said to him, "The disciples of John are always fasting**
and offering prayers, and so are those of the Pharisees, but yours
just eat and drink."
34 And Jesus said to them, "You can't make the groom's friends fast
as long as the groom is around, can you? 35 But the days will come
when the groom is taken away from them, and then they will fast, in
those days."
36 He then gave them a proverb: "Nobody tears a piece from a new
garment and puts it on an old one, since the new one will tear and the
piece from the new will not match the old. 37 And nobody pours young
wine into old wineskins, otherwise the young wine will burst the
wineskins, it will gush out, and the wineskins will be destroyed.
38 Instead, young wine must be put into new wineskins. 39 Besides,
nobody wants young wine after drinking aged wine. As they say,
'Aged wine is just fine!'"

Question of fasting
Lk 5:33–39
Mk 2:18–22, Mt 9:14–17
Source: Mark

Question of fasting. In Mark and Matthew it is the disciples of John who pose the question of Jesus: Why don't your disciples fast? Since the two movements were competitors during Jesus' lifetime, this is not an unreasonable question. And it was to be expected, since Jesus ceased to practice fasting when he left John and began his own program in Galilee. In Luke, however, the narrative context indicates that the question is posed exclusively by the Pharisees (v. 33). To the concern about fasting, Luke has added an interest in prayer, one of his special themes. These changes reflect Luke's interests and context. Thus, although the story in Mark and Matthew was given a gray designation, the modified account here in Luke was colored black: the picture of Jesus has begun to fade and is being replaced by Christian concerns of a later period.

6 **It so happened that he was walking through grainfields on a**
sabbath day, and his disciples would strip some heads of grain,
husk them in their hands, and chew them. 2 Some of the Pharisees
said, "Why are you doing what's not permitted on the sabbath day?"
3 And Jesus answered them, "Haven't you read what David did
when he and his companions were hungry? 4 He went into the house of
God, took and ate the consecrated bread himself, and gave some to his
men to eat. No one is permitted to eat this bread except the priests
alone!"
5 And he used to say to them, "The son of Adam lords it over the
sabbath day."

Sabbath observance
Lk 6:1–5
Mk 2:23–28, Mt 12:1–8
Source: Mark

Sabbath observance. Following the lead of Mark, whose text is here being revised, Luke represents Jesus and his disciples as itinerants who harvest and eat grain by hand as they walk through fields. They engage in this practice on the sabbath day, which is what draws Pharisaic criticism. The Fellows think that the practice of Jesus and the disciples and the objection of the Pharisees has some basis in fact. So they designated vv. 1–2 pink.

What is at stake in this story from the Christian point of view is the abrogation of sabbath restrictions on the authority of Jesus. To be sure, Christians began very early to substitute the first day of the week (Sunday) for the sabbath, but the immediate point is the authority of Jesus (and Christian leaders) to contravene Jewish custom. Christians are free to do so, it is argued, because Jesus as the son of Adam has that authority (v. 5). In addition, exceptions to the sabbath code have their precedent in the story of David who ate the sacred bread in the temple—even though David's act had nothing to do with the sabbath. This line of reasoning of course did not originate with Jesus. In his original response in Mark, Jesus drew on the creation story to suggest that the well-being of Adam and Eve took precedence over the sabbath as a day of rest (the aphorism of Jesus is preserved in Mark 2:27–28).

Man with crippled hand
Lk 6:6–11
Mk 3:1–6, Mt 12:9–14
Source: Mark
Cf. GNaz 4

6 **[6]On another sabbath day, it so happened that he entered the synagogue and taught. A man was there whose right hand was crippled. [7]And the scholars and the Pharisees watched him carefully, to see if he would heal on the sabbath day, so they could find some excuse to denounce him. [8]However, he knew their motives, and he said to the fellow with the crippled hand,** "Get up and stand here in front of everybody." **And he got to his feet and stood there.**

[9]Then Jesus queried them: "I ask you, on the sabbath day is it permitted to do good or to do evil, to save life or to destroy it?" **[10]And he looked right at all of them, and said to him,** "Hold out your hand!" **He did and his hand was restored.**

[11]But they were filled with rage and discussed among themselves what to do with Jesus.

Man with crippled hand. Luke has based his version of the story of the man with a crippled right hand on Mark's version. The setting is a synagogue, as in Mark. However, Luke introduces Jesus' critics by name early in the story (v. 7), thus identifying all the participants at the outset. And Luke makes other minor changes: Jesus is able to discern the "motives" of his critics (v. 8, as in 5:22 and 9:46). He also softens Mark's representation of the plot to kill Jesus because it is still too early in Luke's sequence for an explicit threat against Jesus' life. For the most part, however, Luke has simply reproduced Mark's account.

The Fellows were inclined to the view that Mark's version was mostly fictional so they gave it a gray rating. They took the controversy over the sabbath to be contrived (Pharisees would not have objected to what happened to the crippled man in the synagogue on a sabbath since Jesus' actions consisted entirely of words), and they concluded that Mark's representation of a plot against Jesus' life at that point in the story was unwarranted by the synagogue event. Even though Luke has made Mark more plausible historically speaking, the Fellows nevertheless decided that Luke had added details that further fictionalized the story. The result was a weighted average that fell on the line between gray and black. It should be noted, however, that differences in the votes on the three versions—Mark, Matthew, Luke—were microscopic: in the judgment of the Fellows, there is very little possibility that a single historical event lies behind the narrative.

6 **[12]During that time, it so happened that he went out to the**
mountain to pray, and spent the night in prayer to God. [13]The next
day, he called his disciples and selected twelve of them, whom he
named apostles: [14]Simon, whom he nicknamed Rock, and Andrew
his brother, and James and John, and Philip, and Bartholomew, [15]and
Matthew, and Thomas, and James the son of Alphaeus, and Simon
who was called the Zealot, [16]and Judas the son of James, and Judas
Iscariot, who turned traitor.

Call of the twelve
Lk 6:12–16
Mk 3:13–19, Mt 10:1–4; GEbi 2
Source: Mark
Cf. Acts 1:12–14, 15–26

Call of the twelve. In the Gospel of Mark, Jesus is described as withdrawing to the sea upon being surrounded by crowds of people who want to be healed and rid of their demons (Mark 3:7–12). This narrative summary is followed by the appointment of the twelve (Mark 3:13–19). Luke reverses the order of these two scenes: Jesus first appoints the twelve (6:12–16) and then Luke depicts crowds pressing Jesus for his curative powers (6:17–19). It is not clear why Luke rearranges Mark at this point.

Luke identifies the twelve with the group known as the apostles, but he distinguishes the twelve/apostles from the disciples, who constitute a more inclusive group. Elsewhere in the New Testament, especially in the letters of Paul, the apostles seem a larger group than the twelve: In his list of appearances of the risen Jesus, Paul reports that Jesus appeared to the twelve and then, on another occasion, appeared to "all the apostles" (1 Cor 15:5, 7). Because Luke thinks of the apostles as a closed group, twelve in number, he narrates the replacement of Judas Iscariot by Matthias in Acts 1:15–26. As Luke looks back on the apostolic age, he decides that Paul did not qualify as an apostle. Paul of course would have rejected Luke's definition as too narrow and exclusive because it left him out of the circle of apostles. Like the other lists of the twelve, this one is also largely fictitious.

6 **[17]On the way down with them, Jesus stopped at a level place.**
There was a huge crowd of his disciples and a great throng of people
from all Judea and Jerusalem and the coast of Tyre and Sidon. [18]They
came to hear him and to be healed of their diseases. Those who were
tormented by unclean spirits were cured. [19]And everyone in the
crowd tried to touch him, since power would flow out from him and
heal them all.

Jesus heals the crowds
Lk 6:17–19
Mk 3:7–12, Mt 12:15–21
Source: Mark

Jesus heals the crowds. Luke has based this summary on its counterpart in Mark, but because he employs it for different narrative purposes, he has modified it considerably. In Luke, Jesus is descending from the mountain where he has just appointed the twelve; he is about to deliver the sermon on the plain, the parallel to Matthew's sermon on the mount. As a consequence, Jesus is not beside the sea as he is in Mark's version, and thus Luke has no need for the boat that appears in Mark's account. Luke has also added the note that a throng has come "to hear him" to set the stage for the sermon that lies just ahead. Luke follows the other evangelists in repeating the motif of garment-touching as a means of access to Jesus' healing powers.

The geographical notices of the crowd's origins are supplied by Luke as a way of connecting episodes in his story. They have no independent historical value. The other generalizations are based on particular stories the authors of the gospels have already narrated. We learn nothing new from them. Black is the appropriate designation.

The great sermon
Lk 6:20–49
Mt 5:3–12, 38–48,
7:1–5, 15–20, 24–27
Source: Q

6 [20]**Then he would look squarely at his disciples and say:**

Congratulations, you poor!
God's domain belongs to you.
[21]Congratulations, you hungry!
You will have a feast.
Congratulations, you who weep now!
You will laugh.

[22]"Congratulations to you when people hate you, and when they ostracize you and denounce you and scorn your name as evil, because of the son of Adam! [23]Rejoice on that day, and jump for joy! Just remember, your compensation is great in heaven. Recall that their ancestors treated the prophets the same way.

[24]Damn you rich!
You already have your consolation.
[25]Damn you who are well-fed now!
You will know hunger.
Damn you who laugh now!
You will learn to weep and grieve.

[26]"Damn you when everybody speaks well of you! Recall that their ancestors treated the phony prophets the same way.

[27]"But to you who listen I say, love your enemies, do favors for those who hate you, [28]bless those who curse you, pray for your abusers.

[29]"When someone strikes you on the cheek, offer the other as well. If someone takes away your coat, don't prevent that person from taking your shirt along with it.

[30]"Give to everyone who begs from you; and when someone takes your things, don't ask for them back.

31 "Treat people the way you want them to treat you.

32 "If you love those who love you, what merit is there in that? After all, even sinners love those who love them. 33 And if you do good to those who do good to you, what merit is there in that? After all, even sinners do as much. 34 If you lend to those from whom you hope to gain, what merit is there in that? Even sinners lend to sinners, in order to get as much in return. 35 But love your enemies, and do good, and lend, expecting nothing in return. Your reward will be great, and you'll be children of the Most High. As you know, the Most High is generous to the ungrateful and the wicked.

36 "Be as compassionate as your Father is. 37 Don't pass judgment, and you won't be judged; don't condemn, and you won't be condemned; forgive, and you'll be forgiven. 38 Give, and it will be given to you: they'll put in your lap a full measure, packed down, sifted and overflowing. For the standard you apply will be the standard applied to you."

39 And he posed a riddle for them: "Can one blind person guide another? Won't they both end up in some ditch?

40 "Students are not above their teachers. But those who are fully taught will be like their teachers. 41 Why do you notice the sliver in your friend's eye, but overlook the timber in your own? 42 How can you say to your friend, 'Friend, let me get the sliver in your eye,' when you don't notice the timber in your own? You phony, first take the timber out of your own eye, and then you'll see well enough to remove the sliver in your friend's eye.

43 "A choice tree does not produce rotten fruit, any more than a rotten tree produces choice fruit; 44 for each tree is known by its fruit. Figs are not gathered from thorns, nor are grapes picked from brambles. 45 The good person produces good from the fund of good in the heart, and the evil person produces evil from the evil within. As you know, the mouth gives voice to what the heart is full of.

46 "Why do you call me 'Master, master,' and not do what I tell you? 47 Everyone who comes to me and pays attention to my words and acts on them—I'll show you what such a person is like: 48 That one is like a person building a house, who dug deep and laid the foundation on bedrock; when a flood came, the torrent slammed against that house, but could not shake it, because it was well built. 49 But the one who listens <to my words> and doesn't act <on them> is like a person who built a house on the ground without a foundation; when the torrent slammed against it, it collapsed immediately. And so the ruin of that house was total."

The great sermon. Luke has taken the compendium of sayings known as the great sermon from the Sayings Gospel Q. Verse 20 is his narrative introduction to that sermon. It is how Luke imagined the sermon to have been delivered. Black is the proper designation for the brief narrative setting. The collection of sayings was of course color-coded in *The Five Gospels.*

Officer's slave
Lk 7:1–10
Mt 8:5–13; Jn 4:45–54
Source: Q, John

7 **After he had completed all he had to say to his audience, he went into Capernaum.**

[2]**A Roman officer had a slave he was very fond of but who was sick and about to die.** [3]**So when he heard about Jesus, the Roman officer sent some Jewish elders to him, and asked him to come and cure his slave.** [4]**When they came to Jesus, they pleaded with him urgently, saying, "He deserves to have you do this for him.** [5]**As you probably know, he loves our people, and even built a synagogue for us."**

[6]**So Jesus went with them.**

When he got close to the house, the Roman officer dispatched friends to say to him, "Don't trouble yourself, sir, for I don't deserve to have you in my house; [7]**that's why I didn't presume to come to you in person. Just say the word, and let my boy be cured.** [8]**After all, I myself am under orders, and I have soldiers under me. I order one to go, and he goes; I order another to come, and he comes; and <I order> my slave to do something, and he does it."**

[9]**As Jesus listened to this he was amazed at him. He turned and said to the crowd that followed,** "Let me tell you, not even in Israel have I found such trust."

[10]**And when the emissaries returned to the house, they found the slave in good health.**

Officer's slave. Since Luke has taken this story from Q, the text and commentary for Luke's version are located in the first section of *The Acts of Jesus* (pp. 41–50).

Widow's son at Nain
Lk 7:11–17
No parallels
Source: Luke

7 [11]**And it so happened soon afterward that he went to a town called Nain, and his disciples and a large crowd accompanied him.** [12]**As he neared the town gate, just then a dead man was being carried out, the only son of his mother, who was herself a widow. And a considerable crowd from the town was with her.**

[13]**When the Lord saw her, his heart went out to her and he said to her,** "Don't cry." [14]**And he went up and touched the bier. The bearers paused, and he said,**"Young man, I tell you, get up."

[15]**And the dead man sat up and began to speak; then <Jesus> gave him back to his mother.**

[16]**Fear gripped them all; and they gave God the glory, saying, "A great prophet has been raised up among us!" and "God has visited his people!"**

[17]**And this story about him spread throughout Judea and all the surrounding area.**

Widow's son at Nain. The Fellows of the Jesus Seminar were unanimous in their judgment that this story was the creation of Luke. There are several reasons for this judgment.

The revival of the widow's son at Nain closely resembles the story of Elijah resuscitating the son of the widow of Zarephath (1 Kgs 17:17–24; the text of this story is provided in an adjoining box, p. 290). The Seminar agreed that gospel stories were sometimes created on the basis of Old Testament models.

Luke is familiar with stories of resuscitation. He has copied the revival of Jairus' daughter from Mark (8:40–42a, 49–56). He tells the story of Peter raising Dorcas back to life (Acts 9:36–43) and he describes how Paul revives Eutychus after he falls out of a third story-window (Acts 20:7–12). And of course Luke is familiar with accounts of the resurrection of Jesus.

Jesus is credited with resuscitations in the Infancy Gospel of Thomas. On one occasion Jesus revives the dead infant of a grieving mother (17:1–4). On another he brings a worker who had fallen off a building back to life (InThom 18:1–3). In addition to the model of Elijah mentioned earlier, a resuscitation is attributed to Apollonius of Tyana (the text of this tale can be found on p. 457).

Furthermore, Luke will shortly record a text taken from the Sayings Gospel Q about the dead being raised (7:22). The phrase about the raising of the dead is actually taken from Isaiah (26:19) and interpreted as a prophecy applicable to Jesus. By telling the story of the widow's son, Luke offers concrete evidence that the prophecy has come true.

In resuscitation stories, the earlier status of the patient is often ambiguous. The widow's son Elijah raises is described as so ill that there was no breath left in him (1 Kgs 17:1). The daughter of Jairus is said to be asleep rather than dead (Luke 8:52). Paul finds that Eutychus is not dead after all (Acts 20:10). The daughter Apollonius is said to have revived still has a vapor rising from her lips, according to the report of Philostratus. In other words, accounts of resuscitations are often accompanied by a modicum of skepticism. But that element is entirely absent from this story of the widow's son at Nain: for Luke it is a flat-out miracle, evidence that "God has visited his people."

Luke depicts Jesus as touching the bier of the deceased. Since contact with a corpse rendered one unclean, Jesus may have once been represented as subverting purity codes. But the touch in this case is probably another example of the function of touch therapy in healing stories. It should be recalled that the tellers of these tales did not clearly distinguish resuscitations from other kinds of cures.

The language of the story and its location in the narrative strongly indicate that Luke has created a passage to fit his narrative design and to express the religious meaning he affirms in his gospel: The story is told as the fulfillment of scripture and as foreshadowing the resurrection of Jesus—the one who is destined to be raised from the dead is here depicted as having the power to raise others from the dead. The narrative is the product of his christological imagination and not the transmission of a historical report.

John's inquiry
Lk 7:18–23
Mt 11:2–6
Source: Q

7 [18]**The disciples of John brought reports of all these things to him.** [19]**John summoned a couple of his disciples and sent them to the Lord to ask: "Are you the one who is to come, or are we to wait for someone else?"**

ELIJAH & THE WIDOW'S SON

17 A little later the woman's son, who was the head of the household, got sick, so
sick that he couldn't breathe. 18 And she said to Elijah, "What in heaven's name
have you done to me? Have you come here to draw attention to my sin and kill
my son?"
19 Elijah replied, "Give me your son." And he took him from her breast and he
carried him upstairs to the room where he himself had been staying and placed
him on his own bed. 20 Then Elijah cried out, "Consider, Lord, the testimony of the
widow, with whom I have been staying. You've really done a terrible injustice in
killing her son."
21 And he lay on top of the boy three times, and yelled out to the Lord, "Lord,
my God, return this boy's life to him."
22 And just like that [the Lord] did so and the boy cried out.
23 Next Elijah carried the child from the upstairs bedroom to the main part of
the house and gave him back to his mother. Elijah said, "Look, your son is alive."
24 Then the widow said to Elijah, "Believe me, I now know that you are a man of
God and that when you speak the word of the Lord it is true." 1 Kgs 17:17–24

**20 And when the men came to <Jesus>, they said, "John the Baptist
sent us to you to ask: 'Are you the one who is to come, or are we to
wait for someone else?'"**
**21 Jesus had just cured many of their diseases and plagues and evil
spirits, and restored sight to many who were blind. 22 And so he
answered them,** "Go report to John what you have seen and heard:

the blind see again,
the lame walk,
lepers are cleansed,
the deaf hear,
the dead are raised,
and the poor have the good news preached to them.

23 Congratulations to those who don't take offense at me."

John's inquiry. The color-coded text and commentary on John's inquiry is found in the Sayings Gospel Q (pp. 41–50).

Praise of John
Lk 7:24–28
Mt 11:7–11
Source: Q
Cf. Th 78:1–3; Th 46:1–2

7

**24 After John's messengers had left, <Jesus> began to talk about
John to the crowds:** "What did you go out to the wilderness to gawk
at? A reed shaking in the wind? 25 What did you really go out to see? A
man dressed in fancy clothes? But wait! Those who dress fashionably
and live in luxury are found in palaces. 26 Come on, what did you go
out to see? A prophet? Yes, that's what you went out to see, yet some-
one more than a prophet. 27 This is the one about whom it was written:

Here is my messenger,
whom I send on ahead of you
to prepare your way before you.

28I tell you, among those born of women none is greater than John; yet
the least in God's domain is greater than he."

Praise of John. The color-coded text and commentary for this section is located in the Sayings Gospel Q (pp. 41–50).

Children in the marketplace
Lk 7:29–35
Mt 11:16–19
Source: Q

7 **(29All the people, even the toll collectors, who were listening
and had been baptized by John, vindicated God's plan; 30but the
Pharisees and the legal experts, who had not been baptized by him,
subverted God's plan for themselves.)**
31"What do members of this generation remind me of? What are
they like? 32They are like children sitting in the marketplace and calling
out to one another:

We played the flute for you,
but you wouldn't dance;
we sang a dirge,
but you wouldn't weep.

33"Just remember, John the Baptist appeared on the scene, eating no
bread and drinking no wine, and you say, 'He is demented.' 34The son
of Adam appeared on the scene both eating and drinking, and you say,
'There's a glutton and a drunk, a crony of toll collectors and sinners!'
35Indeed, wisdom is vindicated by all her children."

Children in the marketplace. Verses 29–30 are Luke's editorial comment addressed to the reader by way of explanation. His remarks represent his own point of view; they do not provide us with reliable historical information. The balance of the segment was taken from Q and consists entirely of sayings that were designated gray in *The Five Gospels*.

The anointing
Lk 7:36–50
Mk 14:3–9, Mt 26:6–13;
Jn 12:1–8
Sources: Luke, Mark, John

7 **36One of the Pharisees invited him to dinner; he entered the
Pharisee's house, and reclined at the table. 37A local woman, who
was a sinner, found out that he was having dinner at the Pharisee's
house. She suddenly showed up with an alabaster jar of myrrh,
38and stood there behind him weeping at his feet. Her tears wet his
feet, and she wiped them dry with her hair; she kissed his feet, and
anointed them with the myrrh.**
**39The Pharisee who had invited him saw this and said to himself,
"If this man were a prophet, he would know who this is and what
kind of woman is touching him, since she is a sinner."**
40And Jesus answered him, "Simon, I have something to tell you."
"Teacher," he said, "speak up."

41"This moneylender had two debtors; one owed five hundred sil-
ver coins, and the other fifty. 42Since neither one of them could pay, he
wrote off both debts. Now which of them will love him more?"
43**Simon answered, "I would imagine, the one for whom he wrote off
the larger debt."**

And he said to him, "You're right." 44**Then turning to the woman,
he said to Simon,** "Do you see this woman? I walked into your house
and you didn't offer me water for my feet; yet she has washed my feet
with her tears and dried them with her hair. 45You didn't offer me a
kiss, but she hasn't stopped kissing my feet since I arrived. 46You did-
n't anoint my head with oil, but she has anointed my feet with myrrh.
47For this reason, I tell you, her sins, many as they are, have been for-
given, as this outpouring of her love shows. But the one who is for-
given little shows little love."

48**And he said to her,** "Your sins have been forgiven."

49**Then those having dinner with him began to mutter to them-
selves, "Who is this who even forgives sins?"**

50**And he said to the woman,** "Your trust has saved you; go in
peace."

The anointing. Luke's version of this anointing story is remarkably different from the ones found in Mark and Matthew. Luke relocates the tale from the passion week to a much earlier point in his narrative. Unlike the other accounts, Luke identifies the woman as a "sinner." (On the false identification of this woman with Mary of Magdala, consult the cameo "Mary of Magdala," pp. 476–78.) She intrudes on the symposium as an unwelcome guest. Luke introduces Simon the Pharisee into the tale; Simon wonders why Jesus, who is said to be a prophet, doesn't know the woman's social status (v. 39). Jesus can read minds so he tells Simon a parable to illustrate why sinners are more responsive to forgiveness than the righteous (v. 41–42). Jesus then reminds Simon that he failed to fulfill the proprieties that are normally extended to dinner guests: water for washing dusty feet; a kiss of greeting; oil to anoint the head. This woman, Jesus continues, has served as a true host. As a climax Jesus forgives the woman her sins. These additions to the basic story found in Mark are probably Lukan embellishments. The repentant woman represents one of the many sinners who accepts Jesus' message and is forgiven. As a consequence, Luke introduces and underscores the elements of scandal introduced into the Markan edition.

The percentage of gray and black rose when the Fellows voted on Luke's version of the story. The weighted average still came out gray, but in a deeper shade.

Women companions of Jesus
Lk 8:1–3
No parallels
Source: Luke

8 **And it so happened soon afterward that he traveled through
towns and villages, preaching and announcing the good news of
God's imperial rule. The twelve were with him, 2and also some
women whom he had cured of evil spirits and diseases: Mary, the
one from Magdala, from whom seven demons had taken their leave,**

[3]and Joanna, the wife of Chuza, Herod's steward, and Susanna, and many others, who provided for them out of their resources.

Women companions of Jesus. Luke has created a narrative at this point in his gospel, bringing to a close a series of events he has inserted into Mark's itinerary. Even though the first part of v. 1 is a Lukan creation, it nevertheless summarizes Jesus' activity during his Galilean ministry: he was an itinerant, traveling about from village to village, and his primary role was to proclaim the good news or gospel of God's imperial rule. Red is the appropriate color expressing a high degree of probability.

The notice that the "twelve" were with Jesus may reflect the later notion that there were only twelve in Jesus' intimate circle. Jesus undoubtedly had male companions, but they play a relatively small role in Luke. The gray color expresses reservations about the number twelve.

The Seminar is also relatively certain that Jesus had women in his traveling retinue. Among those women was Mary of Magdala. Mary of Magdala also appears first in Mark's list of women observers at the crucifixion in 15:40–41. Magdala was apparently a thriving fishing village in Jesus' day. There is no evidence in the gospels that Mary was a prostitute. That characterization comes from the traditional identification of Mary of Magdala with the unnamed sinful woman who anoints Jesus' feet (Luke 7:36–50). Jesus did, however, apparently free Mary of demons, demons that were later interpreted by church theologians as "demons of sexuality," following their identification of Mary with the woman in the anointing story. Mary of Magdala has suffered many centuries from that one ill-deserved connection.

The other two women mentioned in v. 3 are mere names. Joanna is mentioned again in Luke 24:10 among the women who went to the empty tomb. She is identified as the wife of the manager of the estate of Herod Antipas, the tetrarch of Galilee. Nothing further is known about her or about Susanna. Mary and Joanna are names of Jewish women that occur in inscriptions in first-century Palestine. Susanna is less common. Whether Joanna and Susanna were companions of Jesus cannot be verified. However, in Acts, Luke pictures leading, prominent women involved in the Christian movement (Acts 17:4, 12). A figure such as Joanna may have been created to anticipate later converts from a higher social class than were Jesus' original peasant followers.

8 **[4]Since a huge crowd was now gathering, and people were mak-
ing their way to him from town after town, he told them some such
parable as this:**

In parables
Lk 8:4–18
Mk 4:1–34, Mt 13:1–53
Source: Mark

[5]A sower went out to sow his seed; and while he was sowing,
some seed fell along the path, and was trampled under foot, and
the birds of the sky ate it up. [6]Other seed fell on the rock; when
it grew, it withered because it lacked moisture. [7]Still other seed
fell among thorns; the thorns grew with it and choked it. [8]Other

seed fell on fertile earth; and when it matured, it produced fruit a hundredfold.

During his discourse, he would call out, "Anyone here with two good ears had better listen!"

[9]**His disciples asked him what this parable was all about.** [10]**He replied,** "You have been given the privilege of knowing the secrets of God's imperial rule; but the rest get only parables, so that

> They may look but not see,
> listen but not understand.

[11]"Now this is the interpretation of the parable. The 'seed' is God's message. [12]Those 'along the path' are those who have listened to it, but then the devil comes and steals the message from their hearts, so they won't trust and be saved. [13]Those 'on the rock' are those who, when they listen to the message, receive it happily. But they 'have no root': they trust for the moment but fall away when they are tested. [14]What 'fell into the thorns' represents those who listen, but as they continue on, they are 'choked' by the worries and wealth and pleasures of life, and they do not come to maturity. [15]But the seed 'in good earth' stands for those who listen to the message and hold on to it with a good and fertile heart, and 'produce fruit' through perseverance.

[16]"No one lights a lamp and covers it with a pot or puts it under a bed; rather, one puts it on a lampstand, so that those who come in can see the light. [17]After all, there is nothing hidden that won't be brought to light, nor kept secret that won't be made known and exposed.

[18]"So pay attention to how you're listening; in fact, to those who have, more will be given, and from those who don't have, even what they seem to have will be taken away."

In parables. Luke has reduced the length of Mark's parables discourse and has provided only the bare minimum of context. The introduction in v. 4 was designated gray because it, like Matthew, particularizes the scene; Mark had made it a form of Jesus' habitual activity to teach beside the sea. The mention in v. 9 that the disciples asked Jesus privately what the parable of the sower meant is a subversion of the intent of the parables. The parables were designed to instruct openly, albeit in highly figurative and oblique modes of discourse. Accordingly, v. 9 received a black designation.

True relatives
Lk 8:19–21
Mk 3:31–35, Mt 12:46–50; Th 99:1–3
Source: Mark, Thomas

8 [19]**Then his mother and his brothers came to see him, but they could not reach him because of the crowd.** [20]**When he was told, "Your mother and your brothers are outside and want to see you,"** [21]**he replied to them,** "My mother and my brothers are those who listen to God's message and do it."

True relatives. Luke has eliminated the implied criticism of Jesus' mother and brothers in Mark's version of this brief episode. In Mark, Jesus' family has come to get him because they think him demon-possessed (Mark 3:20–21, 31–35). Luke has omitted Mark's introduction and edited the contact between Jesus and his family so as to forego any suggestion that they were hostile to him. In Luke's version, his mother and brother cannot reach him because of the crowd (a note Luke may have carried over from Mark 3:20, a verse he has skipped). Further, Luke makes Jesus' saying about true relatives inclusive: everyone who listens to God's message is a true relative, presumably including blood relatives. That is putting a positive spin on a story to which Mark has given a negative interpretation.

The Fellows voted Mark's version pink as a piece of relatively reliable information. But they decided to designate Luke's version gray rather than pink because he seems to be reversing the sense of his source.

The Gospel of Thomas (99:1–3) has knowledge of the same tradition, also detached from the Markan introduction:

> **The disciples said to him, "Your brothers and your mother are standing outside."**
>
> [2]**He said to them,** "Those here who do what my Father wants are my brothers and my mother. [3]They are the ones who will enter my Father's domain."

Jesus' reply in the Thomas version seems to imply, however, some hostility between Jesus and his family: "Those *here* who do what my Father wants . . ." hints that those in Jesus' circle are to be distinguished from his blood relatives standing outside (the house, or group). Of course, the same words could also have been understood to suggest a contrast between Judeans and gentiles, or between true believers and unbelievers, or between those who belong to the Thomas community and those who do not. All of these options are possible interpretations. On the lips of Jesus, however, the contrast was probably between his relatives and his new family of followers.

Jesus stills the storm
Lk 8:22–25
Mk 4:35–41, Mt 8:23–27
Source: Mark

8 [22]**One day Jesus and his disciples happened to get into a boat, and he said to them,** "Let's cross to the other side of the lake."

So they shoved off, [23]and as they sailed he fell asleep. A squall descended on the lake; they were being swamped, and found themselves in real danger. [24]And they came and woke him up, saying, "Master, master, we are going to drown!"

He got up and rebuked the wind and the rough water; and they settled down, and there was a calm. [25]Then he said to them, "Where is your trust?"

Although they were terrified, they marveled, saying to one another, "Who can this fellow be, that he commands even winds and water and they obey him?"

Jesus stills the storm. Luke tells another storm story that involves the apostle Paul (Acts 27:8–44). While Paul does not calm the seas, his presence does ensure the survival of his shipmates (vv. 22–25). In addition, Paul appears to reproduce the miracle of the loaves: the passengers and sailors have been long without food (v. 21), having been blown about for fourteen days (v. 27), when Paul takes bread, gives thanks, breaks it, and begins to eat. The other 276 persons follow suit. They all seem to have had enough (vv. 33–38). In his shipwreck story involving Paul, Luke may be doing no more than giving his readers another version of the stilling of the storm combined with the tale of the loaves and fish (Luke 9:12–17).

For Luke, as for his source, Mark, Jesus is a majestic wonder-worker who has command of the forces of nature. Luke has a "high christology": Jesus' humanity is eclipsed by the powers of a divinity. In the hellenistic world, Luke's story puts Jesus in a class with Zeus, Athena, and Poseidon. He is even the equal of Yahweh in the Jewish world. After all, in the Jewish scriptures, Yahweh has dominion over the chaos of the great sea and has control of the winds (for example, Gen 14:21, Ps 65:5–8, 89:9). The story of the stilling of the storm is accordingly a part of the Christian framework the evangelists have given to the deeds of the sage from Nazareth.

For the view that this story may be part of a collection of miracle stories, consult the cameo essay on "A Gospel of Miracles?"(pp. 388–89). For suggestions that the storm story may have been inspired by the tale of Jonah or by Greek and Roman tales, consult the commentary on the parallel passage in Matthew (pp. 180–81).

Demon of Gerasa
Lk 8:26–39
Mk 5:1–20, Mt 8:28–34
Source: Mark

8 [26]**They sailed to the region of the Gerasenes, which lies directly**
across from Galilee. [27]**As he stepped out on land, this man from the town who was possessed by demons met him. For quite some time he had been going without clothes and hadn't lived in a house but stayed in the tombs instead.**

[28]**When he saw Jesus, he screamed and fell down before him, and said at the top of his voice, "What do you want with me, Jesus, you son of the most high God? I beg you, don't torment me."** (
[29]**You see, he was about to order the unclean spirit to get out of the man. It seems, the demon had taken control of him many times; the man had been kept under guard, bound with chains and fetters, but he would break the bonds and be driven by the demon into the wilderness.)**

[30]**Jesus questioned him:** "What is your name?"

"Legion," he said, because many demons had entered him.
[31]**They kept begging him not to order them to depart into the abyss.**

[32]**Now over there a large herd of pigs was feeding on the mountain; and they bargained with him to let them enter those pigs. And**
he agreed. [33]**Then the demons came out of the fellow and entered the pigs, and the herd rushed down the bluff into the lake and was drowned.**

[34]**When the herdsmen saw what had happened, they ran off and**
reported it in town and out in the country. [35]**And people came out to**

see what had happened. They came to Jesus and found the fellow
from whom the demons had gone, sitting at the feet of Jesus, with
his clothes on and his wits about him; and they got scared. 36Those
who had seen it explained to them how the demoniac had been
cured. 37Then the entire populace of the Gerasene region asked him
to leave them; for they were gripped by a great fear.
So he got into a boat and went back. 38The man from whom the
demons had departed begged to go with him; but he dismissed him,
saying, 39"Return home, and tell the story of what God has done for
you." **And he went his way, spreading the news throughout the**
whole town about what Jesus had done for him.

Demon of Gerasa. Luke has retained more of the Markan flavor and organization of the story than Matthew, although Luke, too, abbreviates. Luke has skipped Mark's reference to the demoniac "howling day and night in the tombs and in the hills" and "bruising himself on the stones" (Mark 5:5), but has otherwise retained the bizarre features of the Markan tale: the demon-possessed had not worn clothes for a long time; he hadn't lived in a house but in the tombs (presumably rock-cut tombs that could function admirably as a shelter); he had been bound with chains and fetters, but to no avail; he had been driven into the wilderness by the demon upon occasion (vv. 27, 29). These details anticipate the fantastic and grotesque dimensions that later Christian miracle tales would develop. Examples of such tales may be found in the Infancy Gospel of Thomas.

Luke's narrative introduction, like those of both Mark and Matthew, is the fruit of his own imagination; it is tailored to fit into his own sequence of events (v. 26). Luke has made the location "directly across from Galilee" more amenable to the requirements of the story—the proximity of the swine to the lake, although Luke probably did not know that both Gerasa and Gadara (the towns mentioned in Mark and Matthew) were miles from the shore. Luke's narrative setting has no independent historical value.

The exchange between the demon and Jesus, together with the story of the unfortunate swine, is colored black, in accordance with the decisions in the case of Mark's tale. A conversation with a demon or demons should be attributed to the inventiveness of some storyteller. It has often been noted that pigs do not form herds, one consequence of which is that they cannot be stampeded as a group. But these features serve the function of the story to portray the victory of Jesus over a "Legion" that resulted in a bevy of pigs drowning in the sea. The word legion invariably called to mind the Roman army and the mention of pigs (unclean animals to Jews) would have suggested gentiles. The combined drowning of pigs and Romans would have entertained a Jewish audience.

Luke has also adopted Mark's missionary conclusion: the ex-demoniac now sits at the feet of Jesus, with his clothes on, and his wits about him (v. 35). He is exhorted by Jesus to recount what God has done for him, which he does (v. 39).

The portion of the story colored gray is supposed to reflect the skeleton of the original tale. It does that only indirectly, of course, because it has been reworked and edited to suit the needs of storytellers marketing Jesus to new and different audiences.

Jairus' daughter
Lk 8:40–42a, 49–56
Mk 5:21–24a, 35–43,
Mt 9:18–19, 23–26
Source: Mark

8 [40]**Now when Jesus returned, the crowd welcomed him, for they were all waiting for him.** [41]Just then a man **named Jairus,** a synagogue official, came up to Jesus. He fell at Jesus' feet and begged him to come to his house, [42]because his only child, a twelve-year-old daughter, was dying.

Jairus' daughter. In imitation of his source, the Gospel of Mark, Luke interrupts the story of Jairus' daughter to relate the cure of the woman with vaginal bleeding. The commentary on the opening verses of Jairus' daughter will be found below in connection with the remainder of the story, vv. 49–56.

Woman with a vaginal hemorrhage
Lk 8:42b–48
Mk 5:24b–34, Mt 9:20–22
Source: Mark

8 [42b]**As <Jesus> was walking along, the crowd milled around him.**
[43]**A woman who had had a vaginal flow for twelve years, and had found no one able to heal her,** [44]**came up behind him, and touched the hem of his cloak. Immediately her flow of blood stopped.**

[45]**Then Jesus said,** "Who touched me?"

When everyone denied it, Peter said, "Master, the crowds are pressing in and jostling you!"

[46]**But Jesus insisted:** "Someone touched me; I can tell that power has drained out of me."

[47]**And when the woman saw that she had not escaped notice, she came forward trembling, and fell down before him. In front of all the people she explained why she had touched him, and how she had been immediately healed.**

[48]**Jesus said to her,** "Daughter, your trust has cured you; go in peace."

Woman with a vaginal hemorrhage. The core of the story is reported in vv. 43–44: the woman's condition and its severity is reported; the cure is effected by touching; the storyteller pronounces her cured. Luke has reproduced the core of the story from Mark, omitting some of the detail. The Fellows agreed to color the gist of the story pink.

However, Luke has also taken over Mark's expansion in vv. 45–48. Jesus apparently knows that power has gone out of him (although Luke omits this element of the Markan tale), but he doesn't know who is responsible. The woman is fearful of this man of power, so she confesses that it was she. These features are not characteristic of the conventional healing story in the gospels; they belong more to the category of tales of magical cures in the ancient world. With respect to the magical element, our story has some affinities with the use of spittle and touch in the cure of the deaf mute (Mark 7:31–37) and blind Bartimaeus (Mark 8:22–26). The elaboration of the core story was designated black here in Luke's version as it was in the case of Luke's source, Mark.

Jairus' daughter
Lk 8:40–42a, 49–56
Mk 5:21–24a, 35–43,
Mt 9:18–19, 23–26
Source: Mark

8 49 **While he is still speaking,** someone from the synagogue offi-
cial's house comes and says, "Your daughter is dead; don't bother
the teacher further."
50 When Jesus heard this, he answered him, "Don't be afraid; just
have trust, and she'll be cured."
51 When he arrived at the house, he wouldn't allow anyone to go
in with him **except Peter and John and James,** and the child's father
and mother. 52 Everyone was crying and grieving over her, but he
said, "Don't cry; she hasn't died; she's sleeping."
53 But they started laughing at him, certain that she had died. 54 He
took her by the hand and called out, "Child, get up!" 55 Her breathing
returned and she immediately got up. **He ordered them to give her
something to eat.**
56 **Her parents were quite ecstatic; but he commanded them not to
tell anyone what had happened.**

Jairus' daughter. Luke has borrowed the story of Jairus' daughter, with the account of the woman with a vaginal hemorrhage intertwined, from Mark.

Scholars currently are inclined to the view that joining the two stories as they are is the work of Mark; scholars had earlier taken the view that the two were combined in the oral tradition because they happened that way. Combining the two tales was prompted originally, in all probability, by no higher motive than catchword association: two "daughters" are involved (v. 42//Mark 5:23; v. 48//Mark 5:34); one is "twelve" years old, the other has been ill for "twelve" years (v. 42//Mark 5:42; v. 43//Mark 5:25). However, Mark seems to have developed the technique of intercalation—inserting one story into another or weaving two stories together—as a basic ingredient in his literary style. For example, he weaves the story of Peter's denial into his account of Jesus' trial in Mark 14:53–72. He inserts a controversy over what is permitted on the sabbath into his tale of the man with the crippled hand (Mark 3:1–6). He frames the Beelzebul controversy with the story of Jesus' family coming to get him (Mark 3:20–35). There are numerous instances of this feature in Mark's gospel. Luke and Matthew usually follow Mark in this practice.

Luke has abbreviated Mark's elaborate tale, but not so much as Matthew. Both Luke and Matthew seemed to have an aversion to Mark's taste for magic and dramatic detail. Luke omits the Aramaic formula, *"talitha koum,"* that Mark has Jesus employ (literally, "Little girl, Get up!" Mark 5:41), and which probably conveyed an aura of magic because it was spoken in Aramaic rather than Greek. However, Luke makes it clear that a resuscitation is involved by having the girl's breath return (v. 55). In Luke's mind, this story is probably related to the raising of the widow's son at Nain (Luke 7:11–17): there it is a woman and her son, here it is a father and his daughter. And both foreshadow for Luke the resurrection of Jesus.

Luke may have been responsible for the name Jairus. Matthew does not mention the name of the synagogue official, and some manuscripts of the Gospel of Mark lack it. After Luke inserted the name, scribes may have copied it into the text of Mark so as to harmonize the two accounts.

The Fellows, and scholars generally, face insurmountable difficulties in sorting through the vagaries of this tradition in search of some historical incident. The Seminar was divided on whether a singular incident gave rise to this tale. That division resulted in a gray color for the gist of the story. Editorial enhancements were given a black designation.

Mission of the twelve
Lk 9:1–6
Mk 6:7–13, Mt 10:5–15;
Lk 10:1–16
Sources: Mark, Q

9 **He called the twelve together and gave them power and**
authority over all demons and to heal diseases. [2]He sent them out to
announce God's imperial rule and to heal the sick. [3]He said to them,
"Don't take anything for the road: neither staff nor knapsack, neither
bread nor money; no one is to take two shirts. [4]And whichever house
you enter, stay there and leave from there. [5]And wherever they do not
welcome you, leave the town and shake the dust from your feet in witness against them."

[6]And they set out and went from village to village, bringing good news and healing everywhere.

Mission of the twelve. Luke has preserved two group commissioning speeches, in addition to the commissioning of Peter in 5:1–11. The first, found here in chapter 9, is based on the parallel passage in the Gospel of Mark. The second, found in Luke 10:1–16, is derived from the Sayings Gospel Q. The first is addressed to the "twelve"; the second is addressed to the "seventy-two." In both cases, the followers of Jesus are sent out in pairs.

The Fellows doubt that Jesus authorized a specific mission on the part of his followers during his lifetime. They doubt that Jesus formed a circle of twelve intimates. Although it seems probable to them that Jesus did encourage his followers to exorcize demons and to help the sick whenever possible, they doubt that he formed them into a special cadre to perform these functions on a regular basis. Gray seemed the appropriate color for a report that exhibits traces of historical memory.

Herod beheads John
Lk 9:7–9
Mk 6:14–29, Mt 14:1–12
Source: Mark

9 [7]Now Herod the tetrarch heard about everything that was happening. **He was perplexed because some were saying that John had**
been raised from the dead, [8]some that Elijah had appeared, and others that one of the ancient prophets had come back to life. [9]Herod
said, "John I beheaded; but this one about whom I hear such things—who is he?" And he was curious to see him.

Herod beheads John. Although Luke has Mark's story of the death of John in front of him, he chooses to abbreviate it to a greater extent than Matthew.

Luke has already reported the arrest of John by Herod Antipas even before he relates John's baptism of Jesus (Luke 3:19–20). As a consequence, he does not need to repeat the story of John's arrest here.

In addition, Luke omits the dramatic details savored by Mark. The one certain event in Luke's account is Herod's beheading of John (v. 9). It is also likely that Herod had heard about the activities of Jesus (v. 7, pink). The speculation about the resurrection of John reflects later Christian preoccupation with the resurrection of Jesus. And the final note in v. 9 is Luke's way of preparing for Herod's meeting with Jesus in Jerusalem during the trial (Luke 23:6–12).

9 [10]**On their return the apostles reported to him what they had done. Taking them along, Jesus withdrew privately to a town called Bethsaida.** [11]**But the crowds found this out and followed him. He welcomed them, spoke to them about God's imperial rule, and cured those in need of treatment.**

The twelve report
Lk 9:10–11
Mk 6:30–34, Mt 14:13–14
Source: Mark

The twelve report. Luke has based his narrative transition on the one he found in the Gospel of Mark. He has abbreviated Mark's version and altered it in one important detail: Jesus and his apostles withdraw to the town of Bethsaida rather than to an isolated place in the wilderness. This alteration makes it difficult to understand the next story, which is the feeding of the five thousand "in the wilderness." Since they were already in a town or city, procuring food should not have been a special problem for the crowd that had gathered around Jesus.

Bethsaida, a fishing village, was located at the north end of the lake, where the Jordan empties into the Gennesaret, the usual name for that body of water, which was also known as the Sea of Galilee and the Sea of Tiberias. The site today is located somewhat inland since the river has silted up the northern shore.

Luke's narrative transition does not shed light on the order of events and was designated black in accordance with the Seminar's judgment on Mark's version.

9 [12]**As the day began to draw to a close, the twelve approached him and said, "Send the crowd away, so that they can go to the villages and farms around here and find food and lodging; for we are in a desolate place here."**

[13]**But he said to them,** "Give them something to eat yourselves."

They said, "All we have are five loaves and two fish—unless we go ourselves and buy food for all these people." ([14]**There were about five thousand men.)**

He said to his disciples, "Have them sit down in groups of about fifty." [15]**They did so, and got them all seated.** [16]**Then he took the five loaves and two fish, looked up to the sky, gave a blessing, and broke**

Loaves & fish for 5,000
Lk 9:12–17
Mk 6:35–44, Mt 14:15–21; Jn 6:1–15
Sources: Mark, John
Cf. Mk 8:1–9, Mt 15:32–39

them, and started handing them out to the disciples to pass around
to the crowd.
17 And everybody had more than enough to eat. Then the leftovers
were collected, twelve baskets full.

Loaves & fish for 5,000. Luke has based his version of the feeding of the five thousand on Mark 6:35–44. While his copy of Mark's gospel undoubtedly contained Mark's second account (8:1–10), he made no use of it because he skipped all the material in Mark from 6:45 to 8:26. Scholars refer to this as Luke's "big omission." Luke's omissions include: the crossing to Bethsaida (Mark 6:45–46), Jesus walking on the water (6:47–52), a Markan narrative summary (6:53–56), the controversy over unwashed hands (7:1–13), a controversy over defilement (7:14–23), the cure of the Greek woman's daughter (7:24–30), the cure of the deaf-mute (7:31–37), Mark's second account of the loaves and fish (8:1–10), the demand for a sign (8:10–13), the discussion of bread and leaven (8:14–21), and the cure of the blind man (8:22–26). What comes next in Mark's sequence of events is Peter's confession (8:27–30).

In omitting this large amount of intervening material, Luke follows the story of the feeding of the five thousand (9:12–17) directly with Peter's confession (9:18–21). No satisfactory explanation has been given for Luke's decision. One reason may have been his tendency to avoid duplicates. While some of the intervening Markan material does not involve duplication, the twin stories of the feeding in the wilderness do.

In this pericope, Luke follows Mark's account of the feeding of the five thousand relatively closely. He adds no new information; he abbreviates Mark here and there without affecting the basic flow of the story.

Since the Jesus Seminar decided that Mark's story was not the report of an actual event in the life of Jesus, they followed suit in evaluating Luke's version as black.

Peter's confession
Lk 9:18–22
Mk 8:27–30, Mt 16:13–20
Source: Mark

9 **18 And on one occasion when Jesus was praying alone the disci-**
ples were with him; and he questioned them asking: "What are the
crowds saying about me?"
19 They said in response, "<Some say, 'You are> John the Baptist,'
while others, 'Elijah,' and still others, 'One of the ancient prophets
has come back to life.'"
20 Then he said to them, "What about you, who do you say I am?"
And Peter responded, "God's Anointed!"
21 Then he warned them, and forbade them to tell this to anyone,
22 adding, "The son of Adam is destined to suffer a great deal, be re-
jected by the elders and ranking priests and scholars, and be killed
and, on the third day, be raised."

Peter's confession. Luke has combined two paragraphs taken from the Gospel of Mark: the first concerns the confession of Peter, the second is the first prediction of the passion of Jesus—his rejection and execution.

Jesus' words in the first segment are a setup for the confession. When asked what people are saying about him, the disciples report that some think of him as Elijah, some as one of the ancient prophets that has come back to life. No one, it seems, has yet thought of him as the Anointed, the Messiah. That makes Peter the first to recognize Jesus as the Anointed. He is thereafter in a privileged position among the disciples. That position is reinforced when Peter becomes the first to have a vision of the risen Jesus (1 Cor 15:5; Luke 24:34). In the judgment of some scholars, the two events actually coincided: Peter had his vision *and* came to the conclusion that Jesus was the Messiah at the same time.

In any case, the story as it has come down to us is a Christian fiction that reads back into the life of Jesus something that developed only after his death. At the same time, this story functions as a kind of authorization story for Peter: as the first to come to the conviction that Jesus was the Anointed, he henceforth holds a pre-eminent position among the disciples. The call of Peter in 5:1–11 anticipates this incident. A comparable story in the Gospel of Thomas (13:1–8) gives the honor to Thomas, as might be expected in a gospel that bears his name. Andrew is the first to recognize Jesus as the Messiah in the Fourth Gospel (1:35–42), although Mary is the first to see the risen Jesus (John 20:18).

Saving & losing life
Lk 9:23–27
Mk 8:34–9:1, Mt 16:24–28
Source: Mark

9 [23]**He would say to everyone,** "If any of you wants to come after
me, you should deny yourself, pick up your cross every day, and fol-
low me! [24]Remember, by trying to save your own life, you're going to
lose it, but by losing your life for my sake, you're going to save it.
[25]After all, what good does it do you to acquire the whole world and
lose or forfeit yourself? [26]Moreover, if any of you are ashamed of me
and of my message, of you will the son of Adam be ashamed when he
comes in his glory and the glory of the Father and of the holy messen-
gers. [27]I swear to you, some of those standing here won't ever taste
death before they see God's imperial rule."

Saving & losing life. Luke's narrative introduction in v. 23 depicts a customary activity of Jesus—speaking publicly to everyone. For that reason it was colored pink by the Seminar. The sayings in this compendium were designated gray and black by the Fellows in *The Five Gospels*.

Transfiguration
Lk 9:28–36
Mk 9:2–8, Mt 17:1–8
Source: Mark

9 **[28]About eight days after these sayings, Jesus happened to take
Peter and John and James along with him and climbed up the moun-
tain to pray. [29]And it so happened as he was praying that his face
took on a strange appearance, and his clothing turned dazzling
white. [30]The next thing you know, two figures were talking with
him, Moses and Elijah, [31]who appeared in glory and were discussing
his departure, which he was destined to carry out in Jerusalem.**

**[32]Now Peter and those with him were half asleep at the time. But
they came wide awake when they saw his glory and the two men
standing next to him. [33]And it so happened as the men were leaving**

him that Peter said to Jesus, "Master, it's a good thing we're here. In
fact, why not set up three tents, one for you, one for Moses, and one
for Elijah!" (He didn't know what he was saying.)
[34]While he was still speaking, a cloud moved in and cast a shadow
over them. And their fear increased as they entered the cloud. [35]And
out of the cloud a voice spoke: "This is my son, my chosen one.
Listen to him!" [36]When the voice had spoken, Jesus was perceived to
be alone. And they were speechless and told no one back then any-
thing of what they had seen.

Transfiguration. Like Matthew, Luke has borrowed the transfiguration from Mark. And, again like Matthew, he has modified it. Luke has added parts of vv. 31–33, 34, and 36. He has also made other minor changes. For example, he has altered Mark's "six days later" to "About eight days after. . . ." In keeping with his special interests, Luke has Jesus and the three intimates ascend the mountain to pray (v. 28). The mention of prayer evidently reminded Luke of the Gethsemane incident: in v. 32, he represents the three associates as falling asleep, just as they do in the garden at the time of Jesus' arrest (22:39–46). However, they awake in time to see the two figures standing next to Jesus (v. 32).

The verses Luke adds make it clear that the transfiguration anticipates Jesus' resurrection (Moses and Elijah appear in "glory," that is, in a resurrected or transfigured state, v. 31). The two figures from Israel's past speak of Jesus' imminent departure, which he is to accomplish in Jerusalem. Jesus' departure refers either to his death or to his resurrection/ascension (v. 31). Finally, Luke adds that the three intimate friends of Jesus kept silent about their experience and told no one in those days anything of what they had seen (v. 36); in Mark, Jesus orders them to tell no one (Mark 9:9//Matt 17:9).

The parallels between the transfiguration and the experience of Moses on Mount Sinai are explored in the commentary on Matt 17:1–8. Luke has increased the similarities between the two events: in the Exodus account, Moses and Jeshua (Jesus) went to the mountain where the Lord appeared as a cloud. The Lord spoke on the seventh day and Moses then (about the eighth day) "climbed up the mountain" (Exod 24:15–18). Afterward "the appearance of Moses' face" was glorified (Exod 34:29).

The role of the transfiguration in the sequence of events in Mark's gospel is sketched in the commentary on Mark. Luke adds nothing to Mark's general picture beyond the suggestions he has taken from the Exodus story.

While Luke takes the story over from Mark and retains the general outline, he feels free to alter it in this or that detail. That liberty suggests that Luke does not have independent knowledge of the event but, like Mark, is indulging the storyteller's license to invent. The appropriate rating is again black.

Man with mute spirit
Lk 9:37–43
Mk 9:14–29, Mt 17:14–20
Source: Mark

9 **[37]On the following day, when they came down from the moun-**
tain, a huge crowd happened to meet him. [38]Suddenly a man from
the crowd shouted, "Teacher, I beg you to take a look at my son, for

he is my only child. [39]Without warning a spirit gets hold of him, and all of a sudden he screams; it throws him into convulsions, causing him to foam at the mouth; and it leaves him only after abusing him. [40]I begged your disciples to drive it out, but they couldn't."

[41]In response Jesus said, "You distrustful and perverted lot, how long must I associate with you and put up with you? Bring your son here."

[42]But as the boy approached, the demon knocked him down and threw him into convulsions. Jesus rebuked the unclean spirit, healed the boy, and gave him back to his father.

[43]And everybody was astounded at the majesty of God.

Man with mute spirit. Like Matthew, Luke has greatly abbreviated the story of Jesus' cure of the epileptic. He has also omitted the elaborate description of his convulsions and has deleted the exchange between the father and Jesus. However, he has retained Mark's narrative context for the story: the failure of the disciples to cure the victim (vv. 40–41). And he has retained Mark's narrative connection in v. 37, which may well be Mark's invention. Those features are designated black as Luke's retelling of events that were the products of Mark's imagination. The core of the story, which may reflect an actual event, was colored gray, following the decisions taken by the Seminar concerning the primary version in the Gospel of Mark.

9 **[43b]While they all were marveling at everything he was doing, he said to his disciples,** [44]"Mark well these words: the son of Adam is about to be turned over to his enemies."

[45]But they never understood this remark. It was couched in veiled language, so they would not get its meaning. And they always dreaded to ask him about this remark.

Jesus predicts his death
Lk 9:43b–45
Mk 9:30–32, Mt 17:22–23
Source: Mark
Cf. Mk 8:31–33, Mt 16:21–23, Lk 9:22; Mk 10:32–34, Mt 20:17–19, Lk 18:31–34

Jesus predicts his death. Luke has reproduced Mark's second prediction of Jesus' death, but in doing so has abbreviated it and modified the narrative context.

In v. 43b, Luke abandons Mark's observation that Jesus and his disciples were passing through Galilee on their way south and links the second prediction rather to the cure of the epileptic boy that has just been narrated: Jesus introduces this ominous note in the midst of his success as a healer.

In v. 45, Luke expands on Mark's comment that the disciples did not understand Jesus and were afraid to ask him what it meant. Luke suggests that the prediction was expressed "in veiled language." It is difficult to see what was veiled about it. Did the disciples not understand that "son of Adam" referred to Jesus? Did they not understand what being betrayed to one's enemies meant? For Luke, as for Mark, the failure to understand is a narrative device rather than a historical note.

Dispute about greatness
Lk 9:46–48
Mk 9:33–37, Mt 18:1–5
Source: Mark

9 [46]**Now an argument broke out among them over which of them was greatest. [47]But Jesus, knowing what was on their minds, took a child and had her stand next to him. [48]He said to them,** "Whoever accepts this child in my name is accepting me. And whoever accepts me accepts the one who sent me. Don't forget, the one who has a lower rank among you is the one who is great."

Dispute about greatness. Luke has collapsed two Markan paragraphs into one by combining a saying about rank with a saying about receiving a child. Luke has revised both the sayings and the narrative setting. Luke's revision is the product of his imagination since he had no historical information at his disposal that was not available to Mark, his source. And Mark's setting was itself already a fiction created by Mark. The Fellows agreed to a black designation without hesitation.

The strange exorcist
Lk 9:49–50
Mk 9:38–41
Source: Mark

9 [49]**John said in response, "Master, we saw someone driving out demons in your name, and we tried to stop him, because he isn't one of us."**

[50]**But he said to him,** "Don't stop him; in fact, whoever is not against you is on your side."

The strange exorcist. Luke has borrowed and abbreviated a complex he found in the Gospel of Mark. The saying in v. 50 was a well-known proverb quoted by others before Jesus, but it is possible, even likely, that Jesus may have quoted it. However, the narrative setting in v. 49 is a Markan invention, in all probability, so the correct color is black.

On the way to Jerusalem
Lk 9:51–56
No parallels
Source: Luke

9 [51]**It so happened as the days were drawing near for him to be taken up that he was determined to go to Jerusalem. [52]He sent messengers on ahead of him. They entered a Samaritan village, to get things ready for him. [53]But the Samaritans would not welcome him, because he had made up his mind to go on to Jerusalem. [54]When his disciples James and John realized this, they said, "Lord, do you want us to call down fire from heaven and annihilate them?" [55]But he turned and reprimanded them. [56]Then they continued on to another village.**

On the way to Jerusalem. Luke has constructed an artificial "travelogue" for Jesus that takes him through the country of the Samaritans on his way to Jerusalem. The journey lasts from 9:51 to 19:27. During this journey Jesus instructs his disciples and performs other acts. Luke has created the sequence mostly from materials he has taken from the Sayings Gospel Q and the oral tradition, until he gets to 18:15, when he resumes copying from Mark.

Mark and Matthew also describe a journey to Jerusalem (Mark 10:1–52// 19:1–20:34), but they have Jesus cross the Jordan into Transjordan and go south on the east side of the river out of Samaritan territory. Given the hostility between Samaritans and Judeans, Galilean pilgrims often preferred this route.

This scene has no counterpart in any of the other gospels and is probably the product of Luke's imagination. The story was inspired in part by an anecdote told about Elijah in 2 Kgs 1:9–12: King Ahaziah sends a captain and fifty men to arrest Elijah as he sits atop his hill for predicting the king's death. Elijah calls down fire from heaven to consume them. Ahaziah sends a second fifty and they meet the same fate. The proposal in v. 54 was derived from the story of Elijah.

As a Lukan fiction, this narrative segment deserves to be colored black.

Foxes have dens
Lk 9:57–62
Mt 8:18–22
Source: Q

9 57**As they were going along the road, someone said to him, "I'll
follow you wherever you go."**
58**And Jesus said to him,** "Foxes have dens, and birds of the sky
have nests; but the son of Adam has nowhere to rest his head."
59**To another he said,** "Follow me."
But he said, "First, let me go and bury my father."
60**Jesus said to him,** "Leave it to the dead to bury their own dead;
but you, go out and announce God's imperial rule."
61**Another said, "I'll follow you, sir; but let me first say good-bye
to my people at home."**
62**Jesus said to him,** "No one who puts his hand to the plow and
looks back is qualified for God's imperial rule."

Foxes have dens. The dialogical framework for these exchanges between Jesus and potential disciples is probably fictive. Yet just such exchanges probably did take place. Not much is to be lost or gained by how they are evaluated, but it seemed wisest to put them in the gray category as possible but not certain events. It is more likely that the remembered sayings of Jesus in vv. 58, 60, 62 prompted the storyteller to supply the corresponding dialogue.

Mission of the seventy-two
Lk 10:1–16
Mk 6:7–13, Mt 10:5–15,
Lk 9:1–6
Sources: Q, Mark

10 **After this the Lord appointed seventy-two others and sent
them on ahead of him in pairs to every town and place that he him-
self intended to visit.** 2**He would say to them,** "Although the crop is
good, still there are few to harvest it. So beg the harvest boss to dis-
patch workers to the fields. 3Get going; look, I'm sending you out like
lambs into a pack of wolves. 4Carry no purse, no knapsack, no sandals.
Don't greet anyone on the road. 5Whenever you enter a house, first
say, 'Peace to this house.' 6If peaceful people live there, your peace will
rest on them. But if not, it will return to you. 7Stay at that one house,
eating and drinking whatever they provide, for workers deserve their
wages. Do not move from house to house. 8Whenever you enter a

town and they welcome you, eat whatever is set before you. [9]Cure the sick there and tell them, 'God's imperial rule is closing in.' [10]But whenever you enter a town and they do not receive you, go out into its streets and say, [11]'Even the dust of your town that sticks to our feet, we wipe off against you. But know this: God's imperial rule is closing in.' [12]I tell you, on that day Sodom will be better off than that town.

[13]"Damn you, Chorazin! Damn you, Bethsaida! If the miracles done in you had been done in Tyre and Sidon, they would have sat in sackcloth and ashes and changed their ways long ago. [14]But Tyre and Sidon will be better off at the judgment than you. [15]And you, Capernaum, you don't think you'll be exalted to heaven, do you? No, you'll go to Hell.

[16]"Whoever hears you hears me, and whoever rejects you rejects me, and whoever rejects me rejects the one who sent me."

Mission of the seventy-two. The program Luke outlines in this passage is almost certainly fictive. Luke has in mind the kind of missionary activity that Peter, Paul, and others initiated later on in the Jesus movement. Here Jesus is represented as sending out his followers in pairs to prepare the way for him in towns he intends to visit. The Greek manuscripts of Luke differ about whether the number was seventy or seventy-two. Seventy is the symbolic number: Moses chose seventy elders to assist him (Exod 24:1) and Jacob had seventy descendants (Exod 1:5). Seventy or seventy-two may also symbolize the number of nations in the world: the Hebrew text of Genesis 10 has seventy nations, the Greek version seventy-two. Luke was probably referring to the Greek rather than the Hebrew version and thus hinting at the world mission of the later church. Calling Jesus "the Lord" in v. 1 is the device Luke uses, especially in the travelogue, to define Jesus' status and thereby add authority to his teachings. Since v. 1 is Luke's creation and does not reflect historical circumstance, black is the correct designation.

The seventy-two report
Lk 10:17–20
No parallels
Source: Luke

10 [17]**The seventy-two returned with joy, saying, "Lord, even the demons submit to us when we invoke your name!"**

[18]**And he said to them,** "I was watching Satan fall like lightning from heaven. [19]Look, I have given you authority to step on snakes and scorpions, and over all the power of the enemy; and nothing will ever harm you. [20]However, don't rejoice that the spirits submit to you; rejoice instead that your names have been inscribed in heaven."

The seventy-two report. This is another Lukan composition with no counterpart in any of the other gospels. It was probably constructed to accommodate the saying of Jesus recorded in v. 18. Luke has arranged the setting so that the remark of the disciples in v. 17 is corrected by Luke's editorial comment in v. 20, here put on the lips of Jesus. Black is the correct designation for the narrative portion of the segment.

Father & son
Lk 10:21–24
Mt 11:25–27
Source: Q

10 [21]**At that moment Jesus was overjoyed by the holy spirit and**
said, "I praise you, Father, Lord of heaven and earth, because you
have hidden these things from the wise and the learned but revealed
them to the untutored; yes indeed, Father, because this is the way you
want it. [22]My Father has turned everything over to me. No one knows
who the son is except the Father, or who the Father is except the son—
and anyone to whom the son wishes to reveal him."
[23]**Turning to the disciples he said privately,** "How privileged are
the eyes that see what you see! [24]I tell you, many prophets and kings
wanted to see what you see, and didn't see it, and to hear what you
hear, and didn't hear it."

Father & son. The narrative location—"at that moment"—is no doubt a fiction of the storyteller. Even though the words of Jesus may have been remembered and transmitted in the approximate form in which they are recorded here, the occasion on which he first spoke them would not have been. Similarly, the notice in v. 23 that Jesus addressed his disciples privately reflects the tradition that the disciples had received privileged information. That tradition was likely invented by the disciples themselves as they vied for position in the new movement. Black is the appropriate evaluation for both narrative elements.

Good Samaritan
Lk 10:25–37
Mk 12:28–34, Mt 22:34–40
Sources: Mark, oral
tradition

10 [25]**On one occasion, a legal expert stood up to put him to the**
test with a question: "Teacher, what do I have to do to inherit eternal
life?"
[26]**He said to him,** "How do you read what is written in the Law?"
[27]**And he answered, "You are to love the Lord your God with all**
your heart, with all your soul, with all your energy, and with all your
mind; and your neighbor as yourself."
[28]**Jesus said to him,** "You have given the correct answer; do this and
you will have life."
[29]**But with a view to justifying himself, he said to Jesus, "But who**
is my neighbor?"
[30]**Jesus replied:**

This fellow was on his way from Jerusalem down to Jericho
when he fell into the hands of robbers. They stripped him, beat
him up, and went off, leaving him half dead. [31]Now by coinci-
dence a priest was going down that road; when he caught sight
of him, he went out of his way to avoid him. [32]In the same way,
when a Levite came to the place, he took one look at him and
crossed the road to avoid him. [33]But this Samaritan who was trav-
eling that way came to where he was and was moved to pity at
the sight of him. [34]He went up to him and bandaged his wounds,

pouring olive oil and wine on them. He hoisted him onto his own animal, brought him to an inn, and looked after him.

[35]The next day he took out two silver coins, which he gave to the innkeeper, and said, "Look after him, and on my way back I'll reimburse you for any extra expense you have had."

[36]"Which of these three, in your opinion, acted like a neighbor to the man who fell into the hands of the robbers?"

[37]He said, "The one who showed him compassion."

Jesus said to him, "Then go and do the same yourself."

Good Samaritan. Luke takes Mark's anecdote in which a friendly scholar asks Jesus which is the greatest commandment and converts it into an introduction to the parable of the Good Samaritan. Luke invents dialogue for Jesus in vv. 26 and 28, and reorders the sequence of the exchange. He has further expanded it with the conclusion in vv. 36–37, which did not go originally with the parable since it contradicts the intent of the parable. The parable poses the question, from what quarter may I expect help when I have been robbed, beaten, and left for dead? The narrative introduction suggests that Jesus is going to answer the question: Who is my neighbor? (v. 29). The narrative conclusion has Jesus reformulate the question to: Who in this story acted like a neighbor? The parable answers neither question.

Luke has taken a narrative context from Mark and remodeled it as a narrative frame for the parable of the good Samaritan; this illustrates the liberties the evangelists took with their material. Black is the only possible designation for what Luke composed.

Mary & Martha
Lk 10:38–42
No parallels
Source: Luke

10

[38]Now as they went along, he came to this village where a woman named Martha welcomed him into her home. [39]And she had a sister named Mary, who sat at the Lord's feet and listened to his words. [40]But Martha kept getting distracted because she was doing all the serving. So she went up <to Jesus> and said, "Lord, doesn't it matter to you that my sister has left me with all the serving? Tell her to give me a hand."

[41]But the Lord answered her, "Martha, Martha, you are worried and upset about a lot of things. [42]But only one thing is necessary. Mary has made the better choice and it is something she will never lose."

Mary & Martha. This episode is the creation of Luke. In the previous segment, a lawyer had asked about what he had to do to inherit eternal life. Jesus responds with the first commandment: love God. In the mind of Luke, the parable of the Samaritan illustrates the second most important commandment, "Love your neighbor as yourself." In this story, Mary's undivided attention to the teaching of Jesus illustrates the first commandment: "You are to love the Lord your God with all your heart, with all your soul, with all your *energy,* and with all your *mind.*" Luke is again creating a narrative context for a teaching of

Jesus. Luke again refers to Jesus as "the Lord," the title current in Luke's community of believers toward the close of the first century. As a composition of Luke, the narrative deserves a black designation.

Lord's prayer
Lk 11:1–13
Mt 6:9–13, 7:7–11
Source: Q

11 **On one occasion he happened to be praying somewhere.**
When he had finished, one of his disciples said to him, "Lord, teach
us how to pray, just as John taught his disciples."
2**He said to them,** "When you pray, you should say:

Father, your name be revered.
Impose your imperial rule.
3Provide us with the bread we need day by day.
4Forgive our sins, since we too forgive everyone in debt to us.
And please don't subject us to test after test."

5**Jesus said to them,** "Suppose you have a friend who comes to you
in the middle of the night and says to you, 'Friend, lend me three
loaves, 6for a friend of mine on a trip has just shown up and I have
nothing to offer him.' 7And suppose you reply, 'Stop bothering me.
The door is already locked and my children and I are in bed. I can't get
up to give you anything'—8I tell you, even though you won't get up
and give the friend anything out of friendship, yet you will get up and
give the other whatever is needed because you'd be ashamed not to.
9"So I tell you, ask—it'll be given to you; seek—you'll find; knock—
it'll be opened for you. 10Rest assured: everyone who asks receives;
everyone who seeks finds; and for the one who knocks it is opened.
11Which of you fathers would hand his son a snake when it's fish he's
asking for? 12Or a scorpion when it's an egg he's asking for? 13So if you,
worthless as you are, know how to give your children good gifts, isn't
it much more likely that the heavenly Father will give holy spirit to
those who ask him?"

Lord's prayer. Luke and Matthew have both provided minimal narrative settings for the Lord's prayer, the words for which were derived from Q. The fact that the two evangelists have slightly different settings indicates how readily they invented contexts. Black is the appropriate color.

Beelzebul controversy
Lk 11:14–23
Mt 12:22–32; Mk 3:22–30
Sources: Q, Mark

11 14**Jesus was driving out a demon that was mute, and when**
the demon had departed the mute man spoke. And the crowds were
amazed. 15**But some of them said, "He drives out demons in the**
name of Beelzebul, the head demon."
16**Others were testing him by demanding a sign from heaven.**
17**But he knew what they were thinking, and said to them: "Every**
government divided against itself is devastated, and a house divided
against a house falls. 18**If Satan is divided against himself—since you**
claim I drive out demons in Beelzebul's name—how will his domain

endure? [19]If I drive out demons in Beelzebul's name, in whose name do your own people drive <them> out? In that case, they will be your judges. [20]But if by God's finger I drive out demons, then for you God's imperial rule has arrived.

[21]"When a strong man is fully armed and guards his courtyard, his possessions are safe. [22]But when a stronger man attacks and overpowers him, he takes the weapons on which he was relying and divides up his loot.

[23]"The one who isn't with me is against me, and the one who doesn't gather with me scatters."

Beelzebul controversy. Since the story of the cure of the (blind) mute and Beelzebul controversy are derived from Q, the evaluation is to be found in the Sayings Gospel Q, which is the first section in this volume (pp. 41–50).

Privileged womb
Lk 11:27–28
Th 79:1–3
Sources: Luke, Thomas

11 [24]"When an unclean spirit leaves a person, it wanders through waterless places in search of a resting place. When it doesn't find one, it says, 'I will go back to the home I left.' [25]It then returns, and finds it swept and refurbished. [26]Next, it goes out and brings back seven other spirits more vile than itself, who enter and settle in there. So that person ends up worse off than when he or she started."

[27]**And so just as he was making these remarks, a woman from the crowd raised her voice and addressed him, "How privileged is the womb that carried you and the breasts that nursed you!"**

[28]"Rather," **he replied,** "privileged are those who hear the word of God and keep it."

Privileged womb. The Fellows of the Seminar thought it possible that the words in v. 28 (and their counterpart in Thom 79:2) may have originated with Jesus. They were dubious, however, that the narrative setting given the words in vv. 27–28 reflects historical reminiscence. Consequently, they designated that setting black.

Demand for a sign
Lk 11:29–30
Mt 12:38–40; Mk 8:11–13, Mt 16:1–4
Sources: Q, Mark
Cf. Jn 2:18; 6:30

11 [29]**As more and more people were crowding around him, he began to say,** "This generation is an evil generation. It insists on a sign, but it will be given no sign except the sign of Jonah. [30]You see, just as Jonah became a sign for the Ninevites, so the son of Adam will be a sign for this generation."

Demand for a sign. The Fellows of the Jesus Seminar were inclined to agree that this Q text correctly represents the source of the demand for a sign. Although it is not specifically stated that the crowds raised the question with Jesus in v. 29, their expectations probably leaned in that direction. Pink is therefore an appropriate designation. The response assigned to Jesus is not likely to have originated with him, but represents the point of view of a later generation. "This generation" in v. 30 was probably the second or third generation after the Jesus movement began—the future from the standpoint of the past.

11 31"At judgment time, the queen of the south will be brought
back to life along with members of this generation, and she will con-
demn them, because she came from the ends of the earth to listen to
Solomon's wisdom. Yet take note: what is right here is greater than
Solomon. 32At judgment time, the citizens of Nineveh will come back
to life, along with this generation, and condemn it, because they had a
change of heart in response to Jonah's message. Yet take note: what is
right here is greater than Jonah.

33"No one lights a lamp and then puts it in a cellar or under a bushel
basket, but rather on a lampstand so that those who come in can see
the light. 34Your eye is the body's lamp. When your eye is clear, your
whole body is flooded with light. When your eye is clouded, your
body is shrouded in darkness. 35Take care, then, that the light within
you is not darkness. 36If then your whole body is flooded with light,
and no corner of it is darkness, it will be completely illuminated as
when a lamp's rays engulf you."

Condemnation of Pharisees
Lk 11:37–54
Mt 23:1–36
Source: Q

**37While he was speaking, a Pharisee invites him to dinner at his
house. So he came and reclined at the table. 38The Pharisee was
astonished to see that he did not first wash before the meal.**

39But the Lord said to him, "You Pharisees clean the outside of cups
and dishes, but inside you are full of greed and evil. 40You fools! Did
not the one who made the outside also make the inside? 41Still, donate
what is inside to charity, and then you'll see how everything comes
clean for you.

42"Damn you, Pharisees! You pay tithes on mint and rue and every
herb, but neglect justice and the love of God. You should have
attended to the last without neglecting the first.

43"Damn you, Pharisees! You're so fond of the prominent seat in syn-
agogues and respectful greetings in marketplaces. 44Damn you! You are
like unmarked graves that people walk on without realizing it."

**45One of the legal experts says to him in reply, "Teacher, when you
say these things you are insulting us, too."**

46And he said, "Damn you legal experts too! You load people down
with crushing burdens, but you yourselves don't lift a finger to help
carry them. 47Damn you! You erect monuments to the prophets whom
your ancestors murdered. 48You are therefore witnesses to and approve
of the deeds of your ancestors: they killed <the prophets> and you
erect <monuments> to them. 49That is why the wisdom of God has
said, 'I will send them prophets and apostles, and some of them they
are always going to kill and persecute. 50So, this generation will have
to answer for the blood of all the prophets that has been shed since the

world was founded, [51]from the blood of Abel to the blood of Zechariah, who perished between the altar and the sanctuary.' Yes, I tell you, this generation will have to answer for it.

[52]"You legal experts, damn you! You have taken away the key of knowledge. You yourselves haven't entered and you have blocked the way of those trying to enter."

[53]By the time he had left there, the scholars and Pharisees began to resent him bitterly and to harass him with all kinds of questions, [54]conspiring to trap him with his own words.

Condemnation of Pharisees. The Sayings Gospel Q evidently included a series of invectives directed against the Pharisees and legal experts. Luke has assembled his own version of that series and given the complex his own narrative framework in vv. 37–38, 45, and 53–54. Since Luke's framework does not match that given to the complex by Matthew, the Fellows concluded that the narrative setting was fictive. They therefore designated it black.

Bread & leaven
Lk 12:1
Mk 8:14–21, Mt 16:5–12
Source: Mark

12 **Meanwhile, a crowd of many thousands had thronged together and were trampling each other.**

He began to speak first to his disciples: "Guard against the leaven of the Pharisees, which is to say, their hypocrisy."

Bread & leaven. Luke has omitted the complex of sayings he found before him in Mark 8:14–21, except for the one saying about the leaven of the Pharisees. Luke then created a new narrative context for that saying (v. 1), plus other sayings he has added to his new complex (12:2–12). In addition, Luke provides readers with an interpretation of the leaven of the Pharisees: leaven symbolizes hypocrisy. As a fiction of Luke, the Fellows agreed the new narrative context should be colored black.

12 [2]"There is nothing veiled that won't be unveiled, or hidden that won't be made known. [3]And so whatever you've said in the dark will be heard in the light, and what you've whispered behind closed doors will be announced from the rooftops.

[4]"I tell you, my friends, don't fear those who kill the body, and after that can do no more. [5]I'll show you whom you ought to fear: fear the one who can kill and then has authority to cast into Gehenna. Believe me, that's the one you should fear! [6]What do sparrows cost? A dime a dozen? Yet not one of them is overlooked by God. [7]In fact, even the hairs of your head have all been counted. Don't be so timid: You're worth more than a flock of sparrows.

[8]"I tell you, everyone who acknowledges me in public, the son of Adam will acknowledge in front of God's messengers. [9]But whoever disowns me in public will be disowned in the presence of God's messengers. [10]And everyone who utters a word against the son of Adam

will be forgiven; but whoever blasphemes against the holy spirit won't be forgiven. [11]And when they make you appear in synagogues and haul you up before rulers and authorities, don't worry about how or in what way you should defend yourself or what you should say. [12]The holy spirit will teach you at that very moment what you ought to say."

[13]Someone in the crowd said to him, "Teacher, tell my brother to divide the inheritance with me."

Disputed inheritance
Lk 12:13–15
Th 72:1–3
Sources: Luke, Thomas

[14]But Jesus said to him, "Mister, who appointed me your judge or arbiter?"

[15]Then he said to them, "Watch out! Guard against greed in all its forms; after all, possessions, even in abundance, don't guarantee someone life."

Disputed inheritance. The Fellows of the Seminar agreed that the saying in v. 14 might conceivably stem from Jesus, but they did not think the moralistic generalization in v. 15 could have been formulated by Jesus. The narrative setting given to the complex (vv. 13, 14, 15, 16, 22) they concluded was the creation of some anonymous storyteller in the oral period since it is reported in roughly the same form by both Luke and Thomas. They designated all parts of it black.

12 **[16]Then he told them a parable:**

Rich farmer
Lk 12:16–21
Th 63:1–3
Sources: Luke, Thomas

There was a rich man whose fields produced a bumper crop. [17]"What do I do now?" he asked himself, "since I don't have any place to store my crops. [18]I know!" he said, "I'll tear down my barns and build larger ones so I can store all my grain and my goods. [19]Then I'll say to myself, 'You have plenty put away for years to come. Take it easy; eat, drink, and enjoy yourself.'" [20]But God said to him, "You fool! This very night your life will be demanded back from you. All this stuff you've collected—whose will it be now?" [21]That's the way it is with those who save up for themselves, but aren't rich where God is concerned.

Rich farmer. Luke's simple narrative introduction in v. 16 indicates that Jesus told the parable of the rich farmer immediately after the discussion of the disputed inheritance (Luke 12:13–15). It is highly unlikely that the two came together in Jesus' actual discourse. Black is thus the proper designation.

12 **[22]He said to his disciples,** "That's why I tell you: Don't fret about life—what you're going to eat—or about your body—what you're going to wear. [23]Remember, there is more to living than food and clothing. [24]Think about the crows: they don't plant or harvest, they don't have storerooms or barns. Yet God feeds them. You're worth a lot more than the birds! [25]Can any of you add an hour to life by fretting

On anxieties
Lk 12:22–31
Mt 6:25–34; Th 36
Sources: Q, Thomas

about it? 26So if you can't do a little thing like that, why worry about the rest? 27Think about how the lilies grow: they don't slave and they never spin. Yet let me tell you, even Solomon at the height of his glory was never decked out like one of them. 28If God dresses up the grass in the field, which is here today and tomorrow is tossed into an oven, it is surely more likely <that God cares for> you, you who don't take anything for granted! 29And don't be constantly on the lookout for what you're going to eat and what you're going to drink. Don't give it a thought. 30These are all things the world's pagans seek, and your Father is aware that you need them. 31Instead, you are to seek <God's> domain, and these things will come to you as a bonus."

On anxieties. The minimal narrative connective in v. 22 is once again Luke's innocent device to connect parables and compendia of sayings into a narrative sequence. Black is the requisite color.

12 32"Don't be afraid, little flock, for it has delighted your Father to give you his domain. 33Sell your belongings, and donate to charity; make yourselves purses that don't wear out, with inexhaustible wealth in heaven, where no robber can get to it and no moth can destroy it. 34As you know, what you treasure is your heart's true measure."

Watchful servants
Lk 12:35–48
Mt 24:43–44; Th 21:5–7, 103;
Mt 24:45–51
Sources: Luke, Q, Thomas

35"Keep your belts fastened and your lamps lighted. 36Imitate those who are waiting for their master to come home from a wedding, ready to open the door for him as soon as he arrives and knocks. 37Those slaves the master finds alert when he arrives are to be congratulated. I swear to you, he will put on an apron, have them recline at the table, and proceed to wait on them. 38If he gets home around midnight, or even around 3 A.M., and finds them so, they are to be congratulated! 39Mark this well: if the homeowner had known what time the burglar was coming, he would not have let anyone break into his house. 40You too should be prepared. Remember, the son of Adam is coming when you least expect it."

41Peter said, "Lord, are you telling this parable just for us or for the benefit of everyone?"

42The Lord said, "Who then is the reliable and shrewd manager to whom the master assigns responsibility for his household staff, to dole out their food allowance at the right time? 43Congratulations to the slave who's on the job when his master arrives. 44I'm telling you the truth: he'll put him in charge of all his property. 45But suppose that slave says to himself, 'My master is taking his time getting here,' and begins to beat the servants and the maids, and to eat and drink and get drunk, 46that slave's master will show up on the day he least expects and at an hour he doesn't suspect. He'll cut him to pieces and assign him a fate fit for the faithless. 47And the slave who knew what his master wanted, but didn't get things ready or act properly, will be flogged

severely. 48On the other hand, the slave who didn't know what his
master wanted, yet did things that deserve punishment, will be
flogged lightly. A great deal will be required of everyone to whom
much is given; yet even more will be demanded from the one to whom
a great deal has been entrusted."

Watchful servants. Luke has inserted a brief narrative reference (vv. 41–42) into this complex of sayings, which he has assembled from various sources. Peter's question does not reflect an actual event, but was conjured up by the imagination of the storyteller. Black is the appropriate color.

12 49"I came to set the earth on fire, and how I wish it were
already ablaze! 50I have a baptism to be baptized with, and what pres-
sure I'm under until it's over! 51Do you suppose I came here to bring
peace on earth? No, I tell you, on the contrary: conflict. 52As a result,
from now on in any given house there will be five in conflict, three
against two and two against three. 53Father will be pitted against son
and son against father, mother against daughter and daughter against
mother, mother-in-law against daughter-in-law and daughter-in-law
against mother-in-law."

Knowing the times
Lk 12:54–56
Mt 16:2–3; Th 91:1–2
Sources: Q, Thomas

54**He would also say to the crowds,** "When you see a cloud rising in
the west, right away you say that it's going to rain; and so it does.
55And when the wind blows from the south, you say we're in for
scorching heat; and we are. 56You phonies! You know the lay of the
land and can read the face of the sky, so why don't you know how to
interpret the present time?"
57"Why can't you decide for yourselves what is right? 58When you
are about to appear with your opponent before the magistrate, do
your best to settle with him on the way, or else he might drag you up
before the judge, and the judge turn you over to the jailer, and the
jailer throw you in prison. 59I tell you, you'll never get out of there until
you've paid every last red cent."

Knowing the times. The narrative connective is v. 54 generalizes on Jesus' customary activity—teaching crowds of people—and so was designated pink by the Fellows.

Repent or perish
Lk 13:1–5
No parallels
Source: Luke

13 **Some who were there at the time told him about the
Galileans, about how Pilate had mixed their blood with their sacri-
fices. 2He answered them,** "Do you suppose that these Galileans were
the worst sinners in Galilee, because they suffered this? 3Hardly.
However, let me tell you, if you don't have a change of heart, you'll all
meet your doom in the same way. 4Or how about those eighteen in
Siloam, who were killed when the tower fell on them—do you suppose

that they were any guiltier than the whole population of Jerusalem? [5]Hardly. However, let me tell you, if you don't have a change of heart, all of you will meet your doom in a similar fashion."

Repent or perish. The incidents in vv. 1–5 are reported by Luke alone. Since there is nothing distinctive about either sayings or setting to connect them with Jesus, the Fellows colored both black. Luke has attached the parable in vv. 6–9 to confirm what happens to the unrepentant. The linking remark in v. 6 is Luke's creation. Black is appropriate.

Barren tree
Lk 13:6–9
No parallels
Source: Luke

13 [6]**Then he told this parable:** "A man had a fig tree growing in his vineyard; he came looking for fruit on it but didn't find any.

[7]"So he said to the vinekeeper, 'See here, for three years in a row I have come looking for fruit on this tree, and haven't found any. Cut it down. Why should it suck the nutrients out of the soil?'

[8]"In response he says to him, 'Let it stand, sir, one more year, until I get a chance to dig around it and work in some manure. [9]Maybe it will produce next year; but if it doesn't, we can go ahead and cut it down.'"

Barren tree. Once again Luke has linked the parable of the barren tree with the preceding group of sayings, thereby suggesting a specific historical sequence. Since Luke did not know the sequence of sayings and parables, his linkage is a fiction, for which black is the appropriate color.

Afflicted woman
Lk 13:10–17
No parallels
Source: Luke

13 [10]**Now he was teaching in one of the synagogues on the sabbath day. [11]A woman showed up who for eighteen years had been afflicted by a spirit; she was bent over and unable to straighten up even a little. [12]When Jesus noticed her, he called her over and said,** "Woman, you are freed from your affliction." [13]**He laid hands on her, and immediately she stood up straight and began to praise God.**

[14]**The leader of the synagogue was indignant, however, because Jesus had healed on the sabbath day. He lectured the crowd: "There are six days which we devote to work; so come on one of those days and be healed, but not on the sabbath day."**

[15]**But the Lord answered him,** "You phonies! Every last one of you unties your ox or your donkey from the feeding trough on the sabbath day and leads it off to water, don't you? [16]This woman, a daughter of Abraham whom Satan has kept in bondage for eighteen long years—should she not be released from these bonds just because it is the sabbath day?" [17]**As he said this, all his adversaries were put to shame, but most folks rejoiced at all the wonderful things he was doing.**

Afflicted woman. The story of the afflicted woman is often taken as the twin of the account of the man with dropsy (14:1–6): both stories are unique to

Luke and both revolve around a sabbath controversy involving an argument from the lesser to the greater ("If you would do this for a sheep or an ox, why not for a human being?"). In the handicapped woman, the cure is narrated in vv. 10–13; the controversy is tacked on to the end (vv. 14–17), as a subordinate feature. In the man with dropsy, on the other hand, the controversy is the featured element, with the healing providing only the minimal occasion.

The first question for scholars is whether there is solid historical evidence that Jesus engaged in practices that infringed sabbath codes, and, if he did so, whether he further engaged in controversies over those practices.

The gospels contain five stories featuring cures that evoke controversy over sabbath practice. The Fellows designated Mark 3:1–6, the man with the crippled hand, gray because Mark has turned it into a plot against Jesus' life. The paralytic by the pool (John 5:1–9a) is another cure framed by a sabbath controversy. The Seminar colored the cure gray, but designated the surrounding controversy black. There is also the account of the man born blind (John 9:1–7), which the author of the Fourth Gospel has again encased in a controversy. The Fellows again voted the cure gray but the framing controversy black. The two remaining stories that combine cures with sabbath controversies are the twin stories unique to Luke: the afflicted woman and the man with dropsy.

It seemed entirely probable to the members of the Seminar that Jesus was faced with a confrontation on a sabbath after healing someone's non-life-threatening condition (a life-threatening condition would automatically have caused sabbath restrictions to be set aside). They also thought it probable that Jesus questioned sabbath regulations and that he occasionally failed to observe them. However, they did not think the story of the afflicted woman supported these probabilities, except as a remote fictive memory. They were inclined, rather, to view it as a Lukan composition based, perhaps, on Mark 3:1–6, but exhibiting Lukan vocabulary, style, and themes, for example, the praise of God in v. 13. In this story Luke also indulges his proclivity to imitate the Greek scriptures (LXX). That was the principal reason for the black designation. E. P. Sanders cites this story but does not say whether he thinks it is historical.[61] John P. Meier concludes that a decision about its historicity is not possible. That probably translates as a gray vote.[62]

13 [18]**Then he would say:**

What is God's imperial rule like? What does it remind me of? [19]It is like a mustard seed that a man took and tossed into his garden. It grew and became a tree, and the birds of the sky roosted in its branches.

[20]**He continued:**

What does God's imperial rule remind me of? [21]It is like leaven that a woman took and concealed in fifty pounds of flour until it was all leavened.

In parables
Lk 13:18–21
Mt 13:31–33; Mk 4:30–32; Th 20:1–4, 96:1–2
Sources: Q, Mark, Thomas

In parables. The narrative links in vv. 18, 20 are Luke's additions as a way of attaching two parables loosely to the story of the afflicted woman. This complex, like many others in his gospel, are of Luke's own devising.

Narrow entrance
Lk 13:22–30
Mt 7:13–14, 22–23, 8:11–12, 19:30, 20:16; Mk 10:31; Th 4:2–3
Sources: Q, Mark, Thomas

13 [22]**On his journey, he passed through towns and villages, teaching and making his way toward Jerusalem.**

[23]**And someone asked him, "Sir, is it true that only a few are going to be saved?"**

He said to them, [24]"Struggle to get in through the narrow door; I'm telling you, many will try to get in, but won't be able. [25]Once the master of the house gets up and bars the door, you'll be left standing outside and knocking at the door: 'Sir, open up for us.' But he'll answer you, 'I don't know where you come from.' [26]Then you'll start saying, 'We ate and drank with you, and you taught in our streets.' [27]But he'll reply, 'I don't know where you come from; get away from me, all you evildoers!' [28]There'll be weeping and grinding teeth out there when you see Abraham and Isaac and Jacob and all the prophets in God's domain and yourselves thrown out. [29]And people will come from east and west, from north and south, and dine in God's domain. [30]And remember, those who will be first are last, and those who will be last are first."

Narrow entrance. Luke set Jesus on his way to Jerusalem in 9:51. He now reminds his readers many chapters later that Jesus is still on that journey. This narrative reference belongs to the weak framework Luke has given the materials he has assembled in this long section. It does not provide any reliable historical information. Black is the correct color.

Jesus & Herod
Lk 13:31–35
Mt 23:37–39
Sources: Luke, Q

13 [31]**About that time some Pharisees approached and warned him, "Get out of here! Herod wants to kill you."**

[32]**He replied to them,** "Go tell that fox, 'Look here, today and tomorrow I'll be driving out demons and healing people, and the third day I'll be finished. [33]Still, today and tomorrow and the day after, I have to move on, because it is impossible for a prophet to die outside of Jerusalem.' [34]Jerusalem, Jerusalem, you murder the prophets and stone those sent to you! How often I wanted to gather your children as a hen <gathers> her own chicks under her wings, but you wouldn't let me. [35]Can't you see, your house is being abandoned? I tell you, you certainly won't see me until the time comes when you say, 'Blessed is the one who comes in the name of the Lord.'"

Jesus & Herod. In *The Five Gospels*, the Fellows designated the saying in v. 32 gray on the grounds that Jesus may have been aware of the threat Herod Antipas posed to him as a successful and popular sage. But they thought the balance of the sayings attributed to Jesus were the composition of Luke. In line with those earlier judgments, they concluded that the narrative setting Luke has given this complex is probably of his own invention, although they conceded that friends may have warned Jesus of Herod's animosity. They gave it a hesitant black.

14 **And so one sabbath day, when Jesus happened to have din-**
ner at the house of a prominent Pharisee, they were keeping an eye
on him. 2This man who had dropsy suddenly showed up.
3Jesus addressed the legal experts and Pharisees: "Is it permitted
to heal on the sabbath day, or not?"
4But they were silent.
So he took the man, healed him, and sent him on his way.
5Then he said to them, "Suppose your son or your ox falls down a
well, would any of you hesitate for a second to pull him out on the
sabbath day?"
6And they had no response to this.

Man with dropsy
Lk 14:1–6
No parallels
Source: Luke

Man with dropsy. Dropsy is a unique complaint in the chart of ailments addressed by Jesus in the gospel stories. Dropsy is known in modern medicine as edema—the accumulation of fluid in the connective tissues that results in abnormal swelling and distention. It is often associated with poor circulation. Whether or not that is actually the ailment of the patient in this story cannot be determined.

The format of the story is basically that of a controversy. Jesus is having dinner in the house of a Pharisee when a man with dropsy suddenly appears. It is unclear whether the man was already among the guests or whether he wandered in from outside. And, of course, in the customary fashion, the Pharisees were keeping an eye on Jesus. The scene begins to look contrived; narrative plausibility is being strained. Jesus takes the initiative: He wants to know whether it is permitted to heal on the sabbath or not. That sounds like the bait for an argument. When his host and guests do not respond, he heals the man and dismisses him. Jesus then pursues the argument.

All of this struck the Fellows of the Seminar as implausible. They doubt that Jesus deliberately provoked arguments about sabbath codes; they doubt that he debated fine points of the law with the Pharisees or others. On the other hand, they were equally confident that Jesus' behavior occasionally provoked criticism about his sabbath practice. They reasoned that his actions spoke more loudly than his words.

In this case the setting in the house of a Pharisee is most likely a Lukan contrivance. The appearance of the patient at a dinner party, as noted earlier, is unmotivated. Taking the initiative in both the cure and the debate is unusual for Jesus, who normally only responds when questioned or addressed and who functions as a healer only when requested. These abnormalities, plus the fact that the story exhibits other traces of Luke's style, suggested a black vote. John P. Meier is more cautious: he opts in this instance for a *non liquet*—the evidence is ambiguous—as he often does in such stories; that conclusion is the equivalent of a Jesus Seminar gray.[63]

Places of honor
Lk 14:7–14
No parallels
Source: Luke

14 7**Or he would tell a parable for those who had been invited, when he noticed how they were choosing the places of honor.**

He said to them, 8"When someone invites you to a wedding banquet, don't take the place of honor, in case someone more important than you has been invited. 9Then the one who invited you both will come and say to you, 'Make room for this person,' and you'll be embarrassed to have to take the lowest place. 10Instead, when you are invited, go take the lowest place, so when the host comes he'll say to you, 'Friend, come up higher.' Then you'll be honored in front of all those reclining around the table with you.

11"Those who promote themselves will be demoted, and those who demote themselves will be promoted."

12**Then he said also to his host,** "When you give a lunch or a dinner, don't invite your friends, or your brothers and sisters, or relatives, or rich neighbors. They might invite you in return and so you would be repaid. 13Instead, when you throw a dinner party, invite the poor, the crippled, the lame, and the blind. 14In that case, you are to be congratulated, since they cannot repay you. You will be repaid at the resurrection of the just."

Places of honor. Luke has created this narrative context for a series of remarks on table etiquette Jesus is supposed to have made, climaxing in the parable of the dinner party (14:1–24). Since the context is a Lukan fiction, black is the appropriate color.

Dinner party
Lk 14:15–24
Mt 22:1–14; Th 64:1–12
Sources: Q, Thomas

14 15**When one of his fellow guests heard this, he said to him, "Congratulations to those who will eat bread in God's domain!"**
16**Jesus told him:**

Someone was giving a big dinner and invited many guests. 17At the dinner hour the host sent his slave to tell the guests: "Come, it's ready now." 18But one by one they all began to make excuses. The first said to him, "I just bought a farm, and I have to go and inspect it; please excuse me." 19And another said, "I just bought five pairs of oxen, and I'm on my way to check them out; please excuse me." 20And another said, "I just got married, and so I cannot attend." 21So the slave came back and reported these <excuses> to his master. Then the master of the house got angry and instructed his slave: "Quick! Go out into the streets and alleys of the town, and usher in the poor, and crippled, the blind, and the lame."

22 And the slave said, "Sir, your orders have been carried out,
and there's still room."
23 And the master said to the slave, "Then go out into the roads
and the country lanes, and force people to come in so my house
will be filled. 24 Believe you me, not one of those who were given
invitations will taste my dinner."

Dinner party. Verses 15–16a are a continuation of the narrative setting Luke inaugurated in 14:7 for Jesus' table talk that ends with the parable of the dinner party. For a Lukan fiction, black is the correct color.

Way of the cross
Lk 14:25–35
Mt 10:37–38, 16:24, 5:13; Th 55:1–2, 101:1–3; Mk 8:34, 9:50a; Lk 9:23
Sources: Q, Thomas, Mark, Luke

14 25 **Once when hordes of people were traveling with him, he
turned and addressed them:** 26 "If any of you comes to me and does not
hate your own father and mother and wife and children and brothers
and sisters—yes, even your own life—you're no disciple of mine.
27 Unless you carry your own cross and come along with me—you're
no disciple of mine.
28 "Consider this: Don't those who plan to build a tower first sit down
and calculate whether they can afford to complete it? 29 Otherwise they
might lay the foundation and not be able to finish, and all the onlook-
ers would begin to make fun of them: 30 'Those people started to build
but couldn't finish.'
31 "Or what king would go to war against another king and not first
sit down and figure out whether he would be able with ten thousand
men to engage an enemy coming against him with twenty thousand?
32 If he decided he could not, he would send an envoy to ask for terms
of peace while the enemy was still a long way off.
33 "On these analogies, then, if you don't say good-bye to everything
that belongs to you, you're no disciple of mine.
34 "Salt is good <and salty>. But if salt loses its zing, how will it be
renewed? 35 It's no good for either earth or manure. It just gets thrown
away. Anyone here with two good ears had better listen!"

Way of the cross. Luke has continued the fiction of Jesus' journey to Jerusalem in v. 25. As a fiction, black is the correct designation.

Lost parables
Lk 15:1–32
Mt 18:12–14; Th 107:1–3
Sources: Q, Luke, Thomas

15 **Now the toll collectors and sinners kept crowding around
Jesus so they could hear him. 2 But the Pharisees and the scholars
would complain to each other: "This fellow welcomes sinners and
eats with them."**
3 **So he told them this parable:**

4 Is there any one of you who owns a hundred sheep and one of
them gets lost, who wouldn't leave the ninety-nine in the wilder-
ness, and go after the one that got lost until he finds it? 5 And

when he finds it, he lifts it up on his shoulders, happy. [6]Once he gets home, he invites his friends and his neighbors over, and says to them, "Celebrate with me, because I have found my lost sheep."

[7]"I'm telling you it'll be just like this in heaven: there'll be more celebrating over one sinner who has a change of heart than over ninety-nine virtuous people who have no need to change their hearts.

[8]Or again, is there any woman with ten silver coins, who if she loses one, wouldn't light a lamp and sweep the house and search carefully until she finds it? [9]When she finds it, she invites her friends and neighbors over and says, 'Celebrate with me, because I have found the silver coin I had lost.'

[10]"I'm telling you, it's just like this among God's messengers: they celebrate when one sinner has a change of heart."

[11]**Then he said:**

Once there was this man who had two sons. [12]The younger of them said to his father, "Father, give me the share of the property that's coming to me." So he divided his resources between them.

[13]Not too many days later, the younger son got all his things together and left home for a faraway country, where he squandered his property by living extravagantly. [14]Just when he had spent it all, a serious famine swept through that country, and he began to do without. [15]So he went and hired himself out to one of the citizens of that country, who sent him out to his farm to feed the pigs. [16]He longed to satisfy his hunger with the carob pods, which the pigs usually ate; but no one offered him anything. [17]Coming to his senses he said, "Lots of my father's hired hands have more than enough to eat, while here I am dying of starvation! [18]I'll get up and go to my father and I'll say to him, 'Father, I have sinned against heaven and affronted you; [19]I don't deserve to be called a son of yours any longer; treat me like one of your hired hands.'" [20]And he got up and returned to his father.

But while he was still a long way off, his father caught sight of him and was moved to compassion. He went running out to him, threw his arms around his neck, and kissed him. [21]And the son said to him, "Father, I have sinned against heaven and affronted you; I don't deserve to be called a son of yours any longer."

[22]But the father said to his slaves, "Quick! Bring out the finest robe and put it on him; put a ring on his finger and sandals on his feet. [23]Fetch the fat calf and slaughter it; let's have a feast and celebrate, [24]because this son of mine was dead and has come back to life; he was lost and now is found." And they started celebrating.

[25]Now his elder son was out in the field; and as he got closer to the house, he heard music and dancing. [26]He called one of the servant-boys over and asked what was going on.

27 He said to him, "Your brother has come home and your father has slaughtered the fat calf, because he has him back safe and sound."

28 But he was angry and refused to go in. So his father came out and began to plead with him. 29 But he answered his father, "See here, all these years I have slaved for you. I never once disobeyed any of your orders; yet you never once provided me with a kid goat so I could celebrate with my friends. 30 But when this son of yours shows up, the one who has squandered your estate with prostitutes—for him you slaughter the fat calf."

31 But <the father> said to him, "My child, you are always at my side. Everything that's mine is yours. 32 But we just had to celebrate and rejoice, because this brother of yours was dead, and has come back to life; he was lost, and now is found."

Lost parables. Luke has coined the transitional connective in vv. 1–2; it has no parallels in either Mark or Matthew. Luke represents the scene as typical of Jesus' public life: toll collectors and sinners continually crowd around Jesus to hear his wisdom, while the Pharisees and scholars complain about the company Jesus keeps. While Jesus' association with sinners at table is well established in the gospel tradition, Luke here features the grumbling of the opposition, which is represented narratively in 5:29–30. In addition, mention of crowds pressing in on Jesus comes in the middle of the long journey to Jerusalem and belongs to one of several Lukan crowd scenes (11:29, 12:1, 14:25).

This summary provides the introduction to the following series of parables featuring things that have been lost—a sheep, a coin, a son—which is also the creation of Luke. In all probability, there never was a banquet at which Jesus said and did the things he is depicted as saying and doing in Luke 14:1–24, any more than there was an occasion on which Jesus delivered the sermon on the mount (Matthew 5–7) or told all the parables linked together in the fourth chapter of Mark. Scenes of this type are the product of the storyteller who is grouping events and stories together by common subjects or themes. The transitional summary, however, depicts behavior typical or characteristic of Jesus, which, in this case, is also probably historically accurate.

The transition marker in 15:11 is also supplied by Luke to give some continuity to the telling of the three parables one after another. Since Jesus probably did not tell the parable of the prodigal immediately after the tale of the lost coin, the Fellows colored this minor narrative notice black.

16 **Or Jesus would say to the disciples:**

The shrewd manager
Lk 16:1–15
No parallels
Source: Luke

There was this rich man whose manager had been accused of squandering his master's property. 2 He called him in and said, "What's this I hear about you? Let's have an audit of your management, because your job is being terminated."

[3]Then the manager said to himself, "What am I going to do? My
master is firing me. I'm not able to dig ditches and I'm ashamed to
beg. [4]I've got it! I know what I'll do so doors will open for me
when I'm removed from management."
[5]So he called in each of his master's debtors. He said to the
first, "How much do you owe my master?"
[6]He said, "Five hundred gallons of olive oil."
And he said to him, "Here is your invoice; sit down right now
and make it two hundred and fifty."
[7]Then he said to another, "And how much do you owe?"
He said, "A thousand bushels of wheat."
He says to him, "Here is your invoice; make it eight hundred."
[8]The master praised the dishonest manager because he had
acted shrewdly; for the children of this world exhibit better sense
in dealing with their own kind than do the children of light.

[9]"I tell you, make use of your ill-gotten gain to make friends for
yourselves, so that when the bottom falls out they are there to wel-
come you into eternal dwelling places.
[10]"The one who can be trusted in trivial matters can also be trusted
with large amounts; and the one who cheats in trivial matters will also
cheat where large amounts are concerned. [11]So if you couldn't be
trusted with ill-gotten gain, who will trust you with real wealth? [12]And
if you can't be trusted with something that belongs to another, who
will let you have property of your own? [13]No servant can be a slave to
two masters. No doubt that slave will either hate one and love the
other, or be devoted to one and disdain the other. You can't be
enslaved to both God and a bank account."
**[14]The Pharisees, who were money grubbers, heard all this and
sneered at him. [15]But he said to them,** "You're the type who justify
yourselves to others, but God reads your hearts: what people rank
highest is detestable in God's estimation."

The shrewd manager. The Seminar colored the narrative connective in v. 1 pink simply because it depicts something typical that Jesus did—tell a parable. It does not point to a specific situation or define the time and place precisely. As a generalization it is very likely accurate.

The characterization of the Pharisees in v. 14 and Jesus' reply are certainly the work of Christian apologists who were seeking to justify themselves by belittling the Pharisees. Neither the characterization nor Jesus' reply accurately reflects historical circumstance. Black is the correct evaluation.

16 [16]"Right up to John's time you have the Law and the Prophets;
since then God's domain has been proclaimed as good news and
everyone is breaking into it violently. [17]But it is easier for the world to
disappear than for one serif of one letter of the Law to drop out.

18"Everyone who divorces his wife and marries another commits adultery; and the one who marries a woman divorced from her husband commits adultery.

19There was this rich man, who wore clothing fit for a king and who dined lavishly every day. 20This poor man, named Lazarus, languished at his gate, all covered with sores. 21He longed to eat what fell from the rich man's table. Dogs even used to come and lick his sores. 22 It so happened that the poor man died and was carried by the heavenly messengers to be with Abraham. The rich man died too, and was buried.

23From Hades, where he was being tortured, he looked up and saw Abraham a long way off and Lazarus with him. 24He called out, "Father Abraham, have pity on me! Send Lazarus to dip the tip of his finger in water and cool my tongue, for I am in torment in these flames."

25But Abraham said, "My child, remember that you had good fortune in your lifetime, while Lazarus had it bad. Now he is being comforted here, and you are in torment. 26And besides all this, a great chasm has been set between us and you, so that even those who want to cross over from here to you cannot, and no one can cross over from that side to ours."

27But he said, "Father, I beg you then, send him to my father's house 28—after all, I have five brothers—so he can warn them not to wind up in this place of torture."

29But Abraham says, "They have Moses and the prophets; why don't they listen to them?"

30"But they won't do that, father Abraham," he said. "But, if someone appears to them from the dead, they'll have a change of heart."

31<Abraham> said to him, "If they won't listen to Moses and the prophets, they won't be convinced even if someone were to rise from the dead."

17

Traps & millstones
Lk 17:1–4
Mt 18:6–7, 15, 21–22; Mk 9:42
Sources: Q, Mark, Luke

He said to his disciples, "It's inevitable that snares will be set; nevertheless, damn the one who sets them! 2You'd be better off if you had a millstone hung around your neck and were dumped into the sea than to mislead one of these little ones. 3So be on your guard. If your companion does wrong, scold that person; if there is a change of heart, forgive the person. 4If someone wrongs you seven times a day, and seven times turns around and says to you, 'I'm sorry,' you should forgive that person."

Traps & millstones. The minimal narrative link in v. 1 is provided by Luke. In the judgment of the Seminar, Jesus did not say the words attributed to him in vv. 1–4. Black is the right color for both sayings and narrative introduction.

Trees into the sea
Lk 17:5–6
Mt 17:20; Mk 11:23,
Mt 21:21; Th 48, 106:2
Sources: Q, Mark, Thomas

17 [5]**The apostles said to the Lord, "Make our trust grow!"**

[6]**And the Lord said,** "If you had trust no larger than a mustard seed, you could tell this mulberry tree, 'Uproot yourself and plant yourself in the sea,' and it would obey you."

Trees into the sea. The narrative frame has been created by the evangelist as he continues to present sayings and parables one after the other in this section of his gospel. For that reason alone the Fellows decided to color the narrative portions black.

17 [7]"If you had a slave plowing or herding sheep and he came in from the fields, would any of you tell him, 'Come right in and recline at the table'? [8]Wouldn't you say to him instead, 'Get my dinner ready, put on your apron, and serve me while I eat and drink. You can eat and drink later'? [9]He wouldn't thank the slave because he did what he was told to do, would he? [10]The same goes for you: when you've done everything you've been told to do, say, 'We're miserable slaves; we've only done our job.'"

Ten lepers
Lk 17:11–19
No parallels
Source: Luke

[11]**And on the way to Jerusalem he happened to pass between Samaria and Galilee. [12]As he was coming into this village, he was met by ten lepers, who kept their distance. [13]They shouted: "Jesus, Master, have mercy on us!"**

[14]**When he saw them, he said to them,** "Go show yourselves to the priests."

And as they departed they happened to be made clean.

[15]**Then one of them, realizing that he had been healed, came back. He praised God out loud, [16]prostrated himself at Jesus' feet, and thanked him. (Incidentally, this man was a Samaritan.)**

[17]**But Jesus said,** "Ten were cured, weren't they? What became of the other nine? [18]Didn't any of them return to praise God besides this foreigner?"

[19]**And he said to him,** "Get up and be on your way; your trust has cured you."

Ten lepers. The story of the ten lepers is probably a Lukan composition. It betrays knowledge of the story found in Mark 1:40–45, which Luke copied into his gospel (5:12–17). In addition, it has been influenced by the account of the leper Naaman, the Syrian general, who was cured by Elisha (2 Kgs 5:1–15: the entire story is reproduced in translation in the facing cameo).

Luke has taken a simple healing story (vv. 11–14) and expanded it formally into a pronouncement story—an anecdote that climaxes in a memorable pronouncement of Jesus (vv. 15–19). However, in this case the story does not preserve a memorable aphorism of Jesus, only his final instruction to the grateful Samaritan leper. It thus appears to be a secondary composition designed to

THE CLEANSING OF NAAMAN

1 Naaman, the leader of the Syrian military forces, was a great man in his master's
eyes and a veritable wonder, because the Lord had given victory to Syria by
means of his prowess. He was a powerful man of courage, and he was a leper.
2 Earlier the Syrians on one of their forays had abducted a young girl from the land
of Israel, and now she was a servant to Naaman's wife. 3 She told her mistress, "I
wish my lord were with the Samaritan prophet of God! He would cure him of his
leprosy." 4 So Naaman went in and said to his lord, "This is what the young girl
from Israel said." 5 And the king of Syria said, "Go now, and I will write a letter on
your behalf to the king of Israel."

7 And when the king of Israel read the letter, he ripped up his clothes and said,
"Am I God, with power over life and death, that someone would send to me a
man to be cured of leprosy? Mark my words, you'll see he's trying to pick a fight
with me."

8 When Elisha heard that the king of Israel had ripped up his clothes, he sent
word to the king, saying, "Why have you torn your clothes? Let Naaman come to
me and let him know that there is a prophet in Israel." 9 So Naaman came along
with his horses and chariots and stood in front of the door to Elisha's house. 10 And
Elisha sent a messenger to him, saying, "Go and bathe seven times in the Jordan,
and your skin will be restored, and you shall be made clean." 11 But Naaman got
angry, and left, saying, "Look here, I was expecting that he would come out to see
me in person, and stand here, and invoke the name of his God, and wave his hand
over the place, and then cure my leprosy. 12 Are not the rivers of Damascus, the
Abana and the Pharpar, better than the Jordan and all the waters of Israel? Could
I not go and wash in them and be made clean?" He then turned and left in a rage.
13 But his servants approached him and said to him, "If the prophet had given you
a great order, wouldn't you have carried it out? And that's just what he said to
you, 'Go wash and be made clean.'" 14 So Naaman went down and immersed him-
self seven times in the Jordan according to the word of Elisha, and his skin was
restored to that of a small child, and he was made clean.

2 Kgs 5:1–5a, 7–14 (LXX)

feature a theological theme dear to the evangelist Luke. Indeed, Joseph Fitzmyer is unequivocal in stating that vv. 11 and 19 are Lukan creations.[64]

The admonition to the ten to show themselves to priests has been borrowed from the Markan tale (Mark 1:44//Luke 5:14). The motif of the return of the grateful foreigner echoes the theme of the Elisha story, in which Naaman returns to thank Elisha and to acknowledge the God of Israel as the only God in the entire world.

The unusual geography represented by v. 11 has frequently been noted. Luke is apparently unacquainted firsthand with the geography of Palestine: He has Jesus traveling between Galilee and Samaria, as though Galilee and Samaria lay side-by-side, west to east (Galilee on the Jordan side), rather than north to south, with Samaria separating Galilee from Judea and Jerusalem.

Like the account of the raising of the widow's son (Luke 7:11–17), this tale is apparently a Lukan invention. The Fellows were virtually unanimous in designating it black.

Coming of God's imperial rule
Lk 17:20–21
Th 113:1–4
Sources: Q, Thomas

17 [20]**When asked by the Pharisees when God's imperial rule would come, he answered them,** "You won't be able to observe the coming of God's imperial rule. [21]People are not going to be able to say, 'Look, here it is!' or 'Over there!' On the contrary, God's imperial rule is right there in your presence."

Coming of God's imperial rule. The Pharisees probably did not ask Jesus the question indicated in v. 20. In any case, the narrative context is the invention of Luke, as it is so often in these extended sayings complexes. Black is appropriate.

The parallel in Thom 113:1–4 is cited in conjunction with Mark 3:11–13. The narrative framework was colored black as the invention of some early storyteller.

There'll come a time
Lk 17:22–37
Various parallels
Sources: Q, Mark, Luke, John, Thomas

17 [22]**And he said to the disciples,** "There'll come a time when you will yearn to see one of the days of the son of Adam, and you won't see it. [23]And they'll be telling you, 'Look, there it is!' or 'Look, here it is!' Don't rush off; don't pursue it. [24]For just as lightning flashes and lights up the sky from one end to the other, that's what the son of Adam will be like in his day. [25]But first it is necessary that he suffer many things and be rejected by this present generation. [26]And just as it was in the days of Noah, that's how it will be in the days of the son of Adam. [27]They ate, drank, got married, and were given in marriage, until the day 'Noah boarded the ark.' Then the flood came and destroyed them all. [28]That's also the way it was in the days of Lot. Everyone ate, drank, bought, sold, planted, and built. [29]But on the day Lot left Sodom, fire and sulfur rained down from the sky and destroyed them all. [30]It will be like that on the day the son of Adam is revealed. [31]On that day, if any are on the roof and their things are in the house, they had better not go down to fetch them. The same goes for those in the field: they had better not turn back for anything left behind. [32]Remember Lot's wife. [33]Whoever tries to hang on to life will forfeit it, but whoever forfeits life will preserve it. [34]I tell you, on that night there will be two on one couch: one will be taken and the other left. [35]There will be two women grinding together: one will be taken and the other left." [37]**Then they asked him, "Taken where, Lord?" And he said to them,** "Vultures collect wherever there's a carcass."

There'll come a time. The narrative frame given this compendium of sayings in vv. 1 and 37 is once again the creation of Luke. Black is the correct evaluation.

18 **He told them a parable about the need to pray at all times and never to lose heart. [2]This is what he said:**

Corrupt judge
Lk 18:1–8
No parallels
Source: Luke

Once there was a judge in this town who neither feared God nor cared about people.

[3]In that same town was a widow who kept coming to him and demanding: "Give me a ruling against the person I'm suing."

[4]For a while he refused; but eventually he said to himself, "I'm not afraid of God and I don't care about people, [5]but this widow keeps pestering me. So I'm going to give her a favorable ruling, or else she'll keep coming back until she wears me down."

[6]**And the Lord said,** "Don't you hear what that corrupt judge says?
[7]Do you really think God won't hand out justice to his chosen ones—
those who call on him day and night? Do you really think he'll put
them off? [8]I'm telling you, he'll give them justice and give it quickly.
Still, when the son of Adam comes, will he find trust on the earth?"

Corrupt judge. Luke has reported a parable that probably originated with Jesus, but he has again provided the narrative context, including the interpretation in vv. 6–8. The editorial introduction in v. 1 emphasizes one of Luke's favorite themes. The Fellows could not avoid a black conclusion.

18 [9]**Then for those who were confident of their own moral superiority and who held everyone else in contempt, he had this parable:**

Pharisee & toll collector
Lk 18:9–14
No parallels
Source: Luke

[10]Two men went up to the temple to pray, one a Pharisee and the other a toll collector.

[11]The Pharisee stood up and prayed silently as follows: "I thank you, God, that I'm not like everybody else, thieving, unjust, adulterous, and especially not like that toll collector over there. [12]I fast twice a week, I give tithes of everything that I acquire."

[13]But the toll collector stood off by himself and didn't even dare to look up, but struck his chest, and muttered, "God, have mercy on me, sinner that I am."

[14]Let me tell you, the second man went back home acquitted but the first one did not. For those who promote themselves will be demoted, but those who demote themselves will be promoted.

Pharisee & toll collector. Luke has again supplied one of his editorializing introductions in v. 9. That introduction reflects Luke's views but not those of Jesus. Black was the inevitable conclusion.

Children in God's domain
Lk 18:15–17
Mk 10:13–16, Mt 19:13–15;
Th 22:1–3
Sources: Mark, Thomas

18 15 **They would even bring him their babies so he could lay
hands on them. But when the disciples noticed it, they scolded
them.** 16 **Jesus called for the infants and said,** "Let the children come
up to me, and don't try to stop them. After all, God's domain belongs
to people like that.
17 "I swear to you, whoever doesn't accept God's imperial rule the
way a child would, certainly won't ever set foot in <his domain>!"

Children in God's domain. Although Luke bases this segment on the Gospel of Mark, in his narrative introduction he agrees with the Gospel of Thomas (22:1–3) that the objects of Jesus' pronouncement are babies rather than children. In the saying, however, Luke uses the same term, "children," as he found in Mark. Whether babies or children, Jesus probably did assign God's domain to them, just as he did to the poor, the hungry, and the mournful. Whether he was in conflict with his male disciples in admitting children to his circle is dubious; disciples ordinarily acquiesced in the opinions of their teachers. Uncertainty about whether Mark created this context or not led to a gray vote. Since Luke is merely copying a gray passage in Mark, Luke's narrative setting was also designated gray.

The man with money
Lk 18:18–30
Mk 10:17–31, Mt 19:16–30,
GNaz 6:1–5
Source: Mark

18 18 **Someone from the ruling class asked him, "Good teacher,
what do I have to do to inherit eternal life?"**
19 **Jesus said to him,** "Why do you call me good? No one is good
except God alone. 20 You know the commandments: 'You are not to
commit adultery; you must not murder, or steal, and you are not to
give false testimony; you are to honor your father and mother.'"
21 **And he said, "I have observed all these since I was a child."**
22 **When Jesus heard this, he said to him,** "You are still short one
thing. Sell everything you have and distribute <the proceeds> among
the poor, and you will have treasure in heaven. And then come, follow
me!"
23 **But when he heard this, he became very sad, for he was
extremely rich.**
24 **When Jesus observed that he had become very sad, he said,**
"How difficult it is for those with real money to enter God's domain!
25 It's easier for a camel to squeeze through a needle's eye than for a
wealthy person to get into God's domain."
26 **Those who heard this spoke up: "Well then, who can be saved?"**
27 **But he said,** "What's humanly impossible is perfectly possible for
God."
28 **Then Peter said, "Look at us! We have left what we had to follow
you!"**
29 **And he told them,** "I swear to you, there is no one who has left
home, or wife, or brothers, or parents, or children, for the sake of
God's imperial rule, 30 who won't receive many times as much in the
present age, and in the age to come, eternal life."

The man with money. The anecdote in vv. 18–23 that Luke has taken over from Mark may vaguely reflect some event in the life of Jesus, in the judgment of the Fellows. As a consequence, they agreed to a gray designation for the narrative context, in spite of the fact that Luke has enhanced the status of the rich man by making him a magistrate.

The compendium of sayings that Mark had affixed to the core anecdote was his own creation. Luke reproduces that compendium in vv. 24–30. Its narrative frame, which Luke has modified in a minor way, is therefore fictive. Black is the correct designation.

The Gospel of the Nazoreans apparently had an alternative version of the anecdote about the rich man who asked Jesus what he had to do to have life (GNaz 6:1–5). It is quoted by Origen, a biblical exegete and theologian who lived in the first half of the third century (ca. 185–254 C.E.):

> **The second rich man said to him, "Teacher, what good do I have to do to live?"**
> 2**He said to him,** "Mister, follow the Law and the Prophets."
> **He answered, "I've done that."**
> **He said to him,** "Go sell everything you own and give it away to the poor and then come follow me."
> 3**But the rich man didn't want to hear this and began to scratch his head. And the Lord said to him,** "How can you say that you follow the Law and the Prophets? In the Law it says: 'Love your neighbor as yourself.'
> 4Look around you: many of your brothers and sisters, sons and daughters of Abraham, are living in filth and dying of hunger. Your house is full of good things and not a thing of yours manages to get out to them."
> 5**Turning to his disciple Simon, who was sitting with him, he said,** "Simon, son of Jonah, it's easier for a camel to squeeze through a needle's eye than for a wealthy person to get into heaven's domain."

The core anecdote (vv. 1–2) has been greatly abbreviated, yet remains essentially true to the version found in the synoptic gospels. The narrative framework for the compendium of sayings Mark had originally attached to the anecdote has been considerably revised. The rich man scratches his head when Jesus tells him he must sell all his goods and give the proceeds to the poor. Jesus addresses the punch line, the authentic saying about a camel squeezing through the eye of a needle, directly to Simon Peter. This version illustrates once again how those who passed the traditions along felt free to modify them.

18

31**<Jesus> took the twelve aside and instructed them:** "Listen, we're going up to Jerusalem, and everything written by the prophets about the son of Adam will come true.
32For he will be turned over to the foreigners, and will be made fun of and insulted. They will spit on him,
33and flog him, and put him to death. Yet after three days he will rise."
34**But they did not understand any of this; this remark was obscure to them, and they never did figure out what it meant.**

Jesus predicts his death a third time
Lk 18:31–34
Mk 10:32–34, Mt 20:17–19
Source: Mark
Cf. Mk 8:31–33, Mt 16:21–23, Lk 9:22; Mk 9:30–32, Mt 17:22–23, Lk 9:43–45

Jesus predicts his death a third time. All that is left of Mark's rather long narrative introduction for Jesus' third forecast of his execution is the short notice in v. 31a. Mark is clearly the source, since Luke retains Mark's idea that Jesus gave this prediction to his followers privately. In addition, Luke goes back to Mark 9:32, the conclusion to Mark's second prediction of Jesus' death, and picks up the note that the disciples did not understand what Jesus was talking about. Luke has retained this same note in his parallel to Mark's second prediction (Luke 9:45), but he repeats it here without any warrant in his source. In any case, the narrative framework is the creation of Mark, so the appropriate color for Luke's version of it is black.

Blind Bartimaeus
Lk 18:35–43
Mk 10:46–52, Mt 20:29–34
Source: Mark
Cf. Mt 9:27–31; Jn 9:1–7

18 35 One day as he was coming into Jericho, this blind man was
sitting along the roadside begging. 36 Hearing a crowd passing
through, he asked what was going on.
37 They told him, "Jesus the Nazarene is going by."
38 Then he shouted, "Jesus, you son of David, have mercy on me!"
39 Those in the lead kept yelling at him to shut up, but he kept
shouting all the louder, "You son of David, have mercy on me!"
40 Jesus paused and ordered them to guide the man over. When he
came near, <Jesus> asked him, 41 "What do you want me to do for
you?"
He said, "Master, I want to see again."
42 Jesus said to him, "Then use your eyes; your trust has cured you."
43 And right then and there he regained his sight, and began to follow him, **praising God all the while. And everyone who saw it gave God the praise.**

Blind Bartimaeus. As in the case of Mark, Luke's source, the narrative introduction was taken by the Fellows to be a secondary formulation that was invented either in the oral tradition or by Mark. As such, it does not provide reliable historical information. Yet because it is plausible, it was colored gray rather than black.

The rest of the story follows Mark close enough to warrant a pink designation, except for the reference to trust in v. 42 and to following Jesus in v. 43—probably Markan motifs Luke has adopted. Luke has added a new narrative conclusion featuring one of his favorite themes: praise to God is a fitting response to a cure. Luke's editorializing is appropriately black.

Zacchaeus
Lk 19:1–10
No parallels
Source: Luke

19 **Then he entered Jericho and was making his way through
it. 2 Now a man named Zacchaeus lived there who was head toll collector and a rich man. 3 He was trying to see who Jesus was, but
couldn't, because of the crowd, since he was short. 4 So he ran on
ahead to a point Jesus was to pass and climbed a sycamore tree to get a view of him.**
5 When Jesus reached that spot, he looked up at him and said,

"Zacchaeus, hurry up and climb down; I have to stay at your house today."

[6]**So he scurried down, and welcomed him warmly.**

[7]**Everyone who saw this complained: "He is going to spend the day with some sinner!"**

[8]**But Zacchaeus stood his ground and said to the Lord, "Look, sir, I'll give half of what I own to the poor, and if I have extorted anything from anyone, I'll pay back four times as much."**

[9]**Jesus said to him,** "Today salvation has come to this house. This
man is a real son of Abraham. [10]Remember, the son of Adam came to
seek out and to save what was lost."

Zacchaeus. The story of Zacchaeus is an invention of Luke inspired by the call of Levi in Mark 2:14 and the parallel passage in Luke 5:27–28. Luke's fiction heightens the elements in the story of Levi's call: Zacchaeus is a chief toll collector and rich. In addition, Luke has formulated Jesus' message in his own words: "The son of Adam came to seek out and to save what was lost." The son of Adam is here a heavenly redeemer figure, and the term "lost" reminds the reader of the status of the coin, the sheep, and the son of Luke's three "lost" parables.

Furthermore, Zacchaeus must make himself "poor" in order to be worthy of Jesus' company. Luke has constructed this scene to counterbalance the story of the rich ruler who has just rejected Jesus' advice that he give his wealth to the poor (18:22). Although the ruler had observed the commandments his whole life, he apparently could not be saved without that final act of obedience (18:26). Zacchaeus is presented as Luke's model for gaining the salvation the rich ruler failed to attain.

Luke's narrative was conceived from the standpoint of early Christian conviction: Jesus came to seek and to save the lost—the poor, the destitute, the diseased. While Jesus did seek out the company of toll collectors and sinners and favored the poor, Luke has incorporated those themes obliquely into a scene built around a more elevated figure—a rich tax agent. Luke is preaching to the choir. The appropriate color for the entire passage is black.

The money in trust
Lk 19:11–27
Mt 25:14–30
Source: Q

19 [11]**While they were still paying attention to this exchange, he proceeded to tell a parable, because he was near Jerusalem and people thought that God's imperial rule would appear immediately.**
[12]**So he said:**

A nobleman went off to a distant land intending to acquire a
kingship for himself and then return. [13]Calling ten of his slaves,
he gave them each one hundred silver coins, and told them: "Do business with this while I'm away."

[14]His fellow citizens, however, hated him and sent a delegation right on his heels, with the petition: "We don't want this man to rule us."

15As it turned out, he got the kingship and returned. He had
those slaves summoned to whom he had given the money, in
order to find out what profit they had made.
16The first came in and reported, "Master, your investment has
increased ten times over."
17He said to him, "Well done, you excellent slave! Because you
have been trustworthy in this small matter, you are to be in
charge of ten towns."
18The second came in and reported, "Master, your investment
has increased five times over."
19And he said to him, "And you are to be in charge of five
towns."
20Then the last came in and said, "Master, here is your money. I
kept it tucked away safe in a handkerchief. 21You see, I was afraid
of you, because you're a demanding man: you withdraw what
you didn't deposit, and reap what you didn't sow."
22He said to him, "You incompetent slave! Your own words
convict you. So you knew I was demanding, did you? That I
withdraw what I didn't deposit and reap what I didn't sow? 23So
why didn't you put my money in the bank? Then I could have
collected it with interest when I got back."
24Then he said to his attendants, "Take the money away from
this fellow and give it to the one who has ten times as much."
25"But my lord," they said to him, "he already has ten times as
much."
26He replied, "I tell you, to everyone who has, more will be
given; and from those who don't have, even what they do have
will be taken away. 27But now, about those enemies of mine, the
ones who didn't want me to rule them: bring them here and exe-
cute them in front of me."

The money in trust. Luke is here continuing the fiction of the journey to Jerusalem that he began in 9:51. Luke takes notice infrequently that Jesus is on his way to the holy city: 9:56–57, 10:1, 38, 11:53, 13:22, 14:25, 17:11, 18:35, 19:1, here in v. 11, and 19:28 and 41. The reader often loses sight of the fact that, according to Luke, Jesus is moving along toward his destiny. Jesus will finally arrive in Jerusalem in 19:45. Verse 11 is Luke's editorializing introduction to the parable of the money in trust. It is Luke's attempt to provide the parable with some plausible narrative setting. As a fiction of Luke, it merits a black rating.

Jesus enters Jerusalem
Lk 19:28–40
Mk 11:1–11, Mt 21:1–11;
Jn 12:12–19
Sources: Zechariah 9:9,
Psalm 118:25–26, Mark, John

19 **28When he had finished the parable, he walked on ahead, on
his way up to Jerusalem. 29And it so happened as he got close to
Bethphage and Bethany, at the mountain called Olives, that he sent
off two of the disciples, 30with these instructions:** "Go into the village
across the way. As you enter it, you will find a colt tied there, one that

has never been ridden. Untie it and bring it here. 31If anyone asks you,
'Why are you untying it?' Just tell them: 'Its master has need of it.'"
**32So those designated went off and found it exactly as he had
described.**

**33Just as they were untying the colt, its owners challenged them:
"What are you doing untying that colt?"**

34So they said, "Its master needs it."

**35So they brought it to Jesus. They threw their cloaks on the colt
and helped Jesus mount it. 36And as he rode along, people would
spread their cloaks on the road. 37As he approached the slope of the
Mount of Olives, the entire throng of his disciples began to cheer
and shout praise to God for all the miracles they had seen. 38They
kept repeating,**

> **Blessed is the king who comes in the name of the Lord!**
> **Peace in heaven and glory in the highest!**

**39But some of the Pharisees, also in the crowd, said to him,
"Teacher, restrain your followers."**

40But he responded, "I tell you, if these folks were to keep quiet,
these stones would break into cheers."

Jesus enters Jerusalem. Luke has taken the story of the triumphal entry over from Mark and revised it. He has provided his own narrative connective in v. 28 and his own conclusion in vv. 39–40. Indeed, all three synoptic evangelists have constructed different conclusions to the story: In Mark (11:11) Jesus goes to the temple area, looks about, and then returns to Bethany with the twelve; in Matthew, the whole city trembles at the arrival of the prophet Jesus from Nazareth (21:10–11); Luke brings the Pharisees onto the scene with the request to Jesus to restrain his followers; Jesus responds by suggesting that if he were to do so, the stones would erupt into cheers (19:39–40). In story after story the authors of the gospels illustrate how freely they revise or augment both narrative introduction and conclusion.

Luke has also added a bit of narrative commentary to the text he found in Mark. Luke depicts the throng of Jesus' disciples cheering and shouting praise of God for the miracles they had witnessed. This is a nice Lukan touch that connects the triumphal entry with earlier stories Luke has related.

Another point at which the evangelists felt free to alter their sources was the quotation of Psalm 118. In the commentary on Matthew, we noted how Matthew revised Mark, who had himself considerably modified Psalm 118:25–26. Now Luke makes further changes. Luke has altered "Blessed is the one who comes in the name of the Lord" to "Blessed is the *king* who comes in the name of the Lord"—a not so subtle change to undergird Luke's messianic interpretation of the event. Luke has furthermore augmented the Psalm with a new version of a refrain he cited in 2:14: "Glory to God in the highest, and on earth peace to people whom he has favored."

Some Fellows thought it possible that Jesus elected to enter Jerusalem on a donkey as a symbolic act, perhaps in contrast to the way Romans entered the cities they had conquered. Others argued that the whole story was suggested by a prophecy from Zechariah that is quoted by both Matthew and the Fourth Gospel. There was general agreement that Jesus did not intend his entry into Jerusalem to be understood as the arrival of the messiah. It is possible that the story was originally a parody of the freedom marches organized by zealots and rebels that occasionally began on the Mount of Olives and descended into Jerusalem during the turbulent days leading up to the Roman siege of Jerusalem (66–70 C.E.). Whatever is left of an actual event has been eclipsed by Christian interests as storytellers sought to interpret the event in messianic terms.

Lament over Jerusalem
Lk 19:41–44
No parallels
Source: Luke

19 [41]**When he got close enough to catch sight of the city, he wept**
over it: [42]"If you—yes, you—had only recognized the path to peace
even today! But as it is, it is hidden from your eyes. [43]The time will
descend upon you when your enemies will throw up a rampart
against you and surround you, and hem you in on every side, [44]and
then smash you to the ground, you and your children with you. They
will not leave one stone upon another within you, because you failed
to recognize the time of your visitation."

Lament over Jerusalem. Luke has again provided a minimal narrative setting for this lament over Jerusalem. He has supplied a novelistic touch by having Jesus weep. Since Luke has made that setting a part of his fictive journey to Jerusalem, the Fellows designated v. 41 black.

Temple incident
Lk 19:45–48
Mk 11:15–19, Mt 21:12–17;
Jn 2:13–22
Sources: Mark, John

19 [45]**Then he entered the temple area and began chasing the**
vendors out. [46]**He says to them,** "It is written, 'My house is to be a
house of prayer'; but you have turned it into 'a hideout for crooks'!"

[47]**Every day he would teach in the temple area. The ranking**
priests and the scholars, along with the leaders of the people, kept
looking for some way to get rid of him. [48]**But they never figured out**
how to do it, because all the people hung on his every word.

Temple incident. Luke has shortened Mark's account of the temple incident even more than Matthew. The Fellows believe that Jesus did demonstrate against the commercialization of the temple cult, perhaps in the manner depicted in v. 45. And he probably uttered some indictment of the temple bureaucracy. But he probably did not say what he is reported to have said in v. 46—which Luke has simply borrowed from Mark (colored gray in *The Five Gospels*).

The narrative conclusion in vv. 47–48 Luke has reproduced, with characteristic revisions, from Mark. Luke pictures Jesus taking over the temple courtyard as his teaching venue (also 20:1), with throngs of attentive listeners. In

Luke, it is Jesus' popularity that threatens the Jerusalem leaders. These features do not reflect knowledge of actual events.

20 **One day as he was teaching the people in the temple area and speaking of the good news, the ranking priests and the scholars approached him along with the elders, [2]and put this question to him: "Tell us, by what right are you doing these things? Who gave you this authority?"**

By what authority?
Lk 20:1–8
Mk 11:27–33, Mt 21:23–27
Source: Mark

[3]In response Jesus said to them, "I also have a question for you: tell me, [4]was John's baptism heaven-sent or was it of human origin?"

[5]And they started conferring among themselves, reasoning as follows: "If we say, 'Heaven-sent,' he'll say, 'Why didn't you trust him?' [6]But if we say, 'Of human origin,' the people will all stone us." (Remember, <the people> were convinced John was a prophet.) [7]So they answered that they couldn't tell where it came from.

[8]And Jesus said to them, "Neither am I going to tell you by what authority I do these things!"

By what authority? Luke has copied this story from Mark, revising it only slightly. One change he does make is in v. 6. In Mark (11:32) the reasoning of Jesus' critics breaks off, while in Luke they blurt out (to themselves) "the people will stone us."

The Fellows determined in their earlier work that the words ascribed to Jesus in this dialogue would not have been faithfully transmitted in the oral tradition. If such an exchange had taken place during the public career of Jesus, it would likely have come much earlier in the story, in closer proximity to the events connected with John the Baptist. In any case, its present location in the passion narrative was triggered by the temple incident and related events; that connection seems contrived. The Fellows decided that it was wise to think of it as the invention of some clever Christian storyteller, in spite of the fact that nothing in the dialogue contradicts what we otherwise know of Jesus.

20 **[9]Then he began to tell the people this parable:**

The leased vineyard
Lk 20:9–20
Mk 12:1–12, Mt 21:33–46
Source: Mark

Someone planted a vineyard, leased it out to some farmers, and went abroad for an extended time. [10]In due course he sent a slave to the farmers, so they could pay him his share of the vineyard's crop. But the farmers beat him and sent him away empty-handed. [11]He repeated his action by sending another slave; but they beat him up too, and humiliated him, and sent him away empty-handed. [12]And he sent yet a third slave; but they injured him and threw him out.

[13]Then the owner of the vineyard asked himself, "What should I do now? I know, I will send my son, the apple of my eye. Perhaps they will show him some respect."

[14]But when the farmers recognized him, they talked it over, and concluded: "This fellow's the heir! Let's kill him so the inheritance will be ours!" [15]So they dragged him outside the vineyard and killed him.

What will the owner of the vineyard do to them as a consequence? [16]He will come in person, do away with those farmers, and give the vineyard to someone else.

When they heard this, they said, "God forbid!"

[17]But <Jesus> looked them straight in the eye and said, "What can this scripture possibly mean: 'A stone that the builders rejected has ended up as the keystone'? [18]Everyone who falls over that stone will be smashed to bits, and anyone on whom it falls will be crushed."

[19]The scholars and the ranking priests wanted to lay hands on him then and there, but they were afraid of the people, since they realized he had aimed this parable at them. [20]So they kept him under surveillance, and sent spies, who feigned sincerity, so they could twist something he said and turn him over to the authority and jurisdiction of the governor.

The leased vineyard. Luke has followed Mark in introducing this parable with an apt remark that correctly characterizes how Jesus taught. Pink is appropriate.

In v. 16, Luke follows Matthew in introducing audience response, which was the invention of some unknown storyteller. Since the remark attributed to Jesus in v. 16 was probably not uttered by him, the response is likewise a fiction. Black is the correct designation.

The narrative conclusion in vv. 19–20 is the product of the storyteller's imagination. As the creation of Luke, v. 20 heightens the tension between the people and the authorities, who now resort to undercover agents to entrap Jesus. Black is an accurate designation.

Emperor & God
Lk 20:21–26
Mk 12:13–17, Mt 22:15–22; Th 100:1–4; EgerG 3:1–6
Sources: Mark, Thomas, Egerton Gospel

20 **[21]They asked him, "Teacher, we know that what you speak and teach is correct, that you show no favoritism, but instead teach God's way forthrightly. [22]Is it permissible for us to pay taxes to the Roman emperor or not?"**

[23]But he saw through their duplicity, and said to them, [24]"Show me a coin. Whose likeness does it bear? And whose name is on it?"

They said, "The emperor's."

[25]So he said to them, "Then pay the emperor what belongs to the emperor, and God what belongs to God!"

[26]And so they were unable to catch him in anything he said in front of the people; they were dumbfounded at his answer and fell silent.

Emperor & God. Luke has employed the narrative conclusion to the parable of the leased vineyard (vv. 19–20) also as the introduction to his next segment, the saying on emperor and God. Whether as a conclusion or an introduction, Luke's treatment of the narrative context deserves a black rating. His narrative setting for the saying in v. 25 is based on Mark, and so deserves the same black designation that was given to that portion of Mark. That is also true of v. 26, the narrative conclusion to the present segment, which Luke has again largely borrowed from Mark.

The Egerton Gospel has preserved another version of the question about paying taxes, but with a different response on the part of Jesus (3:1–6):

> **They come to him and interrogate him as a way of putting him to the test. [2]They ask, "Teacher, Jesus, we know that you are [from God], since the things you do put you above all the prophets. [3]Tell us, then, is it permissible to pay to rulers what is due them? Should we pay them or not?" [4]Jesus knew what they were up to, and became indignant. [5]Then he said to them,** "Why do you pay me lip service as a teacher, but not [do] what I say? [6]How accurately Isaiah prophesied about you when he said, 'This people honors me with their lips, but their heart stays far away from me; their worship of me is empty, [because they insist on teachings that are human] commandments [. . .]'"

The Egerton Gospel consists of five small fragments that belonged originally to another narrative gospel, title unknown. The papyrus fragments can be dated to the first half of the second century and consequently are as old as any physical evidence for the canonical gospels. Chapter 1 of this gospel contains an array of sayings that have parallels in the Gospel of John. Chapter 2 reports the story of the leper Jesus cured (the text and commentary is provided in conjunction with Mark 1:40–45). And Chapter 3, reproduced above, provides another response on the part of Jesus to the question about tribute to Caesar. Chapter 4 reports a miracle at the Jordan, but is too fragmentary to permit firm judgment about its content. Chapters 5 and 6 survive only as a few odd words.

Verses 1–2 of chapter 3 sound very much like the narrative introduction to the question about paying taxes found in Mark and the synoptic parallels. The query in v. 3 is parallel to the question put to Jesus in those same gospels. Jesus' response, however, is quite different than the aphorism reported in the synoptics; it consists of a patchwork of words attributed to Jesus in Q (Luke 6:46) and Mark (7:6–8). This segment of the Egerton Gospel reveals how the oral tradition made use of words ascribed to Jesus first in one configuration and then in another. The setting for this exchange is in all likelihood the work of some early Christian storyteller.

On the resurrection
Lk 20:27–40
Mk 12:18–27, Mt 22:23–33
Source: Mark

20 [27]**Some of the Sadducees—those who argue there is no resurrection—came up to him [28]and put a question to him. "Teacher," they said, "Moses wrote for our benefit, 'If someone's brother dies, leaving behind a wife but no children, his brother is obligated to take the widow as his wife and produce offspring for his brother.' [29]Now let's say there were seven brothers; the first took a wife, and died**

**childless. [30]Then the second [31]and the third married her, and so on.
All seven <married her but> left no children when they died.
[32]Finally, the wife died too. [33]So then, in the 'resurrection' whose wife
will the woman be?" (Remember, all seven had her as wife.)**

[34]And Jesus said to them, "The children of this age marry and are
given in marriage; [35]but those who are considered worthy of partici-
pating in the coming age, which means 'in the resurrection from the
dead,' do not marry. [36]They can no longer die, since they are the equiv-
alent of heavenly messengers; they are children of God and children of
the resurrection. [37]That the dead are raised, Moses demonstrates in the
passage about the bush: he calls the Lord 'the God of Abraham, the
God of Isaac, and the God of Jacob.' [38]So this is not the God of the
dead, only of the living, since to him they are all alive."

**[39]And some of the scholars answered, "Well put, Teacher." [40]You
see, they no longer dared to ask him about anything else.**

On the resurrection. Luke has taken this anecdote over from Mark with very little revision. As in Mark, Luke's source, the question and the response are tightly conceived as a unity, so the words ascribed to Jesus in vv. 34–38 never circulated independently of this story. Yet because the sayings put in Jesus' mouth preserve ideas that may have been close to those held by Jesus, the vote on the fictive narrative setting also produced a gray weighted average.

Son of David
Lk 20:41–44
Mk 12:35–37, Mt 22:41–46
Source: Mark

20 **[41]Then he asked them,** "How can they say that the Anointed
is the son of David? [42]Remember, David himself says in the book of
Psalms, 'The Lord said to my lord, "Sit here at my right, [43]until I make
your enemies grovel at your feet."' [44]Since David calls him 'lord,' how
can he be his son?"

Son of David. Luke has reduced Mark's anecdote to the bare minimum, while retaining the essential point: the Anointed—the messiah—cannot be David's son since David refers to him as his lord in Ps 110:1. Both the narrative context and the words ascribed to Jesus were colored black in both Mark and Matthew; they fare no differently in Luke.

Scholars in long robes
Lk 20:45–47
Mk 12:38–40
Source: Mark

20 **[45]Within earshot of the people Jesus said to the disciples,**
[46]"Be on guard against the scholars who like to parade around in long
robes, and who love to be addressed properly in the marketplaces, and
who prefer important seats in the synagogues and the best couches at
banquets. [47]They are the ones who prey on widows and their families,
and recite long prayers just to put on airs. These people will get a stiff
sentence!"

Scholars in long robes. Luke has taken this segment from Mark but provided it with a slightly altered narrative introduction. Luke's suggestion that

Jesus warned his followers about the scholars "within earshot of the people" gives a furtive cast to Jesus' technique that seems incongruent with Jesus' openness. At the same time, Jesus may well have given instruction to his circle in the presence of other observers. Gray in this instance means that the Fellows thought the evidence ambiguous and therefore inconclusive.

21 **He looked up and observed the rich dropping their donations into the collection box. 2Then he noticed that a needy widow put in two small coins, 3and he observed:** "I swear to you, this poor widow has contributed more than all of them! 4After all, they all made donations out of their surplus, whereas she, out of her poverty, was contributing her entire livelihood, which was everything she had."

Widow's pittance
Lk 21:1–4
Mk 12:41–44
Source: Mark

Widow's pittance. Luke has borrowed Mark's story and both abbreviated it and sharpened the contrast between the donations of the rich and the gift of the poor widow.

Since these anecdotes were circulated during the oral period without narrative connection to other incidents in the life of Jesus, the authors of the gospels placed them where they seemed to fit. In this case Mark located the story among incidents taking place during the passion week because Jesus was in Jerusalem teaching daily in the temple area, which is the scene of the widow's gift. In addition, in the preceding segment (Mark 12:38–40//Luke 20:45–47), Jesus vents an invective against scholars who prey on widows: the reference to widows functioned as a catchword calling to mind the anecdote of the poor widow. If the story does reflect an actual incident in the life of Jesus, we have no idea when it really took place.

Jesus' comment seems consonant with the style of his aphorisms: he regularly endorses the absolute, the ultimate, the ideal. For example, the person who finds a cache of coins in a field sells *all* he or she has in order to purchase that field. The merchant who comes across a priceless pearl sells *everything he owns* and buys that pearl. The widow contributes *all* she has. Jesus seems not to calculate in percentages or degrees. In this respect, the saying ascribed to him in this anecdote accords with other parables and aphorisms that honor a full commitment. The narrative setting seems entirely congruent with the content of the sayings, which suggests that it, too, could be authentic. However, since there are many parallels to the story in common lore, the Fellows thought that gray was the most appropriate color. Jesus' well-known sympathy for the poor would naturally have prompted his followers to attribute a similar sentiment to him, whether or not he had actually given expression to it.

21 **5When some were remarking about how the temple was adorned with fine masonry and ornamentation, he said,** 6"As for these things that you now admire, the time will come when not one stone will be left on top of another! Every last one will be knocked down!"

Temple's destruction
Lk 21:5–6
Mk 13:1–2, Mt 24:1–2
Source: Mark

Temple's destruction. Luke has borrowed Mark's imaginary setting for his apocalyptic discourse, the so-called little apocalypse (short as compared with the book of Revelation, which is an extended apocalypse). Luke's minor alterations do not make it any less a fiction. Black is the correct designation.

Signs of the end
Lk 21:7–36
Mk 13:3–37, Mt 24:3–42
Source: Mark

21 7**And they asked him, "Teacher, when are these things going to happen? What sort of portent will signal when these things are about to occur?"**

8**He said,** "Stay alert! Don't be deluded. You know, many will come using my name and claim, 'I'm the one!' and 'The time is near!' Don't go running after them! 9And when you hear of wars and insurrections, don't panic. After all, it's inevitable that these things take place first, but it doesn't mean the end is about to come."

10**Then he went on to tell them,** "Nation will rise up against nation, and empire against empire; 11there will be major earthquakes, and famines and plagues all over the place; there will be dreadful events and impressive portents from heaven. 12But before all these things <take place>, they will manhandle you, and persecute you, and turn you over to synagogues and deliver you to prisons, and you will be hauled up before kings and governors on account of my name. 13This will give you a chance to make your case. 14So make up your minds not to rehearse your defense in advance, 15for I will give you the wit and wisdom which none of your adversaries will be able to resist or refute. 16You will be turned in, even by parents and brothers and relatives and friends; and they will put some of you to death. 17And you will be universally hated because of me. 18Yet not a single hair on your head will be harmed. 19By your perseverance you will secure your lives.

20"When you see Jerusalem surrounded by armies, know then that its destruction is just around the corner. 21Then the people in Judea should head for the hills, and those inside the city flee, and those out in the countryside not re-enter. 22For these are days of retribution, when everything that was predicted will come true. 23It'll be too bad for pregnant women and for nursing mothers in those days! There will be utter misery throughout the land and wrath <will fall> upon this people. 24They will fall by the edge of the sword, and be taken prisoner <and scattered> in all the foreign countries, and Jerusalem will be overrun by pagans, until the period allotted to the pagans has run its course.

25"And there will be portents in the sun and moon and stars, and on the earth nations will be dismayed in their confusion at the roar of the surging sea. 26People will faint from terror at the prospect of what is coming over the civilized world, for the heavenly forces will be shaken! 27And then they will see the son of Adam coming on clouds with great power and splendor. 28Now when these things begin to happen, stand tall and hold your heads high, because your deliverance is just around the corner!"

29**Then he told them a parable:** "Observe the fig tree, or any tree, for
that matter. 30Once it puts out foliage, you can see for yourselves that
summer is at hand. 31So, when you see these things happening, you
ought to realize that God's imperial rule is near. 32I swear to you, this
generation certainly won't pass into oblivion before it all takes place!
33The earth will pass into oblivion and so will the sky, but my words
will never be obliterated!

34"So guard yourselves so your minds won't be dulled by hang-
overs and drunkenness and the worries of everyday life, and so that
day won't spring upon you suddenly like some trap you weren't
expecting. 35It will descend for sure on all who inhabit the earth. 36Stay
alert! Pray constantly that you may have the strength to escape all these things that are about to occur and stand before the son of Adam."

Signs of the end. Like Matthew, Luke has also borrowed Mark's fictive setting for the compendium of apocalyptic materials he has taken from Mark. Since Mark's setting was a fiction, so is Luke's. Black is the apposite color.

21 37**During the day he would teach in the temple area, and in
the evening he would go and spend the night on the mountain
called Olives. 38And all the people would get up early to come to the
temple area to hear him.**

Jesus' daily routine
Lk 21:37–38
No parallels
Source: Luke

Jesus' daily routine. The fiction that Jesus taught daily in the temple was probably suggested to Luke by the sequence of events in Mark, his source. In 12:35, Mark indicates that Jesus was teaching in the temple during the last week of his life, and at 14:26, Mark reports that after the last meal Jesus and his disciples departed for the Mount of Olives, opposite the city. In any case, verses 37–38 are one of Luke's narrative summaries. Here it is employed to draw the events of the week to a close and mark the transition to the passion narrative. It reiterates the opening frame in 19:47–48 that inaugurates Jesus' activity in Jerusalem. Black is the accurate designation.

Note: For an introduction to the passion narrative, consult the cameo (pp. 132–33). A second cameo has been prepared treating the problem of the sources for the passion story (pp. 246–47).

22 **The feast of Unleavened Bread, known as Passover, was
approaching. 2The ranking priests and the scholars were still look-
ing for some way to get rid of Jesus. But remember, they feared the
people.**

The conspiracy
Lk 22:1–2
Mk 14:1–2, Mt 26:1–5;
Jn 11:45–57
Sources: Mark, John

The conspiracy. Luke has abbreviated Mark's introduction to the passion while retaining its essential elements: the ranking priests and scholars are the culprits in the conspiracy against Jesus. The Jesus Seminar was basically skeptical of the conspiracy theory, although the Fellows did agree that some high-ranking Jewish officials concurred in Pilate's decision to execute Jesus. They observed the tendency, especially in Luke's version, to exonerate the Romans and lay the full responsibility for the death of Jesus at the door of the Jewish officials. This tendency they regarded as the consequence of later Christian attempts to whitewash the Romans. Like its counterparts in Mark and Matthew, Luke's first statement of the conspiracy garnered a black vote.

The contract
Lk 22:3–6
Mk 14:10–11, Mt 26:14–16
Source: Mark

22 **3Then Satan took possession of Judas, the one called**
Iscariot, who was a member of the twelve. 4He went off to negotiate
with the ranking priests and <temple> police officers on a way to
turn Jesus over to them. 5They were delighted, and consented to pay
him in silver. 6And Judas accepted the deal, and began looking for
the right moment to turn him over to them when a crowd was not
around.

The contract. Luke is slightly more creative than Matthew in handling the version he found in Mark. Luke credits Satan with the responsibility for Judas' betrayal (v. 3). During the symposium at the last meal, Jesus warns Peter: "Simon, Simon, look out, Satan is after all of you" (22:31). In this case, Jesus is hinting at Peter's denial about to take place. But it is Judas whom Luke identifies as Satan-possessed. Still, the basic information Luke includes in his brief statement is derived mostly from Mark. Since the Markan account is fictive, the Fellows were obligated to color Luke's revision black as well.

Preparation for Passover
Lk 22:7–13
Mk 14:12–16, Mt 26:17–19
Source: Mark

22 **7The feast of Unleavened Bread arrived, when the Passover**
<lambs> had to be sacrificed. 8So <Jesus> sent Peter and John, with
these instructions: "Go get things ready for us to eat the Passover."
9They said to him, "Where do you want us to get things ready?"
10He said to them, "Look, when you enter the city, someone carry-
ing a waterpot will meet you. Follow him into the house he enters,
11and say to the head of the house, 'The Teacher asks you, "Where is
the guest room where I can celebrate Passover with my disciples?"'
12And he will show you a large upstairs room that's been arranged;
that's the place you're to get things ready."
13They set off and found things exactly as he had told them; and
they got things ready for Passover.

Preparation for Passover. Luke has taken the basic story from Mark and edited it slightly. He has, for example, identified the two anonymous disciples in Mark as Peter and John (v. 8), a verse that has no counterpart in Mark. But those names should not be regarded as additional historical specificity. Rather, their mention reflects the freedom with which the evangelists treated their sources, often adding detail from their own imaginations.

This story, like many others in the passion narrative, does not make sense as an isolated tale that could have been transmitted orally as an anecdote. It gains its meaning entirely from the role it plays in the narrative sequence in which it occurs; it was created as a part of that sequence. It owes its existence entirely to the creator of the first continuous story of the passion, probably the author of Mark. The story is a Markan fiction. Since Luke is dependent on Mark, his version must also be considered a fiction and colored black.

The last supper
Lk 22:14–20
Mk 14:22–26, Mt 26:26–30
Source: Mark
Cf. Jn 13:21–30, 6:48–58; 1 Cor 11:23–26; Did 9:1–5

22 14**When the time came, he took his place <at table>, and the**
apostles joined him. 15**He said to them,** "I have looked forward with
all my heart to celebrating this Passover with you before my ordeal
begins. 16For I tell you, I certainly won't eat it again until everything
comes true in God's domain."
17**Then he took a cup, gave thanks, and said,** "Take this and share it
among yourselves. 18For I tell you, I certainly won't drink any of the
fruit of the vine from now on until God's domain is established!"
19**And he took a loaf, gave thanks, broke it into pieces, offered it to**
them, and said, "This is my body which is offered for you. Do this as
my memorial."
20**And, in the same manner, <he took> the cup after dinner and**
said, "This cup is the new covenant in my blood, which is poured out
for you."

The last supper. Luke's version of the last supper appears to be confused. He has Jesus begin with the cup, whereas Mark has Jesus begin with the loaf. Moreover, here in Luke there are two cups: the cup is mentioned in v. 17 and again in v. 20. What is the source of Luke's information?

Early Christian copyists were puzzled by Luke's version when they compared it with those of Mark and Matthew. As a consequence, variant textual traditions were created by scribes who attempted to fix the problem. One variant text ends with the words "This is my body" in v. 19; the rest of v. 19 and all of v. 20 are omitted. There are several other variations preserved in different manuscripts.

The omission of v. 20 would of course solve the problem of two cups, but it does not deal with the reverse order: first the cup, then the loaf. Both Paul and Mark attest the order: first the loaf, then the cup. In the Didache, an early Christian manual of instruction, the celebration of eucharist also begins with the cup followed by the bread. (The text of the Didache is cited in the commentary on the parallel passage in Matthew.) Perhaps the order of the elements was not fixed in the tradition. It is also possible that Luke is imitating the Seder, the Passover meal, in which *two* cups are drunk: a preliminary cup to sanctify the occasion and a second cup in remembrance of the events of the exodus.

This last explanation gains force, perhaps, when it is observed that Luke specifically identifies the meal Jesus ate with his disciples as the *Pascha*, the Passover meal (v. 15). Of course, Mark and Matthew also assume that it is a Passover meal, but they do not identify it as such during the meal. Luke may have been more conscious of the order of elements in the regular Passover celebration.

The dating of the last meal Jesus ate with his disciples is differently represented in the synoptic gospels and the Gospel of John. The synoptic gospels portray the meal as a Passover meal, which would have been eaten on the evening of Nisan the 14th or, more precisely, at the beginning of Nisan the 15th (for Judeans the day began at sundown; Nisan is the name of first month in the Jewish calendar). In addition, that day was said to be "the day of preparation": in the synoptics it is the day of preparation for the sabbath; in John it is the day of preparation for Passover. The preparation for Passover (and the Feast of Unleavened Bread which followed) and the preparation for a sabbath did not always coincide.

According to the Gospel of John, in the year Jesus died, the two did coincide, which implies that the last meal Jesus ate with his disciples was not the Seder—the Passover meal. According to John (19:14), Jesus was crucified on the day of preparation for the Passover, just at the time the Passover lambs were being slaughtered in anticipation of the meal that evening (Nisan the 14th). The last supper would then have been eaten the previous night. In other words, the Fourth Gospel makes Jesus' death coincide with the slaughter of the Passover lambs, while the synoptic gospels make the last meal coincide with the Seder, the Passover meal. On the synoptic chronology, Jesus was tried and crucified during Passover, a high holy day. Both the synoptic and the Johannine dates cannot be correct; it is possible that both are wrong.

The Fellows of the Jesus Seminar, after reviewing the elements of the meal as depicted in the gospels, concluded that it was not a conventional Passover meal. The date indicated by the synoptic gospels is therefore in error. Paul does not represent the meal Jesus ate on the night in which he was betrayed as a Passover meal (1 Cor 11:23–26), nor does the Didache so portray it. Christian liturgical practice celebrates the last supper on Maundy Thursday, or Holy Thursday, the Thursday before Easter, and conflates that event with the footwashing ceremony (in the Fourth Gospel, Jesus washes feet rather than speak about the loaf and cup as his body and blood). This practice is first attested in 393 C.E. at the Council of Hippo. Liturgical practice thus obscures the conflict.

In view of the discrepancies in date and description of the meal, the Seminar concluded that the synoptic account was not the report of an actual event. Rather, the last supper represents the ritualization of many meals Jesus ate with his followers, including a last meal. At those meals Jesus most likely taught his disciples. And he almost certainly broke bread with people from all social and economic categories, slave and free, male and female. His egalitarianism was another form of his teaching. In the course of time those meals came to be identified with a hypothetical Passover meal in the synoptic gospels. His followers then interpreted the bread and wine theologically as the body and blood of Jesus as the lamb of God.

The narrative frame of the account is therefore properly designated black.

The betrayer
Lk 22:21–23
Mk 14:17–21, Mt 26:20–25;
Jn 13:21–30
Sources: Mark, John

22 21"Yet look! Here with me at this very table is the one who is
going to turn me in. 22The son of Adam goes to meet his destiny; yet
damn the one responsible for turning him in."
23**And they began to ask one another which of them could possi-
bly attempt such a thing.**

The betrayer. In the Gospel of Mark, Jesus' remarks about the one who was to betray him precede his words about the bread and wine; Luke has reversed the order and placed the prediction of the betrayal second. In this new location, Jesus' words about the informer introduce a series of remarks on discipleship—its responsibilities and privileges (22:24–30). Although the remarks he ascribes to Jesus are brief, Luke is following the tradition of having famous men give a farewell speech before they die. The author of the Fourth Gospel follows this same tradition, only his version is four chapters long (John 14–17).

Most scholars consider vv. 21–23 a Lukan revision of Mark 14:17–21. As such, it provides the reader with no independent information. And since the story in Mark is very probably a Markan fiction, its parallel in Luke is also colored black.

Dispute over the greatest
Lk 22:24–27
Mk 10:35 45, Mt 20:20–28
Source: Mark

22 24**Then a feud broke out among them over which of them
should be considered the greatest.** 25**He said to them,** "Among the
foreigners, it's the kings who lord it over everyone, and those in
power are addressed as 'benefactors.' 26But not so with you; rather, the
greatest among you must behave as a beginner, and the leader as one
who serves. 27Who is the greater, after all: the one reclining at a ban-
quet or the one doing the serving? Isn't it the one who reclines?
Among you I am the one doing the serving.
28"You are the ones who have stuck by me in my ordeals. 29And I
confer on you the right to rule, just as surely as my Father conferred
that right on me, 30so you may eat and drink at my table in my domain,
and be seated on thrones and sit in judgment on the twelve tribes of
Israel."

Dispute over the greatest. Luke's report of a feud among those reclining at table with Jesus at their last meal together is reminiscent of an anecdote related by Mark at an earlier point in his narrative and reproduced by Matthew (Mark 10:35–40//Matt 20:20–23). Luke omitted that earlier story in which James and John, the "thunder brothers," request places of honor on Jesus' right and left hands in his coming kingdom. Now he decides to make use of the second part of that earlier anecdote (Mark 10:41–45//Matt 20:24–28), in which a feud breaks out when the ten become annoyed with James and John over their request. Luke borrows that part of the anecdote and uses it as a setting for sayings of Jesus at the last supper.

The Fellows concluded that Mark's setting for the request of the two brothers and the subsequent feud was fictive. Luke has decided to have Jesus give an after-dinner speech at the last supper, unlike Mark and Matthew. He makes the feud over who is greatest a part of that discourse. Luke has obviously invented this new context for material he has taken from Mark. Black is the appropriate designation.

The oath
Lk 22:31–34
Mk 14:27–31, Mt 26:31–35;
Jn 13:36–38
Sources: Mark, John

22 [31]"Simon, Simon, look out, Satan is after all of you, to winnow you like wheat. [32]But I have prayed for you that your trust may not give out. And once you have recovered, you are to shore up these brothers of yours."

[33]**He said to him, "Master, I'm prepared to follow you not only to prison but all the way to death."**

[34]**He said,** "Let me tell you, Peter, the rooster will not crow tonight until you disavow three times that you know me."

The oath. Luke moves the prediction of Peter's denial into the dialogue that takes place during the last meal, unlike Mark and Matthew, who locate it during the transition from the upper room to the Garden of Gethsemane.

In addition, vv. 31–32 are unique to the Gospel of Luke. Luke has referred to Satan earlier in his gospel (10:18, 11:18, 13:16), but he now pictures Satan as the tempter, just as he did earlier in the temptation story of Jesus (4:13). Mark and Matthew both have Jesus call Peter "Satan" for failing to understand (Mark 8:33; Matt 16:23). Moreover, this motif is vaguely reminiscent of statements found in the Fourth Gospel: Satan takes possession of Judas during the last supper (13:27), a move foreshadowed in John 13:2. What these traditions have in common is the connection of Satan or the devil with the defection of the disciples.

Verse 33 may be viewed as a revision of its parallel in Mark (14:29), but it also has something in common with a similar remark in the Fourth Gospel (13:37): "Peter says to him, 'Master, why can't I follow you now? I'd give my life for you.'" Mark suggests only that Peter will lose faith, whereas both Luke and John indicate that Peter will become a martyr.

Luke has drawn on traditional lore in revamping the basic story taken from Mark. And because he has artificially constructed a discourse for Jesus to deliver during the symposium format of the last supper, he moves the exchange with Peter back into that context (for more on the symposium, consult the cameo "Jesus at Table," pp 352–53). The Fellows designated the words of Jesus black in *The Five Gospels,* and they have now voted the narrative context black as well.

Two swords
Lk 22:35–38
No parallels
Source: Luke

22 [35]**And he said to them,** "When I sent you out with no purse or knapsack or sandals, you weren't short of anything, were you?"

They said, "Not a thing."

[36]**He said to them,** "But now, if you have a purse, take it along; and the same goes for a knapsack. And if you don't have a sword, sell your

coat and buy one. [37]For I tell you, this scripture must come true where I
am concerned: 'And he was treated like a criminal'; for what is written
about me is coming true."
[38]**And they said, "Look, Master, here are two swords."**
And he said to them, "That's enough."

Two swords. In *The Five Gospels,* the Jesus Seminar designated the words of Jesus in this passage black. His words reverse earlier instructions given to the seventy when they are dispatched on a mission in Luke 10:4: They were to take no purse or knapsack or sandals and yet they had what they needed. Moreover, the quotation of Isa 53:12 in v. 37 suggests that early Christian scribes are at work: They are preparing for the incident of the sword during the arrest of Jesus (22:49–51). Jesus is about to be treated like a criminal, just as Isaiah predicted. In the view of most commentators, Jesus should be understood here as speaking ironically—his words mean something like the opposite of what they appear to say. But the disciples take him literally.

Luke has invented the narrative context to go with the words. Out of materials gathered from elsewhere in his gospel (22:24–38), he has created a symposium, which has no counterpart in his source, Mark. Black is the proper color for Luke's invention.

Gethsemane
Lk 22:39–46
Mk 14:32–42, Mt 26:36–46
Source: Mark

22 [39]**Then he left and walked, as usual, over to the Mount of**
Olives; and the disciples followed him. [40]**When he arrived at his**
usual place, he said to them, "Pray that you won't be put to the test."
[41]**And he withdrew from them about a stone's throw away, fell to**
his knees and began to pray, [42]"Father, if you so choose, take this cup
away from me! Yet not my will, but yours, be done."
[45]**And when he got up from his prayer and returned to the disci-**
ples, he found them asleep, weary from grief. [46]**He said to them,**
"What are you doing asleep? Get up and pray that you won't be put to
the test."

Gethsemane. Luke has severely abbreviated the account of Jesus' prayers in Gethsemane that he found in the Gospel of Mark, his source. Rather than have Jesus withdraw three times to pray, Luke has him withdraw only once. And Luke is kinder to the disciples: they fall asleep out of grief (v. 45) rather than out of boredom or inattention. Jesus twice admonishes his followers to pray that they won't be put to the test—the final petition of the Lord's Prayer (Luke 11:4). This accords with Luke's interest in prayer. Luke's treatment of his source illustrates once again how freely the evangelists rewrote and remodeled their sources in producing their own versions of stories.

Verses 43–44 were evidently added by some scribe to a manuscript of Luke; they do not appear, however, in the best—the oldest and most reliable—ancient manuscripts. The omitted verses read:

JESUS AT TABLE

When the gospel writers describe meals of Jesus, they picture them as formal banquets in the tradition of symposia. Socrates is featured in two famous *Symposia* in antiquity, one written by Plato, the other by Xenophon. At symposia, famous sages engage in philosophical discourse with their friends and guests, especially during the second part—the drinking party—that follows the meal.

When the evangelists describe the posture at meals, it is reclining rather than sitting (for example, Mark 2:15, 14:18). In this posture, one leaned on one elbow, and ate with the other hand. This was the posture utilized at all formal banquets in the world of Jesus, whether they were Greek, Roman, or Jewish.

Other customs that are common at the reclining banquet are also reflected in the Jesus tradition. When someone hosted a meal at his or her home, as Levi (or Matthew) does for Jesus (Mark 2:15), invitations were normally sent to the guests. Jesus refers to this custom when he speaks of "inviting" (or "enlisting": the Greek word here means both "to invite" and "to enlist") not the righteous ("religious folk") but sinners to the table (Mark 2:17).

Upon their arrival at the meal, guests would have their feet washed by a household servant before they took their positions on the couches. This custom is referred to in Luke 7:44, where Jesus' Pharisaic host is criticized for not providing this basic act of hospitality for Jesus, and in John 13:1–16, where Jesus assumes the role of servant to wash the feet of the disciples.

It was also common to place guests at the table according to their social rank, a custom that forms the backdrop for a parable of Jesus in Luke 14:7–11. Washing one's hands at the table before the meal was a common practice of pagans as well as Jews, but it had been raised to the level of religious ritual in Pharisaic Judaism. Jesus was criticized for ignoring this custom (Mark 7:1–8).

The ancient banquet had two primary courses, the eating course, or *deipnon* ("dinner"), and the drinking course, or symposium. Each course began with a benediction or libation over the food and wine, a custom that was adapted in different ways by Greeks, Romans, and Jews, and which is reflected in Jesus' benedictions at various meals, including the last supper (Mark 8:6, 14:22–25). The distinction between the courses is preserved in the tradition in which Jesus offers

43 An angel from heaven appeared to him and gave him strength. 44 In his anxiety he prayed more fervently, and it so happened that his sweat fell to the ground like great drops of blood.

It is more likely, in the judgment of most textual critics, that these verses are additions to the original form of Luke. That seems more likely than that they were deleted from the original form by some scribe, possibly because he objected to the all too human features portrayed in v. 44 and the divine intervention indicated in v. 43. At all events, they add nothing to our knowledge of the historical Jesus.

The scene on the Mount of Olives (Luke does not mention Gethsemane) was inspired originally by the story of David's flight across the Kidron when his son Absalom revolted (2 Samuel 15–17). Luke may not have been aware of this separate benedictions, first over the bread and then over the wine (Mark 14:22–25). In the Pauline and Lukan versions of the last supper, the benediction over the bread is separated from the benediction over the wine by the phrase "after dinner" ("after the *deipnon*"; 1 Cor 11:23–25, Luke 22:19–20).

The symposium course was intended to last long into the evening and was expected to include entertainment. While some Greeks and Romans tended toward prurient entertainment, giving us the traditional meaning of "orgy," philosophical Greeks and Romans often offered enlightened conversation on philosophical topics as their symposium entertainment; this is the format we find in the *Symposia* of Plato and Xenophon.

Similarly, Jewish tradition preferred discourse on the law at the table (as in Sir 9:15–16). Consequently, it is not surprising to see Jesus teaching at table in the gospels; this is what philosophers and rabbis frequently did (Luke 14 provides an example).

Etiquette at the banquet had been raised to a high level of consciousness among the ancients. It was a regular topic of discourse among Greek philosophers as well as Jewish sages (Sir 32:1–13 offers one example), so it is not surprising to find Jesus also discoursing on meal ethics, as he does in Luke 14:7–14.

Meals functioned as social boundary markers, not only defining by seating arrangement who outranked whom, but relegating to the bottom of the social heap those not invited in the first place. Women and slaves were marginalized by the fact that they were traditionally not allowed to recline, if they were present at the table at all.

Jewish dietary laws tended to produce an even more strictly defined marginalized group—those who for a variety of reasons were considered unclean and unfit table companions. Thus when Jesus is pictured eating with "sinners and toll collectors," or women, or gentiles, he is making a powerful statement about the inclusion of persons of dubious social standing among his associates and, by extension, in "God's domain" (Mark 2:15–17, 8:1–10).

We cannot be sure that these stories are always based on real events. They probably reflect distant memories of what Jesus typically did during his lifetime and thus are an index not only to his social behavior, but to aspects of his teaching.

connection, however. Nevertheless, the sequence of events depicted in Mark, Luke's source, follows the sequence of that earlier story. The parallels are sketched in the cameo, "David and Jesus on the Mount of Olives" (pp. 150–51). Since Luke's source is a fiction, Luke's version belongs to the same category. Black is the correct color.

The arrest
Lk 22:47–54a
Mk 14:43–52, Mt 26:47–56; Jn 18:1–12
Sources: Mark, John

22 47**Suddenly, while he was still speaking, a crowd appeared with the one called Judas, one of the twelve, leading the way. He stepped up to Jesus to give him a kiss.**

48**But Jesus said to him,** "Judas, would you turn in the son of Adam with a kiss?"

49**And when those around him realized what was coming next,**

they said, "Master, now do we use our swords?" [50]**And one of them struck the high priest's slave and cut off his right ear.**

[51]**But Jesus responded,** "Stop! That will do!" **And he touched his ear and healed him.**

[52]**Then Jesus addressed the ranking priests and temple police officers and elders who had come out after him:** "Have you come out with swords and clubs as though you were apprehending a rebel? [53]When I was with you day after day in the temple area, you didn't lay a hand on me. But this is your hour, and the authority darkness confers is yours."

Before the high priest
Lk 22:54
Mk 14:53–54, Mt 26:57–58;
Jn 18:13–14, 15–18
Sources: Mark, John

[54]**They arrested him and marched him away to the house of the high priest.**

Peter followed at a distance.

The arrest. Luke's version of the arrest pictures Jesus as more in charge of the scene than does Mark's account. In the Gospel of John, Jesus will also take command of events. The tendency is thus to make Jesus less of a victim as the story evolves and matures.

Luke has once again abbreviated Mark's account. However, he has retained all the Markan ingredients, except the final one: the flight of the disciples. Luke does not wish to denigrate the disciples, so he has them stick by Jesus: they are there at the crucifixion not far from the cross (23:49) and they never leave the Jerusalem area (24:49).

Luke adds a poignant touch to the story by identifying the ear that was severed and then reattached as the priest's slave's *right* ear (vv. 50–51), a detail found elsewhere only in the Gospel of John (18:10).

Like its Markan counterpart, Luke's version of the arrest is a fiction. The basic elements Luke has simply taken from Mark, so their status in Luke is dependent on their status in Mark. The alterations and additions Luke has made to the story come from his own imagination; he has no additional factual information. The one certain historical event, the arrest, is colored pink in the Lukan text. The appearance of Judas was designated gray in Luke because it received a gray rating in Mark: it is probable that someone who knew Jesus betrayed him to the authorities, but it is less certain that Judas was that person.

Before the high priest. Luke has borrowed these statements from Mark, his source, in preparation for the hearing before the high priest and the denial of Peter. Since the Fellows of the Jesus Seminar are convinced that Jesus was arrested, they think it likely that he was taken to the high priest and the temple authorities following his arrest. The probability factor merits a pink rating.

The behavior of Peter, on the other hand, the Seminar regards as a Markan fiction. Its introduction here is therefore designated black.

Peter's denial
Lk 22:55–62
Mk 14:66–72, Mt 26:69–75;
Jn 18:15–18, 25–27
Sources: Mark, John

22 [55]**When they had started a fire in the middle of the courtyard and were sitting around it, Peter joined them.**

[56]**Then a slave woman noticed him sitting there in the glow of the fire. She stared at him, then spoke up, "This fellow was with him, too."**

57 He denied it, "My good woman," he said, "I don't know him."
**58 A little later someone else noticed him and said, "You are one of
them, too."**
"Not me, mister," Peter replied.
**59 About an hour went by and someone else insisted, "No question
about it; this fellow's also one of them; he's even a Galilean!"**
60 But Peter said, "Mister, I don't know what you're talking about."
**And all of a sudden, while he was still speaking, a rooster
crowed. 61 And the Lord turned and looked straight at Peter. And
Peter remembered what the master had told him:** "Before the rooster
crows tonight, you will disown me three times." **62 And he went out-
side and wept bitterly.**

Peter's denial. Luke has modified Mark, his source, in several minor respects. In Mark, the first two accusers of Peter are female (14:66, 69), the third is a group (14:70); Luke makes the three accusations come from a woman and two men (vv. 57, 58, 60), which more nearly meets the requirements of the Mosaic law that two [male] witnesses are necessary to convict (Deut 19:15). But Luke cleans up Peter's act: Peter does not swear in Luke's version. Luke has added another touch in v. 61: Jesus is able to see Peter just as the rooster crows—the eye contact is something that can have happened only in Luke's imagination. Verse 62 matches Matthew's conclusion to the story precisely: "And he went outside and wept bitterly" (Matt 26:75). Since Mark's concluding statement varies slightly in the manuscripts, we must attribute the adjustment in Luke or Matthew to some early Christian scribe who wanted to harmonize the two gospels.

A very substantial majority of the Fellows of the Seminar voted black on this version of Peter's denial, as in the case of the other synoptic versions. That conclusion was dictated in large part by the conviction that Luke's story is derived largely from Mark, and that Luke's revisions are the result of his own imagination. Black is the appropriate color.

22 **63 Then the men who were holding <Jesus> in custody began
to make fun of him and rough him up. 64 They blindfolded him and
demanded: "Prophesy! Guess who hit you!" 65 And this was only the
beginning of their insults.**

Mocking by the guards
Lk 22:63–65
Mk 14:65, Mt 26:67–68
Source: Mark

Mocking by the guards. These verses in Luke parallel Mark 14:65. However, Luke has relocated this incident from its Markan position. In Mark, the order of events is: arrest, trial before the Council, with the mocking coming at the close of that trial (14:53–65), and Peter's denial (14:66–72). The sequence in Luke is: arrest, Peter's denial (22:54–62), mocking by the police (22:63–65), and trial before the Council (22:66–71). Although Luke reorders the sequence of events, as he does elsewhere—for example, during the last meal—his source here is also certainly the Gospel of Mark.

In Jewish lore, the prophet was supposed to have extra-sensory perception.

When a local woman, a sinner, anoints his feet at supper, Jesus is supposed to know without being told that she is a sinner (Luke 7:36–50). Here a blindfolded prophet is supposed to be able to tell who hit him. The game, a parody of "blind man's buff," is no less cruel because it was the figment of an early Christian storyteller's imagination. Black is the color.

Before the Council
Lk 22:66–71
Mk 14:55–65, Mt 26:59–68;
Jn 18:19–24
Sources: Mark, John

22 66 **When day came, the elders of the people convened, along
with the ranking priests and scholars. They had him brought be-
fore their Council, where they interrogated him: 67 "If you are the
Anointed, tell us."**
But he said to them, "If I tell you, you certainly won't believe me.
68 If I ask you a question, you certainly won't answer. 69 But from now on
the son of Adam will be seated at the right hand of the power of God."
70 **And they all said, "So you, are you the son of God?"**
He said to them, "You're the ones who say so."
71 **And they said, "Why do we still need witnesses? We have heard
it ourselves from his own lips."**

Before the Council. Luke has made major changes in the account of the trial before the Council. Those changes have led some scholars to conclude that Luke had a special source, or a different source, for this episode than Mark, his customary source. The Fellows were divided on this issue. That division did not make a great deal of difference, however, in their final assessment of Luke's account.

Luke has modified Mark's chronology in a fundamental way. Mark has the arresting party take Jesus directly to the high priest where other priests, elders, and scholars are assembled (Mark 14:53). The time was night, after the arrest in the garden. Luke, in contrast, says that they did not bring Jesus before the Council until the next morning, with no mention of the high priest (v. 66). Luke also skips over Mark's account of the false witnesses who testify against Jesus, and he fails to mention the accusation that Jesus had promised to destroy the temple (14:55–60). In addition, there is no mention in Luke of the charge of blasphemy (v. 71; contrast Mark 14:64).

The response of Jesus to the question of whether he is the messiah, the Anointed, also takes a different form in Luke: Luke represents Jesus as responding in his more customary fashion as a clever sage (v. 67). Jesus' claim to be the son of God is sufficient, on Luke's view, to bind him over for Pilate's review (v. 71). In standard Jewish parlance, the epithet "son of God" means simply that one is a creature of God, not that one is divine. For Luke, however, it implies more than that Jesus is one of God's creatures, and more than the title "the Anointed" suggests. Many of the emperors of Rome were considered divine sons of God in a very special sense. In some cases, that meant they were sired by one divine parent. As son of God in the hellenistic sense, Jesus now competes with Caesar and with other hellenistic heroes, such as Plato and Alexander the Great.

Writing more than a half century after the death of Jesus and a decade or two after Mark, Luke has no new information to offer. Even if he is dependent on some additional written source unknown to Mark, his account follows the same basic lines Mark employed in composing his version. The Fellows concluded that Luke's version was also a fabrication and therefore deserved to be colored black.

23 At this point the whole assembly arose and took him before
Pilate, <the Roman governor>. 2 **They introduced their accusations
by saying, "We have found this man to be a corrupting influence on
our people, opposing the payment of taxes to the Roman emperor
and claiming that he himself is an anointed king."**
3 **Pilate questioned him, "You are 'the King of the Judeans'?"**
In response he said to him, "If you say so."
4 **And Pilate said to the ranking priests and the crowds, "In my
judgment there is no case against this man."**
5 **But they persisted, saying, "He foments unrest among the people
by going around teaching everywhere in Judea, and as far away as
Galilee and everywhere between."**
6 **When Pilate heard this, he asked whether the man were a
Galilean.** 7 **And once he confirmed that he was from Herod's jurisdiction,
he sent him on to Herod, who happened to be in Jerusalem at
the time.**

Before Pilate: 1
Lk 23:1–7
Mk 15:1–15, Mt 27:1–2, 11–26; Jn 18:28–19:16; Pet 1:1–2
Sources: Mark, John, Peter

Before Pilate: 1. Luke has introduced massive alterations into the Markan version of the "trial" before Pilate. For this reason, numerous scholars have again argued that Luke had a special source as the basis of his information. (These scholars do not claim that Luke had more reliable information, only that he had a different source.) The Jesus Seminar was divided on whether Luke had an additional source or whether he was heavily editing Mark to achieve his own theological purposes.

Even Raymond E. Brown, who attempts as a rule to locate pregospel traditions behind the narratives, concludes that Luke is not relying on independent sources at this point, but is reworking Mark. Brown argues that the trial narrative is "neither a legal report on the trial nor an eyewitness summary." It does, however, have a historical kernel: Jesus was sentenced to die on the charge that he was a king. The storytellers turned that fact into a "dramatically effective" narrative.[65]

Verse 2 is a Lukan creation intended to prepare the way for the suggestion that Jesus was the king of the Judeans in v. 3. In Mark that suggestion comes as a surprise. Luke imagines how it might have gone: Like Socrates, Jesus was perceived as a corrupting influence on the people. Moreover, he was opposed to paying taxes—not necessarily a capital offense. And he claimed in 22:28–30 that he was himself an anointed king (a king who had been properly crowned in an anointing ceremony). Since God had conferred on Jesus the right to rule, so Jesus can now confer that right on his disciples, who will sit on twelve thrones and judge the twelve tribes of Israel.

Luke now has Pilate render a specific judgment: "There is no case against this man" (v. 4). Luke has Pilate repeat this judgment in v. 14. In Mark Pilate never declares Jesus innocent, although he asks the crowd what Jesus has done wrong (14:14). Nor does Matthew have Pilate reject the charges laid against Jesus. However, Matthew introduces Pilate's wife, who has learned in a dream that Jesus is innocent (Matt 27:19), and he has Pilate wash his hands to symbolize his unwillingness to bear the responsibility for Jesus' death (Matt 27:24–25). But Luke, who is the consummate apologist for the Christian cause to the Romans, wants it known that the Romans held Jesus to be free of blame. In his version of the trial, Luke comes very close to making a Christian out of Pilate. Later tradition completes what Luke inaugurated: in the Coptic church Pilate is revered as a martyr (his feast day is June 25).

Hearing before Herod
Lk 23:8–12
No parallels
Source: Luke

23 **[8]Now Herod was delighted to see Jesus. In fact, he had been**
eager to see him for quite some time, since he had heard so much
about him, and was hoping to see him perform some sign. [9]So
<Herod> plied him with questions; but <Jesus> would not answer
him at all. [10]All this time the ranking priests and the scholars were
standing around, hurling accusation after accusation against him.
[11]Herod and his soldiers treated him with contempt and made fun of
him; they put a magnificent robe around him, then sent him back to
Pilate. [12]That very day Herod and Pilate became fast friends, even
though beforehand they had been constantly at odds.

Hearing before Herod. Luke alone among the gospel writers introduces the trial before Herod (vv. 5–12). In so doing Luke achieves two things. First, he joins a king (Herod) to a governor (Pilate) in fulfillment of Psalm 2:2: kings and rulers are arrayed against the Lord and his Anointed. Second, he has Herod join Pilate in declaring Jesus innocent (v. 15). That is a clean sweep for the Christians: the real authorities had agreed in finding nothing with which to charge Jesus. His death is the sole responsibility of the religious authorities and the mob. His death is also "innocent," so that it functions as the suffering of the righteous one in scripture.

The Herod to whom Luke was referring was supposedly Herod Antipas—the son of Herod the Great—whose title was actually tetrarch of Galilee, and who ruled from 4 B.C.E. to 39 C.E. But there was also Herod Agrippa I—the grandson of Herod the Great—who was appointed king by the Emperor Claudius. He ruled 41–44 C.E. These Herods ruled in the shadow of Herod the Great who had died in 4 B.C.E. When Luke was writing about "Herod" all those years later, he may not have been very clear about which Herod he had in mind. The house of Herod and the house of Annas had held the two posts—king and high priest—for so long that one could claim that one or the other was always in power.

So Luke creates the scene with Herod. That scene is a duplicate of the trial before Pilate: Herod interrogates Jesus, but Jesus remains silent. Meanwhile the ranking priests and scholars accuse Jesus. And Herod duplicates the mocking that had taken place at the trial before the Council (Luke 22:63–65); Luke omits the mocking performed by the soldiers in Mark's version (Mark 15:16–20).

Raymond E. Brown describes the scene with Herod as an added "dramatization drawn from traditions of Herodian opposition to Jesus," in the same way that Luke made the trial "appear more formally proper" by adding the charges against Jesus in v. 2, charges that Brown concedes were drawn "from the atmosphere of Jewish versus Christian polemics of the 70s–80s."[66]

Pilate renders his definitive judgment in vv. 13–16, for which there is no parallel in Mark. Luke then returns to his source, Mark, in reporting the Barabbas incident (vv. 18–19) and then brings his account of the trial before Pilate to a close in vv. 20–25, where he is again drawing on Mark for his information.

Luke does not have an independent source of information that provides him with reliable historical data. He is dependent on Mark for his basic narrative. Beyond that, there is nothing in Luke's story that he did not invent out of his own imagination, either on the basis of hints in scripture or on the grounds of suggestions required by his apologetic aims. Aside from the remark that Jesus was turned over to Pilate, the entire narrative merits a black designation.

Even Raymond E. Brown, who endeavors to salvage as much as he can from the passion narrative, stipulates that Luke 23:6–15 "is scarcely a direct historical account."[67] He thinks Luke has interpolated the memory of Herod's antipathy to Jesus into the trial. That would appear to be a black vote, using the categories of the Jesus Seminar.

Before Pilate: 2
Lk 23:13–25
Mk 15:1–15, Mt 27:1–2, 11–26; Jn 18:28–19:16; Pet 1:1–2
Sources: Mark, John, Peter

23 **13 Pilate then called together the ranking priests, the rulers,**
and the people, 14 and addressed them: "You brought me this man as
one who has been corrupting the people. Now look, after interrogat-
ing him in your presence, I have found in this man no grounds at all
for your charges against him. 15 Nor has Herod, since he sent him
back to us. Indeed, he has done nothing to deserve death. 16 So I will
teach him a lesson and set him free."

18 But they all cried out in unison, "Do away with this man, and set
Barabbas free." (19 This man had been thrown into prison for murder
and for an act of sedition carried out in the city.)

20 But Pilate, who wanted to set Jesus free, addressed them again,
21 but they shouted out, "Crucify, crucify him!"

22 For the third time he said to them, "Why? What has he done
wrong? In my judgment there is no capital case against him. So, I
will teach him a lesson and set him free."

23 But they kept up the pressure, demanding with loud cries that
he be crucified. And their cries prevailed. 24 So Pilate ruled that their
demand should be carried out. 25 He set free the man they had asked
for, who had been thrown into prison for sedition and murder; but
Jesus he turned over to them to do with as they pleased.

Before Pilate: 2. The commentary for this section is included in the commentary on vv. 1–7. Note: Verse 17 does not appear in the best ancient manuscripts and so is omitted in modern critical editions of the Greek New Testament.

Simon of Cyrene
Lk 23:26–32
Mk 15:21, Mt 27:32
Source: Mark

23 [26]**And as they were marching him away, they grabbed some-
one named Simon, a Cyrenian, as he was coming in from the coun-
try. They loaded the cross on him, to carry behind Jesus.** [27]**A huge
crowd of the people followed him,** including women who mourned
and lamented him. [28]**Jesus turned to them and said,** "Daughters of
Jerusalem, do not weep for me. Weep instead for yourselves and for
your children. [29]Look, the time is coming when they will say, 'Congrat-
ulations to those who are sterile, to the wombs that never gave birth,
and to the breasts that never nursed an infant!'

[30]Then they will beg the mountains:
"Fall on us";
and the hills:
"Bury us."

[31]If they behave this way when the wood is green, what will happen
when it dries out?"

[32]**Two others, who were criminals, were also taken away with him
to be executed.**

Simon of Cyrene. When faced with Mark's introduction of Simon of Cyrene into the procession to Golgotha, Luke does his best to make a plausible story out of it. Efforts to explain Mark's snippet as something the Roman soldiers had to do—for example, because Jesus was so weak from his flogging that he couldn't carry his own cross—fail to notice Mark's narrative motive: He has a strange Simon perform what Simon Peter could not perform—Simon Peter was not able to deny himself and take up his cross and follow Jesus (Luke 9:23). In addition, the Markan story contradicts the Gospel of John, where Jesus carries his own cross in the customary fashion (John 19:17). Luke has failed to recognize Mark's touch for what it is and attempted to improve the plausibility, without success. As a fiction black is the appropriate color.

Raymond E. Brown has no way of telling whether Luke has made use of a pre-Lukan tradition about the women lamenting for Jesus (v. 27) or whether he has employed a common motif to supply context for the sayings in vv. 28–31. In any case, "Luke's hand and mind-set are apparent in almost every line."[68] Brown might have voted gray on the lamenting women, in concert with the Fellows; his remarks do not suggest a higher ranking.

The notice in v. 32 of the crucifixion scene anticipates Luke 23:33, which will be discussed in the commentary on the next segment.

Crucifixion
Lk 23:33–43
Mk 15:22–32, Mt 27:33–44;
Jn 19:17–24; Pet 4:1–5
Sources: Mark, John, Peter

23 **33And when they reached the place called "The Skull,"** they
crucified him **there along with the criminals, one on his right and**
the other on his left. 34They divided up his garments after they cast
lots. 35And the people stood around looking on.
And the rulers kept sneering at him: "He saved others; he should
save himself if he is God's Anointed, the Chosen One!"
36The soldiers also made fun of him: They would come up and
offer him sour wine, 37and they would say, "If you're the King of the
Judeans, why not save yourself?"
38There was also this sign over him: "This is the King of the
Judeans."
39One of the criminals hanging there kept cursing and taunting
him: "Aren't you supposed to be the Anointed? Save yourself and
us!"
40But the other <criminal> rebuked the first: "Don't you even fear
God, since you are under the same sentence? 41We are getting justice,
since we are getting what we deserve. But this man has done noth-
ing improper."
42And he implored, "Jesus, remember me when you come into
your domain."
43And <Jesus> said to him, "I swear to you, today you'll be with me
in paradise."

Crucifixion. Unlike Mark and Matthew, Luke makes some mixture of Judean authorities and people responsible for the crucifixion of Jesus. The Romans are basically responsible in Luke's source, the Gospel of Mark. But Luke is apparently concerned to push the Romans into the background and lay the blame on the Judeans. A crowd with the ranking priest, temple police, and elders came to the garden to arrest Jesus (Luke 22:47, 50, 52, 54). The Roman governor, on the other hand, is made to look innocent of the death of Jesus in 23:4, 14, and 16; even Herod Antipas concurred in Pilate's judgment that Jesus did not deserve to die (23:15). Pilate persists in his desire to set Jesus free (23:20 and 22). The demands of the Judeans prevail (v. 23), so Pilate rules that their demand should be carried out (v. 24) and turns Jesus over to them to do with as they please (v. 25). As Luke has it, those who crucify Jesus in 23:33 consist of the same Judean authorities. However, the Roman soldiers are involved to some extent, since they join in the mockery (vv. 36–37). Luke thus joins the Gospel of Peter in assigning responsibility to the Judeans (in Pet 1:1–2, 2:4, Herod and the Judeans crucify Jesus; Pilate washes his hands).

Luke tells essentially the same story as Mark and Matthew, except that he rearranges the elements and develops the role of the two being executed with Jesus (vv. 39–41). In Luke, the two become common criminals rather than "the rebels" of Mark and Matthew.

Luke introduces the two criminals who were crucified with Jesus at the beginning of his story. Mark and Matthew reserve that observation until later in the course of events. Furthermore, Luke includes mention of the inscription on the placard among the taunts (vv. 35–39). In these rearrangements, Luke is merely attempting to improve the flow of the story.

Luke also distributes the taunts between "the rulers" (v. 35) and "the soldiers" (vv. 36–37). In Mark the taunts are made by "those passing by" and by "the ranking priests and scholars" (Mark 15:29, 31). Matthew retains "those passing by" and adds "elders" to "ranking priests and scholars" (Matt 27:39, 41).

Luke gives his imagination free rein in enlarging on the role of the two malefactors. In this Luke has something in common with the parallel passage in the Gospel of Peter (4:1–5). In Luke, one criminal joins in the cursing and taunting, the other is sympathetic to Jesus. The second convict reprimands the first. Then there is an exchange between Jesus and his sympathizer (vv 39–43). That is all the product of Luke's imagination. In the Gospel of Peter, one of the malefactors reproaches the soldiers for their treatment of Jesus, in retaliation for which the soldiers refuse to break his legs and thus shorten his agony (Pet 4:4–5). Raymond E. Brown concludes: "Surely then there was no precise memory about this reviling of Jesus," which suggests no more than a gray designation, were he employing the voting categories of the Fellows.[69]

Some Fellows of the Jesus Seminar think that Luke knew and used the Gospel of Peter; others took the view that the author of Peter may have known the Gospel of Mark; still others think both Luke and the Gospel of Peter were dependent on a common source now lost. The problem of sorting out the relationships between and among the various sources is discussed fully in the cameo on "Sources for the Passion Story" (pp. 246–47). The dispute about sources did not, however, affect the final decision of the Fellows regarding the historical reliability of Luke's version of the execution of Jesus: the vote was black.

The death of Jesus
Lk 23:44–49
Mk 15:33–41, Mt 27:45–56;
Jn 19:25–37; Pet 5:1–6
Sources: Mark, John, Peter

23 [44]**It was already about noon, and darkness blanketed the whole land until mid-afternoon, [45]during an eclipse of the sun. The curtain of the temple was torn down the middle.**

[46]**Then Jesus cried out at the top of his voice,** "Father, into your hands I entrust my spirit!" **Having said this he breathed his last.**

[47]**Now when the Roman officer saw what happened, he praised God and said, "This man was completely innocent!"**

[48]**And when the throng of people that had gathered for this spectacle observed what had transpired, they all returned home beating their chests. [49]And all his acquaintances and** the women who had followed him from Galilee were standing off at a distance watching these events.

The death of Jesus. Luke narrates in abbreviated form six of the seven events Mark reports in the parallel passage: darkness at noon, the destruction of the temple veil, the shout and death of Jesus, the confession of the Roman officer, and the presence of the women. He does not repeat Mark's claim that those standing nearby thought Jesus was calling on Elijah when he shouted (Mark 15:35).

Luke narrates the incidents in a different order than Mark and he adds a couple of touches of his own.

Luke moves the rending of the temple curtain from its position in Mark as an event simultaneous with the death of Jesus (mid-afternoon) and allies it with darkness at noon, which he explains as an eclipse of the sun (vv. 44–45). Luke's explanation makes the incident appear more "scientific," but Luke apparently failed to realize that an eclipse is not possible at Passover, which always takes place during a full moon because the time of its celebration is determined by phases of the moon.

Furthermore, Luke follows Mark in suggesting that it was the way Jesus died that prompted the Roman officer to blurt out his "confession" (v. 47// Mark 15:39: "When the Roman officer . . . saw that he had died like this . . ."), but Luke alters the confession. Rather than have the officer say that Jesus really was God's son, he proclaims Jesus innocent, which sounds appropriate for Roman ears. This also reinforces the exonerating verdicts of Pilate and Herod one final time. Matthew, on the other hand, links the confession of the officer directly to the portents: torn veil, earthquake, tombs opened. The freedom with which the evangelists modify and edit their sources demonstrates that they are exercising their storytellers' theological license rather than aiming at historical precision.

Luke also attributes different final words to Jesus. Luke has Jesus quote Ps 31:5, "Into your hands I entrust my spirit" (v. 46), rather than the complaint of Ps 22:1, "My God, my God, why did you abandon me?" The fourth evangelist proposes yet another version of Jesus' final words.

In v. 48, Luke introduces the note of regret—the throng begins beating their chests as a sign of repentance at the wrong they have done. That note of regret does not appear in Mark or Matthew, but it does show up in the Gospel of Peter (7:1), where the Judeans, elders, and priests beat their breasts, supposing that their sin has brought the judgment and the destruction of Jerusalem on them.

Finally, Luke retains Mark's statement that the women watched the final moments of Jesus' life from a distance. The Jesus Seminar decided that this detail was probably historically accurate: the male disciples disappeared, but the women remained behind to watch. A pink rating was the result. The rest of Luke's account drew a black designation.

The burial
Lk 23:50–56
Mk 15:42–47, Mt 27:57–61; Jn 19:38–42; Pet 2:1–5, 6:1–4
Sources: Mark, John, Peter

23 **50There was a man named Joseph, a Council member, a**
decent and upright man, 51who had not endorsed their decision or
gone along with their action. He was from the town of Arimathea in
Judea, and he lived in anticipation of God's imperial rule. 52This
man went to Pilate and requested the body of Jesus. 53Then he took it
down and wrapped it in a shroud, and laid him in a tomb cut from
the rock, where no one had ever been buried. 54It was the day of

preparation, and the sabbath was about to begin. [55]The women who had come with him from Galilee tagged along. They kept an eye on the tomb, to see how his body was laid to rest. [56]Then they went home to prepare spices and ointments. On the sabbath day they rested in accordance with the commandment.

The burial. Verses 50–51 are Luke's revision of Mark. According to Mark, all the members of the Council agreed to the death penalty (14:64). Luke attempts to rectify what appears to be an inconsistency by depicting Joseph as "a decent and upright man" and suggesting that he did not concur in either the decision or the action of the Council. In other words, Luke cleans up Mark's story. The tomb is hewn out of rock in Mark (15:46), but in both Matthew (27:60) and Luke (v. 53) it is a new tomb, one in which no one had ever been buried. It is also new in the Gospel of John (19:41) and is located in a garden, which is given the name "Joseph's Garden" in the Gospel of Peter (6:4). It is difficult to avoid the double impression that these accounts are all derived from one basic story and that each of the authors feels entirely free to elaborate or alter the details.

Raymond E. Brown concurs with the finding of the Seminar that the note about the women watching the burial of Jesus is a "back-formation" from their presence at the tomb on Easter morning, and is therefore a fiction.[70] However, he believes the women were watching the crucifixion from a distance.

Luke has the women prepare spices for the burial rites on sabbath eve, in anticipation of their trek to the tomb on the first day of the week (v. 56). They cannot make those preparations on Saturday since that is the sabbath. Luke is here only anticipating the continuation of his story in 24:1, a form of narrative continuity that Luke practices more frequently than the two other synoptic writers.

Luke has added nothing to his Markan base that cannot readily be accounted for on the basis of his skill as a storyteller. He has no separate source of information, fictive or historical. Like Mark, his source, Luke's account also deserves the designation black.

Note: Luke's versions of the empty tomb and appearance stories are gathered on pp. 449–95 of *The Acts of Jesus*. Color coding and commentary on Luke 24:1–12, 13–35, 36–49, and 50–53 will be found there.

THE GOSPEL OF JOHN

Prologue
Jn 1:1–18
No parallels
Source: John

1 In the beginning there was the divine word and wisdom.

The divine word and wisdom was there with God,
and it was what God was.
2It was there with God from the beginning.
3Everything came to be by means of it;
nothing that exists came to be without its agency.
4In it was life,
and this life was the light of humanity.
5Light was shining in darkness,
and darkness did not master it.

6There appeared a man sent from God named John. 7He came to tes-
tify—to testify to the light—so everyone would believe through him.
8He was not the light; he came only to attest to the light.

9Genuine light—the kind that provides light for everyone
—was coming into the world.
10Although it was in the world,
and the world came about through its agency,
the world did not recognize it.
11It came to its own place,
but its own people were not receptive to it.
12But to all who did embrace it,
to those who believed in it,
it gave the right to become children of God.
13They were not born from sexual union,
not from physical desire,
and not from male willfulness:
they were born of God.

14The divine word and wisdom became human
and made itself at home among us.
We have seen its majesty,
majesty appropriate
to a Father's only son,
brimming with generosity and truth.

15John testifies on his behalf and has called out, "This is the one I was talking about when I said, 'He who is to come after me is actually my superior, because he was there before me.'"

16From his richness
all of us benefited—
one gift after another.
17Law was given through Moses;
mercy and truth came through Jesus the Anointed.
18No one has ever seen God;
the only son, an intimate of the Father—he has disclosed <him>.

Prologue. John's testimony (v. 15) has been inserted into what many scholars believe is an ancient hymn that has been Christianized. Here John the Baptist is represented as giving direct testimony to the status of the "Father's only son" of v. 14—to Jesus. John probably did expect a figure to appear who would supercede him, but is very dubious that he recognized Jesus of Nazareth as that figure. The fourth evangelist represents the Baptist as giving similar testimony in 1:26–27. The Fellows designated both black because the Baptist has become subservient to Christian interests.

A voice in the wilderness
Jn 1:19–28
Mk 1:1–8, Mt 3:1–12,
Lk 3:1–20; GEbi 1, 3
Sources: John, Mark, Q

1 19This is what John had to say when the Judeans sent priests and Levites from Jerusalem to ask him, "Who are you?"
20He made it clear—he wouldn't deny it—"I'm not the Anointed."
21And they asked him, "Then what are you? Are you Elijah?"
And he replies, "I am not."
"Are you the Prophet?"
He answered, "No."
22So they said to him, "Tell us who you are so we can report to those who sent us. What have you got to say for yourself?"
23He replied, "I am the voice of someone shouting in the wilderness, 'Make the way of the Lord straight'—that's how Isaiah the prophet put it."
(24It was the Pharisees who had sent them.)
25"So," they persisted, "why are you baptizing if you're not the Anointed, not Elijah, and not the Prophet?"
26John answered them, "I baptize, yes, but only with water. Right there with you is someone you don't yet recognize;
27he's the one

who is to be my successor. I don't even deserve to untie his sandal straps."

[28]All this took place in Bethany on the far side of the Jordan, where John was baptizing.

A voice in the wilderness. The early Christian movement had to come to terms with the fact that their Christ, Jesus, had been baptized by John the Baptist. Mark represents John as the prophetic forerunner of Jesus preparing the way for the messiah (Mark 1:1–8). John in the wilderness has or is given the attributes of the great prophet Elijah (a hairy mantle and a leather belt). In Matthew Jesus even openly declares that John is Elijah (Matt 11:14). Luke describes John as the one who precedes the messiah "in the spirit and power of Elijah" (Luke 1:17). But now the author of the Fourth Gospel has John deny that he is Elijah or one of the prophets in a curious reversal. Questions about John's identity become a foil for the question about Jesus' identity. John the Baptist is made to be the star witness testifying to Jesus' identity as the one sent from God. As in Mark, John contrasts his own baptism in water with the baptism in spirit to be practiced by his successor. The belittling of John is designed to enhance the status of Jesus as the messiah. The words in vv. 26–27, although reminiscent of the sayings attributed to John in Mark 1:7–8 and Luke 3:16, are turned into direct confession on the part of John: here John testifies that Jesus is the expected messiah; there John is correctly represented as expecting the messiah to appear but without identifying Jesus as the fulfillment of that expectation. Words of the Baptist that rang true in the synoptic gospels have now been made to serve an entirely different purpose. By common consent the Fellows agreed that this representation of John was thinly disguised Christian propaganda, probably fueled by the continuing competition between the Jesus movement and the Baptist's followers. At the same time, it is a Christian defense of the superiority of Jesus.

1 **[29]The next day John sees Jesus approaching and says, "Look,**
the lamb of God, who does away with the sin of the world. [30]This is
the one I was talking about when I said, 'Someone is coming after
me who is actually my superior, because he was there before me.' [31]I
didn't know who he was, although I came baptizing with water so
he would be revealed to Israel."
[32]And John continued to testify: "I have seen the spirit coming
down like a dove out of the sky, and it hovered over him. [33]I wouldn't
have recognized him, but the very one who sent me to baptize with
water told me, 'When you see the spirit come down and hover over
someone, that's the one who baptizes with holy spirit.' [34]I have seen
this and I have certified: This is God's son."

The testimony of John the Baptist
Jn 1:29–34
Source: John
Cf. Mk 1:9–11, Mt 3:13–17, Lk 3:21–22; GNaz 2; GEbi 4; GHeb 3

The testimony of John the Baptist. The Gospel of John does not report the story of Jesus' baptism by John the Baptist. In this gospel, John the Baptist appears as the first Christian—bearing witness to Jesus as the one sent from God. By consensus, the Fellows view these words of John the Baptist to be the formulation of the author of the Fourth Gospel. However, the words attributed to John the Baptist contain what appears to be an allusion to the story of John's baptism of Jesus, only now John is the one who sees the spirit descending like a dove (v. 32–33).

The Christian community can here be observed erasing whatever memories it may have had of Jesus as subservient to John: an explicit account of Jesus' baptism at the hands of John is omitted; John is made to testify to Jesus; John is represented as observing the descent of the spirit in the form of a dove.

Call of Andrew & Peter
Jn 1:35–42
Source: John
Cf. Mk 1:16–18, Mt 4:18–20; Lk 5:1–11; GEbi 2

1 **35 The next day John was standing there again with two of his disciples. 36 When he noticed Jesus walking by, he says, "Look, the lamb of God."**

37 His two disciples heard him <say this>, and they followed Jesus. 38 Jesus turned around, saw them following, and says to them, "What are you looking for?"

They said to him, "Rabbi" (which means Teacher), **"where are you staying?"**

39 He says to them, "Come and see."

They went and saw where he was staying and spent the day with him. It was about four in the afternoon.

40 Andrew, Simon Peter's brother, was one of the two who followed Jesus after hearing John <speak about him>. 41 First he goes and finds his brother Simon and tells him, "We have found the Messiah" (which is translated, Anointed), **42 and he took him to Jesus.**

When Jesus laid eyes on him, he said, "You're Simon, John's son; you're going to be called Kephas" (which means Peter <or Rock>).

Call of Andrew & Peter. As in the case of the synoptic gospels, John also relates a pair of call stories: this one in which Andrew and Peter are enlisted, and the following narrative segment in which Philip and Nathanael become followers (1:43–51). But John's stories differ considerably from the versions found in Mark and Matthew (Luke has again gone his own way).

The author of the Fourth Gospel has set the stories in Bethany on the far side of the Jordan, where John the Baptist was performing his baptismal rite (John 1:28, 43), not in Galilee along the seashore, as in Mark (1:16). According to John, the first disciples of Jesus had been followers of John the Baptist (John 1:35); this is not mentioned in the synoptic accounts. Jesus seems to have enlisted his first followers soon after his baptism by John the Baptist, while he was still in John's company—this is how matters are represented in the Gospel of John. In Mark, Jesus enlists his first followers only after he has left John the Baptist and returned to Galilee to begin his public work. In the book of Acts, Luke seems to confirm the account of the Fourth Gospel, when Luke has Peter say that Judas' replacement should be someone who was a companion of Jesus during his entire public life, from "John's baptism" until his ascension (Acts

1:21–22). It is not entirely clear what the reference to John's baptism means, although it may indicate that Jesus' first followers were present at his baptism at the hands of John. The Fellows of the Jesus Seminar were agreed, by a substantial majority, that:

- **Jesus was a disciple of John the Baptist**

and

- **Some of John the Baptist's disciples became followers of Jesus.**

On these two points the Fellows determined that the information provided by the Gospel of John was accurate.

In other respects, however, they regarded the story of the call of Andrew and Peter in the Fourth Gospel as unreliable. In that story, John the Baptist acknowledges Jesus as "the lamb of God" and "God's son" (John 1:29–36). And he does so in the presence of Andrew and Peter. This is not historically plausible. In the Sayings Gospel Q (Luke 7:18–20), John the Baptist sends his disciples to Jesus to ask who he is; he evidently had not yet made up his mind about Jesus. Yet in the Fourth Gospel, John the Baptist knew who Jesus was from the moment of his baptism. In addition, in the Gospel of Mark, Peter does not confess Jesus as the messiah until well into the story, while in John Peter hears Jesus confessed as God's son from the beginning. Even so conservative a commentator as Raymond E. Brown can conclude that "we cannot treat John 1:35–51 as historical narrative."[71]

Call of Philip & Nathanael
Jn 1:43–51
Source: John
Cf. Mk 1:19–20, Mt 4:21–22; Lk 5:1–1; GEbi 2

1 43 **The next day Jesus decided to leave for Galilee. He finds**
Philip and says to him, "Follow me."
44 **Philip was from Bethsaida, the hometown of Andrew and Peter.**
45 **Philip finds Nathanael and tells him, "We've found the one Moses**
wrote about in the Law, and the prophets mention too: Jesus,
Joseph's son, from Nazareth."
46 **"From Nazareth?" Nathanael said to him. "Can anything good**
come from that place?"
Philip replies to him, "Come and see."
47 **Jesus saw Nathanael coming toward him, and he remarks about**
him: "There's a genuine Israelite—not a trace of deceit in him."
48 **"Where do you know me from?" Nathanael asks him.**
Jesus replied, "I saw you under the fig tree before Philip invited
you <to join us>."
49 **Nathanael responded to him, "Rabbi, you are God's son! You are**
King of Israel!"
50 **Jesus replied,** "Do you believe just because I told you I saw you
under the fig tree? You're going to see far more than that."
51 **Then he adds,** "As God is my witness before you all: You'll see the
sky split open and God's messengers traveling to and from the son of
Adam."

Call of Philip & Nathanael. The Gospel of Mark records a pair of call stories in which first Peter and Andrew and then James and John are enlisted as disciples (Mark 1:16–20). The Gospel of John has twin stories that are structured very similarly: in the first, Andrew finds his brother Peter and brings him to Jesus (1:35–42); in the second, Philip finds Nathanael and introduces him to Jesus. The parallelism between the two stories in John is striking; the fact that the two gospel traditions—the synoptics and John—have parallel twin stories is also remarkable. The transmitters of the oral tradition must have decided that two stories were sufficient to authorize the appointment of "learners" (a disciple is a learner) and leaders—they did not feel the need to relate the commissioning of every leader. The tradition then developed in two different directions, one of which ended up in the Gospel of Mark, the other in the Gospel of John. In the further process of transmission—handing the stories around and on by word of mouth—the pairs of call stories became stereotyped as they were repeatedly retold.

Philip is introduced into the story abruptly in v. 43, unless he is the second, unnamed disciple of John mentioned in the previous narrative (1:35–39). There is no motivation given for his enlistment, but the assumption is that Philip learned who Jesus was from the testimony of John the Baptist (1:29–34). In any case, when he endeavors to enlist Nathanael (v. 45), Philip is clear that Jesus is the messiah.

Nathanael is skeptical that Nazareth can produce heroes (v. 46), presumably because there was nothing in scripture to warrant high expectations. But Jesus evidently has forms of wisdom that surprise and convince: Prior to the time Philip goes to get Nathanael, Jesus had spotted him sitting under a fig tree and that bit of lore is enough to persuade Nathanael that Jesus is the son of God and king of Israel. Interpreters have labored through the centuries attempting to determine why Jesus observing "sitting under a fig tree" would have impressed Nathanael—without success.

The four who are enlisted as the first followers of Jesus, and presumably as part of an inner circle, include Peter and Andrew, James and John, the sons of Zebedee. In the Gospel of John the four are Andrew and Peter, Philip and Nathanael. The discrepancy in the second pair may represent rivalries in early Christian communities, or it may simply be the result of inexact information that was filled in by storytellers on their own authority. Philip does appear in the list of twelve given by Mark (3:13–19), but Nathanael does not, unless he is to be identified with Bartholomew (perhaps two names for the same person). Bartholomew is paired with Philip in Mark's list, which is the reason some scholars give for identifying the two.

That Peter and Andrew, two brothers, became followers of Jesus there can be no doubt. However, the fourth evangelist demotes Peter as a recruit of his brother Andrew. In this way the author signals Peter's secondary role in his version of the Christian beginnings—the beloved disciple is his hero—in contrast to Peter's starring role in the synoptics. The enlistment of Philip also reflects historical memory, in all probability. It is more difficult to say whether Nathanael is a real disciple since he appears nowhere else in the other gospels.

But beyond the mere names there is nothing in these call stories in the Gospel of John that reflects hard historical knowledge. Black is the correct designation.

The confusion over the lists of followers—whether disciples, apostles, or the twelve—is further exemplified by a citation from the Gospel of the Ebionites by Epiphanius, a fourth-century Christian writer and bishop. Epiphanius refers to it as a gospel written in Hebrew, but that is clearly incorrect: the text he cites follows the Greek text of the synoptic gospels closely. The Gospel of the Ebionites is the modern name scholars have assigned to these fragmentary citations; the ancient name of this narrative gospel is unknown. Our knowledge of its contents depends entirely on Epiphanius (GEbi 2).

1 There was this man named Jesus, who was about thirty years old, who
chose us. 2 And when he came to Capernaum, he entered the house of
Simon, who was nicknamed Peter. He then began to speak as follows:
3 "As I was walking along by the lake of Tiberias, I chose John and
James, sons of Zebedee, and Simon and Andrew and Thaddeus and
Simon the Zealot and Judas the Iscariot. 4 Then I summoned you,
Matthew, while you were sitting at the toll booth, and you followed
me. 5 Therefore, I want you to be twelve apostles, to symbolize Israel."

The Gospel of the Ebionites mentions that Jesus intended the apostles to be twelve in number to symbolize Israel—the traditional twelve tribes. But the gospel in fact list only eight names. Further, Ebionites identifies the former toll collector of the group with Matthew, whereas he is called Levi in the Gospel of Mark (2:14); Mark does not list Levi among the twelve (Mark 3:13–19). The information provided by the Gospel of the Ebionites is no more reliable than the traditions preserved by John and the synoptics.

Miracle at Cana
Jn 2:1–11
No parallels
Source: John

2 **Three days later there was a wedding in Cana, Galilee. Jesus'**
mother was there. 2 Jesus was also invited to the wedding along with
his disciples. 3 When the wine had run out, Jesus' mother says to him,
"They're out of wine."
4 Jesus replies to her, "Woman, what is it with you and me? It's not
my time yet."
5 His mother says to the servants, "Whatever he tells you, do it."
6 Six stone water-jars were standing there—for use in the Jewish
rite of purification—and each could hold twenty or thirty gallons.
7 "Fill the jars with water," **Jesus tells them.**
So they filled them to the brim.
8 Then he tells them, "Now dip some out and take it to the caterer."
And they did so. 9 When the caterer tasted the water, now changed
into wine—he had no idea where it had come from, even though the
servants who had taken the water out knew—he calls the groom
aside 10 and says to him, "Everyone serves the best wine first and
only later, when people are drunk, the cheaper wine. But you've
held back the good wine till now."

[11]Jesus performed this miracle, the first, in Cana, Galilee; it displayed his majesty, and his disciples believed in him.

[12]Then he went down to Capernaum, he and his mother and brothers and disciples; but they stayed there only a few days.

Miracle at Cana. In conventional healing and exorcism stories, there are three structural elements: First, a misfortune or lack is called to the attention of the miracle worker; then the misfortune or lack is somehow overcome; and finally the miracle is certified by the storyteller and/or by witnesses.

In the miracle at Cana, the lack is the failure of the wine supply. The deficiency is called to Jesus' attention by his mother and then is presumably overcome in the first scene, which ends at v. 8 (the servants depart to take some of the water, now turned into wine, to the caterer). The certification that a miracle has taken place occurs in the second scene but only obliquely: the caterer is not aware that a miracle has taken place. In his ignorance, he cites a proverb, otherwise unattested in ancient literature, to the effect that the typical host serves the superior wine first, and only later, when the guests can no longer tell the difference, serves the inferior wine. There is no other testimony in the story proper.

However, the storyteller addresses the reader directly in the epilogue (v. 11): a miracle did occur; it revealed Jesus' "majesty"; his disciples believed in him. Perhaps no one else knew what had happened, except the servants who had taken the water out (v. 9).

Jesus had arrived at the wedding with his disciples (v. 2). Those disciples play no active role in the body of the story. But they are reintroduced at the end, as external and belated witnesses. In the conventional format, one would have expected a person or persons within the story to confirm the miracle.

It is evident that the fourth evangelist is less interested in the miracle itself than in its symbolic value. In the tale of the paralytic by the pool (John 5:1–18), the cure of the lame man is told for the sake of the controversy about the sabbath. In the story of the man born blind (John 9:1–41), the miracle provides the occasion for a theological discourse on blindness and sight. The raising of Lazarus (11:1–57) anticipates the resurrection of Jesus and furnishes some of the motivation for the authorities to kill Jesus. On the other hand, because of the resurrection (of Lazarus and, of course, Jesus), many came to believe in him (11:45).

In the Cana story, the replacement of the water destined for the purification rites with good wine constitutes the symbolic miracle: the new, good wine is Christianity, which replaces the old, ineffective rites symbolized by the imperfect number six—one short of seven—(the number of the beast in Revelation is 666). This of course happens "on the third day," which may be an allusion to resurrection day. There is no comparable story in any of the other gospels. Yet the metaphorical character of the story comports well with Nicodemus' inability to understand that he must be "born again," not from his mother's womb but "from above" (3:1–21); and with the puzzlement of the woman at the well, who has trouble understanding what kind of water quenches thirst forever (4:1–29). Johannine fingerprints are all over the narrative of the miracle at Cana. Scholars commonly conclude that the story is the creation of the author of the Fourth Gospel. John P. Meier belongs to that large company.[72] The Fellows of the Jesus Seminar join in that chorus with a black vote.

The narrative notice in v. 12 is the product of the evangelist's imagination. The particular movements of Jesus had long since been lost, so storytellers made up minor connective splices to give the gospel narrative some semblance of continuity.

Temple incident
Jn 2:13–22
Mk 11:15–19, Mt 21:12–17, Lk 19:45–48
Sources: John, Mark

2 **[13]It was almost time for the Jewish Passover celebration, so**
Jesus went up to Jerusalem. [14]In the temple precincts he came upon
people selling oxen and sheep and doves, and bankers were doing
business there too. [15]He made a whip out of rope and drove them all
out of the temple area, sheep, oxen, and all; then he knocked over
the bankers' tables, and set their coins flying. [16]And to the dove mer-
chants he said, "Get these birds out of here! How dare you use my
Father's house as a public market."

([17]His disciples were reminded of the words of scripture: "Zeal for your house is eating me alive.")

[18]To this the Judeans responded, "What miracle can you show us <to justify> doing all this?"

[19]Jesus replied, "Destroy this temple and I'll resurrect it in three days."

[20]"It has taken forty-six years to build this temple," the Judeans said, "and you can reconstruct it in three days?"

([21]However, he was referring to his body as a temple. [22]When he
had been raised from the dead his disciples remembered that he had
made this remark, and so they came to believe both the written word
and the word Jesus had spoken.)

Temple incident. John's version of the temple incident differs from the synoptic account in both content and context. The episode in John takes place nearly at the beginning of Jesus' public life, whereas in the synoptics it occurs in the last week—the so-called passion week. Furthermore, in the Fourth Gospel Jesus does not quote scripture as he expels the merchants from the area, and, after the incident, there is a challenge from the crowd and a response by Jesus that is not found in the synoptic edition.

Does the version of the temple incident in the Fourth Gospel represent an independent source of information? Scholars are divided on this question. The way Jesus talks and what he says are clearly different in the Gospel of John and are not derived from the synoptic gospels. However, many of Jesus' acts in the Fourth Gospel have affinities with incidents reported in the synoptics, particularly in the passion narrative. Many Fellows of the Seminar count John's version of the temple incident as an independent account; many others regard it as John's distinctive version of an event he knew from the synoptic tradition. This division of opinion does not seem to have affected the way Fellows voted: The Fellows by and large believe that Jesus demonstrated physically against the temple cult, probably against its commercialization, and that he made some correlative pronouncement critical of the temple bureaucracy, whether as reported by John or by Mark. On balance, they tended to be more skeptical of the Fourth Gospel's version than of the synoptic account, and that skepticism is reflected in the gray and black coloring.

It is as part of the Fourth Gospel's preoccupation with signs and miracles that in v. 18 the fourth evangelist has Jesus' interlocutors ask him for some definite proof that he is who he says he is. In John 6:30, Jesus' critics ask him: "What miracle are you going to perform so we can see it and come to believe in you? What 'labor' are you going to perform?" The mention of 'labor' is in all likelihood an allusion to the 'labors' of Hercules. Jesus of course rejects all these requests. Thus, while John reports numerous signs and miracles, both the evangelist represents Jesus as treating an interest in such matters as an inferior form of faith. For the view that the Gospel of John is based on an earlier Gospel of Miracles, consult the cameo on that subject (pp. 388–89).

Many miracles
Jn 2:23–25
Source: John

**2 23When he was in Jerusalem at the Passover celebration, many
believed in him once they saw with their own eyes the miracles he
performed. 24But Jesus didn't trust himself to them, because he
understood them all too well. 25He didn't need to know more about
humanity; he knew what people were really like.**

Many miracles. This segment is a narrative transition and summary created by the fourth evangelist. It is intended to prepare for the dialogue with Nicodemus to follow. The evangelist does not specify what "signs" Jesus did at the Passover celebration to elicit the approval of the crowd. Verses 24–25 are the comments of an omniscient narrator who knows what is in Jesus' heart. None of this provides reliable historical information; it is the work of a storyteller attempting to forge links between episodes in a narrative. Black is the correct designation.

Conversation with Nicodemus
Jn 3:1–21
No parallels
Source: John

**3 A Pharisee named Nicodemus, a Judean leader, 2came to
<Jesus> during the night and said, "Rabbi, we know that you've
come as a teacher from God; after all, nobody can perform the mir-
acles you do unless God is with him."**

3Jesus replied to him, "As God is my witness: No one can experi-
ence God's imperial rule without being reborn from above."

**4Nicodemus says to him, "How can an adult be reborn? Can you
re-enter your mother's womb and be born a second time?"**

5Jesus replied, "As God is my witness: No one can enter God's
domain without being born of water and spirit. 6What is born of the
human realm is human, but what is born of the spiritual realm is
spirit. 7Don't be surprised that I told you, 'Every one of you must be
reborn from above.' 8The spirit blows every which way, like wind: you
hear the sound it makes but you can't tell where it's coming from or
where it's headed. That's how it is with everyone reborn of the spirit."

9"How can that be possible?" Nicodemus retorted.
10Jesus replied, "You are a teacher of Israel, and you don't under-
stand this? 11As God is my witness: We tell what we know, and we give
evidence about what we've seen, but none of you accepts our evi-
dence. 12If I tell you about what's mundane and you don't believe, how
will you believe if I tell you about what's heavenly? 13No one has gone
up to heaven except the one who came down from there—the son of
Adam."

**14In the wilderness Moses elevated the snake; in the same way the
son of Adam is destined to be elevated, 15so every one who believes
in him can have real life. 16This is how God loved the world: God
gave up an only son, so that every one who believes in him will not
be lost but have real life. 17After all, God sent this son into the world
not to condemn the world but to rescue the world through him.
18Those who believe in him are not condemned. Those who don't
believe in him are already condemned: they haven't believed in
God's only son. 19This is the verdict <on them>: Light came into the
world but people loved darkness instead of light. Their actions were
evil, weren't they? 20All those who do evil things hate the light and
don't come into the light—otherwise their deeds would be exposed.
21But those who do what is true come into the light so the nature of
their deeds will become evident: their deeds belong to God.**

Conversation with Nicodemus. Nicodemus is a well-attested name in sources contemporary with the Gospel of John. The Jewish historian Josephus mentions a Nicodemus in both his *History of the Jews* (14.37) and *The Jewish Wars* (2.451). A Nicodemus also appears in the Talmud. But Nicodemus in this episode is really a representative figure, just as Jesus represents the Johannine community: Both speakers use the first-person plural ("we" and "us") and the second-person plural ("you"). In v. 2, Nicodemus says, "Rabbi, we know. . . ." In v. 11, Jesus responds, "*We* tell what *we* know, and *we* give evidence of what we've seen, but none of *you* accepts our evidence." The dialogue is an exchange between those who have seen the signs that Jesus performed but do not fully understand and the Christian community that does understand. Nicodemus is a fictive dialogue partner.

Nicodemus appears three times in the Fourth Gospel. He plays a role here in chapter 3 and reappears in the extended debate about origins and authority in 7:50–52, and then shows up once again at the burial of Jesus (19:38–41). He is depicted, according to many scholars, as a sympathizer, perhaps even as a "crypto-Christian"—one of those secret believers who for fear of their fellow Judeans could not openly declare allegiance to the Jesus movement (19:38: Joseph of Arimathea was just such a secret Christian).

The episode appears to be a typical Johannine construction. Nicodemus is introduced with the barest of narrative settings. He comes to Jesus "by night," which should perhaps be understood symbolically: Nicodemus will not understand, cannot understand, because he is in the darkness. By contrast, the woman at the well in the next chapter encounters Jesus "at noon" and she will be able to "see" the truth. The vocabulary is largely Johannine: it does not therefore represent tradition that had been formulated in earlier terms and taken over by the fourth evangelist. And finally, there is no real outcome to the encounter. Nicodemus is not called on to make a decision, or to perform an action; there is no suggestion that he has begun to get a glimmer of light. Instead, the dialogue devolves into a monologue that goes on for an indefinite time. Since scribes did not use quotation marks, it is unclear, in fact, when Jesus stops speaking and the evangelist continues. The Fellows of the Jesus Seminar put the closing quotation marks at the end of v. 13, and for that reason colored vv. 14–21 black as the interpretive work of the evangelist. Just as the Seminar designated the words of Jesus black in *The Five Gospels*, it decided to color the narrative context black as well. The scene belongs entirely to the imagination of the storyteller.

John's final testimony
Jn 3:22–30
Source: John

**3 [22]After this Jesus and his disciples went to Judea, and he
extended his stay with them there and began to baptize. [23]John was
baptizing too, in Aenon near Salim, since there was plenty of water
around; and people kept coming to be baptized. ([24]Remember, John
hadn't yet been thrown in prison.)**

**[25]A dispute over purification broke out between John's disciples
and one of the Judeans. [26]They came to John and reported: "Rabbi,
that fellow who was with you across the Jordan—you spoke about
him earlier—guess what! He's now baptizing and everyone is flocking to him."**

**[27]John answered, "You can't lay claim to anything unless it's a gift
from heaven. [28]You yourselves can confirm this: I told you I was not
the Anointed but had been sent on ahead of him. [29]The bride
belongs to the groom, and the best man stands with him and is
happy enough just to be close at hand. So I am content. [30]He can only
grow in importance; my role can only diminish."**

John's final testimony. This scene presents a number of difficult historical problems. First, Jesus has just been in Jerusalem and Judea according to 2:13, 23; he now comes to Judea (v. 22). Next, in a narrative aside, v. 24 indicates that John the Baptist had not yet been imprisoned; yet according to the synoptic chronology, Jesus did not begin his public ministry until after John had been arrested (Mark 1:14). A third problem arises with the remark in v. 26 to the effect that John's disciples resent the rise of a competitive baptist movement led by Jesus. In fact, John had already given eloquent testimony to the superiority of Jesus in 1:29–31, something his disciples seem to have forgotten. These discrepancies have prompted some scholars to suggest that this passage is a duplicate of 1:29–31, to which editorial corrections have been made in v. 26 and 28 to adapt the passage to its present narrative location. However that may be, it is clear that this passage in its present form and location does not make historical sense. It is doubtful that it preserves any accurate historical data. As a consequence, the Fellows voted it black.

The one from above
Jn 3:31–36
Source: John

3 **[31]The one who comes from above is superior to everyone.
Earthly things are simply earthly and give voice to their earthliness.
The one who comes from heaven [32]testifies to what he has seen and
heard—little wonder that no one accepts his testimony! [33]Whoever
does accept his testimony can guarantee that God is truthful. [34]In
other words, the one God sent speaks God's language, since the
spirit does not give by half measures. [35]The Father loves the son and
has entrusted everything to him. [36]Those who entrust themselves to
the son have real life, but those who refuse the son will not see life;
no, they remain the object of God's wrath.**

The one from above. This editorial commentary falls in the same category as the remarks in 3:14–21: it could be taken as an extension of the words attributed to John the Baptist in 3:22–30, just as those in 3:14–21 could be mistaken for part of Jesus' monologue to Nicodemus. But in this case, as in the earlier one, the words are undoubtedly those of the evangelist, who frequently editorializes on his narrative material. The theological commentary here represents the point of view of the evangelist. Black is the appropriate category.

The woman at the well
Jn 4:1–44
No parallels
Source: John

4 **Jesus was aware of the rumor that had reached the Pharisees:
Jesus is recruiting and baptizing more disciples than John. ([2]Actually,
Jesus himself didn't baptize anyone; his disciples did the baptizing.)
[3]So he left Judea again for Galilee. [4]His route took him through
Samaria.**

**[5]He came to a Samaritan town called Sychar, near the field Jacob
had given to his son Joseph—[6]that's where Jacob's well was. Jesus
was exhausted from traveling, so he sat down on the edge of the
well. It was about noon. [7]When a Samaritan woman comes to get
water, Jesus asks her,** "Give me a drink." **([8]In fact, his disciples had
already gone off to town to buy food and drink.)**

**[9]The woman replies to him, "You are a Judean; how can you ask a
Samaritan woman for a drink?" (You see, Judeans don't associate
with Samaritans.)**

[10]Jesus answered her, "If you knew what God can give you, and
who just said to you, 'Give me a drink,' you would ask him and he
would give you lively, life-giving water."

**[11]"Mister, you don't have anything to draw water with," she says,
"and the well is deep; where will you get this 'lively, life-giving
water'? [12]Can you do better than our patriarch Jacob? He left us this
well, which used to quench his thirst and that of his family and his
livestock."**

[13]Jesus responded to her, "Whoever drinks this water will get thirsty
again; [14]but all who drink the water I'll provide them with will never
get thirsty again; it will be a source of water within them, a fountain of
real life."

15The woman says to him, "Sir, give me some of this water, so I'll never be thirsty or have to keep coming back here for water."

16Jesus says to her, "Go, call your husband and come back."

17"I don't have a husband," she answered.

"You're right to say that you don't have a husband," **Jesus says.** 18"In fact, you've had five husbands, and the man you are now living with is not your husband; you've told the truth."

19"Master," she exclaims, "I can tell you're a prophet. 20Our ancestors worshiped on this mountain; you people claim Jerusalem is the only place for worship."

21Jesus says to her, "Woman, believe me, the time is coming when you won't worship the Father either on this mountain or in Jerusalem. 22You people worship God-knows-what; we worship what we know—'Judeans are the agents of salvation,' and all that. 23But the time is coming—in fact, it's already here—for true worshipers to worship the Father as he truly is, without regard to place. It's worshipers of this sort that the Father is looking for. 24God is not tied to place, and those who worship God must worship him as he truly is, without regard to place."

25The woman continues, "All I know is that the Messiah, the one called Anointed, is going to come; when he does he'll tell us everything."

26Jesus says to her, "You've been talking to <the Anointed> all along; I am he."

27But just then his disciples returned. They were puzzled that he was talking with a woman, but no one said, "What are you trying to do? Why are you talking with her?" 28At this the woman left her water jar, hurried off to town, and tells everyone, 29"Come, see someone who told me everything I ever did. Could he be the Anointed?"

30They set out from their town and made their way to him.

31Meanwhile the disciples pleaded with him, "Rabbi, eat something."

32He replied to them, "I have food to eat, food you know nothing about."

33The disciples queried each other: "Has someone already brought him food?"

34"Doing the will of the one who sent me and completing his work—that's my food," **Jesus tells them.** 35"You have a saying: 'It's still four months till harvest.' Yet I tell you: Look at the fields, they're ripe for harvesting. 36The harvester is already getting his pay; he is gathering the crop <that sustains> real life, so planter and harvester can celebrate together. 37Here too the proverb holds true: 'One plants, another harvests.' 38I sent you to harvest what you haven't labored over; others have labored, and you've benefited from their work."

39Many Samaritans from that town had believed in him because of the woman's testimony: "He told me everything I ever did." 40So when those Samaritans got to him they kept begging him to stay

> **with them. And he stayed there for two days. [41]And many more believed because of what he said. [42]They told the woman, "We no longer believe because of what you said. Now we've listened to him ourselves and we realize that he really is the savior of the world."**
>
> **[43]Two days later Jesus left there for Galilee. ([44]Remember, <Jesus> himself had observed,** "A prophet gets no respect on his own turf.")

The woman at the well. Verses 1–4 are another narrative transition provided by the fourth evangelist. In verse 1, the author apparently gives the reason for Jesus' departure: his movement has begun to gather even more followers than that of John the Baptist. The reader learned in 3:22 that Jesus had launched a baptizing movement similar to John's. Now, in a parenthetical aside to the reader, we are told that Jesus himself did not actually baptize, only his disciples did (v. 2).

Jesus has been in Jerusalem and now returns to Galilee (v. 3). He goes directly north through Samaria, the shortest route, rather than descend to the Jordan Valley, cross the Jordan River, and travel north in Transjordan, beyond Samaritan territory. In practice, many Jews avoided the direct route via Samaria as a consequence of the hostility that existed between Judeans and Samaritans, who once had their own temple on Mount Gerizim, destroyed 150 years earlier by Judean troops. By having Jesus cross Samaria, the evangelist anticipates that something significant will happen.

When Jesus sends out the twelve in the Gospel of Matthew, he warns them not to travel foreign roads and not to enter a Samaritan town (10:5). The Samaritans and Samaria are not mentioned in the Gospel of Mark. However, Luke and John show some special interest in the Samaritans. Luke's geographical program for the advancement of the gospel in Acts 1:8 begins in Jerusalem and then extends to Judea, Samaria, and the ends of the earth. Like the Fourth Gospel, Luke also has Jesus travel through Samaria, except that, in Luke's case, his movement is from north to south, on his way to Jerusalem (9:51–52). Luke's account is probably a fiction. Luke tells of the cure of ten lepers, only one of whom returned to thank Jesus; he was a Samaritan (Luke 17:15–16). And the hero of one of Jesus' parables was a Samaritan (Luke 10:30–35).

Elsewhere in John's gospel, the Judeans respond to Jesus, "Aren't we right to say, 'You're a Samaritan and out of your mind'?" Jesus responds, "I am not out of my mind" (8:48–49). That exchange prompted St. Augustine to give the parable of the Good Samaritan an allegorical interpretation, in which he identified Jesus with the Good Samaritan. But the focus of John's interest in the Samaritans is this story of the woman at the well.

The reader can be confident the encounter with the woman will turn out well: It was about noon (v. 7). The visit of Nicodemus was at night and for all his apparent sincerity he did not grasp what Jesus was trying to tell him. Now, at high noon, this Johannine theme will assert itself: "We must carry out the work of the one who sent me while the light lasts. Nighttime is coming and then no one will be able to undertake any work" (9:4). The woman does get Jesus' point.

It is possible that the Johannine circle included Samaritans. If so, the story of the woman at the well may be described as an aetiological legend—a story that gives the origin of or reason for something. It is thus an explanation of how there came to be Samaritan converts to the Jesus movement. When the evangelist notes in v. 9 that "they [the Judeans] don't associate with Samaritans," the implication is that we (the Johannine people) do, just as Jesus did. The precedent of Jesus would be enough to warrant this expansion of the original circle of Judeans. So the story turns out to be a legend of the origins of the Samaritan component in the Christian community.

The story itself is a drama in three acts. In the first act, the disciples go off to buy food (v. 8), leaving Jesus alone with the woman with whom he is about to discuss some very intimate matters (vv. 7–26). The climax comes in v. 26 when Jesus informs the woman that he is the messiah.

The second act begins with the return of the disciples and the departure of the woman, who leaves her water jar behind. Does she now have the water that quenches thirst forever? She rushes into town to tell her friends and neighbors of her discovery. Meanwhile, Jesus and the disciples turn to the subject of food (vv. 31–38), which they had gone into the village to buy. As so often in discourses engineered by the author of the Fourth Gospel, this one turns from food to harvest and harvest in a metaphorical sense: enlisting converts to the movement. So Jesus, who knows what is happening in the Samaritan village, interprets the event for his disciples: "Already the harvester is getting his pay; he is gathering the crop" (v. 36).

In the third act, we learn that many Samaritans had believed the testimony of the woman and so presumably became followers of Jesus (vv. 39–42). At their invitation, Jesus visits the Samaritans in Sychar and stays with them. This confirms that the Samaritans are "born of God" (1:13) and that Jesus can trust himself to them (contrast 2:24–25).

All of this is a wonderfully entertaining story, full of misunderstanding, word play, irony and other witticisms. But it is scarcely history. Raymond Brown comments: "It is not at all impossible that even in the conversation we have echoes of a historical tradition of an incident in Jesus' ministry." Echoes are about all he is prepared to claim.[73] As suggested earlier, however, the story is probably an aetiological legend created to explain how Samaritans came to be included in the Jesus movement and to provide the warrant of Jesus for that inclusion. If that assessment is correct, black is the only possible color.

Official's son
Jn 4:45–54
Lk 7:1–10, Mt 8:5–13
Sources: John, Q

4 [45]**So when he came to Galilee, the Galileans welcomed him, since they had seen everything he had done at the celebration in Jerusalem. (They had gone to the celebration too.)** [46]**Then he came back to Cana, Galilee, where he had turned the water into wine.**

In Capernaum there was an official whose son was sick. [47]**When he heard that Jesus had returned to Galilee from Judea,** he approached him and pleaded with him to come down and cure his son, who was about to die.

[48]Jesus said to him, "You people refuse to believe unless you see 'portents and miracles.'"

[49]The official responds, "Sir, please come down before my child dies."

[50]Jesus says, "Go, your son is alive and well."

The man believed what Jesus told him and departed. [51]While he was still on his way home, his slaves met him and told him that his boy was alive. [52]So he asked them when he had begun to recover, and they told him, "Yesterday at one o'clock the fever broke."

[53]Then the father realized that one o'clock was precisely the time Jesus had said to him, "Your son is alive." And he believed, as did all his household. [54]Jesus performed this second miracle after he had returned from Judea to Galilee.

Official's son. In the Johannine version of this story, Jesus has just returned to Cana, Galilee from Jerusalem (vv. 45–46). The Fellows believe that the visit to Jerusalem and the references to Cana in vv. 45 and 47 are editorial fictions of the evangelist. Accordingly, these verses were designated black.

An official approaches him and asks him to cure his son (v. 47). With an occasional exception, it appears to be a general rule in healing stories that someone has to ask Jesus to perform a cure; he does not volunteer to assist people unless they or their representatives request it. In this case, the official approaches Jesus on behalf of his son. Jesus responds with remarks about portents and miracles. The official repeats his plea (v. 49). Then Jesus accedes.

A similar exchange occurs in the dialogue of the Greek woman with Jesus (Mark 7:24–30//Matt 15:21–28): she asks Jesus to exorcize a demon from her daughter (Mark 7:26//Matt 15:22); Jesus responds by saying that children ought to be fed before the dogs; to this the Greek woman pleads for the crumbs that fall from the table (Mark 7:28//Matt 15:27). Jesus then assents and the daughter is cured at a distance.

In both of these cases, the initial request is met with a rebuff on the part of Jesus. But he then assents and the cure is effected without his having to come into contact with the patient.

The Johannine version of the official's son is derived, in all probability, from the Signs Gospel, a collection of miracle stories utilized by the author of the Fourth Gospel in creating his own gospel. (For the reconstruction of the story in the Signs Gospel, consult *The Complete Gospels*, 182–83.) The Fellows of the Jesus Seminar, by a slim majority, took the view that the Johannine version represents an earlier form of the story than the one preserved by the Sayings Gospel Q and recorded by Luke and Matthew. Nevertheless, a gray vote means that while the story may reflect some actual event, the information provided by the storyteller is unreliable. About all that can be said with confidence about this tradition is that an official asked Jesus to heal his son (or servant) and the patient got well. Jesus is given the credit for the cure, although the story does not specifically claim that Jesus was the agent, only that Jesus' assurances and the cure were effected simultaneously.

Jesus' uncomplimentary observation that belief is dependent on portents and miracles (John 4:48) is a criticism of the miracles mentality that reflects the perspective of the Fourth Gospel. Jesus is not made to say anything like that in the Q version preserved by Matthew and Luke. Although the criticism probably was an invention of the fourth evangelist, it may well reflect an old tradition. Jesus rejects a request for a sign in Mark 8:10–13 with what appears to be disgust. And in the temptation story that appears at the beginning of Q, Jesus rejects the suggestion that he should throw himself off the pinnacle of the temple in order to demonstrate his powers (Luke 4:9–12).

The Fellows regarded the Johannine account as slightly closer to the original story than the Q versions: the Q editions were designated black, the version here in John gray. That was an unusual reversal of the general tendency to view reports of events in the Fourth Gospel as less reliable than those in the synoptic gospels.

Paralytic by the pool
Jn 5:1–18
Source: John
Cf. Mk 2:1–12, Mt 9:1–8, Lk 5:17–26

5 **After these events, on the occasion of a Jewish celebration,**
Jesus went up to Jerusalem. 2In Jerusalem, by the Sheep <Gate>,
there is a pool, called Bethzatha in Hebrew. It has five colonnades,
3among which numerous invalids were usually lying around—
blind, lame, paralyzed. 5One man had been crippled for thirty-eight
years. 6Jesus observed him lying there and realized he had been
there a long time.
"Do you want to get well?" he asks him.
7The crippled man replied, "Sir, I don't have anyone to put me in
the pool when the water is agitated; while I'm trying to get in some-
one else beats me to it."
8"Get up, pick up your mat and walk around," Jesus tells him.
9And at once the man recovered; he picked up his mat and started
walking.
Now that was a sabbath day. 10So the Judeans said to the man who
had been cured, "It's the sabbath day; you're not permitted to carry
your mat around."
11But he explained, "The man who cured me told me, 'Pick up
your mat and walk around.'"
12They asked him, "Who is this man who said to you, 'Pick it up
and walk'?"
13Now the man who'd been cured had no idea who it was, since
Jesus had withdrawn because people were crowding around.
14Later, Jesus finds him in the temple area and said to him, "Look,
you are well now. Don't sin anymore, or something worse could hap-
pen to you."
15The man went and told the Judeans it was Jesus who had cured
him. 16And this is the reason the Judeans continued to hound Jesus:
he would do things like this on the sabbath day.
17 <Jesus> would respond to them: "My Father never stops labor-
ing, and I labor as well."
18So this is the reason the Judeans then tried even harder to kill
him: Not only did he violate the sabbath day; worse still, he would
call God his Father and make himself out to be God's equal.

Paralytic by the pool. The author of the Fourth Gospel has taken an older healing story, derived possibly from a written source, and used it as the nucleus of a much larger complex. What begins in vv. 1–9a as a simple healing turns into a dispute about sabbath observance and ultimately into an accusation of blasphemy based on Jesus' references to God as his Father (vv. 9b–18). John concludes that these practices on the part of Jesus led to attempts to kill him.

This passage illustrates the technique of the Fourth Gospel: a single incident functions as the core to which the author adds elements that originally were not part of the underlying narrative event. In this case, the reader does not learn until v. 9b that it was on the sabbath that Jesus told the invalid to pick up his mat and walk around (and so demonstrate that he had been cured). Inappropriate sabbath activity then becomes the theme of the dispute with the "Judeans," who not only object to the violation of sabbath restrictions, but also charge that Jesus makes himself equal to God. This technique of embedding an older piece of narrative tradition in a more elaborate sequence betrays the inclination of the author of the Fourth Gospel to present the story of Jesus in large chunks, in contrast to the synoptic gospels, which narrate the story in short, self-contained episodes. The larger frame, vv. 9b–18, has almost certainly been provided by the imagination of the author of the gospel.

The Fellows were inclined to the view that vv. 2–9a is an old healing story with the usual components: the afflicted person is introduced with some indication of the gravity of the illness; Jesus heals him with a word of command; the victim demonstrates that he has been cured. By way of exception, in v. 6 Jesus initiates a conversation with the paralytic.

There are similarities between this story and the account of the paralytic in Mark 2:1–12, which many scholars take to be alternate versions of the same event: Both victims are crippled or paralyzed; Jesus heals by command; both victims are told to take up their mats and walk; and in both cases some connection is made between their malady and sin.

There are of course differences as well. Mark's account is set in a house in Capernaum; John's at the pool of Bethzatha in Jerusalem. The paralytic in Mark is aided by four friends who bring him to Jesus; the afflicted in John is alone, with no one to help him into the pool when the miraculous stirring of the waters occurs. The man in John does not express his faith; in Mark it is the faith of the four friends that impresses Jesus. The Markan story is not necessarily connected with the sabbath; in John the sabbath is the bone of contention.

The similarities between the two versions, and the possibility that the two stories may derive from a common older source, prompt some scholars to wonder whether one story has developed two faces. In that case, the details are no longer historical. The result was a gray weighted average.

5 [19]**This is how Jesus would respond:** "As God is my witness, the
son can't do anything on his own; <he can only do> what he sees the
Father doing. Whatever <the Father> does, the son does as well. [20]The

Monologue: son & father
Jn 5:19–47
Source: John

Father loves the son, and shows him everything he does. He is going to show him even greater works, so that you'll be amazed. [21]Just as the Father raises the dead and gives them life, the son also gives life to everyone he wants. [22]Not that the Father condemns anyone; rather, he has turned all such decisions over to the son, [23]so that everyone will honor the son, just as they honor the Father. Whoever does not honor the son does not honor the Father who sent him.

[24]"As God is my witness: Those who hear my word and believe the one who sent me have real life and do not come up for trial. No, they have passed through death into life. [25]I swear to God: The time is coming—in fact, it's already here—for the dead to hear the voice of God's son and, because they've heard it, to live. [26]Just as the Father is himself the source of life, he has also made the son to be the source of life. [27]And he has given him the authority to do the judging, because he is the son of Adam. [28]Don't be surprised; the time is coming when all who are in their graves will hear his voice [29]and come out—those who have done good will be raised to life, and those who have done vile acts raised to stand trial.

[30]"I can do nothing on my own authority. I base my decision on what I hear; and my decision is the right one, because I don't consider what I want but what the one who sent me wants. [31]If I give evidence on my own behalf, my testimony is not reliable. [32]Someone else testifies on my behalf, and I am certain the evidence he gives about me is reliable. [33]You've sent <messengers> to John, and he has provided reliable testimony. [34]I'm not interested in evidence from a human source; rather, I make these statements so you will be rescued. [35]<John> was a bright shining light, and you were willing to bask in that light of his for a while. [36]But I have given evidence that is even weightier than John's: the tasks the Father gave me to carry out. These very tasks I am performing are evidence that the Father has sent me. [37]The one who sent me has himself also given evidence on my behalf. You've never heard his voice, you've never seen his image, [38]and his message doesn't find a home in you, since you don't believe the one he has sent.

[39]"You pore over the <sacred> writings, because you imagine that in them there's real life to be had. They do indeed give evidence on my behalf, [40]yet you refuse to come to me to have life. [41]I'm not interested in any human praise; [42]but I <also> know that you have none of God's love in you. [43]I've come in my Father's name, and you don't welcome me; if others come in their own name, you'll welcome them. [44]How can you believe, since you accept praise from each other but don't even consider the praise that comes from the only God? [45]Don't suppose that I'll be your accuser before the Father. You have an accuser, and it's Moses—the one you thought you could trust. [46]But if you really believed Moses, you'd believe me; after all, I'm the one he wrote about. [47]But since you don't really believe what he wrote, how are you going to believe what I say?"

Monologue: son & father. The initiation of the monologue in v. 19a is of course the work of the fourth evangelist. The Fellows colored the entire speech of Jesus in vv. 19b–47 black in *The Five Gospels.* The minimal narrative frame given that speech also merits a black designation.

6 After these events, Jesus crossed to the far side of the Sea of Galilee, <also known as the Sea of> Tiberias. 2A huge crowd was following him, because they wanted to see the miracles he was performing on the sick. 3Jesus climbed up the mountain, and he sat down there with his disciples. 4It was about time for the Jewish celebration of Passover. 5Jesus looks up and sees a big crowd approaching him, and he says to Philip, "Where are we going to get enough bread to feed this mob?" **(6He was saying this to test him; you see, Jesus already knew what he was going to do.)**

7"Half a year's wages wouldn't buy enough bread for everyone to have a bite," Philip said.

8One of his disciples, Andrew, Simon Peter's brother, says to him, 9"There's a lad here with five loaves of barley bread and two fish; but what does that amount to for so many?"

10Jesus said, "Have the people sit down." **(They were in a grassy place.) So they sat down; the men numbered about five thousand. 11Jesus took the loaves, gave thanks, and passed them around to the people sitting there, along with the fish, and all of them had as much as they wanted. 12And when they had eaten their fill, he says to his disciples,** "Gather up the leftovers so that nothing goes to waste."

13So they gathered them up and filled twelve baskets with scraps from the five barley loaves—from what was left over. 14When these folks saw the miracle he had performed they would say, "Yes indeed! This is undoubtedly the Prophet who is to come into the world." 15Jesus perceived that they were about to come and make him king by force, so he retreated once again to the mountain by himself.

Loaves & fish for 5,000
Jn 6:1–15
Mk 6:35–44, Mt 14:15–21, Lk 9:12–17
Sources: John, Mark
Cf. Mk 8:1–9, Mt 15:32–39

Loaves & fish for 5,000. The relation of John's story of the multiplication of loaves to the synoptic accounts is disputed. However, some generalizations can be made. John's account, it appears, is literarily independent of the synoptic account (John did not base his version on the written text of Mark). Yet the stories in John and Mark probably have a common ancestor. Indeed, all six versions of the loaves and fish probably go back to a single oral source, which then developed along slightly different lines.

One way to account for the common ancestry of such stories in the Fourth Gospel is the view that oral miracle stories were collected into a written gospel of miracles, and that one such collection was employed by the fourth evangelist in the creation of his gospel. Seminar Fellow Robert T. Fortna and others have advanced the thesis that the author of the Fourth Gospel found seven "signs" or miracles in his source:

1. Miracle at Cana (John 2:1–11)
2. Cure of the official's son (John 4:46–54)
3. Cure of the paralytic by the pool (John 5:1–9)
4. Loaves and fish for five thousand (John 6:1–15)
5. Jesus walks on the water (John 6:16–21)
6. Cure of the man born blind (John 9:1–8)
7. The resuscitation of Lazarus (John 11:1–44)

It has often been noted that five of these stories have counterparts in Mark's gospel. The story of the paralytic by the pool has its counterpart in Mark's story of the paralytic (2:1–12). The loaves and fish story, of course, has two parallels in Mark (6:35–4, 8:1–10). Jesus walks on the water in Mark (6:45–52). Jesus cures a man of blindness not once (8:22–26) but twice (blind Bartimaeus, 10:46–52). And, if we add the story in Secret Mark to the list, we have a parallel to the resuscitation of Lazarus in SecMark 1:1–11. (For information about Secret Mark, consult the cameo, pp. 116–17; other possibilities for a gospel of miracles are discussed in the cameo, "A Gospel of Miracles?" pp. 388–89.)

It thus appears that both John and Mark knew a sequence of miracle stories from some earlier source. That sequence probably had a checkered history; it may have been transmitted in both oral and written forms. What seems clear is that both Mark and John are at least twice removed from their common source, and thus, while displaying some striking similarities, they deviate in numerous details.

The feeding of the five thousand in the Fourth Gospel is developed as a controversy about the bread of life (6:16–71). Jesus claims that the crowds follow him, not because they had witnessed miracles, but because they had all been well fed (v. 26). Jesus urges them rather to work for food that lasts, real food (v. 27). The real food Jesus has to offer is himself; "I am the bread of life," he proclaims (v. 35). He goes on: "Your ancestors ate manna in the desert, but they still died" (v. 49) The bread that Jesus gives, on the other hand, comes down from heaven; those who eat this bread will never die (v. 50). The bread of which Jesus was speaking, it turns out, is his mortal flesh (v. 51). This pronouncement they find offensive and perhaps incomprehensible. Some of them leave him as a result.

It is clear that John sees a connection between the miraculous multiplication of loaves and the manna "sent from heaven" to feed the Israelites during their Sinai wandering. And this discourse on true bread is his substitute for the synoptic version of the last supper, which is conspicuously absent from the Fourth Gospel. In the synoptic account, the foundation is laid for the eucharist tradition involving bread and wine; John has Jesus wash the feet of his followers at the last supper (13:1–20) rather than interpret the bread and wine as his body and blood.

Seminar Fellow John Dominic Crossan has argued that there were two eucharistic traditions in the early Jesus movement, one combining bread and fish, the other bread and wine. In the earliest iconography of the Christian movement, it is the eleven or seven disciples joined in a common meal of bread and fish that prevails. The last supper with bread and wine does not appear in early catacomb or sarcophagus art.

While the story as John records it does not represent a specific event in the life of Jesus, it probably does represent the narrative ritualization of a common practice: Jesus and his friends sharing a common meal of bread and fish. Like other versions of the story, this one also has to be colored black.

Jesus walks on water
Jn 6:16–21
Mk 6:47–52, Mt 14:22–33
Sources: John, Mark

6 [16]**As evening approached, his disciples went down to the sea.**
[17]**They boarded a boat and were trying to cross the lake to Caper-**
naum. It had already gotten dark, and Jesus still had not joined them.
[18]**A strong wind began to blow and the sea was getting rough.** [19]**When**
they had rowed about three or four miles, they catch sight of Jesus
walking on the lake and coming toward the boat. They were fright-
ened, [20]**but he says to them,** "Don't be afraid! It's me." [21]**Then they**
would have taken him on board, but the boat instantly arrived at the
shore they had been making for.

Jesus walks on water. In the Fourth Gospel, the story of the walking on water is sandwiched between the miraculous feeding of five thousand in the wilderness (6:1–15) and the dispute about the meaning of bread (6:22–71). In this gospel, an event often leads to a controversy related to the event. The miracle of Jesus as a hydropatetic (one who walks on water) appears unrelated to the bread stories. In Mark, too, the connection between the loaves and fish and walking on the water is weak; Mark compensates for the lack of continuity by explaining in Mark 6:52: "You see, the disciples hadn't understood about the loaves; they were being obstinate." The lack of strong connection and Mark's feeble attempt to invent one has persuaded scholars to conclude that the two stories were arbitrarily joined, either in the oral tradition or in some hypothetical written source lying behind both John and Mark—they have simply reproduced the sequence.

Numerous scholars hold the view that a gospel of signs or a gospel of miracles served as the basis for the present Gospel of John. That source may have contained stories of seven miracles altogether, beginning with the miracle at Cana and ending with the resuscitation of Lazarus. Another view is that in the composition of their gospels both John and Mark made use of a source that contained a collection of five miracles. A third possibility is that Mark inherited a double cycle of stories: two sea miracles, two miraculous meals of bread and fish in the wilderness, plus other healing stories, and the Fourth Gospel made use of Mark as a source. (The theory is explored in the cameo "A Gospel of Miracles?" pp. 388–89.)

The setting the Fourth Gospel gives to the walking on the water differs from the one found in Mark. In Mark, Jesus makes his disciples get into the boat and head for Bethsaida at the north end of the lake. Meanwhile, Jesus disperses the crowd and goes off to the mountain to pray (Mark 6:45–46). In the Fourth Gospel, the crowd has just attempted to take Jesus and make him king, so he

A GOSPEL OF MIRACLES?

Several scholars have noted the possibility that collections of miracle stories antedated the creation of the New Testament gospels. Such collections did not survive as separate written texts, to be sure, yet certain features of both the Gospel of Mark and the Gospel of John hint that such collections may have once existed. The possibilities are three in number.

Some scholars have proposed that a Gospel of Signs or Miracles served as the backbone of the first half of the Gospel of John. Attempts have been made to reconstruct such a gospel from the text of the Fourth Gospel. One such attempt has been made by Robert T. Fortna, an active member of the Jesus Seminar. This proposed Gospel of Signs consisted of seven miracles:

1. Miracle at Cana (John 2:1–11)
2. The cure of the official's son (John 4:46–54)
3. The cure of the paralytic by the pool (John 5:1–9)
4. Loaves and fish for five thousand (John 6:1–15)
5. Jesus walks on the water (John 6:16–21)
6. The cure of the man born blind (John 9:1–8)
7. The resuscitation of Lazarus (John 11:1–44)

The primary evidence for this view consists of the deliberate sequence given to the first two events: the miracle at Cana is the first sign that Jesus performed (2:11), and the cure of the official's son is the second (4:54). The remaining miracles, although not given numbers in the Fourth Gospel, add up to seven when combined with the first two. The argument is that a sequence of *seven* miracles cannot have been a coincidence.

The second possibility of a gospel of miracles consists in a double cycle in the Gospel of Mark.

1a. Jesus rebukes the wind & sea (Mark 4:35–42)	1b. Jesus walks on the sea (Mark 6:47–52)
2a. The demon of Gerasa (Mark 5:1–20)	2b. Jesus cures a blind man (Mark 8:22–26)
3a. Jesus cures Jairus' daughter (Mark 5:21–24a, 35–43)	3b. Jesus cures the Greek woman's daughter (Mark 7:24b–30)
4a. Jesus cures the woman with a vaginal hemorrhage (Mark 5:24b–34)	4b. Jesus cures a deaf mute (Mark 7:31–37)
5a. Loaves and fish for five thousand (Mark 6:35–44)	5b. Loaves and fish for four thousand (Mark 8:1–9)

heads for the mountain to get away from them (6:15). Not knowing what to do, the disciples go down to the sea and embark for Capernaum (6:16). These discrepancies, minor though they appear to be, suggest that the introductory setting is the work of the individual evangelist.

In Mark, Jesus approaches the boat by walking on the water at about three o'clock in the morning. He intends to pass them by. The disciples cry out in fear; Jesus reassures them, climbs into the boat, and the storm subsides (Mark

The parallelism between the two series of five miracles is what suggested an underlying source. Two series that begin with a water miracle and end with a miraculous feeding in the wilderness looks like a sequence that Mark borrowed from a source. Alternatively, some scholars take the view that Mark deliberately doubled the series, in some cases creating parallels out of his imagination, in other cases making use of stories known to him from the oral tradition.

A third possible Gospel of Miracles was proposed by John Dominic Crossan; it builds on parallels between the Gospel of Mark and the Fourth Gospel.

1a. Jesus cures a paralytic (Mark 2:1–12)	1b. The paralytic by the pool (John 5:1–18)
2a. Loaves and fish for five thousand (Mark 6:35–44)	2b. Loaves and fish for five thousand (John 6:1–15)
3a. Jesus walks on the sea (Mark 6:45–52)	3b. Jesus walks on the sea (John 6:16–21)
4a. Jesus cures a blind man (Mark 8:22–26)	4b. Jesus cures the man born blind (John 9:1–7)
5a. Jesus raises a young man (Secret Mark 1:1–10)	5b. Jesus raises Lazarus (John 11:1–44)

The cogency of this proposal depends on two assumptions: first, that Secret Mark was the original version of the Gospel of Mark (additional information can be found in the cameo "Secret Mark," pp. 116–17); second, that the order shared by Mark and John is more than a coincidence. Crossan suggests that the five miracles derived from a gospel of miracles were supplemented by the addition of the first and second "signs," the changing of the water into wine (John 2:1–11) and the cure of the official's son (John 4:46–54), to form the Gospel of Signs.

The existence of a Gospel of Miracles would of course move the written record of these stories one step closer to the events they purport to report. At the same time, the existence of such a gospel would reduce the attestation for these stories to a single source, thus weakening the evidence for their historicity. None of these proposals, however, has commanded universal scholarly consent. Scholars are not even agreed that there was a gospel of miracles that preceded the narrative gospels. Unlike the hypothetical Sayings Gospel Q, which rests on impressive verbal agreements between Matthew and Luke, the existence of a gospel of miracles lacks solid textual evidence.

6:47–51). John has a different ending: When Jesus gets into the boat, it suddenly arrives at its destination; nothing further is said about the storm (v. 21).

Like its counterpart in the Gospel of Mark, John's version of walking on the water is also an epiphany or a theophany. The appearance of a divine or heavenly figure, such as an angel, is often depicted as a luminous apparition, as in stories of the risen Jesus or the young man or angel at the empty tomb. In the Fourth Gospel this aspect is not mentioned. In Mark, on the other hand, the disciples think Jesus is a phantom or spook and are terrified (Mark 6:49–50). In John the disciples are frightened until Jesus identifies himself with the formula so common in that gospel: *ego eimi,* "It is I!" which calls to mind other "I am" sayings. But that is as far as the author goes in portraying Jesus as a divine being in this sea story. The evangelist appears more interested in getting to the extended thematic dialogue, in which Jesus claims to be the bread of life (v. 35), the bread that came down from heaven (v. 41), and is thus God's gift to the people. In the Fourth Gospel the major epiphany is the appearance of Jesus as the bread sent from heaven, replicating the miracle of the manna in the wilderness centuries earlier.

Discourse on bread
Jn 6:22–71
Source: John

6 **[22]The next day, the crowd, which was still on the other side of
the lake, remembered that there had been only one boat there, and
that Jesus had not gotten into that boat with the disciples, but that
his disciples had set off alone. [23]Other boats came out from Tiberias,
near the place where they had eaten bread. [24]So when the crowd saw
that neither Jesus nor his disciples were there, they, too, got into
boats and set out for Capernaum to look for Jesus.**

**[25]They found him on the other side of the lake and asked him,
"Rabbi, when did you get here?"**

[26]"I swear to God," **Jesus replied,** "you're looking for me only
because you ate the bread and had all you wanted, not because you
witnessed miracles. [27]Don't work for food that goes to waste, but for
food that lasts—food for real life—which the son of Adam will give
you; on him God the Father has put his stamp of approval."

**[28]So they asked him, "What must we do to set about what God
wants done?"**

[29]"What God wants you to do," **Jesus answered,** "is to believe in the
one God has sent."

**[30]They asked him, "What miracle are you going to perform so we
can see it and come to believe in you? What 'labor' are you going to
perform? [31]Our ancestors had manna to eat in the wilderness. As the
scripture puts it, 'He gave them bread from heaven to eat.'"**

[32]Jesus responded to them: "I swear to God, it was not Moses who
gave you bread from heaven to eat; rather, it is my Father who gives
you real bread from heaven. [33]I mean this: God's bread comes down
from heaven and gives life to the world."

[34]"Sir," they said to him, "give us this bread every time."

[35]Jesus explained to them: "I am the bread of life. Anyone who
comes to me will never be hungry again, and anyone who believes in
me will never again be thirsty. [36]But I told you this: You have even seen
me, yet you still refuse to believe. [37]Every one the Father gives me will
come to me, and I would never reject anyone who comes to me.
[38]Understand, I have come down from heaven, not to do what I want,
but to do what the one who sent me wants. [39]What the one who sent

me wants is this: that I lose nothing put in my care, but that I resurrect it on the last day. 40My Father's intent is that all those who see the son and believe in him will have real life, and I'll resurrect them on the last day."

41**The Judeans then began to grumble about him because he had said,** "I am the bread that came down from heaven." 42**They would say things like, "Isn't this Jesus, Joseph's son? Don't we know both his father and his mother? How can he now say, 'I have come down from heaven'?"**

43**Jesus replied,** "Don't grumble under your breath. 44People cannot come to me unless the Father who sent me takes them in, and I will resurrect them on the last day. 45As the prophets put it: 'And they will all be informed by God.'

"Everyone who listens to the Father and learns from him comes to me. 46Not that anyone has seen the Father; the only one who has seen the Father is the one who is from God. 47I swear to God, the believer has real life. 48I am the bread of life. 49Your ancestors ate the manna in the desert, but they still died. 50This is the bread that comes down from heaven: anyone who eats it never dies. 51I am the life-giving bread that came down from heaven. Anyone who eats this bread will live forever. And the bread that I will give for the world's life is my mortal flesh."

52**At this point the Judeans began quarreling among themselves: "How can this fellow give us his mortal flesh to eat?"**

53**So Jesus told them:** "I swear to God, if you don't eat the son of Adam's mortal flesh and drink his blood, you don't possess life. 54Everyone who feeds on my mortal flesh and drinks my blood possesses real life, and I will resurrect them on the last day. 55For my mortal flesh is real food, and my blood real drink. 56Those who feed on my mortal flesh and drink my blood are part of me, and I am part of them. 57The Father of life sent me, and I have life because of the Father. Just so, anyone who feeds on me will have life because of me. 58This is the bread that comes down from heaven. Unlike your ancestors who ate <manna> and then died, anyone who feeds on this bread will live forever."

59**He said these things while he was teaching in the synagogue at Capernaum.**

60**When the disciples heard this, many responded, "This teaching is offensive. Who can take it seriously?"**

61**Jesus knew his disciples were grumbling about it and said to them:** "Does this shock you, then? 62What if you should see the son of Adam going back up to where he was to begin with? 63The spirit is life-giving; mortal flesh is good for nothing. The words I have used are 'spirit' and 'life.' 64Yet some of you still don't believe." **(Jesus was aware from the outset which ones were not believers, and he knew who would turn him in.)** 65And so he would say, "This is why I told you: People cannot come to me unless the Father has granted it to them."

66 **As a result, many of his disciples pulled out and would no
longer travel about with him.**
67 **Jesus then said to the twelve,** "Do you want to leave too?"
68 **Simon Peter replied to him, "Lord, is there anyone else we can
turn to? You have the words of real life!** 69 **We have become believers
and are certain that you are God's holy one."**
70 **Jesus responded to them,** "Isn't this why I chose you twelve?
Even so, one of you is a devil." **(** 71 **He was of course referring to Judas,
son of Simon Iscariot, one of the twelve, who was going to turn him
in.)**

Discourse on bread. The narrative transition in vv. 22–24 presents scholars with an insoluble puzzle, just as it did ancient scribes and commentators. The large number of textual variants in the Greek manuscripts point to an erratic textual history, probably because the temporal and spatial references do not make good sense. "The next day" in v. 22 probably does not indicate a strict temporal reference, but is a vague marker of sequence: "This is what Jesus did next." The crowd is still on "the other side of the lake" where the feeding took place; the other side was presumably the east side (6:1). There are allegedly 5,000 males involved, not counting women and children (6:10). There was only one boat at the point of embarkation, which the disciples took; Jesus had not gone with them (v. 22). Now we are to think that other boats came out from Tiberias, which is located on the west side of the lake, and that Tiberias is adjacent to the site of the miraculous feeding (v. 23). The crowd sees that Jesus is not there (it is not clear where "there" is) and embarks in boats for Capernaum (v. 24). The geography makes the reader dizzy.

In chapter 5, Jesus is in Jerusalem. In chapter 6, he crosses the lake (6:1) where the feeding takes place. Since the movement of Jesus from Jerusalem to the far side of the Sea of Galilee does not make sense, some scholars have proposed reversing the order of chapters five and six.

The best solution to the problem is to assume that the storyteller is confused and so has garbled the time, place, and order of events. Black is the correct designation for vv. 22–24. Even Raymond Brown, who usually attempts to work out some plausible substratum of history, admits that there seems to be "no facile solution for the difficulties involved."[74]

The crowd catches up with Jesus "on the other side of the lake" and asks him when he got there—a reference, it seems, to the miracle of walking on the water (v. 25). But Jesus does not answer the question of when; he responds instead with remarks about why the crowd has followed him and those remarks do not reflect much credit on his audience: they traipse along after because their bellies were filled with the loaves and fish (v. 26). The group that witnessed the miraculous feeding is apparently the same group that Jesus now addresses. This provides the evangelist with a transition to a long discourse about the bread of life (vv. 27–71).

The discourse is cast in the form of a dialogue set in the synagogue at Capernaum (v. 59). In a second section, an acerbic exchange with the disciples (vv. 60–66) results in many of them leaving his entourage. A final segment devoted to the twelve (vv. 67–71) allows Jesus to observe that even one of the twelve is a devil.

It is inconceivable that the Jesus of the parables, aphorisms, and witticisms formulated the remarks attributed to him in this passage. Jesus makes outrageous claims that he is the bread of life and that unless his listeners eat of the son of Adam's mortal flesh and drink his blood, they cannot possess life (v. 53). Such a claim is inconsistent with the sage who taught that forgiveness is reciprocal and that self-effacement is the only way to real life. In *The Five Gospels,* all these words are colored black. Since the words did not derive from Jesus, the Fellows concluded that the narrative framework was equally the creation of the evangelist. They therefore decided on a black designation.

Not my time
Jn 7:1–9
Source: John

7 **After this, Jesus moved around in Galilee; he decided not to go**
into Judea, because the Judeans were looking for a chance to kill
him. 2The Jewish celebration of Sukkoth was coming, 3so his broth-
ers said to him, "Get out of here; go to Judea so your disciples can
see the miracles you're doing. 4No one who wants public recognition
does things in secret. If you are going to do these <miracles>, let the
world see you." (5Evidently, even his brothers didn't have any confi-
dence in him.)

6Jesus replies, "It's not my time yet. It's always your time. 7The
world can never hate you, but it hates me, because I provide evidence
that its actions are evil. 8You go ahead to the celebration; I'm not going
to this celebration because my time hasn't yet arrived."

9With this piece of advice, he stayed behind in Galilee.

Not my time. Like many of the other narrative segments of the Fourth Gospel, this section, too, is the invention of the evangelist. It has no parallels in the synoptic tradition. The only question is whether it preserves any traces of historical attitudes or events. Apparently it does not.

The evangelist will take Jesus to Jerusalem only when his "time" has come. Jesus' preliminary response to his mother at Cana was that his time had not yet come (2:4). For the Fourth Gospel the time of Jesus is the time of his elevation on the cross, his lifting, his execution. When that time comes he will go to Jerusalem.

According to the storyteller, Jesus elects not to go to Jerusalem at present because he knows of the hostility of the Judeans in that city. His brothers take the worldly view: If you want to be known, if you are going to perform miracles, let the world see you. In a narrative aside, the author tells his readers that Jesus' brothers evidently had no confidence in him.

The approaching feast was that of Sukkoth, also known as Booths or Tabernacles, the fall festival. His "time," according to the Gospel of John was Passover: he was to be executed at the very time the Passover lambs were being slaughtered. Consequently, Jesus was to escape arrest and execution at the feast of Tabernacles (8:59).

This is the last time in the Gospel of John Jesus is depicted as going to Jerusalem. Later he leaves Jerusalem temporarily, but he does not return to Galilee. He goes to Jerusalem secretly (7:10), just as he does in the Gospel of Mark (9:30). Yet the synoptic representations of Jesus' final visit to Jerusalem and that of the Fourth Gospel are very different. For one thing, John has Jesus go to Jerusalem in the fall and stay until the following spring; in the synoptics he arrives in early spring only days before Passover and his arrest and death.

The author of this gospel is creating sequence and setting as he goes along, without reference to historical data of any kind. Black is the only way to represent the information provided in this segment.

Secret visit to Jerusalem
Jn 7:10–13
No parallels
Source: John

7 [10]**After his brothers had left for the celebration, he went too; he didn't go openly but traveled incognito. [11]So the Judeans kept an eye out for him at the celebration, inquiring repeatedly, "Where is that fellow?" [12]and there was a good deal of wrangling about him in the crowd. Some were claiming, "He's a good man," but others dissented, "No, he's just hoodwinking the public." [13]Yet no one spoke openly about him for fear of the Judeans.**

Secret visit to Jerusalem. The evangelist is again freely editorializing on what the Judeans did and thought and how the crowd thought of Jesus. His remarks are fiction, pure and simple. Black is correct.

Lecture in the temple
Jn 7:14–52
Source: John

7 [14]**When the celebration was half over, Jesus went up to the temple area and started teaching. [15]The Judeans were taken aback, saying, "This man is uneducated; how come he's so articulate?"**

[16]**To this Jesus responded,** "What I'm teaching does not originate with me but with the one who sent me. [17]Anyone who sets out to do what God wants knows well enough whether this teaching originates with God or whether I'm speaking solely on my own authority. [18]All who speak on their own authority are after praise for themselves. But as for him who is concerned with the praise of the one who sent him—he is truthful; there is nothing false about him.

[19]"Moses gave you the Law, didn't he? (Not that any of you observes the Law!) Why are you bent on killing me?"

[20]**The crowd answered, "You're out of your mind! Who's trying to kill you?"**

[21]"I do one miracle," **Jesus replied,** "and you're stunned! [22]That's why Moses gave you circumcision—not that it really came from Moses, but from our ancestors—and you can circumcise someone on the sabbath day. [23]If someone can be circumcised on the sabbath day without breaking Moses' Law, can you really be angry with me for making someone completely well on the sabbath day? [24]Don't judge by appearances; judge by what is right."

[25]**Some of the Jerusalemites began to say, "Isn't this the one they**

are trying to kill? 26Look, here he is, speaking in public, and they say
nothing to him. You don't suppose the authorities have now con-
cluded that he is the Anointed? 27But wait—we know where this fel-
low's from. When the Anointed comes, no one is supposed to know
where he's from."

28As a consequence, while he was teaching in the temple area,
Jesus shouted out: "It's true, you know me; it's true, you know where
I'm from. But I haven't come on my own—the one who sent me is
authentic, and you don't have any idea who that is. 29I know who he is,
because I came from him and he is the one who sent me."

30They would have arrested him then and there, but no one laid a
hand on him, because his time had not yet come.

31Many people in the crowd believed in him and would ask,
"When the Anointed comes, is he likely to perform any more mir-
acles than this man?"

32The Pharisees heard the crowd wrangling about him; so the
ranking priests and the Pharisees sent deputies to arrest him.

33Then Jesus said, "I'll be with you a little longer; then I'll return to
the one who sent me. 34You'll look for me, but you won't find me:
where I am you can't come."

35So the Judeans reflected aloud, "Where is this man going to go,
that we won't find him? Will he go to the Greek Diaspora, to teach
the Greeks? 36What is this spiel he's giving us—'You'll look for me,
but you won't find me: where I am you can't come'?**"**

37On the last and most important day of the celebration, Jesus
stood up and shouted out, "Anyone who's thirsty must come to me
and drink. 38The one who believes in me—as scripture puts it—'will be
the source of rivers of life-giving water.'"

(39He was talking about the spirit that those who believed in him
were about to receive. You realize, of course, that there was no spirit
as yet, since Jesus hadn't been glorified.)

40When they heard this declaration, some in the crowd said, "This
man has to be the Prophet." 41"The Anointed!" others said. Still
others objected: "Is the Anointed to come from Galilee? 42Doesn't
scripture teach that the Anointed is to be descended from David and
come from the village of Bethlehem, where David lived?" (43As you
can see, the crowd was split over who he was.)

44Some were in favor of arresting him, but no one laid a hand on
him. 45Then the deputies came back to the ranking priests and the
Pharisees, who said to them, "Why haven't you brought him in?"

46The deputies answered, "No one ever talked like this!"

47The Pharisees came back at them, "Don't tell us you've been
duped too! 48None of the authorities or the Pharisees have believed
in him, have they? 49As for this rabble, they are ignorant of the Law!
Damn them!"

50Then Nicodemus, who was one of their number—he had earlier
paid Jesus a visit—challenges them: 51"Since when does our Law

pass judgment on people without first letting them speak for themselves, and without establishing the facts?"

52 They retorted, "You wouldn't be from Galilee too, now would you? Check for yourself: no prophet has ever come from Galilee."

Lecture in the temple. Jesus has gone to Jerusalem incognito (7:10) and when the weeklong festival is half over, he goes into the temple area, now crowded with pilgrims, and starts teaching. In the dialogue that follows, as the evangelist represents it, Jesus engages various groups in a seesaw conversation focused on his origin. In v. 15 the Judeans question his learning. Jesus responds in vv. 16–18: his teaching does not come from learning but from God.

In v. 19, Jesus asks why "they" are trying to kill him. The crowd now surprisingly answers (v. 20): You must be out of your mind for thinking anyone is trying to kill you. And yet in vv. 25–26, the Jerusalemites are clear that it was the authorities who would like to execute Jesus.

The one miracle Jesus claims to have done is evidently the cure of the paralytic by the pool (5:1–9). The Judeans were apparently angry with him for making someone well on the sabbath, although they themselves are willing to circumcise a newborn boy on the sabbath (vv. 21–24).

Now the exchange switches to "some of the Jerusalemites" (v. 25), who wonder why the authorities have done nothing to Jesus as he speaks in public. They wonder whether Jesus may actually be the messiah, but concede that can't be: everyone knows that Jesus is from Galilee, but no one is supposed to know where the Anointed comes from (vv. 26–27).

That gives Jesus the opportunity to change the subject once again, this time to the question of his origin (vv. 29). Now the narrator tells the reader that they would have arrested him then and there, except that his time had not yet come (v. 30).

The storyteller is an omniscient narrator: he or she knows that many in the crowd really believe in Jesus (v. 31) and this prompts the Pharisees to send deputies to arrest him (v. 32). The Pharisee were a religious party and not temple officials, so they of course did not have this prerogative. Then when Jesus tells the Pharisees that he is going away and that they won't be able to find him (v. 33), the Judeans respond with the literal puzzlement that earlier characterized Nicodemus and the woman at the well: where can he go where we won't be able to find him? (vv. 35–36).

Jesus now changes the subject once again, this time to life-giving water. The evangelist explains that Jesus is talking about the spirit his followers were to receive (vv. 38–39).

The storyteller again assumes his role as omniscient narrator and explains the different views of Jesus in the crowd (40–43). Some of the crowd wanted to arrest Jesus, we are told (v. 44), but the deputies who had been dispatched in v. 32 come back empty-handed. The Pharisees are irate; they think the deputies have been duped, and condemn the crowd as ignorant of the Law (vv. 45–49).

Finally, the evangelist reintroduces Nicodemus, who criticizes the authorities for not letting Jesus tell his side of the story. They respond with a slur on Nicodemus' place of origin (vv. 50–52).

This complicated dialogue involving numerous parties and frequent changes in focus can only have been the creation of the evangelist. The sole trace of historical reminiscence in the whole construction is the notice in v. 15 that Jesus was articulate although uneducated. That piece of information is probably correct because it is confirmed by data from the other gospels. The content of the dialogue expresses the theological interests and perspectives of the Fourth Gospel and its narrative structure is entirely fictive. Except for the notice in v. 15, black is appropriate.

First Stone Gospel
Jn 7:53–8:11
No parallels
Source: John

8 [53]Then everybody returned home, [1]but Jesus went to the Mount
of Olives. [2]Early in the morning he showed up again in the temple
area and everybody gathered around him. He sat down and began to
teach them.
[3]The scholars and Pharisees bring him a woman who was caught
committing adultery. They make her stand there in front of every-
body, [4]and they address him, "Teacher, this woman was caught in
the act of adultery. [5]In the Law Moses commanded us to stone
women like this. What do you say?" ([6]They said this to trap him, so
they would have something to accuse him of.)
Jesus stooped down and began drawing on the ground with his
finger. [7]When they insisted on an answer, he stood up and replied,
"Whoever is sinless in this crowd should go ahead and throw the first
stone at her." [8]Once again he squatted down and continued writing
on the ground.
[9]His audience began to drift away, one by one—the elders were
the first to go—until Jesus was the only one left, with the woman
there in front of him.
[10]Jesus stood up and said to her, "Woman, where is everybody?
Hasn't anyone condemned you?"
[11]She replied, "No one, sir."
"I don't condemn you either," Jesus said. "You're free to go, but
from now on, no more sinning."

First Stone Gospel. This fascinating little anecdote is an intrusion into the Gospel of John. The earliest ancient manuscripts of John do not have it, and modern scholars are virtually unanimous in concluding that it was not an original part of the Fourth Gospel. It does not match the style of John and it breaks the flow of text from 7:52 to 8:12. In ancient manuscripts, moreover, its position is not fixed: It sometimes appears in John between 7:52 and 8:12, but it is also found at other locations in John—after 7:36, after 7:44, and at the end of the gospel; it even appears in one group of manuscripts after Luke 21:38. It does not have a fixed canonical home.

If it is a "stray" or "orphan" text, how is it to be assessed? Is it an old story or a late legend? Can it possibly reflect anything Jesus did or said?

The story appears to have been well known in the ancient church. Eusebius of Caesarea reports that Papias, another early Christian scholar, knew the story of a woman accused of sin, a story that was recorded in the Gospel according to the Hebrews. Eusebius lived in the third/fourth centuries C.E. Papias died ca. 130 C.E. The Gospel of the Hebrews was probably composed some time in the early second century C.E. A third-century document known as the Didascalia Apostolorum ("The Teachings of the Apostles") has an unmistakable reference to the story. The Didascalia originated in Syria, which means that the story was probably known in an oral form in Syria by the late second century. However, Augustine (354–430 C.E.) and Ambrose (339–397 C.E.) regarded it as a part of the Gospel; Jerome (342–420 C.E.) included it in the Vulgate, the official Bible of the Roman Catholic Church. There can be little doubt that the story is quite old.

An impartial evaluation of the story has been impeded by its preservation as a part of the Gospel of John. Since it is known only as a "textual variant" (a textual variant is a kind of footnote to a reconstructed Greek text) in one of the canonical gospels, the argument has been focused on whether or not it was to be considered canonical. Roman Catholic scholars have tended to assume its canonicity because it was included in the Latin Vulgate. They are therefore obligated to treat it as scripture. Critical scholars, both Protestant and Catholic, have tended to exclude it from consideration for the simple reason that it did not really belong to any of the canonical gospels. It has therefore been evaluated and usually rejected as a textual variant rather than as an independent fragment. The incidental fact that it survived only when attached to Luke or John has played a negative role in its treatment by critical scholars.

The beginning of the fragment indicates that it does not belong to the Johannine context into which it was most frequently inserted (John 7:53–8:11): The narrator tells us that everybody returned home, while Jesus went to the Mount of Olives. That much indicates that Jesus was in Jerusalem at the time, and that he and his companions left the city at the end of the day. The next day, the narrator continues, Jesus goes back into the city to the temple area to teach. It was on that occasion that some scholars and Pharisees allegedly present him with a tough judicial decision: Should we stone this woman or not?

The narrative setting—an exit from Jerusalem at the end of the day, a return in the morning to teach—suggests Jesus' final week in Jerusalem when he is reported to have done just that each day. It was for this reason that some scribes inserted the anecdote into the Gospel of Luke after 21:37–38:

> During the day he would teach in the temple area, and in the evening he would go and spend the night on the mountain called Olives. And all the people would get up early to come to the temple area to hear him.

A synoptic-like setting for the story seems much more appropriate than does its position as 7:53–8:11 in the Gospel of John.

Its location in one of the canonical gospels is not, however, the crucial issue. The fundamental question is whether this anecdote is a fragment that survived from an otherwise unknown gospel. Had it been discovered as a separate piece of papyrus, it would have attracted serious scholarly attention in its own right. For this reason, the Fellows of the Jesus Seminar have decided to recognize its independent status and reclassify it as a fragment from a lost gospel. This move puts it in the same category as the Egerton Gospel, Gospel Oxyrhynchus 840, and Gospel Oxyrhynchus 1224. As an independent fragment, it should be assessed without reference to its manuscript connection to either Luke or John.

As the testimony of Eusebius and Papias indicates, the story of the accused woman had been circulating orally in the second century. It was a bit of stray oral tradition, like a few other fragments we know about, that was not captured by one of the larger narrative gospels. Of course, it is possible that it may have been a part, for example, of the Gospel of Peter, assuming that Peter as a passion gospel contained other stories assigned to the passion week. Or it may have belonged to some other collection of anecdotes the traces of which have disappeared from history. We are confident that only a small portion of the literary records of the early Jesus movement have survived.

In the story Jesus is presented with a question designed to trap him: Should we stone her as ordered by the Law of Moses? If Jesus said "No," he would be contravening the Mosaic code; if he said "Yes," he might be endorsing a mob action—especially if the Romans had removed the jurisdiction for capital crimes from the Jewish authorities. Or, Jesus may have been acting against what his opponents perceived as his open association with prostitutes. In either case the trap posed an uncomfortable dilemma. Jesus circumvents the dilemma by inviting his opponents to comply with the ancient codes but to do so only insofar as they are themselves without guilt.

It is unclear why the woman is brought to Jesus in the first place. He had no authority to adjudicate the case. Was he being asked to endorse a mob action? Or is the anecdote a hypothetical problem presented to Jesus that was later turned into a fictional incident?

A second objection is sometimes made against the historicity of the story. It is reminiscent of the story of Susanna, who was falsely accused of adultery by two elders who were also judges. In that story, an addition to the book of Daniel, Susanna is condemned to death. Daniel intervenes and exposes the two judges as frauds who had committed perjury because Susanna had refused to submit to their sexual advances. It is possible that the first stone incident was inspired by the story of Susanna.

As it stands, the scene is an artificial construction. Elements of it may reflect something Jesus did and said, but as a whole it is not the report of a specific event. Yet because it reflects Jesus' open association with sinners and his unqualified willingness to endorse mercy on every occasion, the story merited at least a gray rating.

Discourse in Jerusalem
Jn 8:12–59
Source: John

8 [12]**Jesus spoke out again, saying to them,** "I am the light of the
world. My followers won't ever have to walk in the dark; no, they'll
have the real light."

[13]**The Pharisees came back at him: "You're giving evidence on
your own behalf; your evidence is invalid."**

[14]**Jesus answered them,** "Even if I give evidence on my own behalf,

my evidence is valid, because I know where I came from and where
I'm going. You, on the other hand, don't know where I come from or
where I'm headed. 15You judge by human standards; I pass judgment
on no one. 16But if I do render judgment, my decisions are valid
because I do not render these judgments alone; rather, the Father who
sent me joins me in them. 17Your Law stipulates that the testimony of
two is valid. 18I offer evidence on my own behalf and the Father who
sent me offers evidence on my behalf."

19So they asked him, "Where is your father?"

Jesus replied, "You don't recognize me or my Father. If you recog-
nized me, you would recognize my Father too."

**20He made these remarks while he was teaching near the collec-
tion box in the temple area. But no one arrested him because his
time had not yet come.**

21He spoke to them again: "I am going away. You'll try to find me,
but you'll die in your sin. Where I'm going you can't come."

**22The Judeans then said, "Does he intend to kill himself—is that
what he means when he says, 'Where I'm going you can't come'?"**

23So he would respond to them, "You belong down here, I belong
up above. You're right at home in this world, I'm not at home in this
world. 24I told you you would die in your sins. If you don't believe that
I am <what I say I am>, you will die in your sins."

25So they countered, "Who are you?"

"What I told you from the start," **Jesus replied.** 26"There's a lot I
could say about you and judge you for; but the one who sent me is the
real authority, so I'll tell the world what I've heard from him."

**(27They didn't realize that he was talking to them about the
Father.)**

28Then Jesus continued, "When you elevate the son of Adam, then
you'll know that I am <what I say>, and that I don't act on my own.
Rather, I say what my Father taught me. 29The one who sent me is with
me. <The Father> hasn't left me on my own, because I always do what
pleases <the Father>."

30Many believed in him because he was saying this.

**31Then Jesus began to tell the Judeans who had come to believe in
him,** "If you adhere to my teaching you really are my disciples, 32and
you'll know the truth, and the truth will liberate you."

**33They protested: "We're Abraham's descendants, and we've never
been slaves to anyone; how <can> you say, 'You'll be liberated'?"**

34Jesus answered them, "I swear to God, everyone who commits sin
is a slave. 35No slave is ever a permanent member of the family; but a
son is. 36So if the son liberates you, you'll really be free.

37"I recognize that you are Abraham's descendants, yet you're try-
ing to kill me because my teaching gets nowhere with you. 38I'm telling
you what I saw <when I was> with the Father, and you do <only>
what you learned from <your own> father."

39"Our father is Abraham," they <repeated>.

Jesus says, "If you <really> are children of Abraham, act as
Abraham did. 40As it is, you're trying to kill me, even though I've told
you the truth I heard from God. Abraham never did that. 41No, you're
doing what <your real> father does."

**They replied, "We're not bastards; we have only one father—
God."**

42Jesus responded, "If in fact God were your father, you'd love me,
since I've come from God and here I am—not on my own initiative;
<God> sent me. 43Why don't you understand what I'm saying? <It's>
because you can't hear what I'm saying. 44You are your father's chil-
dren all right—children of the devil. And you intend to accomplish
your father's desires. He was a murderer from the start; he is far from
truth, <in fact,> there's no truth in him at all. When he tells his lies, he
is expressing his nature, because he is a liar and breeds lying. 45But
since I tell the truth, you don't <want to> believe me. 46Which of you
can implicate me in sin? If I speak truthfully, why don't you believe
me? 47Everyone who belongs to God <can> hear God's words. That's
why you don't listen: you don't belong to God."

**48The Judeans replied, "Aren't we right to say, 'You're a Samaritan
and out of your mind'?"**

49"I'm not out of my mind," **Jesus replied.** "What I do is simply
honor my Father; you <on the other hand> dishonor me. (50Not that
I'm looking to be honored; there is one who seeks that <for me> and
who acquits <me>.) 51I swear to God, all who obey my teaching will
certainly never die."

**52To this the Judeans retorted, "Now we're certain you're out of
your mind! <Even> Abraham died, and so did the prophets, and
here you are claiming,** 'All who obey my teaching will certainly never
taste death.' **53Are you greater than our father Abraham? He died,
and so did the prophets. What do you make yourself out to be?"**

54Jesus replied, "If I were to glorify myself, that glory of mine
would mean nothing. But in fact my Father glorifies me—the one you
call your God, 55though you've never known God. But I know him; if I
were to say I don't know <God> I would be a liar like you. I do know
God, and I obey God's teaching. 56Your father Abraham would have
been overjoyed to see my day; in fact, he did see it and he rejoiced."

**57The Judeans said to him, "You aren't even fifty years old and
you've seen Abraham!"**

58Jesus said to them, "As God is my witness, I existed before there
was an Abraham."

**59They picked up stones to hurl at him, but Jesus disappeared
from the temple area.**

Discourse in Jerusalem. The dialogue in 8:12–59 is an extension of the exchange recorded in 7:14–52. And, like the earlier segment, this part of the conversation is also the creation of the fourth evangelist. The intrusion of the story of the woman accused of adultery should not be permitted to obscure the continuity of the two sections.

The dialogues that make up 8:12–59 fall into sections. The first section is an exchange between Jesus and the "Pharisees"; it ends with the narrative remark in v. 20 to the effect that Jesus was teaching in the temple area, but since his time had not yet come, no one arrested him.

The second exchange is between Jesus and the "Judeans" (vv. 21–59), with pauses at vv. 27 and 30, with the narrative conclusion in v. 59. Verse 27 is a narrator aside addressed to the reader. Verse 30 is a narrative remark also aimed at the reader. The final narrative note, v. 59, renews the theme that runs through these conversations: The authorities, the Judeans, and the crowd want to kill Jesus, but he continues to elude them because his time has not yet come.

This narrative framework is of course the product of the evangelist's imagination. Nothing this extensive or detailed could possibly have survived for more than a half century from the death of Jesus to the composition of the Fourth Gospel toward the close of the first century. The Fellows designated all the words of Jesus black in *The Five Gospels.* They colored the correlative narrative framework black for this report.

Man born blind
Jn 9:1–41
Source: John
Cf. Mk 8:22–26

9 **As he was leaving he saw a man who had been blind from birth.**
[2]His disciples asked him, "Rabbi, was it this man's wrong-doing or
his parents' that caused him to be born blind?"

[3]**Jesus responded,** "This fellow did nothing wrong, nor did his parents. Rather, <he was born blind> so God could display his work through him. [4]We must carry out the work of the one who sent me while the light lasts. Nighttime is coming and then no one will be able to undertake any work. [5]So long as I am in the world I am the light of the world."

[6]**With that he spat on the ground, made mud with his spit and treated the man's eyes with the mud.** [7]**Then <Jesus> said to him,** "Go, rinse off in the pool of Siloam" (the name means "Emissary"). **So he went over, rinsed <his eyes> off, and came back with his sight restored.**

[8]**Then his neighbors, and those who recognized him as the one who had been a beggar before, would say, "Isn't this the fellow who used to sit and beg?"**

[9]**Some would agree, "It's him"; others would say, "No, it only looks like him."**

He kept saying, "It's me."

[10]**So they asked him, "How were your eyes opened?"**

[11]**He answered, "Someone called Jesus made some mud and treated my eyes; he told me, 'Go to Siloam and rinse off.' So I went, and when I had rinsed off, I could see."**

[12]They said to him, "Where is this man?"
He says, "I don't know."
[13]They take the man who had been blind to the Pharisees. ([14]It was
the sabbath day when Jesus made mud and opened his eyes.) [15]So
the Pharisees asked him again how he could see.
"He put mud on my eyes, I washed, and I can see," he told them.
[16]Then some of the Pharisees said, "That man is not from God,
because he does not keep the sabbath day." But others said, "How
can a sinner do such miracles?" And there was a rift among them.
[17]So they ask the blind man again, "What do you have to say about
him, since it was your eyes he opened?"
He said, "He's a prophet."
[18]The Judeans wouldn't believe that he had been blind and got his
sight until they called in the parents of this man who had recovered
his sight. [19]They asked them, "Is this your son that you claim was
born blind? So how come he can see now?"
[20]His parents replied, "We know this is our son; we know he was
born blind; [21]but we don't know how he can see now or who opened
his eyes. Ask him, he's an adult; he'll speak for himself." ([22]His par-
ents said this because they were afraid of the Judeans, for the Ju-
deans had already agreed that anyone who acknowledged <Jesus> as
the Anointed would be banned from the synagogue. [23]That's why his
parents said, "He's an adult, ask him.")
[24]So for a second time they called in the man who had been blind,
and said to him, "Give God the credit. We know this man is a sinner."
[25]He replied, "Whether he's a sinner I don't know; the one thing I
do know is that I was blind, and now I can see."
[26]They asked him, "What did he do to you? How did he open your
eyes?"
[27]He answered them, "I told you already and you wouldn't listen
to me. Why do you want to hear it again? You don't want to become
his disciples too, do you?"
[28]They hurled insults at him: "You may be his disciple; we're dis-
ciples of Moses. [29]We know God spoke to Moses; we don't even
know where this man came from."
[30]"Now isn't that wonderful," he responded. "You don't know
where he's from and yet he opened my eyes! [31]God doesn't listen to
sinners; we know that. But if someone is devout and does God's
will, <God> listens. [32]It's unheard of that anyone ever opened the
eyes of someone born blind. [33]If this man were not from God, he
couldn't do anything at all."
[34]"You're a born sinner and you're going to teach us?" they
replied. And they threw him out.
[35]Jesus heard they had thrown him out; so he found him and said,
"Do you believe in the son of Adam?"
[36]He replied, "Master, who is he, so I can believe in him?"

37**Jesus said to him,** "You've already seen him; he's speaking with
you right now."
38**He said, "Master, I believe," and paid him homage.**
39**Jesus said,** "I came into this world to hand down this verdict: the
blind are to see and those with sight are to be blind."
40**When some of the Pharisees around him heard this, they said to
him, "We're not blind, are we?"**
41**Jesus said to them,** "If you really were blind, you would be free of
sin; but now <since> you say, 'We see,' your sin is confirmed."

Man born blind. The color coding of the story of the man born blind indicates how the Fellows of the Jesus Seminar understood its history. John has taken a simple healing miracle (vv. 6–7) and encased it in an elaborate controversy about whether affliction is the consequence of sin, and about the relation of sight to blindness in some metaphorical sense. The framework is the creation of the author of the Fourth Gospel; the core story may have been borrowed from an older tradition.

John Dominic Crossan suggests that the cure of the blind man reported in Mark 8:22–26 and this story in the Fourth Gospel have evolved from the same basic incident in the life of Jesus. His suggestion is based on the conjunction of blindness and spittle. Sara Winter, another Fellow of the Seminar, is inclined to link the story in the Fourth Gospel to the account of blind Bartimaeus as told by Mark (10:46–52). Her reasoning is two-pronged. On the one hand, she takes the story of the blind man in Mark 8:22–26 to be connected to the story of the deaf mute in Mark 7:31–37 (because the two stories have much in common, some scholars have concluded that one is a clone of the other). On the other hand, she thinks the fact that the man born blind is described as a blind beggar (v. 8) provides a link to blind Bartimaeus, who is also a beggar. Of course, in Jesus' society, most blind people were forced to be beggars. Nevertheless, that piece of narrative information is a link, however modest.

The difficulties attendant upon determining the history of these stories, especially their relation to each other, can be pursued in the cameo "A Gospel of Miracles?" (pp. 388–89).

The core of the story in the Fourth Gospel (vv. 6–7) might well have been colored pink had the author not so completely adapted it to the controversy in which it is now embedded. Gray indicates the Fellows' recognition that what is left may yet harbor the memory of an actual event.

Sheep & the shepherd
Jn 10:1–18
Source: John

10 "I swear to God, anyone who does not enter the sheep pen
through the gate, but climbs in some other way, is nothing but a thief
and a robber. 2But the one who comes through the gate is the shep-
herd. 3The gatekeeper lets him in. The sheep recognize his voice; he
calls his own sheep by name and leads them out. 4When he has driven
out the last of his own sheep, he walks in front of them, and the sheep
follow him, because they know his voice. 5They would never follow a

stranger, but would run away from him, since they don't know the
voice of strangers."
**[6]Jesus used this figure of speech with them, but they didn't
understand what he was talking about.**
[7]Jesus went on to say, "As God is my witness, I am that gate for the
sheep. [8]All who came before me are nothing but thieves and robbers,
but the sheep haven't paid any attention to them. [9]I am the gate; who-
ever comes in through me will be safe and will go in and out and find
pasture. [10]The thief comes only to steal and sacrifice and slaughter. I
came so they can have life and have it to the full.
[11]"I am the good shepherd. The good shepherd gives his life for his
sheep. [12]A hired hand, who isn't a shepherd and doesn't own the
sheep, would see the wolf coming and run off, abandoning the sheep;
then the wolf <could> attack the sheep and scatter them. [13]He would
run off because he's a hired hand and the sheep don't matter to him. [14]I
am the good shepherd; I know my sheep and my sheep know me,
[15]just as the Father knows me and I know the Father: so I give my life
for my sheep. [16]Yet I have sheep from another fold, and I must lead
them too. They'll recognize my voice, and there'll be one flock, one
shepherd.
[17]"This is the reason my Father loves me: I am giving up my life so I
can take it back again. [18]No one can take it away from me; I give it up
freely. I have the power to give it up and the power to take it back
again. I have been charged with this responsibility by my Father."

Sheep & the shepherd. The narrator's explanation in v. 6 is for the benefit of the reader: Jesus employs figures of speech that are analogies, and these figures confuse his listeners. In the Fourth Gospel, Jesus is portrayed as offering extended analogies about himself, in contrast to the synoptic gospels, where his parables offer brief metaphors of God's domain. The minimal narrative framing for the analogy of the shepherd is of course the work of the evangelist. Black is appropriate.

Jesus is accused
Jn 10:19–21
Source: John
Cf. Mk 3:22; Mt 12:24,
Lk 11:16; Jn 7:20, 8:48, 8:52

10 **[19]Once more there was a rift among the Judeans because he
made these claims.** [20]Many of them were saying, "He's out of his
mind and crazy. Why pay any attention to him?" **[21]Others would say,
"These aren't the words of someone who is demon-possessed. A
demon can't open the eyes of the blind, can it?"**

Jesus is accused. Once again the narrator speculates that the "Judeans" were divided in their response to Jesus. Some accuse him of madness, of being demon-possessed; others wonder whether his words and cures don't point to a different assessment. It seems likely that his family thought Jesus possessed—the early community would not have invented that charge—and it may well be that many others thought him mad. That would have been grounds for ignoring what he said. For that reason, the Fellows decided to color v. 20 gray. Verse 21, on the other hand, expresses the logic of the evangelist in appealing to his readers.

At the Festival of Lights
Jn 10:22–42
No parallels
Source: John

10 **22It was then the Festival of Lights in Jerusalem, and it was
wintertime. 23Jesus was walking about in the temple area, in
Solomon's Colonnade. 24Judeans surrounded him. "How long are
you going to keep us in suspense?" they kept asking. "If you are the
Anointed, just say so."**

25Jesus answered them, "I did tell you, and you don't believe. The
things I am achieving in my Father's name are evidence on my behalf.
26But you don't believe me, because you're not my sheep. 27My sheep
recognize my voice; I know them and they follow me, 28and I provide
them with real life; they'll never be lost, nor will anyone snatch them
away from me. 29What my Father has given me is greatest of all, and
no one can wrest it from the Father. 30What goes for the Father, goes for
me too."

**31Again the Judeans took stones in hand to stone him. 32Jesus
responded,** "I showed you many wonderful works that were really
the Father's. Which of these works makes you want to stone me?"

**33The Judeans answered him, "We're not stoning you for some
wonderful work, but for blasphemy—you, a mere human, make
yourself out to be God."**

34Jesus answered them, "Isn't it written in your Law: 'I said, You are
gods'? 35The scripture can't be wrong: if God has called people gods—
those who got the word of God—36do you mean to say about the one
the Father set apart and sent to earth, 'You're blaspheming,' just
because I said, 'I am God's son'? 37If I don't do my Father's works,
don't believe me; 38if I do, even if you can't believe in me, believe in the
works, so that you'll fully understand that the Father is in me and I am
in the Father."

39Again they tried to arrest him, but he escaped.

**40He went away once more, to the place across the Jordan where
John had first baptized, and there he stayed. 41Many people came to
him; they kept repeating, "John didn't perform any miracle, but
everything John said about this man was true." 42And many believed
in him there.**

At the Festival of Lights. The occasion for the next dialogue between Jesus and the Judeans is the Festival of Lights, better known as Hanukkah. Jesus is represented as going up to Jerusalem for Passover (2:13–25), and then for another festival, perhaps the Feast of Weeks or Pentecost in 5:1. He had returned to Samaria in the meantime, where he had the discussion with the woman at the well (4:1–42), and then went on to Galilee (4:43), where he cured the official's son (4:45–54). Following the visit to the holy city in chapter 5, he travels once again to Jerusalem, this time for Sukkoth or the Festival of Booths (7:1–13). He is still in Jerusalem when the winter festival, the rededication of the temple called the Festival of Lights, takes place.

The temple had been profaned by the Seleucids during their occupation of it in 167–164 B.C.E. They had sacrificed a pig to make the temple's desecration complete. Mattathias Maccabeus and his five sons rebelled against the Seleucids and drove them from Jerusalem. Judas Maccabeus took over from his father, cleansed the temple, rebuilt the altar, and fabricated new holy vessels. He and his countrymen rededicated the temple on the twenty-fifth of Chislev in 164 B.C.E. by relighting the lamps, from which the eight-day Festival of Lights gets its name.

This colloquy is again between Jesus and the "Judeans." Two themes are preeminent: The Judeans want to know whether Jesus is the Anointed, the messiah (v. 24). And they accuse Jesus of identifying himself with God (v. 33). Jesus responds to the first in vv. 25–30; he answers the second in vv. 34–38. The "Judeans" react to the first by attempting to stone Jesus (v. 31), then to the second by trying to arrest him (v. 38).

The interest in Jesus' status is a central Johannine theme. It plays a lesser role in the synoptics, and never appears in the authentic parables, aphorisms, and witticisms of Jesus. The conversations in chapters 7 and 8 are also preoccupied with Jesus' status—his origin and destination and his relation to Moses and Abraham. The present dialogue, like the earlier ones, is the fabrication of the fourth evangelist or the community before him. The words of Jesus were colored black in *The Five Gospels;* the narrative framework also deserves a black rating as the product of the storyteller's imagination.

The raising of Lazarus
Jn 11:1–44
SecMk 1:1–11
Sources: John, Secret Mark

11 **Now someone named Lazarus had fallen ill; he was from**
Bethany, the village of Mary and her sister Martha. ([2]This was the
Mary who anointed the Master with oil and wiped his feet with her
hair; it was her brother Lazarus who was sick.) [3]So the sisters sent
for <Jesus>: "Master, the one you love is sick."

[4]But when Jesus heard this he said, "This illness is not fatal; it is to
show God's majesty, so God's son also will be honored by it."

[5]Jesus loved Martha and her sister and Lazarus. [6]When he heard
that <Lazarus> was sick, he lingered two more days where he was;
[7]then he says to the disciples, "Let's go to Judea again."

[8]The disciples say to him, "Rabbi, just now the Judeans were
looking for the opportunity to stone you; are you really going back
there?"

[9]"Aren't there twelve hours in the day?" **Jesus responded.** "Those
who walk during the day won't stumble; they can see by this world's
light. [10]But those who walk at night are going to stumble, because they
have no light to go by."

[11]He made these remarks, and then he tells them, "Our friend
Lazarus has fallen asleep, but I am going to wake him up."

12"Master, if he's only fallen asleep," said the disciples, "he'll revive." (13Jesus had been speaking of death but they thought that he meant <he was> only asleep.)

14Then Jesus told them plainly, "Lazarus is dead; 15and I'm happy for you that I wasn't there, so you can believe. Now let's go to him."

16Then Thomas, called "the Twin," said to his fellow disciples, "Let's go along too, so we can die with him."

17When Jesus arrived, he found that <Lazarus> had been buried four days earlier. 18Bethany was near Jerusalem, about two miles away, 19and many of the Judeans had come to Martha and Mary to console them about their brother. 20When Martha heard that Jesus was coming, she went to meet him; Mary stayed at home. 21"Master," said Martha, "if you'd been here, my brother wouldn't have died. 22Still I know that whatever you ask of God, God will grant you."

23Jesus says to her, "Your brother will be resurrected."

24Martha responds, "I know he'll be raised in the resurrection on the last day."

25Jesus said to her, "I am resurrection and life; those who believe in me, even if they die, will live; 26but everyone who is alive and believes in me will never die. Do you believe this?"

27"Yes, Master," she says, "I believe that you are the Anointed, God's son, who is to come to earth."

28At this point she went to call her sister Mary, telling her privately, "The Teacher is here and is asking for you." 29When she heard that, she got up quickly and went to him.

(30Jesus hadn't yet arrived at the village; he was still where Martha had met him.)

31When the Judeans, who hovered about her in the house to console her, saw Mary get up and go out quickly, they followed her, thinking she was going to the tomb to grieve there. 32When Mary got to where Jesus was and saw him, she fell down at his feet. "Master," she said, "if you'd been here, my brother wouldn't have died."

33When Jesus saw her crying, and the Judeans who accompanied her crying too, he was agitated and deeply disturbed; 34he said, "Where have you put him?"

"Master," they say, "come and see."

35Then Jesus cried.

36So the Judeans observed, "Look how much he loved him." 37But some wondered: "He opened the blind man's eyes; couldn't he have kept this man from dying?"

38Again greatly agitated, Jesus arrives at the tomb; it was a cave, and a stone lay up against the opening. 39Jesus says, "Take the stone away."

Martha, sister of the dead man, replies, "But Master, by this time the body will stink; it's been four days."

40Jesus says to her, "Didn't I tell you, if you believe you'll see God's

majesty?" 41**So they took the stone away, and Jesus looked upwards
and said,** "Father, thank you for hearing me. 42I know you always hear
me, but I say this because of the people standing here, so they'll believe
that you sent me." 43**Then he shouted at the top of his voice,** "Lazarus,
come out!" 44**The dead man came out, his hands and feet bound in
strips of burying cloth, and his face covered with a cloth. Jesus says
to them,** "Free him <from the burying cloth> and let him go."

The raising of Lazarus. In its present form, the story of the resuscitation of Lazarus is a Johannine composition. It may share a common ancestor with a similar story preserved in Secret Mark; if so, that core lies behind vv. 33–44. The first thirty-two verses are mostly the product of the Johannine imagination. If there is an earlier tale lying behind vv. 33–44, the author of the Fourth Gospel has reconceived the entire narrative, including that core, along his own particular lines.

The Fellows are uncertain that there were two sisters named Mary and Martha, despite the anecdote in Luke 10:38–42 that features them. They doubted that the two sisters had a brother named Lazarus. They did not think the family was from Bethany. And they were all but certain that the Mary in this story was not the woman who anointed Jesus' feet (Mark 14:3–9//Matt 26:6–13//Luke 7:36–50), in spite of the remark in v. 2.

Some Fellows thought it remotely possible that the story of Lazarus was based on a historical event, but they were certain such an event did not involve the resuscitation of a corpse. The Seminar tested the range of possibilities to determine if there was any consensus, and, if so, where it lay. Most Fellows doubted that Jesus revived a person whom others believed to be dead (the semblance of a resuscitation). They also rejected as remote the possibility that Jesus released from the tomb a man who had been buried prematurely (also the illusion of a resuscitation). If there was an actual event that gave rise to the story, they decided they could not determine what it was.

The Lazarus story has several points in common with its counterpart in Secret Mark (found on p. 117): The story is set in Bethany (John 11:1, SecMk 1:1); the dead man is the brother of a woman (John 11:19, SecMk 1:1); Jesus becomes agitated (John 11:33, 38, SecMk 1:4); they go to the tomb (John 11:38, SecMk 1:4); a loud voice is heard (John 11:43, SecMk 1:5); a stone is taken away from the entrance to the tomb (John 11:39, 41, SecMk 1:6); a young man exits the tomb (John 11:44, SecMk 1:9).

These features provide the bare bones of a common story, although in some instances the motifs take a different form. For example, in Secret Mark, the young man loves Jesus; in John, Jesus loves Lazarus. The loud voice in Secret Mark issues from the tomb; in John the loud voice comes from Jesus. In John, Jesus orders the stone taken away; in Secret Mark, Jesus rolls it away himself. In Secret Mark, Jesus enters the tomb, raises the young man up and brings him out; in John, Jesus calls for him to come out and Lazarus comes out on his own. It is common in folktales for motifs to migrate from one character to another.

John has elaborated the common story by adding a second sister and narrating an exchange between the two of them. He has inserted a discussion of the resurrection faith, so that the story of Lazarus anticipates Jesus' own resurrection. The author of the Fourth Gospel also adds observers he calls "Judeans," who comment on the scene. The author of Secret Mark also expands the story, but does so to a lesser extent and in different ways.

John P. Meier gives this story extended treatment, as he does the other resuscitation reports. He agrees that references backward and forward that tie this story to the larger narrative context are the work of the fourth evangelist. He also concedes that the dialogues in the Johannine version reflect theological themes characteristic of the Fourth Gospel and therefore do not go back to Jesus. He notes that there are seams and inconsistencies in the story. And he agrees that the style and vocabulary of the Lazarus story are predominantly congruent with those of the fourth evangelist elsewhere. All of this leads him to conclude that, while the author has thoroughly adapted his story to his gospel, he has also preserved an older tale. Meier attempts to reconstruct that tale on the basis of the Gospel of John alone (he thinks the parallel in Secret Mark is of no value because it isn't canonical). He concedes that the story may have originated as the healing of a critically ill person. However, he insists in the last analysis that the story originally had to do with raising someone from the dead. This, he insists, is how Jesus' first disciples viewed it. In spite of his extensive, detailed arguments, it is difficult to see how he could have assigned a color other than gray for the core story, just as did the Fellows of the Jesus Seminar.[75] E. P. Sanders, on the other hand, considers the Lazarus story an example of someone who was thought to be dead but later recovered.[76]

The conspiracy
Jn 11:45–57
Mk 14:1–2, Mt 26:1–5, Lk 22:1–2
Sources: John, Mark

11 **45As a result, many of the Judeans who had come to Mary**
and observed what Jesus had done came to believe in him. 46But
some of them went to the Pharisees and reported what Jesus had
done.

47So the ranking priests and Pharisees called the Council together
and posed this question to them: "What are we going to do now that
this fellow performs many miracles? 48If we let him go on like this,
everybody will come to believe in him. Then the Romans will come
and destroy our <holy> place and our nation."

49Then one of them, Caiaphas, that year's high priest, addressed
them as follows: "Don't you know anything? 50Don't you realize that
it's to your advantage to have one person die for the people and not
have the whole nation wiped out?"

(51He didn't say this on his own authority, but since he was that
year's high priest he could foresee that Jesus would die for the
nation. 52In fact, <he would die> not only for the nation, but to
gather together all God's dispersed children and make them one
<people>.)

53So from that day on they began plotting how to kill him. 54As a
consequence, Jesus no longer moved about among the Judeans pub-

licly, but withdrew to a region bordering the wilderness, to a town called Ephraim, and there he stayed with the disciples.

[55]It was almost time for the Jewish Passover, and many of the country people went up to Jerusalem before Passover to purify themselves. [56]They were on the lookout for Jesus, and as they stood around in the temple area, they were saying to one another, "What do you think? He certainly won't come to the celebration, will he?" ([57]The ranking priests and the Pharisees had given orders that anyone who knew his whereabouts was to report it, so they could arrest him.)

The conspiracy. The fourth evangelist has created his own version of the conspiracy against Jesus. Since that version comes on the heels of the raising of Lazarus, it makes use of Jesus' success in raising Lazarus to elevate the concern of the officials over Jesus' growing popularity (vv. 45–48). The continued success of Jesus, it seems, would bring the Romans down on all Judeans. That prompts Caiaphas to propose that it would be more prudent to have one person die for the sake of the nation than to have all of them suffer (vv. 49–50). That fine piece of logic is the fourth evangelist's way of having Caiaphas unwittingly formulate a plank in the platform of Christian doctrine: Jesus is to die for all the people (vv. 51–52). The need for Jesus' saving death becomes the basis for the plot against his life (v. 53).

The imagination of the evangelist now ranges over the narrative possibilities posed by the conspiracy. Since the authorities were now openly seeking to kill Jesus, he would be forced to withdraw to a remote location and not move about in public (vv. 53–54). The town Ephraim mentioned in v. 54 has never been positively identified; it may be a figment of John's imagination. With many pilgrims coming to Jerusalem for the festival, the storyteller puts himself in their place and wonders whether Jesus will show up. The narrator informs the reader—to make matters clear—that the "ranking priests and Pharisees" had put out an all-points bulletin: anyone knowing the whereabouts of Jesus was to report to them so they could arrest him. In the Fourth Gospel this all takes place, of course, prior to the triumphal entry on Palm Sunday. The stage is now set for the betrayal.

In the judgment of the Fellows, all of this is the product of the evangelist's imagination. It warrants a black designation.

The anointing
Jn 12:1–8
Mk 14:3–9, Mt 26:6–13; Lk 7:36–50
Sources: John, Mark, Luke

12 **Six days before Passover Jesus came to Bethany, where**
Lazarus lived, the one Jesus had brought back from the dead. [2]There
they gave a dinner for him; Martha did the serving, and Lazarus was
one of those who ate with him. [3]Mary brought in a pound of expen-
sive lotion and anointed Jesus' feet and wiped them with her hair.
And the house was filled with the lotion's fragrance. [4]Judas Iscariot,
the disciple who was going to turn him in, says, [5]"Why wasn't this
lotion sold? It would bring a year's wages, and the proceeds could
have been given to the poor." ([6]He didn't say this because he cared

about the poor, but because he was a thief. He was in charge of the common purse and now and again would pilfer money put into it.)

[7]"Let her alone," Jesus said. "Let her keep it for the time I am to be embalmed. [8]There will always be poor around; but I won't always be around."

The anointing. John resets the anointing scene in Bethany, just outside Jerusalem, and peoples it with well-known characters from his own gospel. The house is owned by Lazarus, rather than Simon the leper or Simon the Pharisee, as in the Markan and Lukan versions. The women present for the meal, Martha and Mary of Bethany, are sisters of Lazarus. In this version, Mary, one of Jesus' closest friends, anoints his feet (as in the Lukan account; in Mark and Matthew, the woman anoints Jesus' head), although she does so in an odd way by pouring the ointment on his feet and then wiping it off with her hair (normally one washed and dried the feet before treating them with perfume). While Mary is anointing Jesus, her sister Martha, looks after the meal.

In Mark's version, Jesus is anointed in anticipation of his burial. Here in the Fourth Gospel, Mary's care for Jesus' feet anticipates the footwashing of the disciples that Jesus will shortly undertake (John 13:1–20).

The author of the Fourth Gospel has produced a highly revised or alternative version of the story. Although the Johannine version drew a higher percentage of black votes than did its Lukan counterpart, the weighted average was again gray—but a somewhat darker shade.

Jesus enters Jerusalem
Jn 12:9–19
Mk 11:1–11, Mt 21:1–11, Lk 19:28–40
Sources: Zechariah 9:9, Psalm 118:25–26, John, Mark

12 **[9]When the huge crowd of Judeans found out he was there, they came not only because of Jesus but also to see Lazarus, the one he had brought back from the dead. [10]So the ranking priests planned to put Lazarus to death, too, [11]since because of him many of the Judeans were defecting and believing in Jesus.**

[12]The next day the huge crowd that had come for the celebration heard that Jesus was coming into Jerusalem. [13]They got palm fronds and went out to meet him. They began to shout,

> **Hosanna! Blessed is the one who comes in the name of the Lord! <Blessed is> the King of Israel!**

[14]Then Jesus found a young donkey and rode on it, as scripture puts it,

> [15]Calm your fears, daughter of Zion.
> Look, your king comes riding on a donkey's colt!

([16]His disciples didn't understand these matters at the time, but when Jesus had been glorified, they then recalled that what had happened to him matched the things written about him.)

[17]The people who were with <Jesus> when he had summoned Lazarus from his tomb and brought him back from the dead kept repeating <this story>. ([18]That's why the crowd went out to meet him: they heard that he had performed this miracle.)

[19]So the Pharisees remarked under their breath, "You see, you can't win; look, the world has gone over to him."**

Jesus enters Jerusalem. The core of the Johannine version of the story of the triumphal entry is found in vv. 13–15. And that core is built around scriptural quotations from Ps 118:25–26 and Zech 9:9.

All four gospels cite the Psalm in one form or another. The author of the Fourth Gospel is no exception, but his version does not match that of any of the other three. "Blessed is the one who comes in the name of the Lord" is from Ps 118:26, and originally referred to the pilgrim arriving in Jerusalem for one of the festivals. The term "Hosanna" is from Psalm 118:25; "Hosanna" was a call upon God for salvation: "Save us, O Lord" was the cry of the pilgrim. John has added without scriptural warrant: "Blessed is the King of Israel," with reference of course to Jesus.

John joins Matthew in making use of the prophecy from Zechariah, cited here in v. 15. Neither Mark nor Luke quotes Zechariah. The Zechariah quotation was evidently well known among early Christian interpreters as a messianic text that applied to Jesus' entry into Jerusalem. Some of the Fellows were even of the opinion that the entire story was suggested by the prophecy and consequently had no basis in historical fact.

The author of the Gospel of John treats the surrounding narrative terrain with great freedom. He provides his own introduction to the event in v. 12, in which he connects palm fronds to the event (he is the only evangelist to do so). Palm trees are not common on the central ridge where Jerusalem is located; they had to be brought from the Jordan valley around Jericho about fifteen miles away and were usually associated with the feast of Tabernacles or Booths (Sukkoth) in the fall.

The author inserts a narrative aside in v. 16, explaining why the disciples didn't at the time understand what was happening. In vv. 17–18, he connects the crowds that have gathered to greet Jesus as he enters Jerusalem with the resurrection of Lazarus, an event the evangelist has just narrated. And, finally, the author introduces the Pharisees into the scene (as does Luke 19:40), who complain that the whole world has become a supporter of Jesus.

Although some Fellows allowed for the possibility that Jesus may have entered Jerusalem on a donkey as a symbolic act, in contrast to the way Romans entered their cities in triumph, the Seminar generally agreed that the interpretation of this event as the arrival of the new messiah was a Christian fiction.

The time has come
Jn 12:20–36
Source: John

12 **[20]There were some Greeks among those who had come up to
worship at the celebration. [21]These people came to Philip, who was
from Bethsaida, Galilee, and requested of him, "Sir, we want to
meet Jesus."**
**[22]Philip goes and tells Andrew, and both Andrew and Philip go
and tell Jesus. [23]And Jesus responds:** "The time has come for the son
of Adam to be glorified. [24]I swear to God, unless the kernel of wheat

falls to the earth and dies, it remains a single seed; but if it dies, it produces a great harvest. 25Those who love life lose it, but those who hate life in this world will preserve it for unending, real life. 26Whoever serves me must follow me, for wherever I am, my servant must be there also. Whoever serves me, the Father will honor.

27"Now my life is in turmoil, but should I say, 'Father, rescue me from this moment'? No, it was to face this moment that I came. 28Father, glorify your name!" **Then a voice spoke out of the sky: "I have glorified it and I will glorify it further."**

29The crowd there heard this, and some people remarked that it had thundered, others that a heavenly messenger had spoken to him.

30"That voice did not come for me but for you," **Jesus rejoined.** 31"Now sentence is passed on this world; now the ruler of this world will be expelled. 32And if I'm elevated from the earth, I'll take everyone with me." **(33He said this to show what kind of death he was going to die.)**

34The crowd replied to him, "We've learned from the Law that the Anointed will stay forever, so how can you say that the son of Adam is destined to be elevated? Who is this son of Adam anyway?"

35So Jesus said to them, "The light is still with you for a while. Walk while you have light, so darkness won't overpower you. Those who walk in the dark don't know where they're going. 36Since you have the light, believe in the light, so you will become children of light." **When Jesus had said this, he left and went into hiding.**

The time has come. Near the conclusion of Jesus' public ministry, the evangelist reports the visit of some "Greeks" who came to Jerusalem for the festival, presumably that of the Festival of Lights or Hanukkah (v. 20). They want to see Jesus (v. 21).

These people may be Greek-speaking Judeans—after all, the Judeans conjecture in 7:35 that Jesus may go to their kin living in the Greek diaspora, that is, in the hellenistic world; and Greek-speaking Judeans also made their pilgrimages to Jerusalem. However, many scholars judge that the reference here is to gentiles. In Jesus' discourse on the sheep and the shepherd, he remarks that he has "sheep from another fold" (10:16), which may be an indirect allusion to gentiles. Perhaps this visit of Greeks is intended to fulfill the prophecy of Jesus: "they will recognize my voice."

The Greeks approach Philip, a disciple with a Greek name, and a well-known one at that (Alexander the Great's father). Philip turns to Andrew, another disciple with a Greek name. Together they approach Jesus. It seems to be a Greek occasion.

The visiting Greeks never get to see Jesus; instead Jesus addresses Philip and Andrew. This is a clue to the fact that this story is another literary construction, designed to showcase the proverbial saying of Jesus in v. 24: "Unless the kernel of wheat falls to the earth and dies, it remains a single seed; but if it dies, it produces a great harvest." This is meant to be a prophecy that the Christian movement will succeed in a big way. At the same time, it serves a purpose similar to that expressed by the conversation with the woman at the well: It justifies to a later generation the inclusion of non-Jews or diaspora Jews in the community of, or in Christian communities known to, the fourth evangelist.

Once more in this gospel, the reader finds a narrative that supplies no historical data—no event or deed that can be isolated or assessed by historical means. Instead we have here a miniature theological essay, fashioned to legitimate the presence of gentiles in the late first- or early second-century church.

Raymond Brown comments that the narrative treatment of the Greeks suggests that a "poorly known incident from early tradition has been used as the basis for theological adaptation." Then he adds: "There is nothing intrinsically improbable in the basic incident."[77] That would make his vote a gray on the terms adopted by the Jesus Seminar. Brown repeatedly suggests that incidents and details in the gospel stories are "plausible," by which he intends to suggest that they may be historical. But writers of fiction also strive to achieve plausibility. "Plausibility" is therefore not a telling historical criterion in and of itself.

In the dialogue that follows the story of the Greeks, again a conversation between Jesus and the crowd, there is an epiphany. In v. 28 a voice comes from the sky in response to Jesus' prayer. The crowd hears the sound and is divided on whether it is thunder or whether an angel had spoken to Jesus (v. 29). This is a biographical legend in the tradition of the baptismal story, where the spirit descends on Jesus and a voice from the sky identifies Jesus (Mark 1:10–11). An angel speaks to Hagar from the sky in Gen 21:17–18 and to Abraham in Gen 22:11, and God is perceived as thunder speaking to Moses in Exod 19:19. These primitive ways of representing the divine communication have undoubtedly inspired the fourth evangelist to employ them in this context.

Verse 33 is another of the frequent narrator asides addressed to the reader, in this case as in many others to make sure the reader does not miss the allusion: "lifting up" refers, of course, to being lifted up on the cross, but also to Jesus' glorification in being lifted up to heaven.

Jesus' public life now comes to a close, according to the Gospel of John: Jesus goes into hiding (v. 36).

The narrative setting given to the episode of the Greeks (vv. 20–26) and to the closing dialogue of Jesus (vv. 27–36) is contrived; it harbors nothing that qualifies as historical reminiscence. Black is the required designation.

Narrative recap
Jn 12:37–50
Source: John

12 **[37]Although he had performed ever so many miracles before their eyes, they did not believe in him, [38]so that the word the prophet Isaiah spoke would come true:**

> Lord, who has believed our message?
> To whom is God's might revealed?

[39]So they were unable to believe, for Isaiah also said:

> [40]He has blinded their eyes,
> he has turned their hearts to stone,
> so their eyes are sightless
> and their hearts closed to understanding,
> or they would do an about-face
> for me to heal them.

[41]Isaiah said these things because he saw God's majesty, and spoke about it.

[42]Nevertheless, many did believe in him, even many of the ruling class, but because of the Pharisees they did not acknowledge it, so they wouldn't be thrown out of the synagogue. ([43]You see, they were more concerned with human approval than with God's endorsement.)

[44]Then Jesus proclaimed aloud: "Those who believe in me do not
believe only in me, but in the one who sent me. [45]And those who see me
see the one who sent me. [46]I am light come into the world, so all who
believe in me need not remain in the dark. [47]I won't pass judgment on
those who hear my message but don't keep it. You see, I didn't come to
pass judgment on the world; I've come to save the world. [48]But those
who reject me and don't accept my message have a judge: the message
I've spoken will itself be their judge on the last day. [49]For I don't speak
on my own authority, but the Father who sent me ordered me to say
what I have said and will say, [50]and I know that his commandment is
unending, real life. Therefore, I say just exactly what the Father told to
me to say."

Narrative recap. The evangelist now provides a narrative recapitulation of the story and a final summary monologue of Jesus that brings the first part of the gospel to a close.

In the first segment (vv. 37–43), the evangelist explains why so many refused to believe in Jesus in spite of the miracles he had performed. The reason is provided by Isaiah, who insists that God has blinded the eyes of the people and turned their hearts to stone, so they won't understand. Yet, in spite of God's work, many did in fact believe, even members of the ruling Council. That some did find faith in spite of God's efforts constitutes something of a paradox. The Pharisees are also a force in preventing folks from believing: they excommunicate believing persons from the synagogue. These remarks are of course a retrospective reading of the past from the standpoint of events taking place in the present or recent past of the Johannine community. In that community, there seems to have been intense conflict between Jews who became Christian and those who did not—so much so, in fact, that the one group excluded the other from the synagogue. That piece of recent history explains the preoccupation of the Fourth Gospel with the admission of gentiles into the circle of faith and the rancorous depiction of the Pharisees, who were even then attempting to establish a new form of Judaism centered in the synagogue rather than the temple.

The narrative conclusion, like so much in the Fourth Gospel, is the invention of the evangelist and is colored by events that have transpired in his own community in more recent times. Black indicates that fiction is the predominant character of this segment.

The footwashing
Jn 13:1–20
Source: John
Cf. Mk 14:22–26,
Mt 26:26–30, Lk 22:14–20

13 **Before the Passover celebration Jesus knew that the time
had come for him to leave this world and return to the Father. He
had loved his own in the world and would love them to the end.
2 Now that the devil had planted it in the mind of Judas, Simon
Iscariot's son, to turn him in, at supper 3 Jesus could tell that the
Father had left everything up to him and that he had come from God
and was going back to God. 4 So he got up from the meal, took off his
clothing, put it aside, and wrapped a towel around himself. 5 Then he
put water in a basin and began to wash the disciples' feet and to
wipe them off with the towel around his waist. 6 He comes to Simon
Peter.**

Peter says to him, "Master, you're going to wash my feet?"

7 **Jesus replied,** "Right now you don't understand what I'm doing,
but later you will."

8 **"You'll never, ever wash my feet," Peter says.**

Jesus answered him, "Unless I wash you, you won't have anything
in common with me."

9 **"In that case, Master," Peter says, "<wash> not only my feet but
my hands and my head too."**

10 **Jesus says,** "People who have bathed need only to wash their feet;
nevertheless, they're clean all over. And you are clean—but not quite
all of you."

**(11 He knew, of course, who was going to turn him in; that's why he
said,** "You're not all clean.")

12 **When he had washed their feet, he put his clothes back on and
sat down at the table again.** "Do you realize what I've done?" **he
asked.** 13 "You call me Teacher and Master, and you're right: that's who
I am. 14 So if I am your master and teacher and have washed your feet,
you ought to wash each other's feet. 15 In other words, I've set you an
example: you are to do as I've done to you. 16 I swear to God, slaves are
never better than their masters; messengers are never superior to their
senders. 17 If you understand this, congratulations if you can do it. 18 I'm
not talking about all of you: I know the ones I've chosen. But scripture
has to come true: 'The one who has shared my food has turned on me.'
19 I tell you this now, before it happens, so that when it does happen
you'll know that I am <what I say I am>. 20 I swear to God, if they wel-
come the person I send, they welcome me; and if they welcome me,
they welcome the one who sent me."

The footwashing. In the synoptic gospels, Jesus eats a final meal with his followers just before his arrest. At that meal he speaks of the bread and the wine as his body and blood. That cult legend was the basis for the institution of the eucharist. In the Gospel of John, Jesus also eats a final meal with his disciples, but instead of instituting what was to become the eucharist, he washes his disciples' feet. Nothing is said about the bread and the wine.

The synoptics date the last supper on the evening of Nisan 14th, or, more precisely, Nisan 15th (the new day begins at sundown in the Jewish way of reckoning time). That would make the last supper the Seder, the meal that was eaten at the beginning of Passover. In the Fourth Gospel, on the other hand, the final meal occurs one day earlier, on the evening of Nisan 13th, and is therefore not the Passover Seder. That makes it possible for the Fourth Gospel to have Jesus executed just as the Passover lambs were being slaughtered in preparation for the Seder to be eaten that evening. (Without refrigeration, animals were slaughtered on the same day they were to be eaten.)

The synoptics and John thus diverge on these two important matters.

The Fourth Gospel also lacks the story of the preparations for the last supper (Mark 14:12–16//Matt 26:17–19//Luke 22:7–13).

In Mark's account of what transpires at the last supper, Jesus' remarks about the betrayer occur prior to the "words of institution," as they are commonly termed (Mark 14:17–21//Matt 26:20–25). Luke has moved these remarks to *after* the meal and added some additional teaching material, so that the meal becomes a "symposium" in the hellenistic mode—a meal followed by enlightening conversation. John follows Luke's example: he treats the theme of betrayal in 13:21–30 and then appends a series of lengthy discourses that extend from 13:31 to 17:26. John shares the structure of the event with Luke, but has given the constituent parts very different content.

In Luke's version of the symposium, Jesus gives the disciples a lesson in humility. A spat has apparently broken out among the disciples about which of them is greatest. Jesus responds with a series of proverbs about leaders and servants, the greatest of whom behaves as though a beginner (Luke 22:24–27). Similarly, in the instruction that follows the footwashing in John (vv. 12–20), Jesus explains what he has just done: he has set his disciples an example. That is because "slaves are never better than their masters; messengers are never superior to their senders" (v. 16). Jesus fulfills the teaching he set out in Luke's compendium of sayings: "Who is the greater, after all: the one reclining at a banquet or the one doing the serving? Isn't it the one who reclines? Among you I am the one doing the serving" (Luke 22:27). That admonition is acted out by Jesus. In John, we might say, Jesus is portrayed as "practicing what he preaches."

The fourth evangelist evidently provides two interpretations of the footwashing. He may have omitted the traditional account of the last supper found in the synoptics in order to focus on two aspects of Christian discipleship illustrated by this act. The first aspect is treated in vv. 6–10, the second in vv. 12–20.

In the first section, the evangelist emphasizes the role of Jesus in knowing who are "his own" (v. 1). In v. 8, Jesus says to Peter: "Unless I wash you, you won't have anything in common with me." Peter then wants Jesus to wash him all over. By washing their feet, Jesus has made his disciples "clean." That is a powerful word in a society dominated by purity concerns. However, they are not entirely clean—an oblique reference to the betrayer. So the reader won't miss the allusion, the evangelist adds an explanatory aside in v. 11.

The second aspect, treated in vv. 12–20, shifts the perspective from the vertical plane (master to servant) to the horizontal (servant to servant). The Fourth Gospel, which is otherwise notably deficient in ethical instruction, here defines the core requirement of the disciples and, by implication, of all subsequent followers. The command to love one another, so characteristic of the Gospel of John (for example, 13:34), is concerned with relations within the community, not between the community and those outside. For this gospel, those on the outside are already condemned (3:18); they don't belong to God (8:47); they are not a part of the flock for which Jesus will die (John 10:11–16); they are not among the chosen (13:18).

None of this comports with what can be recovered from more primitive tradition about the teaching of Jesus. There is nothing that approaches Jesus' fundamental admonition: "Love your enemies." Instead, it bears the unmistakable imprint of the theological and social vision of the Johannine community. Once more the evangelist has exposed his community as a tight circle of believers for whom the lines are closely drawn: those who are "in" are the chosen and the saved, and those who are "out" are lost without benefit of the grief or compassion of those safely within.

The narrative setting is the product of the evangelist's imagination, and the content of Jesus' instruction reflects the evangelist's theology, not the vision of Jesus. The Fellows designated the entire passage black.

The betrayer
Jn 13:21–30
Mk 14:17–21, Mt 26:20–25,
Lk 22:21–23
Sources: John, Mark

13 [21]**When he had said all this, Jesus became deeply disturbed.
He declared:** "I swear to God, one of you will turn me in."
[22]**The disciples stole glances at each other, at a loss to understand
who it was he was talking about.** [23]**One of them, the disciple Jesus
loved most, was sitting at Jesus' right.** [24]**So Simon Peter leans over to
ask that disciple who it was <Jesus> was talking about.** [25]**He, in turn,
leans over to Jesus and asks him, "Master, who is it?"**
[26]**Jesus answers:** "I am going to dunk this piece of bread, and the
one I give it to is the one." **So he dunks the piece of bread and gives it
to Judas, Simon Iscariot's son.** [27]**The moment <he had given Judas>
the piece of bread, Satan took possession of him. Then Jesus says to
him,** "Go ahead and do what you're going to do."
[28]**Of course no one at dinner understood why Jesus had made this
remark.** [29]**Some had the idea that because Judas kept charge of the
funds, Jesus was telling him,** "Buy whatever we need for the celebra-
tion," **or to give something to the poor.** [30]**In any case, as soon as
<Judas> had eaten the piece of bread he went out. It was nighttime.**

The betrayer. As is his custom, the author of the Fourth Gospel has dealt more expansively and creatively than the synoptic writers with Jesus' remarks at the final meal about his betrayer. First of all, John has replaced the words of institution concerning bread and wine with the symbolic footwashing (13:1–11). At its conclusion Jesus interprets his action for those reclining around the table (13:12–20). During the course of those interpretive remarks, he twice refers to his betrayal. On the first occasion he mentions that not all the disciples are "clean"—an oblique reference to Judas (13:10–11). The second time he cites Ps 41:9—"The one who has shared my food has turned on me"—as the reason his betrayal was necessary: "scripture must come true."

Jesus' remarks about discipleship prepare the way for his symbolic gesture: He takes a piece of bread, dunks it in the bowl, and gives it to Judas. In this sequence, the author again pictures the disciples as unable to fathom what Jesus is talking about (v. 22). (He does so, for example, in 10:6, and again in 13:31–38, where Peter is the dense culprit; lack of understanding is a common narrative device in the Gospel of John.) The moment Judas accepts the morsel, Satan takes possession of him; Jesus' destiny has been sealed. Jesus tells him to go ahead and do what he has to do. The disciples again fail to comprehend (vv. 28–29). Judas eats the bread and disappears into the night.

The themes of betrayal and devil possession run like a thread through the Gospel of John. Jesus remarks, when the disciples want to pull back and leave him, that he chose twelve of them and one of them is a devil. The author then names Judas as that one (6:70–71). At the anointing of Jesus by a woman, in this case Mary, Judas complains about the expense; the author identifies Judas as a common thief although treasurer of the group (12:4–6). In the footwashing scene, Jesus three times makes reference to the betrayer: 13:2, 10–11, and again in v. 18. Then follows the elaborate gesture of footwashing at the last meal. The author has advanced the betrayal theme considerably beyond its synoptic expressions.

All of this is good storytelling, but it is not history. While many Fellows concluded that Judas might possibly be a historical figure, and perhaps was even involved in Jesus' arrest—either by identifying Jesus or by showing the authorities where Jesus could be found—they were convinced that this story and its counterparts are largely inventions of the storyteller, inspired in part by scriptural references like Ps 41:9.

In the judgment of Raymond E. Brown, the notion that Judas was destined from the beginning to betray Jesus is "a theological judgment made in retrospect" and does not tells us anything historical about Judas' personal outlook. The claim that Judas acted to fulfill scripture was clearly a "theological explanation."[78] That puts a good part of the Judas story in the category of fiction, a term Brown avoids.

A new directive
Jn 13:31–35
Source: John

13 [31]**When <Judas> had gone, Jesus says,** "Now the son of Adam
is glorified, and God is glorified through him. [32]If God is glorified
through him, God in turn will glorify him through himself, and will
glorify him at once. [33]My children, I'm going to be with you only a little
while longer. You'll look for me, but, as I told the Judeans, I'm going
where you can't come; it's to you that I say this now. [34]I am giving you
a new directive: Love each other. Just as I've loved you, you are to love

each other. 35Then everyone will recognize you as my disciples—if you
love each other."

A new directive. The evangelist has appended a paragraph on the "new directive" to his account of the final meal of Jesus with his followers. The only narrative remark is in v. 31. Like the other components of the scene, this one, too, is the invention of the evangelist. Verse 31 is therefore colored black to indicate that it does not reflect history but fiction.

13 **36Simon Peter says to him, "Master, where are you going?"**
Jesus answered, "For now you can't follow me where I'm going;
you'll follow later."
**37Peter says to him, "Master, why can't I follow you now? I'd give
my life for you."**
38Jesus responded, "You'd give your life for me? I swear to God:
The rooster won't crow before you disown me three times."

The oath
Jn 13:36–38
Mk 14:27–31, Mt 26:31–35,
Lk 22:31–34
Sources: John, Mark

The oath. Jesus has just told the disciples that he won't be with them much longer, that he is going away (13:33). The author of the Fourth Gospel picks up this theme in rewriting the story of Peter's oath that he would never disown Jesus, which now takes the form of giving his life for Jesus (v. 37). The prospect of martyrdom is a note also struck by Mark (14:31), Matthew (26:35), and Luke (22:33). However, Luke's version of that prospect is closer to the one found here in the Gospel of John. Subsequent events—Peter's actual martyrdom—may have influenced the telling of this story as time passed.

That John is reflecting the same tradition that can be observed in the Gospel of Mark is made clear by v. 38: Mark probably invented the crow of the rooster and the triple denial. The second half of v. 38 concurs with the Markan tradition: it is denial rather than martyrdom that is involved. John has simply melded two traditions. The appropriate color is black since the story is a fiction.

14 "Don't give in to your distress. You believe in God, then
believe in me too. 2There are plenty of places to stay in my Father's
house. If it weren't true, I would have told you; I'm on my way to
make a place ready for you. 3And if I go to make a place ready for you,
I'll return and embrace you. So where I am you can be too. 4You know
where I'm going and you know the way."
**5Thomas says to him, "Master, we don't know where you're
going. How can we possibly know the way?"**
6"I am the way, and I am truth, and I am life," **replies Jesus.** "No
one gets to the Father unless it is through me. 7If you do recognize me,
you will recognize my Father also. From this moment on you know
him and you've even seen him."
**8"Let us see the Father," Philip says to him, "and we'll be satis-
fied."**

Way, truth, life
Jn 14:1–14
Source: John

9"I've been around you all this time," **Jesus replies,** "and you still
don't know me, do you, Philip? Anyone who has seen me has seen the
Father. So how can you say, 'Let us see the Father'? 10Don't you believe
that I'm in the Father and the Father is in me? I don't say what I say on
my own. The Father is with me constantly, and I perform his labors.
11You ought to believe that I'm in the Father and the Father is in me. If
not, at least you ought to believe these labors in and of themselves. 12I
swear to God, anyone who believes in me will perform the works I
perform and will be able to perform even greater feats, because I'm on
my way to the Father. 13In addition, I'll do whatever you request in my
name, so the Father can be honored by means of the son. 14If you
request anything using my name, I'll do it."

Way, truth, life. In the "farewell speeches" the fourth evangelist attributes to Jesus, he occasionally inserts dialogue in order to relieve the monotony of long, uninterrupted monologues. In this segment, Thomas is the foil for the question about the way to the place Jesus is going in v. 5. Philip functions as the dolt in v. 8. These questions and Jesus' answers are both completely alien to the historical Jesus, the crafter of parables, aphorisms, and witticisms. Both the words and the contrived narrative framework deserve a black rating.

The advocate
Jn 14:15–31
Source: John

14 15"If you love me, you'll obey my instructions. 16At my request
the Father will provide you with yet another advocate, the authentic
spirit, who will be with you forever. 17The world is unable to accept
<this spirit> because it neither perceives nor recognizes it. You recog-
nize it because it dwells in you and will remain in you.

18"I won't abandon you as orphans; I'll come to you. 19In a little
while the world won't see me any longer, but you'll see me because
I'm alive as you will be alive. 20At that time you will come to know that
I'm in my Father and that you're in me and I'm in you. 21Those who
accept my instructions and obey them—they love me. And those who
love me will be loved by my Father; moreover, I will love them and
make myself known to them."

**22Judas (not Iscariot) says to him, "Master, what has happened that
you are about to make yourself known to us but not to the world?"**

23Jesus replied to him, "Those who love me will heed what I tell
them, and my Father will love them, and we'll come to them and make
our home there. 24Those who don't love me won't follow my instruc-
tions. Of course, the things you heard me say are not mine but come
from the Father who sent me.

25"I have told you these things while I am still here with you. 26Yet
the advocate, the holy spirit the Father will send in my stead, will
teach you everything and remind you of everything I told you. 27Peace
is what I leave behind for you; my peace is what I give you. What I
give you is not a worldly gift. Don't give in to your distress or be over-
come by terror. 28You heard me tell you, 'I'm going away and I'm going

to return to you.' If you loved me, you'd be glad that I'm going to the
Father, because the Father is greater than I am. 29So I have now told
you all this ahead of time so you will believe when it happens.
30"Time does not permit me to tell you much more; you see, the
ruler of this world is already on the way. 31However, so the world may
know I love the Father, I act exactly as my Father instructed me. Come
on, let's get out of here."

The advocate. As in the previous section, Judas (not the Iscariot) serves to raise a hypothetical question so Jesus can continue his lecture. It is clear from the question and Jesus' answer that the Johannine community, as representative of the Christian community, conceives of itself as a separate, privileged entity vis-à-vis the outside world. In the authentic lore of Jesus, the outsiders—the poor, the hungry, the destitute—are really the insiders, while the insiders are in fact the outsiders. The Johannine community has lost sight of this fundamental perspective. Black is the appropriate color for both words and narrative framework.

15 "I am the authentic vine and my Father does the cultivating.
2He prunes every cane of mine that does not bear fruit, and every cane
that does bear fruit he dresses so it will bear even more fruit. 3You have
already been 'dressed up' by the things I have told you. 4You must stay
attached to me, and I <must stay attached> to you. Just as a cane can-
not bear fruit in and of itself—if it is detached from the trunk—so you
<can't bear fruit> unless you stay attached to me. 5I am the trunk, you
are the canes. Those who stay attached to me—and I to them—pro-
duce a lot of fruit; you're not able to achieve anything apart from me.
6Those who don't remain attached to me are thrown away like dead
canes: they are collected, tossed into the fire, and burned. 7If you stay
attached to me and my words lodge in you, ask whatever you want
and it will happen to you. 8My Father's honor consists of this: the great
quantity of fruit you produce in being my disciples.
9"I loved you in the same way the Father loved me. Live in my love.
10If you observe my instructions, you will live in my love, just as I have
observed my Father's instructions and live in his love.
11"I have told you all this so you will be the source of my happiness
and so you yourselves will be filled with happiness. 12This is my order
to you: You are to love each other just as I loved you. 13No one can love
to a greater extent than to give up life for friends. 14You are my friends
if you follow my orders. 15I no longer call you slaves, since a slave does
not know what his master is up to. I have called you friends, because I
let you know everything I learned from my Father. 16You didn't choose
me; I chose you. And I delegated you to go out and produce fruit. And
your fruit will last because my Father will provide you with whatever
you request in my name. 17This is my order to you: You are to love each
other.

18"If the world hates you, don't forget that it hated me first. 19If you were at home in the world, the world would befriend <you as> its own. But you are not at home in the world; on the contrary, I have separated you from the world; that's why the world hates you. 20Recall what I told you: 'Slaves are never better than their masters.' If they persecuted me, they'll surely persecute you. If they observe my teaching, they will also observe yours. 21Yet they are going to do all these things to you because of me, since they don't recognize the one who sent me.

22"If I hadn't come and spoken to them, they wouldn't be guilty of sin. But as it is, they have no excuse for their sin.

23"Those who hate me also hate my Father.

24"If I had not performed deeds among them such as no one else has ever performed, they would not be guilty of sin. But as it is, they have observed <these deeds> and come to hate both me and my Father. (25This has happened so the saying in their Law would come true: 'They hated me for no reason.')

26"When the advocate comes, the one I'll send you from the Father, the spirit of truth that emerges from the Father, it will testify on my behalf. 27And you are going to testify because you were with me from the beginning."

Jesus departs
Jn 16:1–33
Source: John

16 "I've told you these things to keep you from being led astray. 2They are going to expel you from the synagogue. But the time is coming when those who kill you will think they are doing God a service. 3They are going to do these things because they don't recognize either the Father or me. 4Yet I have told you all this so when the time comes you'll recall that I told you about them. I didn't tell you these things at first because I was with you then. 5Now I am on my way to the one who sent me, and not one of you asks me, 'Where are you going?' 6Yet because I have told you these things, you are filled with grief. 7But I'm telling you the truth: you'll be better off to have me leave. You see, if I don't leave, the advocate can't come to you. But if I go, I'll send the advocate to you. 8When the advocate comes, it will convince the world of its error regarding sin, justification, and judgment: 9regarding sin because they don't believe in me; 10regarding justification because I am going to the Father and you won't see me anymore; 11regarding judgment because the ruler of this world stands condemned. 12I still have a lot to tell you, but you can't stand it just now. 13When <the advocate> comes, the spirit of truth, it will guide you to the complete truth. It will not speak on its own authority, but will tell only what it hears and will disclose to you what is to happen. 14It will honor me because it will disclose to you what it gets from me. 15Everything the Father has belongs to me; that's why I told you, 'It will disclose to you what it gets from me.' [16]After a time you won't see me anymore, and then again a little later you will see me."

[17]Some of his disciples remarked to each other, "What does he mean when he tells us, 'After a time you won't see me, and then a little later you will see me'? And what does he mean by, 'I'm going to return to the Father'?" [18]So they asked, "What does 'a little later' mean? We don't understand what he's talking about."

[19]Jesus perceived that they wanted to question him, so he said to them, "Have you been discussing my remark 'After a time you won't see me, and then a little later you will see me'? [20]I swear to God, you will weep and mourn, but the world will celebrate. You will grieve, but your grief will turn to joy. [21]A woman suffers pain when she gives birth because the time has come. When her child is born, in her joy she no longer remembers her labor because a human being has come into the world. [22]And so you are now going to grieve. But I'll see you again, and then you'll rejoice, and nobody can deprive you of your joy. [23]When that time comes you'll ask nothing of me. I swear to God, if you ask the Father for anything using my name, he will grant it to you. [24]You haven't asked for anything using my name up to this point. Ask and you'll get it, so your bliss will be complete.

[25]"I have been talking to you in figures of speech. The time is coming when I'll no longer speak to you in figures but will tell you about the Father in plain language. [26]When that time comes, you will make requests using my name; I'm not telling you that I will make requests on your behalf, [27]since the Father himself loves you because you have befriended me and believe that I came from God. [28]I came from the Father and entered the world. Once again I'm going to leave the world and return to the Father."

[29]His disciples respond, "Now you're using plain language rather than talking in riddles. [30]Now we see that you know everything and don't need anyone to question you. This is why we believe you have come from God."

[31]"Do you really believe now?" **Jesus countered.** [32]"Look, the time has come for all of you to scatter and return home; you'll abandon me. But I won't be alone, because the Father is with me. [33]I have told you all this so you can possess my peace. In the world you're going to have trouble. But be resolute! I now have the world under control."

Jesus departs. The evangelist continues his practice of interrupting Jesus' monologues with questions from his circle of followers. We have noted examples in 14:5, 8, and 22. He resumes the practice here with remarks of the disciples as a group (the earlier examples were attributed to individuals) in vv. 17–18 and 29–30. It is almost as though Jesus were giving a seminar: he lectures and occasionally his students raise questions, to which he responds. In this instance, those students appear to make some progress in understanding. The reason: Jesus no longer talks to them in "figures," but has begun to speak plainly. The style of Jesus' speech is completely alien to what can be recovered of the more primitive tradition in the Sayings Gospel Q, the Gospel of Thomas, and the Gospel of Mark. The dialogues are contrived and represent the thinking of the evangelist or his community. Black is the only possible rating.

Final prayer
Jn 17:1–26
Source: John

17 **Jesus spoke these words, then he looked up and prayed:** "Father, the time has come. Honor your son, so your son may honor you. [2]Just as you have given him authority over all humankind, so he can award real life to everyone you have given him. [3]This is real life: to know you as the one true God, and Jesus Christ, the one you sent. [4]I honor you on earth by completing the labors you gave me to do. [5]Now, Father, honor me with your own presence, the presence I enjoyed before the world <began>.

[6]"I have made your name known to all those you gave me out of the world <of humankind>. They were yours, you gave them to me, and they have kept your word. [7]They now recognize that everything you gave me is really from you. [8]I passed on to them the things you gave me to say, and they have been receptive <to those things> and have come to know truly that I have come from your presence; they have also come to believe you sent me. [9]I plead on their behalf; I am not pleading for the world but for those you turned over to me because they are yours. [10]Everything that belongs to me is yours, and everything that belongs to you is mine, so I have been honored by them. [11]I am no longer in the world, but they are to remain in the world, while I am going to return to you. Holy Father, keep them under your protection—all those you have given me, so they may be united just as we are united. [12]When I was with them, I kept them under your protection, and I guarded them; not one of them was lost, except the one destined to be lost, since scripture has to come true. [13]Now I'm returning to you, but I say these things while I'm still in the world, so they may fully share my elation. [14]I have passed on your instructions to them, so the world hated them because they are aliens in the world, as I am an alien in the world. [15]I do not ask to have them taken from the world but to have them rescued from evil. [16]They are aliens in the world, as I am. [17]Dedicate them to the service of truth. Your word is truth. [18]I sent them into the world as you sent me into the world. [19]And I now consecrate myself on their behalf, so they too may be consecrated by truth.

[20]"I am not pleading only on their behalf, but also on behalf of those who believe in me as a result of their word: [21]they should all be united, just as you, Father, are with me and I with you; may they be one in us, so the world will believe that you sent me. [22]The honor you granted me I passed on to them, so they may be one, as we are one, [23]I with them and you with me, so they may be perfectly united, so the world will know you sent me and loved them as much as you loved me. [24]Father, I want those you gave into my care to be with me wherever I am, so

they may see my honor—the honor you bestowed on me because you
loved me before the foundations of the world <were laid>. [25]Noble
Father, the world did not acknowledge you, but I acknowledged you,
and these <you gave into my care> acknowledged that you sent me; [26]I
also made your name known to them and will continue to make it
known, so the kind of love you have for me may be theirs, and I may
be theirs also."

Final prayer. The fourth evangelist's final narrative remark appears in v. 1. It is intended to provide a line between the previous speech and Jesus' concluding prayer. It can only be the product of the evangelist's imagination. Since it provides no historical data, black is the correct designation.

The arrest
Jn 18:1–12
Mk 14:43–52, Mt 26:47–56,
Lk 22:47–54a
Sources: John, Mark

18 When he had said all this, Jesus went out with his disciples
across the Kidron valley. There was a garden there where he and his
disciples went. [2]But because Jesus had often gone there with his dis-
ciples, Judas, who was about to turn him in, knew the place too. [3]So
it wasn't long before Judas arrives, **bringing with him the detach-**
ment <of Roman soldiers> and some of the police from the ranking
priests and the Pharisees, armed and with their lamps and torches.
[4]Jesus, of course, knew just what would happen to him, so he
went right up to them and says, "Who is it you're looking for?"
[5]"Jesus the Nazarene," was their reply.
"That's me," **says Jesus.**
And all the while Judas, who was turning him in, was standing
there with them. [6]But as soon as he said, "That's me," they all
retreated and fell to the ground.
[7]So Jesus asked them again, "Who are you looking for?"
"Jesus the Nazarene," they said.
[8]"I told you that's me," **Jesus answered,** "so if it's me you're look-
ing for, let the others go."
([9]This was so the prediction he had made would come true: "I
haven't lost one—not one of those you put in my care.")
[10]Simon Peter had brought along a sword, and now he drew it,
slashed at the high priest's slave, who was called Malchus, and cut
off his right ear.
[11]"Put the sword back in its scabbard," **Jesus told Peter.** "Am I not
to drink from the cup my Father has given me?"
[12]Then the detachment <of Roman soldiers> and their captain,
with the Judean police, arrested Jesus and put him under constraint.

The arrest. There are seven items in Mark's account of Jesus' arrest:

1. Judas as leader of the arresting party
2. The arrival of the arresting party
3. The kiss of identification

4. The arrest
5. The resistance
6. Jesus' reaction to the resistance
7. The flight of the disciples

The author of the Fourth Gospel does not mention item 3, the betrayal kiss, although Judas is still identified as the one who turned Jesus in (v. 5). At the point Mark narrates the kiss and the arrest, the author of John reports the exchange in vv. 4–9. In these verses Jesus is portrayed as being completely in charge of events: He identifies himself as the one they are looking for (v. 4–5, 7–8), which flabbergasts soldiers and police (v. 6). Jesus requests that the officers let the others go, after offering himself (v. 8).

The prediction Jesus had made that not one of his followers would be lost (v. 9) is evidently a reference to 17:12: "When I was with them, I kept them under your protection, and I guarded them; not one of them was lost, except the one destined to be lost, since scripture has to come true." The scripture reference in that earlier prediction is uncertain, although the author may have had in mind Ps 41:9, which he quotes in 13:18 ("The one who has shared my food has turned on me"). In any case, the predictions of Jesus have already begun to take on the authority of scripture in the Fourth Gospel: His prediction in 17:12 becomes the "scriptural" basis of the remark in 18:9.

In vv. 10–12, the author returns to the basic elements of the arrest story and narrates Peter's attempt to defend Jesus, together with Jesus' reaction. John identifies the attacker as Peter, whereas in the synoptic tradition he is just "one of those standing around" (Mark 14:47). The author of John even gives the servant of the high priest a name, Malchus. John joins Luke in identifying the ear as his right ear. Verses 10–11 thus cover items 5 and 6 in Mark's outline. John and Luke do not mention the flight of the disciples from the scene (item 7 in Mark's scheme).

The structures of all four versions of the arrest coincide so closely as to require a common source, in spite of details that only Luke and John share. That common tradition probably stems from Mark. Whatever the ultimate source, the tale of the arrest is a legend that embodies very little history. In the Gospel of John, the arresting party consists of a detachment of Roman soldiers and the temple police, an unlikely assemblage of authorities. The arrest itself is the one item that was colored pink in the synoptic accounts; here it is also, but without the definition of the forces sent to do the job (v. 12). The role of Judas, however, was again given a gray rating: some Fellows doubted that Judas was a historical person but agreed that someone who knew Jesus well led the officials to him at the appropriate time. In this respect, the Gospel of John makes more historical sense in having Judas take the officials to the *place,* rather than having Judas identify Jesus, who was probably well known. The balance of this account, like those in the other gospels, was rated black.

Even Raymond E. Brown identifies details of this narrative as products of the storyteller's imagination, details like the overreaction of the soldiers when Jesus identifies himself (v. 6) and the identification of Peter as the sword-wielder (v. 10). Brown would presumably have voted black on such details had he been a member of the Seminar.[79]

18 [13]They took him first to Annas. (Annas was the father-in-law
of that year's high priest, Caiaphas. [14]It was Caiaphas, you'll remem-
ber, who had given the Judeans this advice: It's to <your> advantage
that one man die for the people.)

Before Annas
Jn 18:13–14
Mk 14:53, Mt 26:57, Lk 22:54
Sources: John, Mark

Before Annas. Annas was high priest during the years 6–15 C.E.; he was removed from office by Valerius Gratus, according to the Jewish historian Josephus. Annas had five sons, all of whom attained the office of high priest. Caiaphas was the son-in-law of Annas; he held the office of high priest from 18 to 36 C.E. The statement in v. 13b is therefore historically accurate.

The references to the high priest in vv. 15, 16, 19, and 22 assume, however, that Annas was the high priest during the hearing, when Peter was in the courtyard denying that he was a follower of Jesus. That is an error. The confusion is perhaps to be explained by the fact that Annas continued to be the patriarch of a high priestly consortium made up of himself, his five sons, and Caiaphas, his son-in-law, although Annas himself no longer held the office of high priest. The confusion in the Johannine account must owe to indistinct memories of who was and who was not the official officeholder. Since the temple had been destroyed by the Romans in 70 C.E., the evangelist may even have forgotten that there could be only one high priest at a time.

Luke has also confused the two high priesthoods of Annas and Caiaphas. In Luke 3:2 he states that both Annas and Caiaphas were high priest at the time John the Baptist began his public work. Luke makes a slightly different error in Acts 4:6: there he says that Annas was high priest at the time Peter and John were arrested for curing a lame man and preaching. To be sure, Luke again groups Annas with Caiaphas, Jonathan, and Alexander, along with other members of the high priestly family.

The question of the hearing before Annas will be considered in the second narrative segment below.

18 [15]Simon Peter and another disciple continued to trail along
behind Jesus. This other disciple, somehow known to the high
priest, went in with Jesus to the high priest's court. [16]Peter was
standing outside the door; so this other disciple, the one acquainted
with the high priest, went out, had a word with the woman who
kept the door, and got Peter in.
[17]The woman who kept watch at the door says to Peter, "You're
not one of this man's disciples too, are you?"
"No, I'm not," he replies.
[18]Meanwhile, since it was cold, the slaves and police had made a
charcoal fire and were standing around it, trying to keep warm.
Peter was standing there too, warming himself.

Peter: first denial
Jn 18:15–18
Mk 14:66–72, Mt 26:69–75,
Lk 22:54b–62
Sources: John, Mark

Peter: first denial. The story of Peter's denial in the Fourth Gospel seems to have been derived from the Gospel of Mark. John Dominic Crossan persuaded the members of the Seminar that the intertwining of denial and interrogation by the high priest in the Gospel of John is literary evidence—Crossan calls it literary DNA—that Mark is the source of the intertwined accounts. If John borrowed his version of the interrogation from Mark, he may have decided to eliminate references to the name of the high priest in John 18:15, 16, 19, 22, who is assumed to be Annas (v. 13): in Matthew the high priest is Caiaphas (Matt 26:3, 57). The author of John resolved a potential discrepancy by eliminating the name.

Mark's view of Peter's denial appears to have been his own invention: It betrays numerous aspects of Mark's literary style, in addition to which the story would not have circulated as an independent anecdote during the oral period. Mark probably created Peter's denial as a climactic parallel to the behavior of disciples who were put to trial in his own time: like Peter, they were inclined to deny their allegiance. John may have borrowed the story without realizing that it compromises his more complimentary assessment of the followers of Jesus. It is black in John because it is black in Mark.

Before the Council
Jn 18:19–24
Mk 14:55–65, Mt 26:59–68, Lk 22:66–71
Sources: John, Mark

18 [19]**Now the high priest interrogated Jesus about his disciples and about his teaching.**

[20]"I have talked publicly to anyone and everyone," **Jesus replied.** "I've always taught in synagogues and in the temple area, in places where all Judeans gather. I've said nothing in secret. [21]Why are you asking me? Ask those who listened to what I told them—you'll find that they know what I said."

[22]**No sooner had he said this than one of the police on duty there slapped Jesus. "So this is how you talk back to the high priest!" he said.**

[23]"If I've said the wrong thing, tell me what's wrong with it," **Jesus said in reply.** "But if I'm right, why do you hit me?"

[24]**At that Annas sent him, under constraint as before, to the high priest, Caiaphas.**

Before the Council. According to the author of the Fourth Gospel, following the arrest, Jesus is taken first to Annas, who is identified as the father-in-law of the high priest Caiaphas (18:13–14). The author then narrates the first denial of Peter (18:15–18) before turning to the interrogation on the part of Annas in our present segment. Annas asks Jesus about his disciples and about his teaching (v. 19). Nothing is said about false witnesses, about blasphemy, or about the desire to concur on the death penalty. In the Gospel of John, Jesus never has a hearing before Caiaphas, unlike Matthew (neither Mark nor Luke mention the name of the high priest).

The exchange between Jesus and Annas is clearly the product of the imagination of the fourth evangelist. Jesus' remarks in vv. 20–21, in response to Annas' question about his disciples and his teaching, pictures Jesus as in complete control: he has always taught in public to anyone and everyone who would listen, so what he said should not be a mystery to so eminent an authority as the high priest (Annas is referred to as the high priest in vv. 19, 22). The slap on the cheek by one of the police was to remind Jesus of the respect he should have for that exalted office; it is also reminiscent of the treatment received by Micaiah when he prophesied truthfully but negatively about King Ahab, in contradiction to what the other court prophets had said. Zedekiah, one of the false prophets, slapped Micaiah on the cheek for speaking contrary to the other prophets and against the king (1 Kgs 22:5–28). In his prophetic vision, Micaiah had seen Israel scattered upon the mountains, like sheep without a shepherd (1 Kgs 22:17), in words that are reminiscent of Jesus' prophecy about his own fate and that of his disciples in Mark 14:27, a prophecy based on Zech 13:7.

The conclusion to the Johannine story returns to the thread of the narrative and has Jesus taken to Caiaphas (v. 24), whence he is taken to Pilate's residence (18:28). The array of authorities and witnesses so prominent in the synoptic version of the hearing before Caiaphas has disappeared entirely.

Since the Johannine account is probably the construct of the evangelist, or of his source, black is the appropriate color.

18 [25]**Meanwhile, Simon Peter was still standing outside, keeping warm. The others there said to him, "You're not one of his disciples too, are you?"**

He denied it: "No, I'm not," he said.

[26]**One of the high priest's slaves, a relative of the one whose ear Peter had cut off, says, "I saw you in the garden with him, didn't I?"**

[27]**Once again Peter denied it. At that moment a rooster crowed.**

Peter: second, third denials
Jn 18:25–27
Mk 14:66–72, Mt 26:69–75, Lk 22:54b–62
Sources: John, Mark

Peter: second, third denials. The Jesus Seminar came to the conclusion that the story of Peter's denial in the Fourth Gospel was based on the Markan account, despite its differences. To be sure, the Johannine account gives the impression that the storyteller has intimate knowledge of the scene. The "other disciple" is present and this other disciple is acquainted with the high priest (vv. 15–16). The fire is a charcoal fire, with people standing around it attempting to keep warm. The high priest's slave who accuses Peter of being one of Jesus' followers (v. 26) just happens to be there in the garden with the arresting party, and to be a relative of the one whose ear Peter had cut off. But that is intimate knowledge generated by a vigorous imagination. As in the case of Mark, this adaptation also merits a black rating.

18 [28]**They then take Jesus from Caiaphas' place to the governor's residence.** By now it was early morning. **They didn't actually go into the governor's residence; otherwise they would become unclean, and unable to eat the Passover meal.** [29]**Then Pilate came out and says to them, "What charge are you bringing against this man?"**

[30]**"If he hadn't committed a crime," they retorted, "we wouldn't have turned him over to you."**

Before Pilate
Jn 18:28–19:16
Mk 15:1–15, Mt 27:1–2, 11–26, Lk 23:1–7, 13–25; Pet 1:1–2
Sources: John, Mark, Peter

31"Deal with him yourselves," Pilate said to them. "Judge him by
your own Law."
"But it's illegal for us to execute anyone," the Judeans said to him.
(32They said this so Jesus' prediction of how he would die would
come true.)
33Then Pilate went back into his residence. He summoned Jesus
and asked him, "*You* are 'the King of the Judeans'?"
34"Is this what you think," **Jesus answered,** "or what other people
have told you about me?"
35"Am I a Judean?!" countered Pilate. "It's your own people and
the ranking priests who have turned you over to me. What have you
done?"
36To this Jesus responded, "Mine is not a secular government. If my
government were secular my companions would fight to keep me
from being turned over to the Judeans. But as it is, my government
does not belong to the secular domain."
37"So you are a king!" said Pilate.
"You're the one who says I'm a king," **responded Jesus.** "This is
what I was born for, and this is why I came into the world: to bear wit-
ness to the truth. Everyone who belongs to the truth can hear my
voice."
38"What is the truth?" says Pilate.
When he had said this, he again went out to the Judeans. "In my
judgment there is no case against him," he says to them. 39"But it's
your privilege at Passover to have me free one prisoner for you. So,
do you want me to free 'the King of the Judeans' for you?"
40At this they shouted out again, "Not him, but Barabbas!"
(Barabbas was a rebel.)

19

Only then did Pilate have Jesus taken away and beaten.
2And the <Roman> soldiers wove a crown out of thorns and put it
on his head; they also dressed him up in a purple robe. 3They began
marching up to him: "Greetings, 'King of the Judeans,'" they would
say, as they slapped him in the face.
4Pilate went outside once more. "See here," he says, "I'm bringing
him out to make it clear to you that in my judgment there is no case
against him."
5Now Jesus came outside, still wearing the crown of thorns and
the purple robe.
<Pilate> says to them, "See for yourselves: here's the man."
6When the ranking priests and the police saw him, they screamed,
"Crucify him! Crucify him!"
"Deal with him yourselves," Pilate tells them. "You crucify him. I
have told you already: I don't find him guilty of any crime."
7"We have our Law," the Judeans answered, "and our Law says

that he ought to die because he has made himself out to be God's
son."
8 When Pilate heard their statement he was even more afraid. 9 He
went back into his residence.
"Where are you from?" he asks Jesus.
But Jesus didn't answer him.
10 "You won't speak to me?" says Pilate. "Don't you understand? I
have the power to free you, and I have the power to crucify you."
11 "You would have no power of any kind over me," **said Jesus,**
"unless it was given to you from above. That is why the one who
turned me in to you has committed the greater sin."
12 At this, Pilate began to look for a way to release him. But the
Judeans screamed at him, "If you free this man, you're not the
emperor's friend! Every self-appointed king is in rebellion against
the emperor."
13 Pilate heard all this, but still he brought Jesus out and sat him on
the judge's seat in the place called Stone Pavement (*Gabbatha* in
Hebrew). 14 It was now the day of preparation for Passover, about
twelve noon. He says to the Judeans, "Look, here's your king."
15 But they only screamed, "Get him out of here! Crucify him!"
"Am I supposed to crucify your king?" asks Pilate.
The ranking priests answered him, "The emperor's our king—we
have no other!"
16 And so, in the end, <Pilate> turned him over to them to be cruci-
fied.

Before Pilate. Scholars generally agree that the fourth evangelist reshapes the lore about the trial and execution of Jesus for dramatic and theological reasons. In the case of the trial before Pilate the Roman governor, he paints a much more complicated picture than the one found in the Gospel of Mark. In Mark, Pilate interrogates Jesus about whether he considers himself king of the Judeans, but Jesus refuses to answer. A crowd then appears on the scene, according to Mark, and Pilate offers to release either Jesus or Barabbas to them; they call for the crucifixion of Jesus, and Pilate accedes to their demand. In the Fourth Gospel, in contrast, the Roman trial is narrated in seven elaborate scenes.

The stage is set in vv. 1–2: Jesus is taken from the high priest to Pilate's residence—a statement that is probably historically accurate and so is colored pink. Then the author explains: the Judeans did not wish to enter the governor's residence since that would make them unclean and disqualify them for participation in Passover, which was to begin, according to the Gospel of John, that evening at sundown (v. 2).

Recall that the Fourth Gospel makes the crucifixion of Jesus coincide with the slaughter of the Passover lambs on the afternoon of Nisan the 14th, in preparation for the Passover Seder that evening, whereas the synoptic gospels, following Mark, identify the last meal Jesus ate with his disciples as the

Passover Seder. In the synoptics, therefore, the trials and execution of Jesus take place on Passover, Nisan the 15th. Scholars are uncertain which of these two chronologies is correct; both cannot be. It is likely that the evangelists did not have any reliable historical information and so imagined how the trial and execution might have happened.

With the Judeans outside and Jesus inside Pilate's residence, the Fourth Gospel has Pilate move back and forth between the two in six scenes. In the middle, as scene four, Pilate has Jesus scourged and mocked. In Mark, the scourging and mocking take place at the end of the trial before Pilate (15:15–20). Just as Jesus' accusers were unable to agree on the charges against him, so the evangelists are unable to agree on the order of events.

Scene one (vv. 29–32) is set outside: Pilate urges the Judeans to deal with Jesus themselves. They respond that they cannot because it is illegal for them to execute anyone. This prompts the narrator to explain, in an aside to the reader, that their response guarantees the manner of Jesus' death, which is something Jesus had predicted. The narrator is presumably alluding to Jesus' words in John 3:14: "In the wilderness Moses elevated the snake [on a standard]; in the same way the son of Adam is destined to be elevated [on a cross]." The evangelist assumes that crucifixion was a form of execution employed only by the Romans. That assumption is not entirely correct, since we know that at least one Judean ruler employed crucifixion as well. In any case, the author has made the crucifixion of Jesus a narrative necessity and thus carried through one of his own themes.

In scene two (vv. 33–38a), Pilate quizzes Jesus inside about his kingship, as in the synoptic accounts. Rather than remain silent, Jesus engages Pilate in a lively exchange in direct discourse. Even Raymond Brown, who tends to give the fourth evangelist the benefit of the doubt, admits that Jesus' words are composed in Johannine style and are therefore fictions.[80] The Seminar colored them black in *The Five Gospels*.

The first two scenes are entirely of Johannine inspiration; they have virtually nothing in common with the synoptic stories. The third (vv. 38b–40) and fourth (19:1–3) scenes, however, have synoptic parallels. The first is devoted to the Barabbas incident, the second to the scourging and mocking. If one has come to the Johannine version from the synoptic account, one expects the trial to end at the end of scene three: the crowd has demanded Barabbas be released and Jesus crucified; Pilate orders Jesus to be flogged. The crucifixion should come next. But it does not.

Mocking. Although the Fourth Gospel relates the mocking of Jesus as something that occurred during rather than after the trial before Pilate, the Fellows of the Seminar agreed that Jesus was probably flogged as a part of the Roman abuse that usually accompanied crucifixion. The Fellows did so on the basis of historical plausibility, not simply because the evangelists report it.

John joins Matthew (Matt 27:27–31) and Peter (Pet 3:1–4) in giving his readers an abbreviated version of the mocking scene found in Mark (15:16–20). (Luke has the arresting party make fun of Jesus prior to his trial [Luke 22:63–5], and later Herod and his troops join in the mockery [23:11].) Investing Jesus in royal robes and putting a crown of thorns on his head was the evangelists' method of having Jesus' enemies proclaim Jesus king. The effect of this form of ritual theater was to make fun of those who rejected Jesus at the very moment they thought they were making fun of him: They thought they were joking but, from the Christian point of view, they were actually telling the truth. For the rhetorician—for the evangelist as propagandist—that is juicy strategy indeed. But the scene is a figment of the Christian imagination. Jesus did not suggest that he was anointed royalty; he did not even hint that he was an anointed messiah. There is a double irony involved: the mocking scene has Jesus' enemies say something they did not intend to say; the intended meaning of the gospel writers—Jesus really *is* king of the Judeans—makes Jesus say something he did not say and did not want to say. A double black would be correct, were that possible.

The trial resumes. The author of the Fourth Gospel constructs three additional scenes that are somewhat confused. In the fifth scene (19:4–9a), Pilate is back outside. He brings Jesus out in due course, clad in the purple robe and crown of thorns he has just acquired. Pilate presents their king to the Judeans. They respond, as expected, by rejecting their king and asking that he be crucified instead. At the conclusion of this scene Pilate goes back inside.

Pilate has another conversation with Jesus inside his residence in 19:9b–12a (scene six). Pilate doesn't like the way things are going, so he seeks some way to release Jesus. But the Judeans suddenly appear again—Pilate must have gone back outside—and resume their shouting (scene seven, 19:12b–16). Now Pilate brings Jesus back out and presents him once again as a king by placing him on the judgment seat—the seat Pilate occupies when he is rendering verdicts. Pilate gives in. The final three scenes are evidently an afterthought of the evangelist: The movements of Pilate and Jesus are muddled, and Jesus is again given Johannine words to mouth.

In spite of the fact that the version of the trial before Pilate is at variance with the synoptic account, the basic ingredients are constant: Pilate's interrogation of Jesus about kingship; the Barabbas incident; the crowd calling for crucifixion; the scourging and mocking. The author of the Gospel of John has just let his imagination roam over the narrative terrain and made a better story out of it. It is riveting drama but poor history. Except for the three points at which the synoptic accounts may touch fact—the transfer of Jesus to Pilate; the time of day; Pilate's order to crucify—the Johannine account merits black coloring as history.

19 **So they took Jesus, [17]who carried the cross for himself, out to**
the place called Skull (known in Hebrew as Golgotha). **[18]There they**
crucified him, and with him two others—one on each side, with
Jesus in the middle.

[19]Pilate also had a notice written and posted it on the cross; it read:
"Jesus the Nazarene, the King of the Judeans." **[20]Many of the**
Judeans saw the notice, since Jesus was crucified near the city and it
was written in Hebrew, Latin, and Greek. [21]The ranking Judean

Crucifixion
Jn 19:17–24
Mk 15:22–32, Mt 27:33–44, Lk 23:33–43; Pet 4:1–5
Sources: John, Mark, Peter

priests tried protesting to Pilate: "Don't write, 'The King of the Judeans,' but instead, 'This man said, "I am King of the Judeans."'"

[22]Pilate answered them, "What I have written stays written."

[23]When the <Roman> soldiers had crucified Jesus, they took his clothes and divided them into four shares, one share for each soldier. But his shirt was woven continuously without seam. [24]So they said to each other, "Let's not tear it, but toss to see who gets it."

(This happened so that the scripture would come true that says, "They divided my garments among them, and for my clothes they cast lots.")

Crucifixion. It is not altogether clear who the agents of Jesus' crucifixion are in the Gospel of John. If we take "them" in 19:16 to refer to the Judean authorities of 19:12 and 15, then they are the agents of Jesus' death in 19:18. But in v. 23, the evangelist states that the Roman soldiers crucified Jesus, and that comports with information that had been reported as far back as 18:3 and 12—the Roman soldiers arrest Jesus, and with the information provided subsequently by 19:24 (the Roman soldiers divide Jesus' clothing) and 19:32 (the Roman soldiers break the legs of those crucified). John has evidently conflated two versions of the trial and crucifixion or woven together two strands of responsibility. In Mark and Matthew, the Romans are clearly responsible, although the Judean authorities concur; in Luke and Peter, the Judeans are to blame.

In other respects, the fourth evangelist mixes a slightly different narrative stew out of the same basic ingredients found in the synoptic accounts. He does not mention the wine mixed with myrrh (Mark 15:23), and he fails to include the extended taunts and jibes at the figure on the cross depicted by Mark (15:29–32). He also has Jesus carry his own cross rather than enlist Simon of Cyrene to do the job (Mark 15:21). But he has the place, Golgotha, and the two co-crucifieds, with Jesus between them (vv. 17–18). He makes a great deal of the placard specifying the crime (vv. 19–22) and the division of clothes (vv. 23–24), both of which he expands.

The Fourth Gospel also has the placard posted on the cross, as in Matthew. The inscription varies slightly from the synoptic version, which read simply, "King of the Judeans" (Mark 15:26) or "This is Jesus the King of the Judeans" (Matt 27:37). The exchange with the ranking Judean priests in vv. 21–22 is the author exercising the storyteller's license.

The use of the placard by the Romans to indicate the crime for which punishment was being given was apparently common. In addition to the examples cited in Matthew's version of the crucifixion, Suetonius, the Roman historian of late first and early second century C.E., relates how the Emperor Caligula (reigned 37–41 C.E.) punished a slave who had stolen a piece of silver: the executioners cut off his hands, tied them around his neck, and took him for a tour of tables at a public dinner, preceded by a placard explaining the reason for the punishment (Suetonius, *Caligula* 32.2).

Dio Cassius, another Roman historian, who spanned the second-third centuries C.E., tells how Caesar Augustus punished a slave who had deserted his son: He paraded him through the Forum with an inscription indicating why he was to be put to death, and then he had him crucified (*Roman History* 54.3.7).

Since the use of the placard in connection with punishment was so common among the Romans, the Fellows allowed that a similar device may have been used for Jesus. The uncertainty of the information contained in the gospel reports prompted many Fellows to choose a gray rating.

The author of the Gospel of John takes the storyteller's approach to the division of Jesus' possessions, in this case, his garments. According to the author, they were divided into four lots, which meant there were four soldiers, each entitled to a share (v. 23). His shirt, the inner garment, was without seam, however, so rather than tear it into four parts, they tossed to see who would get it (v. 24). It was observed in the commentary on the parallel passage in Mark that the event itself had been suggested to some Christian storyteller by a scripture passage, which the author of the Fourth Gospel quotes but does not identify (it is from Ps 21:19 LXX; English 22:18). The original fiction is further enhanced by these additional inventions.

Except for the two items colored red and gray in the text of John, the Fellows persisted in the view that the story of the execution of Jesus did not rest on historical memory but was the product of Christian imagination.

The death of Jesus
Jn 19:25–37
Mk 15:33–41, Mt 27:45–56,
Lk 23:44–49; Pet 5:1–6
Sources: John, Mark, Peter

19 **So while the <Roman> soldiers did this,** 25Jesus' mother, his
mother's sister, Mary the wife of Clopas, and Mary of Magdala
stood by his cross. **26When Jesus saw his mother, and standing
nearby the disciple he loved most, he says to his mother,** "Woman,
here is your son." **27Then he says to the disciple,** "Here is your
mother." **And from that moment the disciple considered her part of
his own family.**

**28Then, since Jesus knew that the course of events had come to an
end, so the scripture would come true, he says, "I'm thirsty."**

**29A bowl of sour wine was sitting there, and so they filled a
sponge with wine, stuck it on some hyssop, and held it to his mouth.
30When Jesus had taken some wine, he said, "It's all over."**

His head sank and he breathed his last.

**31Since it was the day of preparation, the Judeans asked Pilate to
have the legs of the three broken and the bodies taken away.
Otherwise their bodies would remain on the cross during the sabbath day. (That sabbath was a high holy day.)**

**32The <Roman> soldiers came and broke the legs of the first man,
and then of the other who had been crucified with him. 33But when
they came to Jesus, they could see that he was already dead, so they
didn't break his legs. 34Instead, one of the soldiers jabbed him in the
side with his spear, and right away blood and water came pouring
out. (35The one who observed this has given this testimony and his
testimony is true. He knows he is telling the truth, so you too will
believe.) 36This happened so the scripture that says, "No bone of his**

shall be broken," would come true, [37]as well as another scripture that says, "They shall look at the one they have pierced."

The death of Jesus. The death scene in the Fourth Gospel seems to have little in common with the same scene in the Gospel of Mark. In Mark, seven items are narrated:

1. darkness at noon
2. Jesus' shout at 3 P.M.
3. offer of sour wine
4. death
5. curtain of temple torn in two
6. confession of the Roman officer
7. the women at the cross

The author of the Fourth Gospel includes only four items in this scene:

1. the women at the cross (19:25–27)
2. the offer of sour wine (19:28–30)
3. death (19:30)
4. legs of Jesus not broken (19:31–37)

Upon closer inspection, the author actually treats three of Mark's items, but does so in quite a different manner. The women at the cross are moved to the head of the story and a sentimental scene created in an exchange between Jesus and the disciple Jesus loved most. The author gives more narrative body to the offer of sour wine. Mark has Jesus given two drinks, one at the beginning of the ordeal and one just before he dies (15:23, 36). According to the Gospel of Peter, Jesus was apparently given a poisonous drink to hasten the end (5:2–3). The drink is there, in different quantities and for different purposes. In all versions of course, Jesus dies.

As in the crucifixion scene, the author of John elects to emphasize one item. Here he focuses on the fact that Jesus' legs were not broken. This is a motif the Fourth Gospel has in common with the Gospel of Peter and only with that gospel (4:4–5). In John, it is Jesus' legs that are not broken in fulfillment of Ps 34:20:

> The Lord will protect all their bones;
> Not one of them will be broken.

When the soldiers come to break Jesus' legs, he is already dead so his legs remain unbroken. However, one soldier pierces his side with a spear, which might be understood simply as an act of mercy to hasten death, were it not inspired by a statement in Zechariah (12:10): "they will look on him whom they have pierced."

In Peter, oddly enough, it is the good criminal whose legs are not broken in retribution for his rebuke of the soldiers around the cross. The legs of those crucified were broken to hasten death; it was an act of mercy. Failure to break the legs meant a lingering death. The soldiers were angry because the thief has criticized them for gambling over Jesus' clothes. The motif has migrated from one figure in the death scene in Peter to the other in John. It is impossible from this historical distance to know which was first.

The fourth evangelist puts his own personal testimony in v. 35, or rather the fiction of the personal testimony of the disciple whom Jesus loved most. The historian becomes the most skeptical at such claims in documents so far removed from the original events. The testimony here goes with the witnessing hand at the end of the gospel: "This is the disciple who is testifying to all this and has written it down, and we know his testimony is reliable" (21:24). Scholars are confident that chapter 21 of the Gospel of John is the work of a later hand.

Aside from the notice that some of the women were present at the crucifixion in v. 25, the Johannine version of Jesus' death, like the other gospel versions, is the product of imagination laced with scriptural allusions. Black is the correct color.

19 **38 After all this, Joseph of Arimathea—a disciple of Jesus, but**
only secretly because he was afraid of the Judeans—asked Pilate's
permission to take Jesus' body down. Pilate agreed, so <Joseph>
came and took his body down. 39 Nicodemus—the one who had first
gone to him at night—came too, bringing a mixture of myrrh and
aloes weighing about seventy-five pounds. 40 So they took Jesus'
body, and wound it up in strips of burial cloth along with the spices,
as the Judeans customarily do to bury their dead. 41 Now there was a
garden in the place where he had been crucified, and a new tomb in
the garden where no one had yet been laid to rest. 42 Since this tomb
was handy and because of the Judean day of preparation, it was here
that they laid Jesus.

The burial
Jn 19:38–42
Mk 15:42–47, Mt 27:57–61, Lk 23:50–56; Pet 2:1–5, 6:1–4
Sources: John, Mark, Peter

The burial. As in the case of the other evangelists, the author of the Fourth Gospel embellishes the figure of Joseph of Arimathea. Matthew had turned Joseph into a follower of Jesus as well as a rich man (27:57); the Gospel of John now makes him out to be a secret follower because he feared the Judeans (v. 38)—the hostility of the Judeans is a regular feature of this gospel. The author also gives Joseph a partner in Nicodemus, who was introduced into the Fourth Gospel in 3:1. He has an extended conversation with Jesus (3:2–21). Nicodemus is described as a Pharisee, a ruler of the Jews, and a teacher of Israel. He later defends Jesus (7:50–52). Now he joins Joseph in the burial. In the opinion of many of the Fellows of the Seminar, Nicodemus is a Johannine fiction.

Nicodemus provides an unbelievable amount of myrrh and aloes, probably in dry form. Seventy-five pounds would have prepared many corpses for burial. There seems to be a Johannine penchant for exaggerated numbers: Jesus turned more than one hundred twenty gallons of water into wine at Cana (2:6) and there were 153 fish in the miraculous catch narrated in 21:11. These numbers may have symbolic value; they certainly are exaggerations. None of the other gospels mentions spices being put into the tomb on Friday.

In the synoptic gospels, Jesus is wrapped in a shroud for burial. Here in the Fourth Gospel, Jesus' body is wrapped in strips of cloth interspersed with spices. Defenders of the shroud of Turin prefer the synoptic version, since the shroud consists of one continuous piece of cloth. The Johannine version seems to contradict the notion of a shroud.

The location of the tomb in the Fourth Gospel is adjacent to the place of execution and is described as a garden (v. 41). The Gospel of Peter also refers to the tomb as "Joseph's Garden," presumably as a place name. If the place of execution was the location of frequent crucifixions, it is unlikely that a private cemetery was close by. Christian memory, however, did not like the thought that Jesus had been buried in a common grave, so storytellers made it a private burial plot. Christian memory liked even less the notion that Jesus had not been buried at all. The fact is, Christian storytellers may well not have known what happened to Jesus' body.

Scholars have worked hard over the years to reconcile the various accounts of Jesus' burial—without success. The desire to mask unpleasant memories with narrative memorials is unquenchable. The brute facts of history often belie the results of that proclivity. The Johannine version, like those found in the synoptic gospels and Peter, is most likely a product of the Christian imagination. Black is the accurate color.

Note: The stories of the empty tomb, appearance of Jesus, and the ascension have been gathered into a separate section, pp. 449-95. Color coding and commentary on John 20:1–18, 19–23, 24–29, 21:1–14, 15–23 appear there.

20 [30]Although Jesus performed many more miracles for his disci-
ples to see than could be written down in this book, [31]these are written
down so you will come to believe that Jesus is the anointed, God's
son—and by believing this have life in his name.

21 [24]This is the disciple who is testifying to all this and has writ-
ten it down, and we know that his testimony is reliable.
[25]Jesus of course did many other things. If they were all to be
recorded in detail, I doubt that the entire world would hold the books
that would have to be written.

The Gospel of John has two different endings, one concludes chapter 20 and the other chapter 21. In each case the narrator speaks—the same voice addressed to the reader in the parenthetical comment at 19:35 that insisted its testimony was believable.

John 20:30–31 reads like the original ending of this gospel. Whoever later added chapter 21 concluded by speaking in the voice of the earlier narrator and again claiming to provide reliable testimony. This person is never identified by name. Later tradition assumed it was the disciple "John," even though he is not mentioned in this gospel.

THE GOSPEL OF PETER

1 . . . but of the Judeans no one washed his hands, neither Herod nor any one of his judges. Since they were [un]willing to wash, Pilate stood up. [2]Then Herod the king orders the Lord to be [taken away], saying to them "Do what I commanded you to do to him."

Before Pilate
Pet 1:1–2
Mk 15:1–15, Mt 27:1–2, 11–26, Lk 23:1–7, 13–25; Jn 18:28–19:16
Sources: Peter, Mark, John

Before Pilate. The fragmentary Gospel of Peter begins as the trial before Pilate and Herod draws to an end. Peter shares the handwashing scene with the Gospel of Matthew (27:24–25), the only other gospel to mention it. Except that, in this case, Pilate alone presumably washes his hands (the narrative assumes that in v. 1); Herod and his judges refuse. Quite surprisingly, Herod appears to be in charge of the trial (Herod the tetrarch was out of his domain in Jerusalem and would have been subordinate to Pilate the Roman governor). It is he that gives the order to have Jesus crucified (v. 2). This of course contradicts the picture painted by the other gospels.

The Fellows were unable to consider any of this material historical. They designated it black.

2 Joseph stood there, the friend of Pilate and the Lord, and when he realized that they were about to crucify him, he went to Pilate and asked for the body of the Lord for burial. [2]And Pilate sent to Herod and asked for his body. [3]And Herod replied, "Brother Pilate, even if no one had asked for him, we would have buried him, since the sabbath is drawing near. [4]For it is written in the Law, 'The sun must not set upon one who has been executed.'" [5]And he turned him over to the people on the day before their feast, known as Unleavened Bread, began.

Request for the body
Pet 2:1–5
Mk 15:43–45, Mt 27:57–58, Lk 23:50–52; Jn 19:38–42
Sources: Peter, Mark, John

Request for the body. This segment in the Gospel of Peter anticipates the burial of Jesus by Joseph in 6:1–4. Joseph is represented here not only as a friend of Jesus, but as a friend of Pilate. In Mark, Joseph is a respected member of the Council and is looking for the kingdom of God to come (Mark 15:43). Matthew has made Joseph a rich man and a follower of Jesus (Matt 27:57). Luke attempts to correct Mark's inconsistencies: Joseph is a decent and upright man who did not endorse the decision and action of the Council (Mark had reported it as unanimous). Luke also has Joseph looking for the kingdom of God (Luke 23:50–51). In the Gospel of John, Joseph is a secret follower of Jesus because he feared the Judeans (John 19:38); he is joined in the burial of Jesus by Nicodemus, another of the Fourth Gospel's fictitious characters (John 19:39). It seems the fiction of Joseph of Arimathea is adjusted outward with every telling. It is difficult to know which of the stories is the source of all the others, but on balance a majority of the Fellows of the Seminar voted for Mark's version. A somewhat larger majority took the view that Joseph of Arimathea was Mark's invention. It follows that this part of the Gospel of Peter is dependent on Mark for its information.

Verses 2–4 are a continuation of the role of Herod in Jesus' trial and execution. Peter shares this theme with the Gospel of Luke (23:8–12). In Pet 1:2, Herod turns Jesus over to the people for execution. This order is finally consummated in 2:4, after Joseph has requested the body of Jesus.

As a friend of Pilate, Joseph goes to him to ask for burial rights (v. 1). Pilate apparently does not have the disposition rights, so he in turn makes the request of Herod. And it is Herod who sets the stage for the burial before sundown by citing the law. The law referred to in v. 3 is Deut 21:22–23:

> [22]If anyone commits a crime the penalty for which is death and he is put to death and you hang him on a tree, [23]his body is not to be on the tree overnight. Rather, you are to bury him that same day. For anyone hanging on a tree is accursed by God. You must not defile the land which the Lord your God gives you for an inheritance.

This law assumes that someone has been executed and then hung on a tree or cross (v. 22). This would be a case of the crucifixion of someone already dead. The crucifixion of the living, that is, execution by crucifixion, was also practiced. Josephus reports that Alexander Jannaeus (104–78 B.C.E.), one of the successful Hasmonean rulers in the wake of Judas Maccabeus' successful revolt (168–64 B.C.E.), murdered one of his own brothers upon coming to power and became such a tyrant that the Jewish populace rose in revolt against him. Jannaeus retaliated by taking Jewish prisoners, bringing them to Jerusalem, and then crucifying eight hundred of them in the middle of the city. As his victims hung on their crosses, he had their wives and children butchered in front of them, while he dallied with his concubines (Josephus, *Jewish War*, 1.85–98). Crucifixion, it seems, was not practiced only by the Romans.

Whether the deuteronomic law was regularly observed by Herod, or by Pilate, or by other Judean leaders, is not known. Josephus, who is often given to exaggeration, reports that the Idumeans (Herod the Great was an Idumean) tossed out corpses without burial during the fighting in Jerusalem (66–70 C.E.). But the Judeans, he informs us, followed the custom prescribed by Deuteronomy, even for those condemned to crucifixion, and buried the dead before sundown (*Jewish War*, 4.317). It is more likely that the story of Jesus' burial was conceived to fit the law, rather than the law applied to the case of Jesus. So much of the story is fiction that it is virtually impossible to isolate any details that might reflect actual historical memories.

The "he" in v. 4 is of course Herod—which Herod is not clear, but if historical accuracy is involved, it must have been Herod Antipas, the tetrarch who governed Galilee and Perea 4 B.C.E.–39 C.E. There were so many rulers named Herod during the period surrounding Jesus' life that references, especially in fiction, could be to any one of them from Herod the Great (37–4 B.C.E.) to Herod Agrippa I (41–44 C.E.).

The tissue of fictions that constitutes the burial narrative does not breed confidence in historical detail, or even in the fact of burial. The Fellows were not even certain that Jesus was buried. The result is a black designation.

3 They took the Lord and kept pushing him along as they ran;
and they would say, "Let's drag the son of God along, since we have
him in our power." 2And they threw a purple robe around him and
sat him upon the judgment seat and said, "Judge justly, king of
Israel." 3And one of them brought a crown of thorns and set it on the
head of the Lord. 4And others standing about would spit in his eyes,
and others slapped his face, while others poked him with a rod.
Some kept flogging him as they said, "Let's pay proper respect to the
son of God."

Mocking
Pet 3:1–4
Mk 15:16–20, Mt 27:27–31; Jn 19:1–3
Sources: Peter, Mark, John
Cf. Zech 3:3–5 (LX)

Mocking. In this mock investiture of Jesus in the Gospel of Peter, pushing the Lord along was suggested by Ps 117:13 LXX (English 118:13). Robing him with royal robes in jest is derived, of course, from real investiture protocol: the new king, or his vice regent, would be given royal robes, a crown for his head, a staff of authority to be carried in his right hand, and a gold chain for his neck. The king would assume the judgment seat and presumably render just verdicts. That particular aspect of this scene may have been suggested by Isa 58:2. The ritual robing itself is probably derived from the prophet Zech (3:1–5). Spitting and slapping were taken directly from Isa 50:6. Flogging is also mentioned in Isa 50:6, but flogging often preceded crucifixion in Roman forms of punishment and so probably was inflicted on Jesus prior to his execution.

The abuse of Jesus, particularly poking him with a rod (v. 4), may have been suggested by the popular scapegoat ritual. On the Day of Atonement, two goats were selected to bear the sins of the people. One goat was sacrificed on the altar, the second—the scapegoat—was dispatched ritually into the wilderness to die there. In some ancient texts, the priest and the people *spit* their sins on the scapegoat and *nudged* it along with a reed or rod toward the wilderness. Details from various prophetic texts appear to have been combined to produce this strange ceremony now applied to the crucifixion of Jesus.

The mocking scene functions as a piece of Christian apologetic in the Gospel of Peter: for Christians Jesus really is the son of God. The ritual theater depicted here was the evangelists' way of getting Jesus' opponents to confess the truth but to do so indirectly. As a fiction invented in all probability by the author of the Gospel of Mark, it merits a black rating.

Crucifixion
Pet 4:1–5
Mk 15:22–32, Mt 27:33–44,
Lk 23:33–43; Jn 19:17–24
Sources: Peter, Mark, John

**4 And they brought two criminals and crucified the Lord
between them. But he himself remained silent, as if in no pain. [2]And
when they set up the cross, they put an inscription on it, "This is the
king of Israel." [3]And they piled his clothing in front of him; then
they divided it among themselves, and gambled for it. [4]But one of
those criminals reproached them and said, "We're suffering for the
evil that we've done, but this fellow, who has become a savior of
humanity, what wrong has he done to you?" [5]And they got angry at
him and ordered that his legs not be broken so he would die in
agony.**

Crucifixion. The Gospel of Peter has four of the basic elements of the crucifixion reported in the other gospels: the two criminals with whom Jesus was crucified; the inscription on the cross; the division of Jesus' clothes; and words of one of the criminals. The author of the Gospel of Peter elected to feature the last item. The author of the Fourth Gospel chose to focus on the inscription and the division of clothing (John 19:19–22 and 23–24). The Gospel of Mark, on the other hand, seems to emphasize the taunts that come at the end of the scene (15:29–32). Luke comes the closest to Peter in featuring the exchange between the two criminals (23:39–43).

In Luke, one criminal is abusive, the other is sympathetic to Jesus. The good one chastises the abusive criminal and defends Jesus. In the Gospel of John, the two crucifieds are there with Jesus, but they are not identified as criminals (although they must have been so regarded) and they say nothing. Jesus is serenely in charge of events and needs no defense. In Mark and Matthew, where they are called "rebels," both of them abuse Jesus. Peter has his further variation: one criminal defends Jesus to the soldiers who are dividing up his clothing (v. 4).

Peter adds nothing to the story of the crucifixion that can be regarded as independent verification of the event or of any detail. Black is the appropriate color.

The death of Jesus
Pet 5:1–6
Mk 15:33–41, Mt 27:45–56,
Lk 23:44–49; Jn 19:25–37
Sources: Peter, Mark, John

**5 It was midday and darkness covered the whole of Judea. They
were confused and anxious for fear the sun had set since he was still
alive. <For> it is written that, "The sun must not set upon one who
has been executed." [2]And one of them said, "Give him vinegar
mixed with something bitter to drink." And they mixed it and gave
it to him to drink. [3]And they fulfilled all things and brought to completion the sins on their head. [4]Now many went about with lamps,
and, thinking that it was night, they lay down. [5]And the Lord cried
out, saying,** "My power, <my> power, you have abandoned me."

When he said this, he was taken up. 6And at that moment, the veil of the Jerusalem temple was torn in two.

The death of Jesus. The Gospel of Peter has several features in common with the Gospel of Mark: the darkness at noon, which here persists so long that people begin to go to bed thinking it is night (vv. 1, 4); the offer of sour wine mixed with something bitter (v. 2); the shout at the time Jesus expires (v. 5); the rending of the veil of the temple (v. 6). However, the author of Peter adds some wrinkles of his own to the story.

The darkness at noon produces anxiety, as eclipses tend to do, but in this case the anxiety was heightened by the fear that they had broken the law, the law that prohibited the body of an executed criminal to be left exposed overnight (Deut 21:22–23). Peter is the only evangelist to quote the law. He further interprets the drink offered to Jesus as a poison drink intended to hasten death. Peter understands this not as an act of mercy, but as a move inspired by the desire for Jesus to die so they could take him down from the cross in advance of the sabbath just about to begin (vv. 2–3).

The cry of Jesus from the cross in v. 5 is a revision of Ps 22:1, which reads: "My God, my God, why did you abandon me?" The Gospel of Peter may also reflect the very early understanding that Jesus' ascent into heaven took place simultaneously with death (v. 5).

The author of Peter has recounted some of the elements common to the other gospels, but has added unique material. It is possible that all five versions are derived from a single source. Scholars are simply divided about what that source is. Further discussion of this problem can be found in the cameo, "Sources for the Passion Story" (pp. 246–47). The Fellows of the Seminar were fairly certain, however, that the elements of Peter's account are also fictive whatever their source.

The burial
Pet 6:1–4
Mk 15:42–47, Mt 27:57–61, Lk 23:50–56; Jn 19:38–42
Sources: Peter, Mark, John

6 And then they pulled the nails from the Lord's hands and set him on the ground. And the whole earth shook and there was great fear. 2Then the sun came out and it turned out to be 3 P.M. 3Now the Judeans rejoiced and gave his body to Joseph so that he might bury it, since <Joseph> had observed how much good he had done. 4<Joseph> took the Lord, washed <his body> and wound a linen <shroud> around him, and brought him to his own tomb, called "Joseph's Garden."

The burial. The account of Jesus' burial in the Gospel of Peter is anticipated by Joseph of Arimathea, who requests the body in advance of the execution (Pet 2:1–4). In the other gospels, Joseph's request comes after the execution.

The author of the Gospel of Peter pictures Jesus' hands as nailed to the cross, in which case his feet were probably tied (v. 1). The skeleton of the only crucified victim ever discovered in Palestine betrayed the opposite arrangement: feet nailed to the cross, arms lashed to the cross. Peter shares with

Matthew the notion that an earthquake occurred at the time of Jesus' death (v. 1b; Matt 27:51). At 3 P.M. the sun comes out, presumably after the darkness that had fallen on the land around noon (Mark 15:33). The reappearance of the sun prompts the Judeans to shed their fears (v. 1) and begin to rejoice (v. 3). The Judeans give the body to Joseph for burial.

In the Gospels of Mark and Matthew, the crucifixion of Jesus is carried out by the Romans. In the Gospel of Peter, both the order for execution and the execution itself are performed by Herod and the Judeans. Luke also makes the Judeans responsible for the death of Jesus. In Peter and Luke, Jesus is at the mercy of his own people, so to speak, rather than his external enemies. This difference constitutes a fundamental discrepancy in the accounts. John seems to vacillate in assigning primary responsibility as though he were making a poor attempt to weave together two narrative strands.

Joseph's reputation is further enhanced by the acknowledgment that Joseph had observed how much good Jesus had done (v. 3). In Mark, Joseph wraps Jesus' body in a shroud, places him in a tomb, and seals the entrance (Mark 15:46). In the commentary on the other versions of this story, we observed how Joseph's service grew in care and detail. Here in Peter we learn that Joseph washes the body of Jesus before wrapping it in a shroud (v. 4), a detail not found in any of the other gospels. And Peter, like Matthew, identifies the tomb as Joseph's own tomb and Peter even gives it a name (also v. 4). These are all fictions of early Christian storytellers that reflect the hope that Jesus' body was treated in ways appropriate to their memory of him. Black is the correct color.

Mourning & regrets
Pet 7:1–3
Lk 23:48
Sources: Peter, Luke

7 Then the Judeans and the elders and the priests perceived what evil they had done to themselves, and began to beat their breasts and cry out "Our sins have brought woes upon us! The judgment and the end of Jerusalem are at hand!" [2]But I began weeping with my friends. And quivering with fear in our hearts, we hid ourselves. After all, we were being sought by them as criminals and as ones wishing to burn down the temple. [3]As a result of all these things, we fasted and sat mourning and weeping night and day until the sabbath.

Mourning & regrets. Luke introduced a note of regret into his version of the crucifixion (23:48). The author of the Gospel of Peter has developed this same note—whether he got it from Luke or not is uncertain—into a more elaborate account. The Judeans, elders, and priests together confess their sins and accept their guilt, probably at the suggestion of Isa 3:9, where the people confess that they have brought evil on themselves. In Ezek 9:1, the judgment of Jerusalem is said to be at hand, and in Zech 12:10–12, the people mourn for the one they have pierced. These suggestions in ancient prophetic texts were readily reinterpreted as foreshadowing events to occur at a much later time, usually in the reinterpreter's own time.

In any case, the Gospel of Peter not only provides a full description here of regret and repentance, but also anticipates the notice in 11:6, where the elders, who are among those who are guarding the tomb, think they may be stoned for their mistake in crucifying Jesus.

This fiction, like the suggestion in the Gospel of Luke, is regrettable for many reasons, not the least of which is the untold harm it has done to Jewish-Christian relations over the centuries. As a fiction it deserves to be colored black.

Sealing the tomb
Pet 8:1–6
Mt 27:62–66
Sources: Peter, Matthew

8 **When the scholars and the Pharisees and the priests had gath-**
ered together, and when they heard that all the people were moan-
ing and beating their breasts, and saying, "If his death has produced
these overwhelming signs, he must have been entirely innocent!",
[2]they became frightened and went to Pilate and begged him, [3]"Give
us soldiers so that <we> may guard his tomb for three [days], in case
his disciples come and steal his body and the people assume that he
is risen from the dead and do us harm."
[4]So Pilate gave them the centurion Petronius with soldiers to
guard the tomb. And elders and scholars went with them to the
tomb. [5]And all who were there <with> the centurion and the sol-
diers helped roll a large stone against the entrance to the tomb. [6]And
they put seven seals on it. Then they pitched a tent there and kept
watch.

Sealing the tomb. In Matthew's version of this story, it is the ranking priests and Pharisees who seal the tomb and post a guard to make sure Jesus' disciples do not steal his body. The author of the Gospel of Peter has spun this story out into a rather large tale. It was once said of a pastor that he could take the white of one egg and whip it up enough to fill a large church sanctuary with meringue. Peter has filled up four chapters with meringue from the one suggestion that there was a guard at the tomb.

In Peter's version, it is the Pharisees and priests who go to Pilate and ask for a guard (vv. 1–3). Rather than have Pilate instruct them to do their own guarding, as in Matthew (27:65), in the Gospel of Peter, Pilate gives them a centurion named Petronius and soldiers to serve as guards. Elders and scholars representing the Judeans accompany the soldiers (v. 4). All of them join in rolling a huge stone against the entrance; they seal it with no fewer than seven seals. They pitch a tent and post the watch (vv. 5–6). The story has taken on several particulars, including a name for the centurion, who is otherwise unknown.

The evangelist's imagination does not stop there. In the next chapter, we are told the soldiers stood watch, two by two, during the night (9:2). In chapter 10, we learn that the soldiers observed the stone roll away by itself and two young men enter the tomb (9:4 and 10:1). Meanwhile, they wake up the centurion and the elders, who apparently had fallen asleep.

The role of the guards is extended even further. At the beginning of chapter 11, they are all consulting with each other about whether they should report to Pilate. While this conference is going on, a human being descends from the sky and enters the tomb (11:1–2). The centurion and all those around him note this strange sight and rush out into the night to tell Pilate, forgetting that they were supposed to be on guard. As they are relating their story to Pilate, they all blurt out their confession that this man—Jesus—was truly a son of God. So it is not just the centurion, as in the Gospel of Mark (15:39), but everybody in unison reciting the Christian confession (11:3), as in Matthew (27:54).

The function of the guard at the tomb does not stop even there. A crowd had gathered to see the sealed tomb, according to the author (9:1), and they now urge Pilate to order the centurion and his troops to keep quiet (11:5). Pilate obliges them by issuing the order of silence (11:7).

It is not that this version of the tale is more fictitious than its counterpart in Matthew. They are equally the product of the Christian imagination. It is just that the author of Peter has made the Romans a consistent Christian partner and focused the blame even more narrowly on the priests, Pharisees, elders, and any other Judean who happened to be available. Black is quite appropriate.

Note: The resurrection, empty tomb, and appearance stories reported in the Gospel of Peter (chaps. 9–14) are color-coded and evaluated in the next section of *The Acts of Jesus*.

EMPTY TOMB, APPEARANCES & ASCENSION

TABLE OF CONTENTS

The stories of the empty tomb, appearances of the risen Jesus, and the ascension have been gathered in this section. The following is a list in order of appearance of all the texts that will be found here. Multiple texts that report a single event are grouped together for ease of comparison.

INTRODUCTION

In assessing the evidence for the empty tomb, post-crucifixion appearances, and ascension of Jesus, it is essential to determine the approximate age of each source and the probable relation of the sources to each other. Only by so doing is it possible to discriminate primary from secondary data, earlier from derivative traditions. Unfortunately, the lines of development and dependency are not entirely clear. A catalogue of sources and their interrelationships will be useful for the reader encountering this welter of material for the first time.

A simple catalogue of persons and groups to whom the risen Jesus is alleged to have appeared will also come in handy. A concise statement of where and when the appearances are reported to have taken place will indicate some of the problems scholars have to face in evaluating these traditions.

Sources and stories

Evidence for the appearances of the risen Jesus comes in five forms: a list, simple reports, concise stories, intermediate stories, fully developed legends.

List:	1 Cor 15:3–8
Simple reports:	Luke 24:34; Acts 1:3–4, 10:39–41, 13:28–31; John 20:18; Pseudo-Mark 16:9–11, 12–13; Gospel of Mary 7:1–6
Concise stories:	Matt 28:8–10, 16–20; John 20:19–23; Gospel of the Hebrews 9:1–4
Intermediate stories:	John 20:11–17, 26–29; Luke 24:36–49
Legends:	Luke 24:13–35; John 21:1–14; Pet 9:1–14:3; Pseudo-Mark 16:14–18

This may also represent the order in which the tradition developed: lists of witnesses and independent reports of appearances to individuals and groups developed into simple stories; those in return were enhanced and heightened in intermediate tales; finally, full-blown legends were developed. This sequence should be regarded as the *logical* progression of development and not necessarily the actual order in which the tradition developed.

It should be noted that there are no appearance stories in the Sayings Gospel Q, the Gospel of Mark, or the Gospel of Thomas.

The list is provided by Paul in his first letter to the Corinthians (15:3–8). First Corinthians was written in the early 50s, possibly in 54 C.E.

There were also independent statements that God had raised Jesus and that he had appeared to so-and-so. Luke 24:34 is an example: "The Lord really has been raised and has appeared to Simon!" Other examples are: Acts 1:3–4,

10:39–41, 13:28–31; Pseudo-Mark 16:9–11, 12–13. Many of these are derivative: Luke, for example, composes speeches for his characters in the book of Acts, and Pseudo-Mark may be entirely dependent on earlier traditions.

The Gospel of Mark, which originally ended at 16:8, does not narrate any appearances of Jesus. It contains only the story of the empty tomb, which Mark may have created himself. At least there is no early trace of that story, unless Mark and the Gospel of Peter draw on some earlier source. Mark composed his gospel in the 70s, some twenty years after Paul's first letter to the Corinthians and about forty years after the death of Jesus.

The Gospel of Matthew borrows and revises Mark's empty tomb story, and adds concise stories of an appearance to two women and an appearance to the eleven on a mountain in Galilee. Matthew is probably responsible for creating the legend of the guards at the tomb. Matthew's sources beyond Mark may be no more than his fertile imagination.

Appearance stories in the Gospel of Luke and the book of Acts likewise begin with Mark. Luke once again revises Mark's story of the empty tomb, reports an appearance to Peter, and relates an intermediate account of the final appearance to the eleven. He adds the legends of the appearance to the two on the road to Emmaus and the ascension. Luke may have known of some stray oral traditions—tales that had not yet been captured in writing—that he made use of in elaborating his stories, or he may only have drawn on his own imagination.

The book of Acts reports that there were miscellaneous appearances for forty days prior to the ascension, which has now been postponed from the original date announced in Luke 24:51. These reports in Acts (1:1–11), which conflict with the ending to the gospel, are Luke's own creation.

The Gospel of John has two endings. Chapter 20 is the original ending to the gospel; chapter 21 is an appendix supplied by a later hand.

In the earlier chapter, John reports the empty tomb story, which may have appeared in the Signs Gospel, the source used by the author of the Fourth Gospel; it is unclear how John's version of the empty tomb is related to Mark's. However, John expands the empty tomb story with a footrace between Peter and the disciple whom Jesus loved, which is clearly a legendary feature. John has a concise account of Jesus' appearance to Mary outside the tomb, and of the appearance to the eleven that same evening. John also adds an intermediate story of a second appearance to the eleven a week later with doubting Thomas present.

The appendix to John contains an extended legend in which Jesus appears to seven disciples on the Sea of Galilee. This story may have been created by the author of the appendix to the Gospel of John (chapter 21) out of a simpler miracle story about catching fish, like the episode reported in Luke 5:1–11, which originally had nothing to do with Easter or the appearances of Jesus. It is followed by a lengthy dialogue with Peter.

The Gospel of Peter depicts a mythical Jesus emerging from the tomb in the middle of the night. That figure is supported by two other mythical figures. Here we have a fully developed legend. Peter also relates the empty tomb story, which the author may have derived from the canonical gospels.

In the fragmentary Gospel of the Hebrews, Jesus hands his shroud to the priest's slave and then goes and appears to his brother James. This story may be an example of a narrative that has been inspired by the mention of James in a list such as the one Paul records in 1 Corinthians.

The Gospel of Mary reports but does not narrate an appearance to Mary of Magdala.

Pseudo-Mark is an appendix to the Gospel of Mark supplied by a later hand; its purpose was to correct the lack of appearance stories in the original Mark. In Pseudo-Mark the author summarizes the appearance to Mary of Magdala, as well as to two people walking in the country, and reports a legendary appearance and charge to the eleven just prior to the ascension. The stories in Pseudo-Mark appear to be derived from earlier gospels, although some scholars argue that they represent some independent strands of tradition.

In addition to reports of appearances, Luke three times describes the appearance to Paul in the book of Acts. Paul attempts to describe the resurrected body in his first letter to the Corinthians, and in his second letter depicts a vision of his own that may be his account of the appearance to him. These and other epiphanies provide essential clues to the nature of the appearances.

All of these stories will be evaluated in detail in the commentary on individual stories.

Individuals and groups

A canvas of all the surviving reports of appearances yields the following list of persons and groups to whom Jesus is alleged to have appeared (sources are indicated in parentheses):

To individuals:

1. Peter (Paul, Luke)
2. Mary of Magdala (Matthew, John 20, Gospel of Mary, Pseudo-Mark)
3. James, Jesus' brother (Paul, Gospel of the Hebrews, Secret James)
4. Paul (Acts, Paul)

To groups:

5. The eleven or twelve (Paul, Matthew, Luke, John 20, Pseudo-Mark, Secret James)
6. All the apostles (Paul, Acts)
7. Seven disciples on the Sea of Tiberias (John 21)
8. Five hundred at the same time (Paul)

Other appearances:

9. Two on the road to Emmaus (Luke, Pseudo-Mark)
10. The second, unidentified Mary (Matthew)
11. Two soldiers, a centurion, some Judean elders (Peter)
12. Unspecified witnesses (Acts)

Item six in the list, "all the apostles," is probably the same as item five, the eleven or the twelve. The appearance to the seven, item seven, may also be a variant of item five. The appearance to five hundred at the same time, to a second Mary, to soldiers and Judean elders, and to unspecified witnesses are anomalies and may be the consequence of Christian exuberance. That reduces the basic list to six.

When and where

Many scholars have concluded that the earliest appearances were located in Galilee, as forecast in the Gospel of Mark and supported by Matthew, who is dependent on Mark, and by the appendix to John.

Jerusalem is the location of the appearances narrated in Luke, Acts, and the original ending to John. The appearances reported in the Gospel of Peter allegedly also take place in Jerusalem, although Peter breaks off just as the disciples have returned to Galilee, so there may have been additional appearances located in Galilee. Paul's list of appearances does not provide any clues regarding location. However, Luke locates the appearance to Paul on the road to Damascus.

The appearances in Galilee could not have taken place on Easter Sunday. Luke is the first to confine the appearances to Jerusalem and the first Easter Sunday. In Acts, Luke revises that schedule: appearances are extended for a period and the ascension takes place forty days later rather than on Easter Sunday evening.

John starts with the Easter time schedule. But the appearance to Thomas is dated a week later. The appendix to John requires additional time for the disciples to get from Jerusalem to Galilee and resume their lives as fishermen, assuming that the appearances in chapters 20 and 21 were meant to be sequential.

The appearance to Paul is probably to be dated three or four years after the crucifixion and probably in Syria. Secret James, a gospel found among the Nag Hammadi codices, has Jesus continue to appear for 550 days; the Pistis Sophia, a third-century document, prolongs the appearances for eleven years. Reported sightings of Jesus continued for many years, even centuries.

1 COR 15:3–8 [3]**Among the very first things I passed on to you was what I myself also received as tradition:**

The first list of appearances
1 Cor 15:3–8
No parallels
Source: oral tradition

Christ died for our sins according to the scriptures,
[4]**and was buried,**
and rose on the third day
according to the scriptures.
[5]**He then appeared to Cephas**
and later to the twelve.

[6]Next he appeared to a crowd of more than five hundred believers at the same time, most of whom are still alive, although some have died.

[7]Then he appeared to James, **and then to all the apostles.**

[8]Last of all, like the freak of nature I am, he appeared to me as well.

The first list of appearances. The earliest written report of resurrection appearances is found in Paul's first letter to the Corinthians, written about 54 C.E., some twenty years after Paul's conversion. Most Fellows think the components of the list reported there were formed prior to Paul's conversion, which is usually dated around 33 C.E. However, a substantial minority took a more skeptical view that the traditions Paul reports originated over a longer period of time and were collected by him during his missionary travels. In any case, when it came to assessing the reliability of individual items in the list, the Fellows expressed considerable skepticism. Before turning to those items, it will be illuminating to account for the general perspective of scholars.

Scholars are generally agreed that Paul mentions the appearance to him in v. 8 to defend his apostolic authority. Paul cites the list in his letter to the Corinthians as a way of affirming his place among the primary recipients of the revelation. The primacy of Peter in the apostolic group similarly depended on the claim that the risen Jesus had appeared to Peter at an early date. There are, however, conflicting reports about the first appearance, or protophany, as it is called: Paul and Luke award first place to Peter; Matthew and John 20 award the initial appearance to Mary of Magdala; the Gospel of the Hebrews gives the nod to James, the brother of Jesus. These competing claims suggest not so much historical reports as a rivalry among leaders in the early Jesus movement.

There seems to be little reason to doubt that Paul had at least one visionary religious experience that he came to regard as an appearance of the risen Jesus. The Fellows accordingly colored that statement red (v. 8). Although the appearance to Peter is nowhere narrated in any of the gospels, the Fellows were inclined to agree that Peter also had a similar visionary experience. Because Peter does not make the claim for himself—it is always made on his behalf—they designated that statement pink rather than red (v. 5).

Notable is the absence of Mary of Magdala from Paul's list. The Fellows agreed that she, like Peter and Paul, had at least one visionary religious experience of Jesus after his death. Why Paul leaves her name out is not clear.

In view of the competing claims and counter-claims, the Fellows were dubious about the inclusion of the appearances to James, the brother of Jesus, to the "twelve" as a group, and to the five hundred believers at the same time, in spite of the fact that they are in Paul's list (vv. 5–7). The reference to an appearance to "all the apostles" is one the Fellows were inclined to regard as a pious exaggeration to make sure all authorities were included. Part of the skepticism regarding these reports owes to the fact that the names assigned to the twelve vary from list to list, so we cannot establish a firm membership for the twelve, and we do not know who made up the group referred to as "all the apostles." The claim on behalf of James seems to be an attempt to put James on an equal footing with Peter (and perhaps Paul). An appearance to a large crowd, like the five hundred mentioned by Paul, suggests a visionary worship experience, such as the Pentecost experience described in the second chapter of Acts, where the apostles are filled with the spirit and speak in tongues.

Generalized lists of appearances are also found in several of the speeches in Acts, for example, in 10:40–41:

> God raised that one [Jesus] up on the third day and made him visible, not to everyone, but to us whom God had designated witnesses ahead of time—those of us who ate and drank with him after his resurrection from the dead.

These notices were invented by Luke as a part of his theological program. The appearances for Luke are confined to a narrowly defined circle of "apostles"—those who were companions of Jesus during his lifetime (that excludes Paul)—and are terminated by the ascension, which occurred either on Easter (according to the gospel) or forty days later (according to Acts). This means, among other things, that when Luke wrote Acts some thirty years after Paul's letters, he did not regard Paul's Damascus road experience as a bona fide resurrection appearance. Paul would have been surprised at his demotion.

Paul's visions
Acts 9:3–19; 22:1–16; 26:9–18
Sources: Paul, Luke
Cf. 2 Cor 12:1–10;
Exod 3:1–6; Dan 7:9–10;
Rev 1:13–16; Mk 9:2–8,
Mt 17:1–8, Lk 9:28–36;
Lk 5:1–11

ACTS 9:3–19 **[3]As Saul was traveling along and getting close to
Damascus, he was suddenly dazzled by a light emanating from the
sky. [4]He fell to the ground and heard a voice saying to him, "Saul,
Saul, why are you persecuting me?"**

[5]Saul replied, "Who are you, lord?"

**The voice continued, "The one you are persecuting is Jesus. [6]Get
up and go into town. You will be told what you have to do."**

**[7]Saul's traveling companions stood by dumbfounded; they had
heard the voice but said nothing. [8]Saul picked himself up from the
ground but when he opened his eyes he was unable to see anything.
His companions took him by the hand and led him into Damascus.
[9]For three days he was blind and neither ate nor drank.**

**[10]There was this disciple in Damascus named Ananias. The lord
called to him in a vision, "Ananias," it said.**

He replied, "It's me, my lord."

**[11]The lord instructed him, "Get up and go to Straight Street. Ask
for Saul of Tarsus in the home of Judas. You should understand that
he is currently praying; he has had a vision of someone named
Ananias coming in and laying hands on him so he can see."**

**[13]Ananias replied, "Lord, many people have told me about this
man and reported the wicked treatment he has given your followers
in Jerusalem. [14]And here <in Damascus> he has been authorized by
the high priest to arrest everyone who claims your name."**

[15]The lord responded to Ananias, "Go anyway. This fellow is a

special instrument of mine to champion my cause in front of hea-
thens and their royalty and before the people of Israel. 16Understand,
I intend to show him how much has to suffer for my sake."
17So Ananias went, entered the house, and placed his hands on
Saul: "Saul, my brother," he said, "the lord Jesus who appeared to
you on your way here has sent me so you may recover your sight and
be filled with holy spirit." 18Instantly something like scales fell from
his eyes so he could see again. He got up and was baptized. 19Then
he ate something to get his strength back.

ACTS 22:1–16 "Friends and distinguished elders, listen, please,
to the defense I now plead before you."
2When they heard him address them in Hebrew, they quieted
down.
3Paul went on: "I am a Jew. I was born in Tarsus, Cilicia. I was
raised here in Jerusalem. I was trained by Gamaliel in the fine
points of our ancestral law. I was a zealot in my devotion to God,
just as you are on this occasion. 4I persecuted this movement to the
death, arresting men and women alike and turning them over to the
jailor. 5The chief priest and the Council of Elders can testify to this.
From them I received written authorization to our associates in
Damascus. I was on my way there to get prisoners also and bring
them to Jerusalem for punishment. 6As I was going along, this is
what happened to me as I got near Damascus, about noon: an
intense light from the sky engulfed me. 7I fell to the ground and I
heard a voice speaking to me, 'Saul, Saul, why are you persecuting
me?'
8"I replied, 'Who are you, lord?'
"He said to me, 'The one you are persecuting is Jesus the
Nazarene.'
9"My traveling companions saw the light but did not hear a voice
speaking to me. 10I asked, 'What should I do, Lord?"
"The Lord replied to me, 'Get up and go into Damascus. There
you will be told everything you have to do.' 11"Since I could not see
as a consequence of the dazzling light, my companions took me by
the hand and led me into Damascus.
12"Ananias was a devout person by the standards of the law and
all the Jewish inhabitants of Damascus thought well of him. 13He
came and stood before me and declared, 'Saul, my friend, you have
your sight back again!' At that precise moment I opened my eyes
and there he was. 14"He then told me, 'Our ancestral God has des-
tined you to know his will, to lay eyes on the <righteous one>, and
to hear the latter speak. 15On his behalf you are to testify to the
whole world, to everything you have seen and heard. 16And now
why do you hesitate? Get going and get baptized to wash away your
sins by invoking his name."

THE RESURRECTION OF A YOUNG BRIDE

Other sages in Jesus' world were apparently able to raise people from the dead. Among them was Apollonius, contemporary of Jesus and fellow itinerant teacher. As Philostratus reports the story, there is some question about whether the young bride was actually dead when Apollonius revives her. In two similar cases in the gospels—the daughter of Jairus (Mark 5:39) and Lazarus (John 11:11)—Jesus remarks that the patient is not dead, but sleeping.

This is Philostratus' story of how Apollonius revived the young bride:

> It seems a girl had died just as she was getting married. The groom was walking along beside her bier mourning over his unfulfilled marriage, and all Rome was in mourning with him since the girl came from a consular family. When Apollonius happened on this sad scene, he said, "Put the bier down, and I will put an end to the tears you are shedding for this young woman." Then he asked what her name might be. The crowd of course assumed he was launching into a eulogy of the sort given at a funeral to induce mourning, but he did no such thing. Instead, he touched her and pronounced something inaudible over her. All of a sudden the young woman awoke from what looked like death. The girl uttered some sounds and returned to her father's house. This is reminiscent of Alcestis when she was brought back to life by Hercules.
>
> The relatives of the girl wanted to reward Apollonius with one hundred fifty thousand silver coins, but he told them to make a present of them to the young lady.
>
> Whether Apollonius detected some spark of life in her that those caring for her had not noticed—recall the rumor that it was drizzling at the time and a mist rose from her face—or whether she was really dead and Apollonius warmed her up and raised her up has become an inexplicable phenomenon, not just to me, but also to those who happened to be there at the time.*
>
> *Life of Apollonius of Tyana*, 4.45

*Acccording to the old legend, Alcestis agreed to give up her life so her husband, Admetus, might live. Accordingly, she died and the balance of her life was transferred to Admetus. Later, because Admetus had done a kindness to Hercules, the superhero set out to harrow hell and force Hades himself to permit Alcestis to come back to life.

ACTS 26:9–18 9"I myself considered it my duty to do as much as I
could in opposing the name of Jesus of Nazareth, 10and that's what I
did in Jerusalem. I clamped many members of the movement in
prison on the authority of the chief priests, and I concurred in their
condemnation by casting my <black> pebble against them. 11I would
frequently punish them in all the synagogues and try to make them
blaspheme. And in my fury I even pursued them to foreign cities.

12"While I was on my way to Damascus on the authority and
with the approval of the chief priests, 13along the road, about noon,
your majesty, I saw a light emanating from the sky, whose bril-
liance exceeded that of the sun. It engulfed me and my traveling

companions. [14]All of us dropped to the ground, and I heard a voice speaking to me in Hebrew, 'Saul, Saul,' it said, 'why are you persecuting me? You are bringing pain on yourself by resisting the prod.'

[15]"Then I said, 'Who are you, lord?"

"He replied, 'The one you are persecuting is Jesus. [16]But get up on your feet. The reason I have appeared to you is to commission you as my servant and as a witness to the things you have seen and to the appearances I will yet make to you. [17]I will rescue you from your own people, and from the gentiles, to whom I am sending you, [18]to open their eyes so they will turn from darkness to light, and from the power of Satan to God. They will then have their sins forgiven and find a place among those God has made his own through faith in me.

Paul's visions. Paul asks rhetorically, "Am I not free? Am I not an apostle? Have I not seen Jesus our Lord?" (1 Cor 9:1). For him there was an inseparable link between his apostleship and his vision of the risen Jesus. He makes this connection again in the inside address of his letter to the Galatians: "Paul an apostle, commissioned not by mortals nor through human agency, but by Jesus Christ and God the Father, who raised him from the dead" (Gal 1:1). A little later in that same letter (1:15–16), he writes that "God was pleased to reveal his son to me [or: in me] that I might carry his gospel to the gentiles." Earlier he had insisted: "I want you to know, my friends, that the gospel I preached was not a human invention because I did not learn it from my predecessors in the faith nor was I taught it, but I received it through a revelation of Jesus Christ" (1:11–12). The link between appearance, appointment as an apostle, and content of his gospel is unequivocal, at least in Paul's mind.

Paul does not thereby claim that he did not learn summaries of the so-called kerygma—the first creedal statements of the Jesus movement—from his predecessors, summaries like the one he cites in 1 Cor 15:3–8: Christ died, was buried, rose on the third day, and appeared to several of us. He is referring rather to what he calls "the truth of the gospel"—the meaning of the death and resurrection of Jesus for Christian behavior, especially with respect to circumcision and observing kosher. The significance of Jesus' death—that no one is justified by observing circumcision and kosher—he learned, so he claims, not from the Jerusalem leaders, Cephas (Peter), James, and John, but directly from Jesus Christ (Gal 2:1–14).

What was the nature of the revelatory encounter with the risen Jesus that gave him such insights into "the truth of the gospel"? In the book of Acts, Luke three times describes Paul's vision on the road to Damascus. While the three versions differ in details, the basic features are constant: Paul is dazzled by a bright light emanating from the sky; he hears a voice; his companions are not affected the same way he is. In other words, his companions do not share his revelatory experience.

Paul's experience on the Damascus road is akin to other revelatory experiences. Such an experience is an *epiphany,* which means "an appearance, a manifestation" of the divine. If such an appearance is described as that of an angel, it is called as *angelophany.* If it is an appearance of the risen Jesus, it is referred to as a *christophany.* If it is an undifferentiated manifestation of the divine, it is labeled a *theophany.* The appearance to Paul as Luke depicts it was a christophany; Paul himself claims a christophany in 1 Corinthians 9:1 cited above.

In Exod 3:1–6, there is a combined angelophany and theophany:

> Moses was tending the sheep of Jethro his father-in-law, the priest of Midian. He led the sheep beyond the wilderness and came to Mt. Horeb.
> [2]An angel of the Lord appeared to him in the flames that issued from a burning bush. Moses noticed that the bush was on fire but did not burn
> up. [3]Moses said to himself, "I must stop and take a closer look at this unusual sight and try to find out why the fire does not destroy the bush.
> [4]When the Lord noticed that Moses stopped to get a closer look, he called to him out of the burning bush: "Moses, Moses." Moses answered,
> "What do you want?" [5]And the Lord said, "Don't come any nearer. Take your sandals off. The ground on which you are standing is sacred
> ground." [6]And the Lord continued, "I am the God of your fathers, the God of Abraham, the God of Isaac, and the God of Jacob." Then Moses hid his face. You see, he was afraid to look at God.

There is a light of sorts in this story (the burning bush) and there is a communication of God to Moses. Moses of course was alone, so his experience was not shared by others. At first it is announced that an angel appears to Moses in the flames. But then it is the voice of God that Moses hears and on whose presence he is afraid to gaze.

The image of divine radiance in revelatory experience stories has been influenced in part by this description in the book of Daniel (7:9–10):

> While I was watching,
> thrones were set up
> and the Ancient of Days sat down.
> He had a snowy white garment on,
> and the hair of his head was like pure white fleece.
> His throne was a roaring inferno,
> and a stream of fire poured out from his presence.
> Hundreds of thousands stood ready to serve him,
> and he was surrounded by millions of attendants.

The image of God in this scene is brilliant white and emanates fire. He of course communicates with Daniel.

The seer in the book of Revelation is caught up by the spirit and hears a loud voice. When he turns to see who is speaking to him, this is what he sees (Rev 1:13–16):

> One who looked like the son of Adam, in a full-length robe, girded with a golden belt. His hair was as white as snow-white wool, and his eyes were like points of fire; his feet gleamed like burnished brass that had been refined in a furnace; and his voice sounded like a raging torrent. His right hand held seven stars and a sharp, two-edged sword extruded from his mouth. His countenance was like the sun shining in all its power.

The descriptions become more elaborate in Revelation, but they have a clear affinity with the one in Daniel and even with much older epiphanies.

In the transfiguration of Jesus as described by Mark (9:2–8), Jesus' garments become intensely white as Jesus talks with Moses and Elijah. The transfiguration is of course also an epiphany. A voice comes out of the cloud and announces that Jesus is God's son. Moses and Elijah are to be subservient to him. Because this story is an epiphany and because it resembles other resurrection appearances, many scholars have concluded that the transfiguration was originally a resurrection appearance that Mark has deliberately relocated.

In Acts Luke describes a vision of Stephen as he is about to be stoned (Acts 7:54–60). The sky is opened up and the effulgence of God appears, with Jesus as the son of Adam standing on God's right. Stephen's vision is also an epiphany—a combined theophany and christophany. It is difficult to distinguish Stephen's vision of Jesus from other resurrection appearances.

The earliest of the gospels, Mark, does not narrate an appearance of Jesus. But when the women go to the tomb on Easter morning, they find the stone rolled away and a young man in a white robe sitting on the right. He tells them that Jesus will appear to the disciples in Galilee (also promised in Mark 14:28). The women are afraid and don't tell anyone (Mark 16:1–8).

Matthew repeats this story (Matt 28:1–8), except now the young man has become an angel and his garment is dazzling white—it emits a brilliant light. In addition, Matthew has the risen Jesus meet the women as they leave the tomb. It appears that an angelophany is followed by a christophany, which leads some scholars to conclude that, as the tradition developed, angelophanies were gradually turned into christophanies (Matt 28:1–8).

In Luke's revision of Mark, there are now *two* figures. Luke does not have Jesus appear to the women; he evidently did not know Matthew. Instead, the women leave the tomb and tell the disciples everything that has happened. The women get bolder—they are no longer terrified and afraid to relate what they had experienced as they were in Mark—and the number of angels increases. The story grows as it goes (Luke 24:1–12).

Visions of the risen Jesus appear to have taken the form of angelophanies or theophanies. What is the relation of these visions, these revelatory experiences, to the resurrection of the body as the early believers anticipated it? Paul discusses this issue at length in his first letter to the Corinthians.

It is clear that Paul believes in a sort of bodily resurrection. In his discussion of the resurrection in 1 Cor 15:40, 42, he states:

> There are heavenly bodies and there are earthly bodies. But the external appearance of the celestial differs from that of the earthly. . . .
>
> It is the same with the resurrection of the dead. It is planted as something subject to decay, but raised as something imperishable.

The resurrected body is evidently, in Paul's view, something quite different from a revived corpse. This description seems to square with the accounts of the appearances to Paul provided by Luke in the book of Acts. The appearances of Jesus are indistinguishable from the appearances of angels: christophanies, in other words, are indistinguishable from angelophanies (12:1–10).

In his second letter to the Corinthians, Paul describes an experience of someone who was caught up by the spirit into the third heaven and heard things no one is allowed to repeat. Scholars are generally inclined to the view that Paul is reporting his own experience, but are divided on whether this vision and revelation are the same as his Damascus road experience as depicted by Luke. This is how Paul speaks about this unusual occurrence:

> I feel compelled to boast. It does no good, but I will go on to visions
> and revelations of the Lord. 2I know someone in Christ who fourteen
> years ago was transported up as far as the third heaven (whether in the
> body or out of the body I don't know, only God knows). 3And I know that
> this same person (whether in the body or not I can't say, only God
> knows) 4was taken up to Paradise and heard ineffable words that no
> human is allowed to repeat. 5I'll boast on behalf of this fellow, although I
> won't boast on my own behalf, except where my weaknesses are con-
> cerned. 6You see, if I elect to brag, it will not be a fool's braggadocio,
> because I will be telling the truth. But I desist so that no one will think
> more of me than is justified by my words and deeds. 7And, in view of the
> exceptional character of these revelations, in order to keep me from being
> too conceited, I was given a thorn in the flesh, a messenger from Satan, to
> discipline me, to keep me from being too full of myself. 8I prayed to the
> Lord three times to be relieved of this torment, 9but the Lord said to me,
> "My grace is sufficient for you." As you know, power is made perfect in
> weakness. Consequently, I prefer to brag about my weaknesses so that
> the power of Christ may inhabit me. 10As a result, I am content with my
> weaknesses, with insults, with hardships, with persecution and troubles,
> on behalf of Christ, for when I am weak, then I am powerful.

If this visit to Paradise is the same as his conversion experience, then Paul doesn't even know whether his vision was received while he was in his body or out of it. He is tempted here, as elsewhere in his letters, to brag about his credentials. As he begins to cite them, he invariably recalls that he is not supposed to brag; the power of God, he reminds himself, is made perfect in weakness, in Christ as in himself. His heavenly excursions, therefore, really count for nothing—are no basis for boasting.

On the basis of the aggregate evidence of these stories and reports, the Jesus Seminar agreed that:

- **The resurrection of Jesus did not involve the resuscitation of a corpse.**[81]

If the resurrection of Jesus did not involve the resuscitation of a corpse and if a christophany had developed out of an angelophany, it follows that:

- **Belief in Jesus' resurrection did not depend on what happened to his body.**

Since the empty tomb story was a late development, probably created by Mark, the report that Jesus had been buried in a tomb known to the women has come under scholarly suspicion. The tendency to elaborate and enhance the burial stories heightened that suspicion. In view of the nature of the appearances and the late emergence of stories representing the resurrection as physical and palpable, the Seminar concluded:

- **The body of Jesus decayed as do other corpses.**

All the evidence, when taken together, seemed to suggest that

- **The resurrection was not an event that happened on the first Easter Sunday; it was not an event that could have been recorded by a video camera.**

The Seminar followed this trail of evidence to its conclusion, which they formulated as follows:

- **Since the earlier strata of the New Testament contain no appearance stories, it does not seem necessary for Christian faith to believe the literal veracity of any of the later narratives.**

This conclusion, of course, assumes that there were Christians and hence Christian faith prior to the rise of specific appearance stories. The Fellows were unanimous in this judgment; there were no dissenting votes. At the same time, many Fellows hold the view that narratives of the appearances of the risen Jesus are affirmations that Jesus was a living lord. They are confessions of the conviction held by the earliest Christian communities. They are properly understood only when it is recognized that they are not historical reports.

Resurrection
Pet 9:1–10:5
No parallels
Source: Peter

PET 9:1–10:5 Early, at first light on the sabbath, a crowd came from Jerusalem and the surrounding countryside to see the sealed tomb. 2But during the night before the Lord's day dawned, while the soldiers were on guard, two by two during each watch, a loud noise came from the sky, 3and they saw the skies open up and two men come down from there in a burst of light and approach the tomb. 4The stone that had been pushed against the entrance began to roll by itself and moved away to one side; then the tomb opened up and both young men went inside.

10 Now when these soldiers saw this, they roused the centurion from his sleep, along with the elders. (Remember, they were also there keeping watch.) 2While they were explaining what they had seen, again they see three men leaving the tomb, two supporting the third, and a cross was following them.

3The heads of the two reached up to the sky, while the head of the third, whom they led by the hand, reached beyond the skies. 4And they heard a voice from the skies that said, "Have you preached to those who sleep?" 5And an answer was heard from the cross: "Yes!"

THE RESURRECTION OF EURYDICE

Ovid, the Roman poet, was born in 43 B.C.E. and died in 17 C.E. He was educated in Rome, where he studied rhetoric and poetry. He was exiled by the Emperor Augustus in 8 C.E. for some unspecified offense. During his life he composed numerous works, of which the best known is perhaps the *Metamorphoses*. All the stories in this collection have to do with transformations. The story of Orpheus and Eurydice is the story of a failed resurrection that is contemporary with Jesus of Nazareth. It also provides some important clues as to how the underworld was conceived.

> Orpheus was a Thracian minstrel whose playing and singing were so enchanting that the animals were charmed and the stones and trees followed him about. After his marriage, while his wife Eurydice was wandering in the meadows, a serpent bit her ankle and she died. Orpheus mourned her loss. He was so grief-stricken that he boldly descended through the gate of Taenarus to the river Styx, where he attempted to arouse the sympathy of the shades. He wandered among the ghosts, the wraiths of the dead, till he reached Persephone and her lord, the king of the shades. He pleaded with them by singing and playing the lyre. "I beg you," he sang, "weave again Eurydice's destiny, brought too swiftly to a close. We mortals and all that is ours are fated to fall to you, and after a little time, sooner or later, we hasten to this abode. We are all on our way here, this is our final home, and yours the most lasting sway over the human race. If you cannot extend the sojourn of my wife on earth, I do not wish to return myself."
>
> The bloodless ghosts were in tears. The king and queen of the underworld could not refuse Orpheus. They called Eurydice, who walked slowly because of the injury to her ankle. She was given to Orpheus, but only on the condition that he not look back until he had emerged from the underworld.
>
> As Orpheus made his way up the sloping path, when they had almost reached the surface of the earth, out of anxiety that his wife's strength might be failing, he glanced back to make certain she was still there. Immediately she slipped back into the depths. Orpheus reached out to grasp her with his arms, but to no avail. His arms enfolded nothing but air.
>
> Ovid, *Metamorphoses*, Book X

Resurrection. The Gospel of Peter narrates events that allegedly took place on the night prior to Easter Sunday (9:1–11:7), unlike any of the other gospels, with the exception of Matthew. A crowd has gathered on the sabbath to keep watch over the sealed tomb (9:1). As in Matthew (28:4), soldiers keep guard over the tomb during the night (v. 2).

The actual resurrection of Jesus is not narrated in the canonical gospels. In the Gospel of Peter, however, the resurrection itself is depicted in a fantastic epiphany scene in chapters 9 and 10. During the night, a tremendous noise comes from the heavens, the skies open up, there is a burst of light, and two men descend. The huge stone rolls away by itself and the young men enter the tomb (9:1–4). Meanwhile, the centurion in charge has fallen asleep, along with the elders who were assisting in the tomb watch. The soldiers wake their commander up and begin telling him what they have seen.

While they explain, the two men are seen leaving the tomb supporting a third, whom they are leading by the hand. The third figure is presumably Jesus. The enormous size of the figures—their heads reach the skies and beyond—indicates that they are supernatural. The three men are followed by a talking cross (10:1–5). As the resurrection takes place, a voice comes from the skies inquiring whether Jesus has preached to the dead. The cross, which may represent the slain martyrs of Israel, according to John Dominic Crossan, responds affirmatively.

There is another account of the actual resurrection of Jesus. It occurs as a variant reading in one old Latin manuscript (Codex Bobbiensis, fourth century C.E.) at Mark 16:4. It reads:

> **But suddenly at the third hour of the day, there was darkness over the whole circle of the earth, and angels descended from the heavens, and as the Lord was rising in the glory of the living God, at the same time they ascended with him; and immediately it was light.**

As in the Gospel of Peter, in this fragment the resurrection takes place during the night and Jesus is accompanied from the tomb by two angels.

The transfiguration (Mark 9:2–8) may have been a resurrection story relocated by Mark because he did not want to represent Jesus as actually appearing to the inner circle of disciples immediately after his death. Instead, he preferred the story of the empty tomb, which may, in fact, have been his invention. In any case, the transfiguration exhibits several of the motifs connected with resurrection appearances. The clothes of Jesus become intensely white; in Luke's version (9:28–36), the glistening white clothes suggest that Jesus has been "glorified," that is, exalted to heaven (v. 31). He is accompanied by two figures, Moses and Elijah. A voice (noise) issues from the skies. Also in Luke's version, Peter and the other two companions are overcome with sleep (v. 32), as are the centurion and elders at the tomb in the Gospel of Peter.

In Matthew's transfiguration account (17:1–8), the experience terrifies Jesus' three companions (v. 6), as it does the women at the tomb, and, Luke adds, the three tell no one of their experience (Luke 9:36), in imitation, again, of the women in the Gospel of Mark.

If the transfiguration was originally a resurrection epiphany, it is another example of an escorted resurrection appearance—Jesus accompanied by other figures—similar to the one we find in the Gospel of Peter and the Codex Bobbiensis. There is nothing in the fantastic account of the resurrection in the Gospel of Peter, or in the Codex Bobbiensis, that the Fellows of the Jesus Seminar thought warranted the status of historical reminiscence. They therefore designated them black.

The empty tomb
Mk 16:1–8
Mt 28:1–8, Lk 24:1–12; Jn 20:1–18; Pet 12:1–13:3
Sources: Mark, John, Peter

MARK 16:1–8 And when the sabbath day was over, Mary of Magdala and Mary the mother of James and Salome bought spices so they could go and embalm him. [2]And very early on Sunday they got to the tomb just as the sun was coming up. [3]And they had been

asking themselves, "Who will help us roll the stone away from the opening of the tomb?" [4]Then they look up and discover that the stone has been rolled away! (For in fact the stone was very large.)

[5]And when they went into the tomb, they saw a young man sitting on the right, wearing a white robe, and they grew apprehensive.

[6]He says to them, "Don't be alarmed! You are looking for Jesus the Nazarene who was crucified. He was raised, he is not here! Look at the spot where they put him! [7]But go and tell his disciples, including 'Rock,' 'He is going ahead of you to Galilee! There you will see him, just as he told you.'"

[8]And once they got outside, they ran away from the tomb, because great fear and excitement got the better of them. And they didn't breathe a word of it to anyone: talk about terrified . . .

The empty tomb. The earliest of the gospels, Mark, does not narrate any appearances of the risen Jesus. Three women, Mary of Magdala, Mary the mother of James, and Salome go to the tomb on Easter morning carrying spices with them, no doubt for the purpose of carrying out traditional burial rites. Unlike the Gospel of Peter (12:1–3), Mark does not mention that the women had also come to mourn and weep in the customary fashion. By this omission, according to Kathleen Corley, a Fellow of the Seminar, Mark avoids the implication that the women had come to conjure up the spirit of Jesus by magical means; women often attempted to do so in mourning rites in the hellenistic world. The women simply find the tomb empty. Somehow the stone blocking the entrance has been rolled away. Inside they find a young man in a white robe—a heavenly messenger—sitting on the right. The women grow apprehensive. The young man advises the women that Jesus is not there; he has been raised.

The women are instructed to tell his disciples that Jesus will precede them to Galilee, where they will see him, just as he promised (Mark 14:28). But the women run away from the tomb and out of fright don't tell a soul what they have seen.

This story is repeated in Matthew (28:1–8), Luke (24:1–12), John (20:1–13), and Peter (12:50–57) with considerable variation. In all versions it is the first day of the week or the Lord's Day, Mary of Magdala is present, the stone has been removed, the tomb is empty, and the women are given a message by an angelic figure and leave. In other respects the four accounts are hopelessly at variance.

The resurrection of Jesus seems to have developed in two independent traditions. One may be called the "appearance" tradition in which Jesus appears as a luminous apparition to his followers. The other is the empty tomb tradition. The appearance tradition is associated with Galilee (note Mark 14:28 and 16:7, where a Galilean appearance is promised), the empty tomb tradition with Jerusalem. Mark, Matthew, and John 21 reflect the Galilean location; Luke and John 20 belong to the empty tomb branch. The appearances to Peter and Paul mentioned in 1 Corinthians 15, and to Mary in the Gospel of John and the Gospel of Mary, were probably of the luminous apparition variety.

HOW DID THE GOSPEL OF MARK END?

Early copyists of the Gospel of Mark felt that the story ended too abruptly with v. 8. They hankered to fulfill the promise of appearances (16:7) with stories of actual appearances. This they did by appending a string of appearance stories, a compendium they evidently borrowed from some unknown gospel (a fresh composition would have made a better fit with vv. 1–8). This compendium came to be known as the "longer ending" to Mark. The color coding and commentary on the longer ending are to be found under the headings representing its constituent parts: appearance to Mary of Magdala; appearance to two in the country; appearance to the eleven; ascension.

There is also something known as the "shorter ending to Mark"; it is found in manuscripts both as part of and independently of the "longer ending." The longer ending is usually versified as 16:9–20 and the shorter ending as 16:21.

> **All the instructions they had been given they promptly reported to Peter and his companions. Afterwards Jesus himself, using them as agents, broadcast the sacred and imperishable message of eternal salvation from one end of the earth to the other.**

In addition, there also exists an insertion into the longer ending of Mark just after v. 14 known as the "Freer Logion." It is found only in the Codex Washingtonianus, which was discovered by Charles L. Freer (hence its name). The Freer Logion was known to exist by Jerome, a fourth-century scholar and translator of the Vulgate, so it has ancient credentials.

> **And they would apologize and say, "This lawless and faithless age is under the control of Satan, who by using filthy spirits doesn't allow the real power of God to be appreciated. So," they would say to the Anointed, "let your justice become evident now."**

These facts led the Fellows of the Seminar to conclude, in concert with many other scholars, that the empty tomb stories represent a later development of the appearance stories that were originally reports of luminous apparitions. The earliest of the empty tomb stories is that recorded by Mark probably in the decade of the 70s of the first century, approximately forty years after the death of Jesus. The appearance tradition, on the other hand, is reflected in Paul's letter to the Corinthians in the early 50s. The appearance reports may well have originated a few days, or weeks, or months, after Jesus' death. One thing seems clear: the disciples fled from Jerusalem after Jesus was arrested and returned to their homes and line of work in Galilee. How long it was after that flight before the resurrection faith arose is impossible to say, except to note that the conviction that Jesus had risen from the dead had already taken root by the time Paul was converted about 33 C.E. On the assumption that Jesus died about 30 C.E., the time for development was thus two or three years at most.

Fear is a motive for flight, and fear is a common reaction to reports of the appearance of angels or the divine presence in the Hebrew Bible (note, for example, Jacob in Gen 28:17, Moses in Exod 3:6, Gideon in Judg 6:22–23, Isaiah

And the Anointed would respond to them, "The time when Satan is in power has run its course, but other terrible things are just around the corner. I was put to death for the sake of those who sinned, so they might return to the truth and stop sinning, and thus inherit the spiritual and indestructible righteous glory that is in heaven."

The original Gospel of Mark ended with v. 8, in all probability. If it once had another ending, that ending has been lost.

The Freer Logion has no claim to be original, in the judgment of Bruce Metzger, a pre-eminent textual critic: it appears in only one manuscript; it uses words not in Mark's standard vocabulary; and its content has a strong apocryphal or fictional character.

The shorter ending likewise exhibits non-Markan vocabulary and its style does not comport well with that of the Gospel of Mark. Mark is not the author of this ending either.

Although strongly attested in many ancient manuscripts, the longer ending is not the work of Mark. It makes extensive use of words not employed by Mark elsewhere. The decisive argument against its authenticity, however, is the fact that it does not fit with what precedes in genuine Mark: In genuine Mark the women have just fled from the tomb in terror and breathe not a word to anyone; in the longer ending, Jesus has just appeared to Mary, who runs and tells the others who are mourning and weeping at a different location. The fit is so poor that most scholars have come to believe the longer ending was composed for another context and later clumsily appended to Mark.

These variant endings nevertheless attest to the impulse to expand the post-crucifixion stories, without much regard for time, place, and sequence.

in Isa 6:5, and Ezekiel in Ezek 1:27–28). The male disciples of Jesus had fled at the time of his arrest, possibly out of fear for themselves (Mark 14:50; that same fear seems to haunt them in the Gospel of Mary, 5:1–3).

The women disciples are afraid as a consequence of the angelic presence and flee the tomb. The failure of all the disciples is now complete. There is the backhanded recognition of this failure in the young man's instruction at the empty tomb to tell the disciples that Jesus will precede them to Galilee—a kind of permission to return to Galilee after the fact.

The custom of burying executed criminals in common graves, or in the case of crucifixion, of leaving them on their crosses as carrion for crows, provoked initial doubts among the Fellows about the historicity of the burial story. The miracle of the removal of the stone blocking the entrance to the tomb, the appearance of the heavenly messenger, together with the late development of the empty tomb story, convinced Fellows that the empty tomb was an invention of Mark or some other Christian storyteller before him. To top it off, there is no demonstrable interest in Jesus' burial site until the fourth century. That is strange if the location of Jesus' tomb were well known. The story was accordingly colored black.

The empty tomb
Mt 28:1–8
Mk 16:1–8, Lk 24:1–12;
Jn 20:1–18; Pet 12:1–13:3
Sources: Mark, John, Peter

**MATT 28:1–18 After the sabbath day, at first light on Sunday,
Mary of Magdala and the other Mary came to inspect the tomb. 2And
just then there was a strong earthquake. You see, a messenger of the
Lord had come down from the sky, arrived <at the tomb>, rolled
away the stone, and was sitting on it. 3The messenger gave off a daz-
zling light and wore clothes as white as snow. 4Now those who kept
watch were paralyzed with fear and looked like corpses themselves.**

**5In response the messenger said to the women, "Don't be fright-
ened! I know you are looking for Jesus who was crucified. 6He is not
here! You see, he was raised, just as he said. Come, look at the spot
where he was lying. 7And run, tell his disciples that he has been
raised from the dead. Don't forget, he is going ahead of you to
Galilee. There you will see him. Now I have told you so."**

**8And they hurried away from the tomb, full of apprehension and
an overpowering joy, and ran to tell his disciples.**

The empty tomb. Matthew copies Mark's account of the empty tomb, but embellishes it with further fantastic details. Matthew introduces an earthquake, and the women actually witness "a messenger of the Lord" rolling the stone away from the door of the tomb (v. 2). These additions give an apocalyptic cast to the scene. In the first place, earthquakes are associated with "the day of the Lord" and the judgment to come, beginning with such prophetic texts as Isaiah, Jeremiah, Ezekiel, and Joel. In Ezek 38:19–20, for example:

> In my fiery wrath I declare: On that day a gigantic earthquake will most certainly befall the land of Israel. The fish of the sea, the birds of the heaven, the beasts of the field, and all the reptiles that slither along the ground, together with all human beings on the face of the earth, will quake at my presence. The mountains will be leveled, the ravines filled up, and every wall in the land will tumble.

In his little apocalypse in chapter 24, Matthew follows Mark in declaring that "there will be earthquakes everywhere" (24:7). In the book of Revelation, when the angel takes fire from the altar and hurls it to the earth, there follows thunder, thunderclaps, lightning, and an earthquake (8:5). A similar thing happens when the seventh angel pours out his bowl (16:18).

In the second place, Matthew borrows imagery from another apocalyptic book, Daniel (7:9, 10:6), to describe the heavenly messenger: he gave off a dazzling light (perhaps a blinding light) and his clothes were white as snow (glistening white). Such features as glistening white garments and dazzling countenances are stock descriptions in heavenly appearance scenes.

This incredible scene so frightens the Roman guards at the entrance to the tomb that they fall to the ground "as though dead." These are guards Matthew has added to Mark's scene probably to deflect rumors that Jesus' body had been stolen by his disciples (Matt 28:11–13). Remarkably, the women seem unaffected by these traumatic events. The heavenly messenger gives the women a message similar to the one given them in Mark: They are directed to go and tell the other disciples that Jesus is not in the tomb, but is raised, and will appear to them in Galilee.

Although terrified, the women disciples in this instance go with joy to proclaim the news of the resurrection (v. 8). Here, as elsewhere, Matthew improves the image of Jesus' disciples, who appear to be such failures in the Gospel of Mark. Because the empty tomb story developed so late in the gospel tradition, and because of the fantastic elements that embellish the story—the appearance of the angel, the miraculous rolling away of the stone, and the earthquake—the Fellows agreed that the entire scene was the product of early Christian imagination. The designation was accordingly black.

The empty tomb
Lk 24:1–12
Mk 16:1–8, Mt 28:1–8;
Jn 20:1–18; Pet 12:1–13:3
Sources: Mark, John, Peter

**LUKE 24:1–12 On Sunday, at daybreak, they made their way to
the tomb, bringing the spices they had prepared. [2]They found the
stone rolled away from the tomb, [3]but when they went inside they
did not find the body of the Lord Jesus.**

**[4]And so, while they were still uncertain about what to do, two fig-
ures in dazzling clothing suddenly appeared and stood beside them.
[5]Out of sheer fright they prostrated themselves on the ground; the
men said to them, "Why are you looking for the living among the
dead? [6]He is not here—he was raised. Remember what he told you
while he was still in Galilee: [7]'The son of Adam is destined to be
turned over to heathen, to be crucified, and on the third day to rise.'"
[8]Then they recalled what he had said.**

**[9]And returning from the tomb, they related everything to the
eleven and to everybody else. [10]The group included Mary of
Magdala and Joanna and Mary the mother of James, and the rest of
the women companions. They related their story to the apostles;
[11]but their story seemed nonsense to them, so they refused to believe
the women.**

**[12]But Peter got up and ran to the tomb. He peeped in and saw only
the linen wrappings, and returned home, marveling at what had
happened.**

The empty tomb. Like Matthew, Luke retells the story of the empty tomb using Mark's version as the basis. Luke puts his own stamp on the story. Instead of finding a young man in a white robe in the empty tomb, the women find *two* figures in dazzling white clothing (v. 4). The reaction of the women is immediate: they fall to the ground in pure terror (v. 5).

Luke here employs common motifs from the scriptures where heavenly visions are involved. *Fear* is the natural reaction, as in the case of Zechariah, the father of John the Baptist (Luke 1:12–13), and of Mary (1:29–30). The shepherds also respond in fear when they receive the message of Jesus' birth (Luke 2:9–10).

Prostration is a means of veneration when humans are faced with an appearance of God or God's messengers. When God appears to Abram, Abram falls to the ground facedown (Gen 17:3). When three angels appear to Abraham and Sarah at the Oaks of Mamre, he bows prostrate on the ground (Gen 18:2).

Joshua falls to the ground in reverence when confronted by a messenger of the Lord (Josh 5:14). And Manoah and his wife, the parents of Samson, fall on their faces to the ground when the Lord's messenger ascends back into the sky in a flame of fire (Judg 13:20). In the book of Revelation, John catches sight of one like the son of Adam—a figure in dazzling white clothing—and falls down as though dead (Rev 1:17). Even the angels fall face down in the presence of God (Rev 7:11).

Of course, bowing down, falling to one's knees, falling prostrate were gestures of respect from any inferior to a superior in ancient societies. The leper who wants Jesus to heal him falls to his knees with his face to the ground in pleading his case (Luke 5:12). Luke has done nothing more than provide the story with standard motifs.

The instructions of the two figures to the women disciples include reminding them of a prediction Jesus had made much earlier. Luke here quotes his own gospel (v. 7 recalls 9:22). The women who come to the tomb are now identified as Mary of Magdala, Joanna, Mary the mother of James, and other women companions. Luke combines the names of the women from his Markan source with traditions known only to him (Luke 8:1–3).

In Mark, out of fear the women report their experience at the empty tomb to no one. As in Matthew, the women in Luke's version do as they are instructed and inform the male disciples of what has happened (v. 10). However, according to Luke, the disciples do not believe the women (v. 11).

The report in v. 12 that Peter runs to the tomb to check the women's story for himself may have been created by a copyist on the basis of John 20:3–10; v. 12 is omitted in some manuscripts of Luke. In any case, the witness of the women disciples is made secondary to that of the male followers: the male disciples either don't believe or must see for themselves. While Luke has retold the story with new features, we learn nothing that we did not know from Mark. Luke's version is a combination of Mark and his own imagination. Black is the correct designation.

The empty tomb
Jn 20:1–18
Mk 16:1–8, Mt 28:1–8,
Lk 24:1–12; Pet 12:1–13:3
Sources: John, Mark, Peter

JOHN 20:1–18 On Sunday, by the half-light of the early morning,
Mary of Magdala comes to the tomb and sees that the stone has been
moved away. 2So she runs and comes to Simon Peter and the other
disciple—the one that Jesus loved most—and tells them, "They've
taken the Master from the tomb, and we don't know where they've
put him."

**3So Peter and the other disciple went out, and they make their
way to the tomb. 4The two of them were running along together, but
the other disciple ran faster than Peter and was the first to reach the
tomb. 5Stooping down, he could see the strips of burial cloth lying
there; but he didn't go in. 6Then Simon Peter comes along behind
him and went in. He too sees the strips of burial cloth there, 7and
also the cloth they had used to cover his head, lying not with the
strips of burial cloth but rolled up by itself. 8Then the other disciple,
who had been the first to reach the tomb, came in. He saw all this,
and he believed. 9But since neither of them yet understood the**

prophecy that he was destined to rise from the dead, [10]these disciples went back home.

[11]Mary, however, stood crying outside, and in her tears she stooped to look into the tomb, [12]and she sees two heavenly messengers in white seated where Jesus' body had lain, one at the head and the other at the feet.

[13]"Woman, why are you crying?" they ask her.

"They've taken my Master away," she tells them, "and I don't know where they've put him."

[14]No sooner had she said this than she turned around and sees Jesus standing there—but she didn't know that it was Jesus.

[15]"Woman," Jesus says to her, "why are you crying? Who is it you're looking for?"

She could only suppose that it was the gardener, and so she says to him, "Please, mister, if you've moved him, tell me where you've put him so I can take him away."

[16]"Mary," says Jesus.

She turns around and exclaims in Hebrew, "Rabbi!" (which means "Teacher").

[17]"Don't touch me," Jesus tells her, "because I have not yet gone back to the Father. But go to my brothers and tell them this: 'I'm going back to my Father and your Father—to my God and your God.'"

[18]Mary of Magdala goes and reports to the disciples, "I have seen the Master," and relates everything he had told her.

The empty tomb. John's account of the empty tomb is the most novelistic of the several stories, recalling moving scenes from hellenistic romance novels in which lovers return to the graves of their beloved, only to find that the tomb has been robbed, and that their loved one's body has been whisked away by tomb robbers, leaving only their grave clothes behind. Such a story appears to have been the basis of the tale narrated in vv. 1, 11–18 involving only Mary of Magdala. In spite of its novelistic elements, and in spite of the fact that it is undoubtedly a fiction, the Fellows gave this part of the story a gray designation in recognition of an old tradition that Mary was one of the first to come to the Easter faith. She is the first to see the risen Jesus in Matthew (28:8–10) and here in John (vv. 14–18). John contrasts her first with Peter and the beloved disciple (vv. 3–10) and later with doubting Thomas (20:24–29): she believes and confesses, "I have seen the Master" (v. 18); they do not yet believe. It is curious that she is not mentioned in Paul's list in 1 Corinthians 15. In the traditions of the primitive church, she competes with Peter and James, the brother of Jesus, for the honor of having been the first to have had a vision of the risen Jesus. The Gospel of Mary also attests that Mary had a vision of the risen Lord (7:1).

The intervening tale of Peter and "the other disciple," also known as the "beloved disciple," is a Johannine fabrication. It pits Peter and the beloved disciple against each other: the beloved disciple reaches the tomb first in their footrace, but doesn't enter. Peter comes along and goes in. According to the author of the Fourth Gospel, the beloved disciple believed without having seen the risen Jesus (compare v. 8 with 20:29). However, the remark in v. 8 is apparently contradicted by the observation in v. 9 that neither Peter nor the beloved disciple understood that Jesus was to rise from the dead according to some prophecy. Copyists over the years made various attempts to solve the problem, without any real success. According to the Gospel of John, Peter saw the empty tomb but did not believe; the beloved disciple observed the empty tomb and believed. That ranks the beloved disciple above Peter, so to speak.

Because the narrative in vv. 3–10 appears to be at odds with the surrounding narrative context in which Jesus appears first to Mary, many scholars take the footrace to the tomb to be a fiction pure and simple, designed to elevate the beloved disciple at the expense of Peter. The original story must have begun with v. 1 and then continued in vv. 11–13. By inserting the account of the two male disciples into Mary's story, the author of the Fourth Gospel has reduced Mary to a secondary role even though Jesus appears first to her.

The empty tomb
Pet 12:1–13:3
Mk 16:1–8, Mt 28:1–8,
Lk 24:1–12; Jn 20:1–18
Sources: Peter, Mark, John

**PET 12:1–13:3 Early on the Lord's day, Mary of Magdala, a disci-
ple of the Lord, was fearful on account of the Judeans and, since
they were inflamed with rage, she did not perform at the tomb of the
Lord what women are accustomed to do for their loved ones who
die. [2]Nevertheless, she took her friends with her and went to the
tomb where he had been laid. [3]And they were afraid that the
Judeans might see them and were saying, "Although on the day he
was crucified we could not weep and beat our breasts, we should
now perform these rites at his tomb. [4]But who will roll away the
stone for us, the one placed at the entrance of the tomb, so that we
may enter and sit beside him and do what ought to be done?"
[5](remember, it was a huge stone.) "We fear that someone might see
us. And if we are unable <to roll the stone away> we should, at least,
place at the entrance the memorial we brought for him, and we
should weep and beat our breasts until we go home."**

**13 And they went and found the tomb open. They went up to it,
stooped down, and saw a young man sitting there <in> the middle
of the tomb; he was handsome and wore a splendid robe. He said to
them, [2]"Why have you come? Who are you looking for? Surely not
the one who was crucified? He is risen and gone. If you don't
believe it, stoop down and take a look at the place where he lay, for
he is not there. You see, he is risen and has gone back to the place he
was sent from." [3]Then the women fled in fear.**

The empty tomb. The visit of Mary of Magdala to the tomb, accompanied by others vaguely identified as her friends, is narrated in 12:1–13:3. Mary is recognized explicitly as a disciple of Jesus (v. 1). The women, it seems, had not been able to perform the customary rites at the tomb because of the hostility of those who had opposed Jesus. They feared, even a day later, that they might be seen and their mourning rites disrupted. They find the tomb open. A single young man greets them, as in Mark (16:5), the one who had earlier descended from the skies and entered the tomb after the resurrection of Jesus (11:2). The youth tells the women that Jesus has gone back to the place he was sent from, rather than that he will precede them to Galilee, as in Mark (16:7). The women flee in fear, also as in Mark (16:8).

Peter has much in common with the other gospels, but this gospel reflects no knowledge of future appearances in Galilee and makes no mention of the silence of the women. Yet in the final chapter (14:1–3), Peter, Andrew, and Levi the son of Alphaeus are apparently back in Galilee with their fishing nets at work on the sea, as though resurrection had not yet occurred and the women had said nothing of their experience at the empty tomb.

The Fellows of the Seminar could find nothing in the second part of the story that could be designated any color other than black.

The bribing of the guards
Mt 28:11–15
Pet 11:1–7
Sources: Matthew, Peter

MATT 28:11–15 **[11]While they were on their way, some of the
guards returned to the city and reported to the ranking priests every-
thing that had happened. [12]They met with the elders and hatched a
plan: they bribed the soldiers with an adequate amount of money
[13]and ordered them: "Tell everybody that his disciples came at night
and stole his body while we were asleep. [14]If the governor should
hear about this, we will deal with him; you need have no worries."
[15]They took the money and did as they had been instructed. And this
story has been passed around among the Jews until this very day.**

The bribing of the guards. The bribing of the guards is a continuation of the story begun in Matthew in 27:51–54 and 62–66. Verse 15 suggests that a counterclaim was circulating in Matthew's time to the effect that the empty tomb is the consequence of nefarious body snatching. Stationing the guard at the tomb was intended to prevent this counterclaim, but since it hadn't done so, Matthew invents a further rebuttal: the soldiers were bribed to keep quiet about their experiences at the death of Jesus and at the empty tomb. The fiction of the empty tomb bred the fiction of the guards at the tomb, which bred the fiction of the bribing of the guards. This is myth-making at its most prolific. The Fellows were virtually unanimous that this tale is an invention of the evangelist. (See further the cameo essay, "The Guard at the Tomb," p. 474.)

The bribing of the guards
Pet 11:1–7
Mt 28:11–15
Sources: Peter, Matthew

PET 11:1–7 **These men then consulted with one another about
going and reporting these things to Pilate. [2]While they were still
thinking about it, again the skies appeared to open and some sort of
human being came down and entered the tomb. [3]When those in the
centurion's company saw this, they rushed out into the night to
Pilate, having left the tomb which they were supposed to be guard-
ing. And as they were recounting everything they had seen, they
became deeply disturbed and cried, "He really was God's son!"
[4]Pilate responded by saying, "I am clean of the blood of the son of
God; this was all your doing." [5]Then they all crowded around
<Pilate> and began to beg and urge him to order the centurion and
his soldiers to tell no one what they saw. [6]"You see," they said, "it is**

THE GUARD AT THE TOMB

In assessing the details of the passion story, it is important to note which features are derived from the common source (Mark) and which are supplied by the individual evangelists. This procedure is particularly instructive in the account of the Roman officer (centurion) and his troops who are present at the execution of Jesus and stand watch over the tomb.

In Mark, when Jesus died, the curtain of the temple was torn in two and the centurion was made to confess: "This man really was God's son!"

To this version Matthew adds the fantastic details reported in 27:51b–53: there is an earthquake, rocks are split, and the tombs of many sleeping righteous are opened; those dead saints are resurrected and eventually appear in Jerusalem to many. They are not permitted to do so, however, until after Jesus has risen (v. 53). Further, Matthew provides the centurion with troops, all of whom are now terrified at the unusual events and collectively confess (v. 54).

Luke (23:45–49) makes no mention of the fantastic events recorded by Matthew, but repeats the simple story of Mark, except that the Roman officer is provided with a confession more congenial to Roman ears: "This man was completely innocent!" However, Luke elaborates Mark at this point by depicting the response of the assembled throng: Having observed the death of Jesus and the confession of the Roman officer, they returned home beating their breasts as a sign of repentance (Luke 23:48).

The Gospel of Peter seems to know not only the relatively simple account of Mark, but also some elements found only in Matthew and Luke. Like Matthew, Peter knows the story of the Roman guards at the tomb (Pet 8:1–11:7); Mark is not aware of guards and Luke follows Mark in this respect. The Gospel of Peter also has all the elements peculiar to both Matthew and Luke, although not in the same sequence. Peter reports that the elders and priests beat their breasts (7:1) as does the throng in the Gospel of Luke (23:48). Moreover, Peter reports the Roman confession in 8:1 ("He must have been entirely innocent!"), which the author may have learned from Luke 23:47. In addition, he also reports the confession found in Mark and Matthew: in 11:3 Peter has the Roman officer and his troops exclaim, "He really was God's son!"

In both Matthew and Peter, the Roman guards have a vision—in Matthew at the moment Jesus dies, in Peter during the night at the tomb. In that vision there is a secondary resurrection of Jewish saints (Matt 27:53; in Pet 10:2–5 symbolized by the cross following the three men). And finally, Peter knows about the bribing of the guards (Matt 28:11–15), except that as he tells the story, the guards are to keep quiet on the command of Pilate (Pet 11:5–7).

These observations suggest that the final version of the Gospel of Peter is based on information derived from both Matthew and Luke. In addition, the account of the Roman centurion, his troops, their vision, their confession, and other details indicates how the story was augmented and elaborated as it was repeated and edited by the several evangelists.

better for us to be guilty of the greatest sin before God than to fall into the hands of the Judean people and be stoned." [7]Pilate then ordered the centurion and the soldiers to say nothing.**

The bribing of the guards. The Roman guards who witnessed the amazing sights reported in chapters 9 and 10 leave their posts and rush to Pilate, to whom they make a declaration of Jesus' divine sonship similar to that of the Roman centurion in the Gospel of Mark (15:39). As in Matthew (27:24), Pilate declines to take responsibility for Jesus' execution. Pilate orders the centurion and his troops to say nothing about what has happened (11:1–7). In the counterpart to this story in Matthew (28:11–15), it is the chief priests who bribe the tomb guards to say nothing and assure the Roman troops that they will deal with Pilate if the need arises. Peter lays the responsibility for silence at the door of Pilate. Neither version reflects a memory of actual events.

MATT 28:9–10 **[9]And then Jesus met them saying, "Hello!"**
They came up and took hold of his feet and paid him homage.
[10]Then Jesus says to them, "Don't be afraid. Go tell my companions so they can leave for Galilee, where they will see me."

Appearance to Mary of Magdala
Mt 28:9–10
Jn 20:11–18; PsMk 16:9–11
Sources: Matthew, John, Pseudo-Mark

Appearance to Mary of Magdala. In Mark three women come to the tomb on Easter Sunday morning: Mary of Magdala, Mary the mother of James, and Salome (Mark 16:1). In Matthew the number is reduced to two: Mary of Magdala and an unidentified Mary, probably Mary the mother of James. Luke expands the circle: Mary of Magdala, Joanna, Mary the mother of James, and other women (Luke 24:10). The Fourth Gospel reduces the number to one: Mary of Magdala (John 20:1). The Gospel of Peter lists Mary of Magdala and an unspecified number of other women (Pet 12:1–2). Mary of Magdala is the common name in all these reports.

In revising Mark, Matthew appends an appearance of Jesus to the two Marys as they leave the tomb. Matthew may have known an oral tradition that gave warrant for this expansion of Mark. It is possible that the Signs Gospel, the predecessor to the Gospel of John, contained the story of an appearance to Mary of Magdala (John 20:11–18). The Gospel of Mary reports that Mary of Magdala saw the Lord in a vision (7:1). However, connecting Mary's vision with the empty tomb story was probably arbitrary. Since the empty tomb tale is probably Mark's invention, the appearance to Mary at the tomb also has a dubious basis. Of course, the fictive nature of Matthew's narrative in no way discredits the claim that Mary had a vision of the risen Jesus.

JOHN 20:11–18 **[11]Mary, however, stood crying outside, and in her tears she stooped to look into the tomb, [12]and she sees two heavenly messengers in white seated where Jesus' body had lain, one at the head and the other at the feet.**

[13]"Woman, why are you crying?" they ask her.

"They've taken my Master away," she tells them, "and I don't know where they've put him."

Appearance to Mary of Magdala
Jn 20:11–18
Mt 28:9–10; PsMk 16:9–11
Sources: John, Matthew, Pseudo-Mark

MARY OF MAGDALA

Two basic portraits of Mary of Magdala developed over the centuries, each with many variations: one stressed her roles as a prominent disciple of Jesus, a visionary, and a spiritual teacher; the other painted her as a repentant prostitute whom Jesus forgave, a latter-day Eve turned from her sinful ways. While both portraits have legendary aspects, only the first has any claim to historical truth. The portrait of Mary as a repentant prostitute is pure fiction with no historical foundation. The historical Mary of Magdala was a prominent Jewish follower of Jesus and a visionary.

Mary came from the town of Magdala, located on the west shore of the Sea of Galilee, just north of the city of Tiberias. Apparently of independent means, she accompanied Jesus during his ministry and supported him out of her own resources. After his death she became a leader in the early Christian movement. As with so many of the other disciples, the very meagerness of what was known about her life only served to fire the imaginations of later Christians, who elaborated her history in story and art according to their spiritual needs and political aims.

Mary as prominent disciple

Early Christian literature, including the New Testament gospels, portrays Mary of Magdala as a prominent disciple of Jesus. She was present at his crucifixion and was a witness to the resurrection. Indeed, she is portrayed as the first, or among the first, privileged to see and speak with the risen Lord. In the Gospel of John, the risen Jesus gives her special teaching and commissions her as an apostle to the apostles to bring them the good news.

Newly discovered Christian literature from Egypt further develops this portrait of Mary as a prominent disciple. In the Dialogue of the Savior, a late first- or early second-century work from Nag Hammadi, Mary has a vision of the "Son of Man" and is singled out, along with Matthew and Judas (Thomas), in a dialogue with Jesus. Her statements are so insightful that the narrator exclaims: "She spoke as a woman who understood completely."

The Gospel of Mary, an early second-century gospel containing dialogues between Jesus and his disciples after the resurrection, portrays Mary as a woman leader among the disciples. She is the one who takes over leadership after the Savior's departure, comforting the other distraught disciples and providing them with advanced teaching from her own visionary revelation of the Lord.

The Sophia of Jesus Christ, another second-century work from Egypt, presents Mary of Magdala as an equal among the male disciples as they are given special teaching from Jesus and then sent out to preach the gospel. In the Pistis Sophia, a third- or fourth-century work also found in Egypt, Jesus himself says of her: "Your heart is more directed toward the kingdom of God than are all your brothers" (26,19–20).

The prominence of Mary in these texts does not go uncontested, however, nor does her prominence necessarily signal a positive evaluation of femaleness. Often Mary is opposed, usually by Peter. Using her as an example, Peter suggests that women are not worthy of life, and he vociferously rejects any suggestion that Jesus might have favored her over the male disciples. Mary even complains that

Peter hates all women. In every case, however, these works defend Mary and affirm the spiritual value of her understanding. While such controversies do not represent historical events, they do point toward controversies among early Christians over the meaning of Jesus' teachings, his death and resurrection, and issues of early church authority, including women's leadership roles. This literature shows that the name of Mary of Magdala was associated with a theology that focused upon Jesus' teachings, affirmed only his spiritual, not his physical resurrection, and supported women's leadership. This association may have provided one impetus for inventing an alternative portrait of Mary as a prostitute.

Mary as repentant prostitute

From the fourth century onward, the early, positive tone began to shift. The church fathers increasingly tended to explain Jesus' command not to touch him by arguing that Mary, unlike Thomas, was not worthy of touching the resurrected Lord because she lacked a full understanding of the resurrection and hence lacked true faith. She was sent to the male apostles—argued church scholars Ambrose, Jerome, and Augustine—so that her weakness could be supplemented by their strength.

It was nonetheless appropriate, Gregory of Nyssa and Augustine began to argue, that a woman be the first to receive the redemption offered by Jesus through his resurrection, because it was after all—at least in their interpretation of the Genesis story—a woman who had first brought sin into the world. Ambrose wrote of Mary of Magdala as the second Eve, the woman whose faith in the resurrected Jesus overcame the offenses of the first Eve.

That Mary was reported to have received private instruction from the risen Jesus was a more difficult problem. By the end of the second century, she had become closely associated with an interpretation of Jesus' teachings very different from what many of the church fathers were developing. Such teachings are clearly present in the Gospel of Mary, whose content and title both link these "heretical" views with Mary. Discrediting her may therefore have been in part a strategy of the church fathers to counter the interpretation of Jesus' teaching being spread in works like the Gospel of Mary, the Dialogue of the Savior, the Sophia of Jesus Christ, or the Pistis Sophia.

The silence of the church fathers, it turned out, was not an effective strategy, since it left the imaginative field open to their opponents. So starting in the fourth century, Christian theologians in the Latin West invented an alternative story. The first move was to associate Mary of Magdala with the unnamed sinner who anointed Jesus' feet in Luke 7:36–50. The confusion arose when the account in John 12:1–8, in which Mary of Bethany anoints Jesus, was conflated with the anointing by the unnamed woman sinner in the accounts of Luke. From this point, the move to identifying Mary of Magdala with Mary of Bethany is a short one. At the end of the sixth century, Pope Gregory the Great gave a sermon in which he not only identified these figures, but drew the moral conclusion that would dominate the imagination of the West for centuries to come:

> She whom Luke calls the sinful woman, whom John calls Mary, we believe to be the Mary from whom seven devils were ejected according to

> Mark. And what did these seven devils signify, if not all the vices? . . . It is clear, brothers, that the woman previously used the unguent to perfume her flesh in forbidden acts. What she therefore displayed more scandalously, she was now offering to God in a more praiseworthy manner. She had coveted with earthly eyes, but now through penitence these are consumed with tears. She displayed her hair to set off her face, but now her hair dries her tears. She had spoken proud things with her mouth, but in kissing the Lord's feet, she now planted her mouth on the Redeemer's feet. For every delight, therefore, she had had in herself, she now immolated herself. She turned the mass of her crimes to virtues, in order to serve God entirely in penance, for as much as she had wrongly held God in contempt.

The Eastern churches never made this error, and therefore never developed a portrait of Mary of Magdala as a prostitute; there she is honored as an important witness to the resurrection. But in the West, once this initial identification was secured, Mary of Magdala could be associated with every unnamed sinful woman in the gospels, including the adulteress in John 8:1–11 and the Samaritan woman with her five and more "husbands" in John 4:7–30. Mary the apostle and teacher had become Mary the repentant whore.

14 No sooner had she said this than she turned around and sees Jesus standing there—but she didn't know that it was Jesus.

5 "Woman," Jesus says to her, "why are you crying? Who is it you're looking for?"

She could only suppose that it was the gardener, and so she says to him, "Please, mister, if you've moved him, tell me where you've put him so I can take him away."

6 "Mary," says Jesus.

She turns around and exclaims in Hebrew, "Rabbi!" (which means "Teacher").

17 "Don't touch me," Jesus tells her, "because I have not yet gone back to the Father. But go to my brothers and tell them this: 'I'm going back to my Father and your Father—to my God and your God.'"

18 Mary of Magdala goes and reports to the disciples, "I have seen the Master," and relates everything he had told her.

Appearance to Mary of Magdala. The Fellows of the Jesus Seminar decided, after extended debate, to color this version of the appearance to Mary gray. They did so, in a sense, against their better judgment. They agreed that the empty tomb story was probably a Markan invention. Accordingly, the appearance to Mary of Magdala at the tomb must also be fictive. Yet the Fellows felt obligated to acknowledge the claim of Mary to have had a vision of the risen Jesus. They elected to designate the Johannine version gray, rather than that of Matthew, for two reasons: in John it is Mary alone who comes to the tomb and sees Jesus (there are additional women in the other versions); the story in John may derive from the Signs Gospel, an underlying source for the final version of the Fourth Gospel. Among the signs included in the Signs Gospel may have been the story of the appearance to Mary. Gray, it will be recalled, is a muddy category, indicating that the evidence provided by the narrative is remotely possible but unreliable. In a separate vote, however, the Fellows affirmed that:

- **Mary was among the early witnesses to the resurrection of Jesus;**

and

- **Mary was considered a leader in the early Jesus movement along with Peter and Paul.**

In other words, the evidence supports the claims of Mary on a par with those of Peter and Paul. The reliability of other claims diminishes rapidly.

Appearance to Mary of Magdala
PsMk 16:9–11
Mt 28:9–10; Jn 20:11–18
Sources: Pseudo-Mark, Matthew, John

PsMK 16:9–11 **[9]Now after he arose at daybreak on Sunday, he appeared first to Mary of Magdala, from whom he had driven out seven demons. [10]She went and told those who were close to him, who were mourning and weeping. [11]But when those folks heard that he was alive and had been seen by her, they did not believe it.**

Appearance to Mary of Magdala. This account of the appearance to Mary of Magdala at the tomb is part of the so-called longer ending of Mark. The longer ending consists of vv. 9–20; it can easily be divided into three appearance stories: vv. 9–11, the appearance to Mary; vv. 12–13, the appearance to two in the country; vv. 14–18, the final appearance to the eleven. The ascension is narrated in vv. 19–20. (The relation of the longer ending to the original ending of the Gospel of Mark is treated in a cameo essay on pp. 466–67.)

We learn from this report that the resurrection of Jesus occurred at daybreak on Sunday. According to the Gospel of Peter (11:3), the resurrection occurred during the night.

The appearance to Mary is strongly reminiscent of John 20:1–2, where Mary of Magdala runs from the tomb and tells "Simon Peter and the other disciples" that Jesus' body is gone. The note in v. 9 that the Mary in question is the Mary from whom Jesus had exorcized seven demons is a detail derived from Luke 8:2. (Early church writers were understandably confused about the identification of the various Marys in the tradition.) As in the Gospel of Peter (7:3, 14:2), the close followers of Jesus are mourning and weeping at their loss. When they hear Mary's tale, they refuse to believe her, just as they do in the Gospel of Luke (24:11).

This story, like the others in the longer ending, gives strong indications of being secondhand tradition—material derived from known sources, especially the New Testament gospels and the Gospel of Peter. For that reason, the Fellows agreed on a black designation.

The twelve depart
Pet 14:1–3
No parallels
Source: Peter

PET 14:1–3 Now it was the last day of Unleavened Bread, and many began to return to their homes since the feast was over. [2]But we, the twelve disciples of the Lord, continued to weep and mourn, and each one, still grieving on account of what had happened, left for his own home. [3]But I, Simon Peter, and Andrew, my brother, took our fishing nets and went away to the sea. And with us was Levi, the son of Alphaeus, whom the Lord . . .

The twelve depart. This final surviving segment of the Gospel of Peter indicates that seven days have passed since the beginning of Passover and the feast of Unleavened Bread that follows. According to this account, the disciples remained in Jerusalem until the feast was over rather than fleeing at the arrest of Jesus. The sea in v. 3 is probably the Sea of Galilee or Tiberias, where the fishermen were at home. The surviving fragment of Peter breaks off at this point, but it is possible that an appearance to Peter and the group followed in the original form of the gospel. Such an appearance on the sea is recorded in John 21:1–14; it is paralleled by a call story found in Luke 5:1–11, which may also be a misplaced resurrection epiphany.

The use of the first person in v. 3 linked to the name of Simon Peter is the basis for referring to this gospel as the Gospel of Peter.

While the Fellows agree that the disciples fled at the arrest of Jesus, they doubt that the disciples delayed their flight for seven days just to observe the feast of Unleavened Bread. They are inclined to the view that the fishermen in Jesus' circle returned to their jobs in disappointment and frustration. Yet they are skeptical that this gospel represents the words of Peter as v. 3 suggests. Black is the correct color.

Appearance to two in the country
Lk 24:13–35
PsMk 16:12–13
Source: Luke

**LUKE 24:13–35 [13]Now, that same day two of them were traveling to a village named Emmaus, about seven miles from Jerusalem.
[14]They were engaged in conversation about all that had taken place.
[15]And it so happened, during the course of their discussion, that Jesus himself approached and began to walk along with them. [16]But they couldn't recognize him.**

[17]He said to them, "What were you discussing as you walked along?"

Then they paused, looking depressed. [18]One of them, named Cleopas, said to him in reply, "Are you the only visitor to Jerusalem who doesn't know what's happened there these last few days?"

[19]And he said to them, "What are you talking about?"

**And they said to him, "About Jesus of Nazareth, who was a prophet powerful in word and deed in the eyes of God and all the people, [20]and about how our ranking priests and rulers turned him in to be sentenced to death, and crucified him. [21]We were hoping that he would be the one who was going to ransom Israel. And as if this weren't enough, it's been three days now since all this happened.
[22]Meanwhile, some women from our group gave us quite a shock.**

They were at the tomb early this morning [23]and didn't find his body. They came back claiming even to have seen a vision of heavenly messengers, who said that he was alive. [24]Some of those with us went to the tomb and found it exactly as the women had described; but nobody saw him."

[25]And he said to them, "You people are so slow-witted, so reluctant to trust everything the prophets have said! [26]Wasn't the Anointed One destined to undergo these things and enter into his glory?" [27]Then, starting with Moses and all the prophets, he interpreted for them every passage of scripture that referred to himself.

[28]They had gotten close to the village to which they were going, and he acted as if he were going on. [29]But they entreated him, saying, "Stay with us; it's almost evening, the day is practically over." So he went in to stay with them.

[30]And so, as soon as he took his place at table with them, he took a loaf, and gave a blessing, broke it, and started passing it out to them. [31]Then their eyes were opened and they recognized him; and he vanished from their sight. [32]They said to each other, "Weren't our hearts burning within us while he was talking to us on the road, and explaining the scriptures to us?" [33]And they got up at once and returned to Jerusalem.

And when they found the eleven and those with them gathered together, [34]they said, "The Lord really has been raised, and has appeared to Simon!" [35]Then they described what had happened on the road, and how they came to recognize him in the breaking of bread.

Appearance to two in the country. The story of the appearance of Jesus to the two travelers on the road to Emmaus exhibits Luke's storytelling ability at its best. The tale as it stands is a compendium of appearance traditions with a considerable history. The original story may have consisted of the elements found in Pseudo-Mark: Two friends walking in the country encounter a stranger traveling incognito; they eventually recognize him by some characteristic behavior, perhaps when he shares a meal with them.

Abraham is said to have entertained angels unaware (Gen 18:1–15). Three strangers appear whom Abraham entertains according to the laws of hospitality: he has Sarah his wife bake bread (using fifty pounds of flour!) and has a servant slaughter a calf. The three, who turn out to be angels, eat and announce that his wife will bear a son, even though she has entered menopause.

In a similar fashion, Lot entertains two angels without knowing who they are (Gen 19:1–11). Lot insists that they spend the night with him rather than in the public square. He prepares a meal for them, including unleavened bread. When the townspeople insist on looking his guests over, he offers them his two virgin daughters instead. The mob attempts to break Lot's door down; the angels strike the attackers with blindness so they can't find the door.

There is a similar recognition scene in Ovid's tale of Philemon and Baucis (Book 8 of the *Metamorphoses*), who entertain the gods Jupiter and Mercury without knowing it. They provide the best hospitality their limited means afford. Only when the flagon of wine continues to replenish itself do they recognize their visitors as gods, who had come to punish the neighborhood.

Recognition scenes, it seems, often occur while a host is offering hospitality to a stranger. That is the basis of the piece of folk wisdom formulated in Heb 13:2: "Remember to be hospitable. By so doing some have entertained angels unawares."

The appearance to the two travelers is a tale told in the spirit of such popular stories about entertaining divinities without knowing it.

Luke has enhanced the simple story by adding touches that reflect his gospel. Verses 19–20 are in effect a summary of his gospel. He then recapitulates the empty tomb story (vv. 22–24). He further adds his own view of how recent events have been the fulfillment of ancient prophecies (vv. 25–27).

In v. 28 Luke returns to the basic narrative: the two recognize Jesus when he blesses and breaks bread with them. At that moment he disappears (vv. 28–33). The two return to Jerusalem, in accordance with Luke's scheme that Jerusalem is to be the epicenter of the Christian movement. He again goes outside his primary story line and recounts the report of the appearance to Peter and has the two reiterate the experience they have just had. Verses 33b–35 are thus transitional sentences that serve to connect the story of the two in the country to the appearance to the eleven that follows (24:36–49).

Efforts to identify the village of Emmaus have been fruitless, and it has been equally frustrating to connect Cleopas (v. 18) with other known persons. Both may be inventions of Luke. Indeed, the story as it stands is the creation of Luke, except perhaps for a nucleus that he may have known from the oral tradition. The story is so saturated with folk themes and Christian theology that it is not possible to isolate a historical core. The Fellows voted it black by a substantial majority.

Appearance to two in the country
PsMk 16:12–13
Lk 24:13–35
Source: Luke

PsMK 16:12–13 **[12]A little later he appeared to two of them in a different guise as they were walking along, on their way to the country. [13]And these two returned and told the others. They did not believe them either.**

Appearance to two in the country. This brief report looks like a condensed version of the Emmaus road story in Luke 24:13–33a. In both accounts there are two travelers, in both they are presented as walking away from Jerusalem, and in both Jesus is not immediately identifiable. But there is a difference: here the disciples do not believe the tale of the two; Luke, by contrast, preempts their response by having Jesus appear among them. Even so, at first, according to Luke, the disciples were frightened and thought they might have been seeing a ghost (Luke 24:36–42).

The refusal to believe the report of the two travelers (v. 13) is a repetition of the earlier refusal to believe Mary's story (PsMk 16:11).

Since the tale of the two on the road to Emmaus in Luke is colored black, its twin here must also be so designated.

PsMK 16:14–18 [14]**Later he appeared to the eleven as they were reclining <at a meal>. He reproached them for their lack of trust and obstinacy, because they did not believe those who had seen him after he had been raised.** [15]**And he said to them: "Go out into the whole world and announce the good news to every creature.** [16]**Whoever trusts and is baptized will be saved. The one who lacks trust will be condemned.** [17]**These are the signs that will accompany those who have trust: they will drive out demons in my name; they will speak in new tongues;** [18]**they will pick up snakes with their hands; and even if they swallow poison, it certainly won't harm them; they will lay their hands on those who are sick, and they will get well."**

Appearance to the eleven
PsMk 16:14–18
Mt 28:16–20; Lk 24:36–49; Jn 20:19–23
Sources: Matthew, Luke, John

Appearance to the eleven. An appearance to the eleven (or twelve, as a result of confusion arising from Judas' defection) is mentioned in Paul's list in 1 Cor 15:5. It is also narrated in Matthew and John and here in Pseudo-Mark. The version in the longer ending to Mark is dependent on earlier versions.

The appearance to the eleven is the climax of the three appearances reported in the longer ending to Mark. Like the two previous reports, this one is a combination of various elements familiar from other gospels: Jesus appears to the disciples as they are reclining at table—eating a meal in the customary posture—as they are in the Emmaus story related by Luke (24:36–42). Jesus rebukes them for their lack of faith (v. 14), as he does in Luke (24:37–40).

A commission scene follows in vv. 15–18. Now at last the disciples are given their instructions, which at first glance are comparable to those that make up the well-known commission that concludes Matthew's gospel (28:18–20). The promises made to believers in vv. 17–18 are probably borrowed from instructions given to those preparing for baptism. Believers are promised power over demons; the disciples have power to cast out demons in Luke 10:17. Those who have trust are promised the power to speak in new languages; that actually occurs in the story in Acts 2:1–4. Snakes will not harm believers; Paul is apparently immune to the bite of a viper in Acts 28:1–6. They will not be harmed even if they swallow poison; Justus Barsabbas, named in Acts 1:23 as a candidate to succeed Judas the betrayer, is said by later tradition to have survived the consumption of poison. Cures will be effected by the laying on of hands; Paul lays his hands on a man sick with fever and cures him (Acts 28:8).

These are features that define a community of catechumens—people under instruction in connection with baptism—and distinguish them from their social and religion surroundings. There is nothing in these instructions that is directly connected with primitive or authentic Jesus tradition. Indeed, it is probable that an early second-century Christian leader, with access to some or all of the surviving gospels and Acts, has compiled this list of benefits and responsibilities of Christian faith.

Appearance to the eleven
Mt 28:16–20
Lk 24:36–49; PsMk 16:14–18;
Jn 20:19–23
Sources: Matthew, Luke,
John

MATT 28:16–20 **[16]The eleven disciples went to the mountain in Galilee where Jesus had told them to go. [17]And when they saw him, they paid him homage; but some were dubious.**

[18]And Jesus approached them and spoke these words: "All authority has been given to me in heaven and on earth. [19]You are to go and make followers of all peoples. You are to baptize them in the name of the Father and the son and the holy spirit. [20]Teach them to observe everything I commanded. I'll be with you day in and day out, as you'll see, so long as this world continues its course."

Appearance to the eleven. Mark did not relate any appearances of the risen Jesus. Matthew is the first to depict an actual appearance when he has Jesus appear to Mary of Magdala at the tomb (28:9–10). He now adds a second appearance to the first in what will eventually become an extended sequence of appearance narratives.

Matthew was the first to tell the story of an appearance to the eleven disciples, although the report of such an appearance had already been circulated in the list of appearances such as Paul records in 1 Corinthians 15. Paul gives the number as "twelve," which Matthew corrects to "eleven": the discrepancy depends, of course, on whether Judas is to be counted. Since the number twelve had symbolic value (corresponding to the twelve tribes of Israel), Paul uses the symbolic number.

Matthew's account is composed in Matthean style and with words in Matthew's standard vocabulary. It is therefore a Matthean composition based on the promise made in Mark 16:7: "But go tell his disciples, including 'Rock,' 'He is going ahead of you to Galilee! There you will see him, just as he told you.'" This instruction from the young man at the tomb is anticipated by Jesus himself on the way to the Mount of Olives (Mark 14:28). Matthew picks up these clues from Mark and develops them as a relatively simple narrative fulfillment.

The appearance to the eleven in Matthew is a commissioning story: the disciples are given a charge to enlist other followers, to baptize, and to teach what Jesus taught. The location of this final charge is a mountain, which holds special significance for Matthew: A mountain is the place where Moses received the law; it is the scene of the great sermon of Jesus (Matthew 5–7); it is the location of the transfiguration (Matt 17:1–8); and it is on a mountain Jesus commissions his followers to continue his work by forming a new movement. The symbol of the mountain is freighted with meaning for Matthew.

The appearance of Jesus is depicted in the simplest of terms. The disciples "see" him and pay him homage, although some are dubious. The more elaborate confirmation stories of the type we find in Luke and John have apparently not yet arisen. Matthew appears to be narrating simply on the basis of the report that Jesus had appeared to the eleven, without specific guidance about how the appearance should be described.

The Fellows of the Jesus Seminar were doubtful that the eleven as a group ever experienced a vision of the risen Jesus at one time; the general statement received a gray vote. The tradition probably arose as a confirmation of apostolic authority—authority connected to the experience of some of those who had been closely associated with Jesus during his life. An appearance to Peter may well have been generalized as an appearance to the eleven in order to include the whole symbolic circle of associates. In any case, Matt 28:16–20 is a composition created by Matthew; it probably does not rest on historical reminiscence and therefore merits the color black.

Appearance to the eleven
Lk 24:36–49
Mt 28:16–20; PsMk 16:14–18; Jn 20:19–23
Sources: Luke, Matthew, John

LUKE 24:36–49 [36]**While they were talking about this, he himself**
appeared among them and says to them, "Peace be with you." [37]**But**
they were terrified and frightened, and figured that they were see-
ing a ghost.

[38]**And he said to them, "Why are you upset? Why do such**
thoughts run through your minds? [39]**You can see from my hands and**
my feet that it's really me. Touch me and see—a ghost doesn't have
flesh and bones as you can see that I have."

[41]**And while for sheer joy they still didn't know what to believe**
and were bewildered, he said to them, "Do you have anything here
to eat?" [42]**They offered him a piece of grilled fish,** [43]**and he took it and**
ate it in front of them.

[44]**Then he said to them, "This is the message I gave you while I**
was still with you: everything written about me in the Law of Moses
and the Prophets and the Psalms is destined to come true."

[45]**Then he prepared their minds to understand the scriptures.** [46]**He**
said to them, "This is what is written: the Anointed will suffer and
rise from the dead on the third day. [47]**And all peoples will be called**
on to undergo a change of heart for the forgiveness of sins, begin-
ning from Jerusalem. [48]**You are witnesses to this.** [49]**And be prepared: I**
am sending what my Father promised down on you. Stay here in the
city until you are invested with power from on high."

Appearance to the eleven. After encountering the risen Jesus on the road to Emmaus, Cleopas and his companion return to Jerusalem. They report their experience to the eleven. Suddenly Jesus himself appears, and salutes them with a greeting, "Peace be with you." The eleven are terrified: they think they have been confronted by a ghost. Jesus reassures them: You can see from the wounds in my hands and feet that it is really me. A ghost doesn't have flesh and bones as I have.

Jesus then asks them for something to eat. They provide him with fish, which he eats in front of them. Jesus then opens their minds to understand the scriptures: his death and resurrection are the fulfillment of the prophets. In the next segment he commissions the eleven to proclaim the gospel (vv. 50–53).

Luke has adapted the traditional theophany to his own purposes and to the Christian gospel. It is, of course, a christophany rather than a theophany, so it is the risen Jesus rather than Yahweh, the God of Israel, who appears. The risen "body" of Jesus still carries the marks of his crucifixion, just as his hands and feet do in the Johannine version (20:20). In Greek drama, there is a "recognition scene" in which an apparent stranger is revealed as someone well known or hoped for. Recognition is triggered by certain behavior, by congenital marks, or by signs on the body.

Plato (427–347 B.C.E.) has Socrates say in his dialogue *Gorgias:* "If anyone has been a sturdy rogue, and bore traces of his stripes in scars on his body, . . . then after death too his body has these marks visible on it." Luke may have read this account.

In Greek legend, Euridyce, the wife of Orpheus the musician, is bitten by a snake and dies. Orpheus descends to the underworld and begs the gods in charge, by means of song, to allow his wife to return to earth and live out her short life. The gods grant Orpheus' request on the condition that he not look on her until they have reached the surface. As the pair ascends, Euridyce lags farther and farther behind because her ankle is still weak where the snake had bitten her. Orpheus turns to make sure she is still there. Since Orpheus has broken the restriction, Euridyce vaporizes and drifts back into the abode of the shades. The myth of Orpheus and Euridyce provides an example of a resurrection which is not simply the resuscitation of a corpse, yet retains some of the characteristics of the human body.

As a secondary proof that it is really Jesus and that he is not a ghost, he asks for and is given a piece of fish to eat. Luke here echoes the Emmaus road story that he has just narrated (24:30–31), where the two recognize Jesus in the breaking of bread.

Luke's account of Jesus' appearance was constructed, therefore, in a manner consistent with the expectations of his audience and in accordance with his own theological views. The Fellows of the Jesus Seminar were nearly unanimous, however, in judging Luke's narrative to be without historical foundation. Luke's legacy in this passage, as in many others, is not history but affirmation, not a rehearsal of facts but an ingredient of his proclamation.

Appearance to the eleven
Jn 20:19–23
Lk 24:36–49; Mt 28:16–20;
PsMk 16:14–18
Sources: John, Luke, Matthew

JOHN 20:19–23 **19 That Sunday evening, the disciples had locked the doors for fear of the Judeans, but Jesus came and stood in front of them and he greets them: "Peace."**

20 Then he showed them his hands and his side. The disciples were delighted to see the Master. 21 Jesus greets them again: "Peace," he says. "Just as the Father sent me, so now I'm sending you."

22 And at this he breathed over them and says, "Here's some holy spirit. Take it. 23 If you forgive anyone their sins, they are forgiven; if you do not release them from their sins, they are not released."

Appearance to the eleven. The appearance to the disciples in this passage takes the form of a theophany—the appearance of God or an angel—or, more precisely, a christophany—the appearance of a messiah or God's representative. John's story follows the general outline of the call of Isaiah, the great eighth-century B.C.E. prophet, recorded in the sixth chapter.

The Lord appears to Isaiah on a throne high and lofty, so gigantic that the hem of his garment fills the entire temple. Seraphim—winged serpents—with six wings each praise him and the foundations shake. Isaiah is perturbed and confesses that his lips are unclean. One of the seraphs takes a pair of tongs, flies to the altar and retrieves a hot coal, and touches it to Isaiah's lips. Now that he is clean—cleansed by fire from the altar—Isaiah is ready for commissioning: the Lord enlists Isaiah to announce doom on Israel.

Jesus appears to the disciples behind locked doors and greets them: "Peace to you." He shows them his hands and feet for identification. He reassures them with another peace greeting. Then he commissions them. In these few short verses, John has provided an abbreviated commissioning story without the fantastic details of the one found in Isaiah. It is similar to the appearance story found in Luke 24:36–49 and in Ps-Mk 16:14–18.

As in the other versions, the Fellows found nothing in the Johannine account that can be viewed as a historical report. It is therefore designated black.

Doubting Thomas
Jn 20:24–29
No parallels
Source: John

JOHN 20:24–29 [24]**Now Thomas, the one known as "the Twin,"**
one of the twelve, hadn't been with them when Jesus put in his
appearance. [25]**So the other disciples tried to tell him, "We've seen the**
Master."

But he responded, "Unless I see the holes the nails made, and put
my finger in them and my hand in his side, I'll never believe."

[26]**A week later the disciples were again indoors, and Thomas was**
with them. The doors were locked, but Jesus comes and stood in
front of them, and said, "Peace." [27]**Then he says to Thomas, "Put**
your finger here, and look at my hands; take your hand and put it in
my side. Don't be skeptical but be a believer."

[28]**Thomas responded, "My Master! My God!"**

[29]**"Do you believe because you have seen me?" asks Jesus. "Those**
who can believe without having to see are the ones to be congratulated."

Doubting Thomas. The opening verse of the Gospel of Thomas claims that its author is Didymos Judas Thomas, the twin brother of Jesus (Thomas is Hebrew for twin, and Didymos is its Greek counterpart). Thomas is consistently referred to in the Gospel of John as "Thomas the twin" (John 11:16, 14:5, 20:24–28, and 21:2). Yet the real name of one of Jesus' brothers was Judas (or Jude) and he is not identified in the New Testament as a twin. It is unclear what the relation of the two names is. The apostle Thomas may also have been a twin but not the twin brother of Jesus. Judas may have come to be identified with Thomas as a consequence of the fact that they were both twins. Or Judas and Thomas may be the same person. We simply do not know.

The story of doubting Thomas reflects one aspect of a Thomas legend that continued to grow for centuries. Various documents were ascribed to Thomas: the Gospel of Thomas, now known in a recently discovered Coptic text, in addition to three Greek fragments; the Infancy Gospel of Thomas, a work that circulated in the second century; the Acts of Thomas, a third-century composition;

and the Apocalypse of Thomas, which dates to the fourth century C.E. The apostle Thomas is supposed to have carried the gospel to the Parthians and eventually to India, where he is alleged to have founded the Mar Thoma Church; according to the tradition he was martyred there. His name is also associated with Syrian Christianity, which is centered in Edessa; the bones of Thomas were said to have been removed from India to Edessa at the end of the fourth century C.E.

The account of Jesus' appearance to Thomas a week after his appearance to the eleven (John 20:19–23) was not originally connected to the appearance to the eleven. Indeed, the appearance to Thomas is a retelling of the appearance to the eleven (v. 26 recapitulates v. 19, and v. 27 recalls v. 20). When Thomas blurts out "My Master! My God!" in v. 28, we have evidence that this tradition developed very late: in the earlier strata of the New Testament Jesus is never referred to as God. Indeed, what Jesus says to Mary in John 20:17 "I'm going back to my Father and your Father—to my God and your God"—seems to contradict Thomas' confession that Jesus is God.

Although claims have been made for the Thomas story as an independent tradition, the Fellows were inclined to regard it as a late and fictional tale.

Appearance to seven at the Sea of Tiberias
Jn 21:1–14
Source: John
Cf. Lk 5:1–11; Mk 1:19–22, Mt 4:18–22

JOHN 21:1–14 Some time after these events, Jesus again appeared to his disciples by the Sea of Tiberias. This is how he did it:
2When Simon Peter and Thomas, the one known as "the Twin," were together, along with Nathanael from Cana, Galilee, the sons of Zebedee, and two other disciples, 3Simon Peter says to them, "I'm going to go fishing."

"We're coming with you," they reply.

They went down and got into the boat, but that night they didn't catch a thing.

4It was already getting light when Jesus appeared on the shore, but his disciples didn't recognize that it was Jesus.

5"Lads, you haven't caught any fish, have you?" Jesus asks them.

"No," they replied.

6He tells them, "Cast your net on the right side of the boat and you'll have better luck."

They do as he instructs them and now they can't haul it in for the huge number of fish. 7The disciple Jesus loved most exclaims to Peter, "It's the Master!"

When Simon Peter heard, "It's the Master," he tied his cloak around himself, since he was stripped for work, and threw himself into the water. 8The rest of them came in the boat, dragging the net full of fish. They were not far from land, only about a hundred yards offshore.

9When they got to shore, they see a charcoal fire burning, with fish cooking on it, and some bread. 10Jesus says to them, "Bring some of the fish you've just caught."

11Then Simon Peter went aboard and hauled the net full of large

fish ashore—one hundred fifty-three of them. Even though there were so many of them, the net still didn't tear.

[12]Jesus says to them, "Come and eat."

None of the disciples dared ask, "Who are you?" They knew it was the Master. [13]Jesus comes, takes the bread, and gives it to them, and passes the fish around as well.

[14]This was now the third time after he had been raised from the dead that Jesus appeared to his disciples.

Appearance to seven at the Sea of Tiberias. Chapter 21 is an appendix to the Gospel of John. The original gospel undoubtedly ended with chapter 20. A different author has supplemented the story with an additional appearance story, plus an extended dialogue with Peter (21:15–23).

In v. 14 the author of the appendix tells the reader that the appearance to the seven on the Sea of Tiberias (also called the Sea of Galilee) is the *third* appearance. If the author of the supplement is counting the appearances narrated in chapter 20, he has miscounted or has left the appearance to Mary out of account. In the preceding chapter, Jesus appears to Mary, then to the eleven on Sunday evening, and finally to Thomas and the eleven a week later. The omission of the appearance to Mary probably reflects the rivalry among leaders in the early Christian movement.

It is doubtful that the story of the seven on the Sea of Tiberias belongs to the traditions that lie behind the Fourth Gospel. In John, unlike the synoptic gospels, the members of the intimate circle around Jesus are not depicted as fishermen. But here in the appendix they are back at their old trade on the sea. This story is more appropriate as an extension to the appearances promised in Mark and narrated in Matthew than as an appendix to John.

The number of witnesses is given as seven. The appendix lists Simon Peter, Thomas the twin, Nathanael from Cana, along with the two sons of Zebedee (named James and John), and two other unnamed followers. One of the additional disciples must have been the beloved disciple referred in John 20:2 and mentioned again in 21:20–24, unless, of course, the traditional identification of the beloved disciple with John, son of Zebedee, is correct. Simon Peter and James and John, the sons of Zebedee, are known from the synoptic gospels; Thomas and Nathanael are featured in the Fourth Gospel (Nathanael appears in 1:45–49 in a story in which Jesus first spots him sitting under a fig tree).

In addition, Peter, James, and John are participants in the tale of the miraculous catch of fish, which Luke utilizes as the occasion when Jesus enlists his first disciples (Luke 5:1–11). Luke may have borrowed that story from the repertoire of appearances and remodeled it into an enlistment story. He may have done so because he felt that the call stories narrated by Mark (1:16–20) were not sufficiently motivated. (Of course, that transformation may also have taken place in the oral tradition before Luke got hold of it.) Some scholars think that Luke 5:1–11 and John 21:1–14 were originally alternative versions of the same appearance story.

It is impossible to determine where the author of the appendix came up with seven witnesses. He may have started with the three names found in the tale of the miraculous catch of fish, added two names from the Gospel of John, and then jumped to the sacred number seven.

Jesus had already commissioned the disciples in chapter 20 (vv. 20–21) and prepared them for his departure. Yet in chapter 21 they are back in Galilee and have resumed their former occupation as fishermen. That seems an incongruent sequence of events. It is possible that the story in 21:1–14 reflects an older tradition that is an alternative account of the appearance to the eleven in Galilee narrated in Matt 28:16–20. And it is just possible that the appearance to the seven on the Sea of Tiberias, or the account of the miraculous catch of fish in Luke 5:1–11, is a much modified story of the original appearance to Peter, frequently mentioned but nowhere else storied.

Unfortunately, just about everything in this appearance story creates difficult problems and leads to speculative adjustments. Reginald H. Fuller, a distinguished scholar whose work on the formation of the resurrection narratives has been very influential, has concluded that the Gospel of John adds very little to our historical knowledge of what happened at Easter, although he suggests that the stories in John may have been in touch with traditions that are quite old. We are simply unable to untangle those ancient elements from their present narrative contexts.

Conversation with Peter
Jn 21:15–23
No parallels
Source: John

JOHN 21:15–23 **[15]When they had eaten, Jesus asks Simon Peter, "Simon, John's son, do you love me more than they do?"**

"Of course, Master; you know I love you," he replies.

"Then keep feeding my lambs," Jesus tells him.

[16]<Jesus> asks him again, for the second time, "Simon, John's son, do you love me?"

"Yes, Master; you know I love you?" he replies.

"Keep shepherding my sheep."

[17]<Jesus> says to him a third time, "Simon, John's son, do you love me?"

Peter was hurt that he had asked him for the third time, "Do you love me?" and he says to him, "Master, you know everything; you know I love you."

Jesus says to him, "Keep feeding my sheep. [18]I swear to God, when you were young you used to gather your cloak about you and go where you wanted to go. But when you've grown old, you'll stretch out your arms, and someone else will get you ready and take you where you don't want to go."

([19]He said this to indicate with what kind of death <Peter> would honor God.)

And after saying this, he adds, "Keep following me."

[20]Peter turns and sees the disciple Jesus loved most following them--the one who had leaned over on Jesus' right at supper and asked, "Master, who is going to turn you in?" [21]When Peter saw this disciple <following>, he asks Jesus, "Master, what about this fellow?"

[22]Jesus replies to him, "What business is it of yours if I want him to stay around till I come? You are to keep on following me."

([23]Because of this the rumor spread among the family of believers that this disciple wouldn't die. But Jesus had not said to him, "He won't die"; he said, "What business is it of yours if I want him to stay around till I come?")

Conversation with Peter. The triple confession of Peter in this concluding story in the appendix to the Gospel of John corresponds, as is often noted, to the threefold denial of Peter during the trial of Jesus. In other words, this story represents the rehabilitation of Peter.

The extended dialogue with Peter is really an extension of the appearance story narrated in John 20:1–14. In the dialogue that follows the miraculous catch, Jesus assigns Peter the principal role as shepherd of the new community. It therefore corresponds to the story told in Matt 16:13–19 in which Jesus calls Peter the "Rock" (Peter means rock) on which he will build his church. Both of these stories may well belong to the fund of stories that arose after Easter.

Verses 18–19 foreshadow the kind of death, according to tradition, Peter is supposed to have died around 64 C.E. When he was young he went wherever he wanted to go; now his arms have been stretched (fastened to a cross) and he is taken where he doesn't want to go. This was his fate: to share the fate of Jesus. The story was written in retrospect—after Peter had already died—but put in the form of predictions about the future.

The final segment of the appendix to the Gospel of John looks back on the passing of "the disciple Jesus loved most"—whom the author of the appendix attempts to identify as the author of chapters 1–20. The rumor had been spread that some disciples would live to see the son of Adam's return (Matt 16:28). As the disciples died one by one, that prediction became more and more implausible. The one who apparently outlived them all was the beloved disciple, the patriarch of the Johannine tradition, but he, too, had now passed away. That called for a reinterpretation of the earlier rumor. As the author of the appendix has it, Jesus did not say that the beloved disciple would not die before he returned, he only said whether he lives or dies is none of your business (v. 23).

This story, too, is a piece of Christian legend made up of stray bits of tradition, respect for Peter and the beloved disciple, and compounded with hope. But it offers little by way of information about events that occurred at Easter and its aftermath.

GHEB 9:1–4 [After the resurrection of the Savior, the Gospel of Hebrews says:]

[1]**The Lord, after he had given the linen cloth to the priest's slave, went to James and appeared to him.** [2]**(Now James had sworn not to eat bread from the time that he drank from the Lord's cup until he would see him raised from among those who sleep.)**

. . .

Appearance to James, Jesus' brother
GHeb 9:1–4
No parallels
Source: Gospel of the Hebrews
Cf. Thom 12:1–2

[3]"Bring a table and some bread."

. . .

[4]He took the bread, blessed it, broke it, and gave it to James the Just and said to him, "My brother, eat your bread, for the Son of Adam has been raised from among those who sleep."

Quoted by Jerome, *On Famous Men*

Appearance to James, Jesus' brother. Reports of appearances to various people in the early Christian community had political consequences. The recipient of an appearance had received the special endorsement of the source of all authority, Jesus of Nazareth, and was therefore entitled to respect and power in the relatively small circle of leaders. Peter and Mary were both widely reported to have been the recipients of the first appearance. Paul claimed equal validity for his experience of the risen Jesus. To many in the early Christian movement especially those in the Jerusalem community, it was unthinkable that James, the brother of Jesus, would have been left out of that charmed circle. The Gospel of Thomas reflects a tradition in which James was considered preeminent among the apostles (12:1–2):

The disciples said to Jesus, "We know that you are going to leave us. Who will be our leader?"

[2]Jesus said to them, "No matter where you are, you are to go to James the Just, for whose sake heaven and earth came into being."

While the Jesus Seminar does not regard this scene as historical, it is clear that James was highly regarded as a "pillar" among leaders. Paul so represented him in his letter to the Galatians (1:18–20, 2:1–14).

James appears in the list of those to whom Jesus has appeared (1 Cor 15:7). The Gospel of the Hebrews puts body to that reference by supplying a story to support it. The Fellows were virtually unanimous that the scene as described in the Gospel of the Hebrews is a fiction. Jesus is represented as handing his own shroud to the priest's slave. This feature presupposes the story of the empty tomb and it comes very close to depicting an actual resuscitation. In addition, it indicates that Jesus' body was being guarded by representatives of the high priest. All of these features are highly imaginary.

Similarly, Secret James reports an appearance to James and the twelve (2:1–3):

Now the twelve disciples used to sit all together at the same time, remembering what the Savior had said to each one of them, whether secretly or openly, and setting it down in books. [2]I was writing what went in my book—suddenly, the Savior appeared, after he had departed from us, and while we were watching for him. [3]And so, five hundred fifty days after he rose from the dead, we said to him, "You went away and left us!"

This story is equally fictional. It is a continuation and enhancement of the tradition that the risen Jesus had appeared to James.

Fasting seems to have been central in that wing of the early Jesus movement attached to James. So James is represented as fasting until the return of the risen Jesus. When Jesus does appear, he asks for bread that he blesses and breaks, recalling once again the eucharist motif that shows up in a number of appearance stories—a recognition scene connected with hospitality and the breaking of bread.

The Fellows had difficulty assessing whether James should be included among those who claimed that Jesus had appeared to them in risen state. There was less hesitation about Paul, since he makes a claim on his own behalf in his letters. The inclusion of Peter seems less certain because Peter does not make the claim for himself. The evidence for Mary is also secondhand, except that, in the Gospel of Mary, Mary is represented as claiming an appearance to herself (7:1–2). When it comes to James, the Fellows were about evenly divided. On this statement:

- **James, the brother of Jesus, had at least one visionary experience, which he came to regard as an appearance of the risen Jesus.**

the weighted average fell on the line dividing pink from gray. Under the rules of the Seminar, an evenly divided vote falls into the lower category. However, fifty-one percent of the Fellows voted red or pink. Those numbers suggest that although the evidence is ambiguous, a slim majority of the Fellows thought that James may have made such a claim for himself.

LUKE 24:50–53 [50]**Then he led them out as far as Bethany, and lifting up his hands he blessed them.** [51]**And while he was blessing them, it so happened that he parted from them, and was carried up into the sky.** [52]**And they paid homage to him and returned to Jerusalem full of joy,** [53]**and were continually in the temple blessing God.**

Ascension
Lk 24:50–53
PsMk 16:19–20; Acts 1:1–11
Source: Luke

Ascension. Several observations are pertinent to the conclusions of the Seminar regarding reports of the ascension of Jesus, in which he is carried up into the sky and disappears. First, the earliest sequence probably regarded resurrection and ascension/exaltation as a single event: Jesus was raised and taken up into heaven at the same time. The appearances of Jesus would then have been appearances from heaven.

Second, when the appearance stories began to depict the risen Jesus as a resurrected "body," it became necessary to put an end to appearances. A bodily Jesus could not continue to roam the earth—he would have been visible to many people and would have had to die a second time. The ascension was the device by which the appearances were concluded. The ascension story, consequently, comes very late in the development of the tradition.

The third thing to note is that it is only Luke and Pseudo-Mark that narrate the ascension. It does not have deep roots in the storytelling repertoire of early Christians.

In addition to these problems, the Gospel of Luke and the book of Acts, both written by the same author, do not agree on when the ascension took place.

According to Luke 24:50–53, Jesus was taken up into heaven on Easter Sunday evening; according to Acts 1:9 that event occurred forty days later. It is impossible to reconcile the two.

How did this discrepancy arise if the same author wrote both books? Scholars have speculated that Luke-Acts was originally a single book and that, when it was broken into two parts, a conclusion was added to the gospel and a fresh introduction was prepared for Acts. That was when the discrepancy was created. Other scholars have argued that scribes copying the two documents made adjustments to the gospel that created the problem. For example, if one eliminates the reference to "carried up into the sky" and "paid him homage," the ascension is eliminated from the Gospel of Luke and the problem solved. ("Paid him homage" is appropriate only for a Lord already exalted or ascended.) Whatever the solution to this problem, it is clear that the ascension is an invention of Luke to bring the appearances to a close. In so doing, Luke of course excludes Paul from the narrow circle of apostles who had experienced a "real" resurrection appearance, even though Paul is Luke's hero in the second half of Acts.

The verdict of the Fellows was virtually unanimous in designating this story as a fiction.

Ascension
Acts 1:1–11
Lk 24:50–53; PsMk 16:19–20
Source: Luke

ACTS 1:1–11 In my first book, Dear Theophilus, I treated everything Jesus used to do and teach [2]until the time he was taken up <into the skies>. This was after he had given instructions, under the influence of the holy spirit, to the apostles he had chosen. [3]He appeared to these <apostles> and gave ample proof that he was alive following his death. He appeared to them repeatedly during a forty-day period and spoke of God's domain. [4]During these appearances, he instructed them not to leave Jerusalem, but to wait for what the Father promised, as I told you: [5]"John baptized with water, but before many days you will be baptized with holy spirit."

[6]Those who had assembled kept asking him, "Lord, are you going to reestablish the kingdom of Israel at this time?"

[7]He responded to them: "We are not to know the dates or the occasions that the Father has reserved for his own decision. [8]However, you will be empowered when the holy spirit descends upon you, and you will be witnesses for me in Jerusalem, then in the whole of Judea and Samaria, and finally to the ends of the earth."

[9]When he had finished speaking, and while they were still watching him, he was lifted up and a cloud hid him from sight. [10]As they watched him disappear into the sky, suddenly two men in gleaming white apparel appeared at their side [11]and said, "Galileans, why are you standing there gazing up into the sky? This Jesus who was just taken up from you into the sky will come again just as you have seen him go."

Ascension. There is a preliminary reference to the ascension in v. 2, but the ascension itself is not depicted until vv. 9–11. According to Acts, the ascension takes place forty days after the resurrection; according to the Gospel of Luke, it takes place on Easter evening. Luke may have been indifferent to this discrepancy, or the difference may be the result of scribal manipulation.

Luke's conceptual scheme dominates this entire passage. Luke reminds his readers that his gospel tells about what Jesus did and taught and about the command Jesus had given to the apostles whom he had chosen (vv. 1–2). To these same apostles (Paul not included, of course), he appeared for forty days, during which time he continued to instruct them about God's domain (v. 3). Forty days is a symbolic rather than a specific period, suggesting a long but indefinite time. He also ordered them to remain in Jerusalem (v. 4), which we are fairly certain they did not do. They would eventually receive the gift of the spirit (v. 5), which took place on the day of Pentecost, ten days later. The Gospel of John, on the other hand, represents Jesus bestowing the gift of the spirit on the eleven when he appears to them on Easter Sunday evening (John 20: 22–23).

The book of Acts looks back on the early days of the movement, as is indicated by vv. 6–7. Luke here has Jesus respond to questions about the delay of the kingdom's arrival: John the Baptist and his followers had expected it to arrive in the near future. In a California newspaper on 23 January 1997, a quarter-page ad on the editorial page announced eight reasons Jesus was to appear very soon and restore the kingdom. The ad did not explain why the first apostles were mistaken. Luke, however, is aware that early expectations have not been met. So Jesus explains that the times and seasons fixed by God for such epic events are unknown to human beings. The delay is to permit the disciples to spread the Jesus movement from Jerusalem, through Judea and Samaria, and then to the farthest corners of the earth. That is the geographical scheme that forms the backbone of Luke's story unfolded in Acts.

Having laid out his theological program, Luke is ready to have Jesus depart. Jesus does so in vv. 9–11. Jesus ascends into the sky, while two men in white robes (like the two at the tomb) reassure his followers that Jesus will descend again in the same manner at some unspecified date in the future.

All of this is the product of Luke's imagination. Since it is not based on historical events, black was the decisive vote of the Fellows of the Seminar.

PsMK 16:19–20 **[19]The Lord Jesus, after he said these things, was taken up into the sky and sat down at the right hand of God. [20]Those <to whom he had spoken> went out and made their announcement everywhere, and the Lord worked with them and certified what they said by means of accompanying signs.**

Ascension
PsMk 16:19–20
Lk 24:50–53, Acts 1:1–11
Source: Luke

Ascension. The ascension of Jesus—his return to the skies—is narrated in ancient Christian texts only here and in Luke, both the Gospel (24:51) and Acts (1:9), although it is implied in John 20:17: "I have not yet gone back up to my Father." Only Luke depicts the ascension as the kind of event that could have been seen by eyewitnesses. The author of Pseudo-Mark is probably dependent on Luke for his information. Since the stories in Luke and Acts were designated black, this one has been given the same color.

Birth & Infancy Stories

TABLE OF CONTENTS

The stories relating the birth and childhood of Jesus are color-coded and discussed in the order in which they appear in the Gospels of Matthew and Luke.

INTRODUCTION

The Gospels of Matthew and Luke contain three birth and infancy narratives. One is devoted to John the Baptist (Luke 1:5–25, 57–80), the other two to Jesus of Nazareth (Matt 1–2; Luke 1:26–56, 2:1–52, 3:23–38).

The infancy stories were developed rather late in the emerging gospel tradition. The birth and childhood stories recorded by Matthew and Luke were composed late in the first century or early in the second. The Gospel of Luke may originally have begun with chapter 3: There is what appears to be a second prologue in 3:1–7 to match the first prologue in 1:1–4. It is even possible that an early version of Matthew began with 3:1 in that gospel. In any case, the primary source of the two gospels, the Gospel of Mark, opens with the work of John the Baptist rather than with a birth and childhood story. The birth and childhood stories prefaced to Matthew and Luke give the appearance of secondary compositions not originally integral to the gospels they preface.

Popular Christian representations blend the two infancy narratives of Matthew and Luke into one story by selecting elements from each and forging them into an entirely new tale. In so doing, they ignore the discrepancies and contradictions. The historian is not permitted the privilege of a storyteller. Although the two stories have several things in common, the historian finds it impossible to blend the two into a single, consistent narrative.

Both gospels place the birth of Jesus in the reign of Herod the Great, who died in 4 B.C.E. The two agree that Jesus was born in Bethlehem. They also concur in identifying Nazareth as his home village. They have the name Joseph in common as Jesus' father and the name Mary as Jesus' mother. They assume that Jesus was the real name of this remarkable person. The two evangelists believe that Jesus was to be the savior of the people.

In both gospels Mary and Joseph are engaged but not married. Mary is described as a virgin at the time she conceives. They insist that Joseph was not involved in the conception of Jesus. They attribute the pregnancy of Mary to the agency of the holy spirit and they agree that Jesus was born after Mary and Joseph began to live together.

In spite of these remarkable agreements, the two infancy narratives are developed along quite divergent lines. All of the first chapter of Luke and most of the second have no parallels in Matthew. Matthew does not relate the conception and birth of John the Baptist. He knows nothing of the annunciation to Mary, of Mary's visit to Elizabeth, of Elizabeth's greeting. He does not record Mary's hymn of praise, the Magnificat.

Matthew does not mention the journey to Bethlehem to enroll in the census. There is no mention of the swaddling cloth, the feeding trough, and the vision of angels by the shepherds. Matthew does not report the circumcision of Jesus or his presentation in the temple in Jerusalem. Matthew's story does not permit the family to return to Nazareth from Bethlehem.

Luke, on the other hand, is unaware of the visit of the astrologers who play such a significant role in Matthew's version. Luke does not know of the flight to Egypt to escape the wrath of Herod the Great in the slaughter of the babies.

Indeed, the whole of the second chapter of Matthew is unique to Matthew. The table of contents indicates how little overlap there is between the two accounts (see p. 497).

The two accounts report that Jesus was born in Bethlehem. That common feature was undoubtedly inspired by the prophet Micah, who predicted that the messiah would be born there. Both Matthew and Luke are aware of that prophetic text. Both gospels claim that Jesus was a descendant of David because the prophets had said that the messiah would have David as an ancestor.

Annunciations by angels and predictions of greatness were well-established features of other miraculous birth stories. The births of famous persons were often accompanied by portents and signs; Matthew and Luke were cognizant of that tradition. The genealogies of Matthew and Luke also owe their origin to the practice of tracing the ancestors of heroes and heroines to other famous persons and even the gods.

There is very little in the two infancy narratives that reflects historical reminiscence. Four possible facts emerge from the welter of data found in the two stories. Scholars are inclined to the view that Jesus was born during the era of Herod the Great, though that is by no means certain. Jesus' home was almost certainly Nazareth: there seems to be no good reason for that to have been invented. Jesus' mother's name was Mary and we have no reason to doubt that the prophet from Nazareth was named Jesus. These constitute the meager traces of history found in the birth stories. Everything else is fiction.

The Fellows of the Jesus Seminar were certain that Mary did not conceive Jesus without the benefit of human male sperm. But they were uncertain whether Joseph or some unnamed male was the biological father of Jesus. It is possible that Jesus was illegitimate.

The birth stories of Isaac, Samson, and Samuel provided the evangelists with models for their own versions of the birth of Jesus. In Genesis 21:1, for example, Yahweh visited Sarah the wife of Abraham, but that does not imply that God had sex with Sarah—only that Sarah was made fertile by divine agency when she was well past the age of childbearing. Abraham was the biological father of Isaac. Similarly, God blessed Mary, according to the evangelists, but some male contributed the sperm. The hellenistic option of giving heroes one divine and one human parent is not suggested by the gospel accounts: Mary was not impregnated by some god masquerading as a human lover.

In addition to the two infancy narratives in the New Testament gospels, there are two independent infancy gospels. The Infancy Gospel of James depicts the birth and childhood of Mary, the mother of Jesus. The Infancy Gospel of Thomas (not to be confused with the Gospel of Thomas) relates fantastic stories about Jesus' precocious childhood. The two infancy gospels, composed in the second century C.E., are entirely imaginative constructs. Since they contain no reliable historical information, they have been omitted from *The Acts of Jesus.* Modern translations may be found, however, in *The Complete Gospels.*

Family tree
Mt 1:1–17
Source: Matthew
Cf. Lk 3:23–38

MATT 1:1–17 This is the family tree of Jesus the Anointed, who was a descendant of David and Abraham.

[2]Abraham was the father of Isaac, Isaac of Jacob, Jacob of Judah and his brothers, [3]and Judah and Tamar were the parents of Perez and Zerah. Perez was the father of Hezron, Hezron of Ram, [4]Ram of Amminadab, Amminadab of Nahshon, Nahshon of Salmon, [5]and Salmon and Rahab were the parents of Boaz. Boaz and Ruth were the parents of Obed. Obed was the father of Jesse, [6]and Jesse of David the king.

David and Uriah's wife were the parents of Solomon. [7]Solomon was the father of Rehoboam, Rehoboam of Abijah, Abijah of Asaph, [8]Asaph of Jehoshaphat, Jehoshaphat of Joram, Joram of Uzziah, [9]Uzziah of Jotham, Jotham of Ahaz, Ahaz of Hezekiah, [10]Hezekiah of Manasseh, Manasseh of Amos, Amos of Josiah, [11]and Josiah was the father of Jechoniah and his brothers at the time of the exile to Babylon.

[12]After the Babylonian exile, Jechoniah was the father of Salathiel, Salathiel of Zerubbabel, [13]Zerubbabel of Abiud, Abiud of Eliakim, Eliakim of Azor, [14]Azor of Zadok, Zadok of Achim, Achim of Eliud, [15]Eliud of Eleazar, Eleazar of Matthan, Matthan of Jacob. [16]And Jacob was the father of Joseph, the husband of Mary, who was the mother of Jesus. Jesus is known as the Anointed.

[17]In sum, the generations from Abraham to David come to fourteen, those from David to the Babylonian exile number fourteen, and those from the Babylonian exile to the Anointed amount to fourteen also.

Family tree. Mark, the earliest narrative gospel, does not provide Jesus with a family tree. Both Matthew and Luke do in connection with their birth and childhood stories. In Matthew the genealogy opens the gospel; Luke postpones his version until after the baptism of Jesus (3:23–38). The two genealogies differ greatly from one another in form and content. By an overwhelming majority, the Fellows affirmed that these tables of Jesus' lineage are legitimating fictions.

The tables of ancestors were constructed, in the view of the Fellows, for theological reasons and are not, strictly speaking, lists of biological ancestry. Matthew traces Jesus' lineage from Abraham by way of King David, thereby establishing Jesus as a descendant of David and therefore "the Anointed" or messiah. By contrast, Luke claims that Jesus as God's "son" (Luke 3:22) was descended from Adam, who was also God's "son" (Luke 3:38), and thus like Adam represents all humankind, gentile as well as Jew.

As legitimating fictions, the gospel genealogies have much in common with the genealogies strategically placed throughout the Old Testament. But this does not mean that such genealogies reflect family or official records; instead, they echo folklore and popular conceptions of the ancestry of famous persons.

The Fellows do not doubt that Jesus was a descendant of Abraham since he was a Jew. They think it remotely possible that Jesus was a descendant of David. Both Matthew and Luke trace Jesus' lineage back to David, and Mark reports that Jesus was addressed as "Son of David" (Mark 10:46–52). Paul, too, cites an early tradition that Jesus was descended from David "according to the flesh" (Rom 1:3–4). But this tradition may reflect nothing more than popular piety.

The Fellows endorsed the view that "Joseph" was the name of Mary's husband and Jesus' supposed father. They also agreed that Mary was the name of his mother, although references to her name outside the birth and childhood stories are rare (only Mark 6:3 and Acts 1:14). In the Gospel of Mark, Joseph is never mentioned and Jesus is referred to as "Mary's son," which casts some doubt on whether Joseph was Jesus' father, since the convention was to refer to a son by his father's name. Jesus' brothers and sisters were apparently well known in early Christian circles.

The lack of certainty about the father of Joseph stems from a contradiction in the two genealogies: in Matthew the father of Joseph is listed as Jacob, whereas Luke names him Eli.

As legitimating fictions the genealogies are colored black except at specific points where there seemed no good reason to doubt actual family links.

Birth of Jesus
Mt 1:18-25
Source: Matthew
Cf. Lk 2:1-7

MATT 1:18–25 [18]The birth of Jesus the Anointed took place as follows: While his mother Mary was engaged to Joseph, but before they slept together, she was found to be pregnant **by the holy spirit.** **[19]Since Joseph her husband was a decent man and did not wish to expose her publicly, he planned to break off their engagement quietly.**

[20]While he was thinking about these things, a messenger of the Lord surprised him in a dream with these words: "Joseph, descendant of David, don't hesitate to take Mary as your wife, since the holy spirit is responsible for her pregnancy. [21]She will give birth to a son and you will name him Jesus—the name means 'he will save his people from their sins.'" [22]All of this has happened so the prediction of the Lord given by the prophet would come true:

> [23]Behold, a virgin will conceive a child
> and she will give birth to a son,
> and they will name him Emmanuel

(which means "God with us").

[24]Joseph got up and did what the messenger of the Lord told him: he took <Mary as> his wife. **[25]He did not have sex with her until she had given birth to a son.** Joseph named him Jesus.

Birth of Jesus. Ancient literature abounds with infancy narratives about famous men. These narratives characteristically underscore, in various ways, how the divine, or the gods, participated in the generation and protection of

BIRTH OF ALEXANDER THE GREAT

Alexander was a descendant of Hercules on his father's side [Philip], through Caranus; on his mother's side [Olympias] he was a descendant of Aeacus through Neoptolemus. Everyone believes this to be the case. It is said that Philip was initiated into the mysteries at Samothrace with Olympias.

At that time he was still a lad and she was an orphan. He fell in love with her and made her his wife, with the consent of her brother Arymbas.

Now prior to the night they were to be united as husband and wife in the bridal suite, the bride had a dream. There was a peal of thunder and a bolt of lightning struck her womb. The strike produced a great deal of fire, which broke into flames that danced about until they died out. Somewhat later, after they were married, Philip too dreamed that he sealed his wife's uterus; he imagined that the seal bore the image of a lion. Some seers became suspicious as a result of this dream and thought Philip should keep a closer eye on his wife; another seer, Aristander of Telmessus said that Olympias was pregnant, since no one puts a seal on something that is empty, and that the son to be born would be high-spirited and lion-like.

On another occasion, a serpent was observed stretched out at Olympias' side while she slept. And this, they say, cooled Philip's ardor for his wife so that he no longer slept with her as frequently, either because he feared she might cast a spell or work some magic on him, or because he thought she had mated with a higher being, which also made him shrink from his obligations as a husband.

There is another tale about these events: It is said that all the women of the region had practiced Orphic rites and Dionysian orgies from ancient times (known as Klodones and Mimallones), imitating in many respects the practices of the Edonian women and the Thracian women around Mount Haemus. It appears the word *threskeuein* (to act as a Thracian woman) was attached to the unrestrained and superstitious rites. Olympias practiced these rites with greater zeal than other women, and performed the frenzies in a more barbaric fashion. She

these heroes. Portents, often astral in character, frequently accompanied such births. For parallel accounts of miraculous births, consult the boxes on Alexander the Great, Plato, and Apollonius of Tyana (pp. 505 and 507).

The earliest sources—Paul, Mark, and the Sayings Gospel Q—betray no interest in the birth and childhood of Jesus. However, both Matthew and Luke preface their adaptations of Mark with infancy narratives. With some notable exceptions, these narratives are so dissimilar that they must have been composed independently of one another. Yet they do converge on several points:

1. The parents of Jesus, Mary and Joseph, are engaged but have not begun to live together.
2. Mary's conception of Jesus is not through intercourse with Joseph.
3. The birth of the child takes place after the parents begin to live together.
4. The birth takes place at Bethlehem.
5. The birth takes place during the reign of Herod the Great.

used to provide the revelers with a huge tame snake, who would crawl out of the ivy <around the wands they carried> and the mystical winnowing baskets <they carried on their heads>, or would coil themselves around the wands or garlands of the women, and this would fill the men with terror.

After his vision, Philip sent Chairon of Megalopolis to Delphi <to learn the meaning of his vision>. Chairon returned with an oracle from Apollo, who instructed him to sacrifice to Zeus-Ammon and to hold that god in special reverence. He also told him he was to lose one of his eyes—the eye he used to spy on the god through a crack in the door, the god who had slept with his wife in the form of a serpent.

Eratosthenes tells us that Olympias, when she sent Alexander to war, confided in him the secret of his birth and enjoined him to consider <among his goals> only those worthy of his birth. But others claim that she shrugged the whole thing off and said, "Alexander should stop spreading rumors about me to Hera."

Alexander was born early in the month of Hecatombaeon, the Macedonian name of which is Loüs, on the sixth of the month, the same day the temple of Ephesian Artemis burned to the ground. [356 B.C.E.] . . . Hegesias the Magnesian said of this coincidence, "It is no wonder the temple of Artemis burned down—the goddess was too busy bringing Alexander into the world." But all the astrologers, who happened to be gathered in Ephesus, regarded the temple disaster to be a portent of further calamities, and went about flailing themselves and shouting that ruin and great misfortune had that day been inaugurated. In contrast, Philip, who had just conquered Potidea, received three messages simultaneously: the first was that Parmenio had been victorious over the Illyrians in a great battle; the second that his horse had won a victory at the Olympic games; and the third that Alexander had been born. He was delighted with the news and the astrologers gave him more to cheer about by declaring that the son whose birth coincided with three victories would be unconquerable.

Plutarch, *Parallel Lives: Alexander,* 2.1–3.5

These Matthean parallels with Luke are all to be found in Matt 1:18–2:1. The core of the nativity narratives must therefore be based on common lore that circulated widely before Matthew and Luke composed their narratives. The balance of the account of Matthew differs so markedly from the story related by Luke that it is not conceivable that the two had a common source or fund of information.

The infancy story in Matthew is constructed around three dream visions of Joseph and related prophecies, together with two subscenes involving the Zoroastrian astrologers (magi) and related prophecies. In other words, it was important to Matthew to have events correlated with both immediate divine communication and with ancient prophetic texts. The five panels of Matthew's story are:

1. Matt 1:18–25 Joseph's dream to accept Mary (Isa 7:14)
2. Matt 2:1–12 Star in the East, Astrologers (Mic 5:1)
3. Matt 2:13–15 Joseph's dream to flee to Egypt (Hos 11:1)

4. Matt 2:16–18 Astrologers, murder of innocents (Jer 31:15)
5. Matt 2:19–23 Joseph's dream to return to Nazareth (unknown prophecy)

Numerous scholars have noticed that the second chapter of Matthew begins as though this were the beginning of the gospel and nothing preceded: "Jesus was born at Bethlehem, Judea, when Herod was king." Chapter 2 may thus be understood as a second account of the birth paralleling the briefer version, with genealogy, of chapter 1.

Matthew's scenes have obviously been formulated in the light of similar stories in the Old Testament. The events narrated are said to have been in fulfillment of specific texts. The stories themselves—Joseph's discovery of Mary's pregnancy through the medium of a dream, the visitation of the magi, the flight to Egypt, and the massacre of the children—recall stories involving Israel's heroes, principally Joseph, who rose to fame as a vizier of the Pharaoh and interpreter of dreams, and Moses, the renowned lawgiver and emancipator of his people from Egyptian bondage. Tales of Isaac, Samuel, Samson, and even Balaam also play a role. The birth and infancy stories demonstrate the storyteller's art in applying ancient lore and motifs to Jesus. For that reason they are imaginative constructs rather than reports of historical events. They depict how the "son of God" came to be incorporated into the Davidic line and how the events surrounding the infancy of Jesus recapitulated epic events in the history of Israel.

The Seminar doubted, without denying, the possibilities that Jesus was conceived while Mary and Joseph were betrothed and that she was a virgin at the time she conceived. The account in Matthew seems to reflect the marriage customs of first-century Palestine where marriage took place in two stages: first, the engagement, or betrothal, during which time sexual intercourse and conception might occur; and secondly, the marriage proper, which involved the transfer of the bride to her husband's home.

With regard to the manner of Jesus' conception, the Fellows were unequivocal. With a virtually unanimous vote, the Fellows declared that the statement "Jesus was conceived of the holy spirit" is a theological and not a biological statement. They accordingly rejected the notion that Mary conceived Jesus without sexual intercourse with a man. That Jesus was generated by God without human male involvement goes beyond what historical, or scientific, reason allows. Jesus certainly made no such claim about his origin; and there exists no first-person testimony by Mary his mother. Furthermore, not even the theological confession of Jesus as "son of God" requires a virginal conception: Paul, Mark, and John affirm Jesus' divine status without recourse to a miraculous conception. The confession of Jesus as "God's son," in association with Old Testament stories of God's control of the womb, may have been influential in the development of the belief that Jesus was miraculously conceived, in tandem with similar pagan stories in which one divine parent unites with a human counterpart. The New Testament birth stories appear to walk a fine line between the crass pagan versions, such as Plato's conception by Apollo, and the Hebrew accounts in which an infertile womb is somehow made fertile

BIRTH OF APOLLONIUS OF TYANA

Apollonius' hometown was Tyana, a Greek city located in the territory of the Cappodocians.

Apollonius' father had the same name; he came from an old family descended from the original settlers. His family was wealthier than others, although the region was well off generally. As she was about to give birth, his mother had a vision—a vision of Proteus, an Egyptian deity, who changes his form as Homer tells it. She was not in the least afraid, so she asked him, "What am I about to give birth to?"

He replied, "to me."

"And who are you," she asked.

"Proteus," he said, "the god of Egypt."

I need not explain to those who have listened to the poets how wise Proteus is, how kaleidoscopic, now appearing as this, now that, how allusive, apparently having both knowledge and foreknowledge about everything. It is necessary to keep Proteus in mind as the story unfolds, since it will show Apollonius to possess even greater foreknowledge than Proteus. Apollonius proves to be superior to a multitude of difficulties and impossible situations, especially when he is under duress.

It is rumored that he was born in a meadow, close to which now stands a temple erected for him. We should also not fail to mention how he was born. Just as the time approached for his mother to give birth, she was told in a dream to go to this meadow and gather flowers. She had no sooner arrived than she fell asleep on the grass, while her maids spread out over the meadow to gather flowers. There were some swans there for whom the meadow provided sustenance. These swans danced around her as she slept and, as they often do, flapped their wings and honked all at the same time, for there was a light breeze on the meadow at the time. At this sound she jumped up and gave birth since any sudden shock can cause a premature delivery. Those who lived thereabouts claim that a bolt of lightning appeared to strike the earth but then was carried aloft where it vanished. In my judgment, the gods used this sign to reveal and predict that Apollonius would transcend all earthly standards and rival the gods.

Near Tyana there is a spring, sacred to Zeus the god of oaths, that they call *Asbanaion* (the name means unquenchable). The water comes up cold but bubbles like a hot kettle. This water is forgiving and sweet to those who honor their oaths, but it is swift justice for perjurers—it attacks eyes and hands and feet, the body swells and decays, so perjurers are not able to leave but are kept next to the spring moaning and confessing their false oaths. The inhabitants of that region say that Apollonius is a son of Zeus; the sage himself says that he is the son of Apollonius.

Philostratus, *Life of Apollonius*, 1.4–6

by divine decree, such as Sarah's conception of Isaac. In any case, the Fellows of the Jesus Seminar consider Jesus to have had a human father.

The Fellows of the Seminar were divided on who that father was. Roughly half of the Fellows think it probable that Mary conceived by the agency of Joseph, in spite of the explicit denial in the stories themselves. The logic of the genealogies supports the paternity of Joseph. The other half held the view that Mary conceived by some unnamed man through rape or seduction. The latter possibility is suggested by some evidence that the birth stories were designed to cover up some scandal regarding Jesus' paternity. The stories themselves insist that Joseph was not the biological father of Jesus and there is the strange inclusion, in the genealogy of Matthew, of the four disreputable women: Tamar, who conceived twins of her father-in-law after seducing him (Gen 38); Ruth, the Moabite woman who claimed Boaz as her husband under dubious circumstances (Ruth 4); Rahab, the Jericho prostitute who aided the Israelite spies when prospecting for the invasion across the Jordan (Josh 2); and Bathsheba, who was raped by King David (2 Sam 11). There is also the old Greco-Roman and Jewish tradition that Jesus was the son of a Roman soldier named Pantera.

Astrologers from the East
Mt 2:1–12
No parallels
Source: Matthew

MATT 2:1–12 Jesus was born at Bethlehem, Judea, when Herod
was king. Astrologers from the East showed up in Jerusalem just
then. 2"Tell us," they said, "where the newborn king of the Judeans
is. We have observed his star in the east and have come to pay him
homage."

3When this news reached King Herod, he was visibly shaken, and
all Jerusalem along with him. 4He called together all the ranking
priests and local experts, and pressed them for information: "Where
is the Anointed supposed to be born?"

5They replied, "At Bethlehem, Judea. This is how it is put by the
prophet:

> 6And you, Bethlehem, in the province of Judah,
> you are by no means least among the leaders of Judah.
> Out of you will come a leader
> who will shepherd my people, Israel."

7Then Herod called the astrologers together secretly and ascer-
tained from them the precise time the star became visible. 8Then he
sent them to Bethlehem with these instructions: "Go make a careful
search for the child. When you find him, report back to me, so I can
also go and pay him homage."

9They listened to what the king had to say and continued on their
way.

And there guiding them on was the star that they had observed in
the East: it led them on until it came to a standstill above where the
child lay. 10Once they saw the star, they were beside themselves with
joy. 11And they arrived at the house and saw the child with his

BIRTH OF PLATO

Plato was the son of Ariston and Perictone (or Potone) and a citizen of Athens. His mother traced her lineage back to Solon. Solon had a brother, Dropides, who was the father of Critias, Critias of Callaeschrus, Callaeschrus of Critias, one of the Thirty, and of Glaucon, who was the father of Charmides and Perictone. Plato was the son of Perictone and Ariston, six generations removed from Solon. Solon, for his part, traced his lineage back to Neleus and Poseidon. They say his father too is a descendant of Codros, son of Melanthus, both of whom were descendants of Poseidon, according to the account of Thrasylus.

In his work entitled *Plato's Wake,* Speusippus, together with Clarchus in an encomium on Plato, and Anaxilaides in the second volume of his work *On Philosophers,* all report a story circulating in Athens to this effect: Ariston made passionate love to beautiful Perictone but did not succeed <in making her pregnant>. When he stopped assaulting her, Apollo appeared to him in a dream. From then on he left her unmolested until she gave birth.

In his chronology, Apollodorus says that Plato was born in the 88th Olympiad, on the seventh day of Thargelion, which is the day the Delians say Apollo himself was born. He died according to Hermippus at a wedding party, in the first year of the 108th Olympiad, when he was eighty-one. Neanthes says, however, that he died when he was eighty-four. He was thus six years younger than Isocrates. . . . Some say that he was born in Aegina, in the home of Phidiades, son of Thales, as Favorinus states in his *Miscellaneous History.*

If Phoebus <Apollo> did not sire Plato in Greece,
How did he heal the souls of mortals with speech?
Asclepius, you will recall, also the son of the
    god, heals the body,
While Plato makes the soul immortal.

Phoebus <Apollo> conceived Asclepius and Plato
    for the benefit of humankind,
the one to save their bodies,
the other to save their souls.
From a wedding banquet Plato was translated to
    the city he had founded for himself
    and established in the celestial realm of Zeus.

Diogenes Laertius, *Lives of Eminent Philosophers,* 3.1–3, 45

mother Mary. They fell down and paid him homage. Then they opened their treasure chests and presented him with gifts—gold, pure incense, and myrrh. [12]And because they had been advised in a dream not to return to Herod, they journeyed back to their own country by a different route.

Astrologers from the East. The Seminar rejected the claim in Matthew and Luke that Bethlehem, in Judea, was the place of Jesus' birth. The two gospels offer very different explanations about how Jesus came to be born there. The gospel traditions generally point to Galilee as Jesus' home turf and Nazareth as his home village. The Fellows think that the church's claim that Jesus was of Davidic descent led to the story of his birth in Bethlehem, the town associated with David and the Davidic messiah.

The Seminar affirmed the likelihood that Jesus was born during the reign of Herod the Great (37-4 B.C.E.). There appears to be no reason for this particular claim to have been invented by the Christian community. If Jesus were born while Herod ruled, it would have been during his final years, no later than 4 B.C.E.

The three visitors lured by some astrological sign were probably imagined to be Zoroastrian priests from Persia. In the *Travels of Marco Polo,* a thirteenth-century work probably dictated by Marco Polo while he was in prison in Genoa, the three are kings whose tombs Marco visited in Saveh, Persia. He was told by locals that the three kings brought gifts of gold, frankincense, and myrrh in order to learn whether the new child was a king, a god, or a healer. If he accepted the gold, he was an earthly king; if he accepted the frankincense, he was a god; and if he accepted the myrrh, he was destined to be a healer. The baby Jesus accepted all three according to the legend Marco Polo learned on his travels. In return, the story continued, Jesus gave the three kings a small closed chest. They later opened the box and found that it contained a stone. Jesus had evidently made them the present of a stone to indicate that they would be firm and constant in their new faith. Since the kings did not know this, they threw the stone into a well. As soon as the stone fell into the well, a burning fire descended from heaven and filled the well. The kings took some of the fire and carried it to their own country where they worshiped it as a god. This is how they came to be fire-worshipers, explains Marco Polo. This tale is a good example of how myths once launched take on a life of their own and develop strands suitable for the new contexts in which they are alive.

The star in the East has been interpreted as a supernova or new star, as a comet, and as a conjunction of planets. Johannes Kepler (1571–1630), the German astronomer, calculated that the conjunction of Jupiter and Saturn in the constellation Pisces took place in 7–6 B.C.E., and his calculation has attracted wide support. But, of course, that the star led them to Bethlehem and then became stationary over where the child lay is pure fantasy.

The astrologers, like Joseph, are given divine instructions in a dream: they are told not to return to Jerusalem and Herod but to return to their country by another route.

Except for the notice that Jesus was born during the reign of Herod, all this material rates a black designation. It is long on pagan pageantry but short on history. (See the cameo on the comet on p. 128.)

Flight to Egypt
Mt 2:13–15
No parallels
Source: Matthew

MATT 2:13–15 [13]**After <the astrologers> had departed, a messenger of the Lord appeared in a dream to Joseph, saying, "Get ready, take the child and his mother and flee to Egypt. Stay there until I**

**give you instructions. You see, Herod is determined to hunt the
child down and destroy him."**
**14So Joseph got ready and took the child and his mother under
cover of night and set out for Egypt. 15There they remained until
Herod's death. This happened so the Lord's prediction spoken by
the prophet would come true:**

Out of Egypt I have called my son.

Flight to Egypt. In a second dream, Joseph is advised to take the child and flee to Egypt in anticipation of the slaughter of the male babies by Herod. This movement is designed, of course, to fulfill the prophecy of Hosea in v. 15. Israel was called out of Egypt both literally and metaphorically: literally, in the Exodus under the leadership of Moses; metaphorically, the Exodus meant to forsake the worship of idols. Jesus is made to recapitulate the history of Israel, so to speak.

Murder of the babies
Mt 2:16–18
No parallels
Source: Matthew

**MATT 2:16–18 16When Herod realized he had been duped by the
astrologers, he was outraged. He then issued instructions to kill all
the children two years old and younger in Bethlehem and the sur-
rounding region. This corresponded to the time <of the star> that he
had learned from the astrologers. 17With this event the prediction
made by Jeremiah the prophet came true:**

18In Ramah the sound of mourning
and bitter grieving was heard:
Rachel weeping for her children.
She refused to be consoled:
They were no more.

Murder of the babies. The murder of the babies and the flight to Egypt represent the persecution of a potential royal rival by a reigning king. This is a constant feature in hellenistic biographies of heroes and in tales of royal succession the world over: a king attempts to kill or exile successors to protect his own position. Matthew's story is borrowed specifically from the account of Moses' birth in Exodus (1:1–2:10): the Pharaoh orders the midwives to destroy all male children born to Hebrew women because the Hebrews are multiplying and thriving; when the midwives fail to heed the Pharaoh's order, he commands that all male babies be thrown into the Nile and drowned. Once again, Matthew's story is designed to go with a prophetic text, in this case one from Jeremiah.

Although Herod the Great was capable of slaughtering babies wholesale (he had three of his own sons put to death and he wanted his soldiers to execute notable political prisoners at the time of his death to make sure that everyone mourned his passing), the incident Matthew relates is undoubtedly a fiction.

Migration to Nazareth
Mt 2:19-23
No parallels
Source: Matthew

MATT 2:19–23 [19]**After Herod's death, a messenger of the Lord appeared in a dream to Joseph in Egypt:** [20]**"Get ready, take the child and his mother, and return to the land of Israel; those who were seeking the child's life are dead."**

[21]**So he got ready, took the child and his mother, and returned to the land of Israel.** [22]**He heard that Archelaus was the king of Judea in the place of his father Herod; as a consequence, he was afraid to go there. He was instructed in a dream to go to Galilee;** [23]**so he went there and settled in a town called Nazareth. So the prophecy uttered by the prophets came true: "He will be called a Nazorean."**

Migration to Nazareth. In the third of his dream visions, Joseph is told to take the child and his mother and go to Galilee (not Judea). He settles with them in a village called Nazareth. According to Luke and other New Testament sources, Nazareth was actually the home of Joseph and Mary and in all probability Jesus was born there. But Matthew is interested in playing out the scenario that he knew from the story of the Exodus: the Israelites went down into Egypt to escape the famine and did so under the protection of Joseph; after the death of Joseph, Moses led the Israelites out of Egyptian captivity and eventually brought them to Palestine. The holy family is made to recapitulate that epic journey.

The prophecy mentioned in v. 23 is not derived from any known source. Matthew seems to have invented it, or he may be reflecting an oral tradition. The derivation of "Nazorean" is not certain: Matthew evidently understands it to refer to Nazareth, the name of the village, although phonetically the transition from Nazorean to Nazareth is difficult. Some suggest that it may also refer to *nazirite,* the name for someone dedicated to God. Samuel (1 Sam 1:9–11) and Samson (Judg 13:2–7) were *nazirites* from birth. Nazirites did not cut their hair and avoided strong drink. John the Baptist also manifests some traits of a nazirite. Finally, it has been speculated that "Nazorean" is derived from a Hebrew word (*netzer*) meaning "branch":

> There will come forth a shoot from the root of Jesse,
> and from his roots a *branch.* Isa 11:1

In Isaiah the term refers to royal succession and was eventually applied to the messiah, the Anointed One. Matthew clearly had the reference to Nazareth in mind, but he may also have been aware of other nuances.

Family tree of John the Baptist
Lk 1:5–6
No parallels
Source: Luke

LUKE 1:5–6 [5]In the days of Herod, king of Judea, **there happened to be this priest** named Zechariah, **who belonged to the priestly clan of Abijah. His wife, a descendant of Aaron, was** named Elizabeth. [6]**They were both scrupulous in the sight of God, obediently following all the commandments and ordinances of the Lord.**

Family tree of John the Baptist. John the Baptist, like Jesus, requires a genealogy indicating that he comes from illustrious ancestors. Because his status is reduced in comparison to that of Jesus, his lineage is only briefly reported. We are told that his father, Zechariah, comes from one of the four priestly families. These comprised some eighteen thousand priests and levites, according to Joachim Jeremias, who has compiled exhaustive information on Jerusalem in the time of Jesus. Names were often derived from ancient stories based on typological association: John's father was a priest, so his name must have been Zechariah, a priestly name mentioned frequently in Chronicles. However, there is no evidence outside the infancy stories that John's father was a priest. Both vocation and name may be fictions. Elizabeth, the name assigned to John's mother, was the name of Aaron's wife (Exod 6:23): Aaron was the brother of Moses and the first high priest in ancient Israel. That provides John with some illustrious ancestors. Supplying John with Aaronic ancestors and noting the piety of his parents was a way of giving John credibility as the forerunner of Jesus. In other words, we cannot be sure on such slender evidence that the names of John's parents were really Zechariah and Elizabeth. A gray color is appropriate.

There is no hard evidence for dating John's birth. However, because both Matthew and Luke locate the infancy narratives during the reign of Herod the Great (37–4 B.C.E.), and because John the Baptist and Jesus were contemporaries, there is some reason to accept that date. Again, gray is the appropriate designation.

Miraculous conception of John
Lk 1:7–25
No parallels
Source: Luke

LUKE 1:7–25 **[7]But they had no children, because Elizabeth was**
infertile, and both were well along in years. [8]While he was serving
as priest before God when his priestly clan was on temple duty, [9]it
so happened that he was chosen by lot, according to the custom of
the priesthood, to enter the sanctuary of the Lord and burn incense.
[10]At the hour of incense, while a huge crowd was praying outside,
[11]there appeared to him a messenger of the Lord standing to the right
of the altar of incense. [12]When he saw him, Zechariah was shaken
and overcome by fear. [13]But the heavenly messenger said to him,
"Don't be afraid, Zechariah, for your prayer has been heard, and
your wife Elizabeth will bear you a son, and you are to name him
John. [14]And you will be joyful and elated, and many will rejoice at
his birth, [15]because he will be great in the sight of the Lord; he will
drink no wine or beer, and he will be filled with holy spirit from the
very day of his birth. [16]And he will cause many of the children of
Israel to turn to the Lord their God. **[17]He will precede him in the**
spirit and power of Elijah: he will turn the hearts of the parents back
towards their children, and the disobedient back towards the ways
of righteousness, and will make people ready for their Lord."
[18]But Zechariah said to the heavenly messenger, "How can I be
sure of this? For I am an old man and my wife is well along in
years."
[19]And the messenger answered him, "I am Gabriel, the one who
stands in the presence of God. I was sent to speak to you, and to

bring you this good news. 20 Listen to me: you will be struck silent
and speechless until the day these things happen, because you did
not trust my words, which will come true at the appropriate time."
21 Meanwhile, the people were waiting for Zechariah, wondering
why he was taking so long in the sanctuary. 22 And when he did come
out and was unable to speak to them, they realized that he had seen
a vision inside. And he kept making signs to them, since he could
not speak. 23 And it so happened, when his time of official service
was completed, that he went back home.

24 Afterwards, his wife Elizabeth conceived, and went into seclu-
sion for five months, telling herself: 25 "This is how the Lord has seen
fit to deal with me in his good time in taking away the public dis-
grace <of my infertility>."

Miraculous conception of John. Heroes in hellenistic birth stories were regularly given a miraculous conception. This could be provided in one of two ways: either the parents were past the child-bearing age so God had to intervene and make an infertile womb fertile (a characteristic of Hebrew birth stories; it is always the woman who is infertile), or one of the parents was a god (in Greek birth stories: the divine parent was usually male, so the male gets the credit). Luke's suggestion that Zechariah and Elizabeth were quite elderly and had had no children because Elizabeth was infertile (vv. 7, 18, 25) reflects the Hebrew variety of the miraculous birth story. Luke is here drawing on such stories as Sarah's conception of Isaac after she had entered menopause (Gen 18:9–15), or the account of infertile Hannah who eventually gave birth to Samuel (1 Sam 1:1–28), or the tale of Manoah's wife who, after a visit by an angel, gave birth to Samson (Judg 13:1–25). Luke composes the story of John's conception to match that of other ancient heroes.

In the ancient world dream visions were widely thought to be the means of divine communication. Jacob has a vision of a ladder reaching up to heaven which prompts him to erect an altar at the place, which he names Bethel (Gen 28:10–22); Joseph dreams of his ascendancy over his brothers (Gen 37:5–11); later he interprets Pharaoh's dreams as predictions of seven years of plenty and seven of famine, and proposes a plan that endears him to the Pharaoh (Gen 41:1–57). Dreams fell into disrepute among the prophets (Jer 23:28; cf. Deut 13:1–5, where a strict warning is issued against "diviners by dreams"), but the medium was revived in the apocalyptic literature, which began with Zechariah and Joel (2:28):

> I will pour out my spirit on everyone:
> Your sons and daughters will prophesy,
> your old men will dream dreams,
> and your young men will see visions.

Daniel and the book of Revelation in the New Testament are filled with dream visions.

Matthew and Luke have adapted the dream vision to serve their purposes in the infancy narratives. In Matthew's version, the commands to Joseph and the astrologers are communicated through dreams (Matt 1:20, 2:12, 13, 19, 22). Luke makes use of the same device, except that his divine messages are delivered through heavenly messengers (angels). The archangel Gabriel is the messenger that appears to Zechariah in the temple (Luke 1:10–20); it is also Gabriel who appears to Mary and informs her of her impending conception of Jesus (Luke 1:26–38). A heavenly messenger, unnamed, also appears to the shepherds in the fields at night to announce the birth of the savior. That messenger is joined by a whole troop of angels praising God (Luke 2:8–15). As if that weren't enough, the advent of the savior is confirmed by Simeon, who has been advised by the holy spirit (Luke 2:25–35), and by Anna, a prophetess who had spent her life in the temple area (Luke 2:36–38). Luke has almost overdone his narrative by having everything predicted or confirmed by some form of divine communication.

Luke has designed the annunciation to Zechariah to indicate that John will become a prophet like Elijah. Luke has included in Gabriel's speech the attributes of the adult John, which Luke knew from sources he had used in the composition of the body of his gospel. Gabriel predicts that John will lead an austere lifestyle (v. 15; cf. Luke 7:33), will be a charismatic prophet (v. 15), and will call on listeners to repent (v. 16). These traits of John are confirmed elsewhere in the gospel tradition, so the Fellows voted their expression here red, even though the annunciation to Zechariah is Luke's composition (in this case, the accuracy of the statement is not compromised by the context in which it is given).

John is identified with Elijah as the forerunner of the messiah in v. 17. Luke was inspired by statements in Mal 4:4–5 and Sir 48:10 to characterize John as the latter-day Elijah. Like other parts of Luke's elaborate composition, this merits a black designation.

Zechariah is dubious about Gabriel's prophecy. That, too, is a standard feature of ancient birth stories. The words used by Zechariah echo Abraham's doubt when God promises Abram (his earlier name) a new land to possess (Gen 15:8); they also reflect the laughter of Abraham and Sarah when God promises that Sarah will bear a son in her old age (Gen 17:15–17, 18:9–15). In addition to these standard features, Zechariah is struck dumb as an omen—of the sort that often accompanied miraculous births.

Luke interweaves the story of the miraculous conception of John with that of Jesus. When Elizabeth is six months pregnant, the time has come to link the two stories: Luke now turns to Gabriel's visit to Mary and Mary's visit to Elizabeth.

Miraculous conception of Jesus
Lk 1:26–38
No parallels
Source: Luke

LUKE 1:26–38 **[26]In the sixth month the heavenly messenger Gabriel was sent from God to a town in Galilee called Nazareth,** **[27]to a virgin engaged to a man named Joseph, of the house of David. The virgin's name was Mary.** **[28]He entered and said to her, "Greetings, favored one! The Lord is with you."**

[29]But she was deeply disturbed by the words, and wondered what this greeting could mean?

TWO ANNUNCIATIONS

To Zechariah (Luke 1:8–20)	To Mary (Luke 1:26–37)
8 While he was serving as priest before God when his priestly clan was on temple duty, 9 it so happened that he was chosen by lot, according to the custom of the priesthood, to enter the sanctuary of the Lord and burn incense. 10 At the hour of incense, while a huge crowd was praying outside, 11 there appeared to him a messenger of the Lord standing to the right of the altar of incense.	26 In the sixth month the heavenly messenger Gabriel was sent from God to a town in Galilee called Nazareth, 27 to a virgin engaged to a man named Joseph, of the house of David. The virgin's name was Mary. 28 He entered and said to her, "Greetings, favored one! The Lord is with you."
12 When he saw him, Zechariah was shaken and overcome by fear.	29 But she was deeply disturbed by the words, and wondered what this greeting could mean.
13 But the heavenly messenger said to him, "Don't be afraid, Zechariah, for your prayer has been heard,	30 The heavenly messenger said to her, "Don't be afraid, Mary. You see, you have found favor with God.
and your wife Elizabeth will bear you a son,	31 Listen to me: you will conceive in your womb and give birth to a son,
and you are to name him John.	and you will name him Jesus.
14 And you will be joyful and elated, and many will rejoice at his birth, 15 because he will be great in the sight of the Lord; he will drink no wine or beer, and he will be filled with holy spirit from the very day of his birth. 16 And he will cause many of the children of Israel to turn to the Lord their God. 17 He will precede him in the spirit and power of Elijah: he will turn the hearts of the parents back towards their children, and the disobedient back toward the ways of righteousness, and will make people ready for their Lord."	32 He will be great, and will be called son of the Most High. And the Lord God will give him the throne of David, his father. 33 He will rule over the house of Jacob forever; and his dominion will have no end."

18But Zechariah said to the heavenly messenger, "How can I be sure of this? For I am an old man and my wife is well along in years."	34And Mary said to the messenger, "How can this be, since I've not had sex with any man."
19And the messenger answered him, "I am Gabriel, the one who stands in the presence of God. I was sent to speak to you, and to bring you this good news.	35The messenger replied, "The holy spirit will come over you, and the power of the Most High will cast its shadow on you. This is why the child to be born will be holy, and be called son of God.
20"Listen to me: you will be struck silent and speechless until the day these things happen, because you did not trust my words, which will come true at the appropriate time."	36Further, your relative Elizabeth has also conceived a son in her old age. She who was said to be infertile is already six months along, 37since nothing is impossible with God."

30The heavenly messenger said to her, "Don't be afraid, Mary. You see, you have found favor with God. 31Listen to me: you will conceive in your womb and give birth to a son, and you will name him Jesus. 32He will be great, and will be called son of the Most High. And the Lord God will give him the throne of David, his father. 33He will rule over the house of Jacob forever; and his dominion will have no end."

34And Mary said to the messenger, "How can this be, since I've not had sex with any man?"

35The messenger replied, "The holy spirit will come over you, and the power of the Most High will cast its shadow on you. This is why the child to be born will be holy, and be called son of God. 36Further, your relative Elizabeth has also conceived a son in her old age. She who was said to be infertile is already six months along, 37since nothing is impossible with God."

38And Mary said, "Here I am, the Lord's slave. I pray that all you've told me comes true." Then the heavenly messenger left her.

Miraculous conception of Jesus. Although the names of Jesus' parents are not widely attested outside the infancy narratives (Mary only in Mark 6:3, Acts 1:14; Joseph only in Luke 4:22, John 1:45, 6:42), there is no reason to doubt the validity of that information. Accordingly, the Fellows endorsed by a wide majority the statement:

- **Jesus' parents were named Joseph and Mary.**

They did so without prejudice to the question of whether Joseph was the biological father of Jesus. The Fellows were evenly divided on the question of whether or not Joseph was the biological father of Jesus.

- Mary conceived of Joseph

received a gray weighted average, half of the Fellows voting pink and half voting gray or black. Some (sixteen percent) thought that the biological father of Jesus was some unnamed man, who either seduced or raped Mary. What the Fellows were clear about is that Jesus had a human father. On the statement

- **Mary conceived Jesus without sexual intercourse with a man**

ninety-six percent voted black.

In spite of the fact that the Fellows agree that Mary and Joseph were commonly recognized as the parents of Jesus, they deemed it awkward (and technically difficult) to color the names of Joseph and Mary red every time they appeared in the text. Instead, as a general policy they decided to assign special color coding to bits of information only when they appear in significant narrative statements meriting the same color. Verse 27, for example, is colored gray, not because there is doubt about the names Joseph and Mary, but because the Fellows are dubious that Mary was a virgin and that Joseph was a descendant of David.

Gabriel's annunciation to Mary follows the same pattern—the same elements and similar wording—as the annunciation to Zechariah (Luke 1:8–20). That suggests that Luke is following an old literary tradition. Indeed, the two annunciations are an elaboration of similar scenes in the Hebrew scriptures, for example, Judg 13:3–20.

The basic elements can be observed when the two annunciations are laid out side-by-side, as in the box on p. 514. The first item is the arrival of the angel. The appearance of the angel troubles both Zechariah and Mary. The angel reassures them that God has approved. They are then informed of an impending birth. The child to be born is given a name in advance. The angel then predicts that the child will be great. Zechariah doubts that he and Elizabeth are capable of bearing a child; Mary protests that she has not had sex with a man so she cannot be pregnant. The angel responds to their doubts by assuring them once again that God has made the arrangements. The annunciation scene concludes with a confirming sign.

The two annunciation scenes are thus compositions of Luke, who was following an ancient, well-established pattern. They are not based on information that was handed down from Zechariah and Mary until Luke learned of it; they are constructs inspired by scripture. They are therefore colored black.

The report in v. 36 that Mary and Elizabeth were related is historically doubtful for several reasons. For one, it is attested only here in Luke's infancy narrative. For another, it is at variance with reports in the Sayings Gospel Q and the Gospel of John that John did not know who Jesus was when he began his ministry (Luke 7:19; John 1:33). And, finally, identifying John as a relative of Jesus fits with the early Christian attempt to co-opt John's movement by portraying him as the prophesied forerunner of Jesus.

Luke's portrayal of Jesus and John as relatives is his way of christianizing John and the Baptist movement. Another way of linking the two persons and movements is to have Mary visit Elizabeth (Luke 1:39–56). Rather than simply narrating the two births sequentially, Luke has entwined the two stories as a symbolic entwining of the two lives. The result is a symmetrical structure in which the two stories lead up to and then devolve away from Mary's visit to Elizabeth. Viewed as a whole, Luke's infancy story has this finely balanced structure:

1a John's genealogy
2b Annunciation of John's birth
3b Annunciation of Jesus' birth
  4 Visit of Mary to Elizabeth: the fulcrum of the two stories
5c John's miraculous birth
6c Jesus' miraculous birth
7a Jesus' genealogy

The two annunciations are "diptychs"—two panels linked by a common theme—and the two miraculous birth stories are similarly diptychs, while the genealogies serve as the non-narrative frame enclosing the whole. Mary's visit to Elizabeth is the fulcrum of the two finely balanced parts. These features indicate that Luke was a consummate storyteller.

Mary visits Elizabeth
Lk 1:39–56
No parallels
Source: Luke

LUKE 1:39–56 **[39]At that time Mary set out in haste for a town in the hill country of Judah, [40]where she entered Zechariah's house and greeted Elizabeth. [41]And it so happened, when Elizabeth heard Mary's greeting, that the baby jumped in her womb. Elizabeth was filled with holy spirit [42]and proclaimed at the top of her voice, "Blessed are you among women, and blessed is the fruit of your womb! [43]Who am I that the mother of my lord should visit me? [44]You see, when the sound of your greeting reached my ears, the baby jumped for joy in my womb. [45]Congratulations to her who trusted that what the Lord promised her would come true."**

[46]And Mary said, "My soul extols the Lord, [47]and my spirit rejoices in God my Savior, [48]for he has shown consideration for the lowly status of his slave. As a consequence, from now on every generation will congratulate me; [49]the Mighty One has done great things for me, and holy is his name, [50]and his mercy will come to generation after generation of those who fear him. [51]He has shown the strength of his arm, he has put the arrogant to rout, along with their private schemes; [52]he has pulled the mighty down from their thrones, and exalted the lowly; [53]he has filled the hungry with good things, and sent the rich away empty. [54]He has come to the aid of his servant Israel, remembering his mercy, [55]as he spoke to our ancestors, to Abraham and to his descendants forever." [56]And Mary stayed with her about three months, and then returned home.

Mary visits Elizabeth. In his elaborate fiction, Luke has intertwined the stories of John the Baptist and Jesus. It will be helpful to summarize in some detail how he weaves the two together.

The story begins with the genealogy of John (1:5–5) and concludes with the genealogy of Jesus (3:23–38).

In the first section, Luke narrates the annunciation to Zechariah of the conception of John (1:7–25), and follows it with the annunciation to Mary of the conception of Jesus (1:26–38).

Luke now joins the two stories directly by having Mary visit Elizabeth in the hill country of Judah (1:39–56). This scene constitutes the bridge to the second diptych to follow. Moreover, it introduces a fundamental theme of the gospels: John is the prophet who recognizes Jesus as the messiah and his superior, and John does so even as a baby in his mother's womb at the moment the pregnant Mary comes on the scene. Luke represents the visit between Mary and Elizabeth as a dialogue in which Elizabeth first praises Mary (1:42–45) and then Mary praises God (1:46–55).

Luke now narrates the birth, circumcision, and naming of John, followed by Zechariah's hymn of praise and concluding formula of the child's progress (1:57–80). That is the first half of the next diptych.

Luke's version of the birth of Jesus is more elaborate than his account of John's birth and childhood (2:1–52), as one might expect. Luke utilizes a hypothetical census to get the family to Bethlehem where Jesus is born (2:1–7). The birth of Jesus is greeted by an angelic announcement to shepherds attending their flocks at night (2:8–20). Jesus is next circumcised and named on the eighth day (2:21).

Luke continues the story by having the family visit Jerusalem for the rites of purification following Jesus' birth (2:22–24). While there, the messianic role Jesus is to play is confirmed by Simeon who had been promised by the holy spirit that he would not die before he had seen the messiah (2:25–35) and by Anna, a prophetess (2:36–38). The scene is brought to a close by the formula conventional in such infancy tales that Jesus made good progress as a child (2:39–40). This concludes the second half of the diptych treating the births of the two heroes.

Luke has added a further scene that has no parallel in the story of John. On a visit to the temple in Jerusalem, Jesus is depicted as wise beyond his years in anticipation of his coming prowess as a sage (2:41–51); his further progress is noted in a second conventional generalization (2:52). But Luke has not finished with the interweaving of the two stories. He presents the public life of John as prophet of the endtime, which climaxes in the baptism of Jesus. During the baptism, the sky opens up, the spirit descends in the form of a dove, and Jesus is acknowledged by a heavenly voice as God's son (3:1–22). John has now served the purposes for which Luke uses him and disappears from the gospel. It is now time for Luke to draw his infancy story to a close with a genealogy of Jesus, in which he tracks the lineage of Jesus back to Adam and God (3:23–38).

LUKE 1:57–80 **[57]The time came for Elizabeth to give birth and she had a son. [58]Her neighbors and relatives heard that the Lord had shown her great mercy, and they rejoiced with her. [59]And so on the eighth day they came to circumcise the child; and they were going to name him Zechariah after his father.**

[60]His mother spoke up and said, "No; he is to be called John."

[61]But they said to her, "No one in your family has this name." [62]So they made signs to his father, asking what he would like him to be called.

[63]He asked for a writing tablet and to everyone's astonishment he wrote, "His name is John." [64]And immediately his mouth was opened and his tongue loosed, and he began to speak, blessing God.

[65]All their neighbors became fearful, and all these things were talked about throughout the entire hill country of Judea. [66]And all who heard about these things took them to heart and wondered: "Now what is this child going to be?" You see, the hand of the Lord was with him.

[67]Then his father Zechariah was filled with holy spirit and prophesied: [68]"Blessed be the Lord, the God of Israel, for he has visited and ransomed his people. [69]He has raised up for us a horn of salvation in the house of David his servant. [70]This is what he promised in the words of his holy prophets of old: [71]deliverance from our enemies, and from the hands of all who hate us; [72]mercy to our ancestors, and the remembrance of his holy covenant. [73]This is the oath he swore to Abraham our ancestor: [74]to grant that we be rescued from the hands of our enemies, to serve him without fear, [75]in holiness and righteousness before him all our days. [76]And you, child, will be called a prophet of the Most High; for you will go before the Lord to prepare his way, [77]to give his people knowledge of salvation through the forgiveness of their sins. [78]In the heartfelt mercy of our God, the dawn from on high will visit us, [79]to shine on those sitting in darkness, in the shadow of death, to guide our feet to the way of peace."

[80]And the child grew up and became strong in spirit. He was in the wilderness until the day of his public appearance to Israel.

Birth & naming of John
Lk 1:57–80
No parallels
Source: Luke

Birth & naming of John. Since John the Baptist was a real person, he must have had a mother. We are just not certain that her name was Elizabeth. The report that John was circumcised on the eighth day (v. 59) is based on general practice rather than specific historical information: John was a Jewish boy and Jewish boys are supposed to be circumcised on the eighth day (Gen 17:9–14). Jesus was also circumcised on the eighth day (Luke 2:21).

The neighbors and relatives of John's family assumed that the parents would name him after his father, Zechariah (v. 59). Luke, who was writing three-quarters of a century after John's birth, of course had no knowledge of what the neighbors and relatives anticipated by way of a name for the new baby. But Luke is interested in turning the scene into another supernatural sign. So he has both Elizabeth and Zechariah agree, without consulting each other, that his name is to be John. To confirm this agreement as a sign, Luke brings Zechariah's speechlessness to an abrupt end (v. 64)—another omen of the sort that typically accompanies miraculous birth stories.

When Zechariah recovers his speech, he bursts out in a hymn (vv. 68–79), commonly called the Benedictus. The Benedictus is an early Christian composition based on a variety of Old Testament passages. Luke uses it as a prophecy of God's coming redemption through a Davidic messiah (v. 69). Since John was apparently not a descendant of David, the pre-Lukan hymn referred to Jesus; Luke has added the reference to John (vv. 76–77) to make it plausible on the lips of John's father. In this, as in other comparable cases, Luke has adapted traditional material to the setting of the story he is telling.

The conclusion to John's birth story (v. 80) is a conventional formula for ending childhood narratives. Similar endings are found in the stories of Isaac (Gen 21:8), Jacob and Esau (Gen 25:27), Samson (Judg 13:24), and Samuel (1 Sam 2:26). Luke uses a similar formula to conclude the story of Jesus' childhood (Luke 2:52).

Birth of Jesus
Lk 2:1–7
Source: Luke
Cf. Mt 1:18–25

**LUKE 2:1–7 In those days it so happened that a decree was issued
by Emperor Augustus that a census be taken of the whole civilized
world. 2This first census was taken while Quirinius was governor of
Syria. 3Everybody had to travel to their ancestral city to be counted
in the census. 4So Joseph too went up from Galilee, from the town of
Nazareth, to Judea, to the town of David called Bethlehem, because
he was a descendant of David, 5to be counted in the census with
Mary, to whom he was engaged; Mary was pregnant. 6It so happened
while they were there that the time came for her to give birth; 7and
she gave birth to a son, her firstborn. She wrapped him in strips of
cloth and laid him in a feeding trough, because the travelers' shelter
was no place for those things.**

Birth of Jesus. Caesar Augustus was the Roman emperor from 27 B.C.E. to 14 C.E. There is no evidence that he decreed a census of the "whole civilized world" during his tenure, although the Romans did enroll the non-citizens of individual provinces for tax purposes and military service as circumstances warranted. Such was the case in the year 6 C.E. after Archelaus was removed as the ruler of Judea and the region attached to the Roman province of Syria. Quirinius was governor of Syria at that time and probably conducted a census for the purpose of taxation. Since this census is probably historical, the Fellows designated the notice of it pink. However, Luke's reference to the census in connection with the birth of Jesus is inaccurate. Here is why: The claim is made in Matt 2:16 that Jesus was born while Herod the Great was still alive and king. Since Herod died in 4 B.C.E., there is a ten-year discrepancy between a date at the close of Herod's reign and the census of Quirinius that took place in 6 C.E. Luke himself suggests elsewhere that Jesus was born during Herod's reign by dating Mary's pregnancy to the time of John the Baptist's birth (Luke 1:5, 36). Accordingly, the linking of Jesus' birth to the census under Quirinius is erroneous. For that reason, vv. 3–4 and part of v. 5 were designated black.

Jesus is depicted as a native of Nazareth in other passages in the gospels (Mark 6:1–4; John 1:46, 7:41, 52). The prophet Micah (5:2) had predicted that the messiah would come from Bethlehem, the city of David, so Luke borrows the census of Quirinius as the fictional occasion to get Mary and Joseph to Bethlehem in time for the birth of Jesus. In this, as in other instances in the gospels, the story of Jesus is accommodated to prophetic texts. The appropriate color is black.

Two sentences in Luke's story, apart from his contrived context, are no doubt accurate in themselves: Mary was engaged to Joseph when Jesus was conceived; she gave birth to Jesus. The Fellows accordingly colored these two statements red.

The statement that Mary placed Jesus in a feeding trough for animals because a travelers' shelter, or caravansary, was no place for a newborn is another of Luke's fictions. According to the Infancy Gospel of James (22:3–4), Mary wrapped Jesus in strips of cloth and placed him in a feeding trough, probably filled with hay, to hide him from Herod's troops. Luke interprets the child's presence in the feeding trough as a divine sign (2:12). But it is unclear how the feeding trough was to function as a sign that the baby was a savior, although it is just possible that the feeding trough is the link between the shepherds and Jesus the good shepherd, the expected savior.

Visit of the shepherds
Lk 2:8–20
No parallels
Source: Luke

LUKE 2:8–20 **[8]Now in the same area there were shepherds living**
outdoors. They were keeping watch over their sheep at night, [9]when
a messenger of the Lord stood near them and the glory of the Lord
shone around them. They became terrified. [10]But the messenger said
to them, "Don't be afraid: I bring you good news of a great joy,
which is to benefit the whole nation; [11]today in the city of David, the
Savior was born to you—he is the Anointed, the Lord. [12]And this
will be a sign for you: you will find a baby wrapped in strips of
cloth and lying in a feeding trough."

[13]And suddenly there appeared with the messenger a whole troop
of the heavenly army praising God:

> **[14]Glory to God in the highest,**
> **and on earth peace to people whom he has favored!**

[15]It so happened when the messengers left and returned to heaven
that the shepherds said to one another, "Come on! Let's go over to
Bethlehem and see what has happened, the event the Lord has told
us about." [16]And they hurried away, and found Mary and Joseph,
and the baby lying in a feeding trough. [17]And when they saw it they
reported what they had been told about this child. [18]Everyone who
listened was astonished at what the shepherds told them. [19]But Mary
took all this in and reflected on it. [20]And the shepherds returned,

glorifying and praising God for all they had heard and seen; everything turned out just as they had been told.

Visit of the shepherds. In ancient birth stories of heroes it is necessary for bystanders and portents in the heavens to bear witness to the miraculous birth. Matthew employs the astrologers and the star in the East for this purpose. Luke makes use of the shepherds tending their flocks in the field at night: they are suddenly surrounded by the "glory of the Lord," which suggests some kind of astral phenomenon. A heavenly messenger appears and tells them about the baby in a feeding trough. The single messenger is then joined by a whole army of angels praising God for what has happened. Luke probably makes use of shepherds because Micah had predicted that the ruler to issue from Bethlehem was to be a shepherd-king (Mic 5:2–6). Luke has patterned the angel's announcement to the shepherds (2:9–12) on the annunciations to Zechariah and Mary in the first chapter of Luke. Luke doubles the role of external witnesses by adding the choir of angels (2:13–14) to the single messenger. Both human and divine witnesses testify to the arrival of this special child.

All of this is clearly Luke's composition based, not on historical memory, but on Luke's imagination and suggestions derived from scripture.

Dedication of Jesus
Lk 2:21–40
No parallels
Source: Luke

LUKE 2:21–40 **[21]Now eight days later, when the time came to circumcise him, they gave him the name Jesus, the name assigned him by the heavenly messenger before he was conceived in the womb.**

[22]Now when the time came for their purification according to the Law of Moses, they brought him up to Jerusalem to present him to the Lord—[23]as it is written in the Law of the Lord, "Every male that opens the womb is to be considered holy to the Lord"—[24]and to offer sacrifice according to what is dictated in the Law of the Lord: "A pair of turtledoves or two young pigeons."

[25]Now there was a man in Jerusalem, named Simeon, a decent and devout man who was waiting for the consolation of Israel, and the holy spirit was with him. [26]It had been disclosed to him by the holy spirit that he would not see death before he had laid eyes on the Lord's Anointed. [27]And so he was guided by the spirit to the temple area. When the parents brought in the child Jesus, to perform for him what was customary according to the Law, [28]he took him in his arms and blessed God: [29]"Now, Lord, you can dismiss your slave in peace, according to your word, [30]now that my eyes have seen your salvation, [31]which you have prepared in the sight of all the peoples [32]a revelatory light for foreigners, and glory for your people Israel."

[33]His father and mother were astonished at what was being said about him.

[34]Then Simeon blessed them and said to Mary his mother, "This child is linked to the fall and rise of many in Israel, and is destined to be a sign that is rejected. [35]You too will have your heart broken—and the schemes of many minds will be exposed."

**[36]A prophetess was also there, Anna, daughter of Phanuel, of the
tribe of Asher. She was well along in years, since she had married
as a young girl and lived with her husband for seven years, [37]and
then alone as a widow until she was eighty-four. She never left the
temple area, and she worshiped day and night with fasting and
prayer. [38]Coming on the scene at that very moment, she gave thanks
to God, and began to speak about the child to all who were waiting
for the liberation of Jerusalem.**

**[39]And when they had carried out everything required by the Law
of the Lord, they returned to Galilee, to Nazareth, their own city.
[40]And the boy grew up and became strong, and was filled with wis-
dom; and God regarded him favorably.**

Dedication of Jesus. The Fellows of the Seminar assume that Jesus was circumcised on the eighth day in accordance with Jewish custom. They also saw no reason to doubt that Jesus was the name given him. Jesus' name is widely attested in ancient sources and so was colored red. The balance of this narrative segment is once again the product of Luke's imagination.

Luke has confused or conflated two Israelite customs. The first is the consecration to God of every firstborn, both animal and human, in memory of the escape from Egypt when God killed all the firstborn of the Egyptians; firstborn humans were to be redeemed with a sacrifice (these practices are prescribed in Exod 13:1, 11–16 and Num 18:15–16). The second ritual concerns the purification of the mother forty days after the birth of a child by offering the sacrifice of a lamb or a pair of turtledoves or two pigeons (this practice is prescribed in Lev 12:1–8). Luke has evidently created this scene from biblical texts as the means to get Jesus to the temple in Jerusalem; it rests on traditional practices and not on specific historical knowledge.

In Matthew, the birth of Jesus fulfills ancient prophecies. In Luke, the destiny of Jesus is predicted in the oracles of Simeon and Anna in the temple. According to Simeon, Jesus is to be a light to the gentiles as well as glory for Israel (v. 32). Simeon also predicts that Jesus will be rejected and the heart of his mother broken (vv. 34–35). Anna prophesies that Jesus is to liberate Jerusalem, that is, Israel (v. 38). Luke of course believed, from his point in time, that the predictions of Simeon and Anna had been fulfilled: He wrote the gospel and the book of Acts to demonstrate that they were true. Luke composed the oracles of both Simeon and Anna after the fact. The correct color is black.

The story of Jesus' dedication in the temple parallels that of the infant Samuel (1 Sam 1:24–2:11): the infant is presented at a sacred shrine (Samuel at Shiloh, Jesus in Jerusalem), the appropriate sacrifice is made (for Samuel a bull, some grain and wine; for Jesus two turtledoves), there is an encounter with an aged holy man (in Samuel's case, Eli; for Jesus, Simeon), and a canticle of praise is recited. Simeon's prediction that Jesus will be rejected echoes the motif, found frequently in heroic infancy narratives, that the hero has a rival. In Matthew the rival is Herod the Great, who slaughters the male babies since he cannot identify the new king. Luke does not specify who Jesus' rejectors will be.

The young Jesus in Jerusalem
Lk 2:41–52
No parallels
Source: Luke

LUKE 2:41–52 **[41]Now his parents used to go to Jerusalem every year for the Passover festival. [42]And when he was twelve years old, they went up for the festival as usual. [43]When the festival was over and they were returning home, the young Jesus stayed behind in Jerusalem, without his parents knowing about it. [44]Assuming that he was in the traveling party, they went a day's journey, and then began to look for him among their relatives and acquaintances. [45]When they did not find him, they returned to Jerusalem to search for him.**

[46]And after three days it so happened that they found him in the temple area, sitting among the teachers, listening to them and asking them questions. [47]Everyone who listened to him was astounded at his understanding and his responses.

[48]And when <his parents> saw him they were overwhelmed. "Child," his mother said to him, "why have you done this to us? Don't you see, your father and I have been worried sick looking for you."

[49]"Why were you looking for me?" **he said to them.** "Didn't you know that I have to be in my Father's house?"

[50]But they did not understand what he was talking about. [51]Then he returned with them to Nazareth, and was obedient to them. His mother took careful note of all these things. [52]And Jesus, precocious as he was, continued to excel in learning and gain respect in the eyes of God and others.

The young Jesus in Jerusalem. Matthew's gospel skips from the birth of Jesus to his baptism as an adult and the beginning of his public life (Matt 3:1). Luke, on the other hand, relates one childhood episode to indicate the kind of child Jesus is and the kind of leader he will become. In this respect, Luke is imitating the hellenistic biography of the hero, in which a single predictive episode from the hero's youth telegraphs what the hero will achieve as an adult.

According to Pausanias, a traveler and geographer who lived in the second century C.E., that Theagenes was destined to become an Olympic champion was already indicated by his youthful prowess: on one occasion he lugged home a massive bronze statue, thus forecasting his athletic abilities as an adult. Later, he won 1,400 prizes at the ancient Greek Olympics. The single episode from his youth was adequate to forecast his success as an adult.

Luke also includes one episode about Jesus' youth. The episode in the temple indicated that he would become a great religious teacher, exceeding even the wisdom of the temple authorities. The Infancy Gospel of Thomas repeats this episode but magnifies the prowess of Jesus by having him instruct the temple authorities (InThom 19:1–12).

Luke rounds off his infancy narratives with another formulaic notice: Jesus was precocious, excelled in learning, and gained respect in the eyes of God and others (v. 80).

This narrative segment, too, is the creation of Luke without foundation in historical memory, so the correct color is black.

Family tree
Lk 3:23–38
Source: Luke
Cf. Mt 1:1–17

LUKE 3:23–38 [23]Jesus was about thirty years old when he began
his work. He was supposedly the son of Joseph, **son of Eli, [24]son of**
Matthat, son of Levi, son of Melchi, son of Jannai, son of Joseph,
[25]son of Mattathias, son of Amos, son of Nahum, son of Hesli, son of
Naggai, [26]son of Maath, son of Mattathias, son of Semein, son of
Josech, son of Joda, [27]son of Johanan, son of Rhesa, son of
Zerubbabel, son of Salathiel, son of Neri, [28]son of Melchi, son of
Addi, son of Cosam, son of Elmadam, son of Er, [29]son of Joshua, son
of Eliezer, son of Jorim, son of Matthat, son of Levi, [30]son of Simeon,
son of Judah, son of Joseph, son of Jonam, son of Eliakim, [31]son of
Melea, son of Menna, son of Mattatha, son of Nathan, son of David,
[32]son of Jesse, son of Obed, son of Boaz, son of Sala, son of Nahshon,
[33]son of Amminadab, son of Admin, son of Arni, son of Hezron, son
of Perez, son of Judah, [34]son of Jacob, son of Isaac, son of Abraham,
son of Terah, son of Nahor, [35]son of Serug, son of Reu, son of Peleg,
son of Eber, son of Shelah, [36]son of Cainan, son of Arphachshad, son
of Shem, son of Noah, son of Lamech, [37]son of Methuselah, son of
Enoch, son of Jared, son of Mahalalel, son of Kenan, [38]son of Enosh,
son of Seth, son of Adam, son of God.

Family tree. Hellenistic birth stories regularly began with a genealogy. Genealogies either provided more or less continuous lists of ancestors linking the infant to an illustrious progenitor, or simply mentioned two or three such illustrious ancestors without providing intervening names. A famous person could be provided with more than one genealogy, depending on the number of illustrious ancestors to which that person was to be linked. Genealogies were designed, of course, to underscore the special status of the child. Although created after the hero had become famous, the genealogy was supposed to predict the child's fame as an adult.

Both Matthew and Luke provide extensive lists of ancestors for Jesus. Jesus' ancestors connect him with major figures mentioned in the Hebrew Bible. The two lists contain almost identical names from Abraham to David because they both draw on the genealogies given in Genesis and 1 Chronicles. There are, however, some notable differences. Matthew's list is arranged in chronological order from the oldest to the most recent; Luke, on the other hand, has reversed the conventional order, placing Adam and God last. Matthew traces Jesus' lineage back to Abraham, the father of the Israelite people; Luke extends his list all the way back to Adam and God. Naturally, he obtains this additional information from Genesis and 1 Chronicles. The two genealogies deviate after King David: Matthew traces Jesus' ancestors through Solomon to emphasize the royal line, while Luke routes Jesus' lineage through Nathan, perhaps because another Nathan was a prophet during David's reign. Here diverging genealogies serve different functions.

Since these genealogies were either taken from older lists in Genesis and Chronicles, or, in the case of the postexilic names, are otherwise unattested, scholars doubt that they reflect accurate historical records. There is very little evidence that royal genealogies were kept after the Babylonian exile, and there is no other evidence that Jesus' family was of royal descent. As a consequence, scholars are inclined to regard these genealogies as inventions of Matthew and Luke to certify that Jesus was qualified by birth to be the Davidic messiah. As in the case of Matthew, black is the appropriate color for the names in Luke's list with the exception of that of Joseph.

Luke's introductory statement in v. 23 that Jesus was about thirty years old when he began his ministry is a plausible round number if we assume that Jesus was born around Herod's death (4 B.C.E.) and was crucified during the tenure of Pontius Pilate (26–36 C.E.). The pink designation is based on general plausibility rather than on any specific information Luke might have had.

There can be little doubt that Jesus was regarded as the son of Joseph (v. 23) by many in the early Christian community, whether or not Joseph is a fictitious name. That fact warrants a red designation. Whether or not Joseph was the biological father of Jesus is a different matter.

What Do We Really Know about Jesus?

What do we know about the deeds of Jesus? About the shadowy figure depicted in snapshots in more than twenty gospels and gospel fragments that have survived from antiquity?

The short answer is that we don't know a great deal. But there are some stories that probably preserve distant historical memories, and we can infer some deeds from his parables and aphorisms.

This summary is based on the inventories of red and pink summaries and events that appear as appendices to this volume (pp. 565–68).

THE BASIC FACTS

We are quite confident that a person Jesus of Nazareth once existed, in spite of a few skeptics who believe that all the stories about Jesus are pure myth. We are confident that he began as a disciple of John the Baptist, that he quit John at some point and returned to Galilee where he launched his own career as an itinerant sage. We believe he spoke about God's domain or God's imperial rule in parables and short, pithy sayings and attracted a substantial following. There is little doubt that he was also a charismatic healer and exorcist and that he was eventually put to death by the Romans around the year 30 C.E. Paul of Tarsus, who became a disciple after Jesus' death, claimed that the risen Jesus appeared to him in a vision and that he had also appeared to Simon Peter, one of the original circle of followers. Beyond these meager facts, there is very little hard detailed information. Yet it is easy to imagine a story that joins these facts together in a single, sequential narrative. The evangelists did so by asking why Jesus met the fate he did and what his life meant to them. They employed scripture and their own convictions as guides in fashioning a story that accounted for the death of a suffering righteous hero.

The Bible scholar who adopts the role of historian rather than theologian will label the sketchy facts "very probably historical." Probability is the category with which historians must work in verifying ancient reports of deeds and words. The gospels preserve other reports of events and typical activities that are "probably historical" or which, although not accurate in detail, contain some historical information. A third category consists of reports that are "probably not historical"—those which preserve no more than vague historical reminiscence or contain information that is unreliable. Still other reports are very likely the product of some storyteller's imagination and therefore of little use in establishing actualities. These four categories—very probably historical, probably historical, probably not historical, and almost certainly not historical—correspond to the four colors—red, pink, gray, black—employed by the Fellows in their voting procedures.

Time

Jesus is linked with the reign of king Herod the Great (37–4 B.C.E.), during whose incumbency Jesus was allegedly born. We also have the name of Herod Antipas, tetrarch from 4 B.C.E. to 39 C.E., who ruled Galilee during Jesus' life and beheaded John the Baptist; and the name of Pontius Pilate, the Roman procurator (26–36 C.E.) under whom Jesus was crucified. Jesus therefore lived in a period bounded by a date prior to the death of Herod on the one side and by the end of Pilate's tenure in 36 C.E. on the other.

Place

His life was played out on the stage we know as Palestine, consisting, in his day, of Galilee to the north and Judea to the south. Dividing the two provinces was the territory of Samaria, through which Jesus may have occasionally passed on his way to and from Jerusalem. He may also have traveled in the region across the Jordan, on the east bank, since, like other Judean pilgrims, he may have chosen to avoid contact with hostile Samaritans by crossing and recrossing the Jordan on pilgrimages to the holy city.

Jesus' home was semi-pagan Galilee, whose inhabitants, because they were often of mixed blood and open to foreign influence, were not highly regarded by the Judeans living to the south. Since Jesus was a Jew, he belonged to the ethnic group we now more accurately call Judeans, the ancestors of present-day Jews.

John the Baptist

John the Baptist was almost certainly a historical figure. Jesus appears to have been attracted to the movement of John the Baptist at some point prior to the inauguration of his own public career. The Fellows of the Jesus Seminar and scholars generally regard it as highly probable that Jesus was baptized by John the Baptist. Scholars also believe that he quit John and launched his own career in Galilee, and that other of John's followers abandoned John and became disciples of Jesus. These events are not likely to have been invented by Christian apologists.

John the Baptist was popular with the people. Herod Antipas had John arrested for criticizing his marriage to Herodias and because John was a threat to his political control of the people. Herod had John beheaded at the fortress palace of Machaerus located in Perea, east of the Jordan River.

Jesus as itinerant sage

Jesus was evidently an itinerant sage, wandering about from place to place, teaching and healing and living on handouts. Jesus was active during his public career in the towns and hamlets of Galilee, but no mention is made in the written gospels of comparable activity in hellenistic towns in the same region. He and his followers, unlike John the Baptist, did not practice baptism in the beginning.

Jesus and his relatives, disciples, enemies, and the crowds

We are not certain that Jesus deliberately formed a group of disciples, but it is clear that followers, including women, gathered around him. We know the names of a few of these followers, such as Simon Peter, and James and John, the sons of Zebedee affectionately known as the "thunder brothers," whose own stories are sketchy at best. Then, too, we know the names of a few women associates, such as Mary of Magdala, who belonged to his retinue and was later to play such a prominent role in legend. Beyond these few whose profiles are indistinct, we have very little hard information.

Mary was the name of Jesus' mother. Jesus had four brothers whose names were James, Joses, Judas, and Simon (Mark 6:3). According to the Gospel of Mark, Jesus' mother and his brothers were originally skeptical of Jesus' program, but later became part of the Christian movement (Mark 3:21, 31; John 7:5; Acts 1:4; 1 Cor 9:5). Jesus also had sisters (Mark 6:3; Matt 13:56). Joseph was probably the name of Jesus' father.

Jesus was popular with the people, although the evangelists tend to exaggerate that popularity. However, Jesus was not well received in his hometown. He was also opposed by some religious authorities in both Galilee and Jerusalem, although much of the controversy in the gospels between adherents of the new sect and Judaism may reflect later conditions, subsequent to the destruction of Jerusalem and the temple (70 C.E.), when the budding church was competing with the synagogue.

We do not know how long his public career lasted, but the narrative gospels imply a relatively short period, from one to three years. As a final act, Jesus went to Jerusalem, either spoke or acted against the temple and the temple authorities, and was executed by the Romans.

Jesus as social deviant

We are confident that Jesus was a social deviant—he regularly infringed the social codes in force in his society. He consorted openly with social outcasts, with "toll collectors and sinners." He did not observe kosher. He suggested that it was not what goes in to a person's body but what comes out that defiles. He did not practice fasting. He infringed the sabbath codes on occasion. He did not observe other purity codes, such as washing his hands before eating. He was at odds with his family; he advocated adopting "true relatives" as part of his extended family.

These characteristics are derived from nine pronouncement stories that were colored red or pink; all nine of these stories involve controversies over the issues listed above.

Jesus' language skills

Jesus' native tongue was a dialect of Aramaic current in Galilee that Judeans apparently could distinguish from their own form of speech, as suggested by Matthew's account of the confrontation with Peter in the courtyard during Jesus' trial (Matt 26:73). The Gospel of Mark attributes several Aramaic expressions to Jesus (5:41, 7:34, 14:36, 15:34). We do not know whether Jesus could read and write; the story of Jesus in the synagogue reading from Isaiah (Luke 4:16–30) may well be a fiction invented by Luke, the author of the third gospel. The orphan story of the woman caught in an adulterous act pictures Jesus stooping down and "drawing" in the sand while those ready with stones are making up their minds who among them is sinless. This story does not have a fixed home in gospel manuscripts, appearing as it does in various locations; it probably did not belong originally to any of the gospels known to us, but may be a fragment of an unknown gospel. It cannot be taken as evidence that Jesus could read and write. The critical reader must be constantly alert to fictional embellishments in the gospels.

We do not know whether Jesus knew Hebrew, in his day only a literary language. There is now evidence that suggests he may have been bilingual; Greek was probably his second language, learned from the pagan environment that surrounded him in Galilee, especially in Sepphoris, a hellenistic city located only four miles from his home village. In any case, the written gospels were all composed in Greek, and judging by the poetic shape of much of the language, it seems certain that the Jesus tradition took its formative shape in Greek as well. If Jesus did not speak Greek, very few of his original words have come down to us.

Exorcism

The Fellows believe that Jesus practiced exorcism. Yet they colored the six reports of exorcisms (Table 3, p. 13) gray on the grounds that they are not accurate reports of specific events. However, the Fellows are convinced that Jesus was accused of being an agent of Beelzebul, the head demon (Luke 11:15–17) and was consequently believed to be mad. There were other exorcists in Jesus' time whose feats are narrated by Josephus, Philostratus, and others. It should be added that most Fellows doubt that there are such things as demons, although some Fellows think there are such things as spirits.

Healing

During his lifetime, Jesus was considered a healer. From today's perspective, Jesus' cures are related to psychosomatic maladies. Jesus usually healed by the use of words alone; his cures were sometimes effected instantaneously. The Jewish scriptures (Old Testament) provided generative models for constructing healing stories about Jesus as physician. Graeco-Roman tales also served as models for stories about Jesus.

Nineteen cures or resuscitations are attributed to Jesus in the gospels (Table 4, p. 14). The Seminar had difficulty in finding stories it believed to be reports of actual cures. However, the core of six stories are colored pink in *The Acts of Jesus*. The other thirteen are designated either gray or black.

The Fellows believe that Jesus actually cured Peter's mother-in-law of a fever (Mark 1:29–31).

Jesus probably cured someone with a skin rash, thought to be leprosy (Mark 1:40–45).

Jesus may well have cured a paralytic (Mark 2:1–12).

It is entirely plausible that Jesus cured some woman who was afflicted with a vaginal hemorrhage (Mark 5:24b–34).

The Seminar concluded that Jesus might have caused a blind man to see (the blind man of Bethsaida, Mark 8:22–26; Blind Bartimaeus, 10:46–52).

The remaining stories, including the raising of Lazarus, the resuscitation of the widow's son at Nain, the officer's son/slave, and the cure of Jairus' daughter are colored black or gray.

Nature wonders

The Fellows were unable to endorse any of the nature wonders (Table 5, p. 15) as historical events.

The stilling of the storm, walking on the water, the feeding of 5,000 and 4,000 in the wilderness with a few loaves and fish, changing the water into wine, cursing the barren fig tree, and the miraculous catch of fish are all fictions suggested by extra-gospel models. They are color-coded black.

Miracles

The Seminar concluded that both the Pharisees and people generally in Jesus' day expected heavenly signs related to the coming of God's kingdom. They were dubious, however, that the Pharisees asked Jesus for a sign. They think Jesus probably refused to provide heavenly signs, as Mark insists (8:12). On the other hand, it is evident that the evangelists and earlier storytellers regarded Jesus' exorcisms, cures, and other miraculous feats as signs of the kingdom's arrival.

Framework stories

Mark opens his gospel with the appearance of John the Baptist in the wilderness, the baptism of Jesus by John, and return of Jesus to Galilee where he began preaching. The Seminar colored all or most of these stories red. The account of Jesus' temptations in the wilderness they colored gray: as reported, these stories are legendary, although they may reflect some actual experience of Jesus as he pondered his mission and prepared to enter public life.

The stories that form the turning point of Mark's plot were all colored black as projections of the convictions of early believers. Those stories include Peter's confession (Mark 8:27–30), Jesus' predictions of his death (Mark 8:31–33, 9:30–32, 10:32–34), and the transfiguration (Mark 9:2–8).

The stories that form the climax of the gospel narrative appear predominantly in black as well. That assessment calls for more detailed treatment.

Passion narrative

The Fellows are relatively certain that Jesus did not ride into Jerusalem on an ass in order to declare his messiahship in accordance with Zech 9:9. They do think he may have ridden into Jerusalem on an ass as a symbolic act.

The Fellows believe that the temple incident, Jesus' arrest, and his execution were all historical events. Something Jesus said or did against the temple became the occasion for his arrest. The disciples probably fled when Jesus was arrested. He was turned over to the high priest, who in turn handed him over to Pilate for judgment. Pilate probably condemned Jesus out of hand. It is not just the content of the trial but the fact of a trial that lacks historical foundation. The Fellows concluded that most of the trial narrative was created on the basis of Psalm 2.

Jesus was probably flogged in accordance with Roman practice and then crucified. However, the narrative depiction of these events has been so heavily influenced by parallel events in the Jewish scriptures and by prophetic texts, including the Psalms, that we cannot extract hard information from them. As a consequence, most of the details are colored black.

The assertion that the Romans were innocent of Jesus' death and the Jews responsible is pure Christian propaganda, in the judgment of the Seminar.

The conspiracy against Jesus and the role of Judas, as well as Judas himself, are probably fictions. The story of Peter's denial is a fiction. The two trials are fictions; Luke has added a third trial before Herod, which is also a fiction. The mocking may be a fiction. Simon of Cyrene is a fiction. The burial of Jesus is a fiction carried out by a fictional character, Joseph of Arimathea.

Resurrection reports

The Fellows of the Jesus Seminar designated red Paul's claim that Jesus appeared to him, since Paul makes that claim on his own behalf. They colored the assertion pink that Jesus appeared to Simon Peter, since Paul's report in 1 Corinthians is a secondhand report. The other appearances listed in 1 Cor 15:5–8 the Fellows voted gray or black.

The empty tomb stories in all the gospels were colored black. The earlier strata of the gospels contain no appearance stories. The actual resurrection of Jesus is depicted only in the Gospel of Peter, and as a fiction that report merited a black designation. The tale of the bribing of the guard is likewise a fiction.

The Fellows believe Mary of Magdala to have been among the early witnesses to the resurrection, although the stories in Matthew and John about the appearance to her are fictional. In any case, Mary was considered a leader in the early movement alongside Peter and Paul.

On the basis of a close analysis of all the resurrection reports, the Seminar decided that the resurrection of Jesus was not perceived initially to depend on what happened to his body. The body of Jesus probably decayed as do all corpses. The resurrection of Jesus was not an event that happened on the first Easter Sunday; it was not an event that could have been captured by a video camera.

The Seminar concluded that it does not seem necessary for Christians to believe the literal veracity of any of the later appearance narratives.

Birth and childhood

Jesus was probably born in Nazareth, his hometown. Later legends that assign his birth to Bethlehem were invented to satisfy an ancient prophecy.

Jesus was not born of a virgin; the Fellows doubt that Mary conceived Jesus without sexual intercourse. Jesus' father was either Joseph or some unknown male who either seduced or raped the young Mary.

The world census, the trip to Bethlehem, the star in the East, the astrologers, the flight to Egypt and return, the massacre of the babies, the shepherds in the fields, the kinship to John the Baptist are all Christian fictions.

The birth and childhood stories in Matthew and Luke were the last part of the gospel tradition to be created. They were not conceived, in all probability, until toward the close of the first century C.E.

Jesus the teacher and sage

In addition to these meager facts, we also have a compendium of teachings consisting of parables, aphorisms, and dialogues, together with a few dubious anecdotes featuring witticisms told about him by his first admirers. The authentic words of Jesus can be isolated, to a greater or lesser degree, from other words borrowed from the old scriptures or common lore and put on his lips, and from words created by the evangelists under the poetic license exercised by storytellers the world over. The content of this body of authentic speech material tells us a great deal more about Jesus, but it does so indirectly.

Meanwhile, the scattered facts we can muster do not of themselves produce a Jesus who is the Christ of the Christian faith. The authors of traditional Christian faith are Peter and Paul.

Redeeming the myths

The Fellows of the Jesus Seminar are profoundly cognizant that human beings do not live by the bread of facts alone. We live by our stories—by our myths, which is only a fancy word for story—and these fictions are supposed to make sense out of a complex universe of meaning mixed with nonsense. Myths are not true or untrue; as one Fellow puts it, they are either living or dead. Literalism in biblical interpretation in tandem with scientism has helped strangle the myths of the Christian tradition. Historical criticism like that practiced by the Jesus Seminar is intended to release the gospel stories from their literalistic burden. Exposing them to historical assessment relocates them in the realm of story and myth, so they can recover their proper function. When we move them back within that perspective, perhaps new mythmakers and storytellers will once again find voice to celebrate the simple yet enduring story of Jesus of Nazareth.

Notes

INTRODUCTION

1. *The Death of the Messiah,* II 1193.
2. Lucian, *Demonax,* 28, quoted by Vernon K. Robbins in *Ancient Quotes and Anecdotes* (Santa Rosa, CA: Polebridge Press, 1989), 226.

Q

3. *A Marginal Jew,* II, 718–26. Conclusions, 726.
4. *The Historical Figure of Jesus,* 138, 147.
5. *A Marginal Jew,* II 656–7, 661.

GOSPEL OF MARK

6. *A Marginal Jew,* II, 650.
7. *A Marginal Jew,* II, 650.
8. *The Historical Figure of Jesus,* 151.
9. *A Marginal Jew,* II, 708.
10. *A Marginal Jew,* II, 706.
11. *A Marginal Jew,* II, 680.
12. *The Historical Figure of Jesus,* 98.
13. *A Marginal Jew,* II, 681–84, 731 n. 16.
14. *A Marginal Jew,* II, 683–84.
15. *The Historical Figure of Jesus,* 148.
16. *A Marginal Jew,* II, 933.
17. *The Historical Figure of Jesus,* 157.
18. *Life of Apollonius,* IV.13.
19. *A Marginal Jew,* II, 652.
20. *A Marginal Jew,* II, 653.
21. *The Historical Figure of Jesus,* 149–54.
22. *A Marginal Jew,* II, 710.
23. *The Historical Figure of Jesus,* 144.
24. *The Historical Figure of Jesus,* 144–45.
25. *A Marginal Jew,* II, 787.
26. *A Marginal Jew,* II, 986.
27. *The Historical Figure of Jesus,* 156–57.
28. *History of the Synoptic Tradition,* 216.
29. *The Historical Figure of Jesus,* 156–57.
30. *A Marginal Jew,* II, 920–23.
31. *A Marginal Jew,* II, 661.
32. *The Historical Figure of Jesus,* 150, 191.
33. *A Marginal Jew,* II, 714.
34. *The Historical Figure of Jesus,* 145.
35. *A Marginal Jew,* II, 694.
36. *The Historical Figure of Jesus,* 145.
37. *A Marginal Jew,* II, 654.
38. *Four Other Gospels,* 111–21.
39. *A Marginal Jew,* II, 686–90.
40. *A Marginal Jew,* II, 896.
41. *A Myth of Innocence,* 305–6.
42. *A Myth of Innocence,* 305–6.

GOSPEL OF MATTHEW

43. *A Marginal Jew,* II, 728n. 3, 746.
44. *A Marginal Jew,* II, 657.
45. *Death of the Messiah,* I, 225.
46. *Death of the Messiah,* I, 234.
47. *Death of the Messiah,* I, 308.
48. *Death of the Messiah,* I, 482.
49. *Death of the Messiah,* I, 621.
50. *Death of the Messiah,* I, 656–57.
51. *Death of the Messiah,* I, 725.
52. *Death of the Messiah,* I, 860.
53. *Death of the Messiah,* I, 814, 820.
54. *Death of the Messiah,* II, 929.

55. *Death of the Messiah,* II, 943–44.
56. *Death of the Messiah,* II, 968.
57. *Death of the Messiah,* II, 1120.
58. *Death of the Messiah,* II, 1128.
59. *Death of the Messiah,* II, 1133–34.
60. *Death of the Messiah,* II, 1312.

GOSPEL OF LUKE

61. *The Historical Figure of Jesus,* 148–49.
62. *A Marginal Jew,* II, 684–85.
63. *A Marginal Jew,* II, 710–11.
64. *The Gospel According to Luke X–XXIV: Introduction, Translation, and Notes,* Anchor Bible (Garden City, NY: Doubleday, 1981), 1149.
65. *Death of the Messiah,* I, 725.
66. *Death of the Messiah,* I, 860, 739.
67. *Death of the Messiah,* I, 783.
68. *Death of the Messiah,* II, 930.
69. *Death of the Messiah,* II, 1028.
70. *Death of the Messiah,* II, 1277.

GOSPEL OF JOHN

71. *The Gospel According to John (i–xii): Introduction, Translation, and Notes,* Anchor Bible (Garden City, NY: Doubleday, 1966), 78.
72. *A Marginal Jew,* II, 949.
73. Raymond E. Brown, *The Gospel According to John (i–xii),* 176.
74. *The Gospel According to John (i–xii),* 259.
75. *A Marginal Jew,* II, 831.
76. *The Historical Figure of Jesus,* 278 and 311 n. 6.
77. *The Gospel According to John (i–xii),* 470.
78. *Death of the Messiah,* II, 1402.
79. *Death of the Messiah,* I, 268, 308.
80. *The Gospel According to John (xiii–xxi): Introduction, Translation, and Notes,* Anchor Bible (Garden City, NY: Doubleday, 1970), 860.

EMPTY TOMB

81. E. P. Sanders expresses the same opinion in *The Historical Figure of Jesus,* 278.

Roster of the Fellows of the Jesus Seminar

Robert W. Funk, Westar Institute, Co-chair of the Jesus Seminar
A.B., Butler University
M.A., Butler University
B.D., Christian Theological Seminary
Ph.D., Vanderbilt University
Special study: Ecumenical Institute, Bossey, Switzerland; American School of Oriental Research, Jerusalem; University of Tübingen; University of Toronto

John Dominic Crossan, DePaul University, Emeritus, Co-chair of the Jesus Seminar
S.S.L., Pontifical Biblical Institute, Rome
D.D., Maynooth College, Ireland
Special study: Ecole biblique et archéologique française, Jerusalem

Andries G. van Aarde, University of Pretoria
B.A., University of Pretoria
B.D., University of Pretoria
M.A., University of Pretoria
D.D., University of Pretoria
Special study: Institute of Ecumenical and Cultural Research, St. John's University, Collegeville, MN

Richard L. Arthur, Unification Theological Seminary
B.A., Gordon College
S.T.B., Harvard Divinity School
Th.D., Graduate Theological Union

Harold W. Attridge, Yale University
A.B., Boston College
M.A., Cambridge University
Ph.D., Harvard University
Special study: Hebrew University of Jerusalem

Robert Bater, Queen's Theological College
B.A., University of Saskatchewan
M.A., Oxford University
B.D., St. Andrew's College, Saskatoon
S.T.M., Union Theological Seminary, New York
Ph.D., Union Theological Seminary, New York
Special study: University of Tübingen

Edward F. Beutner, Westar Institute
B.A., St. Francis Seminary, Milwaukee
M.A., St. Louis University
Ph.D., Graduate Theological Union

Sterling Bjorndahl, Augustana University College
A.B., Luther College, University of Regina
M.A., Claremont Graduate School
M.Div., Lutheran Theological Seminary, Saskatoon
Ph.D., Claremont Graduate School (candidate)

Anthony Blasi, Tennessee State University
B.A., St. Edward's University
M.A., University of Notre Dame
Ph.D., University of Notre Dame
M.A., University of St. Michael's College
S.T.L., Regis College, Toronto
Th.D., University of Toronto

Marcus Borg, Oregon State University
A.B., Concordia College
M.Th., Oxford University
D.Phil., Oxford University
Special study: Union Theological Seminary, New York; University of Tübingen

Willi Braun, Bishop's University, Quebec
B.A., University of Manitoba
M.A., University of St. Michael's College
Ph.D., University of Toronto

Marvin F. Cain, Mid-Columbia Center for Theological Studies
B.S.E.E., Washington State University
B.D., Gettysburg Lutheran Seminary
Th.M., Union Theological Seminary in Virginia
Ph.D., Duke University

Ron Cameron, Wesleyan University
A.B., Western Kentucky University
M.T.S., Harvard Divinity School
Ph.D., Harvard University
Special study: University of Manchester; University of Tübingen

Bruce D. Chilton, Bard College
A.B., Bard College
M.Div., The General Theological Seminary
Ph.D., Cambridge University
Special study: Institutum Judaicum Delitzschanum, Münster

Kathleen E. Corley, University of Wisconsin-Oshkosh
B.A., Westmont College
M.A., Claremont Graduate School
Ph.D., Claremont Graduate School

Jon Daniels, Defiance College
A.B., Wesleyan University
M.T.S., Harvard Divinity School
Ph.D., Claremont Graduate School

Jon F. Dechow, Westar Institute
B.A., Concordia Seminary, St. Louis
M.Div., Concordia Seminary, St. Louis
Ph.D., University of Pennsylvania

Arthur J. Dewey, Xavier University, Cincinnati
A.B., Boston College
M.Div., Weston School of Theology
Th.D., Harvard University

Joanna Dewey, Episcopal Divinity School
A.B., Smith College
M.A., University of California, Berkeley
M.Div., Church Divinity School of the Pacific
Ph.D., Graduate Theological Union

Dennis C. Duling, Canisius College
A.B., College of Wooster
M.A., University of Chicago
B.D., McCormick Theological Seminary
Ph.D., University of Chicago
Special study: University of Heidelberg; Yale University; Yeshiva University

Robert T. Fortna, Vassar College, Emeritus
B.A., Yale University
M.A., Cambridge University
B.D., Church Divinity School of the Pacific
Th.D., Union Theological Seminary, New York
Special study: Ecumenical Institute for Advanced Theological Studies, Jerusalem; American School of Oriental Research/Albright Institute, Jerusalem

James Goss, California State University, Northridge
B.A., University of Southern California
M.Th., School of Theology at Claremont
Ph.D., Claremont Graduate School
Special study: Boston University

Maurice Hamington, Western Oregon University
B.A., Loyola Marymount University
M.B.A., University of Southern California
M.A., Mount St. Mary's College
Ph.D., University of Southern California
Special study: University of California, Los Angeles; University of Oregon

Walter Harrelson, Vanderbilt University
B.A., University of North Carolina
M.Div., Union Theological Seminary, New York
Th.D., Union Theological Seminary, New York
Special study: Ecumenical Institute for Advanced Theological Studies, Jerusalem; Pontifical Biblical Institute, Rome; Pontifical Oriental Institute, Rome

Stephen L. Harris, California State University, Sacramento
A.B., University of Puget Sound
M.A., Cornell University
Ph.D., Cornell University

Charles W. Hedrick, Southwest Missouri State University
B.A., Mississippi College
B.D., Golden Gate Southern Baptist Seminary
M.A., University of Southern California
Ph.D., Claremont Graduate School

James D. Hester, University of Redlands
A.B., Eastern Baptist College
B.D., California Baptist Theological Seminary
D.Theol., University of Basel

C. M. Kempton Hewitt, Methodist Theological School in Ohio
B.A., Cascade College
B.D., Garrett Evangelical Theological Seminary
S.T.M., Yale University Divinity School
Ph.D., University of Durham
Special study: University of Basel; Kerk en Wereld, Netherlands; Centro de Idioma y Cultura Latinoamcricano, Mexico

Julian V. Hills, Marquette University
A.B., University of Durham
S.T.M., McCormick Theological Seminary
Th.D., Harvard University

Roy W. Hoover, Whitman College
A.B., Pasadena College
Th.D., Harvard University

Michael L. Humphries, Southern Illinois University, Carbondale
B.A., Pacific Christian College
M.A., School of Theology at Claremont
Ph.D., Claremont Graduate School

Glenna S. Jackson, Otterbein College
A.B., University of Dubuque
Ph.D., Marquette University
Special study: Britain and Ireland School of Feminist Theology, Dublin

Clayton N. Jefford, St. Meinrad Seminary
A.B., Furman University
M.A., Claremont Graduate School
M.Div., South Eastern Baptist Theological Seminary
Th.M., South Eastern Baptist Theological Seminary
Ph.D., Claremont Graduate School

Gregory C. Jenks, Anglican Diocese of Brisbane
B.A., University of Queensland
M.A., University of Queensland
Ph.D., University of Queensland

F. Stanley Jones, California State University, Long Beach
B.A., Yale University
B.A., Oxford University
M.A., Oxford University
M.A., Vanderbilt University
D.Theol., University of Göttingen
Ph.D., Vanderbilt University

Larry Kalajainen, The American Church in Paris
B.A., University of Pittsburgh
M.Div., Asbury Theological Seminary
Th.M., Princeton Theological Seminary
Ph.D., Drew University

Perry V. Kea, University of Indianapolis
A.B., University of South Carolina
M.A., Vanderbilt University
Ph.D., University of Virginia
Special study: Oxford University

Chan-Hie Kim, School of Theology at Claremont
B.A., Yonsei University
B.D., Vanderbilt University
Ph.D., Vanderbilt University
Special study: University of Heidelberg

Karen L. King, Harvard Divinity School
A.B., University of Montana
Ph.D., Brown University
Special study: Freie Universität, Humboldt University, Berlin

John S. Kloppenborg, University of St. Michael's College
B.A., University of Lethbridge
M.A., University of St. Michael's College
Ph.D., University of St. Michael's College

Davidson Loehr, Unitarian Universalist Community Church, Portage, MI
B.A., University of Michigan
M.A., University of Chicago
Ph.D., University of Chicago

Sanford Lowe, Santa Rosa Junior College, California
B.S., Cornell University
B.H.L., Hebrew Union College, New York
M.H.L., Hebrew Union College
D.Min., Pacific School of Religion
D.D., Hebrew Union College

John Lown, Francis Parker School, San Diego
B.A., Cambridge University
M.A., Cambridge University
M.A., Vanderbilt University
B.D., Nazarene Theological Seminary
Ph.D., Vanderbilt University
Special study: Publishing Institute of Montana

Gerd Lüdemann, University of Göttingen
D.Theol., University of Göttingen
D. Habil., University of Göttingen

Dennis R. MacDonald, School of Theology at Claremont
B.S., Bob Jones University
M.Div., McCormick Theological Seminary
Ph.D., Harvard University

Brian Rice McCarthy
S.T.Lic., University of Fribourg, Switzerland
S.T.M., Perkins, S.M.U.
Special study: Yale Divinity School

Lane C. McGaughy, Willamette University
A.B., Ohio Wesleyan University
M.A., Vanderbilt University
B.D., Drew Theological Seminary
Ph.D., Vanderbilt University
Special study: University of Tübingen; Harvard Divinity School; Yale Divinity School; Ecumenical Institute, Tantur

Edward J. McMahon II, Texas Christian University
A.B., University of Notre Dame
M.A., Vanderbilt University
Ph.D., Vanderbilt University

Loren Mack-Fisher, the Double Bar A Ranch
A.B., University of Oregon
M.A., Butler University
Ph.D., Brandeis University
Special study: Hebrew Union College, Jerusalem; Collège de France

Marvin W. Meyer, Chapman University
A.B., Calvin College
M.Div., Calvin Theological Seminary
Ph.D., Claremont Graduate School

L. Bruce Miller, University of Alberta, Edmonton
B.A., Carleton University
M.Div., Westminster Theological Seminary
S.T.M., Union Theological Seminary, New York
Ph.D., University of Chicago

Robert J. Miller, Midway College
B.A., St. John's College
M.A., University of California, Santa Barbara
M.A., Claremont Graduate School
Ph.D., Claremont Graduate School
Special study: Vanderbilt University

Robert L'H. Miller, Tufts University
B.A., Tufts University
M.Div., Tufts University
Th.D., Boston University

†Winsome Munro, St. Olaf College
A.B., Witwatersrand University
B.D., Birmingham University
S.T.M., Union Theological Seminary, New York
Ed.D., Teachers College, Columbia University and Union Theological Seminary
Special study: William Temple College, UK

Culver H. Nelson, Founding Minister Emeritus, Church of the Beatitudes, Phoenix
A.B., University of Redlands
M.A., University of Southern California
L.H.D., University of Redlands
D.D., Pacific School of Religion
D.D., Doane College
Special study: Pacific School of Religion; University of Southern California

Stephen J. Patterson, Eden Theological Seminary
A.B., Yankton College
M.A., Claremont Graduate School
M.T.S., Harvard University
Ph.D., Claremont Graduate School
Special study: University of Heidelberg

Robert M. Price, Drew University
B.A., Montclair State University
M.T.S., Gordon-Conwell Theological Seminary
Ph.D., Drew University [1981]
Ph.D., Drew University [1993]

James M. Robinson, Institute for Antiquity and Christianity, Claremont Graduate School
B.A., Davidson College
B.D., Columbia Theological Seminary
D.Theol., University of Basel
Ph.D., Princeton Theological Seminary

†John J. Rousseau, University of California, Berkeley
M.S., Collège Libre des Sciences Sociales et Economiques, Paris
Cambridge Diploma of English Studies
Ph.D., University of Paris
D.Rel., School of Theology at Claremont
Special study: University of Nevada, Las Vegas; University of Haifa; Pacific School of Religion; Saint George's College, Jerusalem

Daryl D. Schmidt, Texas Christian University
A.B., Bethel College
M.Div., Associated Mennonite Biblical Seminaries
Ph.D., Graduate Theological Union

Bernard Brandon Scott, Phillips Theological Seminary, Tulsa Center
A.B., St. Meinrad
M.A., Miami University
Ph.D., Vanderbilt University
Special study: Yale University

Philip Sellew, University of Minnesota
A.B., Macalester College
M.Div., Harvard Divinity School
Th.D., Harvard University

Chris Shea, Ball State University
B.A., University of Illinois at Urbana-Champaign
A.M., University of Illinois at Urbana-Champaign
Ph.D., University of Illinois at Urbana-Champaign

Thomas Sheehan, Loyola University of Chicago
B.A., St. Patrick's College, Menlo Park
M.A., Fordham University, New York City
Ph.D., Fordham University, New York City

Lou H. Silberman, Vanderbilt University, University of Arizona
B.A., University of California, Berkeley
M.H.L., Hebrew Union College, Cincinnati
D.H.L., Hebrew Union College
Special study: University of Basel

Dennis Smith, Phillips Theological Seminary
A.B., Abilene Christian University
M.A., Abilene Christian University
M.Div., Princeton Theological Seminary
Th.D., Harvard University

Mahlon H. Smith, Rutgers University
A.B., Rutgers University
B.D., Drew University
M.S.L., Pontifical Institute of Medieval Studies, Toronto
Special study: Université Catholique de Louvain, Belgium

Michael G. Steinhauser, Toronto School of Theology
A.B., Cathedral College, Brooklyn
M.A., University of Innsbruck
Th.D., University of Würzburg

Johann Strijdom, University of South Africa
B.A., University of Pretoria
B.D., University of Pretoria
M.Div., University of Pretoria
M.A., University of Pretoria
D.Litt. et Phil., University of South Africa (candidate)

W. Barnes Tatum, Greensboro College
A.B., Birmingham Southern College
B.D., Duke University
M.L.S., University of North Carolina at Greensboro
Ph.D., Duke University
Special study: University of St. Andrews; Yeshiva University

Hal Taussig, Chestnut Hill College, Albright College
A.B., Antioch College
M.Div., Methodist Theological School in Ohio
Ph.D., The Union Institute
Special study: Institut Catholique, Paris; University of Basel

James Veitch, Victoria University, Wellington, New Zealand
- B.A., University of Otago, Dunedin, New Zealand
- B.D., University of Otago, Dunedin
- M.Th., University of Otago, Dunedin
- Ph.D., University of Birmingham, UK
- Special study: Westminster College, Cambridge

Paul Verhoeven, Brooksfilms
- Ph.D., University of Leiden

William O. Walker, Jr., Trinity University
- B.A., Austin College
- M.Div., Austin Presbyterian Theological Seminary
- M.A., University of Texas, Austin
- Ph.D., Duke University

Robert L. Webb, Luther College, University of Regina
- M.Div., Northwest Baptist Theological Seminary
- Th.M., Regent College
- Ph.D., University of Sheffield

Theodore J. Weeden, Sr., Colgate Rochester Divinity School, retired
- B.A., Emory University
- B.D., Candler School of Theology
- Ph.D., Claremont Graduate School

John L. White, Loyola University of Chicago
- A.B., William Jewell College
- M.A., Vanderbilt University
- B.D., Colgate Rochester Divinity School
- Ph.D., Vanderbilt University
- Special study: University of Toronto

Walter Wink, Auburn Theological Seminary
- A.B., Southern Methodist University
- B.D., Union Theological Seminary, New York
- Th.D., Union Theological Seminary, New York
- Special study: Oxford University; Peace Fellow, U.S. Institute of Peace, Washington, D.C.

Sara C. Winter, New School for Social Research, New York
- B.A., Bryn Mawr College
- M.S., Drexel University
- M.Div., Princeton Theological Seminary
- Th.M., Princeton Theological Seminary
- M.Phil., Union Theological Seminary, New York
- Ph.D., Union Theological Seminary, New York

SUGGESTIONS FOR FURTHER STUDY

Reports and study instruments produced by the Jesus Seminar

Robert W. Funk, Roy W. Hoover, and the Jesus Seminar. *The Five Gospels. The Search for the Authentic Words of Jesus.* San Francisco: HarperSanFrancisco, 1993.

Robert W. Funk, Brandon B. Scott, and James R. Butts. *The Parables of Jesus: Red Letter Edition.* Santa Rosa, CA: Polebridge Press, 1988.

Robert W. Funk and Mahlon H. Smith. *The Gospel of Mark: Red Letter Edition.* Santa Rosa, CA: Polebridge Press, 1991.

W. Barnes Tatum. *John the Baptist and Jesus: A Report of the Jesus Seminar.* Santa Rosa, CA: Polebridge Press, 1993.

A workbook to go with *The Acts of Jesus* has been prepared by the chair of the Jesus Seminar. Parallel reports of events in the life of Jesus are conveniently arranged on the page for easy comparison and study.

Robert W. Funk. *Acts Parallels: A Workbook for the Jesus Tradition.* Santa Rosa, CA: Polebridge Press, forthcoming.

All the surviving gospels and gospel fragments have been collected into one volume in a fresh, new translation made by the Fellows of the Jesus Seminar:

Robert J. Miller, editor. *The Complete Gospels: Annotated Scholars Version.* Revised and expanded edition. Santa Rosa, CA: Polebridge Press, 1994.

In this workbook, parallels to each section of the Gospel of Mark are printed in facing columns with matching lines to make comparison easier.

Robert W. Funk. *New Gospel Parallels.* Vol. 1, 2: Mark. Third edition. Santa Rosa, CA: Polebridge Press, 1995.

The Jesus Seminar publishes its technical papers in *Forum,* a scholarly journal that will appear in a new series twice yearly. Reports prepared for the general reader are printed in *The Fourth R,* a magazine sponsored by the Westar Institute. Both are published by Polebridge Press, Santa Rosa, CA.

Profiles of Jesus

There have been countless profiles of Jesus. The following brief list represents recent studies of merit. The first several are by Fellows of the Jesus Seminar.

Marcus J. Borg. *Jesus: A New Vision. Spirit, Culture, and the Life of Discipleship.* San Francisco: Harper & Row, 1987.

Marcus J. Borg. *Meeting Jesus Again for the First Time. The Historical Jesus and the Heart of Contemporary Faith.* San Francisco: HarperSanFrancisco, 1994.

John Dominic Crossan. *The Historical Jesus: The Life of a Mediterranean Jewish Peasant.* San Francisco: HarperCollins, 1991.

John Dominic Crossan. *Jesus: A Revolutionary Biography.* San Francisco: HarperSanFrancisco, 1994.

Robert W. Funk. *Honest to Jesus. Jesus for a New Millennium.* San Francisco: HarperSanFrancisco, 1996.

Robert W. Funk. *Jesus as Precursor.* Revised edition. Edited by Edward F. Beutner. Santa Rosa, CA: Polebridge Press, 1993.

Thomas Sheehan. *The First Coming: How the Kingdom of God Became Christianity.* New York: Random House, 1986.

Günther Bornkamm. *Jesus of Nazareth.* San Francisco: Harper & Row, 1960.

John P. Meier. *A Marginal Jew. Rethinking the Historical Jesus.* Vol. II. New York: Doubleday, 1994.

E. P. Sanders. *The Historical Figure of Jesus.* New York: Penguin Books, 1993.

Geza Vermes. *Jesus the Jew: A Historian's Reading of the Gospels.* Revised edition. Philadelphia: Fortress Press, 1981.

The history of the quest for the historical Jesus

Marcus Borg. *Jesus in Contemporary Scholarship.* Valley Forge, PA: Trinity Press International, 1994.

Michael R. McAteer and Michael G. Steinhauser. *The Man in the Scarlet Robe: Two Thousand Years of Searching for Jesus.* Etobicoke, Ontario: The United Church Publishing House, 1996.

Albert Schweitzer. *The Quest of the Historical Jesus: A Critical Study of Its Progress from Reimarus to Wrede.* New York: Macmillan, 1961. (Originally published in German in 1906.)

Russell Shorto. *Gospel Truth: The New Image of Jesus Emerging from Science and History, and Why It Matters.* New York: Riverhead Books, 1997.

W. Barnes Tatum. *In Quest of Jesus: A Guidebook.* Atlanta: John Knox Press, 1982.

The gospels

Rudolf Bultmann. *History of the Synoptic Tradition.* Translated by John Marsh. Revised edition. San Francisco: Harper & Row, 1963.

John Dominic Crossan. *Four Other Gospels. Shadows on the Contours of Canon.* Second edition. Santa Rosa, CA: Polebridge Press, 1992.

Robert T. Fortna. *The Fourth Gospel and Its Predecessor.* Philadelphia: Fortress Press, 1988.

Robert W. Funk. *The Poetics of Biblical Narrative.* Santa Rosa, CA: Polebridge Press, 1988.

Ronald F. Hock. *The Infancy Gospels of James and Thomas.* Santa Rosa, CA: Polebridge Press, 1995.

John S. Kloppenborg, Marvin W. Meyer, Stephen J. Patterson, and Michael G. Steinhauser. *Q-Thomas Reader.* Santa Rosa, CA: Polebridge Press, 1990.

Helmut Koester. *Ancient Christian Gospels: Their History and Development.* Philadelphia: Trinity Press International, 1990.

Burton L. Mack. *The Lost Gospel. The Book of Q & Christian Origins.* San Francisco: HarperSanFrancisco, 1993.

Burton L. Mack. *A Myth of Innocence. Mark and Christian Origins.* Philadelphia: Fortress Press, 1988.

Elaine Pagels. *The Gnostic Gospels.* New York: Random House, 1979.

Daryl D. Schmidt. *The Gospel of Mark.* Santa Rosa, CA: Polebridge Press, 1990.

Graham Stanton. *Gospel Truth? New Light on Jesus and the Gospels.* Valley Forge, PA: Trinity Press International, 1995.

Introduction to the New Testament

Stevan L. Davies. *New Testament Fundamentals.* Santa Rosa, CA: Polebridge Press, 1994.

Burton L. Mack. *Who Wrote the New Testament? The Making of the Christian Myth.* San Francisco: HarperSanFrancisco, 1995.

Women and meals

Kathleen E. Corley. *Private Women, Public Meals: Social Conflict in the Synoptic Tradition.* Peabody, MA: Hendrickson Publishers, Inc., 1993.

Robert M. Fowler. *Loaves and Fishes: The Function of the Feeding Stories in the Gospel of Mark.* SBL Dissertation Series 54. Chico, CA: Scholars Press, 1981.

Dennis E. Smith and Hal E. Taussig. *Many Tables: The Eucharist in the New Testament and Liturgy Today.* Philadelphia: Trinity Press International, 1990.

Passion narrative

Raymond E. Brown, S.S. *The Death of the Messiah. From Gethsemane to the Grave.* 2 Volumes. The Anchor Bible Reference Library. New York: Doubleday, 1994.

John Dominic Crossan. *The Cross That Spoke. The Origins of the Passion Narrative.* San Francisco: Harper & Row, Publishers, 1988.

John Dominic Crossan. *Who Killed Jesus? Exposing the Roots of Anti-Semitism in the Gospel Story of the Death of Jesus.* San Francisco: HarperSanFrancisco, 1995.

Empty tomb and appearance stories

Reginald H. Fuller. *The Formation of the Resurrection Narratives.* Philadelphia: Fortress Press, 1980.

Gerd Lüdemann. *The Resurrection of Jesus. History, Experience, Theology.* Minneapolis: Fortress Press, 1994.

Gerd Lüdemann. *What Really Happened to Jesus. A Historical Approach to the Resurrection.* Louisville: Westminster John Knox Press, 1995.

John S. Spong. *Resurrection: Myth or Reality? A Bishop's Search for the Origins of Christianity.* San Francisco: HarperSanFrancisco, 1994.

Birth and infancy narratives

Raymond E. Brown, S.S. *The Birth of the Messiah. A Commentary on the Infancy Narratives in the Gospels of Matthew and Luke.* New Updated Edition. The Anchor Bible Reference Library. New York: Doubleday, 1993.

Jane Schaberg. *The Illegitimacy of Jesus. A Feminist Theological Interpretation of the Infancy Narratives.* New York: Crossroad, 1990.

John S. Spong. *Born of a Woman: A Bishop Rethinks the Birth of Jesus.* San Francisco: HarperSanFrancisco, 1992.

Archaeology of the gospels

John J. Rousseau and Rami Arav. *Jesus and His World: An Archaeological and Cultural Dictionary.* Minneapolis: Fortress Press, 1995.

Ancient sources other than the gospels

Additional primary sources that bear on the origins of Christianity are the Nag Hammadi Library and the Dead Sea Scrolls. They are available in translation:

James M. Robinson, general editor. *The Nag Hammadi Library in English.* Third, revised edition. San Francisco: Harper & Row, 1988.

Michael Wise, Martin Abegg, Jr., and Edward Cook. *The Dead Sea Scrolls. A New Translation.* San Francisco: HarperSanFrancisco, 1996.

Dictionary of Terms & Sources

allegory A story in which one series of persons and events is intended to stand, obliquely and indirectly, for another series of persons and events. Example: the parable of the leased vineyard, Mark 12:1–8, is thought by some to represent an abbreviated version of sacred history, culminating in the death of the messiah.

androgyny The state of being in which an individual possesses both male and female characteristics.

angel *See* heavenly messenger.

angelophany A type of epiphany, specifically of an angel.

aphorism Aphorisms and proverbs are striking one-liners. An aphorism is a short, provocative saying that challenges the accepted view of things. A proverb embodies common sense. A proverb: "Early to bed, early to rise, makes one healthy, wealthy, and wise." An aphorism: "What goes into you can't defile you; what comes out of you can" (Mark 7:15).

apocalyptic A type of religious thinking characterized by the notion that through an act of divine intervention, the present evil world is about to be destroyed and replaced with a new and better world in which God's justice prevails.

apocalypticism Apocalypticism is the view that history will come to an end following a cosmic catastrophe and a new age will begin. Such views are frequently expressed in an "apocalypse": a revelation through a heavenly vision of events to come.

Apollonius of Tyana Apollonius of Tyana in Cappadocia (Asia Minor) was a Neopythagorean sage: he followed the teachings of the philosopher Pythagoras (born ca. 521 B.C.E.). Apollonius was born about the same time as Jesus and survived until near the end of the first century C.E. Like Jesus, Apollonius was a wandering sage, offering his advice here and there, sometimes without invitation. He was a vegetarian, wore a linen garment, did not bathe, and frequently fasted. He never carried money with him, and one time went without speaking for five years. He professed to know all languages, including the tongues of animals, without ever having learned them. He practiced exorcism, cured the sick, and forecast the future. He is said to have ascended bodily to heaven and to have appeared to some after his demise. Christian folk in the third century regarded him as a direct competitor of Jesus.

apology An apology is the defense or justification of a point of view, usually the Christian perspective.

Apostles' Creed The so-called Apostles' Creed is alleged to have been created by the twelve apostles, each of them contributing one of the twelve articles. In its present form, the creed goes back only to the sixth century C.E., although its content may be much older.

Apostolic Fathers A collection of early Christian writings by authors who were thought to have been associated directly or indirectly with the original apostles. The collection and the title can be traced back to the seventeenth century C.E.

Aramaic A Semitic language related to the Hebrew that was spoken in Palestine at the time of Jesus.

Asclepius The god of healing, whose cult was centered at Epidaurus, near Corinth in Greece. He was called son of Apollo and "savior." According to the myth, he was said not to be content with healing the sick, but undertook to revive the dead. Zeus regarded Asclepius' resurrections as a dangerous precedent and killed him with a thunderbolt.

Augustine Early Christian theologian (354–430 C.E.) who exerted enormous influence on the Christian world as champion of orthodoxy against Manicheans, Donatists, and Pelagians. Originally a Manichean himself, he converted to Christianity and was baptized Easter 387 C.E. He was Bishop of Hippo (396–430). Known for his *Confessions* and *The City of God*.

Augustus Caesar Adopted by Julius Caesar and designated heir (45 B.C.E.) and renamed Gaius Julius Caesar Octavianus. Became first Roman emperor, 27 B.C.E. –14 C.E. The title of *Augustus* was conferred on him in 27 B.C.E. by the Roman Senate. His stepson Tiberius later became emperor.

Barnabas, Epistle of Barnabas is a treatise in letter form, attributed to Barnabas, the companion of Paul. It was written toward the end of the first century C.E. It is included in the collection known as the Apostolic Fathers.

beatitudes Literary or oral formulations that confer good fortune on the recipient. They usually begin with the expression "Congratulations to" (more traditionally translated as "Blessed are"). The most famous beatitudes are said by Jesus at the opening of the sermon on the mount/plain in Luke (Q) 6:20–23.

Beelzebul The head or chief demon (Mark 3:22), under whose control Jesus was accused of operating. Elsewhere Beelzebul is called Satan.

Bultmann, R. Rudolf Bultmann is undoubtedly the most influential New Testament scholar of the twentieth century. He is famous for his demythologizing proposal, which led to worldwide controversy following World War II. His book *Jesus and the Word* summarizes his views of the historical Jesus, which were based on the dissimilarity concept. Bultmann died in 1976.

canon A collection or authoritative list of books accepted as holy scripture. The canon was determined for Roman Catholics at the Council of Trent in 1546 C.E.; it has never been determined for Protestants, except by common consent and the actions of some individual denominations.

catechesis, catechism Religious instruction given to Christian initiates (catechumens) either as preparation for baptism or as a follow-up to it.

C.E. C.E. stands for Common Era; B.C.E. for Before the Common Era. These designations are used rather than the earlier forms (B.C. and A.D.) out of deference to those for whom the birth of Christ marks the beginning of a new era only in a secular sense.

chreia (*plural: chreiai*). The term of hellenistic rhetoricians for what may be called an anecdote or pronouncement story. A chreia is a short story depicting a situation to which a sage or prominent person gives a response, usually in the form of an aphorism or proverb.

christology Teaching concerning the role or identity of Jesus.

christophany A type of epiphany, specifically an appearance of the risen Jesus.

1 Clement A letter written from Clement of Rome to the church at Corinth about 95 C.E. It is included in the collection known as the Apostolic Fathers.

2 Clement A sermon attributed to Clement of Rome. It dates from about 150 C.E. It is also included in the Apostolic Fathers.

Clement of Alexandria The head of an important Christian school for catechumens in Alexandria. Among his many works is the *Stromateis*, which deals extensively with the question of the relationship between Christian faith and Greek philosophy. Also of interest is a letter from Clement that contains the excerpts from the Secret Gospel of Mark.

codex and scroll The earlier form of the book was the scroll. The codex, which is a stack of sheets the same size bound or tied on one side, replaced the scroll in the first century C.E. because codices were easier to use and store. The modern book is a codex in form. Because such sacred books as the Torah originated in the age of the scroll, they have tended to retain the scroll form.

Congratulations/Damn In the Scholars Version, congratulations replaces the archaic term "blessed" and the more recent but less appropriate terms "happy" and "fortunate." Jesus declares the poor to be possessors of God's domain. For that, speakers of

English would say "Congratulations." "Damn" replaces another archaic expression, "woe." When speakers of English want to put a curse on someone they would say, "Damn you."

Coptic The form of the Egyptian language in use at the time of the introduction of Christianity in Egypt.

Council A Jewish high commission, presided over by the high priest, which met regularly in the temple to deliberate and rule on religious matters. Under the Roman occupation it had limited political jurisdiction. In Greek it was called the Sanhedrin, which means simply to "sit together."

critic, critical "To be critical" in the popular mind means "to criticize, to find fault with." But the basic meaning of "critical" is "to exercise careful, considered judgment." Biblical critics are critics in the second, positive sense, as are art critics and literary critics. For biblical scholars "critical" also means exercising judgment independently of all theological dogma.

Dead Sea Scrolls Discovered in 1947, the scrolls were hurriedly hidden in eleven caves along the Wadi Qumran, just above the Essene settlement at Khirbet Qumran on the shore of the Dead Sea, when the Romans arrived in the Jordan valley in 68 C.E. More than thirty thousand fragments of over five hundred documents were found in Cave 4 alone. The scrolls have provided priceless information about sectarian Judaism at the time of Jesus.

Deuteronomic history The Old Testament writings that tell of the history of Israel from the theological perspective of the book of Deuteronomy: obedience to God produces prosperity, disobedience trails disaster in its wake, to put it simplistically. The Deuteronomic history includes Joshua, Judges, 1 and 2 Samuel, and 1 and 2 Kings.

Didache An early Christian compendium of instruction, an incipient catechism, also known as the Teachings of the Twelve Apostles. The final form of the Didache, which was discovered in 1875, dates from the early second century, but its main sections go back to the first century.

Docetism The belief that Christ was not truly human, but only seemed to be so (from *dokeo*, "seem").

double tradition The gospel material not derived from Mark but common to Matthew and Luke. The double tradition is assumed by many scholars to have been taken from the Sayings Gospel Q.

Egerton Gospel This unknown gospel is represented by four fragments of Papyrus Egerton 2 (papyri are given inventory numbers by museums) and a fifth fragment designated Papyrus Köln 255. The five fragments are from the same papyrus codex, which can be dated to the second century C.E., perhaps as early as 125 C.E. This makes the Egerton fragments as old as the earliest fragment of one of the canonical gospels, the Gospel of John.

The Egerton Gospel contains stories of the healing of a leper, a controversy over the payment of taxes, a miracle of Jesus by the Jordan, plus two tiny segments closely related to the Gospel of John.

Enlightenment The Enlightenment refers to a movement in philosophy that advocated the untrammeled use of reason to establish truth. The movement challenged traditional authority, doctrine, and values. Emphasis was placed on the empirical method employed by the sciences.

epiphany An English cognate term for the Greek *epiphaneia* meaning "manifestation," usually of a supernatural being.

eschatology Religious teaching about those events supposed to happen at the end of time.

etiology (aetiology) The science of causes or origins. Etiological myths are stories that endeavor to account for the origin of some practice or name.

Eusebius Theologian, church historian, scholar, father of church history. Became bishop of Caesarea ca. 314. Was a friend of the Emperor Constantine; attended the Council of Nicea as a moderate, but later voted to repudiate the position of Arius. Author of the *Ecclesiastical History*.

Fellow (of the Jesus Seminar) Fellows of the Jesus Seminar have had advanced training in biblical studies. Most of them hold a Ph.D. or equivalent from some of the world's leading graduate institutions. A roster of Fellows is provided on pp. 537–42.

First Stone Gospel A fragment from an unknown gospel that has survived only as a variant attached either to the Gospel of John (7:53–8:11) or the Gospel of Luke (following 21:38). A woman caught in the act of adultery is brought to Jesus by a mob. He is asked whether they should stone her in accordance with the law of Moses. Jesus invites the one without sin to cast the first stone. This charming anecdote features the wit of Jesus in tandem with his espousal of the cause of sinners.

Galileo Galileo (1564–1642), Italian astronomer and physicist, became convinced of Copernicus' theory that the earth revolves around the sun through his work with the telescope. He was forced to recant such heresies.

Gehenna/Hell Gehenna is the place where the dead are punished; Hades is the abode of the dead, otherwise known as *Sheol.* Hell can be used for either term in the gospels.

gnosticism Gnosticism gets its name from the Greek word *gnosis,* meaning "knowledge" or "insight." In antiquity, it was a widespread religious movement, which in general terms focused on the world as a place of fallenness and evil, the illegitimate creation of a rebellious demigod. Gnostics believed that their origin was not of this evil world, but of a higher realm in which dwells the one true God, who, through a messenger or redeemer, has seen fit to communicate to them the knowledge (gnosis) of their true heavenly home. Armed with this gnosis, the Gnostic seeks to break free from this world and its rebellious creator, to be reunited with the Godhead in the heavenly realm above. Gnosticism was very adaptable and manifested itself in numerous forms, attaching to and transforming older traditional religious systems, such as Judaism and Christianity.

God's imperial rule The translators of the Scholars Version decided that "kingdom of God" was more appropriate to the age of King James I (1603–1625) than to the twentieth century. They wanted a term that had twentieth-century overtones, with ominous nuances, since God's rule is absolute. "Empire" seemed to be that term (one thinks of the Japanese empire, the British empire, and the Third Reich). However, some contexts require that a verb be employed, for which empire would not do. The happy solution was to combine "empire" with "rule": God's imperial rule was the result. When a place is called for, the translators employ "God's domain," which echoes the term "dominion," another candidate to replace "kingdom."

Gospel of the Ebionites A Jewish-Christian gospel preserved only in passages cited by Epiphanius, a fourth-century Christian theologian. The original title is unknown. The Ebionites were Greek-speaking Jewish Christians who flourished in the second and third centuries C.E. Their gospel, erroneously called the Hebrew Gospel by Epiphanius, probably dates to the mid-second century C.E.

Gospel Fragment 840 A single vellum leaf from a miniature gospel—the fragment measures approximately 3 x 3.5 inches and contains 45 lines of writing front and back—that can be dated to the fourth century C.E. The otherwise unknown gospel preserves the conclusion of a discourse between Jesus and his disciples and a controversy story arising out of the confrontation between Jesus and a Pharisaic chief priest in the temple court. *See* Oxyrhynchus.

Gospel Fragment 1224 This unknown gospel consists of two tiny fragments from a papyrus codex. The fragments can be dated to the beginning of the fourth century C.E., although the gospel itself is probably older. The few words that have survived are snatches of sayings of Jesus, including one about those who are well not needing a doctor and another about praying for one's enemies. *See* Oxyrhynchus.

Gospel of the Hebrews The Gospel of the Hebrews, preserved only in cited fragments, contains traditions of Jesus' preexistence and coming into the world, his baptism and temptation, a few of his sayings, and an account of his resurrected appearance to James, his brother (cf. 1 Cor 15:7). The provenance of the Gospel of the Hebrews is probably Egypt. It was composed sometime between the mid-first century and the mid-second century C.E. Several early Christian theologians knew and quoted the gospel; it did not survive as an independent text.

Gospel of the Nazoreans The Gospel of the Nazoreans is an expanded version of the Gospel of Matthew. It is preserved in quotations and allusions in early Christian scholars and in marginal notations found in a number of medieval manuscripts. It is evidently a translation of Greek Matthew into Aramaic or Syriac. The Gospel of the Nazoreans is first quoted by Hegesippus around 180 C.E. It probably comes from western Syria.

Gospel of Signs The identification of a signs source for the Gospel of John is based on two prominent miracle stories in John, the miracle at Cana (2:1–11) and the cure of the nobleman's son (4:46–54), which are numbered one and two (2:11, 4:54). Several other miracle stories in John are believed to have derived from this source. Further, see the cameo "A Gospel of Miracles?" (pp. 388–89).

gospel parallels In a gospel parallels or synopsis

the gospels are arranged in parallel columns with matching materials opposite each other. *New Gospel Parallels* (see "Suggestions for Further Study") is a synopsis incorporating the texts of all known written gospels.

Greek Bible The Greek version of the Judean scriptures, including the books of the official Hebrew Bible (Old Testament), along with the so-called apocrypha. The Greek Bible was the Bible of the early Christian movement. Its precise limits varied from community to community and from edition to edition. *See also* LXX.

heavenly messenger This phrase translates the Greek word *angelos,* which is usually translated "angel." Angels are messengers of God or the gods. Since in popular lore the function of angels is unclear, the translators of the Scholars Version thought the longer phrase would be more descriptive.

Hebrew Bible The officially recognized scriptures of rabbinic Judaism (the five books of the Law, the Prophets, and the Writings). Modern translations of the Old Testament for Christians are based on the Hebrew text, rather than on the text of the Greek Bible or LXX.

Hell *See* Gehenna.

Hermas The Shepherd of Hermas consists of Visions, Mandates (Commandments), and Similitudes (Parables). It was composed about 100 C.E. by an unknown author. Hermas belongs to a collection of early Christian documents known as the Apostolic Fathers.

Ignatius Ignatius was bishop of Antioch in Syria. He was arrested and transported to Rome under guard around 110 C.E. On his way he wrote letters to several churches: Ephesians, Magnesians, Trallians, Romans, Philadelphians, and Smyrnaeans. He also wrote a letter to Polycarp, bishop of Smyrna. Ignatius' letters are included in the collection known as the Apostolic Fathers.

Jerome Ca. 340–420 C.E. Secretary to Pope Damascus. Migrated to Bethlehem, Palestine in 382 and devoted his life to biblical scholarship. Published a Latin version of the Bible known as the Vulgate.

John, Gospel of The Gospel of John was allegedly written by John, son of Zebedee, one of an inner group of disciples. According to legend, John lived to a ripe old age in Ephesus, where he composed the gospel, three letters, and possibly the book of Revelation. The legend is highly improbable. The Gospel of John was probably written toward the close of the first century C.E., which makes it a close contemporary of Matthew and Luke. It exhibits evidence of having gone through several editions. Many scholars therefore conclude that John is the product of a "school," which may indeed have been formed by John of the legend.

Its place of origin is unknown. It was clearly created in a hellenistic city of some magnitude with a strong Jewish community. A city in Asia Minor or Syria, or possibly Alexandria in Egypt—all are possible.

It is uncertain whether John knew the synoptic gospels. He may have made use of a "signs" source and possibly a source consisting of lengthy discourses.

Josephus Josephus was a writer and historian, a near contemporary of Jesus (born 37/38, died after 100 C.E.). He wrote two huge works: *The Jewish War,* which is his account of the events leading up to the destruction of Jerusalem in 70 C.E., and *The Jewish Antiquities,* a history of the Jews down to the Roman war in twenty books. The two works are primary sources of information about the period just before and after Jesus.

Judas (the brother of Jesus) Judas is named as a brother of Jesus in Mark 6:3 and Matt 13:55, along with James, Joses, and Simon. Judas (=Jude), "a servant of Jesus and brother of James," is named as the author of the Epistle of Jude. These two figures may be the same person, even though the author of the Epistle of Jude demurs from claiming the status of "brother" of Jesus.

Judeans The religion of the first Jerusalem temple was practiced by the Israelites. The religion of the second temple (520 B.C.E.–70 C.E.) was practiced by Judeans. The religion of the rabbis and synagogue (90 C.E. and continuing) was and is practiced by Jews. The Fellows of the Jesus Seminar have adopted this nomenclature in order to be historically accurate and to avoid confusing the three major periods of Jewish history.

Justin Justin was a Christian apologist who was martyred between 163 and 167 C.E. He composed the First and Second Apologies and the Dialogue with Trypho. These books were produced shortly after 150 C.E.

Kepler, J. Johannes Kepler (1571–1630), German astronomer, established that the planes of all planetary orbits passed through the center of the sun; he also came to the view that the sun was the moving power of the solar system. Kepler is regarded as the founder of modern physical astronomy.

kerygma A technical term of New Testament scholarship deriving from the Greek word for "preaching." It is used to refer to the earliest Christian proclamation about Jesus. Most scholars agree that the gospels were profoundly influenced by the early Christian kerygma, and thus are more a product of early Christian preaching than a desire to preserve history.

L Luke's special source for materials the evangelist did not borrow from the Sayings Gospel Q or the Gospel of Mark.

lacuna *(plural: lacunae)* A gap in a manuscript caused by damage or deterioration.

Levites Descendants of the tribe of Levi who had sacred duties in the Jerusalem temple, but who did not offer sacrifice or conduct worship, duties reserved for priests.

Luke, Gospel of Luke-Acts, a two-volume work by a single author, depicts the emergence of Christianity on the world stage. It was composed around 90 C.E., during the same period as Matthew. Whereas Matthew was concerned with the relation between Judaism and Christianity, Luke is preoccupied with developments among the gentiles.

The tradition that Luke the physician and companion of Paul was the author of Luke-Acts goes back to the second century C.E. It is improbable that the author of Luke-Acts was a physician and it is doubtful that he was a companion of Paul. As in the case of the other gospels, the author is anonymous.

LXX The Greek translation of the Hebrew Bible, together with other miscellaneous works, some of which were composed in Greek. According to the legend, seventy (or seventy-two) translators produced a translation of the Torah (five books of Moses or the Law) under miraculous conditions. Originally the name Septuagint (meaning seventy) referred only to this translation of the first five books of the Bible. The Roman numeral (LXX) was later adopted as an abbreviation of the term Septuagint, and was used to refer to the larger collection of writings regarded as sacred. *Also see* Greek Bible, Hebrew Bible.

M Matthew's special source for materials he did not borrow from the Sayings Gospel Q or the Gospel of Mark.

Mark, Gospel of An anonymous author composed the Gospel of Mark around 70 C.E., which is the date of the destruction of the Jerusalem temple. Mark may be responsible for forming the first chronological outline of the life of Jesus. He may also be responsible for the first connected account of Jesus' passion (Mark 14–16). He reflects the early Christian view that God was about to bring history to an end in an apocalyptic conflagration (Mark 13). Matthew and Luke made use of Mark in creating their own gospels a few years later.

Matthew, Gospel of An anonymous author compiled the gospel of Matthew sometime after the fall of Jerusalem in 70 C.E. and before the council of Jamnia, 90 C.E. This is the period in which the new Christian movement was seeking its own identity separate from rabbinic Judaism, which was also just then emerging. Both were attempting to recover from the loss of the temple in Jerusalem, which had served as the focus of national religious life. Matthew is often dated to about 85 C.E., which is no more than an educated guess.

Matthew was composed in Greek in dependence on Mark and the Sayings Gospel Q, both written in Greek. It is therefore incorrect to identify Matthew with a gospel composed in Hebrew by a disciple of Jesus.

Mishnah The Mishnah is a compendium of rabbinic teaching that presupposes, but does not quote, the Law (the Torah, the first five books of the Bible). The one hundred fifty authorities cited lived from 50 B.C.E. to 200 C.E. The Mishnah serves as the "constitution" of the rabbinic movement, which laid the foundations of modern Judaism.

mnemonic device A device aiding, or intending to aid, memory.

Nag Hammadi The town in Egypt near which a collection of Christian and gnostic documents, known as the Nag Hammadi library, was discovered in 1945.

Ovid A Latin poet (43 B.C.E.–ca. 17 C.E.) who wrote, among other things, the *Metamorphoses* in fifteen books.

Oxyrhynchus An ancient village in Egypt where numerous papyri have been discovered. Among its most important treasures are Oxyrhynchus Gospels

840 and 1224, fragments of otherwise unknown gospels, and POxy 1, 654, 655, Greek fragments of the Gospel of Thomas. *See* Gospel Fragments 840 and 1224.

paleography The study of ancient handwriting. Paleography can often determine the age of a manuscript by the style of its handwriting.

papyrus Papyrus is the predecessor of modern paper. Ancient works were written on animal skins, called parchment or vellum, or on papyrus, made from Egyptian reeds, which were cut in strips, dried, and glued together to form sheets. Thousands of papyrus documents and fragments were retrieved from the sands of Egypt during the last one hundred years. These documents provide invaluable information about everyday life in the ancient Mediterranean world. Papyrus manuscripts are the oldest surviving written records of the gospels.

parable A parable is a brief narrative or picture. It is also a metaphor or simile drawn from nature or the common life, arresting the hearer by its vividness or strangeness, and leaving the mind in sufficient doubt about its precise application to tease it into active thought.

parchment Parchment, which is also known as vellum, is made from the skins of animals, usually sheep or goats, and prepared to receive writing. Parchment is more expensive than papyrus, but is more durable. Manuscripts of the New Testament written on parchment are called uncials. The oldest surviving uncials date from the third century C.E.

parody A parody consists in imitating a style or symbol for comic effect (Mark 4:30–32).

parousia Literally "presence"; in the New Testament it refers to the arrival or coming of the son of Adam, or the messiah, a term meaning simply Anointed, who will sit in cosmic judgment at the end of history. It is thus commonly understood to mean "second coming," as distinguished from the first coming, or advent, of the messiah.

Passion This term traditionally refers to the last two days of Jesus' life, beginning with the last supper and including the so-called agony in Gethsemane, the arrest, trials, crucifixion, death, and burial. It is sometimes used in an abbreviated sense to refer to Jesus' suffering on the cross and his death. In the phrase, "the Passion Week," it includes all the events of the final week of his life, beginning with the entry into Jerusalem.

performance When an orchestra plays a musical score, that is a "performance." When a group of players stage a drama, that is a "performance." The surviving versions of the parables and aphorisms of Jesus are also "performances," for which the original "score" or "scripts" have been lost.

pericope A Greek term literally meaning "something cut out," It refers to a discrete unit of discourse, such as a paragraph in an essay or a segment of a well-ordered story.

Peter, Gospel of The Gospel of Peter is preserved only as a fragment discovered in upper Egypt in 1886–1887; the language is Greek and the fragment dates to the eighth or ninth century C.E. However, two Greek papyrus fragments from Oxyrhunchus, dating to late second or early third century C.E., may also belong to the Gospel of Peter. The gospel contains a passion narrative, an epiphany story, an account of the empty tomb, and the beginning of a resurrection story. In its original form, the Gospel of Peter may have arisen in the second half of the first century C.E.

Pharisees Jewish laymen dedicated to the exacting observance of religion, the rigorous application of the Law to everyday life, and the cultivation of a tradition of teaching not found in the Torah, sometimes called the "oral Torah." The Pharisees are routinely parodied and condemned in the gospels. The polemic more accurately reflects conflicts between the synagogue and the Christian communities that produced the gospels in the last quarter of the first century than it does the situation of the historical Jesus.

Philostratus Flavius Philostratus (ca. 170–245) belonged to a literary circle in Rome patronized by Julia Domna, wife of Emperor Septimius Severus. At her suggestion, he wrote the life of Apollonius of Tyana, a contemporary of Jesus.

Polycarp Polycarp was bishop of Smyrna and a contemporary of Ignatius. His letter to the Philippians actually consists of two letters: chapters 13–14 were written much earlier than chapters 1–12. He suffered martyrdom under Marcus Aurelius, after 160 C.E.

pronouncement story *See* chreia

prooftext A scriptural text adduced as proof for a theological dogma, belief, or practice. Prooftexting often ignores the actual context of words, phrases, or verses used as proof.

proverb *See* aphorism.

Pseudo-Clementines Treatises wrongly attributed to Clement of Rome, consisting of two divisions,

Homilies and Recognitions. The Homilies are a philosophical romance arranged in twenty discourses that Clement is supposed to have sent to James of Jerusalem, the brother of Jesus. The Recognitions comprise ten books; they cover much of the same ground as the Homilies, although they add details about Clement's family and history.

Q (Sayings Gospel Q) *Q* stands for the German word *Quelle*, which means source. Q is the source on which Matthew and Luke draw, in addition to Mark.

rabbinic Judaism The Judaism centered in Jerusalem and the temple was replaced by rabbinic Judaism following the destruction of city and temple in 70 C.E. The Council of Jamnia in 90 C.E. laid the groundwork for the development of learning and worship focused in the synagogue. The rabbinic traditions surrounding the Hebrew Bible and codifying law and lore were later gathered in the Mishnah and Gemara, which together make up the Talmud.

redaction The process of producing a new text by reworking an existing text with a particular purpose in mind. Redaction can include adding or deleting material, rearranging, and rewriting. Redaction criticism is a scholarly method of investigation that seeks to isolate an evangelist's purpose and perspective by analyzing the way the author handles material derived from sources.

Renaissance The Renaissance ("renaissance" means rebirth) was marked by the revival of learning, the invention of the printing press, and other advances that initiated the modern period. With the Renaissance, attention shifted from the divine to the human, from theological speculation to the sciences.

Sanhedrin *See* Council.

scholar The ability to read and write was relatively rare in Jesus' world. Those who could do both usually became petty officials, since they were needed to produce the paperwork that goes with any bureaucracy. Scholars could also be accomplished in the Law or in rhetoric, to mention two other areas that brought special recognition.

Schweitzer, A. Albert Schweitzer (1875–1965), world-renowned organist, biblical scholar, medical doctor, and recipient of the Nobel Peace Prize, gave up a brilliant academic career to found a mission hospital in Africa. He wrote *The Quest of the Historical Jesus* at age thirty-one; it was published in 1906 and remains one of the great critical works on the gospels.

scroll *See* codex.

Secret Gospel of Mark The Secret Gospel of Mark is a fragment of an early edition of the Gospel of Mark containing accounts of the raising of a young man from the dead, a rite of initiation, and Jesus' encounter with three women at Jericho. These stories are presently embedded in a letter of Clement of Alexandria (second century C.E.), the copy of which dates to the eighteenth century C.E. Secret Mark may go back in its original form to the early second century C.E.

Sirach Jesus ben Sira taught in Jerusalem ca. 200–175 B.C.E. His teachings were collected into a book called Sirach or Ecclesiasticus, which was preserved as a part of the Old Testament apocrypha. It belongs to the wisdom tradition of the Old Testament, but it bears the stamp of a highly disciplined individual mind.

son of Adam This phrase is used to refer to any descendant of Adam and Eve. Sons of Adam and Eve are insignificant creatures in the presence of God, according to the Bible, but they are also next to God in the order of creation. "Son of Adam" is also a special term for the figure in Daniel 7, who will come on the clouds at the end of time and sit in judgment.

sophia Greek for "wisdom." Wisdom is often personified in early Jewish literature as a supernatural female figure. See, for example, Proverbs 8 and Sirach 1.

Sophia of Jesus Christ This document is a philosophical-gnostic treatise that takes the form of a revelation discourse in which the risen redeemer instructs the twelve disciples and seven women. It is a Christianized version of a gnostic treatise found at Nag Hammadi under the name of Eugnostos the Blessed. The tractate was probably composed in Egypt in the second half of the first century C.E.

synoptic A term from the Greek *synoptikos*, which means "seeing together," or "having a common view of." It is used specifically of the Gospels of Mark, Matthew, and Luke, which are similar in form, outline, and contents.

SV The Scholars Version is a new translation of the gospels prepared by members of the Jesus Seminar. See pp. xv–xx.

Teachings of the Twelve Apostles Another name for the Didache.

theophany A type of epiphany, an undifferentiated manifestation of the divine.

Thomas, Gospel of The Gospel of Thomas is a new and important source for the sayings and parables of Jesus. It contains one hundred fourteen sayings and parables, but lacks a narrative framework.

Thomas has survived in complete form only in a Coptic translation found among the fifty-two tractates that make up the Coptic Gnostic Library discovered at Nag Hammadi, Egypt, in 1945. Three fragments of a Greek version of Thomas were discovered at Oxyrhynchus, Egypt, about 1900 C.E. The Greek fragments can be dated by the style of writing to about 200 C.E. The first edition of Thomas was probably composed during the decade 50–60 C.E.

Thomas is widely regarded as an independent witness to the sayings of Jesus, comparable in form to so-called Q, a sayings collection believed to function as one of the two sources utilized by Matthew and Luke in creating their gospels.

Torah The first five books of the Bible, often called simply "the Law." These books are also referred to as the Pentateuch.

tradition Tradition is a body of information, customs, beliefs, stories, wisdom, and other material transmitted by word of mouth or in writing from one generation to another. The Jesus tradition is the entire body of lore about Jesus that was transmitted from one generation to another in early Christian communities.

triple tradition Gospel material that Mark, Matthew, and Luke (the synoptic gospels) have in common.

weighted average The weighted average is the numerical value assigned to each item by vote of the Fellows of the Jesus Seminar. Votes are weighted as follows: red (the historical reliability of this item is virtually certain) is given a value of 3; pink (this information is probably reliable) is given a value of 2; gray (this information is possible but unreliable) has a value of 1; and black (this information is improbable) has a value of zero. Each value is multiplied by the number of votes in each category and the sum of values divided by the total number of votes. The Fellows adopted the weighted average because that is the measure they use for determining grades in their classrooms. Had the Fellows adopted majority rule, some Fellows would have lost their votes on each ballot; the weighted average means that every vote counts in the final determination of the color designation.

For an explanation of how this method of assessment was utilized in evaluating reports of the acts of Jesus, see pp. 36–38 of the Introduction.

Inventory of Summaries & Settings

This inventory includes all narrative materials that do not qualify as reports of specific acts or events: summaries, transitions, generalized settings, and genealogies. The color refers only to the narrative portion of the text; for the color of the sayings, consult *The Five Gospels*.

An Index of Red & Pink Summaries and Settings derived from this inventory appears on p. 565.

1. **Cures & exorcisms** (Mark)
   Mk 1:32–34 gray
   Mt 8:16–17 black
   Lk 4:40–41 black
2. **Jesus tours Galilee** (Mark)
   Mt 4:23–25 black
3. **Jesus heals the crowds** (Mark)
   Mk 3:7–12 black
   Mt 12:15–21 black
   Lk 6:17–19 black
4. **In parables** (Mark)
   Mk 4:1–2 pink
   Mt 13:1–3a gray
   Lk 8:4 gray
5. **The secret of the kingdom** (Mark)
   Mk 4:10–20 black
   Mt 13:10–23 black
   Lk 8:9–15 black
6. **The lamp** (Mark)
   Mk 4:21–23 pink
7. **The standard** (Mark)
   Mk 4:24–25 pink
8. **Parable of the weeds** (Mark)
   Mk 4:26–29 pink
   Mt 13:24–30 black
9. **Mustard seed & leaven** (Mark)
   Mk 4:30–32 pink
   Mt 13:31–33 black
   Lk 13:18–21 black
   Th 20:1–4 pink
10. **Only in parables** (Mark)
   Mk 4:33–34 pink
   Mt 13:34–35 black
11. **Departures** (Mark)
   Mk 6:45–46 black
   Mt 14:22–23 black
12. **Many sick are cured** (Mark)
   Mk 6:53–56 black
   Mt 14:34–36 black
13. **Jesus departs for Judea** (Mark)
   Mk 10:1 gray
   Mt 19:1–2 gray
14. **Leased vineyard** (Mark)
   Mk 12:1–12 black
   Mt 21:33–46 black
   Lk 20:9–20 black
15. **Scholars in long robes** (Mark)
   Mk 12:38–40 pink
   Lk 20:45–47 gray
16. **Great sermon** (Q)
   Mt 5:1–7:29 black
   Lk 6:20–49 black

17. **Foxes have dens** (Q)
Mt 8:18–22 black
Lk 9:57–62 gray
18. **Narrative summary** (Matthew)
Mt 9:35 pink
19. **Sheep without a shepherd** (Matthew)
Mt 9:36–38 black
20. **Narrative transition** (Matthew)
Mt 11:1 black
21. **Jesus heals many** (Matthew)
Mt 15:29–31 gray
22. **Scholars and Pharisees** (Q, Mark, Matthew)
Mt 23:1–39 black
23. **Women companions of Jesus** (Luke)
Lk 8:1–3 red
24. **On the way to Jerusalem** (Luke)
Lk 9:51–56 black
25. **Rich farmer** (Luke, Thomas)
Luke 12:16–21 black
26. **On anxieties** (Luke)
Luke 12:22–31 black
27. **Knowing the times** (Q, Thomas)
Lk 12:54–56
28. **Barren tree** (Luke)
Lk 13:6–9 black
29. **Way of the cross** (Luke)
Lk 14:25–35 black
30. **The shrewd manager** (Luke)
Lk 16:1–15 pink
31. **Traps & millstones** (Luke)
Lk 17:1–4 black
32. **Trees into the sea** (Luke)
Lk 17:5–10 black
33. **Coming of God's imperial rule** (Q, Thomas)
Lk 17:20–21 black
Th 113:1–3 black
34. **There'll come a time** (Q, Mark, Luke, Thomas)
Lk 17:22–37 black
35. **Corrupt judge** (Luke)
Lk 18:1–8 black
36. **Pharisee & toll collector** (Luke)
Lk 18:9–14 black
37. **The money in trust** (Q)
Lk 19:11–27 black
38. **Jesus' daily routine** (Luke)
Lk 21:37–38 black
39. **Many miracles** (John)
Jn 2:23–25 black
40. **The one from above** (John)
Jn 3:31–36 black
41. **Monologue: son & father** (John)
Jn 5:19–47 black
42. **Sheep & the shepherd** (John)
Jn 10:1–18 black
43. **Narrative recap** (John)
Jn 12:37–43 black
44. **Way, truth, life** (John)
Jn 14:1–14 black
45. **Family tree** (Matthew)
Mt 1:1–17 black
Cf. Lk 3:23–38
46. **Family tree of John the Baptist** (Luke)
Lk 1:5–6 black
47. **Family tree** (Luke)
Lk 3:23–38 black
Cf. Mt 1:1–17

Inventory of Events

This is an inventory of the 176 acts of Jesus and of the 387 reports of those acts. The acts are listed in the order in which they appear in the primary source, followed by the parallels. The color refers only to the narrative portion and in many cases to the core event of the text; for the color of any sayings involved, consult *The Five Gospels*.

The Index of Red and Pink Events printed on pp. 566–68 is derived from this inventory.

SAYINGS GOSPEL Q

1. **The temptation of Jesus** (Q, Mark)
   Lk 4:1–13 gray
   Mt 4:1–11 gray
   Mk 1:12–13 gray
2. **Officer's slave/son** (Q, John)
   Lk 7:1–10 black
   Mt 8:5–13 black
   Jn 4:45–54 gray
3. **John's inquiry** (Q)
   Lk 7:18–23 black
   Mt 11:2–6 black
4. **Praise of John** (Q)
   Lk 7:24–28 black
   Mt 11:7–11 black
5. **The mute demon** (Q)
   Lk 11:14 gray
   Mt 12:22–23 gray
6. **Beelzebul controversy** (Q, Mark)
   Lk 11:15–23 red
   Mt 12:24–32 pink
   Mk 3:22–30 pink

GOSPEL OF MARK

7. **A voice in the wilderness** (Mark, Q, John)
   Mk 1:1–8 (core event) red
   Mt 3:1–12 (core event) red
   Lk 3:1–20 (core event) red
   Jn 1:19–28 black
   GEbi 1 red
   GEbi 3 pink
8. **John baptizes Jesus** (Mark, John)
   Mk 1:9–11 (core event) red
   Mt 3:13–17 (core event) red
   Lk 3:21–22 (core event) red
   Jn 1:29–34 black
   GNaz 2 black
   GEbi 4 (core event) red
   GHeb 3 black
9. **Jesus proclaims the good news** (Mark)
   Mk 1:14–15 red
   Mt 4:12–17 black
   Lk 4:14–15 gray
10. **Call of Simon & Andrew** (Mark)
    Mk 1:16–18 gray
    Mt 4:18–20 gray
11. **Call of James & John** (Mark)
    Mk 1:19–20 gray
    Mt 4:21–22 gray
12. **The unclean demon at Capernaum** (Mark)
    Mk 1:21–28 gray
    Lk 4:31–37 gray

13. **Peter's mother-in-law** (Mark)
    Mk 1:29–31 pink
    Mt 8:14–15 pink
    Lk 4:38–39 pink
14. **Jesus tours Galilee** (Mark)
    Mk 1:35–39 black
    Lk 4:42–44 black
15. **The leper** (Mark, Egerton)
    Mk 1:40–45 pink
    Mt 8:1–4 pink
    Lk 5:12–16 pink
    EgerG 2:1–4 pink
16. **Paralytic & four** (Mark)
    Mk 2:1–12 pink
    Mt 9:1–8 gray
    Lk 5:17–26 gray
17. **Call of Levi** (Mark)
    Mk 2:13–14 pink
    Mt 9:9 pink
    Lk 5:27–28 pink
    GEbi 2:4 pink
18. **Dining with sinners** (Mark, GosFr 1224)
    Mk 2:15–17 red
    Mt 9:10–13 red
    Lk 5:29–32 gray
    GosFr 1224 5:1–2 pink
19. **Question of fasting** (Mark)
    Mk 2:18–22 gray
    Mt 9:14–17 gray
    Lk 5:33–39 black
20. **Sabbath observance** (Mark)
    Mk 2:23–28 pink
    Mt 12:1–8 pink
    Lk 6:1–5 pink
21. **Man with crippled hand** (Mark)
    Mk 3:1–6 gray
    Mt 12:9–14 black
    Lk 6:6–11 black
    GNaz 4 black
22. **Call of the twelve** (Mark)
    Mk 3:13–19 black
    Mt 10:1–4 black
    Lk 6:12–16 black
    GEbi 2 black
23. **Jesus' relatives come to get him** (Mark)
    Mk 3:20–21 pink
24. **True relatives** (Mark, Thomas)
    Mk 3:31–35 pink
    Mt 12:46–50 pink
    Lk 8:19–21 gray
    Th 99:1–3 pink
25. **Jesus stills the storm** (Mark)
    Mk 4:35–41 black
    Mt 8:23–27 black
    Lk 8:22–25 black
26. **Demon of Gerasa** (Mark)
    Mk 5:1–20 gray
    Mt 8:28–34 black
    Lk 8:26–39 gray
27. **Jairus' daughter** (Mark)
    Mk 5:21–24a, 35–43 gray
    Mt 9:18–19, 23–26 gray
    Lk 8:40–42a, 49–55 gray
28. **Woman with a vaginal hemorrhage** (Mark)
    Mk 5:24b–34 pink
    Mt 9:20–22 pink
    Lk 8:42b–48 pink
29. **No respect at home** (Mark)
    Mk 6:1–6 pink
    Mt 13:54–58 pink
30. **Mission of the twelve** (Mark, Q)
    Mk 6:7–13 gray
    Mt 10:1, 5–15 gray
    Lk 9:1–6 gray
    Lk 10:1–16 black
31. **Herod beheads John** (Mark)
    Mk 6:14–29 (core event) red
    Mt 14:1–12 (core event) red
    Lk 9:7–9 (core event) red
32. **The twelve report** (Mark)
    Mk 6:30–34 gray
    Mt 14:13–14 black
    Lk 9:10–11 black
33. **Loaves & fish for 5,000** (Mark, John)
    Mk 6:35–44 black
    Mt 14:15–21 black
    Lk 9:12–17 black
    Jn 6:1–15 black
34. **Walking on the water** (Mark, John)
    Mk 6:45–52 black
    Mt 14:22–33 black
    Jn 6:16–21 black
35. **Eating with defiled hands** (Mark)
    Mk 7:1–13 pink
    Mt 15:1–9 pink
36. **Private interpretation** (Mark)
    Mk 7:14–23 black
    Mt 15:10–20 black

37. **Greek woman's daughter** (Mark)
    Mk 7:24–30 gray
    Mt 15:21–28 gray
38. **Deaf-mute** (Mark)
    Mk 7:31–37 gray
    Mt 15:29–31 gray
39. **Loaves & fish for 4,000** (Mark)
    Mk 8:1–10 black
    Mt 15:32–39 black
40. **Demand for a sign** (Mark, Q)
    Mk 8:11–13 gray
    Mt 16:1–4 black
    Mt 12:38–40 gray
    Lk 11:29–30 pink
41. **Bread & leaven** (Mark)
    Mk 8:14–21 black
    Mt 16:5–12 black
    Lk 12:1 black
42. **The blind man of Bethsaida** (Mark)
    Mk 8:22–26 pink
43. **Peter's confession** (Mark)
    Mk 8:27–30 black
    Mt 16:13–20 black
    Lk 9:18–22 black
    Th 13:1–8 black
44. **Jesus predicts his death** (Mark)
    Mk 8:31–33 black
    Mt 16:21–23 black
    Lk 9:18–22 black
45. **Way of the cross** (Mark)
    Mk 8:34–9:1 black
    Mt 16:24–28 black
    Lk 9:23–27 black
46. **Transfiguration** (Mark)
    Mk 9:2–8 black
    Mt 17:1–8 black
    Lk 9:28–36 black
47. **Elijah as precursor** (Mark)
    Mk 9:9–13 black
    Mt 17:9–13 black
48. **Man with mute spirit** (Mark)
    Mk 9:14–29 gray
    Mt 17:14–20 gray
    Lk 9:37–43 gray
49. **Jesus predicts his death again** (Mark)
    Mk 9:30–32 black
    Mt 17:22–23 black
    Lk 9:43b–45 black
50. **Dispute about greatness** (Mark)
    Mk 9:33–37 black
    Mt 18:1–10 black
    Lk 9:46–50 black
51. **The strange exorcist** (Mark)
    Mk 9:38–41 black
    Lk 9:49–50 black
52. **Is divorce permitted?** (Mark)
    Mk 10:2–12 black
    Mt 19:3–8 black
53. **Children in God's domain** (Mark)
    Mk 10:13–16 gray
    Mt 19:13–15 gray
    Lk 18:15–17 gray
    Th 22:1–3 black
54. **The man with money** (Mark)
    Mk 10:17–31 gray
    Mt 19:16–30 gray
    Lk 18:18–23 gray
    GNaz 6:1–5 gray
55. **Jesus predicts his death a third time** (Mark)
    Mk 10:32–34 black
    Mt 20:17–19 black
    Lk 18:31–34 black
56. **Revival of the young man at Bethany** (Secret Mark)
    SecMk 1:1–13 gray
57. **Request for precedence** (Mark)
    Mk 10:35–45 black
    Mt 20:20–28 black
58. **Blind Bartimaeus** (Mark)
    Mk 10:46–52 pink
    Mt 20:29–34 gray
    Lk 18:35–43 pink
59. **Jesus enters Jerusalem** (Mark, John)
    Core event gray
    Mk 11:1–11 black
    Mt 21:1–11 black
    Lk 19:28–40 black
    Jn 12:12–19 black
60. **Fig tree without figs** (Mark)
    Mk 11:12–14, 20–25 black
    Mt 21:18–22 black
61. **Temple incident** (Mark, John)
    Mk 11:15–19 pink
    Mt 21:12–17 pink
    Lk 19:45–48 pink
    Jn 2:13–22 gray
62. **By what authority?** (Mark)
    Mk 11:27–33 black
    Mt 21:23–27 black
    Lk 20:1–8 black

63. **Emperor & God** (Mark, Thomas, Egerton)
Mk 12:13–17 pink
Mt 22:15–22 pink
Lk 20:19–26 pink
Th 100:1–4 pink
EgerG 3:1–6 black

64. **On the resurrection** (Mark)
Mk 12:18–27 gray
Mt 22:23–33 gray
Lk 20:27–40 gray

65. **Most important commandment** (Mark)
Mk 12:28–34 gray
Mt 22:34–40 black

66. **Son of David** (Mark)
Mk 12:35–37 black
Mt 22:41–46 black
Lk 20:41–44 black

67. **Widow's pittance** (Mark)
Mk 12:41–44 gray
Lk 21:1–4 gray

68. **Temple's destruction** (Mark)
Mk 13:1–2 black
Mt 24:1–2 black
Lk 21:5–6 black

69. **Signs of the end** (Mark)
Mk 13:3–37 black
Mt 24:3–42 black
Lk 21:7–36 black

PASSION NARRATIVE

70. **The conspiracy** (Mark, John)
Mk 14:1–2 black
Mt 26:1–5 black
Lk 22:1–2 black
Jn 11:45–57 black

71. **The anointing** (Mark, Luke, John)
Mk 14:3–9 gray
Mt 26:6–13 gray
Lk 7:36–50 gray
Jn 12:1–8 gray

72. **The contract** (Mark)
Mk 14:10–11 black
Mt 26:14–16 black
Lk 22:3–6 black

73. **Preparation for Passover** (Mark)
Mk 14:12–16 black
Mt 26:17–19 black
Lk 22:7–13 black

74. **The betrayer** (Mark, John)
Mk 14:17–21 black
Mt 26:20–25 black
Lk 22:21–23 black
Jn 13:21–30 black

75. **The last supper** (Mark, Paul)
Mk 14:22–26 gray
Mt 26:26–30 black
Lk 22:14–20 black
1 Cor 11:23–26 black

76. **The oath** (Mark, John)
Mk 14:27–31 black
Mt 26:31–35 black
Lk 22:31–34 black
Jn 13:36–38 black

77. **Gethsemane** (Mark)
Mk 14:32–42 black
Mt 26:36–46 black
Lk 22:39–46 black

78. **The arrest** (Mark, John)
Core event pink
Mk 14:43–52 gray
Mt 26:47–56 gray
Lk 22:47–54 gray
Jn 18:1–12 gray

79. **Before the high priest** (Mark, John)
Core event pink
Mk 14:53–54 black
Mt 26:57–58 black
Lk 22:54 black
Jn 18:13–14 black

80. **Before the Council** (Mark, John)
Core event pink
Mk 14:55–65 black
Mt 26:59–68 black
Lk 22:66–71 black
Jn 18:19–24 black

81. **Peter's denial** (Mark, John)
Mk 14:66–72 black
Mt 26:69–75 black
Lk 22:55–62 black
Jn 18:15–18, 25–27 black

82. **Before Pilate** (Mark, John, Peter)
Core event pink
Mk 15:1–15 black
Mt 27:1–2, 11–26 black
Lk 23:1–7, 13–25 black
Jn 18:28–19:16 black
Pet 1:1–2 black

83. **Mocking** (Mark, John, Peter)
Mk 15:16–20 black
261. Mt 27:27–31 black
262. Lk 22:63–65 black
Jn 19:1–3 black
Pet 3:1–4 black

84. **Simon of Cyrene** (Mark)
Mk 15:21 black
Mt 27:32 black
Lk 23:26–32 black

85. **Crucifixion** (Mark, John, Peter)
Core event red
Mk 15:22–32 black
Mt 27:33–44 black
Lk 23:33–43 black
Jn 19:17–24 black
Pet 4:1–5 black

86. **The death of Jesus** (Mark, John, Peter)
Core event red
Mk 15:33–41 black
Mt 27:45–56 black
Lk 23:44–49 black
Jn 19:25–37 black
Pet 5:1–6 black

87. **The burial** (Mark, John, Peter)
Mk 15:42–47 black
Mt 27:57–61 black
Lk 23:50–56 black
Jn 19:38–42 black
Pet 2:1–5, 6:1–4 black

GOSPEL OF MATTHEW

88. **Two blind men** (Matthew)
Mt 9:27–31 black

89. **Man with mute demon** (Matthew)
Mt 9:32–34 black

90. **Damn you, Chorazin!** (Q)
Mt 11:20–24 black

91. **Wise & untutored** (Q)
Mt 11:25–30 black
Lk 10:21–24 black

92. **Private interpretation** (Matthew)
Mt 13:36–43 black

93. **End of the parables discourse** (Matthew)
Mt 13:51–53 black

94. **Temple tax** (Matthew)
Mt 17:24–27 black

95. **Traps** (Q)
Mt 18:12–35 black

96. **Castration for heaven** (Matthew)
Mt 19:10–12 black

97. **Two sons** (Matthew)
Mt 21:28–32 black

98. **Wedding celebration** (Q, Thomas)
Mt 22:1–14 black
Lk 14:15–24 black

99. **The death of Judas** (popular lore)
Mt 27:3–10 black
Acts 1:15–20 black

100. **The guard at the tomb** (Matthew, Peter)
Mt 27:62–66 black
Pet 8:1–6 black

GOSPEL OF LUKE

101. **A voice in Galilee** (Luke)
Lk 4:14–30 black

102. **Rejection at Nazareth** (Luke)
Lk 4:16–30 black

103. **Fishing for people** (Luke)
Lk 5:1–11 black

104. **Widow's son at Nain** (Luke)
Lk 7:11–17 black

105. **The seventy-two report** (Luke)
Lk 10:17–20 black

106. **Good Samaritan** (Luke)
Lk 10:25–37 black

107. **Mary & Martha** (Luke)
Lk 10:38–42 black

108. **Lord's Prayer** (Q)
Lk 11:1–13 black

109. **Privileged womb** (Luke, Thomas)
Lk 11:27–28 black
Th 79:1–3 black

110. **Condemnation of Pharisees** (Q)
Lk 11:37–54 black

111. **Disputed inheritance** (Luke, Thomas)
Lk 12:13–15 black
Th 72:1–3 black

112. **Watchful servants** (Luke)
Lk 12:35–48 black

113. **Repent or perish** (Luke)
Lk 13:1–5 black

114. **Afflicted woman** (Luke)
Lk 13:10–21 black

115. **Narrow entrance** (Luke)
Lk 13:22–30 black

116. **Jesus & Herod** (Luke)
Lk 13:31–35 black

117. **Man with dropsy** (Luke)
Lk 14:1–6 black

118. **Places of honor** (Luke)
Lk 14:7–14 black
119. **Lost parables** (Luke, Q, Thomas)
Lk 15:1–32 gray
120. **Ten lepers** (Luke)
Lk 17:11–19 black
121. **Zacchaeus** (Luke)
Lk 19:1–10 black
122. **Lament over Jerusalem** (Luke)
Lk 19:41–44 black
123. **Hearing before Herod** (Luke)
Lk 23:8–12 black

GOSPEL OF JOHN

124. **Prologue** (John)
Jn 1:1–18 black
125. **The testimony of John the Baptist** (John)
Jn 1:29–34 black
126. **The call of Andrew & Peter** (John)
Jn 1:35–42 black
127. **The call of Philip & Nathanael** (John)
Jn 1:43–51 black
128. **Miracle at Cana** (John)
Jn 2:1–11 black
129. **Conversation with Nicodemus** (John)
Jn 3:1–21 black
130. **John's final testimony** (John)
Jn 3:22–30 black
131. **The woman at the well** (John)
Jn 4:1–44 black
132. **Paralytic by the pool** (John)
Jn 5:1–18 gray
133. **Discourse on bread** (John)
Jn 6:22–71 black
134. **Not my time** (John)
Jn 7:1–9 black
135. **Secret visit to Jerusalem** (John)
Jn 7:10–13 black
136. **Lecture in the temple** (John)
Jn 7:14–52 black
137. **First Stone Gospel** (John)
Jn 7:53–8:11 gray
138. **Discourse in Jerusalem** (John)
Jn 8:12–59 black
139. **Man born blind** (John)
Jn 9:1–41 gray
140. **Jesus is accused** (John)
Jn 10:19–21 gray
141. **At the Festival of Lights** (John)
Jn 10:22–42 black
142. **The raising of Lazarus** (John, Secret Mark)
Jn 11:1–44 gray
143. **The time has come** (John)
Jn 12:20–36 black
144. **The footwashing** (John)
Jn 13:1–20 black
145. **A new directive** (John)
Jn 13:31–35 black
146. **The advocate** (John)
Jn 14:15–31 black
147. **Jesus departs** (John)
Jn 16:1–33 black
148. **Final prayer** (John)
Jn 17:1–26 black

GOSPEL OF PETER

149. **Mourning and regrets** (Peter)
Pet 7:1–3 black

EMPTY TOMB, APPEARANCES & ASCENSION

150. **The first list of appearances** (Paul)
1 Cor 15:3–8 red, pink
151. **Paul's visions** (Luke)
Acts 9:3–19 gray
Acts 22:6–16 gray
Acts 26:12–18 gray
Cf. 2 Cor 12:1–10
152. **Resurrection** (Peter)
Pet 9:1–10:5 black
153. **The empty tomb** (Mark, John, Peter)
Mk 16:1–8 black
Mt 28:1–8 black
Lk 24:1–12 black
Jn 20:3–10 black
Pet 12:1–13:3 black
154. **The bribing of the guards** (Matthew, Peter)
Mt 28:11–15 black
Pet 11:1–7 black
155. **Appearance to Mary of Magdala** (Matthew, John)
Mt 28:9–10 black
Jn 20:11–18 gray
PsMk 16:9–11 black
156. **The twelve depart** (Peter)
Pet 14:1–3 black
157. **Appearance to two in the country** (Luke)
Lk 24:13–35 black
PsMk 16:12–13 black

158. **Appearance to the eleven** (Matthew, Luke, John)
Mt 28:16–20 black
Lk 24:36–49 black
Jn 20:19–23 black
PsMk 16:14–18 black

159. **Doubting Thomas** (John)
Jn 20:24–29 black

160. **Appearance at the Sea of Tiberias** (John)
Jn 21:1–14 black
Cf. Lk 5:1–11; Mk 1:19–22, Mt 4:18–22

161. **Conversation with Peter** (John)
Jn 21:15–23 black

162. **Appearance to James, Jesus' brother** (GHeb)
GHeb 9:1–4 black
Cf. Th 12:1–2

163. **Ascension** (Luke)
Lk 24:50–53 black
PsMk 16:19–20 black
Acts 1:1–11 black

BIRTH & INFANCY STORIES

164. **Birth of Jesus** (Matthew)
Core event red
Mt 1:18–25 gray
Cf. Lk 2:1–7

165. **Astrologers from the East** (Matthew)
Mt 2:1–12 black

166. **Flight to Egypt** (Matthew)
Mt 2:13–15 black

167. **Murder of the babies** (Matthew)
Mt 2:16–18 black

168. **Migration to Nazareth** (Matthew)
Mt 2:19–23 black

169. **Miraculous conception of John** (Luke)
Lk 1:7–25 black

170. **Miraculous conception of Jesus** (Luke)
Lk 1:26–38 black

171. **Mary visits Elizabeth** (Luke)
Lk 1:39–56 black

172. **Birth & naming of John** (Luke)
Lk 1:57–80 black

173. **Birth of Jesus** (Luke)
Core event red
Lk 2:1–7 black
Cf. Mt 1:18–25

174. **Visit of the shepherds** (Luke)
Lk 2:8–20 black

175. **Dedication of Jesus** (Luke)
Lk 2:21–40 black

176. **The young Jesus in Jerusalem** (Luke)
Lk 2:41–52 black

INDEX OF RED & PINK SUMMARIES & SETTINGS

This index of the ten red and pink summaries, narrative transitions, and generalized narrative settings—all red and pink items that did not qualify as specific acts or events—is derived from the inventory of summaries and settings on pp. 556–57. The color refers only to the narrative portion of the text; for the color of any sayings involved, consult *The Five Gospels*.

1. **In parables** (Mark)
   - Mk 4:1–2 — pink
   - Mt 13:1-2 — gray
   - Lk 8:4 — gray
2. **The lamp** (Mark)
   - Mk 4:21–23 — pink
3. **The standard** (Mark)
   - Mk 4:24–25 — pink
4. **Parable of the weeds** (Mark)
   - Mk 4:26–29 — pink
   - Mt 13:24–30 — black
5. **Mustard seed & leaven** (Mark)
   - Mk 4:30–32 — pink
   - Mt 13:31–33 — black
   - Lk 13: 18–21 — black
6. **Only in parables** (Mark)
   - Mk 4:33–34 — pink
   - Mt 13:34–35 — black
7. **Scholars in long robes**
   - Mk 12:38–40 — pink
   - Lk 20:45–47 — gray
8. **Narrative summary** (Matthew)
   - Mt 9:35 — pink
9. **Women companions of Jesus** (Luke)
   - Lk 8:1–3 — red
10. **The shrewd manager** (Luke)
    - Lk 16:1–15 — pink

Index of Red & Pink Events

The index of red and pink acts is a list of all the events or specific acts of Jesus that were designated red or pink, in whole or in part, by the Fellows of the Jesus Seminar. (A complete inventory of events from which this is derived is printed on pp. 558–64.) In addition, the index includes forty-three related narrative statements, indicated by bullets, on which a separate vote was taken by the Seminar; statements that received a gray or black weighted average are also reported. The red or pink events and the narrative statements of all colors together provide a profile of what the Fellows of the Jesus Seminar regard as the acts of Jesus.

A separate index contains a list of the red and pink narrative summaries, transitions, generalized settings, and lists.

1. **The Beelzebul controversy** (Q, Mark)
   Lk 11:15–17 red
   Mt 12:24–25 pink
   Mk 3:22–23 pink
- **Some who saw Jesus thought he was mad.**
- **Some who saw Jesus thought he was an agent of Beelzebul.**
2. **A voice in the wilderness** (Mark, Q, John)
   Mk 1:1–8 (core event) red
   Mt 3:1–12 (core event) red
   Lk 3:1–20 (core event) red
   Jn 1:19–28 black
   GEbi 1 red
   GEbi 3 pink
3. **John baptizes Jesus** (Mark)
   Mk 1:9–11 (core event) red
   Mt 3:13–17 (core event) red
   Lk 3:21–22 (core event) red
   Jn 1:29–34 black
   GNaz 2 black
   GEbi 4 red
   GHeb 3 black
- **Jesus was a disciple of John the Baptist.**
- **Some of John the Baptist's disciples became followers of Jesus.**
4. **Jesus proclaims the good news** (Mark)
   Mk 1:14–15 red
   Mt 4:12–17 black
   Lk 4:14–15 gray
- **Jesus was an itinerant teacher in Galilee.**
- **Jesus preached in the synagogues of Galilee.**
- **Jesus proclaimed the kingdom of God.**
- **Jesus cured some sick people.**
- **Jesus drove out what were thought to be demons.**
- **Jesus enjoyed a certain amount of popularity in Galilee and surrounding regions.**
- **Jesus practiced prayer in seclusion.**
5. **Peter's mother-in-law** (Mark)
   Mk 1:29–31 pink
   Mt 8:14–15 pink
   Lk 4:42–44 pink
6. **The leper** (Mark, Egerton)
   Mk 1:40–45 pink
   Mt 8:1–4 pink

Lk 5:12–16 pink
GEger 2:1–4 pink

7. **Paralytic and four** (Mark)
   Mk 2:1–12 pink
   Mt 9:1–8 gray
   Lk 5:17–26 gray
   - **Jesus told a lame man to pick up his mat.**
   - **Jesus cured a lame man.**
8. **Call of Levi** (Mark)
   Mk 2:13–14 pink
   Mt 9:9 pink
   Lk 5:27–28 pink
   GEbi 2:4 pink
9. **Dining with sinners** (Mark, GosFr 1224)
   Mk 2:15–17 red
   Mt 9:10–13 red
   Lk 5:29–32 gray
   GosFr 1224 5:1–2 pink
   - **Jesus consorted openly with social outcasts.**
   - **One label for social outcasts was "toll collectors and sinners."**
   - **Jesus was criticized for eating with social outcasts.**
   - **Jesus justified his practice of sharing an open table in aphorism and parable.**
10. **Sabbath observance** (Mark)
    Mk 2:23–28 pink
    Mt 12:1–8 pink
    Lk 6:1–5 pink
11. **Jesus' relatives come to get him** (Mark)
    Mk 3:20–21 pink
12. **True relatives** (Mark, Thomas)
    Mk 3:31–35 pink
    Mt 12:46–50 pink
    Lk 8:19–21 gray
    Th 99:1–3 pink
13. **Woman with a vaginal hemorrhage** (Mark)
    Mk 5:24b-34 pink
    Mt 9:20–22 pink
    Lk 8:42b-48 pink
14. **No respect at home** (Mark)
    Mk 6:1–6 pink
    Mt 13:54–58 pink
15. **Herod beheads John** (Mark)
    Mk 6:14–29 (core event) red
    Mt 14:1–12 (core event) red
    Lk 9:7–9 (core event) red
    - **Herod Antipas had John arrested for having condemned his marriage to Herodias.**
    - **John the Baptist was popular with the people.**
    - **Herod regarded John as a threat to his political control of the people.**
    - **Herod had John beheaded at his fortress palace of Machaerus located in Perea, east of the Jordan river.**
16. **Eating with defiled hands** (Mark)
    Mk 7:1–13 pink
    Mt 15:1–9 pink
17. **Demand for a sign** (Mark, Q, John)
    Mk 8:11–13 gray
    Mt 16:1–4 black
    Mt 12:38–40 gray
    Lk 11:29–30 pink
    - **The Pharisees probably did expect heavenly signs related to the coming of God's kingdom.**
    - **The crowds who came to hear Jesus expected a sign related to the coming of God's kingdom.**
    - **The Pharisees asked Jesus for a sign.**
    - **Jesus refused to provide heavenly signs.**
18. **The blind man of Bethsaida** (Mark)
    Mk 8:22–26 pink
19. **Blind Bartimaeus** (Mark)
    Mk 10:46–52 pink
    Mt 20:29–34 gray
    Lk 18:35–43 pink
    - **Jesus rode into Jerusalem on an ass as a symbolic act.**
    - **Jesus rode into Jerusalem on an ass in order to declare his messiahship in fulfillment of Zech 9:9.**
20. **Temple incident** (Mark, John)
    Mk 11:15–19 pink
    Mt 21:12–17 pink
    Lk 19:45–48 pink
    Jn 2:13–22 gray
21. **Emperor & God** (Mark, Thomas, Egerton)
    Mk 12:13–17 pink
    Mt 22:15–22 pink
    Lk 20:19–26 pink
    Th 100:1–4 pink
    EgerG 3:1–6 black

PASSION NARRATIVE

- **There was a person named Jesus, who was executed by the authorities during the prefecture of Pontius Pilate (26–36 C.E.)**

- **The disciples fled when Jesus was arrested.**
- **The assertion that the Romans were innocent of Jesus' death and the Jews responsible is pure Christian propaganda.**
- **The underlying structure of the passion story was suggested by prophetic scriptures taken from the Greek Bible (the LXX).**
- **It is not just the content of the trial but the fact of a trial that lacks historical foundation.**
- **The trial narrative was created on the basis of Psalm 2.**

22. **The arrest** (Mark, John)

Core event	pink
Mk 14:43–52	gray
Mt 26:47–56	gray
Lk 22:47–54	gray
Jn 18:1–12	gray

23. **Before the high priest** (Mark, John)

Core event	pink
Mk 14:53–54	black
Mt 26:57–58	black
Lk 22:54	black
Jn 18:13–14	black

24. **Before the Council** (Mark, John)

Core event	pink
Mk 14:55–65	black
Mt 26:59–68	black
Lk 22:66–71	black
Jn 18:19–24	black

25. **Before Pilate** (Mark, John, Peter)

Core event	pink
Mk 15:1–15	black
Mt 27:1–2, 11–26	black
Lk 23:1–7, 13–25	black
Jn 18:28–19:16	black
Pet 1:1–2	black

26. **Crucifixion** (Mark, John, Peter)

Core event	red
Mk 15:22–32	black
Mt 27:33–44	black
Lk 23:33–43	black
Jn 19:17–24	black
Pet 4:1–5	black

27. **The death of Jesus** (Mark, John, Peter)

Core event	red
Mk 15:33–41	black
Mt 27:45–56	black
Lk 23:44–49	black
Jn 19:25–37	black
Pet 5:1–6	black

EMPTY TOMB & APPEARANCES

- **The resurrection of Jesus did not involve the resuscitation of a corpse.**
- **Belief in Jesus' resurrection did not depend on what happened to his body.**
- **The body of Jesus decayed as do other corpses.**
- **The resurrection was not an event that happened on the first Easter Sunday; it was not an event that could have been recorded by a video camera.**
- **Since the earlier strata of the New Testament contain no appearance stories, it does not seem necessary for Christian faith to believe the literal veracity of any of the later narratives.**
- **Mary of Magdala was among the early witnesses to the resurrection of Jesus.**
- **Mary of Magdala was considered a leader in the early Jesus movement along with Peter and Paul.**

28. **The first list of appearances** (Paul)

1 Cor 15:3–5	red, pink

BIRTH & INFANCY STORIES

- **Jesus' parents were named Joseph and Mary.**
- **Mary conceived with the assistance of Joseph.**
- **Mary conceived Jesus without sexual intercourse with a man.**

29. **Birth of Jesus** (Matthew, Luke)

Mt 1:18–25	red, gray
Lk 2:1–7	red, black

INDEX OF FRAGMENTARY GOSPELS

The following fragmentary gospels are quoted in *Acts of Jesus* as shown below. The full texts of these and other fragmentary gospels can be found in *The Complete Gospels*.

THE JESUS SEMINAR

The Jesus Seminar is a project of the Westar Institute, a private, non-profit research institute devoted to improving biblical and religious literacy by making the scholarship of religion available and accessible to the general public. As part of its literacy program, the Institute sponsors seminars, workshops, and publications in the field of religion.

MEMBERSHIP

Membership in the Westar Institute is open to professional scholars as Fellows and to others as Associates. Membership benefits include a subscription to the magazine of the Westar Institute—*The Fourth R*—and notices of national and regional meetings of the Jesus Seminar.

To learn more about the Westar Institute and its projects, please contact:

The Westar Institute
P.O. Box 6144
Santa Rosa, CA 95406
707 523-1323
707 523-1350 fax